Great
Canadian Adventures

Great
Canadian

Reader's Digest

Adventures

The Reader's Digest Association (Canada) Ltd.,
215 Redfern Ave., Montreal, Quebec H3Z 2V9

EDITORS: Hugh Durnford, Peter Madely
ART DIRECTOR AND DESIGNER: Val Mitrofanow
DESIGN ASSISTANT: Betty Jakubowicz
EDITORIAL RESEARCHERS: Eileen McKee (research editor),
    Horst D. Dornbusch, Lynda Leonard, Gayle Nowak
PHOTO RESEARCHERS: Penelope Cowie, Viki Colledge
COPY PREPARATION: Lynne Abell, Gilles Humbert,
    Joseph Marchetti, Anne Racine, Philomena Rutherford
PRODUCTION: Holger Lorenzen, Mark Recher

Book Publication Department
DIRECTOR: Louis Hamel
MANAGING EDITOR: George Ronald
MANAGING ART DIRECTOR: James Hayes
CO-ORDINATOR: Denise Hyde-Clarke

TYPESETTING: The Graphic Group of Canada Ltd./
    Compotronic Inc.
ENGRAVING AND PRINTING: Metropole Litho Inc.
BINDING: Volumex Limited
PAPER: The E. B. Eddy Company

SBN: 0-88850-051-3
Printed in Canada 1 2 3 4 5/80 79 78 77 76

Contents

Foreword

Acknowledgments

Foreword

T HE STORY of Canada is fascinating. It is
an accounting of human attempts
to cope with a vast, rugged, often cruel
environment, and with often conflicting hopes
and ambitions. The great cast of characters
includes explorers, colonizers and pioneers . . .
Indian chieftains . . . soldiers, seafarers, spies,
saints . . . politicians and statesmen, lawmen
and criminals, financiers and remote captains
of industry. There are heroes and villains,
fortune seekers, idealists and pragmatists,
figures of towering stature—and countless
ordinary men and women whose extraordinary
achievements have helped to mold a unique
Canadian culture and way of life.

This anthology of 48 great adventures
in the Canadian experience encompasses a time
that began some 1,000 years ago (when the
Norse attempted to settle in North America)
and extends to the 20th century. The rich
and ever-changing subject matter makes
Great Canadian Adventures a superb volume for
fireside browsing and casual reading.

We have been guided by a conviction that
the authors never intended their stories to be
hidden away in archives or on the "restricted"

shelves of libraries. They surely intended these magnificent adventure stories to be enjoyed by as many readers as possible.

This book reintroduces some Canadian writers whose works have been undeservedly neglected for many years. It contains work by such famous authors and historians as Francis Parkman, Stephen Leacock, Archibald MacMechan, W. O. Mitchell, Bruce Hutchison, Pierre Berton and Farley Mowat. The book is given extra excitement by its wealth of drawings, photographs and maps. Artists have based much of their work on prints from museums and archives across Canada.

For greater clarity and readability we have amended some of the original texts, by rearranging and abridging the material, and by modifying the syntax, punctuation, phraseology and spelling. Each story is as historically accurate as the best contemporary research can make it.

Great Canadian Adventures is a vital, exciting panorama of Canadian history.

The Editors

The

Frontier

I hear the tread of pioneers | Of nations yet to be...

John G. Whittier, 1846

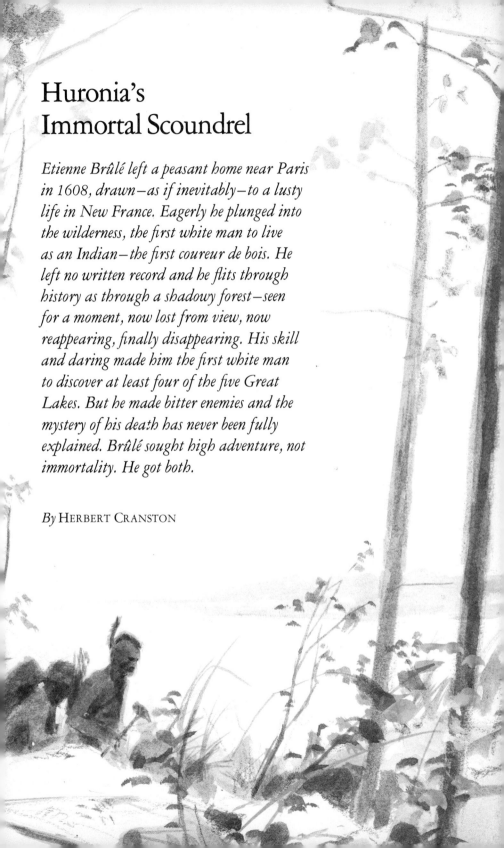

Huronia's Immortal Scoundrel

Etienne Brûlé left a peasant home near Paris in 1608, drawn—as if inevitably—to a lusty life in New France. Eagerly he plunged into the wilderness, the first white man to live as an Indian—the first coureur de bois. He left no written record and he flits through history as through a shadowy forest—seen for a moment, now lost from view, now reappearing, finally disappearing. His skill and daring made him the first white man to discover at least four of the five Great Lakes. But he made bitter enemies and the mystery of his death has never been fully explained. Brûlé sought high adventure, not immortality. He got both.

By HERBERT CRANSTON

ETIENNE BRÛLÉ WAS A STRIPLING of 16 when he found his way to Honfleur, the ancient seaport at the mouth of the Seine, where Champlain was fitting out for a voyage to the New World. The raw country boy, like all Frenchmen, must have been entranced by tales of discovery and profit at the other side of the Atlantic. He joined Champlain's expedition. It sailed April 13, 1608.

During the next two years, at the Habitation at Quebec, Brûlé watched the arrival of Algonkins and Hurons from up the great St. Lawrence River, their canoes laden with beaver pelts. He talked with the Indians and his adventurous spirit yearned to go back with them to their distant homelands and experience the wonders of the wilderness.

In the spring of 1610 Brûlé joined Champlain on an expedition up the St. Lawrence with Indians from Quebec. They were to meet the Algonkin chief Iroquet and the Huron chief Outchetaguin for trading, and to fight the tribes' traditional enemies, the Iroquois. At the mouth of the Richelieu River Champlain's party found and defeated 100 Iroquois. The chiefs arrived the next day, too late for the battle but not too late for trading and a three-day council with Champlain.

Brûlé had confessed his desire to live with the Indians and Champlain was agreeable. He had planned to send young Frenchmen to learn the Indian languages and customs and to explore the land and its wealth. On their return they would act as interpreters and facilitate trade.

Champlain asked Iroquet to take the young man with him for the winter and bring him back in the spring. Iroquet promised to treat Brûlé as his son. But his tribesmen did not like the idea: if some illness or accident befell the lad, would not the white chief make war upon them? Iroquet brought their doubts to the French commander.

Champlain demanded a powwow.

"Why," he asked the assembled warriors, "does Iroquet, whom I looked upon as my friend, refuse to take my boy with him? It is not like a brother or a friend to deny me a thing which he promised, a thing which could only bring good to you all."

Champlain spoke boldly, for he was anxious to get his plan under way. He was certain Brûlé could adapt to the new life and food. The Indians would not be held responsible for accidents, although if they mishandled the lad they would earn displeasure.

Seeing that Champlain was in earnest, and not a little angry, the Algonkins agreed to take Brûlé on condition that the white chief take a young Indian to France. The compromise suited everyone, and a Huron youth named Savignon joined Champlain. Promises were made to meet the following June, when the two youths would be exchanged again.

There is no record of Brûlé's year with the Algonkins. Undoubtedly he first paddled to Iroquet's home, 240 miles up the Ottawa River. Life at Quebec had grown dull but this journey into the wilds rekindled his spirits. Wildfowl and fish were plentiful, quiet stretches of river gave way to foaming rapids, portages led over great rocks and along narrow trails, and the danger of an Iroquois ambush was ever present.

Where the Rideau River plunged into the Ottawa his new friends ran for sheer fun under the archway formed by the cascading water. At the great falls of the Chaudière there was a sacrifice to the spirit of the turbulent waters. Eagerly the lad helped the Indians carry their canoes to the foot of the falls. He contributed his bit of tobacco to the collection taken on a wooden plate, then danced and sang around it with the others. He listened to an orator and learned of the Indian belief that, in return for such offerings, they received protection on their trip. Then, everyone whooping wildly, the tobacco was thrown into the tumbling waters.

Brûlé also probably went with Iroquet and Outchetaguin to Huronia, the land of the Hurons, the fertile area between Nottawasaga Bay and Lake Simcoe. The 18-year-old lad would thus have been the first European to ascend the Ottawa past the future site of Canada's capital, and to follow part of the eventual great route of the fur traders up the unruly Mattawa, across Lake Nipissing and down the fast French River to Georgian Bay in Lake Huron.

After nearly a twelvemonth, during which Brûlé fitted easily into the ways of the Indians, he, Iroquet, Outchetaguin and 200 Indians met Champlain and Savignon at the Lachine Rapids near Montreal. Brûlé was dressed as an Indian and had learned the language so well that he could interpret. He told about his adventures—one was being the first white man to shoot the Lachine Rapids—and Champlain was pleased. He wrote warm reports about "my lad" and "my young man."

The Huron chiefs held a grand council. They told Champlain they wished a close alliance with him. Later they agreed to help him explore Huronia and asked if he would send a young Frenchman to live with them as Brûlé had done with the Algonkins.

Champlain was more than willing. This year three young men returned with the Indians and it seems certain that Brûlé was among them. He travelled with Tregouaroti, Savignon's brother, to Ossossané, the main village of the Hurons' Bear Tribe, on Nottawasaga Bay.

The Hurons, unlike the nomadic Algonkins, lived in villages. They farmed, and traded for furs which they resold to the French. Groups of families lived in windowless bark longhouses up to 200 feet long. Smoke from fires down the middle filled the interior before escaping through a slit along the ridgepole. There was no privacy: adults, children and dogs shared food, utensils and beds. The staple food was sagamité, a mush made of ground corn which one missionary later likened to "the paste we used in France to put on wallpaper." Sometimes the sagamité was flavored with insects or very old fish–the more tainted the better.

Brûlé spent four years at Ossossané, his back happily turned on his countrymen in Quebec. He adopted the Indian language and customs. He could have made a fortune in the fur trade; instead he chose to paddle the wilderness, join the Hurons in the hunt and on the warpath, and take Indian women after feasts and war dances.

The Hurons had few sexual inhibitions. "After nightfall," Champlain wrote, "the young women and girls run about from one lodge to another, as do the young men, possessing them whenever it seems good, yet without any violence, leaving all to the wishes of the women. The husband will do the like to his neighbor's wife, and the wife to her neighbor, no jealousy intervening on that account, and no shame, disgrace or dishonor being incurred." (The custom grew in part because constant warring left the Hurons with more women than men.)

It is scarcely surprising that young Brûlé, alone in the wilderness and with no strong moral training behind him, should accept such a code. Besides, his fine figure and white skin fascinated the Indian women, and they sought his embraces. Yet his adulterous living is one reason for Brûlé being all but lost to history. Some of the missionaries who recorded most of the little we know about him were appalled by his flouting of the religious standards they taught. The kindly and tolerant Gabriel Sagard described him as being "much addicted to women"; Jean de Brébeuf called him an "infamous wretch." Even Champlain is said to have condemned Brûlé to his face for "unrestrained debauchery and libertinism."

Champlain was anxious to explore Huronia himself and had promised his Indian allies he would join them in a new attack on the Iroquois. In 1615, after his four years at Ossossané, Brûlé went with the Hurons to meet Champlain at the Lachine Rapids, then guided his leader back to the land of the Bear tribe on Lake Huron–the *mer douce*, or freshwater sea, as Champlain called it. While the Hurons were gathering forces for an assault on an Iroquois stronghold in the vicinity of present-day Syracuse, N.Y., Brûlé took Champlain on a tour of their villages. Everywhere the great white chief was enthusiastically received with feasts of corn bread, squash and fish.

On Aug. 4 the Frenchmen went to the village of Carhagouha, about 10 miles west of present-day Penetanguishene, Ont. There they met Father Joseph Le Caron, the first missionary to the Hurons, living in a little bark lodge built for him by his Indian hosts. Eight days later Brûlé was an observer as Le Caron celebrated the first Mass in what is now Ontario. Brûlé was probably not impressed. Although he wore a Lamb of God medal around his neck, and may have helped Sagard write his Huron dictionary, Brûlé liked to twit the missionaries. When he noticed how shocked Sagard was to learn of the Hurons' tobacco sacrifices to the mighty rock on the Ottawa, Brûlé mischievously declared that he had once made the offering too—and had experienced his most profitable trip. Sagard rebuked him sharply. Brûlé once told Sagard that when his life was in danger the only prayer he could think of was the *Benedicite,* the grace before meals.

The Hurons decided to ask help from their allies the Susquehannahs, who lived along the north branch of the Susquehannah River in what now is Pennsylvania. The Susquehannahs were great warriors and traditional enemies of the Iroquois, but to reach them quickly it was necessary to go through Iroquois territory. The Hurons chose 12 of their bravest men; Brûlé, excited at the prospect, asked Champlain if he could go too. Sure that his interpreter would bring back valuable information, the commander consented.

Oct. 11 was set as the date for the rendezvous at the Iroquois stronghold, and on Sept. 8 Brûlé and the 12 warriors left the Huron capital of Cahiagué, eight miles northwest of present-day Orillia, Ont. In two canoes they paddled down Lake Simcoe and up the Holland River, then portaged 29 miles to the head of the Humber River. At its mouth Brûlé became the first white man to see Lake Ontario and the site of Toronto.

The party paddled along the shore to what is now Hamilton Bay, then probably east again along the lake's southern shore. Near the mouth of the Niagara River they entered Iroquois country and travelled on foot through dense woods and swamps to avoid ambush. They met one small band of Iroquois; four were killed and two taken prisoner for torturing at the Susquehannah capital of Carantouan.

Champlain wishes Brûlé well as he sets out to cross Iroquois territory.

There Brûlé and his companions were welcomed with frenzied delight. Dances and feasts followed one another in seemingly endless succession. Although war fever grew steadily, Brûlé was unable to impress on his new friends the need for prompt action. At last, however, a grand council was called to debate whether the 500 warriors asked for should be sent.

The decision was favorable but, despite Brûlé's pleas for haste, more delays followed. When the Susquehannahs eventually made the three-day

journey to the Iroquois stronghold they were too late. The Hurons had been discovered before they could launch a surprise attack. A carefully planned assault the next day failed because the undisciplined Hurons fought as a mob. Champlain was wounded. Disheartened by the failure of the white men's guns to ensure victory, and of the Susquehannahs to arrive, the Hurons had fled.

The battle was a turning point. The Iroquois saw that even with French support the Hurons couldn't beat them. Iroquois raids into

Huronia increased over the years, culminating in massacres and the deaths of the Jesuit martyrs in 1649. Whether more effort by Brûlé could have got the Susquehannahs to the Iroquois stronghold on time, and whether they could have tipped the scales of battle, one can only guess.

Brûlé and the Susquehannahs returned to Carantouan. Brûlé, always ready for adventure, then became the first white man to explore the 350 miles of the Susquehannah River from Carantouan to Chesapeake Bay. Around the bay he found many Indians who he reported were "disposed to love the French nation above all others," having been treated harshly by the Dutch. He noted that many warlike tribes lived along the river, but that the climate was mild and there was abundant game.

In the spring of 1616 he returned to Carantouan and the Susquehannahs provided six braves as an escort for his return to Huronia. Along the forest trail the party was attacked by a band of Iroquois. The escort scattered and Brûlé ran for his life. After wandering for days in the forest, he decided surrender was preferable to starvation.

He met three Iroquois, laden with fish, returning to their village. Startled, they were about to flee when Brûlé called to them in their own language. He blurted out his story and laid down his arms, persuading them to do likewise. The Iroquois took Brûlé with them.

At their village a crowd gathered. Who was he? Where did he come from? Was he not one of the French, the men of iron who made war on the Iroquois?

Brûlé blustered that he was of a nation better than the French and that he was a fast friend of the Iroquois.

They didn't believe him. Despite the efforts of their chief, the Indians began to torture him. Reports say he was forced to run the gauntlet between lines of men who beat him with sticks, to jump over a large fire, and to "shake hands" in such a way that his fingernails were pulled out. The Indians burned him with firebrands and pulled out his beard. Finally one of them reached for the Lamb of God medal around his neck.

"Touch that," Brûlé croaked, "and you and your race will die."

The day was hot, the story goes, and Brûlé had noticed a thunderhead in the darkening sky. He pointed to the threatening clouds as symbols of God's anger when the medal was touched. Then the storm broke; thunder and lightning terrified the torturers and they fled. The chief led Brûlé to his lodge and dressed his wounds.

From then on Brûlé was a guest at dances and feasts. He promised he would return as soon as he could to make the Iroquois friends with the French. When he returned to Huronia he was guided for four days by a party of Iroquois.

In 1617, not yet recovered from the sufferings endured at the hands of the Iroquois, he stayed with his friends of the Bear tribe, probably taking minor trips of discovery along the shores of the *mer douce*.

In the spring of 1618 Brûlé went to present-day Trois-Rivières for his first meeting with Champlain since the disastrous attack on the Iroquois. Angrily the commander demanded an explanation of why the Susquehannahs had not arrived on time, and why there had been no report since. Brûlé told his story and showed his mangled hands. Champlain's anger quickly abated. Writing later he said: "He is more to be pitied than blamed."

His faith in his "young man" restored, Champlain sent him on his most important voyage of discovery, to explore farther west than any Frenchman had yet been.

Brûlé returned to Huronia. After delays which apparently lasted several years, he set out with a French companion named Grenolle and probably with some Hurons. Leaving from the Bear village of Toanché, where Brûlé now lived, the party paddled along the North Channel of Georgian Bay, up the St. Mary's River and into Lake Superior. No record of the trip exists, but the lake was apparently traversed from end to end. Brûlé returned with the disappointing news that the great body of water was landlocked and was not salt, but he had become the first white man to see Lake Superior. He also brought back a piece of copper which he apparently found at an Indian mine on the North Channel.

A few years later Brûlé went on the last of his great explorations. Again, there is virtually no written record of his travels, but he is known to have visited the Neutral Indians, a tribe living on the north shore of Lake Erie and named for their ability to survive between the warring Hurons and Iroquois. On this trip Brûlé undoubtedly saw Lake Erie, making him the discoverer of four of the five Great Lakes.

The only lake Brûlé does not get direct credit for discovering is Michigan. Yet Champlain's map of 1632, probably based on information supplied by Brûlé, shows not only the St. Mary's River and Lake Superior but also the beginnings of the Straits of Mackinac and its islands. This could indicate that Brûlé also paddled across the mouth of Lake Michigan on his trip to Lake Superior. Regardless, he had opened the doors of the vast domain which was to become the industrial heart of Canada and the United States.

In 1627 war broke out between France and England, and the English adventurer David Kirke sailed with three ships to capture Quebec. He sank a French supply vessel in the lower St. Lawrence, then pushed upriver and demanded Quebec's surrender. Champlain refused and Kirke sailed away, apparently reluctant to attack the fortified settlement. But he intercepted four more supply ships, and Quebec starved that winter. Some settlers fled to Indian villages for food and safety.

Brûlé apparently spent the grim period in Quebec. In the spring he was sent down the St. Lawrence with men named Le Baillif, Marsolet and Raye to guide the expected new supply fleet up the river. But at Tadoussac Brûlé and his companions found the English in full command. Kirke had returned with nine vessels, and lay waiting for the French ships. Quebec seemed doomed and the four men deserted to the English.

They undoubtedly told Kirke about the plight of Quebec, and, although he probably could have taken the Habitation without their help, they piloted three of his vessels up the river. Champlain, his people starving and in tatters, his supplies exhausted, surrendered.

A few days later he was brought to Tadoussac, from where he was to be taken to England. It was drizzling rain as Champlain came ashore under the dark walls rising from the mouth of the Saguenay River. There he came face to face with Brûlé and Marsolet, who had preceded him downriver. Quivering with anger, he flayed them for their faithlessness to king and country.

"If you realized that this evil thing you have done is both displeasing to God and to man, you would have a horror of yourselves," he told the two interpreters. "To think of you turning round and selling those who put bread in your mouths. May God forgive you. I cannot."

Brûlé and Marsolet flushed but kept silent. The Englishmen standing by guessed the meaning of Champlain's harsh words. Their sympathies were with their aristocratic prisoner.

At last Champlain paused for breath and to hear what defence the two might offer. Brûlé attempted to put on a brave face. He declared that he and Marsolet had been taken by force and had been obliged to do what their captors ordered.

"We know quite well, sir, that if they had us in France they would hang us," he said. "We are very sorry for that, but the thing is done. We have mixed the cup and we must drink it, and make up our minds never to return to France. We shall manage notwithstanding."

The betrayal has been defended by noting that the four were not soldiers, and that patriotism at the time had less influence than personal interest. It has even been suggested that Brûlé's action saved the inhabitants of Quebec from death by starvation.

But Champlain was unforgiving. He was apparently already disillusioned with the interpreters because of their immoral behavior, and he knew they were taking money from the fur traders. He had always considered them employees, not explorers, and his later journals refer to Brûlé not as his "young man" but as his "servant." These attitudes help explain why Champlain's voluminous writings tell so little about Brûlé.

The two men never met again. Champlain sailed across the Atlantic as a prisoner. His betrayer went back to his Indian home by the *mer douce*.

In all probability Brûlé served his new English masters as an interpreter, and urged the Indians to continue trading their furs on the St. Lawrence. He may have made the long journey with the fur flotillas to do some trading on his own. But Brûlé went rapidly to pieces. He realized that the cup he had mixed was filled with a bitter brew. He had no favor with the English; he dared not return to France nor even mingle with the French who had stayed at Quebec, and even his Huron neighbors began to lose respect for him. They may not have known of his treachery, but Champlain had been popular with them and Brûlé must have wondered about his own fate should the French return.

In 1632 the colony was handed back to France, and on May 22 the following year Champlain reached Quebec after nearly four years' absence. Two days later 18 fur-laden Huron canoes arrived at the settlement. The Indians traded with the French but the Huron leader expressed fear, reportedly to Champlain, that "in the association of the French with our people someone may be killed. Then we would be lost. Thou knowest all are not prudent."

What did it mean? Could it be a reference to Brûlé?

When the next band of Hurons approached Quebec in July the fear among them was evident. They were anxious over what the French would do about the grim news which had preceded them down the river. They paused before reaching Quebec.

Earlier that year, learning that their great friend Champlain was returning, and possibly learning the full truth of Brûlé's treachery, the villagers of Toanché had turned on the interpreter. Their contempt became enmity. After the 20-odd years he had lived among them they tortured him, killed him, quartered him, put his mangled remains in a pot, and cooked and ate him.

27

Whatever their reasons, and they will probably never be known, the Indians quickly repented. Gathering the dead man's bones, and in all probability his possessions, they buried them. Champlain might not approve of the killing of one of his servants, even one who was in disgrace. They knew that a Montagnais Indian had been sentenced to death for killing a Frenchman.

But Champlain sent Louis Amantacha, himself a Huron and a former close friend of Brûlé's, to assure the Huron visitors that there was no cause for fear. The French had nothing but good feelings for them, and Brûlé was no longer looked upon as a Frenchman. All doubts vanished. Next day the Hurons arrived at Quebec, where they were heartily welcomed by Champlain himself.

The commander had done everything possible to wipe fear from Huron hearts. He was not, however, able to eradicate superstition. A year later smallpox killed half the population of Toanché. The Indians were terrified. They set fire to their longhouses, but the smoke formed a ghostly shape in the sky which they believed was the spirit of Brûlé's sister seeking revenge on them. In panic they abandoned the village forever.

The remains of Etienne Brûlé are probably still where they were buried, but the exact spot may not be found until there is agreement on the site of Toanché itself. Most authorities place the village on a hilltop on the west side of the entrance to Penetanguishene Bay.

The only hope that the grave will ever be found lies in the probability that his musket, his knives, his pipe and other personal belongings were interred with him, according to Huron custom. Some day, by accident or design, someone may find rusted relics in that sandy soil and identify the resting place of the immortal scoundrel Etienne Brûlé, the first coureur de bois.

The Epic Feud Over Acadia

For 10 bitter, violent years, climaxing in 1645,
two headstrong and ambitious men faced each
other across the Bay of Fundy, grappling
for control of the infant French colony of Acadia.
Installed in forts, each claiming land occupied
by the other, they manipulated ships,
soldiers and New England Puritans in desperate
attempts to gain the advantage. One had
influence at court. The other had an indomitable
wife who became one of our first heroines.

Adapted from The Old Regime in Canada
By FRANCIS PARKMAN

THE FEW DOZEN SOLDIERS at Fort Sainte-Marie, guarding the entrance to the fertile, fur-rich Saint John River Valley, were restless as the spring snows of 1645 melted. Their provisions were inadequate and they had not been paid for weeks. Their commander, Charles Saint-Etienne de La Tour, who claimed to be the governor of Acadia, had gone away and left his fort in charge of his wife Marie. And danger faced them from the Bay of Fundy where Charles de Menou d'Aulnay was cruising with a fleet of armed ships.

The aristocratic d'Aulnay, who commanded a superior force from Port Royal across the bay, also claimed to be governor of Acadia. The King of France himself was not always certain who was his rightful governor in the colony around the Bay of Fundy and what is now southern Nova Scotia. Other matters usually occupied his mind. At this moment, however, he was on the side of the man from Port Royal. D'Aulnay had a royal edict in his favor. All he had to do was carry it out.

It was ironic that La Tour, who had devoted his life to Acadia, should be away from his stronghold at this fateful hour. He had come to the infant settlement of Port Royal in 1610, long before d'Aulnay, and become a friend and lieutenant of the commander. When the settlement was sacked by English colonists in 1613, the 20-year-old La Tour and his chief took to the woods and lived with the Indians. Eventually they were able to rebuild Port Royal, and when the commander died in 1623 La Tour took it over. He expanded French influence with a strong new post at rocky, fog-bound Cape Sable, and eventually moved his headquarters there.

When war broke out between France and England in 1627, his concern for Acadia turned to grave anxiety. The colony was a small thing in the mind of Paris, and little in the way of supplies and military support had ever been sent out. Moreover, his succession as commander had never been given the royal blessing. La Tour begged the King to give him help against the English, and he also begged to command in His Majesty's name. The King, however, decided to give all authority in North America to the Company of New France: La Tour had to be content with a new grant of land on the Saint John River. But his fears proved accurate, and all of New France fell, except for La Tour's stoutly defended outpost at Cape Sable.

In 1632 England returned New France to the French. La Tour hastened to Paris where he was able to obtain another grant of lands at Cape Sable and the titles there of lieutenant-general for the King and commander for the Company of New France. But that was all. The lion's share of Acadia the King entrusted to Isaac de Razilly, a distinguished naval officer who had been instrumental in persuading Cardinal Richelieu to found the Company of New France. Razilly reached Acadia in August 1632 accompanied by his cousin Charles de Manou d'Aulnay, a naval officer destined to become La Tour's worst enemy.

D'Aulnay helped consolidate and expand the colony, and when Razilly died three years later d'Aulnay assumed authority. He made Port Royal his capital and reigned like a feudal lord, which in fact he was. He joined his tenants at their work, and his confessor described him as returning to his log manor house drenched with rain and bespattered with mud, but in perfect good humor, after helping mark out a field. He borrowed large sums, built ships, bought cannon, conscripted soldiers and brought over immigrants. He is reported to have had 300 fighting men at Port Royal, and 60 cannon mounted on his ships and forts.

Now La Tour, who previously had felt himself the chief power in Acadia, was confronted by a rival higher in rank, superior in resources and court influence, proud, ambitious and masterful. To strengthen himself against so formidable a neighbor La Tour built Fort Sainte-Marie on the land granted to him at the mouth of the Saint John River. By 1635 he had moved there from Cape Sable, and Fort Sainte-Marie became his chief station.

Now grew a bitter feud between the two chiefs, each claiming lands occupied by the other, and each claiming leadership of the colony. They differed widely in position and qualities. D'Aulnay came of an old and distinguished family, and prided himself above all on being a *gentilhomme français*. His father had been a councillor of state under Louis XIII. La Tour was of less conspicuous lineage; his father was said by his enemies to have once been so reduced in circumstances that he carried on the trade of a mason in rue Saint-Germain in Paris. Both La Tour and d'Aulnay carried on the fur trade—which in France would have derogated from their claims as gentlemen.

The Royal Court in Paris interposed to settle the dispute, but in its ignorance of Acadian geography its definitions were so obscure that the question was more embroiled than ever.

And La Tour and d'Aulnay had to worry not only about each other, but also about New Englanders. Small parties occupied trading posts at Machias and Pentagouet (now Castine) on the Penobscot River in present-day Maine. As they were competitors in trade no less than foes of God and King Louis, and as they were few in number, both La Tour and d'Aulnay resolved to expel them.

In 1633 La Tour attacked Machias, killed two of the five men he found there, carried off the other three, and seized all the goods. Two years later d'Aulnay took Pentagouet. He had called on La Tour to help him but the latter, unwilling to cede command, had refused. He still hoped that d'Aulnay would become discouraged with his Acadian venture and go back to France.

D'Aulnay did go to France in 1638, but in due time he reappeared, bringing with him an aristocratic bride. He installed Jeanne Motin at Port Royal—a sure sign, as his rival thought, that he meant to make his permanent home there. Disappointed and angry, La Tour lost patience. He tried unsuccessfully to stir the Indians against d'Aulnay, then seized one of his small ships and held nine of its crew prisoner.

And as d'Aulnay had taken a wife, so too would La Tour. He

31

The bold Marie arrives from France to become La Tour's bride.

charged an agent to bring him one from France. The agent acquitted himself of his delicate mission, and sent to Acadia one Françoise-Marie Jacquelin, a woman destined to become one of the first heroines of whom Canadian history has record. She was evidently a Protestant, but her origins are obscure. According to one version her father was a barber of Le Mans and she a Paris actress. Another has it that she came from a family of the lesser nobility. Whatever the case, she was already a woman of 38 when, in 1640, she accepted La Tour's proposal and sailed for the New World. She joined La Tour at Fort Sainte-Marie and proved to be a prodigy of mettle and energy, espousing her husband's cause with passionate vehemence.

Soon after, the feud erupted into fighting. Returning to Port Royal from Pentagouet with two small vessels, d'Aulnay met La Tour with two of his own. In the resulting battle one of d'Aulnay's vessels was dismasted, but La Tour's chief officer was killed and La Tour and his new wife were captured and taken to Port Royal.

D'Aulnay compelled La Tour to sign a promise to keep the peace, but at the request of Port Royal's Capuchin friars he set the couple free.

32

Both parties now laid their cases before the French courts, and whether from the justice of his cause or from superior influence, d'Aulnay prevailed. La Tour's commission was revoked and he was ordered to report in France to receive the King's commands.

Trusting to his remoteness from the seat of power, and knowing that the King was often ill served and worse informed, he did not obey. D'Aulnay's father, however, from his house in Paris, watched over his son's interest and took care that La Tour's conduct should not be unknown at court.

A royal decree was thereupon issued for d'Aulnay to put the old fort at Cape Sable in the hands of "faithful personages." He seized and burned it, keeping the booty for himself. And when he learned that La Tour, cut off from French supplies, had appealed to Boston for mercenaries and the right to trade, d'Aulnay returned to France and accused La Tour of treason.

On Feb. 21, 1642, the powerful Royal Council ordered that the offender be brought prisoner to France, and d'Aulnay was required to execute the decree. La Tour was now in the position of a rebel.

D'Aulnay sailed for Acadia with four ships, and in August 1642 anchored at the mouth of the Saint John. He sent three gentlemen in a boat to read the decree to Fort Sainte-Marie's owner. La Tour snatched the papers, crushed them between his hands, abused the envoys roundly and put them and their four sailors into prison.

His position was now desperate, for he had placed himself in open revolt, and d'Aulnay threw up a blockade. Thoroughly alarmed, La Tour's intrepid wife managed to run the blockade and return to France where she arranged for reinforcements and supplies from the Huguenot stronghold of La Rochelle. The relief ship *Saint-Clément* arrived in the Bay of Fundy in May 1643, only to encounter d'Aulnay's blockade. There was nothing for it but to stand off and wait.

The desperate La Tour now decided to go himself to the heretics of New England. True Catholics detested them as foes of God and man, but La Tour was prepared to accept help where he could find it. The bold Marie, who had already run d'Aulnay's blockade both ways, joined him as he slipped out to the *Saint-Clément* under cover of fog and darkness. The captain agreed to take them to Boston.

As a supposed "papist," La Tour was sorely prejudiced in Puritan eyes, while his plundering of the Machias trading post some years before, and killing of two of its five tenants, did not tend to produce impressions in his favor. But, it being explained that all five were drunk and had begun the fray by firing on the French, the ire against him cooled a little. He was lodged under a hospitable roof, he went to church on Sunday, and the gravity of his demeanor gave great satisfaction—a solemn carriage being of itself a virtue in Puritan eyes.

La Tour was indeed a doubtful Catholic, but when he tried to pass himself as a Protestant his professions were distrusted, notwithstanding the patience with which he listened to long-winded sermons. As to his wife, however, there appears to have been but one opinion: Marie La Tour was a sound Protestant "of excellent virtues" and her denunciations of d'Aulnay no doubt fortified the prejudice that was already strong against him for his seizure of Pentagouet.

La Tour asked only for help to bring his own ship to his own fort, and as his papers seemed to prove that he was a recognized officer of his king, the Massachusetts governor and magistrates thought they might permit him to hire such ships and men as were disposed to join him in his endeavor.

The La Tours, with the *Saint-Clément* and four New England vessels, sailed on July 14. D'Aulnay's three vessels fled before them and his men ensconced themselves in a fortified mill at Port Royal. They were driven out with some loss and the mill was burned.

But this attack totally discredited La Tour in France, and now his wife's efforts to help him landed her in jeopardy. She had sailed again for France and labored strenuously in La Tour's cause. But the influence of d'Aulnay's partisans was far too strong, and, being charged with complicity in her husband's misconduct, she was forbidden to leave France on pain of death. Defying the royal command, Marie escaped to England in the spring of 1644 and boarded the *Gillyflower,* whose captain agreed to carry her to her husband at Fort Sainte-Marie.

The voyage took six months. The captain decided to go fishing on the Grand Banks of Newfoundland. When d'Aulnay stopped the vessel off Cape Sable, Marie narrowly escaped detection by hiding in the hold. Finally they reached Boston, where she sued the captain and won £2,000 damages. With the money she hired three ships, ran d'Aulnay's renewed blockade, and sailed majestically home in late autumn.

In France, meanwhile, the Royal Council had again, by decree dated March 6, 1644, ordered that La Tour be seized and his goods confiscated, and that he be brought home a prisoner. D'Aulnay was empowered to execute this decree if he could. He was incensed at the support given by the Puritans to his enemy, but King Louis had charged him not to offend them since they had helped La Tour in the belief that he was commissioned as lieutenant-general for the King.

D'Aulnay therefore made overtures of friendship. Early in October 1644 the Puritans were visited by one sieur Marie, probably a Capuchin in civilian clothes. He left no doubt which of the rival chiefs had the King of France on his side. He said that if La Tour would give himself up his life would be spared, but if he were caught he would lose his head as a traitor. Marie La Tour was worse than her husband, the envoy said, being the mainspring of his rebellion. The talk ended in a provisional treaty of peace between d'Aulnay and the men of Massachusetts.

Peace with La Tour, however, was the last thing on d'Aulnay's mind. Determined to win in battle the victory that the Royal Council had given him on paper, d'Aulnay attacked Fort Sainte-Marie in February 1645 while La Tour was away on a fur-trading mission. To his surprise the defenders rallied under the resolute leadership of Marie and drove him off with heavy losses. Indeed, d'Aulnay's flagship was so badly damaged he had to run it ashore, out of range of the fort's guns, to keep it from sinking.

While d'Aulnay was repairing his ship and bringing reinforcements over from Port Royal, Marie gave events a fateful turn. Her husband had returned and she now advised him to go to Boston, declare himself a Protestant, ask for a minister to preach to his men, and promise that if the Bostonians would help him to master d'Aulnay and conquer Acadia he would share the conquest with them. La Tour admired the sagacious counsels of his wife, and sailed for Boston to put them in practice.

Shortly thereafter two Récollet friars in the fort, convinced that the La Tours were both rebels and heretics, persuaded eight soldiers to their views. The 10 men set out in a small sailing vessel and were picked up by d'Aulnay.

The master of Port Royal was delighted to hear of La Tour's absence and the weakness of the defending force. Surely this was his chance to destroy his rival and settle their feud once and for all.

He called his officers to council. All were of one mind. On April 13 d'Aulnay reappeared off Fort Sainte-Marie and sent an envoy under a white flag, promising La Tour's men "pardon" and all the wages due them if they would return to the service of the King. Curses and insults were his answer.

The red flag of combat was hung from the fort, and d'Aulnay

Marie La Tour leads the defence of Fort Sainte-Marie against d'Aulnay's attackers.

opened fire. Soon his salvos were battering the earthworks and palisades. Then he landed two cannon and a large force of soldiers to assault the fort from land. For three days Marie, clad in steel breastplate, led the defenders against odds of five to one. Losses were heavy on both sides, and part of the fort's parapet was carried away by cannon fire.

The final assault began on Easter, April 16, while most of the exhausted defenders were in the fort's chapel.

The attackers climbed the palisade where the sentry, a Swiss mercenary, was in the pay of d'Aulnay. Before the garrison could throw up a line of defence attackers were pouring into the enclosure. Animated by their intrepid mistress, the defenders fought back in desperate hand-to-hand combat and again killed or wounded many of their assailants, though not without severe losses.

D'Aulnay then withdrew temporarily beyond the palisades, but Marie could be in no doubt as to the hopelessness of her position. Wearily, she surrendered to the vastly superior force, hoping in that way to spare the lives of her husband's loyal supporters. Indeed, d'Aulnay had promised "quarter to all" if she capitulated without further fighting. But worse was to come.

Marie La Tour, standing, according to one account, with a rope about her neck, had to watch in helpless torment as the men who had fought so bravely at her command were hanged one by one. Only one soldier survived, a man who had agreed to act as the executioner of his comrades. Marie did not long suffer the memory of this grisly spectacle. Put into confinement, she died within three weeks. D'Aulnay was the undisputed master of Acadia.

La Tour, stranded in New England, had lost his fort, and worse, his indomitable wife. By 1647, the year in which a royal decree declared d'Aulnay the hereditary master of Acadia, La Tour was struggling to establish himself in trade in Quebec. But in one of history's strangest reversals of fate La Tour was to have the last word.

On May 24, 1650, a dark and stormy day, d'Aulnay and his valet were in a canoe in the basin of Port Royal not far from the mouth of the Annapolis River. The craft capsized and d'Aulnay drowned. According to one account the valet was rescued but d'Aulnay was towed ashore with his head under water by an Indian whom he had beaten severely three days earlier.

At the news of his enemy's fate a new hope possessed La Tour, who still had agents in France interested in helping him. An extraordinary document appeared in February 1651, less than a year after d'Aulnay's death, completely reversing the decree of 1647. The lately proscribed "rebel and traitor" was confirmed as governor and lieutenant-general in Acadia. The paper went on to say that La Tour would have converted the Indians and conquered Acadia for the King if d'Aulnay had not prevented him.

Unless this document was a fabrication in the interest of La Tour, it suggests strange reflections on the colonial administration of the time. Genuine or not, La Tour profited by it, and after a fruitful visit to France he returned to Acadia with revived hopes.

D'Aulnay's destitute widow, left with eight children, returned Fort Sainte-Marie to him and soon thereafter he married her. Together they had five more children. And even when New Englanders took Acadia in 1654 La Tour persuaded England's Oliver Cromwell that he still had land rights in Nova Scotia. He and his wife apparently retired to Cape Sable, where he is believed to have died in 1666.

John Gyles' Amazing Ordeal

*Wanton savagery filled Acadia and
New England with hate and fear at the end of
the 17th century as France and England
waged a bloody struggle for a new continent. Each
side recruited Indians to sack enemy villages and
murder their inhabitants. John Gyles,
a nine-year-old Puritan boy, was seized by
Malecite Indians during one such raid and spent
nine years as a slave in present-day New Brunswick.
This is a slightly fictionalized account of his
amazing ordeal, based on memoirs he wrote many
years later.*

By STUART TRUEMAN

AMONG THE PURITANS who left the religious persecution of England for the freedom, space and opportunity of the New World was a farmer named Thomas Gyles, Sr. By 1689 he had settled with his wife, four sons and two daughters at Pemaquid, midway between the Kennebec and Penobscot rivers in present-day Maine. The colony's governor, glad to recognize such a reputable gentleman, appointed Gyles chief justice of the region.

On the bright morning of Aug. 2 Judge Gyles decided to take his two oldest boys to help the laborers at his farm near Fort Charles, the little redoubt that guarded the sea approach to the village.

"You might as well come along too, John," he called out, restraining a smile. "We could use an extra man today."

The boy was nine. Neither tall for his age nor broad of frame, he did not always fill out his handed-down clothes. Yet he insisted he could work as hard as his bigger brothers.

The farm was a sight to warm the heart of its owner. There beside Pemaquid Falls were a sea of lush hay waiting to be cut, and rows of corn coming into ear. Surveying his first bumper harvest, the judge was a proud and happy man.

"Hark!" he said suddenly. "Did you hear that?"

A boom reverberated across the fields. Then another and another.

"Is it thunder?" asked John.

"The great guns of the fort! It surely is good news—the Great Council has sent back the soldiers who deserted."

Only a few months ago Fort Charles had been at full strength with 156 soldiers. Then the council had withdrawn all but 30 of the garrison to reinforce other outposts facing French Acadia. That was bad enough, but then a dozen more men quit their posts.

Lately there had been ominous rumblings. One settlement had been attacked by Indians from Acadia the previous autumn, another in January. Rumor said a third in New Hampshire had been ravaged only a few weeks before. But now, thank the Almighty, the guns were apparently signalling all was well at Pemaquid.

Apparently no one saw the eyes glinting from the forest or knew that war parties of Malecites, Micmacs, Passamaquoddys and Penobscots had secreted their canoes two miles away and crept stealthily through the woods.

What happened next can best be told by young John Gyles' journal of years afterward:

"To our great surprise, about 30 or 40 Indians discharged a volley of shot at us from behind a rising ground near our barn. The yelling of the Indians and the whistling of their shots so terrified me that I endeavored to make my escape. My brother ran one way, and I another; and looking over my shoulder I saw a stout fellow, painted, pursuing me with a gun, and a cutlass glittering in his hand, which I expected every moment in my brains. I presently fell down and the Indian seized my arms, lifted me up and led me away. As we went we crossed where my father was, who looked very pale and bloody."

Where moments before the air had been filled with war cries, musket blasts and screaming, now there was eerie silence, punctuated by the moans of the dying and the crackling of flames from the buildings.

Beside young John now, herded along by the Indians, were other captives—two laborers, his 14-year-old brother James and, at the end of the line, his father. There was no sign of 16-year-old Thomas.

After a quarter of a mile the Indians called a halt. Judge Gyles, shocked, stumbling, obviously too badly wounded to keep up, was pushed forward by a brave.

"You must die," said the Indian simply, in English.

Judge Gyles, with an effort, spoke to his captors: "I am a dying man. I want no favor of you but to pray with my children." The warriors drew away.

"To the protection and blessing of God Almighty I recommend you," Judge Gyles said in an encouraging, almost cheerful voice. "I have given you my best advice, and I know you will follow it perseveringly. I take my leave of this life, hoping we shall meet in a better land."

John Gyles' journal related: "The Indians led him aside. I heard the blows of the hatchets, but neither shriek nor groan! I heard afterward that he had five or seven shot holes through his waistcoat, and that he was covered with boughs."

They trudged into a thick swamp where John and James found their mother and sisters and numerous other captives. From snatches of conversation the prisoners learned what had transpired. The war party, numbering about 100 braves led by French officers, had cached their canoes at New Harbour, east of Pemaquid, where 12 fishermen's huts had been abandoned months before. The invaders had dispatched spies who observed that Pemaquid's men were generally at work at noon, leaving only women and children at home. The Indians divided themselves into several parties, attacking the farthest off men first. Then they moved toward the town, killing and capturing as they went.

Mrs. Gyles reassured John and James that their little brother Tad was probably safe for the moment. He had been playing about the fort and had scampered in.

The village was in flames but thunderclaps from the cannon at Fort Charles still resounded in the swamp. The commander was putting up a resolute defence. For two days he held out. Then the firing ceased.

After a night at New Harbour, the Indians and captives paddled up the coast toward the Penobscot River. John Gyles wrote later: "About noon the canoe in which my mother was, and that in which I was, came side by side. She asked me how I did. I think I said, 'Pretty well.' Then she said, 'Oh, my child! How joyful and pleasant it would be if we were going to old England to see your Uncle Chalker and other friends there! Poor babe, we are going into the wilderness, the Lord knows where!'"

After a night on an island the Indians and their dishevelled captives landed at Pentagouet (now Castine), the French outpost at the Penobscot River. John's captor took him to see the missionary of the place, Abbé Louis-Pierre Thury. For the Puritan boy it was like being invited to call on Satan.

The missionary looked smilingly on John, and from his robes brought forth several pieces of gold. He was offering them for the lad's ransom: an Indian who took a prisoner was accounted his master and could sell or kill him at will.

Unimpressed, the warrior shook his head.

"Wait, then," said the priest as he rummaged in a cupboard. He came back and offered John a biscuit.

"Thank you," said the boy, and stuffed it in his pocket.

On his return to the captives' camp, famished though he was, John hid the biscuit under a log. He feared it contained some potion to make him susceptible to the blandishments of popery.

"My mother heard talk of my being sold to a Jesuit," he recorded later. "She said to me, 'Oh! my dear child, if it were God's will, I had rather follow you to your grave or never see you more in this world, than you should be sold to a Jesuit; for a Jesuit will ruin you, body and soul.'"

John's Indian master now paddled and poled his canoe up the forest-lined Penobscot. The boy had been separated from his family but he was no longer in mortal fear for he sensed he had some value. He would not be killed—not yet.

John and his master presented quite a contrast: the boy small, fair and blue-eyed, in muddy English clothing; the Indian stalwart and swarthy, jet-black of hair and eyes, his bare back glistening in the sun as sweat ran down to his loincloth.

"Where are we going?" John asked, forgetting that not a word would be understood. Around Pemaquid all the Indians had known English. The warrior grunted incomprehensibly.

Eventually they came to an Indian village. John's journal recalled: "At home I had ever seen strangers treated with the utmost civility, and being a stranger I expected the same kind of treatment here. But I presently saw a number of squaws get together in a circle, dancing and yelling. An old, grim-looking one led me into the ring where some seized me by the hair and others by the hands and feet, like so many furies; but my master presently laying down a pledge, they released me.

"A captive among the Indians is exposed to all manner of abuse and tortures unless his master lay down a ransom such as a bag of corn, a blanket or the like, which redeems him for that dance."

Next morning, through a cathedral-like forest of pines, they branched up a tributary of the Penobscot. At the first portage the Indian carried the canoe easily on his shoulders while John trotted at his heels trying to keep up. Through a series of lakes they reached the Meductic River which flowed into the Saint John.

His master's name was O-ski-tchin, John had decided. In one of his rare communicative moods the Indian had pointed to himself and said the word repeatedly. Later John discovered that O-ski-tchin really meant Indian or human being. But the name stuck. In turn, he became Chon—the best the Indian could pronounce John.

The final portage was six miles long. O-ski-tchin went ahead, leaving John in the care of an old Indian who, to the boy's elation, spoke some English. "By-and-by come to a great town and fort," he said.

But Meductic, the Indian settlement on the Saint John River 40 miles above present-day Fredericton, was a squalid disappointment—a hut about 35 feet long and a few wigwams encircled by a stake wall and a deep ditch.

John was led to where 30 or 40 yelling Indians were dancing around five or six captives who had been taken some months before. He was whirled inside the circle, and "we prisoners looked on each other with a sorrowful countenance."

Presently four Indians grasped one of the captives by the hands and feet. Swinging him high, they let his back crash on the ground, then repeated this procedure with prisoner after prisoner. John knew his turn was next. He tried to smile at the Indians but no face showed any semblance of pity. Then a squaw laid a bag of corn in the ring as a ransom, and a grave Indian handed him a short pipe.

"Smoke it," he said in English. John puffed and choked, then was led away by the wrist. Now he felt sure his last hour had come. He was too scared to walk, and the Indian carried him to a hut a mile away owned by a Frenchman. While the Indian and the Frenchman's squaw talked, the boy watched apprehensively. Two hours later the Indian led him back to the village and gave him food.

It was a puzzling episode, but it dawned on John that in some inexplicable way he had been shown kindness.

The country in which John found himself looked far different than it does now. Great white pines towered everywhere. Along the broad, winding Saint John the dense forest was rarely broken by field or meadow. Wild flowers splashed color on the riverbanks but there were no dandelions, daisies, clovers or even burdocks. These, along with cultivated grasses, were yet to be brought from Europe and New England.

The river and its tributaries teemed with fish—striped bass at times jammed the smaller streams until their backs arched out of the water—but there were not yet any black bass or rainbow trout.

In Acadia in 1689—a domain embracing present-day New Brunswick, Nova Scotia, Prince Edward Island, part of Quebec, and Maine to the Penobscot River—lived some 900 French settlers and four Indian tribes. Along the Saint John River were 1,000 Malecites, like John's mas-

ter, who raised corn, beans and pumpkins. Two thousand migratory Micmacs, hunters and paddlers of great stamina, ranged from the Gaspé Peninsula down eastern New Brunswick into Nova Scotia. In Maine were
the Penobscots, and around Passamaquoddy Bay the Passamaquoddys.

At Meductic John found a slave his own age, curly-headed Jack Evans.
They were able to adapt to their predicament better than the adult prisoners, but escape was never far from their minds. It was what all the captives
had to live for—escape, or liberation by English forces. They talked it,
dreamed it, ate it, drank it, and it buoyed their spirits. Even one as young
as John could hope, as he watched his master pack food for a trip, that
this would somehow lead to freedom.

"Am I going too?" he asked. The big Malecite pointed to a heavy
packsack, and John willingly wrestled it up on his back.

They paddled up the Saint John—a party of 10—until fall gave way
to winter and travel was hampered by ice. Then they laid up their canoes
in bushes near Chikunikabit (the place that destroys), as the Indians
called Grand Falls, and set out on foot into the uncharted wilds.

For a boy brought up in the sheltered home of a New England
judge it was unbelievably rigorous. John staggered under back-breaking
loads. He had to discipline his body to go without food for days.

But the Indians did not abuse him, and they underwent the same
privations he did. They tried to encourage him by muttering in broken
English: "By-and-by many moose." But he could not converse with them
for he was only beginning to grasp a few Malecite words.

They trekked through forests and over icy clearings; they built
rough rafts to ford open rivers. As they moved deeper into the unknown
John marvelled at the risks the Indians took as a matter of course. He
estimated they must be 60 miles from the nearest settlement—10 persons
with but two guns, on which they wholly depended for food.

Sometimes the hunters shot a bear and once they had the great
luck to get a bear and four cubs, all very fat. Then the party feasted. When
food was eaten, they fasted until the next success. They sometimes preserved meat by smoking it, but large game was rarely so plentiful they
could plan for tomorrow.

The hunters were not always considerate of John. On one occasion
he and a young Indian were sent to fetch a big moose which had been
killed some miles from camp. The pair set forth on a cold morning; the
skies were promising, but dull slate clouds gathered as the day advanced.

It was late in the evening when they found the moose. Soon there was a swirling blizzard.

"We made a small fire with what rubbish we could find around us," John recorded later. "The fire, with the warmth of our bodies, melted the snow upon us as fast as it fell and so our clothes were filled with water.

"Early in the morning we took our loads of moose flesh and set out. We had not gone far before my moose-skin coat (which was the only garment I had on my back, and the hair chiefly worn off it) was frozen stiff around my knees like a hoop. My snowshoes and snow-clouts [moccasins] were frozen to my feet. At first I was in great pain, but then my flesh became numb. My Indian companion, being better clothed, left me behind. At times I felt extremely sick, and after long travelling was very drowsy and had thoughts of sitting down—which had I done, without doubt I would have fallen on my last sleep. But my spirits revived as much as if I had received the richest cordial, and thus I marched the whole day without fire or food.

"Some hours after sunset I reached the wigwam and crawled in with my snowshoes on. The Indians cried out, 'The captive is frozen to death!' They took off my pack, and the place where it lay against my back was the only one that was not frozen. They cut off my snowshoes and stripped the clouts from my feet, which were as void of feeling as any flesh could be.

"I had not sat long by the fire before the blood began to circulate, and my feet to my ankles turned black and swelled with bloody blisters and were inexpressibly painful. The Indians said one to another, 'The feet of Chon will rot and he will die.' Yet I slept well at night. Soon after, the skin came off my ankles whole, like a shoe, leaving my toes naked with a nail and the ends of my great toe bones bare, which in a little time turned black so that I was obliged to cut the first joint off [under the nail] with my knife.

"The Indians gave me rags to bind up my feet and advised me to apply fir balsam, but withal added that they believed it was not worth while for I should certainly die. But by the use of my elbows and a stick in each hand, I shoved myself sitting from one tree to another till I got some balsam. This I burned in a clam shell till it was of a consistence like salve, which I applied to my feet and ankles, and by the divine blessing within a week I could go about on my heels with my staff.

"We had provisions enough so that we did not have to remove

under 10 or 15 days. Then the Indians made two little hoops in the form of snowshoes and sewed them to my feet. I was able to follow their tracks on my heels, although sometimes up to my knees in snow and water which gave me the most acute pain. But I must walk or die.

"Within a year my feet were entirely well, and the nails came on my great toes so that a very critical eye could scarcely perceive any part missing or that they had been frozen at all."

Even when moose were rarely seen, Nature sometimes provided bounteous other fare. With long spears the Indians at Meductic harvested the bass that thronged the rivers in the spring, and harpooned huge, lazy sturgeon. The younger slaves often competed to get the biggest catch of smelt, gaspereau or eels from their traps: with the resilience of youth they made their own fun.

There were strange bird calls to listen to and animal tracks to follow. For hours on end, when they were supposed to be scouring the forest for medicinal roots and herbs, John and Jack Evans would crouch motionless in the riverbank shrubbery watching a family of beavers build a dam.

One sun-drenched summer afternoon Indian youngsters were revelling in a pool below the 15-foot falls on the Meductic River where the Indians speared salmon. A Puritan boy couldn't help but notice how proper the youths were. "Although both male and female go into the water together, they have each of them such covering on that not the least indecency can be observed."

"Come in, Chon," ordered Sa-pa-tis, a heavyset young brave.

"I cannot swim," the boy explained fearfully.

"Dive!" demanded the Indian, advancing. "Dive across the deep place—if you meet trouble, we will help you."

John threw himself in awkwardly, flailing his arms and legs, and choking as he sank. He felt his knees scrape the pebbly bottom, and blindly he moved straight into the deep place.

Suddenly he felt himself pulled upward; strong arms held his chin above water as he spluttered, his eyes still tight closed. He started to gasp thanks to Sa-pa-tis but the strong arms, he was embarrassed to discover, belonged to a girl named Kat-lin. Sa-pa-tis and his friends were farther along the beach, guffawing.

After that John noticed that Sa-pa-tis bore him a grudge, almost as if the Indian were provoked at him for not having drowned. One day at the village when John was cutting wood, a shadow fell and he glanced up to see Sa-pa-tis. Without warning the Indian threw John backward, straddled his chest and pulled out a knife.

"I am going to kill you," he hissed, "for I have never yet killed one of the English." He slashed John several times across the chest.

John yelled and seized Sa-pa-tis by the hair, wrenching mightily and tumbling him off. The boy flew at his assailant, lashing him with furious fists and driving a knee hard into the Indian's fat stomach.

"Enough! Enough!" cried Sa-pa-tis.

Breathing hard, John straightened up—but seeing the blood flowing down his chest he went berserk and battered the Indian back to the ground. "Get up!" he ordered. "Don't lie there like a dog!"

The Indian, his face in the mud, could only shake his head.

Now John feared there would be trouble. At best he would be tortured, at worst burned at the stake. He might as well get it over with quickly. Seeing his master and some other Indians returning from a hunt, the boy hurried to them and admitted everything.

"You did well!" said O-ski-tchin. He looked almost proud.

"Sa-pa-tis is a bad Indian," agreed another. "He is a puffed-up dog who wants to be a wolverine."

"Come in the wigwam, Chon," said O-ski-tchin, taking his arm. "We will put red ochre on your wounds to stop the blood."

Of Sa-pa-tis, John recorded in his journal: "I do not remember that ever he offered me the least abuse afterward, though he was big enough to have dispatched two of me."

One spring day O-ski-tchin and his squaw paddled upriver on a journey. As it was the proverbial time to seed corn—"when the maple leaf is as big as a squirrel's foot"—O-ski-tchin had sent John down to Meductic's planting land where the Indians grew their corn, beans and pumpkins.

No sooner had the boy stepped from his canoe than four Indians grabbed him and dragged him to a great wigwam where strange Indians were dancing around a white captive named James Alexander.

The boy was stunned. What was happening? He had never seen the cavorting Indians before but he knew from their appearance they must be Micmacs.

The strangers were working themselves to a frenzy. A Malecite standing near John explained: "They are two families from Cape Sable who have lost some friends to English fishermen. They have travelled hundreds of miles to revenge themselves on our white captives!" He said it as if John would readily comprehend—and perhaps even comment on what a remarkable journey they had undertaken for such an understandable purpose.

John described what followed: "They tossed me about till I was almost breathless and repeated their barbarities on my fellow captive. Then three Indians seized me by the hair, and, bending me down, one beat me on the back and shoulders so long that my breath was almost beat out of my body. Then others put a tomahawk into my hands and ordered me to sing and dance Indian, which I performed with the greatest reluctance."

The strangers were not through yet. They converged again "like bears bereaved of their whelps," one shouting: "Shall we, who have lost relations by the English, suffer an English voice to be heard among us?"

They beat him again, this time with an axe.

John wrote: "Not one of them showed the least compassion. I saw tears run down the cheeks of a Frenchman who sat behind, but it did not relieve the tortures that poor James and I were forced to endure, the most severe I met with in the years I was a captive."

Finally the two prisoners were yanked to their feet and thrown headlong outside. Bruised, swollen, bleeding, they dragged their bodies along, spurred by the fear that if they did not disappear they might be hauled back. It was days before either could walk without his legs buckling.

It might be supposed that after such abuse the captives would be broken in spirit. Yet John and James Alexander were soon to get their own back and dupe the whole Meductic community.

Nobody could live long among the Malecites without learning of their dread of the Mohawks—vicious fighters whom the Malecites insisted were also cannibals. One day, when many Indians had gathered at Meductic, John and James were kept busy fetching water from a cold spring about three quarters of a mile away. On into the night, lugging big iron kettles, they had to cross a large cornfield, descend to a valley then climb a hill. The hill seemed to get higher and higher, until James had an inspiration.

The next night when he went for water he carefully set his kettle on the descent to the valley, then ran back to the village "puffing and blowing as though in the utmost surprise."

"I have seen Mohawks near the spring!" he shouted. He could not have precipitated greater alarm if he had touched off a cannon. But James' master was a courageous warrior. "Show me," he demanded.

When they crept to the edge of the valley James pointed to distant silhouettes of tree stumps in the semidarkness and at the same moment nudged the poised kettle with his toe.

"I saw them move," he whispered.

At first the kettle rolled silently over moss but soon it sounded properly menacing, its handle clattering at every turn. Without a word the Indian wheeled and ran, James after him. At the village they found the Indians jumping into their canoes and paddling away.

Wrote John later: "They did not return under 15 days. I never heard that the Indians understood the occasion of their fright, but James and I had many a private laugh about it."

When John was first brought to Meductic he had imagined the Indians to be little more than savages—vain, treacherous, lazy, immoral, completely unskilled and untutored. But he discovered they possessed many virtues. They were loyal to one another. They followed a strict moral code in relations between the sexes, and they obeyed tribal laws. They loved light-hearted jokes, stories and singing. They respected the animals of the wild. They were kind to their children and made them behave with exemplary courtesy toward their elders. And, after their fashion, they were able primitive doctors.

During a gale on one hunting expedition an old spruce came crashing down on a hunter's right leg. He lay prostrate, pounding his fists on the ground in agony. After eight Indians lifted the tree off, O-ski-tchin went to work as deliberately as a surgeon in Pemaquid.

Using sphagnum moss as a swab, he cleaned the wound of blood, then dried it with soft maple leaves. He drew the ruptured skin together, sealed it with fir balsam, and for a dressing dusted on cedar bark ash. A splint was fashioned from heavy white pine bark. O-ski-tchin clamped it tightly around the limb, tying it with rope which was made from roots and fibres.

"The sap will help heal the wound and the bone," he reassured the victim.

But the man tossed and turned that night, getting no sleep. In the morning O-ski-tchin found some bloodroot, steeped the root, and made a tea which he forced down the patient's throat. Soon the Indian snored peacefully. The following day he was hauled back to the village on a sled of evergreen boughs—and when John next saw him, weeks afterward, he was walking around as if nothing had happened.

49

One winter John and his slave-friend Jack Evans were on separate hunting trips. Jack had taken a little pet white dog. In the spring John's party returned first and he waited days, then weeks, for the other group. When at last it came in view John was one of the first standing on the riverbank. But there was no sign of Jack. John ran to an Indian he knew.

"What is delaying Jack?"

The Indian was silent for a moment. Then he explained. One day Jack had been carrying a heavy burden on his back. He was weak from hunger, as they all were. A gale was blowing. Descending an icy hill, Jack broke through, cutting his knee badly. He tried to keep going, urging his dog to catch up. But the cold north wind bludgeoned him. Sleet was falling. His legs were plunging ever more slowly into the snow.

"Wait for me!" he called to the Indians. *"Un-ko-wuts!"* (I am cold!)

But, sore beset themselves, they plodded on without heeding his pleas. The last anyone remembered of Jack he was sitting on an ice ledge, legs immersed in water, holding out his arms to them.

Some Indians walked back the next morning. They found Jack still on the ledge, encased in ice, looking sightlessly ahead. In his arms was his little dog, also frozen dead.

One day, nearly six years after his capture, John was approached by a troubled O-ski-tchin. "I have tidings for you," he announced. "We will go hunting tomorrow and we will talk."

Next morning they paddled many miles upstream and squatted on the shore to eat before following some bear tracks. As O-ski-tchin stirred the fire he said abruptly: "You had a brother, Chon. He was seized with you at Pemaquid."

"Yes—James! Have you word of him?"

"He is dead," the Indian told him matter-of-factly. He had heard it from a Penobscot just two days before. James Gyles and another English youth had escaped after three years' captivity. They were overtaken by the Indians at New Harbour (only two miles from home, John thought sadly) and brought back.

"And they slew my brother?"

O-ski-tchin spared him nothing. The Penobscots had tortured the pair with fire; then their noses and ears were cut off, and they were made to eat them. After that they were burned to death at the stake.

John Gyles was too numbed by grief and horror to observe that O-ski-tchin had more to say—something, to him, even more important.

"Chon, I have sold you to Husa. I am going to move with my squaw to Canada [present-day Quebec] and you are better to live here than in such a far-off land."

For a fleeting moment John thought that O-ski-tchin was being considerate—wanting him to stay in Acadia where he might be rescued or traded to his own people. But grief for his brother, and despair and resentment, washed the thought away. He had never before hated O-ski-tchin so much, not even that fateful day at Pemaquid.

Next morning he gathered his meagre belongings. With a perfunctory good-bye to O-ski-tchin and his squaw, but no thanks for their good treatment of him, he strode to Husa's wigwam.

Husa was a sickly Indian. He needed a slave as well as a squaw to look after meals and fires, and to collect medicinal herbs and roots. But by now John was hardened to work. He was almost 15, strong and slim, and his only regret was that he had no opportunity to hunt or fish with his new master, and only rarely to paddle a canoe.

Not long after, however, Husa died. John now became the centre of a heated controversy. Was he the property of the widow or did his ownership revert to his first master? O-ski-tchin had unexpectedly returned and he pressed his claim. Husa's widow argued back. When the claimants chanced to meet one day the dispute boiled over. Spectators crowded in on them, muttering, spoiling for trouble. "The slave is causing enmity between you!" said one brave. "Get rid of him and you will fight no more."

"Kill him!" shouted another, drawing his knife.

At that moment Father Simon Girard, the Récollet missionary at Meductic, came running up, his brown robes flapping about his bare legs. "Hear me!" cried the good man, thrusting his way between the contestants. "You are about to commit a heinous crime. This boy has harmed no one."

The throng paused. Father Simon groped for inspiration. "Why not," he asked, "sell the slave to the French? Then you can divide the money and neither of you will have trouble!"

The widow promptly agreed. O-ski-tchin nodded assent. The crowd quieted. Everyone was satisfied—except John, who could hardly believe his ears. To be sold to the French, to the alien race his mother had warned against, who could ruin him not only in body but also in soul! He stood paralysed, incredulous.

O-ski-tchin placed a hand on his arm. "It is better for you, Chon.

51

You will be with white people. Some day . . ." The boy could not bring himself to reply. After a moment O-ski-tchin dropped his hand and went away.

Soon word came up the river that a French man-of-war was at Mena-goueche (present-day Saint John). This event was greeted with jubilation by Indians for hundreds of miles around. In addition to provisions for the Acadian settlers, such ships always brought gifts and trading goods—guns, blankets, kettles and gaudy trinkets.

Father Simon, John, O-ski-tchin and 40 Indians hurriedly pushed off in canoes. The boy marvelled at the broadening vistas of the great river as he skimmed seaward. And then, after climbing a hilly portage past the seething, roiling rapids known now as the Reversing Falls, the party descended to the harbor of Menagoueche.

As his canoe finally nudged the warship's hull, John felt dwarfed. Officers in colorful uniforms looked over the rail as a heavy rope ladder plummeted down. The priest and the Indians went to the great cabin, from which John heard muffled French voices. Then came the moment John dreaded: he was called in to be put on display. He wrote later: "I, who was dressed in an old, greasy blanket, without cap, hat or shirt, was invited into the great cabin where many well-rigged gentlemen were sitting. I endeavored to hide myself behind the hangings for I was much ashamed, thinking how I had once worn clothes and lived with people who could rig as well as the best of them."

When the interest of the assemblage turned to other things, O-ski-tchin said in a quiet aside: "Tell me, Chon, do you choose to be sold to the people of the man-of-war, or to the inhabitants of the country?"

John preferred to be sold to a settler, certain that if he ended up on the warship he would never be able to return home. After a few days they started upriver again. They stopped briefly at a French estate at Jem-seg, where a small river from what is now called Grand Lake joins the Saint John. The estate's well-attired seigneur, Louis Damours, addressed John pleasantly in Malecite—for the man knew no English and the boy very little French—then beckoned him into the kitchen of the home. There stood Madame Marguerite Damours, tall, pretty and slender. John could hear small children in another room. The woman looked at him and then, smiling, invited him in Malecite to eat.

Silently John walked to the table. At her urging he sat down, but he had neither the appetite nor the inclination to eat the plateful of fish and corn. Then, noticing O-ski-tchin waiting outside, he hurried to him.

That night John learned he had been sold to Damours. Father Simon took the boy to one side. "I bid you not to grieve, John," he said. "This gentleman will not ill-treat you. He is of good humor, and he formerly bought two captives, both of whom he later sent to Boston."

John was silent.

"I shall pass this way again in about 10 days," added Father Simon, "and if you do not like to live with the French better than with the Indians, I will buy you back again." The following day Father Simon and O-ski-tchin headed upstream toward Meductic and John settled into his new home at Jemseg.

Next morning Madame Damours seemed delighted to greet him. "Good day, Little English," she said smiling.

"I am glad that you would wish to buy me," John replied. "I do not deserve your favor. But I shall be a good worker, as I was for the Malecites."

"Ah!" She clapped her hands, turning to her husband. "He speaks! He speaks! And in such a gentlemanly manner for a savage! Now stand still, Little English, for I am going to make you some civilized clothes."

Within a week Madame's deft fingers had fashioned him the beginnings of a new wardrobe including a coat, a homespun shirt and a tuque. Often on a Sunday he glanced sideways as he passed the mirror—not out of vanity, which his religion forbade, but out of wonder after years of near-nakedness. With his tanned face, so like those of the dark-complexioned French youths, visitors assumed he was Acadian—and were puzzled when he could not understand them.

After two months, his tuque tight under his arm, John sought Madame Damours at the door of her sewing room. He felt ill at ease. "I would beg a favor," he started.

Madame regarded him quizzically. "If it is within my power to grant, Little English . . . ."

"I would ask," he said seriously, "that you and Monsieur cease to address me in Malecite. In order to work in my master's trading post I must speak your language, but I have acquired little more than 'oui' and 'non.'"

Madame seemed pleased. "Granted. And I am sure that as a young gentleman of New England you would not wish to receive value for nothing. So you shall teach us some of your English in return. Agreed?"

The Damours took John at his word. He was sometimes privileged to dine with them—and if he wanted the bread, butter or salt passed, he had to ask in French. As he was a healthy, hungry boy, he learned fast.

John had a facility with languages. One day he and his master were stacking casks of wine in the log trading post when they noticed two Indians outside, arguing animatedly over beaver skins.

"They are strange Indians from another territory, which is why their talk is gibberish," explained Damours.

The boy listened a moment. "They have agreed not to take fewer than four knives for their pelts," he said, "and as many more as they can get. One has told the other to keep the poorest pelt on the bottom."

"How could you possibly know this?"

"They are Micmacs and I met many of them at Meductic, sometimes to my pain. I am fluent in their tongue."

The Indians were plainly puzzled when, after they demanded eight knives, the proprietor insisted on four, and when he flipped over the top three pelts and shook his head over the last one. They took the four knives.

John wrote later: "My French master had a great trade with the Indians, which suited me very well. I had not lived long with this gentleman before he committed to me the keys of his store etc., and my whole employment was trading and hunting, in which I acted faithfully for my master and never knowingly wronged him to the value of one farthing."

Now nearly 17, John found life at Jemseg gracious compared with that at Meductic. But he was quick to sense vague undercurrents which disquieted Monsieur and his wife.

John learned that Damours and Joseph Robinau de Villebon, the headstrong governor of Acadia, were old enemies. Villebon's policy toward New England was one of violent harassment. Since John's capture the fort at Pemaquid had been rebuilt and now Villebon was planning to destroy it. He had gathered a mighty force of French and Indians at Nashwaak, his headquarters opposite present-day Fredericton, and was keeping the Indians in a ferment of hatred toward the English.

Damours, distrustful of the governor for personal reasons, sceptical about an attack and worried about the retaliation it might bring on his own estate, went with John to the fort at Nashwaak. There they saw Villebon put on an astonishing performance.

As the braves' emotions were stirred by exhortations from their chiefs, Villebon thrust his way among them, cleared a space, tossed a hatchet into the air and expertly caught it. Then, shivering, shaking, chanting and howling like a wolf, he began an erratic but rhythmic war dance. Whoops and screams of approval greeted the transmutation of the governor into a bloodthirsty warrior. A twisting, snaking line of braves formed behind him. The din was so loud that John thought his eardrums would burst.

But the wild scene depressed him, and the subsequent meeting between Villebon and Damours baffled him, unused as he was to European etiquette which decreed that enemies should exchange pleasantries in public. The two men talked far into the night, and Damours came away convinced that an attack was feasible.

Back at Jemseg, Damours stayed only long enough to prepare for his role in the assault. Gyles was left behind with Madame, and although they both tried to keep occupied with language lessons, the wait was a long one.

One day shouts and whoops were heard and Damours burst in with news of a French triumph. Pemaquid had fallen and the English had been humiliated.

But the elation was short-lived. An English counter-blow had to be expected, and tension rose along the Saint John as Villebon prepared for it. Damours, meanwhile, was packing his baggage for the long trip to France where he was to defend himself at Versailles against accusations made by the governor. He showed no apprehension as he cheerily bade his wife good-bye, and he promised to bring her presents in the latest Paris modes. John was entrusted with the care of Jemseg, and it did not occur to Damours to doubt his loyalty.

The news came straggling through the wilderness less than a fortnight later: "Little English!" Madame came running to the dairy where John was churning butter. "The English are upon us—they have burned our villages at Chignecto!" At the head of the force sailing up the river, Madame said shakily, had been a portly, commanding figure—none other than Maj. Benjamin Church, the legendary bane of the Indians, now the scourge of New France.

But John was thrilled. The fantastic boldness of it! The English were daring the reversing falls, the long winding river and its uncharted shoals, and the hazards of an early winter snowstorm or an Indian ambush.

Suddenly, unbelievably, the distraught Madame Damours found

herself thrown on the mercy of her English slave. If he would help save her home and family, she pleaded, he would be free to go to Boston at the first opportunity.

English ships were only hours away—freedom was within John's grasp. Unhesitatingly he gave his answer: "Madame, it is contrary to the nature of the English to requite evil for good. I shall endeavor to serve you and your interest. I shall not run to the English; but if I am taken by them shall willingly go with them and yet endeavor not to disserve you either in your person or goods."

John printed a message in English for her, and nailed it to the front door: "I entreat the General of the English not to burn my house or barn, nor destroy my cattle. I don't suppose that such an army comes up this river to destroy a few inhabitants, but for the fort above us. I have shown kindness to the English captives as we were capacitated and have bought two captives of the Indians and sent them to Boston. The one now with us shall go also when a convenient opportunity presents and he desires it." Then John, the family and the farm hands took refuge on the far shore of Grand Lake.

The New Englanders moved on to Nashwaak, and when the siege began the dull roar of the guns reverberated to the fugitives huddled in a makeshift shelter. The fort proved impregnable. The English were forced to withdraw, but defiantly they took their time, burning farms as they went.

John and Madame waited for the furor to die. Then: "Hearing no report of the great guns for several days," he related, "I with two others went down to our house to make discovery." The estate was untouched.

Officers came from the governor's headquarters to remark at the seeming miracle and to shake their heads. From Chignecto to Nashwaak French homesteads were in ruins—all but this one, apparently succored by a scrap of paper.

On his return in the spring Damours thanked John profusely and assured him he would fulfil Madame's promise. Soon after he called John with news that an English sloop was due at the mouth of the river with ransom for another prisoner. "You are free to go on this vessel," the Frenchman said, "or, if you choose to stay, I will gladly take you for my own son. Madame and I are extremely desirous that you stay."

"I thank you earnestly," John replied, "but I choose to go to Boston, hoping to find some of my relations yet alive."

Neither spoke much on the trip down to Menagoueche. John's heart leaped as he saw the English flag in the harbor. Damours escorted him aboard, shook hands, and bade him good-bye and good fortune.

The morning after the sloop sailed into Boston, John was still eating breakfast when a crewman announced the arrival of a message-bearer. The big, well-dressed young fellow was waiting on deck.

"You are John Gyles, the former Indian captive?"

"I am—and I hope you bring me news of my family, for I have not seen them for so long I would not know any but my mother."

"She is dead," said the messenger quietly. "She did not live many years after the savages released her, though she was unharmed."

"And my two sisters with her?"

"They were also freed; they are alive and well."

"But my brothers! James was slain. But was Thomas also? And the smallest boy?"

"Thomas is at his home on shore, and his wife is making ready a great banquet to welcome you back."

"But wait—the little fellow, Tad; is he . . . ?"

The messenger grinned. "I did not know how to tell you before—but I am 'the little fellow,' John."

And so, at a festive dinner, surrounded by merry family members, John was initiated back into the life of a New England colonist.

The years of slavery were not in vain. John bore no grudge against any race, and his knowledge of French and Indian languages and customs served him well as an interpreter, trader and soldier. In 1719 he and O-ski-tchin had a joyful reunion in Fort George, at present-day Brunswick, Me., which John commanded. As the British soldier walked his former master to the gate a sentry sprang to attention, saluted and opened the door.

O-ski-tchin smiled. "I always wanted to bring up a warrior," he said.

"*A-ti-u, un-sa-kum-um,*" John replied. Good-bye, my chief.

And the Indian was gone in the night.

Years later John penned in his journal: "On the 2nd of August, 1689, I was taken, and on the 19th of June, 1698, I arrived at Boston, so that I was absent eight years, 10 months and 17 days. In all which time, though I underwent extreme difficulties, yet I saw much of God's goodness."

Escape From Michilimackinac

June 1763. Outside the big British fort at Michilimackinac, on the strait between Lake Huron and Lake Michigan, were hundreds of apparently peaceful Indians. But they were restless—loyal to the recently defeated French and resentful of rigid English trading rules. Inside, supposedly guarding nearly 300 French-Canadian inhabitants, were about 35 soldiers of the 60th Royal American Regiment.

Also inside was Alexander Henry, a 23-year-old Montreal fur trader who later wrote this classic account of his experiences when the general Indian uprising known as Pontiac's Conspiracy engulfed Fort Michilimackinac.

By ALEXANDER HENRY

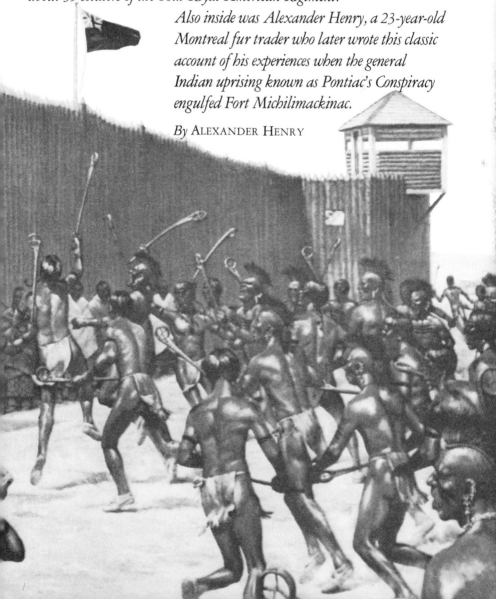

THE MORNING OF June 2 was sultry. A Chippewa came to tell me that his nation was going to play at *baggatiway* [lacrosse] with the Sauks, another Indian nation, for a high wager. He invited me to witness the sport, adding that the commandant [Capt. George Etherington] was to be there and would bet on the side of the Chippewas. In consequence of this information I went to the commandant and expostulated with him a little, representing that the Indians might have some sinister end in view, but the commandant only smiled at my suspicions.

I did not go to see the match, which was to be played without the fort, because, there being a canoe prepared to depart on the following day for Montreal, I employed myself in writing letters to my friends. Even when a fellow trader, a Mr. Tracy, happened to call upon me, saying that another canoe had just arrived from Detroit and proposing that I should go with him to the beach to inquire the news, I still remained to finish my letters, promising to follow him in a few minutes.

Mr. Tracy had not gone more than 20 paces from my door when I heard an Indian war cry and a noise of general confusion. Going instantly to my window, I saw a crowd of Indians within the fort, furiously cutting down and scalping every Englishman they found.

The game of *baggatiway* is necessarily attended with much violence and noise, and the ball may be struck in any direction. Nothing could be less liable to excite premature alarm than that the ball should be tossed over the pickets of the fort, nor that it should be followed on the instant by all engaged in the game. Nothing could be more happily devised than such a stratagem by which the Indians could obtain possession of the fort. To be still more certain of success they had prevailed upon as many as they could to come voluntarily without the pickets, particularly the commandant and garrison themselves.

I had in the room a fowling piece loaded with swan-shot. This I immediately seized and held for a few minutes, waiting to hear the drum beat to arms. In this dreadful interval I saw several of my countrymen fall, and more than one struggling between the knees of an Indian who, holding him in this manner, scalped him while yet living.

At length, disappointed in the hope of seeing resistance made to the enemy, and sensible that no effort of my own unassisted arm could avail against 400 Indians, I thought only of seeking shelter. Amid the slaughter which was raging I observed many of the [French] Canadian inhabitants calmly looking on, neither opposing the Indians nor suffering injury, and I conceived a hope of finding security in their houses.

Between the yard door of my own house and that of M. Charles Langlade, my neighbor, there was only a low fence, over which I easily climbed. I found the whole family at the windows, gazing at the scene of blood before them. I addressed myself immediately to M. Langlade, begging that he would put me into some place of safety until the heat of the affair should be over. But M. Langlade, who had looked for a moment at me, turned again to the window, shrugging his shoulders and intimating that he could do nothing for me: "*Que voudriez-vous que j'en ferais?*"

This was a moment for despair, but the next, an Indian slave woman of M. Langlade's beckoned to me to follow her. She brought me to a door which she opened, desiring me to enter and telling me that it led to the garret where I must go and conceal myself. I joyfully obeyed and she, having followed me up to the garret door, locked it after me and with great presence of mind took away the key.

This shelter obtained, if shelter I could hope to find it, I was naturally anxious to know what might still be passing without. Through an aperture, for there were no windows, I beheld in shapes the foulest and most terrible, the ferocious triumphs of barbarian conquerors. The dead were scalped and mangled, the dying were writhing and shrieking under the unsatiated knife and tomahawk, and from the bodies of some ripped open, their butchers were drinking the blood, scooped up in the hollow of joined hands, amid shouts of rage and victory. I was shaken, not only with horror but with fear. The sufferings which I witnessed I seemed on the point of experiencing. No long time elapsed before there was a general cry of "All is finished!" At the same instant I heard some Indians enter the house in which I was.

The garret was separated from the room below by a layer of single boards. I could therefore hear everything that passed; and the Indians were no sooner in than they inquired whether any Englishman were in the house. M. Langlade replied that he did not know of any, an answer in which he did not exceed the truth, for the slave woman had kept my secret and her own. M. Langlade was therefore, I presume, as far from a wish to destroy me as he was careless about saving me. He added that the Indians might examine for themselves, and he brought them to the garret door.

Some delay was occasioned by the absence of the key, and a few moments were thus allowed me in which to look for a hiding place. In one corner was a heap of birch-bark vessels used in maple sugar making.

The door was unlocked and opening before I had completely crept into a small opening at one end of the heap. Four Indians entered, all armed with tomahawks and besmeared with blood upon every part of their bodies.

The die appeared to be cast. I could scarcely breathe, but I thought that the throbbing of my heart occasioned a noise loud enough to betray me. The Indians walked in every direction about the garret, and one of them approached me so closely that had he put out his hand he must have touched me. Still I remained undiscovered, a circumstance to which the dark color of my clothes and the corner in which I was must have contributed. After taking several turns in the room, during which they told M. Langlade how many they had killed and how many scalps they had taken, they returned downstairs and I heard the door locked for the second time.

There was a feather bed on the floor, and on this, exhausted as I was by the agitation of my mind, I threw myself down and fell asleep. In this state I remained till the evening, when I was awakened by a second opening of the door. A shower of rain having begun to fall, M. Langlade's wife had come to stop a hole in the roof. She was much surprised at finding me but advised me not to be uneasy, observing that she hoped I might escape. On her going away I begged her to send me a little water to drink, which she did.

I continued to lie on the bed, ruminating on my condition but unable to discover a resource from which I could hope for life. A flight to Detroit had no probable chance of success. The distance from Michili-mackinac was 400 miles, I was without provisions, and the whole length of the road lay through Indian countries where the first man whom I should meet would kill me. To stay where I was threatened nearly the same issue. As before, fatigue of mind and not tranquillity suspended my cares and procured me further sleep.

At sunrise I was again on the rack of apprehension. I heard the family stirring, and presently after, Indian voices informing M. Langlade that they had not found my hapless self among the dead and that they supposed me to be somewhere concealed.

M. Langlade appeared by this time acquainted with the place of my retreat, of which no doubt he had been informed by his wife. The poor woman, as soon as the Indians mentioned me, declared to her husband in the French tongue that he should no longer keep me in his house but deliver me up to my pursuers, giving as a reason that should the

Indians discover his instrumentality in my concealment they might revenge it on her children, and it was better that I should die than they. M. Langlade resisted at first this sentence of his wife's, but soon suffered her to prevail, informing the Indians that I had come there without his knowledge and that he would put me into their hands. This was no sooner expressed than he began to ascend the stairs, the Indians following.

I now resigned myself to the fate with which I was menaced, arose from the bed and presented myself full in view to the Indians. They were all in a state of intoxication and entirely naked except about the middle. One of them named Wenniway, whom I had previously known and who was upward of six feet in height, had his entire face and body covered with charcoal and grease except for white spots, of two inches in diameter, encircling his eyes. This man seized me by the collar with one hand, while in the other he held a large carving knife as if to plunge it into my breast. His eyes, meanwhile, were fixed steadfastly on mine. After some seconds of the most anxious suspense he dropped his arm, saying, "I won't kill you!" To this he added that he had been frequently engaged in wars against the English and had brought away many scalps, that on a certain occasion he had lost a brother whose name was Musinigon, and that I should be called after him.

A reprieve, upon any terms, placed me among the living, but Wenniway ordered me downstairs and there informed me that I was to be taken to his cabin. There, and indeed everywhere else, the Indians were all mad with liquor; death was again threatened, and not as possible but as certain. I mentioned my fears to M. Langlade, begging him to represent the danger to my master. M. Langlade, in this instance, did not withhold his compassion, and Wenniway immediately consented that I should remain where I was until he found another opportunity to take me away.

Thus far secure, I reascended my garret stairs in order to place myself the farthest possible out of the reach of drunken Indians. But I had not remained there more than an hour when I was called to the room below, in which was an Indian who said I must go with him out of the fort, Wenniway having sent him to fetch me.

This man I had also seen before. In the preceding year I had allowed him to take goods on credit for which he was still in my debt. Some short time previous to the surprise of the fort he had said, upon my upbraiding him with want of honesty, that he would pay me "before long!"

This speech now came fresh into my memory and led me to suspect that the fellow had formed a design against my life. I communicated the suspicion to M. Langlade; but he gave for answer that I was not now my own master, and must do as I was ordered.

The Indian directed that before I left the house I should undress myself, declaring that my coat and shirt would become him better than they did me. His pleasure, in this respect, being complied with, no alternative was left me than to go out naked or to put on the clothes of the Indian which he freely gave me in exchange. His motive for thus stripping me, as I afterward learned, was that my apparel might not be stained with blood when he should kill me.

I was now told to proceed, and my driver followed me close until I had passed the gate of the fort and turned toward the spot where I knew the Indians to be encamped. This, however, did not suit the purpose of my enemy, who seized me by the arm and drew me violently in the opposite direction to the distance of 50 yards. Here, finding that I was approaching the bushes and sandhills, I determined to proceed no farther, but told the Indian that I believed he meant to murder me and that he might as well strike where I was.

He replied with coolness that my suspicions were just, and that he meant to pay me in this manner for my goods. He produced a knife and held me in a position to receive the intended blow. Both this, and that which followed, were necessarily the affair of a moment: by some effort too sudden to be explained I was enabled to arrest his arm and give him a sudden push, by which I released myself. I ran toward the fort with all the swiftness in my power, the Indian following me, and I expecting every moment to feel his knife.

On entering the fort I saw Wenniway, and to him I hastened for protection. Wenniway desired the Indian to desist but the latter pursued me round him, making several strokes at me with his knife and foaming at the mouth over the repeated failure of his purpose. At length Wenniway drew near to M. Langlade's house, and the door being open I ran into it. The Indian abandoned the pursuit.

Preserved so often and so unexpectedly, I returned to my garret with a strong inclination to believe that through the will of an overruling power no Indian enemy could do me hurt. But new trials were at hand. At 10 o'clock in the evening I was roused from sleep and once more desired to descend the stairs. To my satisfaction and surprise, however, I was summoned only to meet Captain Etherington, Lieut. William Leslie and a trader named Henry Bostwick.

Alexander Henry and other Michilimackinac prisoners are marched into captivity.

These gentlemen had been taken prisoner while looking at the game without the fort, and immediately stripped of their clothes. They were now sent into the fort under the charge of Canadians because the chiefs were apprehensive that they would be murdered by the drunken Indians without. Twenty-one soldiers had been killed, and about 20 Englishmen, including soldiers, were still alive. These were all within the fort, together with the Canadians.

Myself and others proposed to Captain Etherington to make an effort for regaining possession of the fort. The Jesuit missionary was consulted, but he discouraged us by his representations of the merciless treatment we must expect should the Indians regain their superiority and of the little dependence to be placed upon our Canadian auxiliaries. Thus the fort and prisoners remained in the hands of the Indians, although the prisoners and whites were in actual possession the whole night and the Indians were outside the gates.

My fellow prisoners shared my garret, and the greater part of the night was passed in mutual condolence. In the morning, being again called down, I found my master Wenniway and was desired to follow him. He led me to a small house within the fort, where in a narrow and almost dark room I found a trader from Montreal named Ezekiel Solomons, an Englishman newly arrived from Detroit, and a soldier, all prisoners. With these I remained in painful suspense till 10 o'clock in the forenoon, when an Indian marched us to the lakeside. There we found a canoe in which we were to embark.

Our voyage would have commenced immediately but one of the Indians who was to be of the party was absent. This occasioned a very long delay during which we were exposed to a keen northeast wind. An old shirt was all that covered me: I suffered much from the cold, and in this extremity, M. Langlade coming down to the beach, I asked him for a blanket, promising if I lived to pay any price he pleased. But the answer I received was that he could let me have no blanket unless there were someone to be security for the payment. For myself, he observed, I had no longer any property in that country.

I had no more to say to M. Langlade, but seeing another Canadian, John Cuchoise, I addressed to him a similar request and was not refused. But for that blanket I must have perished.

At noon our party was all collected and we steered for the Isles du Castor [45 miles west of Michilimackinac] in Lake Michigan, in the company of seven Indians.

The soldier was made fast to a bar of the canoe by a rope tied round his neck, as is the manner of the Indians in transporting prisoners. The rest were left unconfined, but paddles were put into our hands and we were made to use them.

This was the third day of our distress and the second since I had eaten. Now I was offered bread—but bread with what accompaniment. The Indians had a loaf which they cut with the same knives they had employed in the massacre—knives still covered with blood. The blood they moistened with spittle, and rubbing it on the bread offered this for food, telling their prisoners to eat the blood of their countrymen.

A thick fog came on, on account of which the Indians deemed it safer to keep the shore close under their lee. Every half hour they gave their war whoops, one for every prisoner in the canoe. This is a general custom, by which all other Indians within hearing are apprized of the number of prisoners.

In this manner we travelled 18 miles until we reached Waugoshance, a long point stretching westward into the lake, which the Ottawa [Indians] make a carrying place to avoid going around it. After the war whoops an Ottawa appeared on the beach, making signs that we should land. The Ottawa asked the news and kept the Chippewas in conversation till we were within a few yards of the land and in shallow water. At this moment 100 men rushed from the bushes and dragged all the prisoners out of the canoes amid a terrifying shout.

We now believed that our last sufferings were approaching, but no sooner were we fairly on shore than the chiefs of the party advanced and gave each of us their hands, telling us that they were our friends, whom the Chippewas had insulted by destroying the English without consultation. They added that the Chippewas had been carrying us to the Isles du Castor only to devour us.

It was not long before we were embarked again in the canoes of the Ottawas, who the same evening relanded us at Michilimackinac. They marched us into the fort and took possession of it. The Chippewas were confounded at beholding the Ottawas espouse a side opposite to their own. We, who had changed masters but were still prisoners, were lodged in the house of the commandant and strictly guarded.

Early the next morning a general council was held. The Chippewas complained much of the conduct of the Ottawas in robbing them of their prisoners, alleging that all the Indians, the Ottawas alone excepted, were at war with the English, that Pontiac had taken Detroit, that the King of France had awoke and repossessed himself of Quebec and Montreal, and that the English were meeting destruction in every other part of the world. From all this they inferred that it became the Ottawas to restore the prisoners and to join in the war. The speech was followed by large presents, being part of the plunder of the fort.

The Indians rarely make their answers till the day after they have heard the arguments offered. They did not depart from their custom on this occasion, and the council adjourned.

We, whose fate was thus in controversy, were unacquainted with this transaction and enjoyed a night of tolerable tranquillity. Which of the arguments of the Chippewas were deemed valid by the Ottawas I cannot say, but after the council was resumed in the morning, and after several speeches had been made, the prisoners were returned to the Chippewas.

They marched us to their village below the fort and put us into a lodge, already the prison of 14 soldiers tied two and two, each with a rope about his neck and made fast to a pole.

I was left untied, but passed a sleepless and wretched night. My bed was the bare ground, and I was again reduced to an old shirt, as the blanket which I had received through the generosity of M. Cuchoise had been taken from me among the Ottawas. I was besides in want of food, still having ate nothing.

Such was my situation on the following morning, but a few hours produced an event which gave yet a new color to my lot.

Shortly after my first arrival at Michilimackinac the preceding year, a Chippewa named Wawatam had begun to come often to my house, betraying in his demeanor strong marks of personal regard. On a certain day he brought his whole family and a large present consisting of skins, sugar and dried meat. He informed me that some years before he had observed a fast, devoting himself to solitude and the mortification of his body in the hope of obtaining protection from the Great Spirit. He had dreamed of adopting an Englishman as his son, brother and friend, and had recognized me as the person whom the Great Spirit had been pleased to point out. He hoped I would not refuse his present, and he would forever regard me as one of his family.

Wawatam was about 45 years of age, of an excellent character among his nation, and a chief. I could do no otherwise than accept the present and declare my willingness to have so good a man for my friend and brother. I offered a present in return, which Wawatam accepted.

Two days before the fateful game of *baggatiway* which had precipitated our troubles, Wawatam came again to my house in a state of mind visibly melancholy. He wished me to go to the Sault [Ste. Marie] with him and his family the next morning, and joined an inquiry whether or not the commandant had heard bad news. Finding himself unable to prevail with me he withdrew, but early the next morning he came again, bringing with him his wife and expressing again his apprehension. Unfortunately I turned a deaf ear to everything, leaving Wawatam and his wife to depart alone with dejected countenances and not before they had each let fall some tears.

Now, toward noon, when the great war-chief Minweweh was seated at the opposite end of the lodge, my friend and brother Wawatam suddenly came in. During the days preceding I had often wondered what had become of him. In passing he gave me his hand, but went immediately toward the great chief, by the side of whom he sat down. The most uninterrupted silence prevailed; each smoked his pipe, and this done, Wawatam arose and left the lodge saying to me as he passed, "Take courage!"

An hour elapsed, during which preparations appeared to be made for a council. At length Wawatam re-entered followed by his wife, and both loaded with merchandise which they laid in a heap before the chief. After some moments of silence Wawatam pronounced a speech which, to me, was of extraordinary interest:

"Friends and relations," he began, "what is it that I shall say? You know what I feel. This case is mine. See there," pointing to myself, "my friend and brother among slaves—himself a slave.

"He is my brother, and because I am your relation he is therefore your relation too. And how, being your relation, can he be your slave?

"On the day on which the war began you were fearful lest on this very account I should reveal your secret. You requested that I would leave the fort and even cross the lake. I did so but I did it with reluctance, notwithstanding that you, Minweweh, who had the command in this enterprise, gave me your promise that you would protect my friend.

"The performance of this promise I now claim. I come not with empty hands to ask it, but I bring these goods to buy off every claim which any man among you may have on my brother."

The pipes were again filled, and after they were finished a further period of silence followed. At the end of this Minweweh arose and gave his reply:

"My relation and brother," said he, "what you have spoken is the truth. I promised to take care of your friend, and this promise I performed by desiring my son, at the moment of assault, to seek him out and bring him to my lodge. He went accordingly but could not find him. The day after I sent him to Langlade's, when he was informed that your friend was safe; and had it not been that the Indians were then drinking the rum which had been found in the fort, he would have brought him home according to my orders.

"I am very glad to find that your friend has escaped. We accept your present, and you may take him home with you."

Wawatam thanked the assembled chiefs, and taking me by the hand, led me to his lodge. My entrance appeared to give joy to the whole family; food was immediately prepared for me, and I now ate the first hearty meal which I had made since my capture. I found myself one of the family, and I felt as happy as the situation could allow.

Henry spent the winter with Wawatam and his family in the wilds of present-day Michigan. In the spring he returned with them to Michilimackinac to trade, and was taken to Sault Ste. Marie by friendly French Canadians. He joined Indians travelling to a peace conference at the English stronghold of Fort Niagara and there, at the end of June 1764, he finally found freedom more than a year after his capture.

The Birchbark Brigades

*Paddling, sweating, singing, carrying enormous loads as they trotted over
steamy portages, carousing like madmen at every journey's end,
voyageurs were the blood and muscle of the great transcontinental canoe
system of the late 1700s and early 1800s. Each summer these small, wiry
and incredibly tough French Canadians moved hundreds of tons of
trade goods from Montreal to western Lake Superior. They were back by
autumn, their brigades of fragile birch bark canoes laden with furs
that other voyageurs had taken to Lake Superior from the
remote Northwest. Together these men conquered distance and
climate with a system unmatched anywhere.*

By THE EDITORS

FOR WEEKS BEFORE the spring break-up, agents for the North West Company invaded parishes up and down the St. Lawrence River, from La Prairie to Rivière-du-Loup, seeking voyageurs. The agents were voyageurs themselves—spirited, reckless "old prairie wolves" in picturesque buckskins. They wore moccasins, silk sashes and red caps with the feathers that were the mark of a Northman, one who had passed a winter in the Northwest.

They lounged in taverns, spent money like water, spun yarns of fortune and adventure, flirted with the girls and danced the nights away. Little wonder that a poor country buck who had never been beyond his parish was dazzled. When he timidly expressed a wish to share such a life a contract was produced instantly, along with half the wages in

advance. The recruit passed the next few weeks strutting and boasting at the public house, then one May morning found himself sobering up at the launching spot on Montreal Island above the Lachine Rapids.

The advance wages had melted away and, with a summer of toil ahead, the occasional recruit might beg for release from the contract. But the *bourgeois* (company partners) were not to be softened by tears: a beaver skin was the only thing that could touch their hearts.

A few recruits were too drunk or hung over to appear, and while agents secured substitutes the other men were down by the water making up 90-pound packages of supplies and trade goods. Each *pièce* had two little ears by which a voyageur could lift it easily in the manner of a flour bag. He was expected to carry two, but many a voyageur showed his strength or endurance by carrying three or four. Voyageurs boasted around their campfires that there were even men who had borne eight.

Each 36-foot, 600-pound *canot du maître* (Montreal canoe) was gummed for leaks in its birch bark skin, and eased into the water. Now the trade goods were loaded, along with liquor for each man, kegs of shot, oilskins, tarpaulins, rope, an axe, a cooking pot, spare birch bark, and a big sponge to mop up water. Each canoe held a payload of three tons in addition to the crew of eight or 10 men and their gear. Even such things as pigs and cookstoves were carried to Lake Superior and beyond.

The voyageurs, some weeping but most talking vociferously, bade farewell to parents, wives, lovers, children, relatives, officials. As one writer put it: "All Montreal, it seemed, moved to Lachine on the day when the first canoes set out for the Northwest."

Loaded canoes, their freeboard a scant six inches, circled offshore until the four to eight which made a brigade were assembled. Standing at each stern, steering with a nine-foot paddle, was a *gouvernail.* At the bow stood an *avant,* in charge of the canoe and the key man in shooting rapids. In between were six to eight paddlers. *Commis*—company clerks in training to become *bourgeois*—were wedged in along with any other passengers.

At a signal from the head steersman the canoes were off, each flaunting a flag, the men's voices carrying across the water with the pulse and swing of songs they had inherited from their Gallic forefathers, songs such as "En Roulant Ma Boule" ("A-Rolling My Ball") and "C'est l'Aviron" ("Pull on the Oars") which gave rhythm and drive to their strokes. Lighter canoes carrying the *bourgeois*—all ruffles, lace and gold braid—darted ahead to ensure reaching the trading posts before the goods.

By tradition, the first leg of their journey took them only a few miles, to present-day Sainte-Anne-de-Bellevue on the western tip of Montreal Island. Here in a chapel they paused to pray for aid and protection.

"This Church," wrote Peter Pond, a *bourgeois* and one of the earliest explorers of the Northwest, "is Dedacated to St. Ann who Protects all Voigers. Heare is a small Box with a Hole in the top for ye Reseption of a Little Money for the Hole [holy] father or to say a small Mass for those Who Put a small Sum in the Box. Scars a Voiger but stops hear and Puts in his mite and By that Meanes they Suppose they are Protected. . . ." After a "Sarumony of Crossing them selves and Repeating a Short Prayer" they were ready to depart.

About the same time, 3,000 miles to the west, other brigades of canoes left Fort Chipewyan on Lake Athabasca. They bore furs from the valleys of the Mackenzie, Liard and Peace rivers, thick, far-northern pelts better than any others, prized in Europe for the fashionable beaver hats that made the fur trade viable. From less remote posts, other canoes also headed east. In a race delicately balanced against time and distance and weather, the voyageurs set out for their annual rendezvous at Fort William (now Thunder Bay) on the north shore of Lake Superior. Here the furs would be exchanged for trade goods—knives, pots, pans and the like—with which the Northmen would buy more furs during the following season. The voyageurs, a century before the railway, worked for the ruthlessly efficient, Scots-run, French-manned North West Company, whose transcontinental system of canoe routes became, in the words of one historian, "the backbone of modern Canada." To another author, Hugh MacLennan, it was "an operation in which the supply lines were stretched to a limit which would make any normal hard-headed man of commerce turn pale."

From Montreal, the voyageurs paddled the Ottawa River for 350 miles to its junction with the Mattawa, making 18 portages and encountering roughly the same number of *décharges,* shallow places where the canoes had to be unloaded and towed by the voyageurs—walking on land if possible, otherwise in the water.

They passed falls and rapids bearing names coined by explorers and fur traders in the days of New France, names like La Chaudière (the kettle), Les Allumettes (the matchsticks) and Le Calumet (the peace pipe). At such places they saw simple wooden crosses—memorials to men who had perished in the treacherous swirls and eddies. At each cross or group of crosses the voyageurs pulled off their caps and a man in each canoe uttered a prayer. The river bank at one spot was said to be marked by 30 crosses.

A few miles above Lac des Allumettes, the voyageurs reached the Precambrian Shield and left civilization behind. On long, sandy Pointe au Baptême, near today's Chalk River atomic energy plant, all novices, including clerks, were baptized as Nor'Westers—regular employees of the North West Company—and obliged to treat all the other men with a round of brandy.

On the Ottawa and the 35-mile Mattawa the brigades toiled upstream, using poles as well as paddles against the swift currents. As they approached Lake Nipissing and the French River—whose current would be with them—the voyageurs expressed their joy in a ceremonial throwing away of the poles.

Dashing down wild sections of the French River toward Georgian Bay the men took delight in guiding their frail craft through foaming rapids, counting on lightning thrusts of their silent bowman's nine-foot paddle to save them from the deadly rocks.

So fragile and delicately balanced were the *canots du maître* that it was almost impossible to shift even one's feet. Passengers found this almost unendurable, especially for the first few days. Voyageurs benefited from their small size. If a French Canadian grew much over five feet six inches, wrote Thomas L. McKenney, "it forever excludes him from the privilege of becoming a voyageur. There is no room for the legs of such people, in these canoes. But if he shall stop growing at about five feet four inches, and be gifted with a good voice, and lungs that never tire, he is considered as having been born under a most favorable star."

When rain threatened, these men stripped off upper garments, stowing them where they would remain dry, and paddled exposed to the elements. Passengers sought the protection of oilcloths or tarpaulins.

Though sometimes the going was good and, in relays, the voyageurs paddled all night, they usually stopped about twilight—in spring about nine o'clock. One passenger recalled suggesting two hours earlier than usual that the voyageurs might want to make camp. They had paddled almost 60,000 strokes that day but insisted they were still fresh. When finally they stopped, they had covered 80 miles.

When a brigade halted for the night, fires were lighted, the canoes were unloaded and hauled ashore, the clerk's tent was set up (custom in many a brigade decreed that he must do this without help), and supper was heated and eaten. Although a clerk could indulge in luxuries such as tea, voyageurs ate dried peas or beans until reaching the Lake Huron area; after that, from the Indians, they obtained lyed corn (maize soaked in an alkaline solution to soften it). Peas, beans and corn were cooked with salt pork. Voyageurs who never went beyond Lake Superior–and therefore did not eat the western staple, pemmican–were called *mangeurs de lard* (porkeaters).

The peas and beans had usually been cooked the previous night in a manner "simple but very good," according to one clerk. "The tin kettle, which held eight or 10 gallons, was hung over the fire, nearly full of water, then nine quarts of peas were put in. When they were well bursted two or three pounds of pork, cut into strips, were added. All was allowed to boil or simmer for hours, when the cook added four biscuits, broken up, to the mess. The swelling of the peas and biscuit filled the kettle to the brim, so thick that a stick would stand upright in it." When the meal had been heated, "the men squatted in a circle, the kettle in their midst and each one plying his wooden spoon or ladle from kettle to mouth with almost electric speed. Then the pipes were brought into full smoke."

The voyageurs added whatever they could to their rations. When pinned down by bad weather they sought birds' eggs and honey trees, and tried to catch a fish, a muskrat or a turtle, or to kill a deer or a bear. A beaver tail was an especially dainty morsel, and permission was obtained to eat it even during Lent–apparently on grounds that beaver, like fish, swam.

On the rare occasion when there was flour the cook made a form of bread called *galette*. The flour bag was opened and a small hollow made in the flour, into which a little water was poured. The dough was mixed in the bag, and nothing was added unless the voyageurs were lucky enough to find a nest containing the unhatched eggs of a ruffed grouse, or perhaps a Canada goose. The cook kneaded the mixture into flat cakes which were baked before the fire in a frying pan or cooked in grease.

Pemmican–sun-dried, pounded buffalo meat mixed with fat–was used west of the Lakehead. Pemmican had the double advantage of being compact and nourishing, but one passenger dryly noted that hair, sticks, bark, leaves, stones and sand also entered into its composition.

The voyageurs also liked rubaboo, a classic dish of the Northwest. Some flour was boiled in two and a half quarts of water; then about a

pound of pemmican was cut into pieces, thrown into the kettle and stirred quickly so that the grease of the pemmican would dissolve in the hot flour soup. Men in a hurry poured rubaboo on smooth, hollow rocks where it quickly cooled enough to eat.

When the rest slept, the cook worked alone at the campfire, making meals for the next day. A clerk took to his tent and possibly a mattress of fir boughs. The voyageurs simply pushed a canoe on its side, pulled on a single blanket apiece, and slept on sand or rocks, whatever nature provided. Neither mosquitoes nor rain, heat or cold disturbed them.

They were up before dawn, roused by the guide's shouts of *"Alerte!"*

or *"Lève! Lève, nos gens!"* (Get up! Get up, boys!) Often the voyageurs tried to plague a clerk by dumping his tent on him, using the excuse that the tent poles had to be used in the canoes to balance the cargoes as they were stowed.

The voyageurs left without breakfast and paddled for about 45 minutes before they heard the word *"Allumez!"* It was the signal to stop for five or 10 minutes, to crack jokes, to banter, to dig their pipes from their *ceintures* (sashes) and into their *sacs à feu*, to have a smoke. Then they were off again, singing.

It took three such "pipes" and 15 to 20 miles of travel before they moored their canoes and went ashore for breakfast, a meal like that of the evening before. They had an hour to eat and rest, and they ate in the knowledge that there would be no noon meal unless they had a particularly hard day ahead. If so they were allowed less time for breakfast.

Portages were laborious and difficult. Before the canoe even touched shore, the voyageurs leaped into the water in lithe ritual. While the two ends of the craft were held firm, men grabbed the *pièces* to carry them ashore. Female passengers were almost always carried ashore on voyageurs' backs. To the voyageurs, it was simply a touch of gallantry they felt a woman's due, just as they felt it fitting that when she ate there should be a bouquet of flowers beside her plate.

One traveller described a portage scene: "The goods are unloaded and conveyed across, while the canoe is carried by the stern and bowman [and two others in the case of a *canot du maître*]. As soon as they have reached the end of the portage, it is launched and reloaded without any loss of time. An obstruction of 100 yards does not detain them more than 20 minutes. We had occasion, however, more than once, to regret their speed, which caused them to toss our baggage very unceremoniously, using it as they would packs of furs. . . . The whole care and attention of a voyageur seems to center in his canoe, which he handles with an astonishing degree of dexterity and caution."

Each man was responsible for about six *pièces,* which he normally carried two at a time. In order to shorten carrying periods, long portages were divided by *poses* (put downs) into laps of 500 to 800 yards. The canoe and first load of goods were dropped at the first *pose*—a guard might be stationed in case of an Indian raid—and the men went back for the second load. When the final load was at the first *pose*, everything was carried to the second, and so on to the end of the portage. But the most striking thing of all was how the voyageurs did it. They didn't walk. Sweating, panting, followed by clouds of insects, they trotted—so fast that passengers had to run to keep up. Small wonder that many were afflicted with hernias, or suffered from spastic backs, before they were 40. Small wonder that many died young.

At *décharges,* where it was necessary only to tow the canoes, ropes sometimes broke and canoes plunged down rapids or over falls. In strong currents, one or two men got into the cold northern waters, often up to their waists, and guided the canoe, grasping for footing on unsympathetic rocks. When they reached clear water, they climbed in, soaking wet, and went on.

There were times when men rebelled against all this, and a prison for "refractory voyageurs" was maintained at Fort William. The voyageurs jocularly called it their *pot au beurre* (butter tub). Duncan McGillivray, a trader and explorer, told of a voyageur strike at Rainy Lake in 1794. The men were demanding better wages and working conditions, "yet a timidity was observed in their behaviour which proved very fortunate for their Masters, who took such good advantage of it that before night they prevailed on a few of the most timid to return to their duty, and the rest, being only ashamed to abandon their companions, soon followed the example.... A few of the most resolute were obstinate enough to hold out and were sent down to Montreal in disgrace."

If not often rebellious, voyageurs were still inclined to do things their own way. They paid little attention to company orders forbidding them to shoot certain especially dangerous rapids, despite the certainty that hitting a rock at high speed would smash a canoe.

There was one paradoxical touch to the voyageurs' character. They were not noted for keeping themselves clean en route but if they were approaching a fort the canoes had to stop to allow them to dress up. They put on clean shirts and fancy leggings and belts. The Northmen added the bright feathers which were their sartorial right. Then the canoes went on, as fast as they could go and with the men singing at the top of their lungs.

This they would do, for instance, at Sault Ste. Marie where they got their first major break. The partners needed time to make deals with other traders. There were supplies to take aboard. For the voyageurs it was a chance to occupy themselves in their own way. Eating, drinking, singing and boisterous dancing hardly stopped until the day of departure.

Now came Lake Superior, a great inland sea subject to quick and violent squalls. If the weather was bad, the men might have to wait for days before venturing out. When they did, they made respectful haste, keeping close to the hard, dramatic shoreline whenever possible. At times, however, they had to cross broad stretches and if a storm caught them far from land the voyageurs were hard pressed to keep the canoe's back from breaking, and its sharp nose from going under a wave. When water poured in, the men bailed with the large sponge kept for that purpose.

But the winds of Superior could be gentle too, and then it was a happy time. The voyageurs cast into the water tributes to *"La Vieille,"* the old woman of the wind, some tobacco or a trinket to invite her blessing. *"Souffle, souffle, la vieille,"* they would chorus. (Blow, blow, old woman.) Then they would sit back, asleep or smoking, while makeshift sails of oilcloths or blankets did their work.

Then, at last, they were at palisaded Fort William. Its main building in the centre of the enclosed square boasted a high balcony, a great hall with paintings of the company's main partners, and rooms for the partners. Other buildings served as servants' quarters, storehouses, clerks' lodgings and a powder magazine. Outside the fort an Indian village of little log houses scattered along the Kaministikwia River.

Here, from 1803 on, was the great central warehouse of the North West Company, chosen when the United States began to charge customs duties at Grand Portage, some 50 miles down the lake, on the border of present-day Minnesota.

At Fort William the voyageurs went ashore as dandies raring for celebration and rendezvous, for liquor and Indian women, for fights with the Northmen coming in from the west. At the canteen they were fed and each man was given a keg of rum. Almost all the voyageurs lived outside the fort with the Indians, to whom more liquor was distributed. Then, in the words of a missionary, "the furies of Hell were set loose." Native women were sold to the voyageurs. The drinking lasted for days, and up to a dozen murders might result.

The *bourgeois,* meanwhile, barred the doors to the main building where they lived and held their two-week meeting with the *hivernants* (wintering partners) from the west. Business cares were laid aside at night. There were ruffles, lace and silver-buckled shoes as the partners dined, drank and danced to bagpipes, flutes and violins. The rafters rang till dawn with laughter, applause and Scottish song.

In work hours the trade cargoes from the east were stowed into the small *canots du nord* from the west, the furs from the west into the big canoes from the east. At the end of July it was time for most of the eastern voyageurs to head back to Montreal; from there ships would take the furs to the markets of Europe on the last leg of a transportation system that stretched, in all, over 6,000 miles.

Some easterners elected to become Northmen, to head deeper into the *pays d'en haut,* where the North West Company had driven a great wedge into the domain of the Hudson's Bay Company. Still others went west only as far as Rainy River to get the rich furs of Northmen from the Athabasca country—who could go no farther east if they expected to get back to their wintering grounds before the rivers froze.

Before reaching Rainy River the brigades stopped at the height of land where water flows north to Hudson Bay, east to the Atlantic and south to the Gulf of Mexico. Here every would-be Northman was initiated by sprinkling him with a cedar branch dipped in water. The ceremony ended with a dozen gunshots and a round of brandy from the new members. They took an obligatory vow never to kiss a voyageur's wife without her consent.

Now, while the easterners turned back, the Northmen and would-be Northmen paddled on through the labyrinth of waterways that led west. On the Lake of the Woods canoes were at times lashed together and sails hoisted and they drifted placidly among its many islands. At times, it has been written, hundreds of canoes might be spread out in a great wilderness flotilla, and at night the granite shores would sparkle with the reflections of many fires.

Then on into the swift, wild Winnipeg River with its spectacular rapids and falls, its tortured rock, a river where many voyageurs were drowned in seething cataracts. It had 26 portages and seven of these were visible on one stretch alone. Duncan McGillivray has written of one incident here:

"One of the canoes imprudently advanced too near the Fall to load. After the goods were debarked, the upper end through some negligence was suddenly carried out by the current with the steersman suspended after it, and the foreman attempting to retain his end, which was also carried away. . . . They were hurled down through three successive cascades, the canoe several times overwhelmed with water and threatened every moment with being dashed to pieces on the rocks. After arriving at the dreadful whirlpool it remained a considerable time under water. At length the current drove it to shore, with the men still hanging on. Tho' they at first seemed insensible, after a little assistance they recovered and before night resumed their labours as if nothing had happened."

From this river of heartbreak the brigades entered Lake Winnipeg, 280 miles long and up to 65 wide, which has been called probably the worst lake in Canada for small craft because of its winds and waves. Here they split up to go to various destinations in the network of forts, trading and supply posts the North West Company had built along the rivers of a vast area which extended at its peak to the Pacific Ocean and far into the north.

But before they divided there was another ritual: a race between the haughty Athabasca men and those going to less remote places, whom they treated with great disdain. It was an event much talked about for weeks before and after, and at times, it has been written, as many as 100 canoes participated, each brigade in formation.

Perhaps the most memorable description comes from Duncan McGillivray and concerns a race between a few Athabasca canoes and three of his own:

"The two Bands, instead of camping according to orders, entered the Lake at sunset, the one animated with the expectation of victory, and the other resolved, if possible, not to be vanquished. They pursued the Voyage with unremitting efforts, without any considerable advantage on either side, for 48 hours during which they did not once put ashore.

"On the second night of the contest one of our steersmen being overpowered with sleep fell out of the Stern of his Canoe which being under sail advanced a considerable distance. The poor fellow almost sinking with the weight of his cloathes cried out to two Canoes that happened to pass, within a few yards of him to save his life *pour l'amour de Dieu,* but neither the love of God or of the blessed Virgin, whom he powerfully called to his assistance, had the least influence on his hard-hearted Countrymen. He must have certainly perished if his own Canoe had not returned in time enough to prevent it.

"At length, being entirely overcome with labour and fatigue, they mutually agreed to camp and cross the rest of the Lake together."

The newcomer to all this, the embryo Northman, found himself in another world, a primitive, largely lawless, far-flung world where the two main companies confronted each other almost like contending states, where "winterers" spent months in isolation, manning outposts of the trade, where the Indians enjoyed what one historian calls their "palmy days" because they could play one company off against the other in selling their furs, where a new breed, a new "nation" had gradually emerged from decades of intermarriage between French Canadians and Indian women, a phenomenon going back to the fur trade days of New France. Indeed, it has been said that most of the Northmen were these *Métis.*

Eventually the newcomer was apt to throw in his lot with these half-breed people, to find his own Indian woman. He might work on with the company or with its rival. He might, once his contractual obligations were fulfilled, join in the great hunts for the prairie buffalo which sustained the North West Company and its voyageurs.

The North West Company lasted until 1821 when its name vanished abruptly in an amalgamation with the Hudson's Bay Company. But until then Northmen spread west and north, as the *canots du maître* headed back to Montreal, often overloaded because the *bourgeois* were reluctant to leave any furs behind. The brigades reached Montreal at the end of September about the time that great formations of geese were honking their way south—birds and men alike abandoned the lakes and streams to the first film of ice.

The voyageur's ordeal was over—but he would probably return next year. As one old-timer, long past 70, put it:

"I could carry, paddle, walk and sing with any man I ever saw. I have been 24 years in service; no portage was ever too long for me. Fifty songs could I sing. I have saved the lives of 10 voyageurs, have had 12 wives and six running dogs. I spent all my money in pleasure. Were I young again, I should spend my life the same way."

Susanna Moodie, born into a genteel English family in 1803, was a most reluctant pioneer. In 1832, a year after their marriage, she and her husband settled in Upper Canada, near Cobourg. Two years later they moved to Douro Township, northeast of Peterborough, where Susanna's brother and sister were already carving homesteads from the primeval forest. Reluctant though she was, Mrs. Moodie endured her new life with grace and humor, later describing her experiences in a classic book, ROUGHING IT IN THE BUSH. *These excerpts begin with her description of the 35-mile journey from Cobourg to the backwoods.*

Roughing It in the Bush

By SUSANNA MOODIE

I T WAS A BRIGHT, FROSTY February morning when I bade adieu to the birthplace of my baby Agnes who, nestled beneath my cloak, was sweetly sleeping on my knee, unconscious of the long journey before us into the wilderness. The sun had not yet risen. Our own fine team had been sold the day before and one of our neighbors, a Mr. D——, was to convey us and our household goods to Douro for the sum of $20. During the week he had made several journeys with furniture and stores; all that now remained was for us and the remaining possessions to be conveyed to the woods in two large lumber sleighs, one driven by himself, the other by a younger brother.

It was not without regret that I left our old place. It was a beautiful, picturesque spot and I had learned to love it; indeed, it was much against my wish that it was sold. But all regrets were now useless. Happily unconscious of the life of toil and anxiety that awaited us in those dreadful woods, I tried my best to be cheerful and to regard the future with a hopeful eye.

Our driver took charge of the living cargo, which consisted of my husband Moodie, our maidservant, the two little children and myself—besides a large hamper of poultry, a dog and a cat.

The day was so bright that we suffered no inconvenience from the cold. Little Katie, who was just two, was enchanted with the jingling of the sleigh bells and, nestled among the packages, kept singing or talking to the horses. Trifling as these incidents were, before we had proceeded 10 miles they revived my drooping spirits and I began to feel a lively interest in the scenes we were passing.

The first 20 miles were over hilly and well-cleared country. Deep snow makes all roads alike, and we glided as swiftly and steadily as if they had been the best highways. Anon, the clearings began to diminish and tall woods arose on either side of the path, the deep silence that brooded over their vast solitudes inspiring the mind with a strange awe. Not a breath of wind stirred the leafless branches and it seemed as if Nature was sleeping in her winding sheet upon the bier of death.

"I guess you will find the woods pretty lonesome," said Mr. D——, whose thoughts had been evidently on the same subject. "We were once in the woods, but emigration has stepped ahead of us and made our'n a cleared part of the country. When I was a boy Peterborough was unknown; not a settler had ever passed through the great swamp, and some of them believed it was the end of the world."

"What swamp is that?" asked I.

"Oh, the great Cavan swamp. We are just two miles from it, and I tell you that 10 years ago if pigs or cattle strayed into it they fell prey to the wolves and bears and were seldom recovered. The horses will need a good rest, and ourselves a good dinner, by the time we are through it."

In summer, we were informed, the road through the swamp presents for several miles a bridge of rough and unequal logs, all laid loosely so they jump up and down when pressed by wheels, like the keys of a piano. The snow, however, hid from us all the ugly features of the road and Mr. D——, with his odd stories and Yankeefied expressions, amused the tedium of our progress. He steered us through the swamp in perfect safety and landed us at the door of a little log house which crowned the steep hill on the other side.

It was now two o'clock. We had been on the road since seven and men, women and children were all ready for the good dinner that Mr. D—— had promised us at this splendid house of entertainment.

"Well, Mrs. J——, what have you got for dinner?" said the driver, after seeing to his teams.

"Pritters [potatoes] and pork, sir. Nothing else to be had in the woods. Thank God we have enough of that!"

Mr. D—— shrugged his shoulders and looked at us.

"We've plenty of that same at home. But hunger's good sauce. Come, be spry, widow, and see about it, for I am very hungry."

I inquired for a private room for myself and the children, but there were none. The apartment we occupied was like a cobbler's stall and I was obliged to attend upon the children in public.

"You have much to learn, ma'am, if you are going to the woods," said Mrs. J——.

"To unlearn, you mean," said Mr. D——. "To tell you the truth, Mrs. Moodie, ladies and gentlemen have no business in the woods. Eddication spoils man or woman for that location. So, widow," turning to our hostess, "you are not tired of living alone yet?"

"No, sir; I have no wish for a second husband. I had enough of the first."

I was very hungry, but I felt no appetite for Mrs. J——'s fried pork. It proved salt, hard and unsavory; Mr. D—— pronounced it very bad, and the whiskey still worse. I asked for a cup of tea and a slice of bread, but they were out of both. For this disgusting meal we paid a quarter of a dollar a head. I was glad when we escaped from the rank odor of the fried pork and were once more in the fresh air.

"Well, did you not grudge your money for that bad meat?" said Mr. D——. "But in these parts, the worse the fare the higher the charge."

"I would not have cared," said I, "if I could have got a cup of tea."

We now entered the woods again. It was near sunset and we were rapidly descending a steep hill when one of the traces that held our sleigh suddenly broke. Mr. D—— pulled up to repair the damage, but his brother's team was close behind and came upon us before the brother could stop it. I received so violent a blow from the head of one of the horses that I was stunned and insensible. When I recovered I was in the arms of my husband and Mr. D—— was rubbing my hands and temples with snow.

"There, Mr. Moodie, she's coming to. I thought she was killed. I have seen a man before now killed in the like manner." We resumed our places in the sleigh but all enjoyment of our journey was gone.

When we reached Peterborough, Moodie wished us to remain at the inn all night, as we had still 11 miles to go and that through a forest road, little travelled and very much impeded by fallen trees. But Mr. D—— was anxious to get back to his own home, and he urged us very pathetically to proceed.

The moon arose during our brief stay at the inn, and gleamed upon the straggling frame houses which then formed Peterborough. We crossed the wild, beautiful Otonabee River by a rude bridge and soon found ourselves journeying over the thinly wooded plains beyond the village. Far below, to our right, we heard the rushing river whose waters never receive curb from the iron chain of winter. Even when the rocky banks are coated with ice, and the frost-king suspends from every twig the most fantastic crystals, the black waters rush foaming along, a thick steam rising as from a boiling pot. The shores vibrate and tremble beneath the force of the impetuous flood. We now and then caught the silver gleam of the river tumbling in moonlight splendor, while the hoarse chiding of the wind in the lofty pines gave a fitting response to the melancholy cadence of the waters.

The children had fallen asleep. A deep silence pervaded the party. Night was above with her mysterious stars, and the ancient forest stretched around us. I gazed through tears upon the savage scene, and secretly marvelled, "What brought me here?"

"Providence," was the answer which the soul gave. "Not for your own welfare perhaps, but for the welfare of your children. Look up with confidence to Heaven, and the sun of hope will yet shed a cheering beam through the forbidden depths of this tangled wilderness."

The road became so bad that Mr. D—— was obliged to dismount and lead his horses through the more intricate passages. The animals were weary with their long journey, and the moon had deserted us.

"It will be past midnight before we reach your brother's clearing," (where we expected to spend the night) said Mr. D——. "I wish, Mr. Moodie, we had followed your advice and stayed at Peterborough. How fares it with you, Mrs. Moodie, and the young ones? It is growing very cold."

We were now in the heart of a dark cedar swamp and my mind was haunted with visions of wolves and bears, but beyond the long, wild howl of a wolf, no sound broke the sepulchral silence.

"What a gloomy spot," said I to my husband. "In the old country, superstition would people it with ghosts."

"Ghosts! There are no ghosts in Canada!" said Mr. D——. "The country is too new for ghosts. It is only in old countries like your'n, that are full of sin and wickedness, that people believe in such nonsense. No human habitation has ever been erected in this wood and the red man would not pitch his tent in such a place. Now, ghosts, as I understand the word, are the spirits of bad men made to haunt the spots where their worst deeds were committed. It is more than probable that no person ever ended his days in this forest, so it would be folly to think of seeing his ghost."

This theory of Mr. D——'s had the merit of originality. The belief in ghosts, so prevalent in old countries, must have had its foundation in the consciousness of guilt.

After clearing this low, swampy portion of the wood with much difficulty and the frequent application of the axe to cut away the fallen timber, our ears were assailed by the roar of falling water.

"That is Herriot Falls," said Mr. D——. "We are within two miles of our destination."

Oh, welcome sound! But those two miles appeared more lengthy than the whole journey. Thick clouds that threatened a snowstorm had blotted out the stars, and we now groped our way along the edge of the river in almost total darkness. I felt the chillness of midnight and the fatigue of the long journey with double force, and envied the servant and children, who had been sleeping since Peterborough. We now descended the steep bank and prepared to cross the foaming waters on a miserable, insecure log bridge. "This is an ugly bridge over such a dangerous place," said Mr. D—— as he stood and urged his tired team across. Darkness and death raged below, and one false step of his jaded horses would have plunged us into both. I must confess I drew a freer breath when the bridge was crossed.

We continued along the other bank, but when we were in sight of my brother's clearing a large pine, newly fallen across the narrow path, brought us to a standstill. The mighty trunk was too large to chop with axes, and after laboring half an hour, which seemed an age, the males abandoned the task in despair. To go round was impossible; the roots were concealed in an impenetrable wall of cedar jungle, and the huge branches hung over the precipitous bank of the river.

"We must try to make the horses jump over," said Mr. D——. "We may get an upset but there is no help for it; we must either make the experiment or stay here all night. I am too cold and hungry for that—so here goes."

He urged his horses to leap the log, restraining their ardor for a moment as the sleigh balanced on the top so that a straw would almost have overturned it, and we cleared the obstacle in safety.

He now gave directions to his brother to follow the same plan, but whether the young man had less coolness, or his horses were more difficult to manage, the sleigh overturned with a loud crash. All my household goods and chattels were scattered over the road. Alas, for my crockery and stone china! Scarcely one article remained unbroken.

"Never fret about the china," said Moodie, "thank God the man and the horses are uninjured." I should have felt more thankful had the crocks been spared too for, like most of my sex, I had a tender regard for china and I knew that no fresh supply could be obtained in this part of the world.

Leaving his brother to collect the scattered fragments, Mr. D—— proceeded. We left the road, and wound our way over a steep hill covered with heaps of brush and fallen timber. As we reached the top a light gleamed cheerily from the windows of a log house, and the next moment we were at my brother's door.

I was about to quit the sleigh and seek the warmth of the fire when I was told that I had yet farther to go. My brother's wife was visiting friends, and it had been arranged that we were to stay with my sister and her husband. Their house was only on the next lot, but when a hound sprang up on the sleigh to lick my face and hands, I buried my face on its neck and wept.

My sister and brother-in-law had retired, but they instantly rose to receive the way-worn travellers. I never enjoyed more heartily a warm welcome after a long day of intense fatigue than I did that night of my first sojourn in the backwoods.

Three years after our arrival in Douro the winter was very severe. The morning of Feb. 7 was so intensely cold that when we awoke everything liquid in the house was frozen. The wood for the Franklin stove in the parlor was green, and it ignited too slowly to satisfy the shivering impatience of women and children; I vented mine in grumbling over the wretched fire, at which I endeavored to thaw frozen bread and dress my crying children, now four in number.

The day before, I had hired a young Irish girl. Her friends were only just located in our vicinity, and she had never seen a stove until she came to our house. After Moodie had gone on an errand to my sister's I suffered the fire to die away in the Franklin stove, and went into the kitchen to prepare bread for the oven.

The girl, who was good-natured, had heard me complain of the cold and the impossibility of getting the green wood to burn, and she thought that she would make a good fire for me and the children. Without saying one word she slipped out to the yard, filled her lap with cedar chips and, not knowing the nature of the parlor stove, filled it entirely.

Before I had the least idea of my danger I was aroused by the crackling and roaring of a large fire and a suffocating smell of burning soot. To my dismay I found the parlor stove red hot, from the front plate to the topmost pipe through the roof.

My first act was to plunge a blanket from the servant's bed, which stood in the kitchen, into cold water. This I thrust into the stove, and upon it I threw water until all was cool below. I then ran up to the loft and, by exhausting all the water in the house, contrived to cool down the pipes which passed through the loft. I then sent the girl out of doors to look at the roof. She quickly returned, stamping and tearing her hair and making a variety of uncouth outcries, from which I gathered that the roof was in flames.

This was terrible news, with my husband absent and the closest habitation a mile and a quarter away. I ran out and found that the fire had melted off all the snow. A ladder, which for several months had stood against the house, had been moved two days before to the barn; there was no reaching the fire through that source. I got out the dining table and placed a chair upon it from which I tried to throw water on the roof, but I only expended water without reaching the fire. The girl continued weeping and lamenting.

"You must go for help," I said. "Run as fast as you can to my sister's and fetch your master."

"And lave you, ma'arm, and the childher alone wid the burnin' house?"

"Yes, yes! Don't stay one moment."

"I have no shoes, ma'arm, and the snow is so deep."

"Put on your master's boots; make haste, or we shall be lost before help comes."

The girl put on the boots and started, shrieking "Fire! Fire!" the whole way. This was utterly useless and only exhausted her strength.

After she had vanished into the wood I paused to reflect what had best be done. The house was built of cedar logs; in all probability it would be consumed before any help could arrive. *"What shall I save first?"* was the thought uppermost in my mind. Bedding and clothing appeared the most necessary, and I set to work to save all I could. While little Agnes, Dunbar and baby Donald filled the air with their cries, Katie assisted me in dragging trunks and boxes up the hill. How many anxious looks I gave toward the woods as the fire increased and large pieces of burning wood began to fall about the lower rooms where we were at work.

The children I had kept under a large dresser in the kitchen, but it now appeared necessary to remove them to safety. To expose them to the direful cold was almost as bad as leaving them to the mercy of the fire. At last I hit upon a plan to keep them from freezing. I emptied all the clothes out of a large, deep chest of drawers and dragged the empty drawers up the hill. These I lined with blankets, then placed in each one a child, covering them well with the bedding. The baby I gave to little Agnes, to hold between her knees and keep well covered until help should arrive.

I soon found that I should not be able to take many more trips for goods. As I passed out of the parlor for the last time, Katie looked up at her father's flute, which was suspended upon two brackets, and said, "Oh, dear mama! Do save papa's flute; he will be so sorry to lose it."

God bless the dear child for the thought! The flute was saved; and as I succeeded in dragging out a heavy chest of clothes and looked once more despairingly to the road, I saw a man running at full speed. It was my husband. My heart uttered a deep thanksgiving as another and another figure came upon the scene.

I had not felt the intense cold, although without cap, bonnet or shawl and with my hands bare. The intense excitement, the anxiety to save all I could, had so totally diverted my thoughts that I had felt nothing of the danger to which I had been exposed. But now that help was near, my knees trembled, I felt giddy and faint, and dark shadows seemed dancing before my eyes.

The moment my husband and brother-in-law entered the house, the latter exclaimed, "Moodie, the house is gone. Save what you can of your winter stores and furniture."

Moodie thought differently. Prompt and energetic in danger, and possessing admirable presence of mind and coolness when others yielded to agitation and despair, he sprang upon the burning loft and called for water. Alas, there was none.

"Snow! snow! Hand me up pailfuls of snow!"

Oh, it was bitter work filling those pails, but my brother-in-law and I worked as fast as we were able.

The violence of the fire was greatly checked by covering the boards of the loft with this snow. More help had now arrived. Two neighbors had brought the ladder from the barn, and were already cutting away the burning roof and flinging the flaming brands into the deep snow.

"Mrs. Moodie, have you any pickled meat?"

"We have just killed one of our cows and salted it for winter stores."

"Well, fling the beef into the snow and let us have the brine."

This was an admirable plan. Wherever the brine wetted the shingles the fire turned from it.

But I had not time to watch the brave workers on the roof. I was fast yielding to the effects of overexcitement and fatigue when my brother's team dashed down the clearing, bringing an excellent old friend of mine and the servant girl.

My brother wrapped me in one of the large blankets scattered about. In a few minutes I was seated with the dear children in the sleigh, and on the way to a place of warmth and safety. Katie alone suffered from the intense cold. The dear little creature's feet were severely frozen, but were fortunately restored by her uncle, who rubbed them well with snow.

The friends we had left so actively employed at the house succeeded in getting the fire under control before it had destroyed the walls. The only accident was to a poor dog that Moodie had called Snarleyowe. He was struck by a burning brand, and crept under the barn and died.

It was some weeks before Moodie succeeded in repairing the roof because of the intense cold, but beyond the damage to the building, and the loss of our potatoes and two sacks of flour, we had escaped in a manner almost miraculous.

The news of our fire travelled far and wide. I was reported to have done prodigies and to have saved the greater part of our household goods before help arrived. Reduced to plain prose, these prodigies shrink into the simple and by no means marvellous fact that I dragged out chests which, under ordinary circumstances, I could not have moved; and that I was unconscious both of the cold and of the danger while working under a burning roof which, had it fallen, would have buried both the children and myself. These circumstances appeared far more alarming, as all real danger does, after they were past.

The fright and overexertion gave my health a shock from which I did not recover for several months, and made me so fearful of fire that it haunts me like a nightmare. Let the night be ever so serene, all stoves must be shut up and the hot embers covered with ashes before I dare retire to rest; and the sight of a burning edifice, so common in large towns in this country, makes me really ill.

By the summer of 1837 our fortunes had improved, we were all in high spirits and everything promised fair, until Moodie was asked to attend a bee which was called to construct a corduroy bridge over a very bad piece of road. He and John E——, a young Irish gentleman who was assisting him on the farm, were obliged to go that morning with wheat to the mill, but Moodie lent his yoke of oxen for the work.

The driver was a savage Irishman noted for his ill treatment of cattle, especially if the animals did not belong to him. He gave one of the oxen such a severe blow over the loins with a handspike that the creature came home perfectly disabled, just as we wanted his services in the harvest.

Moodie had no money to purchase, or even hire, a mate for the other ox, but he and John hoped that by careful attendance upon the injured animal he might be restored to health in a few days. They conveyed him to a deserted clearing where he would be safe from injury from the rest of the cattle, and early every morning we went in the canoe to carry poor Duke a warm mash and to watch his recovery.

Ah, ye who revel in this world's wealth, how little can you realize the importance which we, in our poverty, attached to the life of this valuable animal! Yes, it even became the subject of prayer, for the bread for ourselves and our little ones depended greatly upon his recovery. We were doomed to disappointment. After being nursed with the greatest attention for some weeks, the animal grew daily worse and suffered such intense agony that John shot him to put him out of pain.

A neighbor who had an odd ox kindly lent us the use of him when he was not employed, and John and Moodie gave their own work for the occasional loan of a yoke of oxen for a day. But even with this, and also the assistance of old Jenny (an Irish woman we had taken into our service) and myself in the field, a great deal of produce was damaged before it could be secured.

Still, with all these misfortunes, Providence watched over us in a signal manner. We were never entirely without food. Some days later Moodie came running in for his gun. A great she-bear was in the wheat field, busily helping to harvest the crop. There was but one bullet and a charge or two of buckshot, and Moodie started to the wood with the single bullet in his gun, followed by a little terrier dog that belonged to John. Old Jenny was busy at the washtub, but the moment she saw her master running up the clearing and knew the cause, she left her work. Snatching up the carving knife she ran after him, so that in case the bear should have the best of the fight she would be there to help.

A few minutes after came the report of the gun, and I heard Moodie halloo to John, who was cutting stakes in the wood. I ran to the door to listen. The children were all excitement, which the sight of Moodie and John carrying the black monster on poles, followed by old Jenny brandishing her carving knife, increased to the wildest demonstrations of joy.

The rest of the evening was spent in skinning and cutting up and salting the ugly creature, whose flesh filled a barrel with excellent meat, in flavor resembling beef and with the tenderness of mutton. This was quite a godsend, and lasted us until we were able to kill two fat hogs in the fall.

A few nights after, Moodie and I had occasion to visit my friend Emilia who lived in the very depth of the wood. Her parents had come on a short visit and she wanted us to meet them. The evening passed so pleasantly that it was near midnight before the little party prepared to separate. The moon was down. The wood was very dark, the ground being low and swampy and the trees thick and tall. There was, in particular, one very ugly spot where a small creek crossed the path. This creek could only be passed by scrambling over a fallen tree which, on a dark night, was not very easy to find. I begged a torch but none could be found. Emilia laughed at my fears: still, knowing what a coward I was in the bush at night, she found about an inch of candle, which was all that remained from the evening's entertainment. This she put into an old lantern.

"It will not last you long, but it will carry you over the creek," she said.

This was something gained and off we set, preceded by our dog Hector, although our dim candle looked like a solitary red spark and scarcely served to show us the path. We went along, talking over the news of the evening, when I saw a pair of green, bright eyes glare upon us from the edge of the swamp.

"Did you see those terrible eyes, Moodie?" and I clung trembling to his arm.

"What eyes?" said he, feigning ignorance. "It's too dark to see anything. The light is nearly gone, and if you don't quicken your pace you will perhaps get your feet wet."

"Good heavens! I saw them again! And do just look at the dog."

Hector stopped suddenly and, stretching himself along the ground, his nose between his forepaws, began to whine and tremble. Presently he ran back to us and crept under our feet. The cracking of branches and the heavy tread of some large animal sounded close beside us.

Moodie turned the open lantern in that direction and shouted as loud as he could. Just at that moment the candle flickered and expired. We were left in perfect darkness alone with the bear—for such we supposed the animal to be.

My heart beat audibly; a cold perspiration was streaming down my face but I neither shrieked nor attempted to run. I don't know how Moodie got me over the creek. One of my feet slipped into the water but, expecting as I did every moment to be devoured by Master Bruin, that was of no consequence. Glad was I when I saw the light from our little cabin, and the moment I got within the clearing I ran until I was safely within the house. John heard with great interest of our adventure, and thought that Bruin was very good to let us escape without one affectionate hug.

"Perhaps it would have been otherwise had he known, Moodie, that you had not only killed his good lady but were dining sumptuously off her carcass every day."

But the bear was determined to have something in return for the loss of his wife. Several nights after this, our slumbers were disturbed about midnight by an awful yell, and old Jenny shaking our chamber door violently.

"Masther, masther dear! Get up wid you this moment or the bear will desthroy the cattle intirely."

Half asleep, Moodie sprang from his bed, seized his gun and ran out. I threw my large cloak round me, struck a light and followed him to the door. The moment the latter was opened some calves rushed into the kitchen, closely followed by the larger beasts who had come bellowing down the hill pursued by the bear.

It was a laughable scene: Moodie, in his nightshirt, taking aim at something in the darkness, surrounded by the terrified animals; old Jenny, a large knife in her hand, holding on to the white skirts of her master's garment and making outcry loud enough to frighten away all the wild beasts in the bush.

Moodie fired. The bear retreated up the clearing with a low growl. Moodie and Jenny pursued him but it was too dark to discern any object at a distance. I, for my part, stood at the open door laughing until the tears ran down my cheeks.

By daylight, Moodie and John started in chase of the bear, whom they tracked some way into the bush; but here he entirely escaped their search. Moodie put his gun away.

From the early 1700s, when they acquired horses, until the 1870s, when they were forced onto reserves, the Plains Crees lived a wild, free, fierce existence hunting buffalo and fighting their Blackfoot neighbors. The rich folklore of those times was passed on only verbally but in 1923 a young Cree named Edward Ahenakew wrote down the stories of 74-year-old Chief Thunderchild, an honored tribal elder who had lived through the last unrestricted years. In these tales, from the North Saskatchewan River area, it is Thunderchild who speaks.

Tales of the Plains Crees

By EDWARD AHENAKEW
Edited by RUTH MATHESON BUCK

ONE WINTER, when it was very cold, the Crees came from all over the plains to meet near the place where high platforms had been built for the bodies of their dead. They gathered to take revenge against the Blackfoot who had killed 15 women of the Crees that past summer when they went for water. One of these women was Broken Wing and another was her sister, and their father had gone through all the camps of the Crees, crying for his daughters and stirring up the people to avenge them.

Thunderchild (opposite) remembered the great days of unchecked freedom on the plains—and of intertribal war, as between the Blackfoot and the Crees.

It was January [1867] when all the people gathered in a great encampment, and there were women there and many young boys. I was one of these. It was my first expedition and I felt like a man, but the men said to us, "You are not old enough to fight, and if the Blackfoot surprise us you must run away."

The northern lights were bright above the encampment, and for three nights the people danced before we moved out in long, long lines through the deep snow. Scouts went out before us on both sides, and there was a general shout when three riders appeared. Two of them were scouts, the third was a Blackfoot woman, very pretty. The scouts had killed her husband, and they gave her to Short Tail, the brother of Ermine Skin. But they warned us that one Blackfoot had escaped and would give the alarm, and that there might be an attack that same night.

It was cold, cold. Everyone was running, some of them on snow-shoes; everyone was watchful. We camped in the centre of wooded hills, and across the creek there were stands of poplar and the Blackfoot camp. Some went ahead of the main body, and those who reached the Blackfoot camp stole horses and brought them back to our encampment late in the night. With all the other boys, I was made to take my place well back in the circle of our encampment.

When the shooting began, it was as though fire was thrown in streaks into the camp, and shots answered from the tents. I made my way forward toward the lines of firing, and I heard someone moan and strike the ground in his pain. This was Ma-che-num (Good Looking Man) and he was one of us though his name was Blackfoot. He had been hit in the leg, a bad flesh wound, and he thought he would be left alone to die. My father said to him, "That is not the way to act, my son. You are a man." And he was shamed to the quick. My father took him back out of the cold and the snow to where there was a fire.

By now the Blackfoot had fled back to their camp, and there were war yells and the cries of women and children. I ran forward to the line of Crees facing the Blackfoot camp. One of the Crees ran into the camp and hit a Blackfoot tent, shouting, "I am called the son of O-ka-mai-ka-na-wa-sis." Then the others ran forward too, one after the other, and I ran with them.

They began to cut the tents open and pull them down, but the Blackfoot had run among the trees where there were more tents, and they were digging pits in the soft ground of the fire places. They shot and killed some of the Crees at the edge of the bush.

I saw one man rush forward, and when he was hit he shouted, "Come for me. I am killed." Two of our men went forward while the others covered them, and they dragged him back. Those two were As-kā-chas and Ka-ya-sa-yis, a Stoney. Ka-ya-sa-yis said to me, "Come, boy, and bid me good-bye." He had been hit in the stomach. He was a man who had always been kind to me, and I felt sad.

Someone began to yell, "If anyone can take that shield near the tents, he can have all these women." And another sang, "I am O-pe-po-noik. Cover me, fellow children. I will take it." And he walked over and took it; but it was a drum, not a shield.

Again there was much noise, for someone had found Father [Albert] Lacombe's robes in a tent. His horse was taken too. No one would tell where the priest was, and A-chin put on the robes and called out, "Here is the priest." Then there was a cry that a Cree was being scalped, and men rushed to the rescue.

The battle raged all that night; Crees were killed and wounded; the women wailed for their dead.

One of the Crees—he was Mi-sa-ti-mois—had been looking for horses all night, and he called out, "Cover me and I will try to get them from the corral at the centre." He moved slowly toward it, and he had a hard time lifting one big log. At last it was off and he led out three horses, one of them a beautiful gray racer.

The morning was coming, and the wounded and dead were carried back to our encampment although the dead who were close to the Blackfoot tents we had to leave. I walked beside my wounded friend and wet his lips with snow. The Blackfoot followed us, but they were afraid to come near and their shots fell short.

Mi-sa-ti-mois raced part way back on the gray horse that he had taken, crouched low on its back, his robe flying; the Blackfoot shot at him again and again but they could not hit him. Then a Blackfoot did the same and was not hit; as he rode he sang, shouting out to us, "Crees, go back home quickly. We have two other camps close by and we will fight you to them." But the Crees shouted back that he was lying, and we went on to our camp.

There my friend died of his painful wound. His father said, "My son has been in the games and has been beaten. We will leave his body here." And we dressed him in his finest clothes and stood him up to face the Blackfoot proudly.

The Cree who had been scalped and stabbed also died at the camp.

101

Before he died he gave his three horses to his aunt, and he asked her to care for his dog which had waited at the camp for him and had stayed beside him as he was dying. Then the woman sang of her nephew, of his manliness and of the love that his dog had for him. She wept for him, and the women mourned aloud. And the dog searched the camp for the man he had followed faithfully.

We returned the way we had come, having taken our revenge and killed many Blackfoot.

I had only one horse when I first hunted buffalo. I remember how hard that made it for me in the summer of 1869 when we hunted in the country south of Fort Pitt [in present-day Saskatchewan]. Our hunters had been chased by the Blackfoot, and we rode back and forth along our line of carts watching the mirror signals that they flashed from the hills. Our Chief said, "Don't run at them. Don't run at them yet."

Then Mis-ta-wa-sis (Big Child) rode out from the line. He crouched low on his horse and raced about, shouting, "Mount, mount, you horse-fellows, mount. This is no child who goes. He will not stop. After him!" And the hunters all raced after Mis-ta-wa-sis, who was far in the lead.

A Blackfoot riding a white horse came in sight and turned to flee, but we were close upon him, and Wē-zo shouted, "Go on, go on!" The Blackfoot jumped off his horse, and the hunters all shot at him but could not hit him in the confusion of riders as the Crees swept past. His horse raced on with the others, and one of our party grabbed it. Someone else got his blanket and shield, and all I got were two arrows. The Blackfoot was killed and I got there too late. My horse had played out, and I had to stop and could only watch how the fight went in the sandhills below.

Then someone suddenly shouted, "Stop! Stop! The Blackfoot have smallpox. Get away! Get away!" But those of us whose horses had played out could not go on, and we stayed together. We saw five men appear from the north, and we watched them riding back and forth. We thought they might be Blackfoot but we could not tell. Afterward we knew it was Gabriel Dumont and some of his hunters. [This could refer to Louis Riel's lieutenant during the 1885 Northwest Rebellion or to his uncle, who was also named Gabriel Dumont.] They shouted at us in the Black-foot tongue, telling us to come to them, but one of our party was sure they were Blackfoot and he tried to run away. They chased him, and it was Gabriel Dumont who killed him and took his horse. We could do nothing to help.

When I got back to camp I stayed there, for I had only that one poor horse. Then Ka-mā-cha-wās-kis said that he could go with me to the Blackfoot country for horses.

An Old Man [tribal elder] who was a conjurer told us to wait while he prayed for a blessing. We built a lodge for him out of young green trees, and we lashed and braced it firmly. Then we tied the conjurer securely with ropes, carried him into the lodge and left him there alone. He began to chant a song that his spirits had taught him, and we heard other sounds as we waited outside. The lodge began to shake, and it shook until the green poles were loosened and the whole structure leaned. Then the ropes that had bound the conjurer were thrown out with the knots intact. There was silence until the conjurer walked out. He said, "In my dream Thunderchild told me that if I want a horse he will give it to me."

Nine of us started for the Blackfoot country, and one evening we looked down upon a camp, a great circle of Blackfoot tents, with all the best horses inside the ring. It was the time of the full moon and there was too much light; but big clouds came up, as the conjurer had said, and we knew that was our opportunity.

Cha-che-ses and I went around to the other side of the camp and got ready, for there was need to hurry. My gun was big and heavy and I left it, taking only a club. As I went down among the tents I felt afraid, and then the fear left me although the moon was bright again. I saw a white horse near the centre tent, and I cut his rope and began to lead him away. He pulled back at first, but I put my robe on him and rode him out of the camp. He smelled good—a springy horse—his head high. Two other horses followed us.

When Cha-che-ses made his try some Blackfoot went past, and he hid among the horses until they had gone. Then he led a horse in the other direction out of the camp, and more horses followed him. We had just the right number to give one horse to each of the men who had none, and there were two for the Old Man. I had three for myself.

That was the beginning of owning things.

Sometimes we had to camp where there was water but no wood, and the women would go to find it. The men rode out to keep guard. One day I went out with them, and I was riding a fine horse. The women scattered to gather wood and dry leaves. I sat on a little hill, holding my horse, watching, and after a while I stretched out on the grass.

Suddenly I heard a yell from the north and I knew that it could not be buffalo, that something else had been sighted. A rider was coming, too far away for me to see him clearly, but I could hear the shouting and saw that he was being chased. He came racing toward us, lying low on his horse, and those who were chasing him turned their horses and raced away.

It was Mis-ta-tim's father, and he was greatly excited. His partner had been killed not far from where we were, near a big stone that had Indian markings on it. The two of them had thought they had seen buffalo and they moved in slowly, hiding as they went. But it was the Blackfoot, not buffalo and those who went to chase were chased themselves.

Mis-ta-tim's father was riding a fast horse and he had been able to escape, although the Blackfoot got so close that one of them raised his club to knock the Cree from his horse, while the others raced around pretending to shoot at him. Then they saw us on the hill and raced away.

One of our number rode fast to the camp to bring help, but the rest stayed where we were, riding back and forth. When the others came, we rode to find the partner of Mis-ta-tim's father. He had been scalped, and there was a bullet in his back and a stab wound in his shoulder.

We were many now, and we said, "Let us chase the Blackfoot," but when we went to the top of the hill we could see no one. "Wait," someone said, "there may be many of them too." And we stopped where we were while two rode to see from the next hill. To and fro, they rode. "They can see," someone shouted, and we all rode forward.

From the top of that hill we could see many Blackfoot, some of them preparing to fight and others farther away. I felt a fearful delight. We were all singing as we went forward, some keeping back those who were too eager. From the other side of a hill we could hear the voices of the Blackfoot, and one of our number called out, "Wait, wait."

Now one of the Crees, a noted warrior though he was no longer young, was riding a fine gray horse that pranced as it went; he was wearing beaded clothes and carrying the bag that held the sacred symbols of his spirit power [one or more objects which the Indians believed protected them]. He was singing but his voice was weak; when he rode his horse to the top of the hill he leaned down by the horse's neck, not facing the Blackfoot. They missed him when they shot, and he came back to us at full speed. He had done all that to encourage the rest of us.

Then another, one who was later killed in the Rebellion, did the same, riding a short-tailed fine black horse, his red blanket flying, but riding sideways again so that he made less of a target.

Ee-yi-nieu, a Swampy Cree, decided to try. He was riding a low, fairly swift horse, and he had a bit of dog skin for a robe. His face was painted and his hair tied in two knots on his forehead, like ears standing up. Away he went, low on his horse and heavy looking, singing a song out of tune. He clattered up the hill and then his horse stumbled forward, its tail flying into the air while Ee-yi-nieu slid over its head. His legs gave under him and he fell in a heap. The Blackfoot yelled. They thought that he had broken his legs and they rushed toward him. But Ee-yi-nieu stood up. "How! My horse stumbled," he said, and he looked so grotesque that everyone laughed. Suddenly it was all a game.

Now the Blackfoot did as the Crees did, first one side and then the other riding to the hilltop, chasing up and down the hills, making targets of themselves for brief moments. No one was killed but everyone was shooting. It was wild fun. One young Blackfoot rode up, his horse jumping from side to side. He yelled that his name was Black Arrow and he acted like a crazy wolf. He was wearing a short, white coat and he had his hair pulled high up on his head and tied, all thick with mud.

We yelled, "Wait, wait, see how brave this one is. Don't shoot him." We were all excited by the game. One of the Crees who could speak Blackfoot raced his horse up to meet Black Arrow. He held his gun high in the air and shouted in Blackfoot, "If you are a man, drop your gun and come for this one." Each rider let his gun drop and raced for the other's, snatched it from the ground and raced away with the new gun.

At last the Blackfoot rode away. A few of the Crees chased after them, just to make sure they were going. They had many women with them and that was why they fled. We watched until they had crossed the river, and we went on to the Cypress Hills.

Buffalo would attack people only during the mating season. When we chased them we always let the horses have their heads free or there could be accidents. The closer one raced to the buffalo the better it was, because of the dust. Some men were afraid to go close up to a buffalo, but I—we all boast when we talk of the chase—I raced close up and my pony was well trained.

The bulls had great agility in turning to fight. Up would go the tail first. I saw one hunter chasing a bull when it turned on him like that. The horse swerved aside but the bull's horn caught the man's belt just enough to pull him off. Then it was like a ball—toss, catch, toss, catch—twice before he fell to the ground. The second time the horn caught him back of the thigh, and it was as if a knife had cut him. I was ahead and I had to go on, but the riders behind me stopped to help him and they killed the bull.

Our powder horns were small, holding just enough for one shot. We kept the bullets in our mouths so that they were wet with saliva and needed no wadding when we dropped them into the muzzles of our guns.

Once when we had finished chasing buffalo near a coulee—not far from the place that is now called Wilkie [Sask.]—some of the men decided to go back to the hunt. Lightfoot's father was one of them, and he was a good man in the chase. That time he did not return to the camp when it was night, but in the morning his horse was there and the saddle was twisted under its belly. We went to look for him. Many of us looked. He was never found. Much later, hunters came on a wounded bull and the buckle of his belt was round the bull's horn.

In the days when the buffalo were many, there were Old Men who had the gift of "making pounds." Poundmaker's father was such a one, and he gave the name to his son [a famous Cree chief]. Another was Eyi-pā-chi-nas, and when it was known that he was "sitting at pound"—seeking supernatural power to bring the buffalo—hunters would gather.

One winter there were 10 teepees just for these hunters. Working all together, they cut trees to make a circular pound about 70 yards across. The trees were big, and they braced them on the outside for extra strength. They set heavy gateposts with a crossbar above, and they hung an old buffalo skull there that rattled in the wind. The gate was 14 feet wide, and out from it they laid two long lines of tufted willows that spread farther and farther apart, to channel the buffalo into the pound. In the centre they set a great lobbed tree.

When everything was ready, other Old Men joined Eyi-pā-chi-nas and sang the buffalo song. Far on the plain a herd of buffalo was sighted and two young men rode out to watch. They were to blow their whistles as soon as the buffalo started to move in the early morning. Other men went out to hide behind drifts of snow, and when the sun was high we heard yells that the buffalo were coming. Scab Child went out on horseback yelling "*Yei! Yei! Yei!*" [A herd always swung toward a rapidly approaching rider to cut him off, and could thus be decoyed toward the pound.] Others hid themselves along the way.

The buffalo were spread out in a long line, and the noise of their coming was like thunder. Whenever they swung too far one way or the other, the men who were hidden on that side would jump up and yell, *"O-oh-whi!"* and fire their guns. The buffalo came on between the lines of willow and through the gate, and they circled round and round the lobbed tree at the centre until the pound was filled. Then the hunters closed in and stopped the gateway with poles and buffalo robes.

Sometimes it was evening before the pound was filled, and no one was permitted to shoot a gun or arrows until it was daylight once more and the slaughter could begin. Then it was all the same—yell and shoot ... shoot ... snatch arrows from the dead and dying buffalo ... shoot again ... all wild ... terror of animals ... lust of killing ....

We would cut up the meat till late at night, and haul it with dogs to the encampment. It was fat and good but there was more, much more, than we could use. Young animals we cached, to freeze. Other bands came to join us and to feast. Their hunters wanted to make a larger pound for greater slaughter, but Eyi-pā-chi-nas would say nothing, just sit and drink the berry soup that the women made for him from the bones.

Toward spring we took the hides to Fort Pitt, and the skins of many wolves that followed the herds. For 12 wolf skins or three good buffalo hides we got one blanket in trade. Chiefs who were chosen by the Hudson's Bay Company were given more than that, and their men brought them their furs to trade. Traders came to our encampments too, and it was always buffalo hides and pemmican they wanted. Hides. Hides. Shoot. Shoot. See who can shoot most. A curse upon man's greed and on the Cree for that inordinate slaughter.

Pay-mo-ta-ya-siu (Walking Wind) was young the summer that he went with his uncles into a big patch of saskatoons [berries] and found a grizzly there. This is his story:

"We saw signs of bear, and I wouldn't go into the bush, but stayed near the edge. One of my uncles went around to the other side. A sound came to us on the wind, but my uncle made no noise and I followed to see what it was. I came face to face with a grizzly standing over my uncle, his feet on either side and my uncle was killed. The bear looked at me and I saw the blood dripping from its jaws. I turned and ran, and it chased me. I thought I could jump over the creek but it knocked me down. I lay without moving, my eyes closed tight, but it bit me through the shoulder and the chest and blood dripped over me. Then the bear moved aside and cuffed my head with its paw. Blood flowed into my eyes but still I dared not move although I knew the bear had gone back into the bush.

"Then I heard my other uncle's voice, 'A-a-a-ah! A bear has killed my brother.' A rider saw me. He seemed far, far away, but he came nearer and heard my breath whistling through the hole where the bear had bitten. I tried to speak: 'My uncle?' He would not tell me that my uncle was dead and that the bear had partly eaten him.

"Other men came. They wanted revenge, and they followed the tracks and killed the bear, but they would not eat the flesh for the bear had killed a man.

"They said that I could not live but I did. Since then I have been named for the sound of my breathing."

This country lasted long with only Indians here, and then the white men came, and they came with might. That was permitted by God. Yet see how they treat the nation that is weaker. Surely our nation is not to be wiped out. In the days that I remember, an Indian would prepare himself to go on a long and difficult journey. So must all be ready for this road of life.

Isaac Barr's Fiasco

*Clustered in their grimy cities in 1902, Britons could stare at bright
Canadian immigration posters and imagine themselves masters on a golden,
bountiful prairie. When a Canadian-born clergyman made it seem
almost a duty, the response was overwhelming. But the Rev. Isaac Barr's
colonists found the journey arduous, the land harsh and their expectations
shattered. Barr, they concluded, was a deceiver, a thief, a blunderer.*

By W. O. MITCHELL

THE REV. ISAAC MONTGOMERY BARR, a short, full-mustached and
thick-set Anglican clergyman, was responsible for the largest group
of settlers ever to leave England in one company. A dreamer, he
had a talent for igniting dreams in others; centuries earlier he might
have led a children's crusade. He would have made an excellent con man,
but the professional rascal never cons himself. Because of his temperament
Barr did precisely that—closing his mind and senses to reality.

*Barr had told them: "Many of the comforts
of England you must leave behind."*

Barr was born March 2, 1847, in Hornby, Halton County, Ont., and claimed missionary experience in the Northwest as early as 1875. Inspired by Cecil Rhodes' African colonization, he moved to England and touted a scheme for a British colony on the North Saskatchewan River, around what is now the city of Lloydminster, with himself as founder and leader.

The land of Barr's dreams was the vast sea of grass between the Great Lakes and the softly swelling foothills of the Rockies, a land where man was an accident in emptiness—a two-legged surprise for the squeaking gopher, the circling goshawk and the slapstick badger in his baggy hide.

This was a country of forbidding excesses: bitter cold, desert heat, amplitude of space and totality of sky—all insisting on humility. The land was too new for gods, too blunt for mystics, with one lesson for intruding man: mortality. Again and again this was reiterated—in the dried husk of a dead gopher, the clean ribs of a coyote, the bleached bones of a buffalo.

The true prairie offered nothing to break the full thrust of wind, no shred of compassionate shade; a salient man became a sunlight rod drawing upon his vulnerable head all the sun's merciless rays. Because of this, and the torment of mosquitoes, homesteaders often ploughed by moonlight. But worse than the elements and the insects was the loneliness unrelieved by mail or neighbor, particularly when a husband was gone for days to get supplies.

There was terror too. Tinder grass could be ignited by a homesteader's careless match, the coals of a settler's campfire, a spark from a train. "Lightning started three fires," one woman's diary noted, "east, west and north of us." When it had gone, no prairie wool remained to feed horses, oxen or cows; sheds and barns smouldered in ruins; homes were destroyed.

The prairie was forbidding but not unlovely. Northern lights tinting white and green and blue, shaded and faded and died only to be reborn. Millions of migrant fowl lifted in slapping take-offs to assault dawn and rose-stained evening skies. But most of the beauty was in miniature; furred crocuses when snow had barely vanished; tiger lilies in July; lupin and brown-eyed susans, fat buffalo beans and wild violets. When a man walked with breaking plough, he was the first human to have persisted on this particular earth beyond a camp for the night, and that furrow had never before been turned up to the light of day!

With the completion of the Canadian Pacific Railway in 1885 a trickle of immigration became a flood. Across the Atlantic men stopped before posters, circus bright. They stared at fields of stooks and read the promises of 160 acres free. They dreamed the oldest dream, the promised land dream: the Saskatchewan, a river of Jordan draining a land of milk and honey, and they imagined the pot of freehold gold.

It wasn't a dream of self-delusion. The ocean had to be crossed, a wilderness entered. For some the crossing was a lark; for more, a cramped hell. Most rode half a continent in colonist coaches, on wooden slat seats over which hay or straw-filled ticking was spread for the night.

After the train came the trip to the homestead site. Moosomin, Weyburn, Moose Jaw, Swift Current, Maple Creek, Calgary, were alive with oxen, horses, and wagons loaded with children, pots and pans, supplies, furniture, crated chickens, pigs, and covered with a canopy of canvas or oilcloth, often a cow behind. They travelled usually in spring with no road; sometimes over snow laid down by the April blizzards, more likely across sodden prairie mired with rain, the gumbo gluing wheels and balling underfoot. With poignant infrequency they passed tents and sod huts and wooden shacks with roof camber so gentle it seemed borrowed from the earth's great curve. Finally they reached the spot of their new home.

First there was a tent, but soon they went to ground like the gopher, the badger and the burrowing owl. Sods were cut and piled against a frame of poles; some might boast a wooden roof with shingles or even a board floor.

A sod shack gave superb insulation, but as one pioneer put it, "a three-day rain outside meant a five-day rain inside." A woman's diary explained that "... the only dry place was under the table which had an oilcloth on, and I put sugar, flour, etc., under it to keep dry." Another woman brought her piano, an awkward miscalculation for the chatelaine of a sod hut; her husband built a hay stack over it and two years later when a more permanent house was up the hay came off the piano. One homesteader's two canaries arrived in a February blizzard: they thawed above the stove and sang out the night while the wind howled.

Until seed drills were available some homesteaders sowed their first crop by hand, cut it with a mower, combed it with a horse rake, tied it into bundles and thrashed it with a flail. Water was often a problem. In winter, snow was melted; in summer creeks or sloughs gave something that quenched, although it tasted of mud and cat-tail and had to be drunk

111

Isaac Barr: "I do not desire to present a picture that is highly rose-colored."

with careful scrutiny for mosquito larvae and pond skaters. No desert dweller was more careful with water. After potatoes were boiled it was used to wash the dishes, then it washed hands and slaked thirsty pansies, geraniums or sweet peas.

The trek pattern formed and reformed all over the Prairies, yet there was one immigrant group paradoxically typical and atypical: the Barr Colony. Isaac Barr's campaign of newspaper advertisements, lectures and pamphlets began in August 1902 while he was still curate of St. Saviour's Church in London. He told of free land grants on the Prairies and promised: "Before the party arrived at its destination, a commodious and inexpensive building—simply a shell of rough lumber—would be constructed to shelter people, until they get their log or frame cabins, or houses, built upon homesteads . . . ."

His first circular, published in September 1902, indicates that he expected a small party of immigrants to follow him. It was entitled BRITISH SETTLEMENT IN NORTH WESTERN CANADA ON FREE GRANT LANDS–CANADA FOR THE BRITISH. The pamphlet was masterfully persuasive:

> I do not desire to present a picture that is highly rose-colored. There are difficulties and drawbacks to be encountered, but for the brave man obstacles are something to be overcome and stepping stones to victory and success. Britons have ever been the great colonizers. Let it not be said that we are degenerate sons of brave and masterful sires.
>
> Let me say, in brief, you cannot pick up nuggets of gold on the surface of the soil; you must dig for the wealth of the land. Hard work, and plenty of it, lies before you; more or less of hardship, and not seldom privations. You must sweat, and sometimes suffer from the cold. You shall not always find everything to your hand. Many of the comforts of England you must leave behind.

His pitch was peerless. To resist it was an admission that you were *not* brave, Britons were *not* great colonizers, you *were* a degenerate son of a brave and masterful sire, *not* interested in victory or success. Sweat distressed you: you could not stand cold. You preferred to stay at home in England with cowards.

It worked. Instead of the modest number anticipated, thousands applied.

Barr sailed for Canada to select the colony site and make transportation and other arrangements. On his return, at Christmas, he published a second pamphlet explaining his plans in detail, his co-op to buy settlers' supplies, his transport company to carry gear to the homestead site, and a projected agricultural college.

In February he outlined his hospital insurance plan–Canada's first medicare:

> After exhaustive investigation I have come to the conclusion that the principle of insuring against sickness is the one most suitable for my Colony, and I therefore wish to notify those who are joining my Settlement that if they will undertake to contribute under the following scale to this Hospital, they

will be protected against and guaranteed full treatment in sickness and accident:

ADULTS (Male or Female)–£1 per head per annum (in maternity cases an extra £2 2s per week will be charged).

CHILDREN (under 15 years)–10s per head per annum.

FAMILY TICKETS–In case of families over five, there will be, where all insure, a reduction of 20 per cent. Annual tickets will be issued, which will entitle the holder to hospital care, medical attendance and nursing, board and lodging: the only extra will be for medicines, and these will be supplied at wholesale prices.

From Land's End to north of the Tweed they came, for the most part city sparrows: clerks, artisans, merchants, hatters, ironmongers, greengrocers, butchers, laborers and domestics. They came by foot, by train, by horse-drawn buses. All were beginning a great adventure: the pursuit of wealth in a rich land, green and lawn-like, rolling soft as the Weald of Kent, lovely as the Lake District, kinder than the Highlands–land clumped with trees, watered by pure streams, abounding with game. Many males were South African War veterans, armed for the wilderness and Indians–with side arms, shotguns, knives. They were fit and ready in riding breeches, puttees, broad-brimmed stetsons or African veldt hats. In their hearts was Barr's slogan: "Let us take possession of Canada! Let our cry be, 'Canada for the British!' "

Two thousand sailed from Liverpool on the 21-month-old *Lake Manitoba* on March 31, 1903. There was one great cabin below decks. Single men were herded forward, the older and married ones aft, and the women and younger children amidship. Seasickness lived in all quarters. Sanitation facilities were inadequate. On deck was the headquarters cabin of Mr. Barr, whose troubles had just begun. There were 11 fights, seven incipient mutinies, three riots and 22 violent interviews with Barr during the 13-day voyage. Once he made it to the bridge a jump ahead of an angry crowd and threatened to turn the fire hose on them. The Rev. George Exton Lloyd, chaplain for the party, had early moved down with the people below: again and again he was a steadying influence, not only during the voyage but on the CPR trip to Regina and on the Canadian Northern from Regina to Saskatoon, the end of steel.

But problems mounted. When the colonists reached Saskatoon on a cold, wintery April 17 they discovered that virtually no arrangements had been made for their reception. Women and children slept in the immigration shed, kept awake by the roar of a river filled with broken ice. Baggage on another train failed to arrive. When it finally showed up, freight bills had been lost and the keys of the cars could not be found.

The overwhelming response to Barr's appeal had been more than he could manage. His accomplishment in getting 2,000 people from England to the Northwest was staggering, but he had been working against a tight deadline: Canada was being flooded with immigrants, and the government would not promise to reserve the land beyond April 15, 1903. Barr was also betrayed by his naïve trust in official promises (including that of a railway) to meet the needs of such a large group—needs which were impossibly demanding in such a vast, unorganized territory. The colonists became increasingly angry and Barr became more and more defensive, isolating himself from them. He attended indignation meetings guarded by a Mounted Police constable.

There was confusion as to the allotment of homesteads, with no regard for Barr's intended procedure for relocating the dissatisfied. Barr adamantly opposed R. F. Chisholm, agent of Dominion Lands at Battleford, who wanted settlers to go ahead to locate for themselves. He warned James A. Smart, Deputy Minister of the Interior, "If there is bloodshed and destruction of the colony as a result I throw the whole blame on you."

Saskatoon prices became inflated as settlers bought horses, oxen, wagons, harnesses, groceries, ploughs and tools. There were rumors that Barr was demanding a percentage from Saskatoon merchants on all goods sold to the colonists.

Cree Indians watched at corrals as horse gypsies spat and dealt and closed sales, turning over barely broken cayuses to proud owners who had never before held lines in their hands. With great regularity wild-eyed, mane-flying, foam-stringing horses bolted and, belly to the ground, pounded through the emcampment, wagons spewing bucksaws, canned goods, nail kegs and kerosene, collapsing tents and scattering terrified colonists. Men stumbled over guy ropes after dark, felt for tent flaps they thought were theirs, sprang back at male curses and strange female shrieks.

Barr's tent office was completely disorganized. The colonists abandoned his original plan to go west in a caravan. Some left the party for already existent communities or took construction jobs on the Canadian Northern. But most set out individually over the 170 miles of prairie

Barr colonists at Saskatoon, the end of steel, in April 1903.

they must cover to the colony site. Top-heavy Bain wagons tipped and tilted on the ruts made by earlier wheels, flipped and had to be reloaded. A dozen or more bogged down in a slough within sight of Saskatoon. Some settlers, encumbered with women, children and the old, and held up by late blizzards and steep ravines, took weeks to travel the 100 miles to Battleford. Flour sacks were punctured, groceries fouled by kerosene.

Horses were stricken with slough fever from alkali water and overwork. The complicated double harness was a puzzle some uninitiated

teamsters solved with tailors' chalk, drawing the outline on the horses' hides so that they would know how it went back on. One couple who couldn't afford chalk left the harness on the horses for the entire 170 miles. Veteran Westerners suggested that each family be issued a galvanized washtub for the man of the family to stand in for protection when he chopped wood.

The Dominion government had erected large tents at about 20-mile intervals along the trail to Battleford, each supplied with stoves and fuel.

At Battleford the colonists rested a few days in other government-supplied tents and an immigration hall. Barr himself arrived on May 2 and left for the settlement five days later. The *Saskatchewan Herald* said, "Mr. Barr has come. The colonists are dissatisfied with his arrangements. There is every chance now of a hot spell. There is no more connection between these interesting items than the fancy of the reader may invest them with."

In fact a general exodus from Battleford had begun on the day Barr arrived. The trail was better now, much of it through gently undulant land softened by poplar and willow. A last heavy storm hit the earlier travellers but the snow melted soon under strong sun. Violets and peavine and wild roses bloomed. A person could almost walk up and club the unsophisticated ducks nesting on slough edges. Colonists discovered that garter snakes were harmless, became used to the ululation of coyotes at night. Capt. Jacob Tweedale and his partner wakened in their dark tent to the bumping of drums and the song of savage throats, sat the rest of the night with shotguns at the ready, "prepared to sell our lives dearly." In the morning they found they were camped on the Thunderchild Indian Reserve.

By the second week in May the prairie's hot breath turned the grass to tinder. When fire sprang up, Captain Tweedale drove his team and wagon into a slough, unhitched the oxen and ponies, and tied them to the wheels. "We covered the animals' heads with wet sacks, threw water over the canvas cover of our wagon, and started to fire the grass to create a burned area toward the oncoming fire," he recorded later.

"By the time we had completed our task dusk was falling, and a great flickering line was rapidly closing in on us. Dense clouds of choking smoke and sparks filled the air, birds of all kinds went shrieking past, and the ground was alive with panic-stricken rabbits, gophers, an occasional antelope and other creatures. We had just waded into the slough and covered our own heads when the fire reached us with a roar and a crackling. The heat was terrific and it was almost impossible to breathe; our oxen became panicky and tore at their ropes and bellowed. It was only a matter of minutes before the worst of the fire had raced past us, but it was some time before the smouldering grass had cooled sufficiently, and the smoke abated, for us to remove our head covering and venture out of the water. Next day we travelled through a sea of black dust that covered everything."

By the middle of May between 300 and 400 wagons had finished their journey. But once again Barr's promises were not being fulfilled.

The tent hospital had no equipment; the store was stocked only with what the colonists did not need. In Barr's office tent was hopeless confusion and anger. People were unable to locate on allotted homesteads. They demanded the return of money paid for shares in non-operative co-ops. With the hospital's three nurses, Barr left the colony for Battleford. Finally a committee headed by Lloyd presented Barr with papers to sign, agreements cutting him free from all leadership of the colony. When Barr left Battleford the Saskatoon *Phenix* said "Britons never will be slaves." In Regina he was rotten-egged by some Englishmen.

But he had left just as the tide was turning. By Oct. 21 two general stores had been built, two cafés, a butcher and a blacksmith shop and a vicarage for Lloyd, whose name was now given to the settlement. By August 1904 a log church was dedicated by a bishop, its pews made from the salvaged lumber of a Saskatchewan River scow. Each log had been "bought" by a member of the congregation and the donor's name was carved in the wood. The Lloydminster *Times* printed its first edition in 1905. Three large hotels opened for business, as well as a bank and a drugstore. That was the year the railway came through and flour dropped from $5 per 100 pounds to $2.80.

Yet Isaac Barr had done the unforgivable. His mismanagement and stubborn pride had threatened his people's dream. They in turn blamed him for difficulties resulting from their own inexperience and unrealistic expectations, and this he made easy by withdrawing instead of reasoning with them. Barr never recovered from this enormous personal failure and the injustice he felt he received. He paid off his creditors and moved to the United States. His demand for a court investigation of the colony's affairs was rejected by the Canadian government. Two years later he married Christina Mellberg, the secretary he had hired back in London in the heady winter of 1902-03, and a few years after that they and their two sons settled in Australia. There Barr died Jan. 18, 1937, a victim of the visions that moved him to frontiers and the weaknesses that destroyed him.

Exploration

and Discovery

...not only to go farther than any man had ever been before, but as far as it was possible for any man to go....

Capt. James Cook, 1768

To 11th-century Greenlanders, descendants of the Norse Vikings, Vinland was a mysterious land somewhere west across the Labrador Sea. Leif Eriksson had found it not many years before — about A.D. 995 — and had brought back timber and dried fruit that made him rich. Content with his wealth and renown, Leif never returned to Vinland and jealously guarded the secret of its exact location. But others longed to go there. The author, out of long fascination with "the proud and violent ghosts" of the Norse, has drawn from ancient sagas and his own research to construct this version of what probably was the white man's first attempt to establish a colony in North America.

The Quest for Vinland

Condensed from Westviking
By FARLEY MOWAT

B Y THE YEAR 1000 the settlements founded on the southwest coast
of Greenland by Leif's father, Erik the Red, were some 15 years
old. Sheep and cattle had multiplied and distant pastures had come
into use. Summer hunting absorbed the younger men, and their walrus
ivory and hides, narwhal tusks and white falcons (prized for hawking)
brought traders from Iceland and Norway. The trading ships doubtless
continued to supply Greenland with timber, although the price would
have remained high and the supply limited.

About 1003 – the date is arbitrary – two big Icelandic ships arrived
not just for trading but apparently for settlement. Commanding one

was the able and energetic Thorfinn Karlsefni, a daring seaman with a resounding genealogy. About 25 years of age, he was descended on one side from an Irish king named Kiarval, on the other from the legendary Ragnor Shaggypants who was claimed as a forebear by innumerable high-ranking Icelanders and Norwegians.

Although Thorfinn was a trader, his 70-foot *knorr* (a tough, broad, one-sailed cargo vessel developed from the traditional Viking longship) was filled with some 40 would-be settlers. So was the one commanded by Thorhall Gamlisson, another trader.

But soon after the Icelanders reached Greenland, they must have become aware of a distressing fact: virtually all the habitable land had been taken up. Eventually someone seems to have made the electrifying proposal that they seek land in the new country to the west. This would have fired the imagination not only of the Icelandic land-seekers but of many Greenlanders who had heard stories of the richness and goodness of Leif's Vinland with its forests, grapes, berries, pastures, and multitudes of fish and game, not to mention a good climate.

Thorfinn and Thorhall decided to outfit their vessels for an expedition west. (Thorfinn had married Gudrid, the widow of one of Erik's sons.) Now two shiploads of Greenlanders joined the expedition, one led by Thorvald, Erik's youngest son, the other by Freydis, Erik's daughter.

The more people talked about the voyage, the more irresistible it must have seemed. Indeed, many more Greenland settlers might have gone if there had been more ships. The four available could have carried, at most, about 160 adults plus cattle and supplies.

Incipient distrust between the Icelanders and Greenlanders is suggested by an agreement between Thorfinn and Freydis that each ship should carry only 30 men of fighting age, together with an unspecified number of women. This was obviously an attempt to keep both sides nearly equal; but the unscrupulous Freydis smuggled aboard five extra Greenland men.

The leaders doubtless spent long hours discussing the problems they would face but chiefly the question of route. The choice would have been governed by the fact that in the ships would be women and children, whose physical endurance was limited, and livestock, for which a large supply of fresh water was required.

Leif's direct southwesterly route would have been the shortest. But he apparently refused to tell the new expedition how far south Vinland was, or where to expect a landfall—just as he seemingly had withheld these clues from his father Erik, who had tried unsuccessfully to reach Vinland in the year 999.

The leaders of the new expedition finally decided to go up the west coast of Greenland and across the narrowest part of Davis Strait to the Vestri Obygd (Western Wilderness), the Cumberland Peninsula of Baffin Island. These were familiar hunting and fishing grounds to the Greenlanders, and ships making the short crossing needed never be far from fresh water or shelter in storms. Drift ice was apparently little threat in those milder times.

The four ships put out one day in early summer and headed north under the towering ramparts of the west Greenland coast. They crossed to the Vestri Obygd, then sailed south into the unknown. They reached the granite snout of northern Labrador; passed by Helluland (Flagstoneland), the rugged coast where the winds from the Torngat Mountains burst out through narrow fiords even in summer; saw higher and higher mountains, snow-crested and glaciered; and came to what they called Markland (Land of Forests). More than halfway down the Labrador coast, they explored Groswater Bay at the entrance to Hamilton Inlet. This bore some similarity to descriptions of Leif's Vinland, but they went on, past 30 miles of coastline composed largely of a 50-yard dark yellow sand beach now called Porcupine Strand. Soon they entered Sandwich Bay and stopped for three days to explore. This bay, too, appeared to resemble Vinland and might have been considered as a site for the winter. But still they went on—into what must have been a severe shock. For the land which had been generally trending southeast now began to fall off sharply toward the southwest.

When they rounded Cape Charles they would have seen to the south what looked like open ocean (the mouth of the Strait of Belle Isle) with, far away to the southeast, the loom of an island or an isolated headland. Now we can suppose that the skippers followed Norse practice and sent someone to climb the 700-foot peak on Cape Charles. From it an observer with ideal viewing conditions would have seen about 35 miles. He would have seen that the distant land to the southeast was a big island (Belle Isle). He would have seen no land beyond, nor to the south, and would have confirmed that the coast of Markland continued out of sight to the southwest.

Doubtless some people clamored to return to Sandwich Bay or Groswater Bay. Some may have been willing to venture farther into the unknown, but along the coast. The more resolute must have argued for investigation of the distant island—and they won the day.

Leaving the Labrador coast, the ships crossed the 18 to 20 miles to Belle Isle, which rises almost sheer from the sea. The visitors called it Straumey (Island of the Strong Currents). If it was a clear day they would have been rewarded by a stupendous view from its plateau, looking nearly 60 miles down the Strait of Belle Isle. But the impression of the strait which one gets from the island's crest is that of a very deep fiord narrowing away into the distance. Consequently the Norse probably mistook the northern tip of Newfoundland for a continuation of the Markland coast, as their name for the strait—Straumfiord (Fiord of the Strong Currents)—indicates.

They must have felt great hope as they looked south. The sagas describe the approaches to Leif's Vinland in terms which closely resemble the Belle Isle area. It seems likely the voyagers were convinced that they had at last reached the portals of Vinland.

But by now the colonists must have become increasingly concerned about their livestock and their women and children, and must have been clamoring to be put ashore, if only temporarily. Thorfinn, for personal reasons, may have been willing to agree to their demands; his wife Gudrid was at least six months pregnant. What was needed was a temporary campsite from which explorations could be launched while the colonists looked after their stock.

The sagas tell us only that after leaving the island they sailed into Straumfiord, went ashore and established a wintering camp.

There is only one small stretch of coast which could have been sufficiently attractive. It lies at the extreme northern tip of Newfoundland between Cape Bauld and Cape Norman, and includes Sacred Bay.

Looking down into Sacred Bay the Norse could have observed the tempting grasslands between the beach and the encroaching forests. The decision was made. The precise landing place seems to have been in Epaves Bay, within Sacred Bay, near present-day L'Anse aux Meadows—where the remains of houses and household implements have been excavated—the only known proof of Norse settlement in North America.

Epaves Bay was no ideal location. The Norse preferred for settlement the inner reaches of protected fiords or bays—what they called *hops*. On the open shore at Epaves Bay there was no harbor and the ships could have been secured only by hauling them several hundred feet above the high-water mark. If the Norse had intended to remain, all hands ought

126

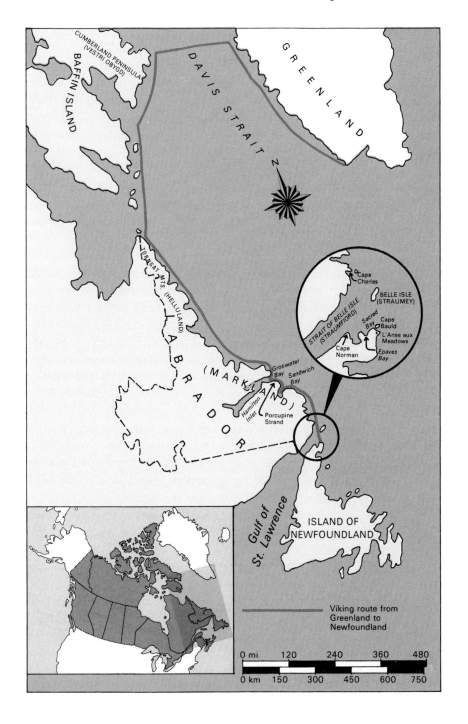

Viking route from
Greenland to
Newfoundland

127

to have prepared for winter. Yet the sagas say they did nothing but explore.

This was a task for the *knorrs'* boats. The larger boats were about 20 feet long and could carry 20 people in an emergency, eight or nine on a long voyage. Equipped with oars and sails, they were lightly built, finely fashioned and fast and easy to handle. With their shallow draft they could enter almost any body of water. The expedition probably possessed six or eight boats and we assume most were used in the exploration.

When all had returned into Epaves Bay, and their skippers had reported, the hope of locating Vinland that season would have failed. By then it would probably have been too late to think of seeking another site; so Epaves Bay, where temporary shelters (called booths) had doubtless already been erected, would have become the wintering camp.

Even so, the colonists may have been satisfied. This was fine berry country, there was no shortage of firewood, and the shore fishery would have been excellent and harbor seals and whales relatively abundant. The adjacent islands were breeding grounds for ducks and other sea birds.

But animal life would have been scarce, and the land itself disappointing. There were no hardwoods of any size. Nor were there any grapes. Winter in this area today is not only cold, it is about as wild as it can be. The low coast is exposed and winds blow over the strait at hurricane strength for days. There would have been long periods when the settlers could not go fishing. They were probably not starving or they would have begun butchering their cattle, but they were hungry enough to call on their gods for help.

Presumably the few Christians among the settlers started praying according to their faith, while an intractable pagan—named Thorhall the Hunter—decided to call on Thor. One did not pray to Thor. The way to gain his aid was to go to some lonely place, as Thorhall did for several days, and alternately argue, bribe, threaten and cajole him into providing assistance.

Christian clerics who transcribed and preserved the Norse sagas during the Middle Ages must have been distressed by the original version of what happened next, for it is clear that Thorhall the Hunter was answered and the Christians were not. Shortly after he got back to camp, a whale blundered into the bay or was found dead in the ice. Great fires were lit and everyone gathered while the cooks filled pots and hung strips of meat to roast.

It was a long, hard winter but one event makes it historic: Thorfinn's wife, Gudrid, gave birth to a son. He was named Snorri, possibly in honor of Snorri Thorbrandsson, who seems to have been Thorfinn's closest comrade and the expedition's wise man. Presumably he was the first child born in North America of white parents.

With the approach of spring, boats could get out whaling and perhaps sealing, yet the people seem to have remained discontented. There was evidently a good deal of bickering over what to do when summer released them.

Dissatisfaction with the Straumfiord camp was probably general. The Greenland colonists were inured to hardship but the Icelanders were not as toughened and were influenced by Thorfinn and by Thorhall Gamlisson. The two shipowners were not settlers; their interest lay in gathering valuable products to trade. For them Straumfiord would have been a major disappointment, and Thorfinn seems to have been convinced that Vinland could still be found and that the expedition ought to search for it.

Leaders of the Greenland contingent, particularly Erik's son Thorvald, evidently shared this view. But there were divergent opinions as to the direction the search should take.

One group of Greenlanders apparently believed they had already passed Vinland on the Markland coast. Another thought it lay along the north coast of Straumfiord (the Strait of Belle Isle). Both appear to have wanted to maintain a base camp at Epaves Bay during the search for Vinland.

The Icelanders, however, felt that Epaves Bay should be abandoned and the hunt for Vinland continued down the south shore of Straumfiord. This divergence led to three exploring expeditions.

Nine Greenlanders under Thorhall the Hunter put out in a boat, intending to return to Markland and hoping to find Vinland at the west end of Groswater Bay. But they were blown out to sea by a westerly gale and probably their small craft was dismasted. Had she kept her sailing capabilities she ought to have been able to run before the wind and make a steady course for Iceland, if not Greenland; without her sail, or with only a makeshift rig, she would have been largely at the mercy of the North Atlantic.

Thorhall and his men reached Ireland but there their luck ran out. The sagas say that the Irish, who were then rebelling against Norse domination, put Thorhall to death.

The second expedition was led by Thorvald. His boat, also manned by about nine Greenlanders, doubtless crossed Straumfiord near Cape Norman, then coasted southwest under the bluff and forbidding north shore of the Gulf of St. Lawrence. How far west they got we do not know. Chances are they wasted days on end in the labyrinth of islands; if they made anything like a thorough examination of the innumerable river mouths and inlets along the way they would have been lucky to make 200 miles up the St. Lawrence River (almost halfway to present-day Sept-Iles) before concluding that Vinland did not lie in this direction.

But when, after about three months, Thorvald's party arrived back at Straumfiord they would have had marvellous tales to tell. The coast they had seen offered any number of attractive settlement sites. The possibility of moving west may have been discussed, but nothing could have been done until Thorhall the Hunter returned—and he never did.

Nor, as the second winter closed in, was there any word of the ships which had sailed south that summer under Thorfinn Karlsefni. This expedition evidently included Thorfinn's Icelanders and the party of Greenlanders led by Erik's daughter Freydis. The ship commanded by Freydis was owned by two Icelandic brothers who accompanied her on the voyage, having been offered half of any profits. She, they and Thorfinn were interested in the same things—furs and hardwood for trading.

Sailing down the west coast of Newfoundland, they came to what is now called St. Pauls Bay. It ran back about two miles into mountains, and just within it, on the south side, was a *hop* or lagoon broadly fringed with grassy meadows. The bay was shallow but there was sufficient water, even at half-tide, for the ships to follow the channel which runs through it. It led to a narrow opening in a limestone ridge where a freshwater lake known as St. Pauls Inlet drains into the bay.

The colonists in the group would have concluded quickly that, Vinland or not, this was an excellent place to settle. Pasture around the shore would have supported far more animals than they had with them. The bay and the inlet behind it teemed with birds and harbor seals. Shellfish, salmon and flatfish abounded. Grapes were apparently plentiful. Some men would have rowed through the breach in the limestone ridge and entered the six-mile-long lake. They would have noticed innumerable caribou trails in the open bogs and they probably saw the animals. The area would have provided everything Vinland offered, except stands of big mixed timber.

130

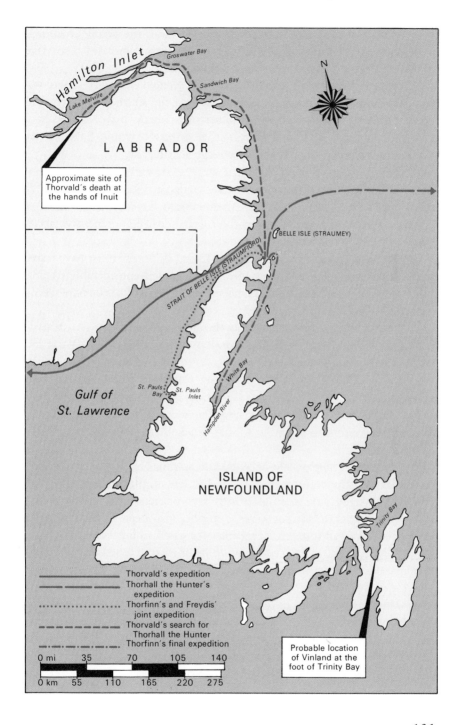

Approximate site of
Thorvald's death at
the hands of Inuit

Hamilton Inlet

Groswater Bay

Sandwich Bay

Lake Melville

L A B R A D O R

N

BELLE ISLE (STRAUMEY)

STRAIT OF BELLE ISLE (STRAUMFIORD)

White Bay

St. Pauls
Bay

St. Pauls
Inlet

Hampden River

Gulf of
St. Lawrence

ISLAND OF
NEWFOUNDLAND

Trinity Bay

——————— Thorvald's expedition
– – – – – – Thorhall the Hunter's
              expedition
.... Thorfinn's and Freydis'
              joint expedition
– - – - – - – Thorvald's search for
              Thorhall the Hunter
–·–·–·–·– Thorfinn's final expedition

0 mi	35	70	105	140
0 km	55	110	165	220	275

Probable location
of Vinland at the
foot of Trinity Bay

Securing the ships under the lee of the land, the people may have built shelters. The cattle were turned loose with someone to see that they didn't stray into the great bog meadow nearby.

No watch was kept; presumably none seemed necessary. There was almost unlimited visibility to seaward and to the south and north. The view inland was obstructed by the limestone ridge, which rose to about 150 feet. But a surprise attack from that direction would have seemed a remote possibility, since behind the ridge lay the lake.

One morning during the third week some early riser glanced out over the estuary—and must have been startled to see a flotilla of small boats approaching. His shout of alarm would have brought the men pouring out, hastily strapping on their gear, tensely apprehensive about this first contact with natives.

And how the approaching Dorset Inuit (Eskimos) must have stared at the ships and the men! They too must have felt considerable trepidation. Their skin canoes seemed to hover on the surface of the bay, reflecting their owners' indecision.

The Dorsets—or Skraelings, as the Norse called them (for reasons now unknown)—began whirling wooden objects that made a noise like flails. These were probably what now are called bullroarers or whizzers, wooden instruments common to many primitive peoples going back to Neolithic times. They make a strange and disturbing noise which seems to come from all sides, rising and falling in pitch and volume. The visual impression is similar to that of a helicopter propeller spinning in bright sunlight.

Some Inuit apparently believed the sound would thwart a variety of unpleasant supernatural spirits. The Dorsets might have thought they had encountered supernatural beings and brandished bullroarers as a matter of prudence. Or the objects might have been used as warning devices or have had some ritual significance when strangers met.

Whatever the facts, Thorfinn and his men concluded that the noisy display was a sign of peace and responded by showing a white shield. The Dorsets landed.

The Norse seem to have been acute enough to treat these uncouth, fur-clad, dark-skinned and almond-eyed strangers with some degree of friendliness. They would have had no way of knowing how great the Skraelings' numbers were or how much of a threat they posed. Regardless of their prowess as fighting men, the Norse were far from home and friends and it behooved them to walk softly.

Good relations seem to have been established and the groups parted in friendly style. The Norse evidently laid the basis for what they hoped would be lucrative trading, perhaps by giving small gifts and indicating that they would appreciate furs in return.

The meeting does not seem to have deterred the Norse from erecting permanent houses. We can assume that the settlers were busy with colonizing chores: we are told that the winter was mild and open.

The Skraelings came again early in the new year, probably an advance group of northbound seal hunters, some of whom had been among the previous visitors.

Trading seems to have begun immediately, the shrewd Norsemen manoeuvring the Dorsets into exchanging furs and skins for crude cheese. Thorfinn forbade the selling of arms: it could not have occurred to him that the Skraelings were superior in weaponry.

While the bargaining went on, some Skraelings seem to have been investigating their surroundings. We can imagine them staring apprehensively but with fascination at the buildings and ships and at the awe-inspiring Norsemen with their great swords and axes, their long beards and their strange clothing. Then something took place which was of paramount importance both to this Norse expedition and to the whole history of Norse attempts to establish colonies in North America.

The settlers had a bull, apparently a singularly intractable and evil-natured beast, which was allowed to run free. He suddenly appeared out of nearby woods, bellowed, pawed the ground, and perhaps charged the nearest Dorsets. The sagas say he "terrified" them "and they ran." Some probably fled to their boats. Some bolted for the Norse houses. The sagas say some "turned toward Thorfinn's house and tried to enter but he defended the door against them."

The Norse seem to have lost their heads too. Suspicious by nature, not realizing that the bull was the cause of the sudden melee, they evidently thought they had been tricked and that this was an attack.

Then the rest of the Skraelings "raced to their boats and rowed away leaving behind their packs and goods." The Norse picked up the abandoned goods and perhaps congratulated themselves on a profitable day's work. Nevertheless they felt considerable apprehension. Thoroughly experienced in the ritual of the blood feud, they expected to be attacked again. They were so convinced of this that they committed their second major blunder—and thereby doomed Norse colonization.

Stockades were built around some houses. A council of war was called and the leaders worked out a plan to catch attacking Skraelings off guard.

Ten men were ordered to show themselves as bait, probably on the low, sandy point at the south side of the bay's entrance. The Skraelings were expected to pounce on this small group before attacking the main camp. But the rest of the Norse warriors would be ambushed in scrub spruce fringing the southern end of the point. Paths were cleared to the seaward edge of the woods, along which cattle could be driven ahead of the attacking warriors.

Nothing happened for three weeks. Then a guard came pounding into camp with news that Skraeling boats were approaching.

What followed was a compounding of errors. The Norse took it for granted that this was an attacking force, although it is most unlikely that the Dorsets of the bull episode would have returned. It is far more likely that they fled north to the sealing grounds, not the least anxious to try another round with the devilish strangers.

This second party of Dorsets may well have appeared from the south, also bound for the sealing grounds but unaware of what had happened earlier. They saw some aliens—about whom they had doubtless heard during the winter—waving their arms in what may have seemed to the Dorsets an invitation to land. It was probably bravado calculated to goad them into attacking.

The Dorsets pulled for shore and hauled their light vessels well up on the beach. Then the 10 men on the spit presumably charged while the main body of the Norse burst out of the forest, driving the cattle ahead of them and yelling fiercely.

The Skraelings would have been momentarily paralyzed but at the first flash of a raised sword or axe they would have reacted instinctively, for they had their sealing weapons such as slings and harpoons. On the other hand most of the Norse weapons were intended for thrusting, hacking or bludgeoning in close combat. The Norse armament was practically useless against people who fought from a distance. The Norse cut down three or four Skraelings but soon were themselves in full flight.

To justify this retreat the sagas make a great deal of strange, bladderlike objects which came flying overhead, implying that they were supernatural weapons of such potency that not even Norsemen could have been expected to stand against them. Unfortunately for Norse pride there is a simpler explanation. The Skraelings would have had inflated bladder floats attached to their sealing harpoons. When attacked, they simply snatched up the harpoons, bladders and all, and let fly.

The flight of the Norse warriors did not cease until they stood with their backs to a rocky cliff–probably the limestone ridge separating St. Pauls Bay from the lake. They did not even attempt a defence of their stockaded houses or of the women and children. Most of the non-combatants probably joined in the wild flight and it seems certain that if the Skraelings had pursued vigorously they could have slaughtered many Norse. That they did not do so is confirmed by the sagas, which state that the Norse lost only two people during the battle, both evidently warriors.

The Norse records say that Freydis, in an advanced state of pregnancy, could not keep up with the other fugitives but that she flung stinging rebukes at the backs of the fleeing men. Then she snatched up a sword. The sagas say she "prepared to defend herself. The Skraelings came closer, whereupon she let fall her shift and slapped her breasts with the naked sword."

There is no other record in Scandinavian history of a woman attempting to protect herself in the face of armed attack by exposing her breasts. Why Freydis did it is a matter for conjecture. The fact remains that the Skraelings did not attack her.

But the final stages of the "battle" make it clear that, far from being aggressors, the Dorsets were the victims of a surprise attack and concerned only with defending themselves until they could escape. They did not pursue the Norse warriors to the cliff, and they did not loot or burn the abandoned settlement. Yet from this encounter emerged a fearsome myth which was to haunt the Greenland Norse for centuries. Later records portray the Skraelings as implacable and supernaturally formidable enemies, impossible to overpower in open battle and dangerous to attack unless caught off guard or heavily outnumbered.

Their pride demolished, their security shaken, the Norse decided to abandon the settlement.

When Thorfinn's expedition arrived back at Straumfiord (after encountering and killing five Skraelings en route) they found "an abundance of everything they needed," not only food and other supplies, but the solace and sense of security that came from being with their own kind again.

After exchanging experiences, the leaders would have called a council on what to do next. Erik's son Thorvald had apparently decided to voyage north in search of Thorhall the Hunter but from the sagas we gather that some colonists wished to go home immediately. Others may have favored one more attempt to find a suitable and safe site for a colony. Still others may have been willing to settle in the Straumfiord area, which was better than anything Greenland had to offer.

The trader-skippers may have still hoped to acquire a cargo of hardwood. Perhaps with this in mind, Thorfinn decided to make one last voyage in search of Vinland, in the only direction which had not yet been explored—down the east coast of Newfoundland. He and 40 men were to voyage south in one ship while the balance of the Icelanders remained at Straumfiord with those Greenlanders who did not accompany Thorvald in his search for the Hunter.

Thorvald went to the head of Groswater Bay, then entered Lake Melville, a salt-water inlet 150 miles long and up to 20 miles wide. On its shores the Norse surrounded and slaughtered eight Dorsets, apparently caught asleep under their skin boats. One native escaped.

The Norse returned victoriously to their ship and sailed on. That evening they pitched camp on the shore and slept.

But the escaping Dorset had spread a warning. At dawn a flotilla of boats filled with hostile men appeared on the horizon. The Greenlanders rushed to their *knorr*. Behind the oaken bulwarks and the rows of shields hung over them, the Norse were reasonably protected. The Dorsets made no attempt to board, and after firing stones and arrows with no apparent results, they withdrew.

They had done better than they knew: Thorvald had been mortally wounded by an arrow.

He seems to have died well, in the Viking tradition. Being great givers of death, the Norse could accept it without demur. Thorvald was buried, according to his wishes, on a headland which had caught his fancy. Then, giving up both the search for Vinland and for Thorhall, his shipmates made for Straumfiord, convinced that the Hunter's disappearance could be laid at the door of the Skraelings. They would have wondered if there was any safety in all this hostile land.

Meanwhile, Thorfinn's ship had headed south along a bald and forbidding coast whose cliffs became more and more formidable, rising 1,000 feet from the sea in places. Occasionally they passed little fiords, most of them mere slits in the sheer face of the cliffs.

Eventually they would have realized that they were sailing into the mouth of a big sound (White Bay). This may have led to renewed hopes that they had found the great fiord which ran south to terminate at Leif's Vinland. Excitement must have been intense as they passed down the last few miles and saw the end of the fiord before them.

Their hopes would have climaxed as the ship reached a sand and gravel bar which extended across the mouth of the Hampden River. A party would have rowed through the gap in the bar into a tiny lagoon, not much more than 100 yards in diameter yet large enough to provide a harbor for the *knorr*.

This was a *hop,* but a minute one. It could have borne no comparisons with the fabulous harbor of Leif's Vinland, nor even with the *hop* that Thorfinn had discovered in St. Pauls Bay. But there were compensations. The hard and soft timber must have been everything that Thorfinn ever hoped to find. There was open land and quite probably it was grassland; if so, the colonists may have hoped they had found a new settlement site. During the next few days they would have been busy investigating their surroundings while the traders' men began lumbering. The location of the camp is not given in the sagas but it would logically have been on the lagoon shore.

At this site the Norse met a people they had never seen before—the Beothuk Indians.

Beothuks used to leave their wintering grounds in the interior of Newfoundland in June and migrate to the coasts for the summer. Those journeying down the Hampden River in birchbark canoes, heading for campsites along White Bay, doubtless discovered the strangers at the river mouth long before the Norse knew there were Indians about. The sounds and sights of men lumbering would have alerted the Indians, and they would have hidden their canoes while one man went forward to reconnoitre. The sight of the *knorr,* of the Norse shelters and of strange men would have amazed the Indian scout but perhaps did not frighten him. The Beothuks seem to have been a friendly and unsuspicious people.

There is no way of knowing whether the scout deliberately revealed himself or was spotted. In any event the Norse seem to have shouted at him and the Beothuk came down. The sagas say he limped or hopped to the ship.

His appearance seems to have tempted the Norse into folly. Instead of trying to make friends, they apparently tried to seize him. Crippled or not, he escaped and vanished up a valley to the north. The Icelanders, with bitter memories of the Skraelings, now doubtless gave up hope of settling and made haste to complete their lumbering. Every man would have gone about alert to the dangers of a surprise attack.

It may have taken several days for the Beothuks to decide what to do about the strangers who were camped astride the main route to their summer camps. Eventually they seem to have decided on a peaceful confrontation.

When the day came, a large company of Beothuks, their bodies glistening with oil and red ochre, advanced slowly out of the forest. We assume that the Beothuks made overtures of peace, probably by offering gifts of sable and other rich furs. The Norse began trading, although the Beothuks probably thought they were simply exchanging gifts.

During the exchanges some of the Beothuks seem to have been indulging their curiosity. One woman peeked into a shelter where the Norse women had doubtless been told to remain until danger was past, and saw Gudrid, Thorfinn's wife, sitting beside the cradle of her 18-month-old son Snorri. Gudrid appears to have tried to make friends by asking the alien woman her name, and by repeating her own. The Beothuk woman tried to imitate the unfamiliar words, whereupon Gudrid beckoned her in.

One wonders what might have happened if the two women had established some sort of rapport. The sagas tell of many proud Norsemen who listened meekly to the outspoken criticisms and suggestions of their women. But at that moment there was a "loud noise" and the Beothuk woman vanished. Blood was flowing once again.

We do not know the cause. Perhaps one of the Beothuks picked up a Norse axe and began to examine it: he may have handed it about among his friends. Probably the Norse reacted in possessive fury. The sagas record that one native was killed "because he seemed about to take" a Norse weapon.

Panic ensued among the Indians. The sagas say that in "the battle" which followed many natives were slain and the rest ran wildly for the woods. There is no mention of Norsemen being killed or wounded.

The Norse hurried to Straumfiord because, as the sagas say, they were "unwilling to risk men's lives any longer" in this place.

The Norse had conducted four exploring expeditions: to the north, west, southwest and southeast. They had not found Vinland. Nor had they found any unoccupied country. Dangerous natives were all around, and sooner or later they could be expected at Straumfiord.

If the Icelanders needed any additional persuasion to go home, it would have been provided by the impending departure of Thorfinn and Thorhall Gamlisson. Having laden their ships, the two men had every reason to sail as soon as possible, for summer was drawing to an end.

En route home Thorhall Gamlisson's worm-eaten ship sank, but he survived (along with half his company) and lived for many years in Iceland where he became known as The Vinlander. The ship bearing Thorfinn and Gudrid reached Greenland. They spent the winter with Erik the Red, then went to Iceland where, the saga literature says, "many great people" descended from them.

The Greenlanders, however, decided to stay the winter at Straumfiord. Since Thorvald's death they had apparently been led by the ruthless Freydis, who had also taken over Thorvald's ship. She may have been anxious to make one more attempt to find Vinland or at least to get a profitable cargo of hardwood.

It was a grim winter. The sagas say "the men began to form in factions and to quarrel over the women ... and there was serious trouble." Freydis apparently provoked a fight with the Icelandic brothers whose ship she was using and with whom she had agreed to share profits. They and their crew were killed. Freydis herself slaughtered five of their women.

Soon after the massacre Freydis and her people sailed home in the brothers' big ship. (Perhaps she used Thorvald's ship as a funeral pyre for the corpses of the Icelanders.) In Greenland she must have threatened her crew to suppress talk of the slaughter but eventually the rumor reached Erik. His torturing of three of Freydis' men revealed the full story, but he himself would have had to try to hush it up or be held responsible—together with Freydis and her people—by the relatives of the dead Icelanders.

Thus ended a brave and hopeful voyage into a new world. But it was brought to nothing as much by human stupidity as by the ill will of those implacable fates in which the Norse had such an unshakable belief. Nor had it come even close to Vinland, which apparently was on the east coast of Newfoundland at the foot of Trinity Bay in a lagoon called Tickle Bay—as lovely a place as one could wish to see.

*Samuel de Champlain stands where the uninterrupted history of Canada
begins. Explorer, fighter, lover of good food and drink, he was
the first European of stature who chose to live and die in Canada.
He first came in 1603 as a private observer with a fact-finding and
fur trading expedition. His imagination fired, he returned again
and again, thrusting himself onto the warpaths and trade routes of the
wilderness, overcoming treachery, pain and defeat to consolidate his vision
of New France—a vision that was to become Canada.*

Champlain, The Father of Canada

By MORRIS BISHOP

THE SHIP *La Bonne Renommée* sighted Newfoundland on May 7, 1603. Beating her way among icebergs and floes, she entered the Gulf of St. Lawrence, then sailed upstream to the mouth of the Saguenay River. There, on May 24, she dropped anchor near Tadoussac, a rendezvous of French and Indian fur traders. Champlain and the leader

Champlain superintends the construction of the habitation at Port Royal on the Annapolis Basin—in what now is Nova Scotia. Left: a map of New France drawn by Champlain.

of the expedition, an adventurer named François Pont-Gravé—an old hand at the fur trade—went ashore making signs of amity.

"We went to the lodge of the Grand Sagamore [chief]," Champlain recorded, "and found him and some 80 of his companions making a feast. He received us very well and made us sit down beside him. When they had ended their feast they began to dance, taking in their hands, as a mark of rejoicing, the scalps of their enemies. They were celebrating a victory over the Iroquois, of whom they had slain about 100."

This was the aftermath of but one battle in an old war. The Algonkian nations of the Ottawa River, the lower St. Lawrence and the Saint John River Valley had joined in common cause against the Iroquois to the south, an aggressive, well-organized confederacy that was raiding the St. Lawrence country, taking plunder and captives.

The French wanted furs and fish, for which the favor of the Algonkians was necessary, so offered them an alliance against the Iroquois. The alliance lasted a century and a half and determined the character of the French penetration of America.

After the feast, the French and the Indians spent a fortnight in polite conversations and fur trading. Champlain attended a victory ball. The Indians, their faces painted like French maskers at carnival time, performed a solemn cotillion. "They arranged all their women and girls side by side, and themselves stood behind, singing all in unison. Suddenly all the women and girls proceeded to cast off their mantles of skins, showing their privities but retaining their beads and braided cords made of porcupine quills, dyed of various colors. After they had made an end of their songs they cried all with one voice: 'Ho, ho, ho!'"

On June 18 Champlain began a journey up the St. Lawrence in a 12-ton pinnace brought from France in parts and assembled at Tadoussac. In four days he reached the narrow spot (a *kébec* in Algonkian) where Quebec City now stands. It was beautiful country, covered with oak, cypress, birch, fir, aspen, fruit trees and vines. The soil, if tilled, would be as good as that of France.

The explorers went up Lac Saint-Pierre, penetrated the nest of islands at its head and came to the mouth of the River of the Iroquois (the Richelieu). An Algonkian camp here was the base for operations against the Iroquois. Champlain went a dozen miles up the Richelieu to the rapids of Saint-Ours. From his guides he learned that farther south lay a long lake—the one destined to be known by his name. Beyond this lay another (Lake George), and at its end dwelt the terrible Iroquois.

The French returned to the St. Lawrence and continued upstream to where Montreal is today. They inspected the great Sault Saint-Louis, now called the Lachine Rapids. "I assure you I never saw any torrent of water with such force," Champlain reported. Only by canoe could he proceed farther, and time was short. On July 4 the party renounced further exploration and went downstream to Tadoussac. Six weeks later the French sailed for home with a cargo of furs.

It had been a successful trip, promising well for the future. Champlain had found the country fit for colonization. The fur trade promised immediate profits. The natives were cordial. There was, to be sure, a lurking Iroquois danger to the south, but the French had made an alliance with the Algonkians and would defend their fur trade routes.

It was to be five years, however, before Champlain again set foot on the shores of the St. Lawrence. He did sail to the New World in 1604 in an expedition headed by the sieur de Monts, who had agreed to establish colonies in return for a 10-year monopoly in the fur trade, but de Monts chose a more southern location on the Bay of Fundy: Acadia. He made unsuccessful attempts to found permanent colonies, first on an island in the St. Croix River, then in 1605 at Port Royal on the Annapolis Basin—where Champlain founded the Order of Good Cheer to help pass the long winters. The settlement had to be abandoned when de Monts lost his monopoly and ran into financial difficulties in 1607.

In Paris that October Champlain found de Monts deeply discouraged. He had lost more than 100,000 livres (almost a quarter of a million dollars) and was on the edge of ruin. Under the King's new system of free trade he could think no more of planting colonies.

Champlain summoned up all his eloquence. The settlement in Acadia had been a mistake, he told de Monts. The area had few furs, few minerals, no entry by water to the interior and no passage to China. The thing to do was to return to the St. Lawrence, the great channel of the fur trade, and establish a permanent warehouse and colony at the strong point where Quebec now stands. The colony would be a fort to protect the river against the terrible raids of the Iroquois. Thence the company's traders could go in summer up to the great rapids, get the first choice of furs, buy them cheaply and bring them downriver in security.

De Monts was persuaded. He and Champlain laid their proposal before King Henry IV. The monarch was interested. He had observed that the Dutch East India Company was paying dividends of 75 per cent, that the English had established trading posts in India and were preparing a settlement in Virginia. France too should have colonies. He regretted cancelling the monopoly and agreed to restore it.

De Monts appointed Champlain his lieutenant and raised money to equip three vessels. One went to Port Royal. A second, under Pont-Gravé, was to spend the summer trading in the St. Lawrence and return to France in the autumn. The third carried Champlain and a little band of artisans with supplies for a northern winter.

Champlain arrived July 3, 1608—our date for the founding of Quebec. He selected land near the water's edge, approximately on the site of the present church of Notre-Dame-des-Victoires.

Champlain drove his men hard. Sluggish from long idleness at sea, they grumbled at clearing ground and digging ditches in the summer heat of the St. Lawrence Valley. They were tormented by flies and mosquitoes. Jean Duval, a locksmith, sounded out four of his companions whom he knew to be troublemakers. One was Antoine Natel, another locksmith. They should rise and cast off tyranny, said Duval. After inciting the other workmen, one by one, they would give a false alarm some night and shoot Champlain as he came out of his hut. Then they would make overtures to the outlaw Basque traders at Tadoussac, sell them the new fort and go back to Europe very rich.

But while the malcontents were working on their mates, Antoine Natel, unable to bear the weight of his secret, confessed. Champlain summoned him, "all trembling with fear. I told him that I forgave him provided he told the whole truth on every point."

Champlain sent Natel back to his work. He then arranged for a trusty sailor to invite the conspirators on board his pinnace to enjoy some wine. At 10 in the evening, when the plotters were carousing below decks, Champlain and his faithful sailors appeared, well armed, and commanded them to surrender.

The jury of ship's officers and men voted to put Duval to death—as a punishment and as an example. He was hanged and his head was placed on a pike and set up at the highest spot of the fort. The others were sent back to France in irons "to receive fuller justice."

Now the other settlers set to work with a will to make their winter home. Champlain called it his Habitation. It consisted of three buildings, each 19 by 13 feet and two stories high, a single-storied warehouse of the same dimensions, and a separate dovecote to shelter pigeons. Around the continuous wall of the buildings ran an exterior gallery for defence.

Outside was a moat with a drawbridge, then an exterior palisade. Beyond the palisade were gardens. Atop the structure were a sundial and a flagstaff flying the lilies of France.

When his buildings were tight against the weather, Champlain put some of his men to clearing the gardens and planting wheat, rye and grapevines, at which activity the friendly Indians gaped and wondered.

Eels that the Indians preserved that autumn – they did nothing else to prepare for winter – were gone before the end of January. The natives ate their dogs and gnawed at their moccasins. By February, Champlain recorded, "so hungry were these poor wretches that in the hope that I would succor them, some made their appearance on the other side of the river. This was out of our power on account of the large amount of ice which was floating down the river. We could hear them screaming so much that it was pitiful." The Indians finally swam to a big floe and landed at the settlement, "so thin and emaciated that they looked like skeletons, most of them being unable to stand.

"I ordered bread and beans to be given to them. They could not wait for these to be cooked before eating them. They noticed some carrion which about two months previously I had thrown out to attract foxes. When the weather was mild it stank so strongly that one could not stay near it. Nevertheless they carried it off to their new wigwam where they devoured it half-cooked."

The snow lay five feet deep about the palisade. During cold spells the trees split with a sound like musket shots. The wine, the ink and the medicines froze. A colonist lost the surface tissue of his tongue by attempting to lick snow from his axe. Eighteen men contracted scurvy, and 10 died. Three more died of dysentery. The surgeon died. Every man was down with one disease or the other.

On April 8, 1609, there was a sudden thaw. Trees and bushes began to put forth their green. The survivors nibbled at new shoots, and little by little the scurvy disappeared. But of 24 men only eight remained, and four were still tottering with illness.

On June 7, at Tadoussac, Champlain met Pont-Gravé, who had just arrived with news from France. De Monts' monopoly had expired but he was ready to continue his support of the Quebec colony. Champlain was ordered to return to France at the end of the summer to report to de Monts.

"And now," said Pont-Gravé, "what is to be our plan for the summer?"

Champlain's decision was to push farther upstream, to meet the Indians from the interior nearer to their hunting grounds and thus get the pick of the furs. The obvious place was the Lachine Rapids but the region was dangerous, being exposed to the marauding Iroquois. Champlain decided to make a raid into the hostile land. A dozen men with firearms would be the equal of an Iroquois army.

After his consultation with Pont-Gravé, Champlain paused in Quebec, then continued upstream to where he found an encampment of Algonkians and Hurons near present-day Batiscan.

This was his first meeting with the tall, handsome Hurons, the aristocrats of Canada's Indian tribes. Hurons had met Jacques Cartier some 75 years earlier. Even then they had been at war with the Iroquois and by 1603 they had migrated to Huronia, just south and east of Georgian Bay. They sold corn, tobacco and fish to other tribes, and bought furs, which they traded to the French or to intermediaries for European goods. In 1609 the Huron trading empire was still abuilding, and Champlain knew the commercial importance of the race. He was glad to welcome their representatives and to entertain them.

There were solemn greetings and exchanges of presents. Champlain smoked in ritual silence with the chiefs, then told them that he and Pont-Gravé wished to help the northern tribes against their enemies. The whole party repaired to Quebec, and there feasted and danced for several days before some set out for the land of the Iroquois.

Champlain, with 11 Frenchmen and 60 Indians, ascended the St. Lawrence to the mouth of the Richelieu. But when they reached the roaring rapids at Chambly they found no passage for the Frenchmen's shallop and no possibility of cutting a road to move the boat through the dense woods. Champlain decided to proceed regardless, "in order to carry out my promise and also to fulfil my desire." He called for French volunteers. Two, whose names we do not know, stepped forward, and the others were sent back to Quebec in the shallop.

Now the warriors, white and red, by-passed the Chambly Rapids. The Indians carried their 24 canoes; Champlain and his men their heavy arquebuses (primitive, heavy muskets), powder, match and shot. They wore steel corselets.

By nightfall July 13 they stood at what we call Lake Champlain. For two weeks the party felt its way along the lake through hostile terri-

Near Ticonderoga, shots that inspired a tradition of French treachery.

tory, travelling by dark, hiding by day in the deep woods. Champlain was stirred by the beauty of the summer nights on this lovely lake, lying among monstrous mountains in the velvet darkness.

At 10 o'clock on the evening of July 29, paddling softly, the invaders came to a cape, probably near present-day Ticonderoga, N.Y. Out of the dark came shouts and cries—a war party of Iroquois, heading north. Startled, the Iroquois pulled in to shore and built a barricade. The invaders lay offshore.

Two Iroquois canoes paddled out for a parley, "to learn from their enemies whether they wished to fight. These replied that they had no other desire, but that it was necessary to wait for daylight in order to distinguish one another. [The Iroquois] said that as soon as the sun should rise they would attack us, and to this our Indians agreed."

Champlain's party spent the night in their canoes. In the first dawn they went ashore and formed in battle array. At the agreed time the Iroquois marched solemnly out of their barricade. They outnumbered the Hurons and Algonkians by more than three to one.

"They came slowly to meet us with a gravity and calm which I admired, and at their head were three chiefs. Our Indians likewise advanced in similar order, and told me that those who had three big plumes were the chiefs, and that I was to kill them.

"Our Indians began to run toward their enemies, who stood firm and had not yet noticed my white companions who went off into the woods. Our Indians began to call to me with loud cries; they divided into two groups and I marched on until I was within some 30 yards of the enemy who, as soon as they caught sight of me, halted and gazed at me. When I saw them make a move to draw their bows, I took aim with my arquebus and shot straight at one of the three chiefs. With this shot two fell to the ground and one of their companions was wounded. I had put four bullets in my arquebus. Our people began to shout so loudly that one could not have heard it thunder, and meanwhile the arrows flew thick on both sides. The Iroquois were much astonished that two men should have been killed so quickly. As I was reloading my arquebus, one of my companions fired a shot from within the woods, which astonished them again so much that they took to flight into the depths of the forest, whither I pursued them and laid low still more of them. Our Indians also killed several and took 10 or 12 prisoners."

So, on the shore of Champlain's lake, were fired the first shots in France's long war against the Iroquois and their Dutch and English allies. Champlain's arquebus inspired among the Iroquois a tradition of French treachery never to be forgotten.

The victors danced, sang and feasted. Then the flotilla headed northward. "The Indians, toward evening, took one of the prisoners, to whom they made a harangue on the cruelties which he and his friends had practiced upon them, and that he should resign himself to receive as much. They ordered him to sing, if he had the heart. He did so, but it was a very sad song to hear.

"Meanwhile our Indians kindled a fire and, when it was well lighted, each took a brand and burned this poor wretch a little at a time . . . . Sometimes they would leave off, throwing water on his back. Then they tore out his nails and applied fire to the ends of his fingers and to his privy member. Afterward they scalped him and caused a certain kind of gum to drip very hot upon the crown of his head. Then they pierced his arms near the wrists and with sticks pulled and tore out his sinews by main force and, when they saw they could not get them out, they cut them off. This poor wretch uttered strange cries, and I felt pity at seeing him treated in this way. Still he bore it so firmly that sometimes one would have said he felt scarcely any pain.

"When they saw that I was not pleased, they told me to give him a shot with the arquebus. I did so and with one shot caused him to escape all the tortures he would have suffered."

This was Champlain's first view of Indian torture. He had never seen such delight in agony. He now knew what it would mean for a white man to fall into the hands of Indian enemies. At Chambly Rapids the Hurons and Algonkians left. "We all separated with great protestations of mutual friendship, and they asked me if I would not go to their country and aid them continually like a brother. I promised them I would."

Champlain busied himself for the rest of the summer with the fur trade and work on the Habitation. He sailed from Tadoussac Sept. 5, arrived in France Oct. 15, and went to see de Monts, who was camped outside the King's palace at Fontainebleau. He presented to the King a belt of porcupine quills, two scarlet tanagers, the skull of a monster garfish from Lake Champlain, and an Iroquois scalp.

For two years Champlain strove to develop the colony, spending the summers in Canada and the winters in France endeavoring to stir up interest in exploration and in a crusade against the Iroquois.

During this period, on Dec. 30, 1610, the 43-year-old explorer married 12-year-old Hélène Boullé, the daughter of a secretary in the King's household. His need for love had become paternal, and the marriage contract provided that the union not be consummated for two years. Hélène did spend the years 1620-24 in Canada, but the couple had no children and after Champlain's death she became a nun.

Meanwhile, things were going none too well for de Monts and his partners. Without the fur trade monopoly, profits declined, yet all the expenses of the Habitation at Quebec remained.

At a meeting with de Monts in France in the fall of 1611, Champlain dwelt on the importance of the alliance he had formed with the Hurons and Algonkians, on the presumed wealth of the interior, and on the discoveries waiting to be made. He spoke of a promise he had made to return the following year with a force of 50 men. Surely the new king, Louis XIII, could be persuaded to provide such an insignificant army to win an empire for France!

De Monts' imagination took fire. "I must attend to this myself.

It will need influence at court. As soon as I can get away, I shall go to Fontainebleau. I shall meet you there."

But on the highway toward Paris, Champlain's horse stumbled and fell and nearly killed him. Champlain lay in a dismal roadside inn through autumn and winter. When he was well enough to ride on he found that de Monts' partners refused to have anything more to do with New France. Free trade, they said, would be their ruin.

But de Monts had faith. He bought out his partners' shares and in the spring of 1612 sent Pont-Gravé to carry on the settlement of Quebec. Champlain, unable to go because of his injury, grieved to think of the disappointment of his Indian friends, who would expect to see him again at the head of a little army.

He proposed that, since free trade was proving ruinous and there was little chance of a renewal of de Monts' own monopoly, all the law-abiding traders should get together and form a common company. De Monts consented, and to Champlain handed the whole duty of obtaining authorization at court.

Champlain turned for help to the Prince de Condé, a cousin of Louis XIII. The prince was induced to become viceroy of New France, and Champlain became his lieutenant – the effective ruler of the colony.

Meanwhile, the ships that had gone to Canada for the summer of 1612 returned. Among the passengers was young Nicolas du Vignau, who had wintered with Chief Tessouat and the Allumette Island tribe of the upper Ottawa River near present-day Pembroke, Ont. He brought exciting news.

"I have seen the northern sea [Hudson Bay]," he said. "The Ottawa comes from a lake [Nipissing] which has an outlet northward into that sea. In 17 days one can go from the [Lachine] Rapids to that sea and back again. On the shore of the sea I saw the wreck of the English ship."

Champlain knew that Henry Hudson [see p. 160] had been cast adrift in James Bay in 1611. Vignau's story seemed reasonable, and nothing would spur the French king so much as a suggestion of English commercial rivalry. It justified Champlain in making a serious attempt to find a good overland route to this northern sea.

There was, however, something vaguely suspect in Vignau's words and manner. "Tell me all the truth, so that I may inform the king," said Champlain. "I warn you that if you are telling a lie, you are putting a rope around your neck." Vignau took the greatest of oaths that his story was true, and drew up a written account of it.

Searching for the northern sea, Champlain uses an astrolabe to determine latitude.

On March 6, 1613, Champlain sailed in Pont-Gravé's ship on his sixth voyage to Canada. He arrived at the Lachine Rapids on May 21 to find trading already in progress.

Some Algonkians from the Ottawa told Champlain that in the previous summer they had been badly treated by merchants. The story had been spread that Champlain was dead. The Indians had concluded that no military aid was to be expected from the French; they had decided to go on the warpath unaided, and perhaps come no more to the trading fairs.

This intelligence pleased Champlain, for it chimed with his purpose

151

to explore the Ottawa River and find the northern sea. "I resolved to make my way into their country to encourage those who had stayed at home with an assurance of the good treatment they would receive, as well as of my desire to help them in their wars, " he wrote.

He obtained from the Indians two canoes and a guide. On May 27 he loaded the craft with food, arms and presents. He also carried his precious copper astrolabe, with which to calculate latitudes. He had with him four Frenchmen, sturdy paddlers. One was Nicolas du Vignau.

Above present-day Hawkesbury, Ont., Champlain met Indians who tried to dissuade him from continuing. "The way is bad," they said. "Hitherto you have seen nothing like it." Champlain pushed on.

He came, on June 4, to the future site of Ottawa and it captivated him.

Near present-day Portage-du-Fort, Que., the Indians warned that the rapids would now get much worse. They urged Champlain to portage west to an easier route through a chain of lakes.

"Not at all," said Nicolas du Vignau. "Stay with the river."

The Indians scoffed and Champlain looked at the young man with suspicion. Vignau had said the northern sea was only eight days from the Lachine Rapids: they had already been out for 10 days and had not even reached Allumette Island where Nicolas had spent the winter with Tessouat.

Champlain took the Indians' advice. Ahead lay a seven-mile portage over high, heavily wooded ground. Champlain's load was three arquebuses, three paddles, his cloak and his astrolabe. The portage took them "through more difficult country than we had yet seen, on account of the wind having blown down pine trees one on top of the other."

(While floundering among the trees Champlain lost his astrolabe. Where it fell, it lay for 254 years. It was discovered in 1867 by a sharp-eyed farmer and is now in the collection of the New York Historical Society.)

When the party finally reached Allumette Island, Champlain was welcomed with shouts of delight from his old friend Tessouat, and taken to the chief's village for a banquet the following day. Afterward Champlain addressed the tribal council, telling them through an interpreter of his desires to aid them in their wars and to visit Lake Nipissing. "I request of you, therefore, four canoes and a crew of eight men to make this expedition."

The Indians warned that the way was hard and that the tribes to the west were sorcerers, but Champlain pointed to Vignau: "This youth," he said, "has been in that country; he did not notice all the difficulties you speak of . . . ."

Tessouat stared at the youth. "Nicolas, is it true that you have said you were in the Nipissing country?"

After a silence Vignau spoke. "Yes, I was there."

"You are a liar!" cried Tessouat. "You know very well that every night you slept alongside of me and my children, and every morning you got up in the same place. If you went to those tribes, it was in your sleep. How have you been so impudent as to tell lies to your chief, and so wicked as to try to risk his life among so many dangers?"

Vignau hung his head.

"Nicolas," said Champlain sternly, "what is your answer? You must make a reply to these accusations."

"I was there," said Vignau.

"Liar," the Indians all shouted. "Put him to death! Let him name the person who took him! Let him name the lakes, rivers and trails on the way!"

"I have forgotten the name of my guide," said Vignau. "I have shown the route on the map I gave to the sieur de Champlain."

Champlain drew out the map and showed it to the Indians. They questioned Vignau regarding it, but he would not make any reply.

Champlain demanded again to know the truth and vowed that if he was deluded into proceeding farther on a vain mission he would have Vignau hanged.

"After some reflection," Champlain wrote later, "he fell on his knees and asked me for pardon, declaring that all he had stated regarding this sea was false; that he had never seen it and had never been farther than Tessouat's village." There was no point in travelling farther. On June 10 Champlain took leave of Tessouat, promising that he would come the following year, ready to go on the warpath. Tessouat promised to collect great numbers of Indians for that enterprise.

Forty canoes, loaded with furs, set off downstream to the Lachine Rapids where there was an act of justice to be done. Champlain assembled all the Frenchmen and the Indian chiefs. Nicolas du Vignau confessed that he had lied because he wished to return to New France and make the journey to the northern sea. If Champlain would let him, he said, he would visit this sea and in the following year would bring back news concerning it. On this condition Champlain granted him his pardon. We never hear of him again.

In Paris, Champlain made his report to the Prince de Condé and to the company owners. They decided to carry on in accordance with the terms of their concession. The company—soon known as the *Compagnie de Champlain*—became the recognized power of New France.

Champlain had another task on this visit—to recruit missionaries to work among his Indian friends. "They were living without law," he wrote, "without religion, like brute beasts. So I exerted myself to find some good friars, with zeal and affection for the glory of God, whom I might persuade to come with me to plant the faith."

The Récollets, accepting poverty, the rudest of garments and the extreme of self-denial, volunteered to a man to go to Canada. Champlain raised enough money to buy food and equipment for four missionaries.

The Prince de Condé had obtained an 11-year renewal of the company's monopoly, as well as an extension of his control to the Gaspé Peninsula. The 10 merchants agreed to take out six families of colonists each year. Champlain was to have at his disposal, for military purposes, four men from each of the five licenced trading vessels on the river.

The supervision of these arrangements was of such importance that Champlain dared not depart for the trading journey of 1614. The Indian chiefs to whom he had promised to return with an army were disappointed again.

Champlain and his party, including the four missionaries, sailed April 24, 1615. At Quebec the Récollets began building a chapel. Champlain's Indian friends at Lachine told him Iroquois raiders were becoming increasingly bold as the Huron trade developed. The Dutch on the Hudson River encouraged the Iroquois warriors, paying well for captured furs from the north. It was time the Hurons strike the enemy in his own country.

Champlain told the chiefs he was ready to assist. Overjoyed, they promised to raise an army of 2,500, and Champlain pledged to bring as many men as he could. On July 9 he began the long journey to Huronia, with interpreters Thomas Godefroy and Etienne Brûlé [see p. 16] and 10 Indians. With six men in one canoe and seven in another, they could carry only their arquebuses, a scanty supply of powder, some trade goods, a minimum of clothing and the barest provision of food.

They ascended the Ottawa, portaging endlessly around rapids, and on July 26 Champlain stood on the shore of Lake Nipissing. After two days of rest and canoe repair he was on the move down the French River, past falls and rapids, and finally into Lake Huron, the *mer douce* (freshwater sea) of which he had first heard 12 years before, of which he had dreamed ever since.

He went southeast along Georgian Bay and on Aug. 1 came to shore in Huronia, a region of comfortable rolling hills and rich forests of maple, oak and elm. Some 30,000 Hurons lived in villages surrounded by cleared lands whereon they grew corn, beans and squash. On Aug. 17 Champlain arrived at the chief village, Cahiagué, and here the great campaign against an Iroquois stronghold in the area of present-day Syracuse, N.Y., was planned.

Champlain's concern to invade the Iroquois country was chiefly commercial. Every Iroquois wanted a steel tomahawk and knife for himself, an awl and needle for his wife. The easiest way to get them was to ambush a Huron canoe carrying the treasures. Almost as easy was the capture of a cargo of furs bound for the trading fair on the St. Lawrence. These could be carried to the Dutch at Fort Nassau (today's Albany, N.Y.) and bartered for the precious trade goods.

Champlain's strategy was to put the enemy on the defensive so he would desist from his raids.

At length some 500 warriors assembled, not the promised 2,500. Champlain had his two interpreters and 12 Frenchmen who had come to Huronia earlier.

Twelve Indians and Etienne Brûlé went ahead on a dangerous mission through enemy country to enlist the aid of the Huron's allies, the Susquehannahs, in present-day Pennsylvania. They were to ask the Susquehannahs to meet the Huron-French war party on a fixed date for a joint assault on the Iroquois stronghold.

The war party reached enemy territory, on the south side of Lake Ontario, in October. Hiding their canoes near the water, they walked south in single file. It took them four days to cover 50 miles.

On Oct. 9 the Hurons made their battle plan. They would creep up on the enemy, hide in the woods for the night, and attack at dawn.

Next day, as the war party came close to the fortified village, Iroquois braves surprised some of the Hurons. The others ran to the rescue. The battle was on, the plan of attack forgotten. When Champlain and the other Frenchmen let fly with their arquebuses, the Iroquois quickly retreated to their stronghold.

Champlain made a reconnaissance of the fort. Protected by open water on one side and running streams on two other sides, it was walled

155

with stout palisades 30 feet high and supporting galleries. It could not be carried by storm.

Furious that the advantage of surprise was lost, Champlain called a council of his chiefs. He persuaded them to construct a movable tower overtopping the walls of the fort, from which the attackers could fire down on the defenders. At the same time they would make wooden screens to be moved close to the fort by men who, thus protected, could set fires and breach the palisade.

At dawn the Hurons set to work. They chopped down tall trees which were fixed in position by crosspieces. Long trunks were lashed to the base to serve as carrying poles. At the top of the structure a platform for sharpshooters was fitted with heavy breastworks. It was a triumph of primitive engineering.

"We advanced to attack this village," Champlain wrote later, "having our tower carried by 200 of the strongest men who planted it about a pike's length in front of the village, and I ordered three of the arquebusiers to mount upon it. Meanwhile, the enemy did not cease to shoot a great many arrows which did not miss their mark, and they threw a great quantity of stones over their palisades. Nevertheless, the arquebus fire compelled them to move from their galleries.

"Now our Indians abandoned the screens under which they were to lay the fires, and began to shout, shooting arrows into the fort which did no great harm. But they must be excused, for they will not submit to discipline. One man set a fire against the fort, but it was in the lee of the wind and produced no effect.

"I shouted and showed them the danger they ran, but they heard nothing on account of the great noise they were making. Seeing that I was troubling myself to no purpose, I determined with my own people to fire at those we could see. Meanwhile the enemy took advantage of our confusion to go for water and put out the fire, and this without ceasing to shoot their arrows which fell upon us like hail.

"We were engaged in this fight about three hours. Two of our principal chiefs were wounded, and some 15 others of ordinary rank, so we withdrew. I received two arrow wounds, one in the leg, the other in the knee, which gave me extreme pain. When we were all assembled I addressed several complaints to them for the confusion which had occurred, but all my discourses availed little. They said they would wait another four days for the Susquehannahs, and that when these had come they would make a second attempt against their enemies.

156

"On the following day a violent wind arose, very favorable for setting fire to the fort; whereupon I urged them strongly but they would do nothing.

"Some skirmishes took place and our men could only retreat under cover of our arquebusiers. These the enemy greatly feared, saying to us that we should not interfere in their battles, and that their enemies had very little courage to call us in to assist them."

Finally, little knowing that their allies were en route and only two days away, the frustrated invaders gave up. On Oct. 16 they set out on the long retreat home after making harnesses for the transport of the wounded. A frame of hickory or elm rested against the carrier's back; at right angles to the frame a seat projected, held by straps of hide or plaited bark. The wounded man sat on the precarious seat, his back to the bearer's back, his legs hunched under his chin and tightly bound.

"It was impossible to move any more than does a little child in its swaddling clothes," wrote Champlain, who was carried for several days because of the arrow wound in his knee. "The pain from the wound was nothing in comparison with what I endured tied and bound on the back of one of our savages."

Champlain's war enterprise, so long promised, so long desired, had failed. As he was tossed and buffeted, helpless, on his bearer's back, whipped by branches, beaten by snow, half immersed in forded streams, he had need of all his fortitude.

The party covered 60 miles in two days, found their canoes intact, and prepared to cross Lake Ontario.

"Now," said Champlain to the chiefs, "I must ask you to let me have a canoe and a crew of paddlers. It is of the utmost importance that I return to my settlement for the winter."

"We cannot spare a canoe," said the chiefs.

Humiliated, Champlain took his place with the Hurons. He headed west, away from Quebec. He had no warm clothing, no equipment for the approaching winter. Wounded and in pain, he could walk only with difficulty. The nights were cold; he must sleep without a blanket on wet ground or in snow. At 48 he felt old and tired and discouraged.

The defeated Huron army crossed Lake Ontario at its northeast corner. To facilitate further travelling over marshy country, they decided to wait for the frost: north of present-day Kingston they built a camp and hunted deer for winter food.

With Quebec in English hands, a good man feels "the dying of his dreams."

By Dec. 4 the lakes were well frozen. The Indians made snowshoes and toboggans for their loads of venison and hides. They headed for home and on Dec. 23 came at last to their village of Cahiagué.

The winter passed, and on May 20 Champlain and 14 Frenchmen set out for the Lachine Rapids. There Champlain found Pont-Gravé,

158

"who had almost despaired of seeing me again." In Quebec there was a moving meeting between the French of the Habitation and those who had returned from the wilderness.

With his expedition to Huronia, Champlain's work as an explorer reached its climax. Now he concentrated on the development of Quebec. It was not always a rewarding task. The fur trade prospered, and the Jesuits began to reinforce the missionary efforts of the Récollets, but there was little official interest in promoting French settlement.

European quarrels, however, crossed the Atlantic. Quebec, inadequately armed and supplied, fell to an English expedition under David Kirke in July 1629. Watching an alien flag raised over his fort, and foreign soldiers patrolling the beloved town where he had ruled for 20 years, Champlain felt the dying of his dreams.

Fortunately, King Charles I of England was in such need of money that in 1632 he permitted the French to buy back New France. Champlain returned to Quebec the next year to find the settlement in a woeful state. Undaunted, he began to build anew. And now came the happiest period of his life. He was in sole command of Quebec and of all the great country to the west. His works were recognized in France, his purposes endorsed. Honest, pious families were coming out to settle. Peace had come and life was ordered. Champlain's heart was gladdened as he looked upon the growing prosperity and activity of his colony.

Little time was left to him. In October 1635, at 68, he was smitten by a paralytic stroke. He died on Christmas Day at the height of his prestige. In France he was soon forgotten. But in New France his memory lingered and grew. Today Champlain is termed the Father of Canada. Canada was his child, the only great love of this lonely, visionary, good man.

Mutiny in James Bay

*Henry Hudson had a strangely assorted crew
when he sailed from England in 1610 and
discovered Hudson Bay. Among those aboard
his 55-ton barque* DISCOVERY *were such potential
troublemakers as a cantankerous first mate
named Robert Juet, who had tangled with
Hudson on previous voyages, and Henry Greene,
the dissolute, arrogant son of a well-to-do family.
Also on board were Hudson's 19-year-old son
John, and Abacuk Pricket, a servant of one
of the voyage's backers and apparently an
unfrocked priest. Pricket, in his own words, "lived
to come home" and wrote this account of one
of the most famous voyages ever.*

By ABACUK PRICKET
Edited by FARLEY MOWAT

ABOUT THE LAST OF JUNE, some 10 weeks from home, we raised land
[Resolution Island] to the north and passed into a great rippling
current until we met with ice. We cast about to the south and
cleared ourselves, and then stood into a great sound [Ungava Bay]
amongst floating ice on which there was a store of seals.

One day we had a great storm and were driven in amongst the ice,
there to lie. Some of our men fell sick; I will not say from fear, although
I saw no other symptoms to explain their sickness.

The storm ceasing, we stood on to the west as the sea and the ice
would suffer us. The Master [Hudson] tried to seek to the south, but
the more he strove the worse he was, for he was fast enclosed by ice and
began to despair.

Henry Hudson, in the DISCOVERY, *sailed into history—and to a mysterious death.*

He showed us by his chart that we were 100 leagues [300 miles] farther than any English man was before us in this place, and asked us whether to proceed farther or no. Some of our people wished themselves at home; others wished themselves anywhere else so long as it was away from the ice; and in this perplexity there passed hot words between some of the people.

Well, to work we went and with much labor got the ship clear of the ice. We continued west until we raised an island [off the northwest tip of present-day Quebec] having a very fair headland to the west which the Master named Digges Island [after one of the voyage's backers].

We sent a boat to the island. In this place bred great quantities of wild fowl, and here also the men found the best grass [apparently edible sorrel] they had seen since leaving England. Also they found huts built by the natives, and like to haycocks, within which were great stores of fowls hanged by the necks. They took many of these fowls to their boat.

Our people tried to persuade Master Hudson to stay here for a time so that we might refresh ourselves with sorrel grass and fowl, but he would not, and sailed to the south.

Full many days later we came into the bottom of a bay, and thence we stood to the north along the western shore. [This was probably James Bay, but Pricket was no navigator and experts don't agree on the course he describes beyond this point.]

Several days later there fell some arguments about the reasons for coming into this last bay, and the Master took occasion to revive old matters of the following nature, which were writ down by Thomas Woodhouse of our company:

> The 10th of September, 1610, after dinner, the Master called all the company together, it having been the request of Robert Juet, the mate, that the Master should redress some abuses and slanders made against himself [Juet].
>
> After the Master had heard Juet, there were proved—by others of the company—so many great abuses and mutinous matters and actions by Juet against the Master that there was danger in suffering them any longer, and it was therefore a fit time to punish Juet and cut off further occasions of his mutinies.
>
> It was first proved by Bennet Mathew, our trumpeter, that, upon our first sight of Iceland, Juet confessed that he expected the outcome of the voyage would be manslaughter.
>
> Secondly, at our coming from Iceland, he did, in the hearing of the company, threaten to turn the ship's head home; but at that time he was pacified by the Master in hopes of amendment of his conduct.
>
> Thirdly, it was deposed by Philip Staffe, our carpenter, and Arnold Lodly that Juet had persuaded them to keep muskets charged with powder, and swords ready in their cabins, and that he said the muskets would be charged with shot before the voyage was over.
>
> Fourthly, at the time we were driven to lie amongst the

ice and were sore beset thereby, he had used many words tending to mutiny, discouragement and slander of the voyage, which easily took effect on the timorous. And now, being in a deep bay which the Master had desire to see, for some reasons known to himself, Juet's words tended altogether to put the company into a fright of extremity.

For these and divers other base slanders against the Master, Juet was deposed, and Robert Bylot was placed master's mate in his stead.

Also the Master promised that if the offenders yet behaved themselves honestly, he would be a means for their good and would forget the injuries.

On Michaelmas Day [Oct. 11] we went in and out amongst certain islands and thence stood to the north and came into shoal water. The weather being thick and foul, we anchored and lay eight days. Then, the wind ceasing (but the seas still running very high), the Master would have raised the anchor against the opinions of all who knew what would follow. And when the anchor was up, the ship took such a sea that it threw them all from the capstan and some men were hurt. We lost the anchor, but saved most of our cable.

We stood to the southwest for a time until we came to the westernmost bay of all that we had yet discovered. There we ran upon the rocks and sat for 12 hours, but by God's mercy we got off again unhurt, though not unafrighted.

We then stood to the east, into another bay and anchored, and the Master sent the carpenter and me to look for a place to winter; it being the last of October, the nights long and cold, the earth all covered with snow, and ourselves wearied, having spent three months in the labyrinth of this bay.

The next day we found a place unto which we brought the ship and hauled her on shoal ground, and on Nov. 10 she was frozen in.

Now we looked to the lengthening of our provisions. We had been victualled for six months, and might have brought more from home had the Master wished. But God dealt mercifully with us, for in the space of three months we killed at least 100 dozen of a kind of fowl as white as milk [ptarmigan].

Our gunner, John Williams, died about the middle of November and note what followed:

163

There was a young man aboard named Henry Greene who was not known to those who sent out our ship, but came privily aboard at Gravesend. At Iceland he fell out with the surgeon, and when they went on shore beat him. There was much ado to get the surgeon to come back on board. I told the Master of it, but he bade me let the matter alone. But Robert Juet must needs put *his* fingers in the embers, and said that the Master had brought Greene along to spy on those who should displease him. For his part, Greene stood upright, and was a serviceable man in every way.

Now the gunner being dead, his things (as is the order in such cases) were brought to the mainmast and sold to them that would give the most for them. The gunner had a gray cloth gown and Greene prayed the Master to let him have it. The Master agreed.

Now, though it was past the season, the Master called upon the carpenter, Philip Staffe, to put in hand the building of a house on shore. On our first coming here, when it might have been done, the Master would not hear of it. The carpenter told him that now the snow and frost were such that he could not go ahead with such work. Whereupon the Master called the carpenter by many foul words and threatened to hang him.

The next day the carpenter took his fowling piece and went hunting with Henry Greene. This did anger Master Hudson so much against Greene that he decided Robert Bylot, the mate, must have the gunner's gown, and he had it delivered to him. Greene, seeing this, charged the Master to keep his promise. Then the Master did rail against Greene, telling him that his friends dared not trust him, and therefore why should he? As for wages, he was to have none. You shall see hereafter how the Devil so wrought out of this, that Greene did the Master what mischief he could.

In the spring of 1611 we searched the woody hills and valleys for food, however vile. The moss on the ground and the frog in his engendering time were not spared.

When the time came to make ready for the homeward voyage, the Master delivered to the company all the bread in the foreroom. It came to a pound apiece, and he wept that it was so little. The boat went to fish, but after two days brought back only 80 small fish for 18 hungry bellies. Whereupon we weighed anchor and came away from our wintering place, into the sea.

Our bread being gone, that store of cheeses which we had must stop the gap, though they were but five. The company grumbled, for they had made account that there were nine cheeses. But those five were equally divided by the Master, although some counselled him to the contrary because there were those who could not govern their appetites.

I know that at one time William Wilson, the boatswain, ate 14 days' bread in one day, and thereafter lay in his bed for two or three days for his pains.

We stood to the northwest but on Monday night, June 18, we fell into the ice and lay fast within sight of land.

Now the Master told the boy Nicholas Simmes that there would be a breaking open of sea chests, and a search for bread, and willed him if *he* had any, to bring it to him, and he delivered to the Master 30 cakes.

On the following Saturday, at night, Wilson the boatswain and Henry Greene came to my cabin and told me that they and their associates would turn the Master and all the sick men into the shallop [small boat] and let them shift for themselves, since there were not 14 days' victuals left aboard the ship even at the poor allowance we were getting. They further said that here we lay in the ice, the Master not caring to go one way or the other, and that they had not eaten anything these three days past. Therefore they were resolute, and what they had begun they would go through with or die.

I told them I marvelled to hear so much from them, considering that they had wives and children. Why should they banish themselves from their native country by thus putting themselves outside the law?

Greene said he would rather be hanged at home than starved abroad, but considering the good will they bore me they would let me stay in the ship.

I gave them thanks but told them that I came into the ship not to foresake her, nor yet to hurt myself and others by any such a deed. Greene then told me that I must take my fortune in the shallop. "If there be no remedy," quoth I, "the will of God be done." Then away went Greene in a rage, swearing to cut the throat of any who tried to thwart him. I had some conference with Wilson but to no avail, for he was persuaded to go on with the action while it was hot.

Greene came back. I tried to persuade him to delay three days; I said I would so deal with the Master that all would be well. Being refused this I begged for two days, nay, for 12 hours. But they still said no.

Then I told them that if they would delay till Monday I would join them and I would also justify the action to the authorities when we came home. But this would not serve either, wherefore I told them it must be some worse matter they had in hand than they admitted, and that it was blood and revenge Greene sought. Greene took my Bible and swore that whatever he did was for the good of the voyage and for nothing else, and the like did Wilson swear.

Greene went away and presently in came Juet. Because he was an ancient man I hoped to have found some reason in him, but he was worse than Greene and swore plainly that he would justify the deed upon our homecoming. After him came John Thomas and Michael Pierce, birds of a feather indeed. Then came Motter and Bennet, of whom I demanded if they were well advised in what they had taken in hand. They answered that they were, and had therefore come to take their oath.

Now because I was later much condemned for preparing this oath, as one that plotted with them, I think it good to set it down in writing to the view of all men. And thus it was: "You shall be true to God, your Prince and Country. You shall do nothing but to the glory of God and to the good of the voyage in hand, and harm to no man."

I asked Henry Greene whom he would put out of the ship with the Master. He said Philip Staffe, the carpenter; John King, whom the Master had made mate, replacing Robert Bylot; and the sick men. Staffe and his friend King were condemned for wrongdoing in the victuals, but the chief complaint against King was that he could neither read nor write. It was feared the Master and his ignorant new mate would carry the ship whither the Master pleased, the Master having forbidden any man to keep account of courses sailed, and having taken from all men whatever might serve them for that purpose.

However, I obtained consent of Greene and Wilson that the carpenter should stay. By his help I hoped that the Master and the rest might be taken back into the ship.

It was not long ere it was day, and then came Bennet to me for water for the kettle. I went into the hold to get the water and they shut the hatch on me.

In the meantime Henry Greene and another went to the carpenter and held him in talk until the Master should come out of his cabin, which he soon did. Then Thomas and Bennet appeared before the Master while Wilson came behind and bound his arms behind his back. The Master asked what they meant to do, and they told him that he should know when he was in the shallop.

While this was doing, Juet followed John King into the hold, but

Hudson watches in the shallop as the DISCOVERY, *manned by the mutineers, sails away.*

King had got a sword, and kept Juet at bay and might have killed him had not others come to help him. King was brought up beside the Master.

Then was the shallop hauled up to the ship's side. The Master called to me, for I had come up as well as I could to the hatchway to speak to him. On my knees I besought them, for the love of God, to remember themselves, and do as they would be done unto. They bade me get myself into the cabin, not suffering the Master to speak to me.

The carpenter, being at liberty, asked them if they wished to be hanged when they came home. As for himself, he said, he would not stay in the ship unless they forced him so to do. They bid him go. "I will," said he, "if I may have my chest and all that is in it." They put it in the shallop and he came to take his leave of me.

I tried to persuade him to stay aboard, saying that he might so work that all might be well. But he answered that he thought the mutineers would be glad to take them back in any case, for the Master had convinced him that there was no one else who could tell them how to sail home. "But," said he, "if the ship and the shallop should separate—which we will not willingly allow, for we will follow the ship—then, when you come to Digges Island, leave some token that you have been there, near

167

to the place where the fowls breed." He said that he would do the like for us if he should come there first, and so I parted from him with tears.

Now were the sick men driven out of their cabins. However Francis Clements had been a friend of John Thomas, and the cooper a friend of Bennet, and so there were words between these two and Henry Greene, he swearing the two sick men must go, and Thomas and Bennet swearing that they should stay, until at last Greene was forced to give way to them.

In the meantime there were some that acted as though they had leave to pillage, breaking up chests and rifling all places.

Now were all the poor men loaded in the shallop, being Henry Hudson, Master; John Hudson, his son; Arnold Ladlo, Sydrack Fenner, Philip Staffe, Thomas Woodhouse, Adam Moore, John King and Michel But. The carpenter had persuaded the villains to give them a musket, powder and shot, some pikes, an iron pot with some meal, and a few other things.

Now the ship stood out of the ice (the shallop still being fast to the stern) but when they were almost clear of the ice the mutineers cut the line. Then out went the topsails, and the ship stood to the east until we lost sight of the shallop. Then they took in the topsails, righted their helm, and lay under foresails only while they ransacked the ship.

In the hold they found one whole vessel of meal and another half spent. They found also two firkins [small casks] of butter, some 27 pieces of pork and half a bushel of peas. In the Master's cabin they found 200 biscuit cakes, a peck of meal and a butt of beer. But now the lookout said the shallop was again within sight, so they let fall the mainsail and broke out the topsails and fled as if before an enemy.

At last, coming near the east shore, they anchored in 16 fathoms and tried with the net for fish, but could not use it because of rocks. Michael Pierce killed two fowls, and here we found a good store of grass, which we gathered and brought on board. We lay there that night and most of the next day, in which time we did not see the shallop, nor did we see it ever after.

Greene was now the captain. He told me that it was the company's will that I should go to the Master's cabin and take charge thereof. I told him that it was more fit for Robert Juet, but Greene said Juet should not come into it, nor meddle with the Master's chart and journals. So up I went and Greene gave me the key to the Master's chest. The bread was also delivered into my keeping. [This was apparently Greene's way of implicating Pricket as a conspirator.]

We stood northeast and this was Bylot's course, contrary to that proposed by Juet, who would have gone northwest.

Now they began to talk that England was no safe place for them, and Greene swore that the ship should stay at sea until he had the King's hand and seal to show for his safety.

Not long after, with great joy, we raised Digges. This day, July 27, 1611, the boat was sent ashore to kill fowl but we saw seven boats filled with savages come about the eastern point toward us. Our men made ready for anything, but the savages came to us and we grew familiar so that we took one of their men into our boat, and they took one of ours into theirs.

Now our boat went to the place where the fowls breed and their man showed us how the savages killed fowls. They take a long pole with a snare on the end which they cast about the fowl's neck and so pull it down. But our men knew of a better way, and so showed the savages the use of our pieces, which at one shot would kill seven or eight.

At last we returned to the cove to receive our man back, and to deliver theirs. When we came to them they made great joy, dancing, leaping and beating their chests, and offering divers things to our men. But we only took some walrus tusks in exchange for a knife and two glass buttons.

Now we came aboard the ship, rejoicing that we had met the most simple people in the world. And Greene, more than the rest, was so confident of gulling them that by no means would he have us stand upon our guard. God blinded him, so that he received more than he looked for from this people.

Two days later we made haste ashore again and made our boat fast to a great stone in the cove. Because I was lame it was agreed that I was to stay in the boat and take charge of such things as we had for trading. The people came to us to barter, but Henry Greene swore they should have nothing until we had some venison from them.

Now Michael Pierce and Andrew Motter climbed upon the rocks to gather sorrel grass, while Greene and William Wilson stood at the head of the boat, with John Thomas, showing looking glasses, jews'-harps and bells to the savages. Not one of them had any weapon save Greene, who had a piece of a pike in his hand.

One of the savages came into the boat and I made signs to him to get out, but he made as though he had not understood and drew my attention to the shore by pointing. While I was thus distracted, another savage stole to the stern of the boat and suddenly I saw the legs and feet of a man beside me. I cast up my eyes and saw this savage striking down over my head with a knife. I cast up my arm and the knife wounded me in the arm and then struck into my breast under the right pap.

The savage struck a second blow which I warded with my left hand, but it struck into my thigh and also nigh cut off my little finger. But I got hold of the string which hung from the knife and, wrapping it around my left hand, so pulled the savage down that his side lay open to me. I reached for the dagger at my side and struck the savage in the body and in the throat.

Meantime, on shore, Thomas and Wilson had their bowels cut. With Greene and Pierce, who had not strayed far, they came tumbling into the boat, which Pierce manfully defended with a hatchet while Greene laid about him with a truncheon. Motter, who was farther away, came running down the rocks, leaped into the water and swam to the boat's stern, crying to be taken in.

The savages then sent so many arrows among us that we received many wounds and Greene was slain outright. But Pierce had cleared the boat, and now he put it from the shore, then helped Motter into it. Only Pierce and Motter had strength to row.

When we had gone a good way from shore Pierce fainted. Then Motter stood in the bow and waved to the ship which at last took us up.

That same day Wilson died, cursing and swearing in a most fearful manner. Pierce lived two days more, then died, as did Thomas. And thus you have the tragical end of Greene and his three mates, the lustiest men in all the ship.

We nine who were yet alive stood to and fro in the straits, for we dared not leave until we had procured more fowl. So we killed 400 fowls and then a west wind drove us homeward, but not without many days of troubles with the fogs and rocks before ever we came clear of the strait and into the sea.

Now Robert Bylot was the Master and he shaped course for Ireland, though Juet spoke for Newfoundland, thinking that we would there find relief among our countrymen upon the fisheries.

We sailed many days, and none knew with certainty where we were. In this time we were fain to fry the bones of the fowls in candle tallow, putting vinegar thereto, and every man had a pound of candles each week to eat, as a great dainty.

Then Juet died, and the rest despaired, saying we were past Ireland. The last fowl in the ship was eaten and then the men cared not which end of the ship went down first. In this extremity it pleased God to give us sight of land and to espy a boat which piloted us into Bear Haven [present-day Castletown Bearhaven] in County Cork. Here we stayed several days hoping to deal with the Irish for relief, but we found neither bread nor drink, for these people would do nothing without having money first.

In the month of September we came at last to Gravesend, and so brought our voyage to its end.

The eight survivors were imprisoned briefly, but released after apparently convincing authorities that the mutiny had been justified. Nothing more was heard of Hudson and his companions, although traces of settlement found at James Bay suggest they might have survived for years.

Down the Roaring Fraser

*At the start of 1808 Britain was already in
a contest with the United States for the western
half of North America. When explorer and
fur trader Simon Fraser headed for the Pacific
that spring, seeking a practicable western trade
route for the far-flung North West Company,
he carried Britain's blessing. With 23 men, the
intrepid Fraser descended a turbulent river never
travelled by Europeans. The river would bear
his name and the dangerous route would become
the main artery of an infant British Columbia.*

By BRUCE HUTCHISON

NO ONE STANDS beside the Fraser River without sensing man's precarious hold upon the earth. This grisly trench, bored out of solid rock through unimaginable time by the scour of brown water, holds him in contempt. It crushes his vessels. It tugs and chews at his bridges. It heaves its avalanches against his fragile railways. It gnaws his little plots of habitable land, overwhelms his dikes, silts up his harbors, and awaits the day of his going.

As recently as 1800 the maps of European man gave no indication of the Fraser's existence. Alexander Mackenzie, the greatest explorer of his time, saw its headwaters before travelling overland to the Pacific in 1793, but *thought* he saw the upper Columbia River.

In any case, Mackenzie had crossed the continent (to near present-day Bella Coola, B.C.) too far north to mark out the bulk of the West for Britain. Where lay the boundary between the United States and British North America? No one knew, but the Columbia would largely fix the ultimate line.

Led by Simon Fraser (left) and John Stuart, four Nor'Wester canoes challenged the "Great River."

The Americans were pressing hard. President Thomas Jefferson bought Louisiana in 1803 and seemed to think his purchase included everything between the original colonies and the Pacific. To nail down his claim he sent Meriwether Lewis and William Clark overland to the Columbia. They reached its mouth near present-day Astoria, Ore., in Nov. 1805.

Thus two thin corridors of exploration and rival ambition stretched clear across the continent—Mackenzie's line far to the north, and the line of Lewis and Clark to the Columbia. Between them lay who knew what furs, minerals, timber and farmlands.

Having lost half of America by its own folly, Britain decided to hang on to anything that was left. The first move was to follow the Columbia to the sea and make sure that every acre down to the mouth was saved from the Yankees.

It was work for another man of Mackenzie's breed. Simon Fraser, by his portrait in the Parliament Buildings at Victoria, was a dour and homely person of bullet head, sloping brow, tangled hair, heavy eyebrows and massive chin—a solid man with infinite patience and courage but no poetry.

He was a *bourgeois* (full partner) in the North West Company, who had come west to establish trading posts and, in the process, extend British authority. In 1806, from his base near Rocky Mountain Portage, on the Peace River west of modern Fort St. John, B.C., he wrote to Montreal for supplies and for permission to descend the "Great River" that Mackenzie had believed to be the Columbia.

The supplies arrived in the fall of 1807, with instructions for Fraser to get to the sea as soon as he could.

It was too late that year. But one day in May 1808, from a fort at what is now Prince George, B.C., he set out on what was to prove perhaps the most desperate expedition in the history of western exploration.

Four canoes headed out into the river. They carried Fraser, his aide John Stuart, a Nor'Wester clerk named Jules Quesnel, 19 paddlers and two Indians. Fraser had no idea what lay between him and salt water. The going was easy at first, as Mackenzie had found, but in the narrow swirl of the canyon some 18 miles downriver from Fort George the canoes became almost unmanageable.

They passed Indian villages in which the sight of white men caused wild excitement. At some point below Mackenzie's most southern penetrations the Indians had gathered in such numbers that Fraser paused to parley with them. Their news was not good. Fraser recorded in his diary:

"According to accounts we received here, the river below is but a succession of falls and cascades. The Indians' opinion was that we should discontinue our journey and remain with them. I remarked that our determination of going was fixed; they then informed us that at the next camp the Great Chief of the Atnah [Shuswap] nation had a slave who had been to the sea and which he might probably give us as a guide."

The slave was produced the following day, along with gifts of dried salmon and evil-tasting roots. Distrusting the man's knowledge of the lower river, Fraser spread out an oilcloth and asked him to draw a map on it: "We could plainly see in his sketch a confirmation of what had been told us of the difficulties of the navigation, and the necessity of leaving our canoes with as much of our baggage as we could spare in order to continue our journey by land."

Fraser was now below the present village of Soda Creek. The river's rage was just beginning. Nevertheless, Fraser resolved to run it rather than portage—a foolish and almost fatal decision as it turned out. From the diary of June 1:

"This morning at an early hour Mr. Stuart, six men and myself went to visit the rapids, which were about two miles long with high and steep banks which contracted the channel in many places to 40 or 50 yards. An immense body of water passed through this narrow space, forming numerous gulfs and cascades and making a tremendous noise and an awful appearance.

"I ordered the five best men into a canoe lightly loaded, which was in a moment under way. After passing the first cascade she lost her course and was whirled about, seemingly in suspense whether to sink or swim. However, she was led from this dangerous vortex, and in this manner she continued, flying from one danger to another, until the last cascade but one where the whirlpools forced her against a low projecting rock. The men debarked, and contrived to save the property, but the greatest difficulty was still ahead."

From the shore Fraser watched the wreck. Then, risking his own life, he slid down the bank to help. It was "extremely high and steep and we had to plunge our daggers at intervals into the ground to check our speed. We cut steps in the slope and fastened a line to the front of the canoe. Some of the men ascended in order to haul it up, while others supported it upon their arms. The failure of the line or a false step by one of the men might have hurled the whole of us into Eternity. How-ever, we fortunately cleared the bank before dark."

Wrestling the canoe out of the water and up the bank had taken all day. This was Fraser's first real glimpse of the river's power as it gath-ered speed for its final journey to the coast. It sobered but did not daunt him, although he decided to abandon one canoe and some supplies. He consulted the Indians again. They urged him to travel south by horse at least until he reached calmer waters near a great eastern tributary (the Thompson). From there on, they said, navigation was easy. Actually, the worst hazards began at this point. But, wrote Fraser, "going to the sea by an indirect way was not the object of this undertaking; I therefore would not deviate."

It meant a three-day portage. The canoes and baggage were lugged along the riverbank by hand and no sooner had the canoes been launched again than the waters closed in as before. But the paddlers, tired of pack-ing, shot the new rapids. They were almost swamped, and landed with their canoes half full of water.

Worse lay ahead. Again Fraser reconnoitred a current: "Having found it very strong and full of tremendous whirlpools, we were greatly at a loss how to act."

He was halfway down to the sea and thought himself even closer to it. To turn back now would be to lose the whole gamble. To advance farther was to risk his own life and the lives of his men. Looking at this maelstrom, he must have wondered whether the entire expedition would not disappear completely in the next half hour. But there could be no retreat.

Fraser watched the canoes head into the rapids. His description of the exhausting ordeal among the rocks and whirlpools is character-istically dry, but at the end he admitted "it was a desperate undertaking!"

Somewhere north of the present town of Lillooet—where the canyon gets so narrow that the modern road is carved out of solid rock—the canoes had to be abandoned. Fraser stored them, with some provisions, under a pile of brush. The expedition advanced on foot but still followed the river.

The walking was harder, if anything, than the paddling, and the river lay ready to receive anyone who stumbled. One of the men got wedged between rocks so that he could not move or unload his pack. Wrote Fraser, "I crawled, not without great risk, to his assistance and saved his life by causing his load to drop from his back over the precipice into the river. This carrying place, two miles long, so shattered our shoes that our feet became quite sore and full of blisters."

On June 19 they reached the capital of the Thompson Indians on the high shelf near modern Lytton where the clear Thompson joins the muddy Fraser. As usual, he was told that the route ahead was impassable by water alone. This time, though he did not believe them, the Indians spoke the truth.

Next day, in two dugout canoes and with Indian guides, Fraser began the final descent. As you look down from the present highway upon the brown line of the river, boiling up here and there in its cauldrons of white foam, you find it hard to believe that men in their senses would attempt to run any part of these waters.

For a few miles the canoes would slide down a navigable current. Then, just in time, they would be pushed ashore before they could be sucked into a whirlpool. Now canoes and baggage would be dragged up and along the side of hill, sometimes far above the river.

The canyon still narrowed. The river, compressed by its walls of rock, churned with a force that often hurled salmon clear of the water and flattened them, dead, against the bank. But the Indians had learned a way around. Their trail utilized every flat ledge, and when a ledge ended they built a ladder of tree trunks and branches to the ledge above. Strung from ledge to ledge, all naked, wet and slippery, this crazy series of ladders hung from rocks and stumps like some monstrous vine.

Fraser had seen nothing like this before but, abandoning the canoes, he led his men up the ladders, 90 pounds on his back, the mountains straight above, the clamor of the river below. At last his diary caught the feeling of the Black Canyon:

"Near the top, where the ascent was perfectly perpendicular, one of the Indians climbed to the summit and by means of a long rope drew us up one after another. This work took three hours. Hanging rocks and projecting cliffs at the edge of the river made the passage so small as to render it difficult even for one person sideways. The natives went boldly with heavy loads in places where we were obliged to hand our guns from one to another."

Thus they climbed and crawled on the Indian web through the deepest gorges of the Fraser. Gazing upward, they could see a country disordered as by a sudden convulsion. Compared with this welter of mountains, these twisted caverns and senseless heaps of stone, the Rockies were disciplined and regular. This was nightmare country, black with shifting shadow, hung with mist, and thunderous with the steady beat of water.

What lay ahead? Fraser could never guess from hour to hour. The river narrowed, deepened and grew in fury, for it was now fighting its way through the central substance of the Coast Mountains. Then, in a final spasm, it broke through the contracted gut of Hells Gate and cleared the last barrier to the sea.

The worst was over. A little farther down, Fraser was able to use Indian dugouts again. He paused at Spuzzum, one of the few quiet spots along the river, to examine an Indian burial ground.

The canyon was beginning to widen out now toward the broad coastal delta. But if travel was relatively comfortable, the river's course planted an alarming suspicion in Fraser's mind. At present-day Hope the current turned sharply west, yet Fraser knew that the Columbia lay far south of this latitude.

For the first time he guessed the truth—that this was another river. If it was, the purpose of the expedition would be defeated after all these weeks of misery. The line of exploration that was to contain the Americans might be drawn too far north.

The mountain waters calmed, almost in a single mile, then broadened and oozed gently west through a thick forest of cedar, fir and hemlock. Now Fraser noticed that the river was rising and falling in regular tides. He was near the sea but far from the Columbia. When the river forked into a maze of channels between islands of silt there could be no more doubt. This was a river that no white man had travelled before.

The sea had been reached, the map of the continent had been revised, a second great river had been discovered, but Fraser could not pause to weigh his triumph against his disappointment. The coastal Cowichan Indians were much more dangerous than their relatives of the interior. They beat drums and chanted war songs, "howling like wolves and brandishing war clubs." Besides, supplies were running out and there was no chance to purchase more.

Reluctantly he turned upstream. His troubles were not over yet. The Cowichans, who had expected the whites to perish on their downward journey, were now determined to prevent their return. More recklessly than ever, the braves harassed the expedition, ramming the canoes and attempting to overturn them.

Details of these attacks we do not know, probably because Fraser was too busy to maintain his diary. They must have been serious since they almost broke the nerve of his men, who by this time were hardened to peril.

On July 6 the paddlers threatened to desert. Maddened by the Indians' attacks, the men proposed to abandon the river channel altogether, head overland and escape through the mountains. This was madness indeed. No trail was known, no map covered the wilderness between there and the prairies. By winter everyone would be swallowed up in the unexplored recesses of the Rockies and the results of the expedition would be lost. Fraser met the crisis:

"I endeavored to persuade the delinquents of their infatuation; but two of them declared in their own names and in the names of the others that their plan was fixed and that they saw no other way by which they could save themselves from immediate destruction than by flying out of the way of danger. I remonstrated and threatened by turns, and the other gentlemen [Stuart and Quesnel] joined me in my endeavors. After much debate on both sides, they yielded and we all shook hands, resolved not to separate during the voyage."

There they were, two dozen ragged, hungry men, in the canyon of an unknown river, far from any settlement, surrounded by savages, half mad with fear. Two dozen men who had altered the history of a continent, and fixed the shape of British North America. Two dozen men who, standing on a rock beside the river foam, raised up their hands and shouted their binding oath above the roar of water: "I solemnly swear before Almighty God that I shall sooner perish than forsake in distress any of our crew during the present voyage."

That sworn, they paddled on, singing their voyageur songs while Indians watched from the bank. The last real peril had passed. Climbing the canyon ladders again, reaching the friendly Thompson country, and finding their own canoes in perfect condition, the men pushed upstream with astonishing speed. Though they had to fight the current all the way, they retraced in 34 days the course they had taken downward in 35, a feat almost beyond belief but attested in Fraser's scrupulous record.

On Aug. 5, 1808, everyone was safe back at Fort George and the second great river of the West was named the Fraser.

John Ross, proud veteran of the Napoleonic Wars, would learn "what poverty can be."

Winter Without End

In 1829 the coastal packet VICTORY *became
the first steam-powered ship to be used in the
search for the Northwest Passage. In command
was 52-year-old Royal Navy Capt. John Ross.
His privately financed 23-man expedition relied
in part on supplies abandoned in 1825 by the
explorer William Parry when the sailing ship*
FURY *was wrecked on Somerset Island, across
Prince Regent Inlet from the west end of Baffin
Island. This extract from Ross' journal begins
on Aug. 13 with the* VICTORY *moored
off Fury Beach.*

By SIR JOHN ROSS
Edited by FARLEY MOWAT

WE PROCEEDED to the only tent which remained entire. This had been the mess of the *Fury*'s officers and it was evident that bears had been paying frequent visits. But where the preserved meats and vegetables had been deposited we found everything entire. Although quite exposed to all the chances of the climate for four years, they had not suffered in the slightest degree.

This was indeed no small satisfaction; wine, spirits, sugar, bread, flour and cocoa were in equally good condition. The lime juice and the pickles had not suffered much, and even the *Fury*'s sails were not only dry but seemed as if they had never been wetted. Boats from the *Fury* also were found intact.

The powder magazine was unroofed but the patent cases had kept the gunpowder dry. We selected what we thought we should require, and then caused the remainder to be destroyed lest it should prove a source of injury to any Esquimaux [Inuit] who might chance to visit this spot. We proceeded to where the *Fury* had been abandoned, but not a trace of her hull was to be seen.

Aug. 14. It had been nearly calm for two days; but at eight in the evening a fresh breeze sprung up from the north and the ice in the harbor began to break. The boats were hoisted up and secured and we made for Cape Garry.

Sept. 12. Let those who have not seen a northern ocean storm remember that ice is stone, a floating rock, not less solid than granite. Imagine, then, these mountains of crystal hurled through a narrow strait by a rapid tide; meeting, as mountains in motion would meet, with the noise of thunder, breaking from each other's precipices huge fragments, or rending each other asunder till they fall over headlong, lifting the sea in breakers, and whirling it in eddies. The flatter fields of ice, forced against these masses or against the rocks by the wind and the stream, rise out of the sea till they fall back on themselves, adding to the indescribable commotion and noise.

Under such conditions we had learned that in reality our ship was aught more than a sailing vessel and whatever advantage we had derived from our machinery was not greater than we might have obtained from our two rowing boats by towing. The engine was a serious encumbrance since it occupied with its fuel two thirds of our tonnage, and demanded the services of four persons who were landsmen, not sailors.

Moreover, as the engine had originally been the essential moving power in the vessel, the masting and sailing had been reduced accordingly. It was presumed that the sails would only be required in stormy weather.

It now seemed most needful that she be a sailing vessel and nothing more. I therefore determined to lighten her of the boilers as soon as we should be frozen in, although we thus reduced ourselves to a degree of power far inferior to that of any preceding crew in these Arctic services.

Oct. 1. During the night, the thermometer threatened us with having reached our last position for this season. Toward daylight the weather became cloudy with snow, which continued all day. We were pleased to find that if we should really be frozen up in this spot, we should find it safe, after sawing our way into the bay ice, which was now six inches thick.

A very recent stone fox trap was found on the shore; and as the seals were very shy, while numerous, I concluded that the Esquimaux

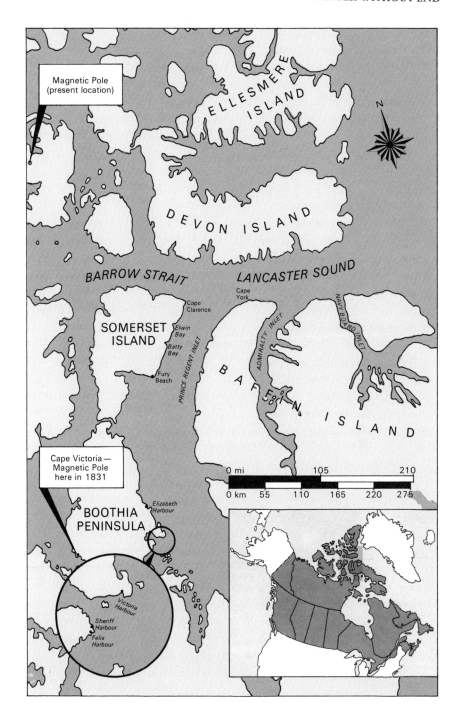

had not long quitted this place. [It was Felix Harbour, on the east side of the Boothia Peninsula some 185 miles south of Fury Beach.]

Oct. 6. A fresh breeze made the last night colder than any preceding. We now proceeded to cut the ice so as to get the *Victory* into safety for the winter.

Oct. 8. There was now not an atom of clear water to be seen. Wearisome snow was visible all round the horizon. Amid all its brilliancy, the land of ice and snow was a dull, dreary, heart-sinking, monotonous waste, under the influence of which the very mind was paralysed, ceasing to care or think. Nothing moves and nothing changes. All is forever the same, cheerless, cold and still.

The work in the ship was continued, and a place for a powder magazine selected on the island near us. The fuel was measured and found to amount to 700 bushels of coal and coke, sufficient for ordinary wants during the same number of days. A complete examination of provisions we had taken from the *Fury*'s stores also took place. There was sufficient for two years and 10 months on full allowance. The quantity of oil and tallow promised equal duration, presuming on captures of bears and seals.

Oct. 13. The brass guns and part of the engine were put on the ice. They who valued omens were left to speculate on the prophesying of a raven which flew round the ship.

Oct. 22. We cut away the ice round the ship, in consequence of her having been so much lightened, and she rose nine inches. We proceeded to build a bank of ice and snow around her, reaching to the gunwale. This joined the sides of a [snow-covered canvas "roof" over the upper deck], forming a perfect shelter from wind.

The upper deck was covered with snow two and a half feet thick, which was trod down till it became a solid mass of ice and was then sprinkled with sand to put on the appearance of a rolled gravel walk.

The galley was moved to the centre of the men's berths so that the heat from the fire might be more equally distributed. During the day the kitchen was found sufficient both for warmth and cooking, and in the night the baking oven served the same purpose.

Apertures were made in the upper deck on which were placed iron tanks with their openings downward. In these the vapor was immediately condensed. By thus keeping the apartment of the crew dry, we saved the necessity of forcing the temperature above 50 degrees (10°C).

The men slept in hammocks which were taken down at six in the morning. The lower deck, being the dwelling floor, was then covered with hot sand and scrubbed till eight, when the men breakfasted on cocoa or tea. Dinner was at noon. When the weather permitted, the men worked outside after that till three or four o'clock. When that was impossible, they were obliged to walk for a certain number of hours on the deck, beneath the roof. Their tea was at five o'clock. At 10 the hammocks were slung and the men retired.

There was only one year's allowance of spirits, a subject rather of congratulation than otherwise, since there can be no question of their pernicious effects in these climates, one being to increase the tendency to scurvy. It was necessary, however, that what we had should be reserved for land excursions or in case of shipwreck and our being condemned to take to the boats. This would then be valuable not merely as an article of diet but as fuel. Orders were accordingly given to stop the use and allowance of grog, and these were received without remonstrance.

On Sunday no work was allowed. The men were mustered and inspected in their best clothes, after which there were prayers and a sermon. To occupy the remainder of the day there was a collection of tracts which had been presented to us by Mrs. Enderby of Blackheath. At six there was a school, while the day was concluded by psalms and the lessons appointed in the liturgy.

Jan. 9, 1830. On my going ashore this morning, one of the seamen informed me that strangers were seen. I soon saw about 30 Esquimaux near a small iceberg about a mile from the ship. They retreated behind it as soon as they perceived me; but as I approached, the whole party came suddenly out of their shelter, forming in a body of 10 in front and three deep, with one man detached on the land side, apparently sitting in a sledge. I sent back for my nephew [Cmdr. James Ross, who had learned to speak Inuit on previous voyages to the Arctic], together with some men, who were directed to keep well behind him. Proceeding then alone to within 100 yards, I found that each Esquimaux was armed with a spear and a knife.

Knowing that the word of salutation was *tima tima,* I hailed them in their language, and was answered by a general shout of the same. The rest of my party now coming up, we advanced to within 60 yards and then threw our guns away, with the cry of *aja, tima,* being the usual method of opening a friendly communication. On this they threw their knives and spears into the air, returning the shout *aja* and extending their arms to show that they were without weapons. We advanced and embraced them, stroking down their dress and receiving from them in return the same ceremony of friendship. This seemed to produce great delight expressed by laughing and clamor and strange gestures.

When James Ross informed them that we were Europeans, *Kablunae,* they answered that they were men, *Inuit.* Two were lame and, with an old man, were drawn on sledges; one of them having lost a leg from a bear and the other having a broken or diseased thigh. They were all well dressed, in excellent deerskins chiefly, and with their immense superstructure of clothes they seemed a much larger people than they really were. All bore spears formed of small pieces of wood or of the bones of animals. The knives consisted of bone or reindeer's horn without point or edge, forming a very inoffensive weapon; but we soon discovered that each had, hanging at his back, a much more effective knife pointed with iron, and some edged with that metal.

Having had no foresight of these visitors, we had no presents for them and we therefore sent a man back to the ship for pieces of iron hoop. But in the meantime they consented to accompany us on board, as we soon arrived at our snow wall. At this they expressed no surprise; it was, indeed, too much like their own work to excite any; nor did they show any astonishment at either the ship itself or the quantity of wood and iron before them. But the present of the iron excited universal delight. In return they offered us their spears and knives which, to their equal astonishment and satisfaction, we refused.

Three men were introduced into the cabin where at length they showed abundant signs of wonder. The engravings representing their countrymen, selected from several of our former voyages, gave them great delight. The looking glasses, as usual, were the chief source of astonishment. Scarcely less surprise was excited by the lamp and the candlesticks; but they never once showed a desire to possess themselves of anything, merely receiving what was offered with signs of thankfulness. They did not relish our preserved meat: one who ate a morsel seemed to do it as a matter of obedience, saying it was very good but admitting, on being cross-questioned, that he had said what was not true; on which all the rest, on receiving permission, threw away what they had taken. But the same man drank some oil with much satisfaction, admitting that it was really good.

A short race was run between one of them and an officer of our party, but with so much politeness that there was no victor to be declared. The violin being afterward produced, they joined our men in dancing.

Jan. 10. After Divine Service we proceeded to visit the Esquimaux,

though the day was very cold. Their village consisted of 12 snow huts at the bottom of a little bight on the shore, about two and a half miles from the ship. They had the appearance of inverted basins, and were placed without any order, each having a long crooked appendage in which was the passage, at the entrance of which were the women with the female children and infants. We were soon invited to visit these, for whom we had prepared presents of glass beads and needles, a distribution of which soon drove away the timidity displayed at our first appearance.

It being then time to think of returning, many of the men offered to accompany us, and we invited the man who had lost a leg to come on the following day that he might be examined by our surgeon.

As we were returning to the ship a very cold blast of wind came down a valley. One of the men observed that the frost had seized one of my cheeks, on which he immediately made a snowball and rubbed it, thus certainly saving me from a disagreeable sore. After this he continued always near me, frequently reminding me to put my hand to the same part, for fear of a recurrence of the attack.

Jan. 11. At one o'clock the man who had lost his leg arrived, with another drawing him on a sledge. On examining the stump, the surgeon found it a sound one, long healed, on which there would be no difficulty in applying a wooden leg. The carpenter was therefore sent for to measure him. We explained that the new leg would be ready in three days, when we hoped for the pleasure of trying it on.

Jan. 14. The thermometer fell last evening and the breeze made it very cold. I doubted if our patient would keep his appointment. He came, however, accompanied by a friend, together with two women, four other men and two boys. The wooden leg was then fitted, to ascertain whether the length was correct, and the man was desired to return after it was finished.

Jan. 15. The two men of yesterday came alone; it was understood that the rest had gone to hunt for seals. The promised leg was fitted on, and there was little time lost in finding its use and value as the disabled person began to strut about the cabin in apparent ecstasy. The leg was inscribed with the name of the ship.

Jan. 28. A fox was taken in a trap, in a state of extreme starvation, and an unfortunate raven, approaching the ship, was shot. It had been a companion of our stay all the winter and deserved to have been spared.

Half the village arrived while we were engaged in our church service, and we learned that they had found a bear, torpid in its den, and had killed it with their knives. One man having a sore on his leg begged to have a wooden leg made, expecting thus to gain a piece of timber. It was easily explained that the first condition was to cut off the sore leg, which put an end to this application.

188

During that winter the explorers purchased three dogs, two seals and many skins from the Inuit, learned how to build a snow hut and obtained helpful information on geography. In January and February it was so cold (40 below) that they could hardly leave the ship. But they built sledges, did some trapping and shooting, and conducted scientific experiments. In March and April, with Inuit guides, Cmdr. James Ross made three sledge trips, establishing that Boothia was a peninsula and thus eliminating the likelihood of a Northwest Passage route south of Felix Harbour. Future exploration would therefore be toward the north and overland to the west coast of Boothia. The events of April 27 and 28 are described by James Ross:

April 27. A large party of Esquimaux had come to the ship the previous day and one of them was engaged to conduct me on a sledge journey with our second mate. We departed accordingly, and on approaching the Esquimaux village were exceedingly disappointed at not hearing the cheerful shouts with which we had usually been greeted. That was succeeded by finding that the women and children had been sent out of the way—a signal of war—and that all the men were armed with knives.

An old man named Pow-weet-yah rushed out of a hut brandishing the large knife used in attacking bears, while tears were streaming down his aged and furrowed face. He lifted his arm to throw his weapon at myself and the surgeon, who were then within a few yards of him. But the sun dazzled him, causing him to suspend his arm for an instant, when one of his sons laid hold of his uplifted hand, giving us time for reflection. My companions and I retired to the sledge, where I had left my gun.

The ferocious old man was still held fast, now by both his sons. They had pinioned his arms behind him, though he strove hard to disengage himself. The rest of the party, however, seemed in readiness to second any attempt he might make on us. They separated to surround us, cutting us off from the ship. Finding that further forbearance would be hazardous, I was about to fire but the threat alone was enough to give them a check.

The state of suspense and perplexity continued for nearly half an hour, when one of the women came out of the hut just as I was again raising my gun, and called to me not to fire. From this woman we soon learned the cause of the hubbub. One of Pow-weet-yah's adopted sons, a fine boy of seven or eight years, had been killed the night before when a stone fell on his head. This they had ascribed to us, through the supernatural powers they believed us to possess.

189

I had much difficulty in persuading the woman that we were totally ignorant of this catastrophe, and that we were sorry for the misfortune. After some conversation among themselves their grim visages began to relax and the knives were put up; becoming at last convinced that we had no concern in the death of this boy, they seemed anxious to remove the unfavorable impression which their conduct had made on us.

Our Esquimaux guide, Poo-yet-tah, offered to accompany me, provided his son Il-lik-tah, a lad of 16 or 17, could come too. The baggage and provisions were then placed on two sledges, each drawn by six dogs, and we travelled off.

April 28. We halted at five o'clock [Cmdr. James Ross continued] to make the necessary observations for longitude. As eating is ever in the minds of Esquimaux, Poo-yet-tah's inquiries took this very natural turn. Should we see any musk-oxen by means of our inexplicable brass instruments?

I was by no means desirous of passing for a conjurer and I therefore declared total ignorance of musk-oxen and their ways. At this he seemed greatly disappointed, but in less than half an hour his sharp eyes observed the tracks of two of these animals on a steep hill. He took his bow and arrows and set off, with two of his dogs, desiring me to follow with my gun and favorite dog. The dogs went off at full speed and were soon out of sight. We went on laboriously enough for two hours over a very rugged country until, on turning the angle of a hill, the sight of a fine ox at bay before the three dogs cured our fatigue in an instant. Poo-yet-tah kept the lead and was in the act of discharging his second arrow when I came up. We saw that it had struck on a rib and had fallen out without even diverting the attention of the animal from the dogs.

I was pleased, therefore, to show him the superiority of firearms, and I fired with two balls at a distance of about 15 yards. The animal fell but rising again made a sudden dart at us. We dodged behind a large stone on which it struck its head so violently that it fell to the ground with a crash.

My guide now attempted to stab the animal with his knife, but failing in this he sought shelter behind the dogs, which again came forward to the attack. The animal's long hair was matted with blood, yet its rage and strength seemed undiminished.

I had reloaded my gun behind the stone and was advancing for another shot when the creature rushed toward me. But I had time for a cool aim; and on the discharge of both barrels it immediately fell within

five yards of me. My companion screamed and danced with joy. He was lost in astonishment at the effect of the firearms, carefully examining the holes which the balls had made, and pointing out to me that some had passed through the animal.

Captain Ross and his 21 men (one had died in January) were still waiting in late August for the break-up that would free the VICTORY *from the ice. The captain's narrative continues:*

Aug. 24. The ice was in rapid motion after the previous day's gale from the north. The inner part of the harbor was cleared, but afterward a pack of ice streamed in and filled all except the place where we lay.

Aug. 30. The ice continued moving till four o'clock. We made ready for hauling the ship into a pool to the north of us, that we might leave when the ice should fairly open. The end of August left us 11 months fixed to that spot. We might have circumnavigated the globe in the same period.

Sept. 4. The weather being fine, and we expecting high tide at two in the morning, we attempted to cross the bar in front of our harbor. But before we could warp [pull the ship] out, the tide fell so much that we remained aground in only 14 inches of water. We repaired several small damages received from the ice and proceeded to lighten the ship by discharging four tons of water and putting 10 tons of other articles in the boats, that we might float her off at the next tide.

Sept. 5. At two o'clock in the morning we attempted again to heave the ship over the bar, but in vain. The wind had shifted [packing ice against the ship], and the tides were diminishing. It became necessary to unload the vessel of all stores, together with the remaining ironwork of the engine.

Sept. 6. A shift of wind produced such a tide as enabled us to heave off the bar very early in the morning. Yet we could not advance far enough to avoid grounding ourselves again when the tide should fall, and did not therefore dare to bring on board much of what had been landed.

Sept. 7. It blew a gale from the north during the night but the ice did not move. Toward morning we contrived to heave out so as to get a foot more water, which enabled us to proceed with the reloading of the ship. After this we gained depth sufficient to allow us to reload and that took us two days.

Sept. 16. At daylight we could see that the ice had drifted off the land but there was still a ridge between the ship and a lane of water which led to the north. By afternoon, however, it seemed to be breaking up; we immediately cast off, warped through the bay ice around us, and in half an hour our ship was in clear water and under sail.

Under sail! We scarcely knew how we felt, or whether we quite believed it. We advanced about three miles but, finding a ridge of ice, were obliged to make fast in a harbor between two icebergs, where we passed the night.

Sept. 18. The wind came round to the south, and by morning our passage was blocked. There was much snow.

Sept. 20. The ice opened so slightly under a westerly breeze that it rendered us no service. We were frozen round by new ice, and so obliged to cut around the ship. Our detention was more perfectly assured next day by a southeasterly wind bringing the ice in upon us.

Sept. 29. The thermometer fell and the clear water of yesterday was covered with newly formed bay ice. The surrounding hummocks were also cemented together in such a manner that nothing but a storm could separate them. Our hopes of a liberation were fast passing away.

Sept. 30. The whole sea was now covered with ice. There was no longer occasion either to hope or fear. Our winter prison was before us again; and all that we had now to do was to reach it, set up our amphibious house, and "take patience to ourselves."

October. The whole month was employed in making a worse than tortoise progress toward harbor, the entire amount of which, after all our toils, was but 850 feet. Some of us could not help calculating the number of centuries it would require to make a single northwest passage at this rate.

Our place [they were barely two miles north of Felix Harbour at a place now called Sheriff Harbour] was by no means a desirable one. Yet it was a great gain, since had we remained in the shallow water the ship would have been almost uninhabitable from her motions and change of position, and might have been destroyed.

The winter of 1830-31 was a repetition of the previous one and even Ross lost heart a little. By February he and his men were groping desperately for ways to ease their long imprisonment.

Feb. 28, 1831. The summary of this month is more barren than usual. It had been very cold, particularly toward the end. It was little more than a schoolboy's experiment, to fire a ball of frozen mercury through an inch plank; but possibly this had not been done before. Not having yet seen the Esquimaux, we now gave up hope of their joining us.

March 31. The continuance and degree of the cold began seriously to attract our attention. Nearly the entire surface of the land was a mass of ice and snow. In March of the preceding year, during several days, the water was running down in streams. Yet the men were in perfect health. There had been none on the sick list, and there was no appearance of scurvy.

April 20. The weather being favorable, James Ross and five men left with sledges on a journey of exploration.

April 21. The temperature increased almost to the thawing point, and we were agreeably surprised by a visit from three of the natives, who came over the western hills with their dogs and stopped about a quarter of a mile off, holding up their hands to show they were unarmed. We welcomed them to dinner and to sleep. They carried a note from James Ross to the effect that he had purchased some salmon from them, and we arranged to fetch this acceptable supply the next morning.

April 22. I left the ship at four in the morning, with the surgeon, three seamen and our Esquimaux guests. When we reached their village after a 16-mile walk over very rough ice they began immediately to erect us a house, which they finished in 45 minutes. We were not long in cooking a warm meal, which was very acceptable.

We were very kindly received by the women and found an old one sick, to whom the surgeon administered some medicine. They offered us water, which is scarce at this season, as it requires much oil to melt any quantity of snow.

A recent widow, we were informed, had immediately obtained a new husband because she had five children. Here children are a source of profit instead of loss, and of happiness instead of vexation. Even at eight they begin to be serviceable; in a few years they are able to maintain more than themselves; and it is on them that the helpless aged depend for support.

It is a Utopian state when she of five children is the best of wives and can take her choice of the young men. It is more than Utopian when population is not poverty but wealth. Let the wise of wiser lands travel hither and take lessons from the savages in sealskins, who drink oil and eat their fish raw.

With Inuit to guide them, sledge parties could now resume extensive exploration of the Boothia Peninsula. James Ross found the North Magnetic Pole. And as summer drew on, the men again waited with terrible uncertainty for the release of the VICTORY *from her frozen harbor.*

Aug. 13. Today was as yesterday, and so will be tomorrow. Of course the ice remained unaltered. We were ever waiting to rise and become active, yet ever to find that nature was still asleep and that we had nothing more to do than to wish and groan and hope.

Aug. 28. The wind had blown strong from the west and the ice begun to drift out of the bay. The ship was warped a quarter of a mile into a convenient place for taking advantage of the first opening. As soon as this was done we got under sail but unfortunately we failed in weathering a large iceberg and ran aground. We hove the ship off by hawsers to the shore, but the lower rudder iron was broken, so that was an end to our progress for this day.

Aug. 29. Early in the morning, the rudder was repaired, and the wind remained steady and strong with occasional snow. It was the very wind that we wanted and we felt that we were at last liberated: liberated, though not yet free. We cast off soon after four, and with a reefed topsail stood for some islands through loose ice. Unluckily the wind came to the northwest and we were unable to fetch within a mile of them. Shortly after nine we were close to shore after having run four miles.

A heavy shower of snow coming on, we were obliged to stand in for a little bay where a baffling breeze nearly laid us on the rocks. We warped to the head of this new harbor [now Victoria Harbour, only 14 miles northeast of Felix Harbour] and immediately made fast to the shore with two hawsers. No sooner had we done this than a violent gale came on with a heavy fall of snow, which compelled us to carry out more hawsers. We saw the ice passing to the southwest with considerable rapidity, and had occasion to be very thankful that we were so secure.

Aug. 31. The wind fell, and we went on shore to examine the state of things. The strait was blocked up with ice.

Sept. 15-17. There was now no open water to be seen. It was exceedingly cold but not unpleasant in the sun. It is little to notice but a great many ptarmigan had been killed in the last week. In such a life as ours, even the capture of an Arctic mouse was an event.

Sept. 30. Our prospects of freedom were becoming less every day. The worst prospect, however, was that the ship would never be extricated and that we should be compelled to abandon her. In any case, it was apparent that she must soon sink in consequence of her leaks.

The first of our future objects was to economize in provisions, still more in fuel, and of course to take all possible care of the health of the men. Their spirits were to be kept up, and we could at least point out that we were really on our return, and there was no reason why it should not be complete in the following year. There were still before us the *Fury*'s remaining stores; and there were [the *Fury*'s] boats to carry us into Davis Strait (should we be obliged to abandon the ship) where we should either meet a whaler or reach the Danish settlements in Greenland. Alas, the hopeful did not hope more and the despondent continued to despair.

Oct. 25. A storm blew so violently as to tear into rags the canvas of our housing, which had now gone through a long service. We could not attempt to save it, from the great danger of exposing the men to the cold.

The summary of October cannot be much in detail. It was now our plan to go next April by land [approximately 180 miles] to the place of the *Fury*'s stores.

A chain had been passed twice around the *Victory* amidships to provide the means of raising her again should any other vessel return to the place. Of this provision for a future as unlikely as a season of spring and roses in Boothia Felix, I have not much to say; but it is probably our nursery education which induces us to do all that we can in prevention of waste. [Boothia Felix is Ross' name for what now are called Somerset Island and the Boothia Peninsula—for Felix Booth, a London distiller who financed the *Victory* expedition.]

Nov. 27-30. Our allowance of bread and salt meat had been necessarily reduced. Notwithstanding the use of spruce beer, six men were slightly afflicted with scurvy. This, however, was checked by lemon juice. Their despondency seemed to have ceased.

Dec. 25. Christmas was made a holiday in all senses. We ate a round of beef which had been in the *Fury*'s stores for eight years and which, with veal and vegetables, was as good as the day it was cooked. The men were much reduced in strength but the scurvy had been kept in check. One man alone, being afflicted with a complication of disorders, was not expected to live very long. [Stoker James Dixon died 16 days later.]

Jan. 31, 1832. Our medical report now begins to be very different from what it had been. All were much enfeebled and there was a good deal of ailment without any marked diseases. An old wound in my side had broken out, with bleeding, and I knew that this was an indication of scurvy. We had not caught much fresh meat and our rations were still reduced.

Feb. 1-4. The month began with a furious storm which continued for two days. The ice was cut through and its thickness found to be five feet and upward. The weather rendered it seldom possible to show ourselves beyond the roof or deck.

Feb. 19-20. Sunday was cold and Monday much worse. In the morning, a wolverine came on board and began to devour the dog's meat. It was inhospitable to kill the starving wretch, but it was the first specimen of this creature we had been able to obtain. The seaman [Anthony] Buck, who had unexpectedly suffered a recurrence of epilepsy with an unusual degree of violence, had become blind.

The plan now was to proceed to Fury Beach, not only for supplies but also to get possession of the *Fury*'s boats there. We would first haul our own boats on sledges to Elizabeth Harbour, with provisions for six weeks at full allowance. There we would deposit the boats and half the provisions, and proceed with the sledges and the other half of the provisions till we reached the latitude of 71°. From there we would send a party of five to Fury Beach. If things there seemed satisfactory the whole party would continue to that place, but if [the *Fury*'s boats were unusable] we could fall back on the depot at Elizabeth Harbour.

March 30-31. The month was very cold in consequence of the frequent winds; our comparative weakness and the alteration in our diet made us feel it more severely. This had retarded the work on the sledges; but we had been busy arranging our several travelling necessaries—arms, ammunition, tools and fuel to thaw snow for drinking, besides instruments and our personal accommodations.

In our crew we had now one blind man, and the [third] mate, [George] Taylor, was so lame that he could walk but a very little way. Three other men were in very indifferent health. The prudent conduct now seemed to be to restore the whole to full food allowance and this was done.

April 23. Though the temperature was low, it was clear and calm. We therefore set out at nine, proceeding with great labor and difficulty through rough ice. We were at length obliged to take but one load at a time, returning for the others alternately; in consequence of which we were no more than seven miles from the ship after five hours' work. It then began to blow so hard, with drift snow, that we were obliged to halt and build snow huts. These were covered with canvas and, by means of the deerskin beds and our cooking apparatus, the whole party of 14 was well accommodated, though the temperature of our house at night was 15 below (−26°C).

After almost a month the men had walked nearly 330 miles and advanced the boats and provisions about 30 miles. They returned to the VICTORY *for the last time.*

May 29. We had now secured everything on shore which could be of use to us. The colors were therefore hoisted and nailed to the mast. We drank a parting glass to our poor ship, and having seen every man out I took my own adieu of the *Victory*, which had deserved a better fate.

May 30. The snow was harder and our road improved, yet the heavy loads made our progress slow. We ended the month at 70° 21′ latitude, leaving us 16 miles more to reach Elizabeth Harbour. Though our crew were in a very indifferent condition, even the blind man and the lame were obliged to exert themselves, contriving thus to keep up their spirits.

June 3. The men seemed much fatigued, and the [first] mate, [Thomas] Blanky, intimated their desire to abandon the boats and spare provisions at this place and proceed direct to Fury Beach. I not only expressed my refusal but ordered the party to proceed, in a manner not easily misunderstood. It was the first symptom approaching to mutiny which had yet occurred.

June 9. Everything was brought forward to the depot in Elizabeth Harbour. It was clearly impossible to carry the boats any farther so I determined to proceed with the people and three weeks' provisions for 20 or 30 miles, leaving the boats and the rest of the supplies here as a reserve, and sending an advance party on to Fury Beach.

June 12. James Ross, with [the second mate, Thomas] Abernethy, and [a seaman, John] Park, departed for Fury Beach, taking with them a sledge, 15 days' provisions and a tent. We calculated on taking double their time with our load.

June 25. We met James Ross' party returning from Fury Beach. He reported that the sea there had risen high and carried three of the *Fury's* boats to the north along the shore. One of them was seriously damaged. All else was in the same condition as we had left it; and the bread and other provisions were in abundance and in good order.

June 30. We resumed our journey, being now obliged to carry the lame man. We had shot several ducks in the last few days and they were somewhat better than a luxury to us.

July 1. The water was now, at last, running down the large cracks in the ice, and everything was hourly changing in appearance. We encamped on Fury Beach at 10 o'clock.

July 2. We were once more at home, for a time at least. The stores were scattered in every direction and it was difficult to prevent the half-starved men from getting access to them, in consequence of which many suffered smartly for their imprudence. Excepting the damage done by the sea, the only important loss was the candles, which had been devoured by foxes.

July 4. A house 31 by 16 feet and covered in canvas was finished. It received the nickname Somerset House. The carpenters were then set to work strengthening the *Fury*'s boats.

Aug. 1. On the last day of July the ice had unexpectedly broken up and we now prepared to depart with the hope of being able to reach Baffin Bay before the departure of the whaling vessels. The boats were stored with provisions to last till Oct. 1, besides the bedding and other needful things, and each carried seven men with an officer.

We left the beach at four in the afternoon, but found the channels in the ice crooked and impeded by floating pieces, so that it was difficult to use our oars. Our progress was therefore slow, and after coming eight miles we stopped at nine o'clock under the very precipice where the *Fury* was wrecked.

The boats were unloaded as quickly as possible and hauled up on the beach. It was not a minute too soon, since the ice had changed direction and closed the channel just offshore. Two floes near us were broken to pieces with a violent crash. We experienced this narrow escape on the same day that the *Fury* was lost eight years before.

Aug. 2. We were unable to proceed on account of ice and found that the vicinity of this precipice, which was 470 feet high, was a position of the utmost danger, due to falling rocks. We might all have been overwhelmed without notice, or the brains of any individual among us might have been knocked out. But we were fully tried by hazards and had become somewhat careless.

Aug. 28. The gale of the last few days moderated at noon and we embarked under sail along the shore, exposed to very heavy squalls from the precipices. Passing Batty Bay, we reached Elwin Bay at midnight. We then stood for a beach about a mile farther north, and pitched our tents amid a storm of snow which, in the night, covered all the land.

Aug. 29. In the morning we embarked again but soon ran into another storm. This evening we were unable to reach land because heavy ice was all around us.

Aug. 30. We were obliged to sleep in our boats, in no comfortable position, and we re-embarked at six in the morning with a southerly wind. We ran along the ice pack but there was no exit anywhere. We therefore stood back to the shore near Cape Clarence and found a good position for pitching the tents and hauling up the boats. [Cape Clarence was the northernmost point of the route. From here the party would sail east toward Baffin Bay.]

Aug. 31. By now we had been detained so long by the state of the ice that it became doubtful if we should succeed during the present season. Our allowance of food consisted of half a pound of meat, with a pound of bread and a pint of cocoa, divided into breakfast and supper. All game was considered extra and luxurious, but for the entire month of August it amounted to just three foxes and as many hares, with a couple of ducks.

The boats, being made of mahogany, gave us great trouble to haul them up on the beach. The whole party was required to draw up one, often requiring the assistance of tackle.

Sept. 17. Two foxes were killed, with some ptarmigans. In the beginning of our sojourn we had thought the fox bad eating but now it was preferred to other meat.

Sept. 20. It was still colder but, as the ice appeared to be loosening, we embarked our things, leaving an account of our proceedings in a tin case beneath a cairn. Putting off at noon, we reached the pack edge of the ice at the junction of Barrow Strait and Prince Regent Inlet. It was a solid mass, giving no hopes of breaking during the present season.

Sept. 24. Everyone agreed that we should return to Fury Beach.

Sept. 27. Our return journey was making very slow progress through heavy ice. Then a gale forced us to put ashore under the most terrific precipice that we had yet seen, two miles from the north cape of Batty Bay. We had but six feet of beach beneath cliffs which rose 500 feet, and were detained by an easterly wind bringing the bay ice on us. We were now reduced to half allowance of provisions.

Anxious as the preceding months had been, we yet found some occupation for our minds in the discussion of our chances and hopes.

Each of our three tents formed a kind of separate deliberative party, or a little society. James Ross, who had always been the most sanguine, was the leader of the hopeful. The contrary opinion prevailed in the party of Mr. Thom [Purser William Thom, RN], whose estimable qualities in all other points were not accompanied by a spirit of confidence. My own tent was one of divided opinions.

Our situation had become truly serious. We began to experience the greatest sufferings we had yet endured from the cold. We had been unable to carry with us our usual quantity of clothes and of canvas, so that we were most in want of protection from the weather when we were least able to bear up against its severity.

Oct. 4. There could be no further hope of getting to Fury Beach in the boats. We therefore determined to leave them for next year's use and proceed pulling sledges. The carpenter made three from empty bread casks, and his chips became welcome fuel, serving to cook a couple of foxes.

The sledges were loaded amid heavy snow, which then rendered our way nearly impassable. The lame man, Taylor, could neither walk with his crutches nor ride on the sledges, which were perpetually upsetting on the rough ice. We gained a resting place at seven o'clock after making but four miles.

Oct. 5. We passed a miserably cold night, but escaped frostbite. In the morning, one of our sledges being broken, we were compelled to leave some stores. But thus having stronger parties to draw them than on the preceding day, we gained seven miles in spite of a strong, cold wind and constant snow. We were enabled to carry Taylor by returning for him with an empty sledge.

Oct. 6. Heavy ice was pressed up to the precipices and we were often obliged to quit a tolerable track to get round in the best manner we could. But the labor kept us warm and we pitched within sight of our winter home, killing several foxes on the way.

Oct. 7. We reached Somerset House and found it occupied by a fox, which soon made its escape. Everything was as we left it and as we were not less hungry than cold, having finished our last morsel at breakfast, the men were treated with a good meal. Two of the men were found to have frostbites, and I had been deeply cut in the leg.

Oct. 13. There was no cessation to a most uncommon storm. The snow gained admission to our beds and everything was frozen. We had great difficulty in keeping ourselves warm by crowding round the stove; but had the good fortune to take three foxes in the traps, a matter now of great congratulation.

Oct. 22-27. A snow wall, four feet thick, was built round our house; and further spars and ropes were applied to support the roof for the purpose of covering it with snow.

Oct. 28. The men had their last dinner on full allowance.

Oct. 29-31. With respect to the present rations, the men were allowed pea soup, alternately with one made of carrots and turnips, out of the stores of the *Fury*. Instead of bread, which we could not now furnish to a sufficient extent, they were provided with dumplings of flour and water. They were, indeed, sufficiently fed, since it was observed that they had become in much better condition since our return to this place.

November. The month was very severe and the men could seldom work out in the open. We made our house tolerably comfortable, each of the men having a bed place with a canvas bottom, a mat for a bed, and a blanket.

December. Half a dozen foxes were taken, and afforded us an excellent meal on Christmas which was the first that we had spent without tasting spirits or wine, these luxuries having been exhausted. [Chimham] Thomas the carpenter was now the only person on the sick list, the scurvy under which he suffered not yielding to our lime juice.

January, 1833. The 29th was very fine, the first time we had seen the sun during 74 days.

February. The carpenter being in a hopeless state, an appropriate sermon was read on Sunday the 10th. On the following Saturday morning he died. The ground was so hard that we had great difficulty in making a grave.

My own condition from the state of ancient wounds brought into troublesome action by a tendency to scurvy, was somewhat threatening. I had reason to suppose that I might not survive.

March. A want of sufficient employment, the short allowance of food, and the inevitable lowness of spirits combined to reduce us all to a state of very indifferent health. We were very weary of this miserable home.

April. Our plan was to carry to the boats we had left at Batty Bay, by stages, sufficient provisions to last us from July 1 till Oct. 1. Thus we would be in readiness for moving whenever the ice should open. On April 21 James Ross and a party of men set off with two loads. They returned about midday on the 24th, having seen a bear and killed a seal. In the evening another bear was killed after having pulled down our flagstaff. During the rest of the month we got our provisions forward eight miles, or a quarter of the way to the boats.

May. The transportation of all our provisions to the boats compelled the parties to travel the same ground eight times, making a total distance of 256 miles. Consequently it was not till May 24 that we arrived with

the first load at the place of the boats, which we could not at first discover, so deeply was the ground covered with snow. By May 29 all provisions were at the place of the boats.

June 1. Having carried forward all that could be spared from our actual wants, we had now to occupy ourselves as best we could at our Somerset House till it was time to move again.

July 4. Our preserved meat was expended. The roof of the house was repaired and strengthened in case we should be obliged to return to it for the ensuing winter though we were at a loss to know how we were to subsist under such an unfortunate event.

July 8. Everything was ready. The sick, who formed our great difficulty, bore the first journey well, and we reached our first station before midday. In the afternoon we proceeded again with infinite toil through nearly impassable ways. So hard was the labor that we were obliged to work in our shirts even at night.

July 14. Sunday at Batty Bay, whence we had at last arrived, had been made a day of rest.

July 15. The ice was examined from the hills, but was not yet breaking. About 100 dovekies [small sea birds] were killed, so that our supply of fresh meat was respectable, if not great.

Aug. 3. We made an attempt to move round the southern point of the bay. Even this fruitless labor kept up the spirits and hopes of the people. We made work when we had ceased to find it. Better was it that the men work themselves into utter weariness, than that they should so hunger as to think only of nothing but a better dinner.

Aug. 14. A lane of water was seen leading northward and not many, I believe, slept, under the anticipation of what the next day might bring.

Aug. 15. All were employed in cutting the ice which obstructed the shore. Then, the tide having risen, with a fine westerly breeze, we launched the boats, embarked the stores and the sick, and at eight o'clock were under way.

It was our business to forget that we had been in the same circumstances the year before; to feel that the time for exertion was now come, to see in the mind's eye the whole strait open before us, and our little fleet sailing with a fair wind through that bay which was now, in our view, England and home.

Aug. 16-17. We rounded the north cape of Batty Bay and crossed Elwin's Bay at midnight, reaching that spot where we had pitched our tents on Aug. 28 in the preceding year. The difference in time was but 12 days, and should those days pass as they had done in the former year, it might still be our fate to return to our last winter's home, and there to end our toils.

But the lane of water still extended toward the north. As we proceeded, the open water increased in breadth and at eight in the evening we reached our former position on Cape Clarence. A view from the hill showed that the ice to the northeast was in such a state as to admit of sailing through it, but as the wind blew too hard to venture out at night, we pitched our tents.

At three in the morning we embarked once more. It was calm, and we held to the east by rowing, until a southerly breeze sprang up. This enabled us to reach the eastern shore of Prince Regent Strait at three in the afternoon.

It was a change like that of magic to find that solid mass of ocean ice which we had looked at for so many years suddenly converted into navigable water. We ran quickly along the shore as the breeze increased, to take shelter on the beach 12 miles west of Cape York, having made on this day a run of 72 miles.

Aug. 18. The wind moderating, and at length becoming calm, we were obliged to take to the oars. At midnight we rested at the cape to the east of Admiralty Inlet.

Aug. 19. We were nearing Navy Board Inlet when, the men being exhausted with nearly 20 hours' rowing, we stopped and pitched our tents. We were soon driven from this exposed place by an easterly wind, and rowed along among icebergs till we arrived at an excellent harbor, having gained five miles more.

Aug. 24. We were imprisoned for several days by a gale, with fog and rain, that had sprung up of the 19th. It had become prudent to reduce ourselves once more to a two-thirds allowance.

Aug. 26. At four in the morning the lookout man discovered a ship in the offing. All hands were immediately out of their tents and on the beach, discussing her rig, quality and course though there were despairers who maintained that it was only an iceberg.

No time was lost, however. The boats were launched and signals made by burning wet powder, and we left at six o'clock. Our progress was tedious, owing to alternate calms and light airs blowing in every direction, yet we made way toward the vessel. Unluckily, a breeze just then sprang up, and she made all sail to the southeast, by which means the boat that was foremost was soon left astern.

About 10 o'clock we saw another ship to the north, which appeared to be lying-to for her boats. We thought at one time, when she hove to, that she had seen us, but she soon bore up under all sail and was fast leaving us. It was the most anxious moment we had yet experienced, to find that we were near no less than two ships and that we should probably reach neither.

It was necessary to keep up the courage of the men by assuring them that we were coming up with the second ship. Most fortunately, the weather fell calm and we really gained so fast that at 11 o'clock we saw her heave to and lower down a boat which rowed immediately toward our own.

The mate addressed us by presuming that we had met with some misfortune and lost our ship. This being answered in the affirmative, I requested to know the name of his vessel, and expressed our wish to be taken on board. I was answered that it was the *Isabella,* once commanded by Captain Ross, on which I stated that I was the identical man in question, and my people the crew of the *Victory*. The mate was astonished; with the usual blunderheadedness of men on such occasions, he assured me that I had been dead two years. I easily convinced him, however, that this was a somewhat premature conclusion.

He immediately went off to communicate his information on board, and in a minute the rigging was manned. We approached slowly after him and were saluted with three cheers as we came within cable's length. We were not long in getting on board, where we were received by the captain with a hearty seaman's welcome.

Never was seen a more miserable looking people than our party. No beggar could have outdone us in exciting the repugnance of those who have not known what poverty can be. Unshaven since I know not when, dirty, dressed in the rags of wild beasts, and starved to the very bones, our gaunt and grim looks, when contrasted with those of the well-dressed and well-fed men around us, made us all feel, I believe for the first time, what we really were.

But serious thought was impossible in such confusion. It was washing, dressing, shaving, eating, all intermingled with interminable questions on all sides, the adventures of the *Victory*, our own escapes, the politics of England, and the news which was now four years old.

But all subsided into peace at last. The sick were accommodated, the seamen disposed of, and all was done which care and kindness could perform. Night brought quiet and serious thoughts; and I trust there was not one man among us who did not then express his gratitude for that interposition which had brought us back from the very borders of a not distant grave, to life and friends and civilization.

Franklin's Last Voyage

Sir John Franklin sailed from England with
two ships in 1845, confident that he was about
to discover the legendary Northwest Passage.
Never before had an Arctic expedition been fitted
out at such expense. Never had crews been so
carefully selected. Never had an entire party
carried greater expectations of success. Never has
one ended in such grievous failure. The
disappearance of Franklin and his 129 men
remains the Arctic's most tantalizing puzzle.

By FRED BODSWORTH

O N MAY 19, 1845, the guns of Greenwich boomed in farewell and
two Royal Navy sailing ships dropped down the Thames on
a voyage that was to take them in search of the Northwest Passage. Striding his scrubbed deck, gallantly waving to the crowds, was
a bald, aristocratic hero, Sir John Franklin, an imperious sea dog who
had fought with Nelson at Copenhagen and Trafalgar, a veteran explorer
who twice had led overland explorations into the Canadian Arctic.

In their Whitehall offices Britain's bewigged Lords of the Admiralty
congratulated themselves that at last, after a 350-year struggle, the elusive
passage from the Atlantic to the Pacific must now certainly be found.
Franklin's ships, the *Erebus* and the *Terror,* heavy with provisions to last
three years, would make the most ambitious assault yet against the Arctic
seas. Their bows were iron-plated and they had steam engines to keep
them moving in calm weather. They carried the latest scientific instruments for observing plants, animal life and celestial bodies, as well as
a complete outfit for taking "sun pictures"—what we call photographs—
and a mechanical organ that played 50 popular tunes.

In those days, at all costs, an officer had to live like a British gentleman, so Franklin and his officers tackled the grinding Arctic floes equipped with mahogany writing desks, initialled silverware, a library of religious books, silk handkerchiefs and swords. Buttons were kept polished by batmen.

Officers and men had been schooled in Royal Navy discipline and courage but, tragically, not one knew how to build a snowhouse or hunt a seal. These were the healthiest, best-trained men Britain could recruit and they had the most modern guns and equipment. Yet they died, evidently of starvation, in a land where Inuit [Eskimos] had survived for centuries with Stone Age weapons.

The expedition served as a grim reminder that Arctic survival depended on leaders who could appreciate such mundane things as learning how to travel light and live off the land, on leaders whose imagination went further than saluting the quarterdeck and keeping buttons polished.

Ten weeks after leaving Britain, the *Erebus* and the *Terror* were met off western Greenland by a whaling vessel which brought back letters from Franklin and his men. They were confident, enthusiastic letters. "Do not worry if the voyage should last longer than anticipated," Franklin wrote his wife. "We can hold out for five years." Officers advised their wives to address future correspondence to Petropavlovsk Kamchatskiy, a Russian seaport on the Pacific.

The *Erebus* and the *Terror* headed west into the maze of Canada's Arctic islands—and disappeared.

Three years later, when no further word had been received, history's greatest quest got under way. In six years more than 40 expeditions combed the Arctic—at a total cost of $4 million, a staggering amount in the mid-19th century. In 1850 alone 14 ships sailed on the search. The Franklin expedition, in failure, accomplished more for Arctic exploration than it could have with success. The searchers mapped more of Canada's Arctic than had been covered in the previous 300 years: as the great blanks were filled in, not *the* Northwest Passage but two or three such passages were found.

The search problem was immense. There were no reliable charts, and compasses spun crazily because of the nearness of the Magnetic Pole. The searchers left great caches of food and clothing on the chance that Franklin's men might find them. They painted messages on rocks visible to ships at sea. They even trapped foxes alive and released them with collars and messages, hoping that one of the animals might fall into the hands of the lost.

In 1850 a reckless whaling captain named William Penny, in charge of a search ship and fed up with the red tape of his expedition leader, struck out on his own. On tiny Beechey Island in Barrow Strait he stumbled across the remains of Franklin's first winter camp. Weeks were spent searching the area. Three graves were found, the remains of several huts, rope, sailcloth and empty food tins, but not a scrap of paper containing a written record. Franklin, in defiance of every exploration custom, had sailed away without leaving a clue to his direction.

There were no more clues for four years. But there was more drama than in a library of dime novels. Ships were crushed in the ice and sank. Men starved and died. One crew was saved when it stumbled across supplies abandoned by explorer Sir William Parry 30 years before; another was itself rescued after being lost for three years.

In 1854 Britain was saddled with a bigger worry—the Crimean War. Franklin and his crews were stricken from Navy rolls and pronounced dead. The search was officially closed.

Then the mystery began to unravel.

The Admiralty had failed to reckon with some searchers who were still out—a Hudson's Bay Company land party under Dr. John Rae in the area of the Boothia Peninsula.

In October 1854 Rae reached England with startling news. He had talked to Inuit who had heard from other Inuit that, several years before, 40 white men had been encountered on King William Island to the west. The men's ships had been crushed in the ice and the party was heading south afoot, starving and ill with scurvy. Later, according to Inuit rumor, 30 white bodies were found 100 miles farther south on the east side of Adelaide Peninsula, at a place which came to be called Starvation Cove.

Said Rae's report to the Admiralty: "From the mutilated state of the corpses, and the contents of the kettles, it is evident that our wretched countrymen had been driven to the last resource—cannibalism—as a means of prolonging existence." Rae's news was authenticated by relics he purchased from the Inuit, mostly silverware bearing the initials of Franklin and his officers.

The suggestion of cannibalism among British officers and men horrified Britain, and the Lords of the Admiralty, in spite of the initialled silverware, were reluctant to accept Rae's story.

But there was now no question that the *Erebus* and the *Terror* had come to grief somewhere between Victoria and King William Islands,

Sir John Franklin, officer and gentleman. Right: the EREBUS *in the ice.*

an area never searched because the Admiralty had bullheadedly insisted Franklin couldn't have reached that far south. Confronted with proof of its mistake, with humiliating hints of cannibalism, and with suggestions that Franklin and his officers had bungled things, the Admiralty reaffirmed its decision to drop the whole business.

Lady Franklin, however, clung to hope that her husband and some of his men might be alive. At the very least, Rae's findings should be

followed up. She fitted out the *Fox,* a ship of her own, and sent it out in 1857 under Leopold McClintock, an officer who had been on earlier search expeditions and had learned something about Arctic survival.

McClintock heard grim Inuit tales of the many white men who years before had left their ships off northern King William Island and staggered down its western coast dragging great sledge loads of equipment. Many of the whites, weak and starving, dropped in their tracks and were left to die. The two ships, Inuit said, remained in the ice for several years and finally sank.

McClintock and his men searched 100 miles of the King William Island coast. They found an amazing assortment of abandoned equipment—a 750-pound boat mounted on a 650-pound sledge, watches, guns, ammunition, silk handkerchiefs, soap, toothbrushes, tools of all sorts including pickaxes and shovels, iron barrel hoops, rolls of sheet lead and a lightning conductor.

Said McClintock later, "A quantity of articles truly astonishing in variety and such as, for the most part, modern sledge travellers in those regions would consider a mere accumulation of dead weight, very likely to break down the strength of the sledge crews."

McClintock found three skeletons, and his lieutenant, Robert Hobson, discovered the only written Franklin record that has been found to this day. It was at the northern tip of King William Island in a stone cairn of the type explorers erect to protect written documents. Inside was this brief message:

28 May, 1847. H.M. Ships Erebus and Terror wintered in the ice in 1846-7 at Beechey Island after having ascended Wellington Channel and returned by the west side of Cornwallis Island. Sir John Franklin commanding the expedition. All well. Party consisting of 2 officers and 6 men left the ships on Monday. 24th May, 1847. Gm. Gore, Lieut. [and] Chas. F. Des Voeux, Mate.

The wintering date 1846-47 was an error, for it was the winter of 1845-46 which Franklin spent at Beechey Island. And scribbled around the margin of the yellowed paper was a later and far less cheerful entry:

April 25, 1848. H.M. Ships Erebus and Terror were deserted on the 22nd of April, 5 leagues NNW of this, having been beset since 12 of September, 1846. The officers and crews, consisting of 105 souls, under the command of Captain F. R. M. Crozier, landed here . . . . Sir John Franklin died on June 11, 1847, and the total loss by deaths in the expedition has been to this date 9 officers and 15 men. F. R. M. Crozier, Captain and Senior Officer. James Fitzjames, Captain H.M.S. Erebus. And start tomorrow 26th for Back's Fish River.

But the mystery was still far from solved. Only three skeletons had been discovered. Eleven years had passed. Could some men be still alive?

One optimist who so believed was a husky American journalist-turned-explorer, Charles Francis Hall (also destined to leave his bones in an Arctic grave when he attempted to reach the North Pole 12 years later). Between 1860 and 1869 Hall lived with Inuit, learning their dialects, questioning them about the Franklin tragedy. In an 1864 letter he told a startling tale.

A few years before, he wrote, Inuit had encountered an officer and two men on Boothia Peninsula. The men were in good health, the officer weak and starving; the men had eaten the flesh of dead companions but the officer had refused to turn cannibal. Inuit fed them for many months and eventually they struck out with an Inuit guide for the south. They still had guns and ammunition. The Inuit did not hear of them again but felt they were still alive.

In 1869 Hall went to King William Island, where he found several additional skeletons and numerous new Franklin relics. Some of the skeletons showed bones that had been cut by saws—further evidence of cannibalism. Inuit told tantalizing stories of many books and diaries they had given to children to play with. Arctic history's greatest story was probably torn into bits and scattered by the winds.

Little of importance has been added to the story revealed by Rae, McClintock and Hall. Later parties picked up Inuit legends about "the great man" being buried in an opening of rock and covered with something that "after a while was all same stone." From this has sprung the belief that somewhere on King William Island is a concrete vault containing Sir John Franklin's remains.

The Hudson's Bay Company sent investigators to King William Island in 1934 and 1936. In 1946 there was an unsuccessful aerial search for Franklin's cemented grave. In 1947 Lawrence Learmonth, a Hudson's Bay Company employee and Arctic veteran, examined the area again and found more skeletons and relics.

From Inuit accounts, skeletons, abandoned equipment and the messages found, much of the Franklin story can be reconstructed. This is probably what happened:

The *Erebus* and the *Terror* passed through Lancaster Sound, turned up Wellington Channel, probably found ice to the north too heavy, and came south again along the western coast of Cornwallis Island—proving for the first time that it was an island. The ships spent the winter of 1845-46 in the protection of Beechey Island. It had been a successful first season. Three men died that winter, but this was nothing to get alarmed about in a party of 130, and spirits were probably high.

The following summer they encountered an uncharted waterway opening invitingly to the south—Peel Sound. The ships turned into it, travelled 400 miles to the neighborhood of King William Island, and there sailed into the ice-choked bottleneck of Victoria Strait, now recognized as one of the Arctic's deadliest traps. In September that year *Erebus* and *Terror* became imprisoned in the floes.

On May 24, 1847, Franklin sent a sledge party under Lieut. Graham Gore to see if a southern outlet from Victoria Strait existed. Gore apparently reached Simpson Strait, separating King William Island from the mainland, an area which had just been charted from the west by Thomas Simpson of the Hudson's Bay Company. Gore would thus have completed the missing link in the Northwest Passage, albeit over ice, and it is possible that he reported his accomplishment to Franklin on his return. It was on this trip too that Gore deposited the "all well" message found 12 years later by McClintock's lieutenant, Hobson.

But on June 11 that year Franklin died, apparently unexpectedly. The ships lay imprisoned for a full year, during which 21 more men died and food would have run low. Francis Crozier, now the leader, decided the remaining officers and men must retreat overland to save themselves.

Here the tragic errors begin. By this time a few adaptable Britons such as Rae and McClintock were prepared to copy the Inuit and survive in the Arctic. But men such as Franklin's officers, puppets of naval discipline and tradition, couldn't forget that they were British gentlemen.

Crozier knew they were about 250 miles from "Back's Fish River," the present-day Back River known then to the Inuit as the Great Fish River. He planned to drag two or three of the ships' 28-foot boats to its mouth and then follow it into the Canadian interior. The leader evidently had visions of returning to civilization in a style befitting an expedition of Her Majesty's Navy; he doesn't seem to have considered the idea of navigating the Back River on driftwood rafts. And the boats had to be in good repair—a rigid naval requirement—so he loaded the sledges with hundreds of pounds of tools, boat siding, sheet lead and other equipment.

Scurvy was probably sapping the strength of the 100 crewmen, yet they staggered across the ice with cookstoves, bags of coal, the religious books, silverware and even curtain rods. Officers' batmen apparently travelled with full kits of brushes and polishes. Inuit found swords that

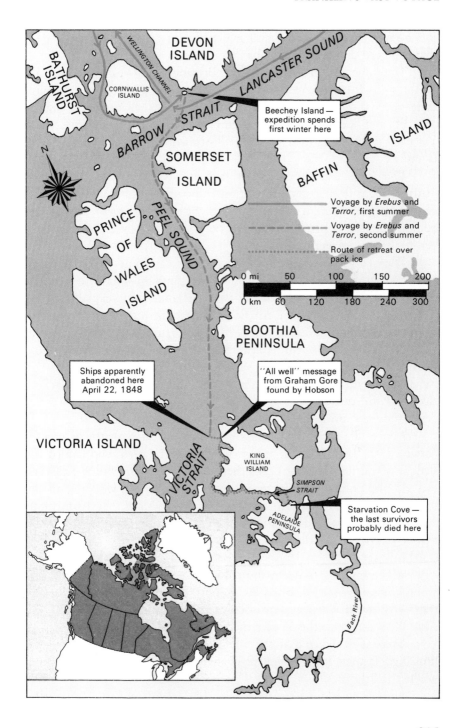

DEVON ISLAND

BATHURST ISLAND

CORNWALLIS ISLAND

WELLINGTON CHANNEL

LANCASTER SOUND

BARROW STRAIT

Beechey Island — expedition spends first winter here

SOMERSET ISLAND

BAFFIN ISLAND

PRINCE OF WALES ISLAND

PEEL SOUND

Voyage by *Erebus* and *Terror*, first summer

Voyage by *Erebus* and *Terror*, second summer

Route of retreat over pack ice

| 0 mi | 50 | 100 | 150 | 200 |

| 0 km | 60 | 120 | 180 | 240 | 300 |

BOOTHIA PENINSULA

Ships apparently abandoned here April 22, 1848

"All well" message from Graham Gore found by Hobson

VICTORIA ISLAND

VICTORIA STRAIT

KING WILLIAM ISLAND

SIMPSON STRAIT

ADELAIDE PENINSULA

Starvation Cove — the last survivors probably died here

Back River

had been carried 100 miles, and Hall found a mahogany writing desk that had been drawn by sledge for 150 miles.

The famed charge of the Light Brigade a few years later was no greater folly. It is estimated that the sledges started with 10 tons of equipment—200 pounds per man. It seems unbelievable that intelligent officers on a life-and-death dash would attempt to carry such loads with them. Yet the evidence was there on the junk-strewn beaches of King William Island.

The Arctic has never seen as grim and tragic a march. Men died in their tracks from scurvy, starvation and overwork. For a few days the dead were given decent burial, then, as the survivors grew weaker, the bodies were left where they fell, to be pounced upon by Arctic foxes before the sledges were out of sight.

There are no diaries describing the last days, but we can gain an idea of how the retreat down King William Island must have been carried out by studying the diaries of the two overland Arctic expeditions led by Franklin. In 1819-21 on a trip down the Coppermine River and along Coronation Gulf, provisions had been inadequate and his 20-man group was overloaded with scientific gear. Starvation and mutiny claimed nine lives before Indians rescued the survivors. In 1825 Franklin did arrange for enough food, but his expedition west from the mouth of the Mackenzie River still carried huge amounts of equipment (including a writing desk) and made no attempt to learn how to live off the land.

Above all, these early Franklin diaries reveal a sharp distinction between "the officers" and "the men." It was the men who hauled the sledges or carried on their backs their own equipment and the officers' too. At one point, Franklin recorded, "Because of the weakness of the men the officers have begun carrying such a portion of their own things as their strength would permit." One man was so weak, Franklin noted, that it was necessary to reduce his load "to little more than his own personal luggage."

When starving to death and reduced to eating shoe leather, officers still maintained social distinctions. In one account Franklin records how they were saved when a man discovered an edible form of lichen. He adds: "It was used in the officers' mess."

There is evidence that the typical naval officer of 1850 considered hunting his own food a menial, degrading task. Like other chores, it was left to "the men."

The last Franklin retreat was probably no different from the earlier ones. Rae recorded what Inuit had told him about the 40 men they saw on King William Island: "None of the party could speak the [Inuit] language so well as to be understood but the natives were led to believe that they were going to where they expected deer to shoot." The Inuit were willing to help but apparently the white men were still determined to do things their own way. Only as some of them died was the reluctant ditching of the "less essential" equipment begun.

The party crossed Simpson Strait to the mainland, the last 30 survivors dying at Starvation Cove. Their skeletons were found by Danish explorer Knud Rasmussen in 1923.

The other 65 men of the 105 who started out for the Back River may have been lagging behind or they may have broken away and headed in another direction. One ship's boat and a sledge discovered by searchers were facing toward where the ships were abandoned, so it is probable that this second party attempted to retrace its steps.

The rest is sheer speculation. The second party may have reached the ships and died waiting for the ice to release them. A few may have mastered the Inuit way of life sufficiently to survive for many years. On Victoria Island, in the 1920s, explorer Vilhjalmur Stefansson found "blonde" Inuit with European facial characteristics. Could they have been descendants of survivors who married Inuit? Some experts believe so.

There is no doubt, though, that many of Sir John Franklin's men died like helpless kittens with loaded guns beside them. Probably they met death unflinchingly–disciplined and courageous British gentlemen to the last.

Wooden Ships

and Iron Men

There is no strength where there is no strain;
seamanship is not learned in calm weather,
and born of the vicissitudes and struggles of life
are the wisdom, the dignity, and the consolations.

Joseph Howe, 1872

A Voyage to the New Land

Storms, icebergs, sickness and bad food made life
rough and dangerous in 19th-century immigrant sailing ships.
On April 5, 1817, a Presbyterian minister named William Bell,
his wife and six children boarded the ROTHIEMURCHUS
in the east-coast Scottish port of Leith. They were bound for
Quebec City, and Perth in Upper Canada. From his new home Bell
wrote this account of his voyage, confessing that the recollection
"still presents a gloomy picture to my mind."

By WILLIAM BELL

ALL WAS HURRY AND BUSTLE getting ready for sailing. The passengers, young and old, amounting to 105, were all on board. Some appeared lively and cheerful, some thoughtful and serious—while a few, by the tears which they shed, showed that they were not leaving their country and their friends without a struggle.

About half an hour before we sailed a messenger at arms came on board with a warrant to apprehend and carry ashore a man who had forgotten to discharge his debts before he came away. But after searching half an hour below with a lighted candle he was forced to return disappointed. After he was gone the man he had been seeking crawled out of the coal-hole below the lower deck, to the no small astonishment of his fellow passengers; many congratulated him on his narrow escape from the hands of justice.

At five in the evening the captain came on board and gave orders to get ready for proceeding. Before six we had weighed anchor and were under sail with a fair wind. But in half an hour the wind came round to the east and blew rather fresher so that about seven we were forced to come to anchor not far from the place we had just left.

The accommodations which the ship afforded were not of the first order. She was fitted for the timber trade and had no cabin except a small one on the quarterdeck, but as there was a good deal of room between decks, and as we were not overcrowded with passengers, we expected, at this season of the year, to make a tolerable shift. We were accompanied by the Reverend Mr. Taylor and his family who were proceeding with us to Canada. Mr. Taylor and I had engaged a part at the stern, in which were the two windows which usually light the cabin. For this we paid £120. The captain had engaged to divide it from the rest of the ship by a temporary partition; this, however, he never performed.

On each side of the ship were ranged two tiers of berths, the passengers providing their own bedding. Along the open space in the middle were placed two rows of large chests which were sometimes used as tables and at other times as seats. A good deal of noise and confusion took place before all the passengers were arranged in their berths, and in the evening the captain was obliged to interpose his authority and to determine which bed everyone was to have.

We now began to feel what it was to be at sea with so much company. The crying of the children, the swearing of the sailors and the scolding of the women who had not got the beds they wanted produced a concert in which it was difficult to discover any harmony. Its disagreeable effect was heightened by the darkness of the night and the rolling of the ship on a sea becoming somewhat rough. I almost envied the happiness of many a poor but pious cottager who, at that moment at his peaceful fireside and surrounded by his family, was worshipping the God of his fathers.

Next morning, which was the Sabbath, I got up at seven and found that we were still at anchor. The wind was easterly and blowing a fine breeze so that numbers began to be affected with seasickness. I had agreed with both the captain and the passengers that we should have worship morning and evening every day, and preaching twice on the Sabbath. This morning we met at eight o'clock for the first worship, the bustle and confusion having prevented us the evening before. Most of the passengers and sailors attended and behaved with the greatest propriety, with the exception of two young gentlemen who were passengers, and two or three of the sailors.

After breakfast I began to be sick but, by the advice of a sailor, I took a draught of salt water which operated as an emetic, and I soon got better.

I was just about to commence preaching when the captain requested me to defer it till the afternoon as he wished the passengers' luggage put below and the decks cleared. With this request we found it necessary to comply. But what annoyed us even more was the arrival of boats from the shore with persons who brought liquors on board that they might have a parting glass with their friends. The sailors were always sure to have their shares, so that some of them became quite intoxicated.

In the afternoon, the necessary arrangements being made, Mr. Taylor preached between decks. All the passengers and most of the sailors attended. Not an instance of levity was observed excepting in the conduct of the young gentlemen above alluded to. At six we met again for worship. The evening was delightful, and my feelings at the moment were such as I am not able to describe. The service in which we were engaged, the sight of our native shore, and the recollection that many prayers had that day been presented to God on our behalf produced emotions of an unusual nature.

At five next morning we weighed anchor and set sail with a fair wind. The morning was fine and the ebbing tide in a few hours carried us out of the river. During the day the wind, though light, continued favorable. Every heart was light and every face wore a smile. Some were reading books, and some conversing about their prospects or the friends they were leaving; between decks a party of young people were dancing. We scudded rapidly along the coast of Fife, and its numerous towns and well-cultivated fields were soon left far behind. About sunset we were opposite Stonehaven, and before midnight passed Aberdeen.

The following morning I was awakened early by the violent motion of the ship and an unusual bustle on deck. A gale blew from the northwest, the sea roared and foamed around us, the passengers became sick, and everything began to wear a discouraging aspect. As we entered the Moray Firth both wind and sea increased; two thirds of our people were sick and in a very uncomfortable condition. Consternation and alarm were soon visible in every countenance; children were crying and women wringing their hands and wishing they had remained at home. What a change a short time produces! Fiddling and dancing were never once proposed.

Our ship had little ballast and mounted on the waves like a feather. But sometimes a head sea broke over her with a shock that made everyone stagger, and swept the deck of everything movable. The gale continued all day, and about sunset began to blow more violently than before. The sea roared and ran tremendously high. The ship rolled so much that we were often dashed from one side of our beds to the other. She sometimes lay so long on one side that I feared she would never rise more. Those who had young children found it difficult to avoid crushing them in their beds. About midnight a woman lately married was taken with premature labor and added much to the horror of the scene by her dismal cries. The surgeon's situation during her labor was scarcely less embarrassing than her own; he was several times thrown down by the violent motion of the ship. At one time the berth in which the woman lay went to pieces with a crash which made some people think that the good *Rothiemurchus* herself had uttered her last groan. But before morning the woman was safely delivered of a male child, and in a few days was as well as before.

After a sleepless night in which we received many a bruise and uttered many a groan I was informed that a squall had carried away our main yard and damaged the rigging, and that we were on our way back to Leith to refit. The ship was going smoother, it is true, for she was going with the wind, but the gale was not in the least abated. What a sight was now presented between decks! Clothes and vessels of all descriptions; spoons, knives, broken bottles, basins and jugs, shoes and hats, with provisions of all sorts, were strewed over the decks or lying in heaps. At one time when the ship lay on her side several of the chests, though strongly lashed to the deck, had broken from their moorings and carried destruction to everything on which they fell. Now and then we were alarmed by a sea breaking over us and pouring down the hatches, which could not be entirely shut for fear of suffocating the people below.

At the mouth of the Dee, the river on which Aberdeen is situated, the captain went ashore to try to procure a main yard. The wind was northwest and the hills were covered with snow; we were continually assailed with showers of rain and sleet. We could not meet for worship, most being sick and no one able to stand on deck.

On the 10th the wind and weather became a little more moderate. About midday the captain returned with a main yard dragging behind the boat. As soon as it was taken on board we bent our course once more northward, but the wind being still against us we found it necessary to stand out to sea during the night.

On the morning of the 11th, finding that we were a great way to sea, we put about and stood for the shore. When we reached it we found that we had not advanced an inch to the north.

Next day the ship had a narrow escape from destruction by fire. A party of the passengers had supplied their own provisions. One of them was melting tallow in a pot when it caught fire and, the flame rising to a great height, the ship would have been in a blaze had not the captain heaved the pot, tallow and all, into the sea.

Although the next day was the Sabbath we had no sermon, the storm being so great that no person could keep his place without holding fast. For myself, I was very sick and compelled to keep to my bed the whole day. Some were now, however, getting clear of their sickness and able to move about. At sea it is easy to discover the natural disposition of your fellow travellers. They soon lay aside all reserve. Some conduct themselves as seriously and consistently as on the last Sabbath while others are more profligate and regardless.

The morning of the 14th was fine and I rose refreshed with a good sleep. The wind had fallen during the night, the sea was becoming calm, and all our passengers were well and hungry for their breakfast. This being dispatched, the captain gave orders to prepare and rig our new main yard, a work which had hitherto been prevented by the storm. In a few minutes as many carpenters, including passengers, as could get round it were at work. About two o'clock it was finished and in its place, and from that time till six in the evening we sailed with a fine favorable breeze. But when we entered the Moray Firth the wind veered to the northwest as before, and began to blow a gale, so that we were obliged to stand out to sea during the night, carrying very little sail.

After a rough and tempestuous night in which sleep was out of the question we tacked and made for the shore. On the appearance of land it was found that we had drifted southward and were still between Aberdeen and Peterhead. As the gale increased we carried but little sail and stood to the northeast during the whole day.

On the morning of the 16th we tacked and stood for the shore, or rather drove before the storm, for it had now become so violent that sailing was out of the question. Indeed not a sail was up except a staysail to steady the ship. One wave nearly carried a sailor overboard, and two or three of the passengers also had very narrow escapes. I could have enjoyed the sublime aspect which the sea at this time presented could I have obtained a firm station from which to view it, but the violent vibrations of the ship produced so much corporeal uneasiness that the mind could enjoy nothing. The waves, capped with foam, resembled hills covered with snow and separated by green valleys.

The storm continued all day, attended with hail and rain: the passengers spent their time below, some of them as quiet as possible and others either grumbling about the provisions or groaning under the influence of uneasy feelings.

The provisions, indeed, were none of the best, and produced much altercation. The captain himself admitted the bread was more than a year old and the beef much older; indeed I have never seen anything like the latter presented to human beings. The pork, however, was tolerable, and the oatmeal, of which there was a considerable quantity, proved excellent.

The first complaints about the beef were made to the cook, who was a cross, ill-natured old man and swore shockingly. He treated them in a very unceremonious way and it was painful to hear his language. For some time after this storm of human passions the old man would not allow female passengers to approach the fireplace to prepare food for their children, and he kicked some who dared to disobey.

On the morning of the 17th, our 12th day at sea, we found ourselves near a rugged, rocky shore a few miles south of Wick. The wind having moderated the evening before, we had not only got a sound sleep but advanced a good many miles during the night. Most of us were free from sickness, and joy was visible in every countenance at the happy change in our circumstances. I called the people together to worship, and we offered our grateful adorations to the Being who sets bounds to the raging of the sea and hushes the storm into a calm at his pleasure. I had been using every endeavor, from the first day I came on board, to get both the passengers and crew to leave off swearing. I reminded them now of the disagreeable and even dangerous circumstances in which we had been placed for eight days, and that something worse might await us if this vice should be still indulged. From this time forward none were heard to swear except for two or three of the sailors and as many of the passengers.

At sunset we arrived at John o' Groat's, the northeast point of the mainland of Scotland. The tide not being favorable we waited until three in the morning to enter the Pentland Firth. Here the tide runs with inconceivable fury, and having at this time to oppose the wind, the conflict was tremendous. We made many a tack and were sometimes within the ship's length of the rocks; the wind blew a strong breeze, the sea foamed and the rain fell in torrents; but both sailors and passengers exerted themselves so well that before noon they brought the ship to anchor in a spacious natural harbor in front of the town of Stromness in the Orkney Isles. Here we were resolved to remain until the wind shifted. Some ships had arrived before us and others came afterward, all more or less damaged by the late gales. We were quickly surrounded by islanders in boats eager to take the passengers on shore: being asked how much they charged, they replied sixpence each person; but a competition taking place, most got ashore for a penny.

Mr. Taylor and I went ashore and waited upon one of the ministers. He treated us with civility but appeared rather embarrassed and seemed pleased when we took our leave. We purchased a few articles of which we were in want and took a walk in the country. On our return we found that farmers had been to the ship with provisions. Fowls they sold at ninepence each, butter at ninepence a pound, and eggs at fivepence a dozen. They had also a small quantity of milk which they sold at threepence a quart, but no bread could be obtained.

On the morning of the 22nd we finally prepared for leaving Stromness. A shower in the morning, followed by a thick fog, hindered us from putting to sea till the afternoon. In the meantime we were employed warping out of the harbor, as the little wind we had blew directly in. Toward evening the fog cleared off and we proceeded to sea in company with 15 other vessels, most of them bound for America. After sunset the wind died away and left us rocking among the waves which still rolled in from the western ocean.

All night it continued calm but about midday on the 23rd a breeze sprang up. It was indeed in a wrong direction, but being now in the open sea and all alone we had room to tack. All day we stood to the north. As the breeze freshened and the motion of the ship increased, many became sick and despondency again took the place of cheerfulness. An inquiry was set on foot to ascertain why the wind was generally against us. Some imputed it to the stowaway who had forgotten to pay his debts, others to a party of smugglers on board who had escaped from the clutches of the excise, but the cook determined the question by affirming in the strongest manner that it was the unchristened newborn child that occasioned our detention. The man who owned the child, however, did not ask for baptism. He was one of the smuggling party, a desperate character, and it was discovered that he and the mother of the child were not married, although they had said they were. The wind becoming fair about sunset, we had a comfortable sleep and all night ran seven or eight miles an hour—a velocity which we seldom exceeded.

In the afternoon of the 24th there was much grumbling about the provisions. A new act had been passed a few weeks before we sailed, providing that a certain quantity of butter, flour and oatmeal should be allowed to each passenger. None of these articles had been served out and, the beef and biscuit being too long kept, dissatisfaction became quite general.

On the 25th a rebellion was like to have broken out, the captain persisting in his refusal to serve out butter, flour, &c. It was ascertained that he had been required to lay in these articles and that they had been taken on board. One of the passengers produced a printed copy of the act which he handed about. A meeting was held and a deputation was appointed to wait upon the captain and request that he grant the passengers the allowance due them. But he denied that any such provision had been made and threatened to make the passengers' situation much worse. They offered to show him the copy of the act but he refused to look at it and ordered them to leave the quarterdeck immediately. This produced a serious fermentation, and some few even proposed resorting to violent measures. These, however, were rendered unnecessary by our worthy commander's order to serve out *immediately* a week's provisions. This not only restored peace but gave general satisfaction, these articles being of good quality. At noon we were 225 miles west of Stromness. The weather was fine and the air mild.

A new difficulty arose on the 26th. The daily allowance of soup hitherto furnished was withheld from the passengers in consequence of their dispute with the captain. Some of them went to him to remonstrate, but he not being in a listening humor a serious altercation took place and much threatening and abuse followed. I had been sick and in bed for some time, but after inquiring what was the matter I went to the scene of action, and having learned the merits of the case, proposed an accommodation to which both parties agreed. The captain, however, appeared to be a good deal mortified; during the rest of the passage he was more harsh and unaccommodating than before and seldom attended our morning and evening worship. Some even said that he wished to throw obstacles in the way of others.

Be this as it may, on the morning of next day, which was the Sabbath, the captain ordered all the beds and bedding to be brought on deck and aired. As this was the first time such an order had been given it excited both surprise and indignation. The greater number of the passengers requested me to endeavor to persuade the captain to defer the work till another time, and to assure him that they would willingly attend to it on Monday or any other day except the Sabbath, which they wished to devote to religious purposes. I delivered their message but the captain, having taken at least his usual allowance of grog, was not in an accommodating humor. He told me he was determined to enforce the order, as an act of Parliament required the beds to be aired and it was usual to have it done on the Sabbath. I observed that, as another day would answer equally well, I thought it would be better to comply with the wishes of the passengers. They were at that moment met for our morning worship: it was my turn to officiate, and I proceeded to perform my duty.

Worship being over, the captain came forward and made a speech which was intended to remove our scruples. Among other things he said, "Although I am not so well up to religion as you (directing a look to Mr. Taylor and me) I know that airing the beds is a work of necessity and I declare to God there is no harm in it." He then walked off, repeating his order to turn out the beds and air them. A few complied immediately but the majority determined to wait till next day. About two hours after, the captain ordered all the passengers off the quarterdeck and onto the foredeck, swearing that as master of his ship he was determined to have some respect shown him. Those who had carried their bedding on deck lost part of their blankets soon after by a sudden gust of wind which carried them overboard. In the afternoon the sailors cleaned the decks and sprinkled them with vinegar. The cleaning of a ship is very necessary for the health of the passengers, but surely this work might be performed on any other day but the Sabbath.

The wind was fair on the 29th but light and unsteady. We went, however, six miles an hour all day. A large herd of porpoises passed us, tumbling along in a very odd manner. We saw, soon after, a few of the petrels called Mother Carey's chickens. They resembled swallows at a distance but were much larger. The day was fine and everyone cheerful and free from sickness.

May 2 and 3 were stormy but the Sabbath, May 4, was perhaps the most dismal day we had during the voyage. We had both snow and hail, and the storm was so great that we could neither sit nor stand; there was no alternative but to lie in bed. Even there no ease was to be obtained for we were knocked from one side to the other till our sides ached. No cooking could be accomplished and no provisions were served out except rotten Dutch cheese, as bitter as soot, and bread partly alive. Luckily we had brought some provisions along with us. About noon the gale began to abate although the swell did not. The aspect of the sea was grand to any who could contemplate it without terror. One moment we were placed upon an eminence from which we could see in all directions the waves curling their monstrous tops to the sky; the next we descended into a gulf which seemed opening its mouth to swallow us. At sunset the wind was become quite moderate but the swell was still prodigious. During worship I was thrown down by the rolling of the ship but not hurt.

On May 7, 15 days after we had left Stromness, I arose much refreshed after a good sleep. Health is sweet after sickness, and rest after toils. For some days I had not only been affected with seasickness but in other respects was very unwell. Whenever we had stormy weather or a head wind I was affected with a qualmish sickness, a headache and an aversion to food of every kind. The best remedy I found was a little vinegar and sugar.

About noon on May 8 we passed a quart bottle floating on the water. Perhaps it was the bearer of a letter, but we could not persuade the captain to lower the boat and take it up, though we passed very near it.

Our water for some time past had been very bad. When drawn out of the casks it was no clearer than that of a dirty street gutter after a heavy shower of rain, so that its appearance alone was sufficient to sicken one. But its dirty appearance was not its worst quality; it had a rancid stink that was enough to turn one's stomach. Judge then, what its taste must have been. I do not know what I would not have given at this time for a draught of good water. What we brought from Stromness was good to the last, but what came from Leith was now horrid. Some said that its being put in port wine casks was the reason it was so bad; others that Leith water is always bad after it has been some time at sea. But the ship's boy informed us that it had been in the casks near six months.

On May 9 many of our passengers were seized with dysentery in consequence of eating putrid beef. It had been fresh when we left Leith but they were not allowed to taste it till it was unfit for use. Three or four seemed almost in a dying condition and were placed under the doctor's care.

What took place on the 10th I cannot inform you as I was too sick to get out of bed. It was a favorable circumstance, however, that Mrs. Bell was a little better so that she could take care of the children.

I would not be a sailor for the world. The 11th was fine but I did not enjoy it, still not being able to quit my bed. As I grew worse and worse, the doctor attended and gave me some medicine in the evening. Of the captain I saw nothing, but Mr. Richmond, the first mate, paid me every attention in his power, as indeed he had done to all the family during their protracted illness. I was told that two sharks were seen near the ship, and at some distance a whale was observed.

During the 12th the wind was fair although light, and we sailed four miles an hour. Being somewhat better I sat up about an hour on deck. We passed a Danish ship coming from St. Thomas in the West Indies, the first we had seen since we entered the ocean.

On the 15th we were surrounded with fog, which indicated we were near the banks of Newfoundland. We sounded but found no bottom with a line of 120 fathoms. The fog made the weather cold and uncomfortable.

At sunrise on the 16th we sounded and found the bottom with a line of 70 fathoms. Two hours later we sounded again and found the bottom, a coarse gravel, at 43 fathoms. We tried to fish but took nothing. At nine o'clock a mass of ice appeared about 200 yards ahead. We instantly altered course a little. The novelty of the ice's appearance brought on deck every person who was able to get out of bed. The ice was oval in shape and appeared to be half a mile in length. We had scarce time to look at it when another, larger mass was announced. It was as high as our topmast and probably reached near the bottom of the sea. In the course of the day we passed about 30 other masses, none of them large excepting four. They were all moving to the southeast with a velocity which showed that the current in this place is very considerable. About noon we shortened sail and again tried fishing but were not very successful. After three hours with five lines we had taken only 22 cod. These, however, filled a barrel and afforded a very seasonable refreshment.

The wind was fair on the 18th but so light that we advanced only about four miles an hour. The ship went so smoothly that we could scarcely perceive her moving. Six vessels were in sight and still more as we approached the entrance of the Gulf of St. Lawrence.

On the 21st, the 46th day of our voyage, the coast of Newfoundland was discovered and we had it some hours in view. Being entirely covered with snow it had a very uninviting appearance; a dreary waste extended as far as the eye could reach. The cold was so intense that one could seldom remain more than a few minutes on deck.

At daybreak on the 22nd we discovered the island of Cape Breton distant only five or six miles. The coast, for several miles from the shore, was lined with pack ice. The wind being northerly, it was very cold and we made but little progress. Some of the passengers being still dissatisfied about the provisions, one of them filled a bottle with soup which he said he would carry to Quebec where he intended to make a complaint against the captain for the manner in which he had treated us. He said the soup was merely stinking water in which stinking beef had been boiled, which no dog would taste unless he was starving. In the evening the air became mild and pleasant and we were becalmed on a sea as smooth as glass. Twenty-seven vessels were in sight.

On the morning of the 23rd we prepared to enter the Gulf of St. Lawrence by a strait between Cape North and St. Paul's Island. Our course appeared to be blocked with ice, several masses of which were covered with sea birds; seals lay on others like so many shipwrecked mariners. Two men were stationed at the helm, eight at the bow with cushioning devices, and the first mate at the masthead to look for openings in the ice and give directions. We soon discovered that the ice was merely an immense assemblage of loose masses. By dexterous steering and the calmness of the sea we got through in safety, striking only one large piece, although this knocked some splinters off the bow and nearly threw us down with the shock.

After about two hours we reached open sea. The breeze increasing, we ran before it with every sail set and the sea running high although the fog soon grew so thick we could not see the ship's length before us. We had sailed two hours without seeing any ice and were beginning to congratulate ourselves that we were out of danger when the man stationed at the bow vociferated, "There is ice ahead!" We were within a few yards of a group of enormous masses like ragged rocks which would probably have stove in the side of the ship if we had been dashed upon them. Everything was let go and the ship was brought about with the utmost dispatch; a few moments of awful suspense necessarily elapsed but Providence mercifully preserved us and we got around in safety.

The evening of the 25th being fine, several whales were seen spouting near us. They are very numerous in the Gulf. They, and I suppose all we saw on the passage, were fin whales, called finners by the sailors.

At four on the morning of the 26th we passed Cap-des-Rosiers and approached the continent of America. About noon the wind became squally and shifted to the west. This soon brought sickness and a violent headache to many of us, for the ship was rather tumbling among the waves than sailing. In the ocean we had seen much larger waves but never a more stormy and boisterous sea. One squall carried away the maintopmast of a brig near us before her sails could be lowered. The situation of my family at this time gave me no little uneasiness, most of them

Like shipwrecked mariners, seals on the Gulf ice.

being so reduced by protracted sickness as to be unable to come out of bed even in fine weather. One of the boys was nearly blind and we were much alarmed lest he should become entirely so.

Just after noon on the 29th we took on a pilot who had a cask in his boat from which we tasted the first American water; I can state that wine would not have afforded me half the pleasure. The pilot also gave me a little maple sugar. In color it was something like bees' wax and in taste it resembled honey.

At daybreak on the 31st we passed Ile du Bic. As we approached the south bank of the St. Lawrence we observed that the land was cleared and inhabited. The neatness of the farmhouses and the aspect of the fields, which were assuming a verdant hue, revived our spirits and afforded sensations no less new than agreeable. Being favored by both wind and tide we glided along with great rapidity. At dusk we dropped anchor

30 miles below Quebec. All were in high spirits, encouraged by the hope of soon getting ashore.

On the morning of June 1 we weighed anchor at three o'clock and proceeded with the tide. It being the Sabbath we had a sermon as usual, but the fine day and the novelty of the scene around us induced a few of the more irreligious part to absent themselves. At a bend of the river a short distance below Quebec, that city gradually presented itself to our view. The spires of the churches and many roofs of the houses are covered with tin, which causes them, when the sun shines, to glitter like silver. Just as the evening gun was fired at the fort we dropped anchor before the town.

At eight o'clock on the 2nd we got ashore at Quebec, the first time we had been on land for six weeks. Perhaps prisoners liberated from a dungeon never felt more joy on the event.

Ensign Prenties' Dispatches

*The American Revolutionary War was
nearing its climax when Walter Prenties
of the 84th Regiment of Foot sailed
from the bastion of Quebec on Nov. 17, 1780,
with dispatches from Gen. Frederick
Haldimand for the British commander in
New York. Prenties, in his twenties, was
one of six passengers on the leaky brigantine*
ST. LAWRENCE, *which was manned by a
drunken captain and 12 inept seamen. This
is Ensign Prenties' account of his shipwreck on
Cape Breton Island and his amazing efforts to
reach help and deliver the dispatches. It begins
as the* ST. LAWRENCE *is battered by storms
off Anticosti Island.*

By WALTER PRENTIES
Edited by G.G. CAMPBELL

O N NOV. 29 THE WIND CAME ROUND to the northwest and we proceeded down the Gulf of St. Lawrence, with two feet of water in
the ship's hold, in company with a schooner carrying duplicates
of General Haldimand's dispatches. The wind kept gradually increasing
till Dec. 1 when it blew a perfect gale from the northwest. The ship's
crew being almost overcome with cold and fatigue, and the water having
increased to four feet in the hold, they left off working the pumps and
declared themselves quite indifferent about their fate. By the force of
persuasion and promises, together with the timely distribution of a pint
of wine per man, which I had fortunately brought on board, they were
diverted from this desperate resolution. The delay, though not exceeding

a quarter of an hour, had increased the depth of water another foot; but the men added to their exertions, being encouraged by the wine which was issued to them every half hour, and reduced the water in two hours to less than three feet. The captain remained in his cabin.

During Dec. 2 and 3 the gale seemed to increase rather than diminish. The ice formed so thick on the ship's sides as to impede her way very much, which furnished us with a new labor, that of cutting it off as fast as it formed, with saws and axes. The leaks continued to gain ground. The schooner that was in company, far from being able to afford us any assistance, was in as leaky a condition as our own vessel, having struck some rocks at Ile aux Coudres. A heavy snow beginning to fall, it was with the utmost difficulty we could get sight of each other, though at no great distance, and in order not to part company we fired a gun every half hour. The schooner at length made no answer, whence we concluded she had foundered; nor were we wrong in our supposition, I learned later. There were 16 persons on board, every one of whom perished.

On the following day the gale increased prodigiously and the sea began to run high, with a heavy fall of snow so as to prevent our seeing 20 yards ahead of the vessel. The men being excessively fatigued, the water had risen to between four and five feet. The mate, an intelligent young man and well acquainted with his profession, judged that we could not now be far from the Magdalen Islands, which have been fatal to many vessels. In less than two hours we heard the sea breaking upon the rocks and soon after discovered one of the islands, called the Deadman, close under our lee. We weathered the point with the greatest difficulty, and being unable to see many yards ahead we were obliged to leave the vessel to the direction of Providence through the rest of the islands. Fortunately, I might say almost miraculously, we ran through them without damage. The sailors had nearly determined a second time to quit the pumps when, acquiring fresh spirits from the danger we had escaped, they agreed to continue their efforts a little longer, toward which they were not a little encouraged by the wine which I distributed to them occasionally.

About five on the morning of Dec. 5 a large wave broke on the ship's quarter, which stove in our deadlights [windows], filled the cabin and washed the master out of his bed, where he had remained ever since the commencement of the gale.

We soon discovered from the increase of the leaks that the sternpost had been parted by the impulse of the sea. No resource was left but that of attempting to stop the leaks with beef, which we cut into small pieces for that purpose; but this expedient we soon found ineffectual, and the water continued to gain on us faster than ever. The sailors, finding all their labors fruitless and the leaks irreparable, abandoned themselves to despair and again refused to work at the pumps. They were soon persuaded to make another effort, when, to our great surprise and consternation, we found the pumps so hard frozen that it was impossible to move them.

In a very short time the ship filled to the water's edge, and we resigned ourselves to our fate. Notwithstanding, when the vessel was quite full, we observed she was very little deeper in the water than before.

Recollecting that we had a quantity of lumber on board, we immediately accounted for the phenomenon of her not sinking beyond a certain depth, and began to recall hopes of saving our lives if we could make the Island of St. John's [now Prince Edward Island] or some other island in the Gulf.

We contrived to prevent the ship from oversetting by steering directly before the wind, although not without some difficulty as the waves frequently washed clear over the decks. We used every precaution to secure the ship's small boat from being washed overboard, the loss of which would have been a dreadful misfortune. The cabin, being above the level of the main deck, was tolerably clear of water and afforded us some little shelter. Thither we retired, leaving only one man upon deck to govern the helm, who was fastened by a rope to prevent his being carried away by the waves.

In a few hours we observed the waves grow shorter and break higher, which is always the case on approaching the shore. I thought it incumbent on me to take every precaution to save the dispatches I was charged with, and therefore ordered my servant to open my trunks and collect all the letters they contained, which I put into a handkerchief and fastened about my waist. He, at the same time, offered me the money he found in the trunks, to the amount of 180 guineas, which I desired him to dispose of as he thought proper, thinking it in the present emergency rather an encumbrance. My servant, however, thought otherwise and took care to secure the cash, which was afterward of more service to us than I could possibly have imagined.

The weather continued thick till about one in the afternoon when it suddenly cleared and we discovered land at about 10 miles' distance. Taking it at first to be the Island of St. John's, inhabited by several French and English families from whom we might have expected some assistance, we found from a nearer view that it had not the least appearance of that island. We observed the sea break high and have a very dismal appearance about three miles from the land. It was necessary for us to pass through those breakers ere we could gain the shore, but contrary to our expectations there was a considerable depth of water, so that we went over the reef without touching.

The land now began to have a dreadful appearance, seeming to be high and rocky, but on approaching within a mile of it we had the pleasure of decrying a fine sandy beach and a clear shore [at the mouth of the Margaree River]. The sea ran high, but not to such a degree as on the reef we had passed. We advanced to within 50 or 60 yards of the beach before we struck: the mainmast went out of the step, and then the foremast, but neither of them fell, the boards in the hold being stowed so close together; at the same time the rudder was unshipped with such violence as to be near killing one of the sailors. Each wave lifted the ship four or five feet nearer the shore. The stern was beat in by the sea, and then, having no shelter in the cabin, we were obliged to go upon deck and hang by the shrouds lest we should be washed overboard. In this uncomfortable situation we remained till the vessel was beat so high by the waves that we could venture to walk upon deck. We now perceived that the ship's keel was broken, which we imagined would occasion her to go to pieces: this however did not happen, which I can only attribute to the boards in the hold being so interwoven and frozen together as to provide a degree of solidity.

Our first care now was to launch the ship's small boat. Our vessel was broadside to the wind so that she afforded some shelter for the boat to the lee. Having, with much labor, cleared the boat of ice and prepared her for launching, I ordered some liquor to be distributed to those who were yet sober, and asked if any were willing to embark with me in the attempt to gain the shore. All who offered themselves were the mate and two sailors, together with my servant and a boy who was a passenger.

At length we got the boat into the water, and having thrown into it an axe and a saw, I leaped in followed by my servant and the mate. The boy followed but, not springing far enough, fell into the water; we contrived to drag him into the boat, but not without difficulty, our fingers being so benumbed that we had scarcely the power of using them; and this accident was later of fatal consequence to the unfortunate youth. The two sailors who had agreed to go with us next leaped into the boat, and all the rest seemed ready, notwithstanding their former hesitation, to follow. I found it necessary to shove off from the ship's side, for the boat certainly would have sunk had so many persons crowded in together. The surf broke over us every moment, and the intense cold froze every drop of water immediately so as to cover our clothes with ice. The ship was about 40 yards from the shore, but before we got halfway to it we were overtaken by a wave that almost filled the boat, and the next drove us on the dry sand.

To find ourselves once more safe upon the land gave us no small satisfaction; the joy made us for a few moments forget that we had escaped one species of death, probably to undergo another more lingering and painful. What most affected us was the distress of our companions whom we had left on board: their lamentations and cries for help we could hear distinctly but it was not in the power of a human being to relieve them.

The night was now approaching and we found ourselves getting stiff with cold; the gale continuing as severe as ever, we were obliged to wade up to our waists in snow to the shelter of a thick wood about 250 yards from the beach. This afforded some relief from the piercing northwest wind, yet a fire was still wanting to warm our frozen limbs.

We had put a tinderbox in the boat but the water had rendered it useless. I recommended it to the men to move about, being better acquainted with the nature of cold climates than any of my companions. My advice was strictly adhered to for about half an hour, when the young passenger, being overcome with the severity of the weather, threw himself down in order to sleep. I used my utmost endeavors both by persuasion and force to rouse him, but all to no purpose.

After walking about for half an hour longer I went to where the boy lay, and putting my hand on his face and finding it quite cold, I observed to the mate that I believed he was dead. The youth answered immediately that he was not yet dead but would be so very shortly; he requested I would write, if I survived, to his father at New York, and inform him of his son's misfortune. In about 10 minutes he had expired.

The death of the boy could not deter three of my fellow sufferers from giving way to this drowsy sensation. Finding it impossible to keep them on their legs, I broke a branch and, desiring the mate to do the same, our employment during the remainder of the night was to prevent them from sleeping by beating them continually with the branches. At daylight I desired the men to let me examine their legs, as they had no feeling in them: I perceived that they were frozen at least halfway up.

I then went with the mate to see if we could discover any traces of the ship, and to our great surprise and satisfaction found she had not yet gone to pieces although the wind continued with unabated severity. The vessel had by this time beat much closer to the shore, so that the distance was but very small at low water.

When the tide was out we advised the persons on board to fasten a rope to the jib boom, by which they might swing themselves one by one toward the shore. By watching the motion of the sea they all got safe on the land except a carpenter who was a passenger in the vessel.

He did not think proper to venture in this manner, or was unable, having the night before made rather too free with the bottle. I was informed that a Captain Green, a passenger, had fallen asleep on board and been frozen to death.

The ship's captain had put some materials for striking a light in his pocket. We therefore made a fire with all possible expedition, and were happy for some time in hovering about it and warming our benumbed limbs. But this gratification was, to several of my companions, followed by the most excruciating pain as their frozen parts began to thaw.

This night we passed a little better than the last, yet we found extreme inconveniency from the total want of covering, as well as from hunger, a new misery that we had hitherto been unacquainted with.

The next morning we persuaded the carpenter to come on shore in the same manner as the others had done; but this he accomplished with much difficulty, being very weak, and frozen in different parts of his limbs. We began to be reduced in strength for want of nourishment.

The gale continued as boisterous as ever, and in the night between Dec. 8 and 9 the ship went to pieces from the stern to the mainmast. We obtained some provisions which washed on shore, viz. some pieces of salt beef, some fresh meat that hung over the stern, and a quantity of onions that the captain had on board for sale. This relief was very seasonable, it being now the fourth day since we had eaten. Having no utensils, we dressed our meat in the best manner we could and made what we thought a most delicious repast.

The sense of hunger being assuaged, we collected all the provision we could find scattered upon the beach, which amounted to between 200 and 300 pounds of salt beef and a considerable stock of onions. Our next care was to get ourselves under cover; this task was not an easy one, so many of our company being unable to move, and of the remainder none but the mate and myself capable of any active exertion. A quantity of boards had floated on shore from the wreck: of these we carried about 250 into the wood, and by 10 at night completed a kind of house about 20 feet long and 10 wide. It was constructed in the following manner: we cut two poles of the above-mentioned length and, having no nails, tied them at a proper height on the outside of two trees 20 feet from each other: against these cross poles we placed boards with a slope of about 60 degrees, which constituted the sides. The interval between the poles, which was equal to the breadth of the trees, served for the smoke of our fire to go through, the fire being laid in an oblong position nearly the whole length of the house. The ends were composed of boards placed perpendicular, the trunks of the trees being taken in and forming part of each end: on the end that looked toward the southeast we left a vacancy for the entrance.

On the sixth day after we landed the gale abated and gave us an opportunity to get on board what remained of the vessel. Three of us went to work at opening the hatches, and having but one axe, and the cables being frozen over them in a solid lump of ice, it took the whole day to accomplish it. The next day we got out two casks of onions, a small barrel of beef containing about 120 pounds, and what we believed to be three barrels of apples shipped by a merchant of Quebec. We likewise found a quarter cask of potatoes, a bottle of oil which proved very serviceable to the men's sores, another axe, a large iron pot, two camp kettles and about 12 pounds of tallow candles. On opening the apple casks we found, to our great surprise, that they contained bottles of Canadian balsam salve, a more valuable commodity to be sure than apples, but one we would gladly have exchanged for something more friendly to the stomach. This disappointment extorted a few hearty good wishes toward the merchant, yet we found afterward some use for his Canadian balsam, although different from what he intended.

We went on board once more on the 14th and cut as much of the sails as possible from the bowsprit, with part of which we covered our hut and made it tolerably warm and comfortable notwithstanding the severity of the weather.

By this time the sores of the men who had been frostbitten began to mortify, and caused their toes, fingers and other parts of the limbs affected to rot off, the anguish being almost intolerable. The carpenter, who came on shore after the others, had lost the greatest part of his feet, and at night became delirious, in which unhappy state he continued till death released him the following day. We covered him with snow and branches, having neither spade nor pickaxe to dig a grave for him; nor would it have been possible if we had been provided with them, the ground being so hard frozen. Three days after, our second mate died in the same manner.

We felt but very little concern at the death of our companions; we considered it rather a happiness than a misfortune to be deprived of life in our present wretched situation, and there became the fewer mouths to consume our little stock of provisions. But what affected me

243

more than all our other miseries was the quantity of vermin proceeding from the men's sores, and continually increasing, which infested us in every part and rendered us disgusting even to ourselves. Several, however, who had been but slightly frozen, recovered in a short time with the loss of a few toes and fingers; no one having entirely escaped the frost but myself. On the 20th another sailor died, having been some time in a delirium.

About a fortnight after we had fixed ourselves in the hut, the mate and I, on one of our frequent trips to search for any traces of inhabitants, discovered a wigwam where Indians had recently left the skin of a moose. This we took away after erecting a sign pointing toward our hut.

Twenty days after the shipwreck, our provisions being very much reduced, I began to entertain a suspicion that there was some foul play during our absences in search of inhabitants. By keeping a constant watch at night I at length discovered that the depredators were no other than the captain and two sailors, who had consumed no less than 70 pounds, besides a quantity of onions, in so short a space of time. To prevent such unfair practices for the future, the mate and I never went out together.

Giving up at length all hopes of seeing any inhabitants, having provisions only for six weeks longer, and a few of our men together with the captain being recovered, I proposed leaving with as many as could work in the ship's small boat, in search of inhabitants. This proposal was unanimously assented to, although we discovered that the boat had been beat in such a manner by the sea that every seam was open.

We attempted to stop them with dry oakum but it would not answer the intended purpose, and having saved no pitch from the wreck we began to despair. I at length thought of the Canadian balsam which had been shipped for apples. We accordingly boiled a quantity of the balsam in the iron kettle and soon brought it to a proper consistence. We turned up the boat and gave her a coat of the balsam, which effectually stopped up all crevices for the present.

By Jan. 1 we got our boat in tolerable condition, likewise our mast and sail rigged, although we could not often expect a fair wind on this coast at the present season of the year. We had agreed to take six in the boat, viz. the captain and mate, two sailors, myself and my servant; of the others none were equal to the fatigues we might expect.

Our shoes being all nearly worn out, my employment during the whole of the next day was to make moccasins of canvas. My needle was the handle of a pewter spoon which I had fashioned for the purpose, and the canvas also supplied me with thread. As soon as I had made two pairs for each man in our party, we divided the provisions that remained into 14 equal parts, which amounted to a quarter of a pound of beef per day for six weeks; those who were to stay behind sharing equally.

The wind blowing fresh from the northwest, we were obliged to remain where we were till Jan. 4, by which time the ice, floating in prodigious quantities on the coast, rendered our undertaking extremely hazardous. On the afternoon of the 4th, the wind moderating, we set off. Eight miles from the place of our shipwreck the wind began to increase and blow very hard from the southeast, which was immediately off the shore. We were on the point of being blown out to sea, but by the dint of rowing made shift to get into a deep bay about a mile ahead where we thought we might pass the night with safety. We hauled our boat up as high as our strength would permit and set to work in lighting our fires and cutting our wood. We cut some pine branches, the smaller of which served to lie on, and the larger, in the form of a wigwam, to shelter us.

The place we had landed on was a fine sandy beach [joining Chéticamp Island with the mainland] with little or no snow. Having observed some pieces of wood that had been cut with an axe, I thought there might be some inhabitants near at hand. As soon as we had taken a little refreshment I set out with two of the men to a point of land, at about two miles' distance, which was clear of wood and appeared to be cultivated. Having gained the top of it we descried to our inexpressible joy a few houses about half a mile distant, but on coming up to them found they were only the remains of some old storehouses built for the curing of cod. As we walked along the point we gathered about a quart of cranberries, some of which we ate, preserving the remainder for our companions.

By the next day the wind had come round to the northwest, and blew with such violence as to prevent us from proceeding on our voyage. It continued so for two days when, happening to get up in the middle of the night, I was astonished on observing that while the wind continued blowing, the sea was entirely without agitation. I awoke the mate, and, going down to the beach, we found the sea covered with ice for leagues around. This alarming circumstance seemed to preclude all possibility of proceeding farther, and might give us cause even to regret having left our habitation.

At length, on Jan. 9, it became perfectly calm. Next morning the wind came round to the southeast and in a short time blew extremely hard, so that by four in the afternoon there was not a piece of ice to be seen, the whole of it being blown out to sea. However, the violence of the wind prevented us from moving till Jan. 11 when, the weather being moderate and a fine light breeze blowing along the coast, we launched our boat. Having got round the point of the land, we hoisted our sail and put before the wind.

We had not proceeded far before we descried an extremely high point [Cap Rouge] about 20 miles ahead, with a continued precipice along the coast so that it was impossible to land before we came to that headland. This made it very dangerous to attempt the passage, for if the wind should come round to the northwest we must infallibly perish among the rocks. But danger was no longer considered by us; so we got out two oars, not being able to use any more as two men were constantly employed in keeping the boat clear of water, and with the assistance of a fair wind made the point at about 11 o'clock at night. Finding no place that we could possibly land on, we were obliged to keep along the coast till two in the morning when, the wind increasing and a stony beach appearing on which we should not have thought it expedient to land had the wind been moderate, we put ashore. The sea had beat the gravel up into a kind of bank which rendered it impossible for us to haul our boat up: we were obliged to leave her to the mercy of the sea.

The place where we landed [Pigeon Cove] was a beach of about 400 yards in length, bounded at the distance of about 50 yards from the water's edge by an insurmountable precipice of at least 100 feet.

On Jan. 13 the wind came round to the northwest, and the sea beat with such violence against the shore as to drive our boat 20 yards higher than she was. Surrounded by precipices which prevented us from sheltering ourselves, and having no firing but some pieces of timber which floated accidentally upon the shore, we could but just keep ourselves from freezing. The same weather continued for eight days with a prodigious fall of snow.

On the ninth day we contrived to turn our boat over in order to examine the damage she had received. We found the coat of balsam entirely rubbed off, and several holes in her bottom. We had no pitch or balsam left, and but little dry oakum, which was of no service without the former. I at length thought of throwing water over the oakum and letting it freeze into a cake of ice. The men in general made light of my undertaking and assisted with much reluctance; however I soon convinced them, for by four in the afternoon we froze up every seam and hole in such a manner that not a drop of water could enter as long as the weather continued freezing.

On Jan. 27, the weather being moderate and a light breeze directly off the shore, we got our boat very carefully launched and set off early in the morning from this ill-omened bay. We had the pleasure to observe that the boat made little or no water, so that we were enabled to keep our four oars continually at work.

A shower of rain the next day melted all the ice off our boat: we were therefore prevented from going any farther till a return of the frost, and had the mortification to lose the benefit of a fine day in the course of which we might have proceeded a good distance more on our journey. Our provisions were now reduced to two pounds and a half of beef for each man.

On the morning of Jan. 29 the mate, having wandered a little distance from our fire, returned in haste to inform me that he had discovered a partridge on the bough of a tree. I immediately went to the place and observed that the bird was very tame and not above 14 feet from the ground. I cut a long pole, and taking part of the rope yarn that fastened my canvas shoes, made a running loop of it and fixed it to the end of the pole. Walking softly under the tree and lifting the pole gently up, I fixed the loop about the partridge's neck; giving it a sudden jerk, I closed the loop and secured the bird. The mate, as well as myself, laughed very heartily for the first time since our shipwreck. Having boiled the bird in some melted snow with a little salt water, we divided it into six equal parts and all sat down to what we found a delicious meal; the only one, excepting the quart of cranberries, for which we were indebted to chance or Providence since we had been cast upon the island.

On Feb. 3 we discovered an exceeding high land [Cape North], appearing to be about 20 miles distant, with several other mountains and large bays between. It being yet early in the day, with a fine wind and no great sea, we were in hopes if the wind should not increase too much we should be able to reach it before night. But the prodigious height of the land led us into an erroneous computation of its distance, and it was almost dark by the time we reached it. Finding no place to land, we were obliged to double the cape and continue our journey. Our course now lay in a very different direction, so that we were obliged to strike our sail and take to the oars. The wind blew so hard off the high land that had we not been assisted by a heavy swell from the northeast we must certainly have been blown out to sea.

We continued rowing as close as we could to the rocks till about five in the morning when, hearing the sea run on the shore very long and heavy, we rowed toward the land. At the distance of 50 yards, for it was yet dark, we discerned a beach at least four miles in length.

Having landed [in Aspy Bay, one month after leaving the scene of the shipwreck], our first care was to haul up the boat that she might meet with no further damage from the sea. We then got into the woods, which lay close to the shore, and contrived to kindle a fire. It was with the greatest difficulty we kept ourselves awake before the fire, so that we were under the necessity of watching in turn lest, all being asleep together, the fire should go out and we should be frozen to death.

Our provisions were now entirely consumed, and having not the most distant prospect of getting any more, we were ready to abandon ourselves to despair. I was of the opinion, as was the mate, that it would be most advisable to sacrifice one for the preservation of the rest; and that the most proper method would be by casting lots to decide which should be the unfortunate victim. But this shocking, though prudent, resolution we agreed to put off to the last extremity.

We contrived at length to gather about two quarts of hips, or wild rose pods, from under the snow. Having with this sorry food allayed in some degree the keen sense of hunger, and the wind having become somewhat more moderate, we got into our boat and pushed off, the day already drawing toward a conclusion. Our progress was soon impeded by ice which obliged us to put ashore on another part of the same beach. In landing I had the misfortune to let the tinderbox fall from my bosom into the water, by which means we were unable to kindle a fire. We therefore thought it best to get into our boat again as fast as possible and return to the spot from whence we came, in hopes of finding some fire still remaining.

It was with the greatest difficulty we got back, being the whole way under the necessity of breaking through the ice, which had by this time formed almost into a solid sheet. We had the satisfaction to find that the fire was not extinguished, otherwise we must have perished in the course of the night.

In landing on Feb. 8 we had the misfortune to lose two of our oars, which were washed overboard by the surf.

On Feb. 13 about a dozen tallow candles remained of those which we had hitherto employed in stopping the leaks of our boat. We divided a small part among us, which gave us some relief for the present from our hunger. We began now to be fully sensible of our desperate situation, and to expect that our fate would be that of perishing with hunger, yet what gave me the most uneasiness was that my friends would probably forever remain uninformed of our wretched catastrophe. I took every occasion of cutting my name on the bark of the largest trees. The fatigue of cutting, as well as the preservation of my knife, which was the only one among us, would not allow me to be more particular. But on the walls of the storehouses which we had discovered in the beginning of our progress, I wrote a short account of our disasters in English and French and requested, if any persons should fall in with it, that they would transmit it to my father at Quebec.

On Feb. 17 we made another division of a part of the tallow candles that yet remained, and on the following day, the wind being favorable, we proceeded about five miles. Finding a fine, flat country [St. Ann's Bay] and a sandy beach that extended for a considerable way, we put on shore with a resolution to perish on this place unless some unforeseen accident should bring us relief. To attempt drawing up our boat would, in our present weak condition, be a vain undertaking, so all that we could preserve was our axe, a saw and the sail of the boat, which we generally made use of as a covering.

We cleared away the snow from a spot in the entrance of the wood and, having cut some small branches of pine to lie upon, together with some larger for shelter, which we stuck into the bank of snow that surrounded us, we made our fire. We had the good fortune to find about a pint of hips which, boiled up with a couple of tallow candles, afforded us a tolerable meal.

The next day we passed without any kind of provision, and being apprehensive that our little remaining strength would soon desert us, we employed ourselves in cutting and piling as much wood as we were able, to supply the fire. Meanwhile the waves had beat our boat so high upon the beach as to deprive us of the power of putting to sea again had we been disposed to do it, for our strength was by no means equal to the task of moving her a single foot.

We found ourselves so much weakened the following day that we could make no further use of our axe, and were under the necessity of creeping about to gather rotten branches for our fire. As we had not a proper quantity of fuel, the fire that we kept up was but just sufficient to preserve us from freezing.

Having now no more than two tallow candles remaining, and being too weak even to search for hips, we thought we might derive some nourishment from the kelp lying upon the shore. We accordingly collected a little of it and boiled it for a few hours in a kettle, but found it very little tenderer than at first. We then melted one of our tallow candles in the liquor, and having supped it up and eat a quantity of the weed, our appetite became somewhat satiated; but in about two hours we were all affected with a very uneasy sensation and were soon after seized with a fit of vomiting without being able to bring the offending matter entirely off the stomach. This vomiting having continued for about four hours, we found ourselves tolerably easy but exceedingly exhausted.

On Feb. 22 we made use of some more kelp and our last tallow candle. It operated in the same manner, but not to so violent a degree as before.

We were now under the necessity of boiling the kelp without the mixture of tallow; however nauseous at any other time, it afforded us not only nourishment but an exquisite relish.

Having for three days tasted of no other food but the kelp, we began to swell to an alarming degree. Notwithstanding the little flesh we had upon our bones, we could sink our fingers two inches deep on the skin and the impression remained visible for above an hour. Hunger still obliged us to make use of the kelp. [The kelp acted to retain an abnormal amount of water in the starving men's bodies.] After a few days more we were so much swollen as to be almost deprived of our sight, and so reduced in strength that it was with the utmost difficulty we could keep our fire in.

The time was now arrived when I thought it highly expedient to put the plan before mentioned into execution; I found that although my companions objected to the proposal of casting lots which should be the victim, yet all concurred in the necessity of someone being sacrificed. By a kind of reasoning more agreeable to the dictates of self-love than of justice, it was agreed that as the captain was so reduced as to be the first who would sink under our present misery; as he had been the person to whom we considered ourselves in some measure indebted for all our misfortunes; and as he had been the most remiss in his exertions toward the general good, he was undoubtedly the person who should be first sacrificed.

I must confess that I was not a little shocked at the captain's intended fate, although I had more reason than anyone else to be incensed against him, and not only on account of his neglect of duty and his purloining our provisions at the hut. After our shipwreck I had discovered by some papers washed on shore that although the captain's pretended destination was New York, his real one was the West Indies if he could possibly effect it. Thus would he have baffled General Haldimand's intentions in sending me with dispatches that might be of the first consequence, and also have defrauded me of the money which I paid him for my passage.

The determination now made was kept secret from the captain, and it would have been impossible for us to live many days longer without putting it into execution had we not happily met with relief from a quarter whence we little expected it. On Feb. 28, as we were lying about our fire, we thought we heard human voices in the woods, and soon after descried two Indians with guns in their hands. This sight gave us fresh strength and so, getting up, we advanced toward them with the greatest eagerness imaginable.

As soon as we were perceived by the Indians they started back and seemed fixed with surprise and horror. This indeed is not to be wondered at, our appearance being enough to alarm the most intrepid. Our clothes were almost entirely burnt off, our limbs swollen to a prodigious bulk, our eyes from the same cause almost invisible, and our hair in a confused and dishevelled state. Some of us wept while others laughed.

Being a little recovered from their surprise, the Indians did not show much inclination to accost us till I got up to one of them and took him by the hand; he shook it for some time very heartily, the usual mode of salutation among Indians. They then walked with us to our fire and, sitting down, one of them who could speak a little broken French desired we would inform him whence we came and the particulars of the accident that brought us there. I gave him as concise an account as possible, during the relation of which he seemed very much affected at our sufferings.

Having finished my narration I asked the Indian if he could furnish us with any provisions, to which he answered in the affirmative. Observing that we had very little fire he suddenly started up and took our axe in his hand; when looking at it and laughing heartily, I suppose at the badness of it, he threw it down again, and taking his tomahawk from his side he went and in a short time cut a quantity of wood which he threw upon our fire. This done he took up his gun and, without saying a word, went off with his companion.

251

This would have been very alarming to persons ignorant of Indian manners, but I doubted not but they were gone for some provisions. I must confess that I felt but little inclination to eat; the fire which the Indian had made was the greatest refreshment to us as we had been for many days without a good one.

After about three hours we perceived them coming round a point in a bark canoe. Being arrived, they took out some smoked venison and a bladder of seal oil. They put some of the meat into our kettle and boiled it, then gave each of us a very small quantity together with some oil. I knew very well their reason for being so sparing of their meat: eating a quantity of gross food in our present state might be attended with fatal consequences. It gave me no small pleasure to find that the Indians were so careful of us.

This light repast being ended, the Indians desired three of us to embark in their canoe, that being all she could carry at a time, and proceed to their hut which lay five miles farther by water and about a mile from the shore in the middle of the woods. We were received at the seaside by three other Indians and about 12 or 14 women and children. We were conducted by these last to their habitation, which consisted of three wigwams, there being that number of families among them. We were treated with the greatest humanity by these people; they gave us broth to sup but would not suffer us to eat meat or any kind of substantial food whatever. Meanwhile the same Indians as had brought us went back in their canoe for the remaining men of our party.

Having provided for our own immediate wants, our thoughts recurred to those unfortunate men whom we had left by the wreck. We were under much anxiety for them, and I asked the Indians if it was possible to go to their relief.

From the description I gave, the Indians said they knew the place perfectly well; that it was above 100 miles distant through difficult paths and over rivers and mountains; and that if they undertook the journey they must expect some compensation. This indeed was but reasonable, for it could not be expected that the Indians should leave their hunting, by which alone they subsisted their wives and families, through pure benevolence.

I then informed them that I had some money and would pay them for their trouble. They seemed much pleased, and showed an eagerness in their countenances at the sight of the coin which I had little expected among Indians. I made an agreement with them that they should receive

25 guineas at their departure and the same sum on their return. Three of them went off the next morning.

After these people knew that I had money they became as mercenary as they had hitherto been charitable, and exacted above 10 times the value for every little necessary they furnished. I was under constant apprehension lest they should be incited by this extraordinary passion for money to plunder us and leave us destitute. The only circumstance on which I founded my hope was their religion, for they were Christians, having been converted by the French. But perhaps it was this very circumstance of their communication with Christians that had inspired them with that vehement love of money.

After near a fortnight the Indians arrived with three men who were the only survivors of the eight who had been left behind at the hut. They were in a very reduced and miserable condition, and informed me that after having consumed all the beef they lived for some days on the skin of the moose which we had left. This being consumed, three of them died in a few days and the others were under the necessity of subsisting on the flesh of the dead men till they were relieved by the Indians. One of the remaining five was so imprudently ravenous when the Indians came to their assistance as to eat such a quantity of meat that he expired in a few hours in the greatest agonies imaginable; and another soon after shot himself accidentally with one of the Indians' guns. Thus was our number, which originally consisted of 19 persons, reduced to nine; and I rather wonder how so many persons could, for the space of three months, go through such distresses from excessive cold, fatigue and hunger.

The Indians led Prenties to an army outpost on Sydney Harbour. There he recovered his health. Taken by other Indians to Halifax, he boarded a ship to New York and delivered the tattered dispatches, for what they were still worth, to Sir Henry Clinton on Aug. 19, 1781—nine months and two days after he left Quebec.

253

The Saga of "Rudder" Churchill

*George Churchill was already known as an intrepid
shipmaster when he sailed the raging North Atlantic
in the winter of 1866-67. He and his ship
were from Yarmouth, N.S., a town famous for
the stamina of its mariners and its vessels.
But on that stormy voyage Churchill's determination
met its sternest test. This is the story of how
he saved his stricken ship and earned himself
a proud nickname.*

By Archibald MacMechan

O N THE NIGHT OF NOV. 26 the full-rigged ship *Research,* bound late
in the season for Greenock, Scotland, with a load of timber from
Quebec, had cleared the Strait of Belle Isle. As she moved slowly
into the Atlantic the wind almost died away and the barometer fell to
28 inches—ominous hints of trouble to come.

The captain, George Churchill, 29, had a gentle, almost dreamy
face but there was nothing vague about his seamanship or his iron determination. He braced the yards and reduced sail to close-reefed topsails.
With all made snug, the *Research,* stripped like a gymnast, awaited the
onslaught.

All night the uncanny lull continued, but with morning the tempest
broke. It came out of the northwest, a furious storm that smote the
Research like the hammer of Thor. It ripped the topsails from the yards
and flung them on the waves, leaving only whipping streamers of canvas.
A tremendous sea fractured the rudder stock just below its casing under
the stern. The chains which linked the back of the rudder to the rail
of the ship snapped, and the vessel was suddenly out of control.

George Churchill, no man to resign himself to calamity, tried to

After an uncanny lull, a tempest like the hammer of Thor. George Churchill's ordeal had begun.

hobble the rudder by passing a hawser over the stern. But the rope chafed through and the pounding rudder began to break up.

How to fetter the massive piece of mechanism and prevent further damage? If rope-and-pulley tackles could be fastened to the ringbolt on the back of the rudder, it could be controlled and the ship steered from the deck. But the rudder of a loaded vessel is practically all under water, and the *Research* was wallowing in mountainous seas. The first thing to do was to lighten the ship aft and so bring the ringbolt to the surface. The carefully stowed deck load had to be unpacked and the fresh-cut boards thrown overboard. It was a long and dangerous job but it was done. And all the time the gale blew harder, the billows swept the deck, and the spray froze where it fell.

Next morning came the task of fastening the tackles to the ringbolt. There was but one way: a man must go into the water. The first mate of the *Research* was Aaron Flint Churchill, the captain's nephew and a handsome giant of 16 who had earned his post by his ability, not by any Board of Trade certificate. On that bitter winter morning Aaron Churchill stripped to the buff and went over the side slung in a rope.

With one hand he held the tackle. With the other he tried to save himself from being battered to death against the vessel. On the deck above, men watched and lifted the rope when waves swept over him. The huge, heavy rudder was beating continually against the sternpost with terrifying violence. Mother-naked, frozen, blinded, half-strangled, Aaron had to watch for the favorable instant when the ringbolt was near enough for him to slip the hook of the tackle into it. He was fighting for the lives of all on board. After an hour and a half he succeeded in hooking the tackle into the ringbolt. He was hauled up insensible and laid on the deck to recover. Half a pint of brandy was poured down his throat. Slowly his strength returned. Then he went over the other side of the ship with a second tackle.

This time he was down for an hour and three quarters before he managed to fasten the second tackle in the ringbolt. The dangerous rudder was securely hobbled; the *Research* could be steered by the ancient device of hauling on the tackles. Aaron Churchill was dragged back to the deck more dead than alive.

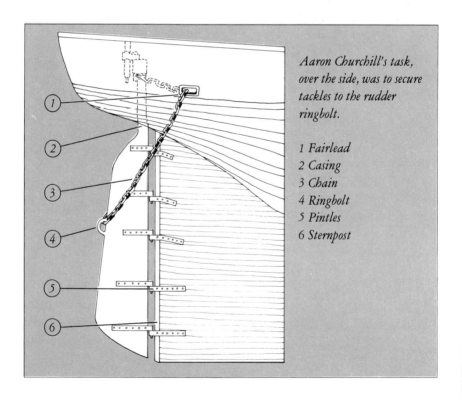

Aaron Churchill's task, over the side, was to secure tackles to the rudder ringbolt.

1 *Fairlead*
2 *Casing*
3 *Chain*
4 *Ringbolt*
5 *Pintles*
6 *Sternpost*

But wind and wave are pitiless antagonists. The next day what was left of the rudder was torn from the pintles and swept away. Even a damaged rudder was better than none; now the *Research* was rudderless.

For two days and two nights the big, impotent timber ship was driven before the storm while officers and men constructed a makeshift rudder. Using some of the remaining deck load of boards, they measured, sawed and hammered on the icy, reeling deck, stopping only to snatch a mouthful of food or an hour's sleep.

On the morning of Dec. 2 the rudder was finished. The whole heavy, clumsy contrivance, with all its trailing ropes, had to be lowered over the stern and then the stock had to be drawn up through the casing into the ship. As the rig was being lowered a wicked cross sea snapped the hawser like a thread. Away floated the rudder.

Now George Churchill made a steering oar. To one end of a spare topmast, about 60 feet long, he bolted a huge square of boards. This would be lashed to the rail, and moved to and fro by lines fastened to the blade. It was ready for use the next day, but it was a failure. Lightening the *Research* aft, in order to get at the ringbolt on the rudder, had lifted her stern too high out of the water.

Part of the forward deck load was jettisoned in order to restore the vessel's trim, but now the oar could not be sunk deep enough in the water. It was weighted with chain but the weight was too much and the spar fractured. Nonetheless, with their damaged oar and such scanty canvas as they dared to set in that living gale, the sailors sent the *Research* storming ever eastward toward their destination.

The storm grew worse. Moving hills of water broke over the helpless *Research,* smashing the forward deckhouse where the crew lived and wrecking the provision locker. The men went on short rations.

No stauncher vessels ever sailed than the best products of Nova Scotia shipyards, but after weeks of battering the *Research* began to leak. Although a timber-laden vessel cannot sink, she can become waterlogged, an unnavigable hulk below the level of the waves. Officers and men labored at the pumps day and night. They kept the water down, although they could not prevent it from coming in.

In spite of wet and cold and the heartbreaking labor at the pumps, the men of the *Research* built a third rudder, and during a lull on the morning of Dec. 14 they got it tied on. For a whole day this clumsy contrivance functioned and the vessel answered to her helm, but on the 15th the violent seas smashed the stock, and the new rudder was useless.

For nearly another week they could do nothing but hold on and work the pumps. One pump broke down. But on Dec. 21 a new rudder, Number Four, was begun. On Jan. 2, the 53rd day out of Quebec, Number Four was wrestled into place.

It held but it was not powerful enough to control the direction of the vessel. Another steering oar, rudder Number Five, was put over the stern.

Navigating a leaking ship in hurricane weather with two makeshift rudders, the men pulling and hauling on two sets of tackles at the word of command, presented difficulties, but Churchill kept his vessel on course until Jan. 5, when rudder Number Four was carried away.

By about the turn of the year the leaking, crippled *Research* had travelled from the Strait of Belle Isle to within 50 miles of Tory Island at the north of Ireland. This was about 100 miles, as the gull flies, from her destination. Then the gale came round to eastward, dead in her teeth. Hurricanes and heavy seas drove her back and back, south and west, out into the Atlantic, until she was 1,800 miles off her course, in the neighborhood of the Azores.

On Jan. 10 Churchill sacrificed his main yard to form the stock of a new rudder, and three days later rudder Number Six was in place. It was not large enough to be really effective, but with it Churchill pointed the *Research* back toward Greenock.

Ever since the blizzard struck her on the morning of Nov. 27, the big timber ship had been alone on the waste of waters. But now she was nearing the great traffic lanes between the old world and the new. On Jan. 16 she met the *Empress Eugenie,* Liverpool-bound from San Francisco, and across the stormy sea, told her story in whipping signal flags. Both ships hove to and the small boat of the *Research* rowed off for provisions. The *Empress Eugenie* had little beef and biscuit to spare but she gave what she could. The next day the steamer *Palmyra,* on her way to Liverpool from New York, stopped to assist the *Research.*

The captains of both vessels offered to take Churchill and his crew off the battered *Research* with its crazy steering gear, but Churchill refused despite the entreaties of his starving, exhausted crew. Pride and duty forbade him to take the easy way out.

On Jan. 25 Churchill began work on rudder Number Seven. It was shipped two days later, but the last line was hardly taut when the stock broke.

The *Research* had now clawed back from the Azores to the south of Ireland. Churchill built another rudder and on Feb. 1, about 185 miles southwest of Cape Clear, it was shipped without mishap. Rudder Number Eight was a success and with this triumph the luck of the *Research* changed: a favorable wind urged her up the Irish Channel. At Ailsa Craig she fell in with a tug and accepted a tow. It was no disgrace. After a voyage of 88 days under her own sail, with the aid of her eight improvised rudders, the *Research* reached Greenock on Feb. 5.

Her main yard, forward deckhouse and wheelhouse were gone. Great ragged gaps showed in her bulwarks. Her deck was encumbered with strange gear, and astern was her homemade rudder. But her hull was sound and the cargo in her hold was intact. Insurance would cover all repairs.

Aaron Churchill was given a silver chronometer, a watch and chain and a sextant by the underwriters of the ship and its cargo. Capt. George Churchill was given a gold watch and chain and a purse of 60 sovereigns. From the underwriters' association he received an engraved silver salver and warm expressions of appreciation. The chairman of Lloyd's commended his "indomitable perseverance" and *The Times* of London published an account of his exploit under the title "An Example to Shipmasters."

Churchill's achievement is unique in the annals of the sea: to the end of his days he was famous among his brother captains as "Rudder" Churchill.

The Wreck of the *Codseeker*

*On a stormy night in 1877
the brand-new fishing schooner
CODSEEKER capsized east of Cape Sable,
the rocky southern tip of Nova Scotia
and one of the graveyards of the Atlantic.
Of the 13 men aboard five were left clinging to a windswept
gunwale and two more were trapped in the forecastle.
All were given up for dead.*

*Adapted from an account
By* WILLIAM M. MURPHY

B Y THE NIGHT OF MAY 9, the easterly wind which had been increasing all afternoon along Nova Scotia's south shore had become a gale. Offshore, sometimes in sight of land but more often not, a slender fishing schooner was flying down the coast with all sails set and her two masts straining.

She was the *Codseeker,* 58½ feet long and the first of the "toothpick" schooners whose speed and seaworthiness were to dominate the area's fishing fleets for decades. But this was her maiden voyage and neither Capt. Philip Brown nor anyone else realized that a craft of such slender lines required unusually careful trimming. Brown had stowed her ballast without any particular delicacy.

When the wind became strong the vessel began rolling heavily to leeward and recovering only slowly. As the seas driving under her stern grew higher the pounding and careening became more marked. Brown seemed heedless of the danger but by 9 p.m., as the ship passed the Shelburne light, his crew was worried. James Edwin Smith, in his late teens and the adopted son of the ship's owner, recorded later that he "didn't like the look of things"—especially when he heard some of the older men asking Brown to reef in and lie low.

The *Codseeker* had been launched only 20 days before at Port Clyde, close to Cape Sable. Captain Brown, owner Reuben Stoddart and all but one of the crew were from nearby Bear Point, a tiny fishing settlement on the peninsula of the same name.

Early in May the *Codseeker* had sailed for Halifax, both to stock up on provisions and to give the captain and crew the feel of her. On Tuesday, May 8, she left Halifax on what was to be her first fishing expedition. In the afternoon Brown put in at Prospect, near Peggy's Cove, for bait. But bait was scarce, and the following morning he decided to strike for home where it could be obtained more easily.

After passing the Shelburne light, with the wind still increasing in ferocity, Brown finally ordered the mainsail hauled down, then headed for land. About 10:30 the lookout sighted the Baccaro light, nine miles northeast of Cape Sable. The jib was hauled down halfway and the course held for the light, but even so the older hands among the crew stayed prudently close to the deck or clung to the rigging.

Three crew members were below deck, however, and James Smith decided to join one of them, Samuel Atwood, for a dipperful of water in the forecastle. As he reached the bottom of the companionway he saw a box containing a picture of his girl shoot out from his berth and strike the floor. Smith hastened to retrieve it, then made toward the water bucket. "Before I could raise the dipper to my lips," he recorded later, "the schooner gave a wild lurch and flung over on her beam-ends [side], and I went sliding to leeward. The light went out, there was a great racket of pots and pans fetching away, and a weird lot of noises as the barrels and boxes in the hold rolled up against the turn of the deck."

Smith reached his feet and made toward the companionway, now lying at a crazy angle, but as he reached it a flood of water poured through, splaying his fingers apart and smashing him back. In a few seconds he found himself, in pitch darkness, floating in icy water amidst a jumble of flotsam with only a pocket of air above him. He heard Atwood floundering about but couldn't see him. When he shouted, Sam didn't answer. Further aft, the two other men below deck had died almost instantly.

Above, the tilted deck was a jungle of tangled rigging, but at length seven men, including the captain, found themselves lying across the weather side of the hull clinging to the rail. As the sea broke over them one sailor lost his hold and was swept away, never to be seen again.

Brown, in desperation, fought his way aft to try to clear the small dory from the stern. Crouched in her he found two more sailors.

Although one of the davits was under water the three men finally cleared the flooded boat and cut it loose. They launched it and found themselves almost swamped in the angry sea: feverishly they bailed with their hats, but by the time they had rendered the dory navigable they were far to the west of the *Codseeker*. Then, as Brown noted in the official report, "the night being exceedingly dark, we lost sight of the vessel."

Brown and his companions tried to find the schooner but there were no thole pins to hold the oars, the wind was constantly increasing and the sea was breaking into the boat. They had no choice but to head for Cape Sable Island a few miles to the west. Providentially, the dory drifted near some net buoys and Brown, fearing the dory might be smashed to pieces if they attempted to land on the rough shore in such a heavy sea, succeeded in catching on to a buoy and tying up for the night. At dawn Thursday the wind diminished slightly so Brown untied the dory and allowed the heavy swells to carry her ashore at Cape Sable Island South Side. By seven o'clock the three weary men had trudged the four miles to Clark's Harbour, where they spread the news of the disaster.

The local fishermen sought immediately to undertake a rescue. Lying at hand was the schooner *Matchless,* commanded by Capt. Job Cro-well. Her crew was scattered but nine volunteers, headed by Captain Brown's brother Henry, quickly came forward. At 10 o'clock, in the teeth of the newly increasing gale, the *Matchless* sailed under double reefs on her errand of mercy.

For two days that was all anyone knew. The *Matchless* failed to return and the *Codseeker* seemed to have been swallowed by the sea. On Saturday morning Philip Brown appeared before the Receiver of Wrecks for the Port of Barrington and filed his report. Brown told the story as he knew it, certifying at the close that of the 13 men who set out from Halifax all but three had been drowned. For all he knew the would-be rescuers of the *Matchless* were lost too.

Captain Crowell and his crew had sailed with no very clear notion of where they were going. But, as Reuben Stoddart was to write later, they were "determined to save the sufferers or perish in the attempt."

They headed into the wind, tacking toward the south, calculating from Captain Brown's story that the *Codseeker* must lie somewhere west of the rock where the steamship *Hungarian* had foundered 17 years before with the loss of 205 lives. When they had sailed about eight miles south-west of Cape Sable, "the storm grew so violent and the weather so thick with mist and spray that the search was considered hopeless." But just as the spirits of the would-be rescuers were at their lowest they sighted the wreck about half a mile away, wallowing helplessly on her side, five figures clinging to the bulwark.

The seas and wind made it impossible to bring the large rescue vessel close to the *Codseeker*. Fortunately the *Matchless* carried a big boat and this put out with Henry Brown in charge of a picked crew.

The five men left on the gunwales of the *Codseeker* were in constant fear of being swept away, particularly when shifting ballast tilted the vessel violently. With difficulty they had strung a lifeline between the points where the fore and main shrouds fastened to the hull, and had hung on grimly.

Even in midsummer the waters off Cape Sable are cold; in early May they are almost arctic. Mountainous seas tossed the hull and sprayed the numbed fingers of the desperate men. Heavy waves still broke over them. Gradually their strength ebbed.

About noon on Thursday, even as the boat from the *Matchless* rowed unseen toward them, a towering comber carried away Crowell Nickerson. When the water subsided for a moment the others saw him tangled helplessly in the cordage just below the surface of the water. With terrified eyes they watched him drown.

Now the survivors all but abandoned hope. Will Kenney, oppressed by the sense of impending death and moved by the awful spectacle of his friend's drowning, began to sing "Jesus, Lover of My Soul." His shipmates joined in, certain that the end was not far off. Then, when rescue seemed impossible, they saw the *Matchless*.

The rescuers, aiming for a point between the *Codseeker*'s bowsprit and foremast where the sea was least dangerous, had seen Nickerson swept from his perch, and redoubled their efforts. As they drew near, a line was thrown to the wreck and made fast. Then, as the sea allowed, the boat was hauled slowly toward the middle of the *Codseeker*'s deck. Once the fore shrouds caught over the bow of the boat, almost trapping her, but the crew pulled her free. Finally she lay rising and falling under the slanting deck, and the four survivors were taken aboard.

Before casting off Brown asked whether there might be other survivors but was assured there were not. Leaving the wallowing wreck to the swells and the gale, the boat made her way back to the *Matchless*. But now the wind and sea were so violent that Captain Crowell found it impossible to return to land. The only recourse was to ride out the

storm, and by the time it abated later that day he found himself becalmed well out to sea.

So it was that the *Matchless* and her crew were also given up for lost. They did not return to Clark's Harbour until late on Saturday after Philip Brown had filed his report.

Meanwhile, inside the abandoned wreck, an even more terrifying drama was being enacted. James Smith and Samuel Atwood, alive in the forecastle, had each eventually found the side of a berth to cling to. Below them the icy sea water surged back and forth as the vessel pitched, pouring out the companionway door only to return with the next wave, though always bringing new air as it came. In the darkness the men could only feel their way about, hanging on in the hope that the morning would bring calm seas and rescue. The roar of the ocean and the pressure of the trapped air deafened them so that neither could hear the other while the storm lasted.

Let Smith describe their situation: "The schooner had settled as the water got into her and, happily for us, the bows were the highest part. She was still on her side, but listed a little past her beam-ends so that her spars sloped into the sea at an angle of about 20 degrees. As she wallowed, the bows were sometimes lifted much higher out of water and at other times nearly submerged.

"The round of her starboard bow was the highest part, and we were in the bunks built against the bulge of the bow. The face or side board of the bunk on which I was lying was only about 12 inches wide, and I had to hold on with hands and knees, especially when she took a roll, to keep from slipping into the black abyss on either side. Atwood, lying on the face board of the lower bunk, was in a somewhat better position as he could only slip off one side. About two and a half feet above us was the side of the ship; right under us, usually three or four feet down, was the surging flood and a litter of floating things. Outside, the waves were crashing against the hulk, roaring dreadfully.

"We were afraid she would sink or turn turtle altogether. When the bows fell the water would surge forward, then back up and overwhelm us. At such times we had to hold our breath and cling to our perches for dear life, or sit up and brace our shoulders against the side of the ship."

During the night, despite the noise and danger, Smith dozed off. He dreamed that he saw his friend Will Kenney washed overboard, and dived after him. Instantly he awoke to find himself submerged in the icy water. He fought to get to the surface but found his head trapped as in a vice. The more he struggled the harder he was held. But he realized his mouth was just above water, and after a few gasps his brain cleared. He discovered he was caught between two steps of the companionway ladder. Backing out gingerly, he drew himself round it and floated free again.

Thursday's dim light, filtering through the doorway, gave some cheer to the men but also made them aware of acute hunger and thirst. Breaking into a compartment which lay above the water line, they found five doughnuts soaked with salt water and kerosene; they devoured them hungrily. But their thirst grew, and when a water barrel floated by Smith he held it fast and sucked out the contents with a barrel pump. Foolishly he gulped down a large quantity before discovering that the water was salt. All the other barrels that bobbed past were similarly spoiled.

Smith suffered badly from thirst. By Thursday afternoon he had grown so "wild," to use his own term, that he cut the ends of his fingers and sucked the blood. But this brought no relief. Nor was their hunger further assuaged. Once a barrel of biscuits came floating through a hole in the bulkhead and Smith got a finger on it. But he failed to hold on, the barrel floated back through the hole, and they never saw it again.

Toward evening the sea grew calm and the prisoners were able to take stock of their position. For one thing, the water was no longer surging in and out bringing fresh oxygen; their air supply was now limited. Smith, still tortured by terrible thirst, became aware that he could feel nothing below his knees. Reaching through the water to remove his sea boots, he found his feet so swollen that the boots were stuck fast. And to their other afflictions was added the most horrible of all, the knowledge that they were trapped in an abandoned, overturned schooner with an ever-diminishing chance of being rescued. "That night," said Smith, "I knew what fear is, the stark, fierce, angry fear of a long-drawn-out and terrible death."

On Friday, by a brighter light from the doorway, they could see that it was about eight feet under water. "A good swimmer might have dived out," Smith acknowledged later, "but we felt too stiff to try it, and it would have been a desperate job the way the water was still surging and swirling." Both men preferred their little pocket of fetid air to the risks of the eight-foot dive. And even had the dive succeeded, who could tell whether they would reach the surface through the tangled skein of rigging?

"After Saturday noon," according to Smith, "it was just suffering and endurance. We seldom talked; our parched throats and our swollen tongues made speech painful and our voices sounded weird and unnatural. Nor did we think much. Most of the time we lay in a stupor. Now and then we dreamed of beautiful ships all around us, all coming to our rescue, and we would wake with a start to wonder if we were going mad. We lived as in a nightmare, lost count of time, felt as if we had suffered through eternity."

On Saturday, as the trapped men abandoned hope and settled back to die, the schooner *Ohio*, under the command of Capt. Edward Dorr, sailed out of Bucksport, Maine, on her way to the Grand Banks. About four o'clock on Sunday afternoon, about 36 miles southwest of Cape Sable, the lookout sighted what some took to be a floating wreck and others a dead whale. A heated argument ensued. Finally the captain sent a party

in a small dory to investigate, some of the men armed with axes for securing any salvage.

The sea was calm and the sun had baked the side of the *Codseeker*
dry. One of the men clambered aboard to find the name of the ship while
another began to strike with an axe at the lanyards of the forerigging.
Suddenly the axe struck an iron strap and there was a clang. From within
the vessel, directly beneath the feet of the man walking on her, came
the cry, "Help! Help! Help!"

The American leaped with terror. "She's haunted!" he cried. "For
God's sake, let's get into the boat." He jumped aboard, and the oarsmen
pulled away feverishly. Then, sheepish at their cowardice and superstition,
they rowed back and circled the wreck warily. Now they heard rapping
against the side. One of the party, taking courage, jumped aboard, rapped
three times and received three raps as an answer. "In the name of God,"
he called, "are you ghosts, living men or the devil?"

Smith and Atwood shouted that they were indeed living men. After
a few more questions and answers the Americans sent the dory back to
the *Ohio* for more men and axes, and started chopping a hole in the side
of the *Codseeker*. At length they broke through. As Smith was to tell the
story later, "the eruption of imprisoned air acted like a whirlwind, and
the water leaped through the hole in a solid stream 50 feet into the air.
Small sticks which had been floating in the forecastle whizzed by our
heads. One man was knocked over as if by an explosion." The *Ohio* crew
reported that the escaping gases "gave off a sickening stench." Inside,
the sea rose through the companionway to fill the space left by the discharged air, and the trapped men almost drowned before the hole was
big enough for them to escape. Atwood, being slim, was drawn out easily.
Smith, more portly and slightly hunchbacked, stuck when he had his
head and one shoulder clear. It took four men to tug him through, and
in the process he parted with his vest and several strips of skin. After
89 hours in their dark prison Smith and Atwood finally stood, shaken
and wobbly, in the open air.

"The sun was nearing the horizon," said Smith later, "glowing
softly amid a glory of rose and gold. Never have I seen such beauty in
the heavens."

Their trials were by no means ended, for several days of painful
thirst were to follow. In keeping with the custom of the time water was
carefully rationed to the men, first a spoonful every 15 minutes, then
every five minutes. By midnight, in his berth in the *Ohio,* Smith was

raging for water. At the change of watches he and Atwood found themselves alone. Smith crawled to the water jug and began to drink. Atwood, too weak to move, called, "Give me a drop—just one drop." But, related Smith, "that was too much of a gift." He drank it all and promptly swelled up. The horrified *Ohio* crewmen gathered round to watch him die, but he confounded them by staying alive although he felt as thirsty as ever.

For Smith there was additional agony as circulation returned to his swollen feet. His sea boots had to be cut off, and the stuff beneath "looked like the flesh of a drowned person who had been many days in the water."

By eight o'clock Monday morning they were making into Shag Harbour. As Smith and Atwood were being rowed ashore Smith spotted Tanny Knowles, one of the sailors who had been saved with Captain Brown, rowing Smith's small skiff. Knowles had seen it lying in a cove: believing Smith dead, and reluctant to leave the boat to rot, he was taking it to Shag Harbour.

"Hello, Tanny Knowles! Where are you going with my boat?" Smith called. Knowles recognized the voice, dropped his oars and turned white at the sight of the men who had apparently come back from the dead.

The miraculous survival of Smith and Atwood drew national attention to the disaster. Parliament awarded a gold watch to Captain Crowell of the *Matchless*.

Smith and Atwood's ordeal was discussed for years in Bear Point, with embellishments provided by local poets. One story still circulating is that the *Codseeker* sank, then rose again when her salt ballast dissolved. But the unloaded vessel's buoyancy makes such an event unlikely, and Smith nowhere speaks of the ship scraping the bottom.

The *Codseeker*'s history was not ended with the rescue. On May 22 she was seen floating south of Yarmouth, and later was towed into Green Cove. The hole in the hull through which Smith and Atwood had been rescued proved her greatest wound, and by July she was at sea again. Properly ballasted she proved seaworthy, and in the great Newfoundland gale of 1885 she was one of only five ships from a fleet of 35 to return to port.

Among the crew on her second maiden voyage was James Edwin Smith, who sailed in her till Christmas, sleeping in the same berth he had clung to during his extraordinary ordeal.

The Great Ship

The WILLIAM D. LAWRENCE, *launched at Maitland, N.S., in 1874,
was the biggest ship in the Bluenose fleet of Canadian vessels that
roamed the world in the late 19th century. She cost more than
$107,000 – half as much again as most ships of the day. Sceptics had
said she couldn't be built; if built, they added, she wouldn't sail, and
if she sailed she would never pay. But a memorable round-the-world
maiden voyage proved the sceptics wrong.*

By JOSEPH SCHULL

*W.D. and his dream ship, on the stocks
at Maitland. A teetotaller, he launched her
with cider.*

WILLIAM D. LAWRENCE had done pretty well in Maitland. He was 52 years old, stood six feet three in his boots, and had lived his life amid the clatter of shipyards. His early years with the broadaxe and the maul had been spent in Dartmouth. Then he had gone to Boston to learn something of ship design from the famous Donald McKay, the Nova Scotia boy who was building clippers for the Americans. After a few years he had come north again and settled at the head of the Bay of Fundy, ready to build his own ships. Somewhere, he had learned to play the fiddle.

For his first little ship he had gone into the woods himself, chopped down the trees he wanted and carried out the timber on his shoulders. Soon other men were doing his fetching and carrying. Carpenter sheds

and blacksmith shops and stores of seasoning timber stood beside the W.D. Lawrence house along the banks of the Shubenacadie River. By 1868 six able vessels had come down his slipways and put to sea.

He was a widower now, but his daughter Mary had married Jim Ellis of Shubenacadie, and there were three young grandchildren. It was a fine little family. The only trouble was that W.D. didn't see much of them. Jim was captain of the Lawrence ship *Pegasus,* Mary and the children sailed with him, and grandfather was left at home. In the evenings, when W.D. sat alone in his study scraping away at his fiddle, with the housekeeper wincing in the kitchen, he did a lot of thinking.

He thought about ships, he thought about the sea and he thought about Jim and Mary and the children. He was growing no younger, and still the far places of the earth were nothing to him but names on bills of lading. He was missing something.

In the summer of 1868 the sea-going Ellises were home for a spell and Captain Jim found his father-in-law preoccupied. There was no vessel building outside this year but there were a lot of papers and drawings cluttering up the study. W.D. would shuffle them around and talk a little evasively of the need for bigger ships, ships that would carry twice the cargo with the same crew. When he walked with Jim in the woods and talk turned to the next voyage of the *Pegasus* he seemed more concerned than usual about profits. His son-in-law looked at the empty yards and thought of the plans in the study. By the time he gathered up Mary and the children and left to join the *Pegasus* again he had a pretty good idea what was in W.D.'s mind.

The *Pegasus* sailed from Saint John, N.B., in September with lumber for Liverpool, England. Then she took coal from Cardiff to Yokohama and sailed in ballast for the Chincha Islands off the west coast of South America. After waiting with scores of other ships she finally moved under the chutes running out from the cliffs and opened her hatches to load guano, the hardened droppings of sea birds. Guano was in heavy demand in Europe as a fertilizer, and carrying it was an industry in itself. For days the *Pegasus* lay amid clouds of evil-smelling dust while coolies shovelled thousands of tons of the ancient substance into her hold. At last she sealed her hatches, scrubbed her decks, and rolled away around the Horn for Antwerp. Next she carried coal from Cardiff to Montevideo, more guano to Hamburg, coal again to Hong Kong, and sugar from the Philippines to Boston. There, after four years and three months, her voyage ended with a profit of $82,716.

Jim Ellis had known he would see a ship building when he got back to Maitland. Bluenose captains had come into Hamburg, Calcutta, San Francisco and Manila with rumors of it. Bluenose ships had hailed him on the high seas to retail the gossip that was running through the Maritime ports and out around the world. But even with all that, he hadn't quite realized what his father-in-law was up to.

The mighty thing towered beside the house, overshadowing the chimney tops. The framework of the hull ran like a wall down the length of the lawn to the edge of the Shubenacadie. Seventy-five workmen swarmed about the stocks. The neighborhood echoed to the rasp of saws, clink of caulking mallets and thud of mauls driving home bolts in timber.

Ellis and W.D. passed under the loom of the bows, climbed the scaffolding and paced off the 275 feet of her deck. Its timbers were 18 inches through, and beneath them ran two more decks with timbers just as huge. Ellis looked over the roof of the house toward the woods where this timber had grown. He ran his hand along the inner wall of the hull. The broad spruce planks were a foot thick and held with black iron bolts as thick as a man's two thumbs. The massive vertical ribwork was spaced so closely that it was almost another wall, and bolted to the outside was the heavy timber of the planking. With one hand on the inner wall Jim Ellis reached across to touch the outer planking. He couldn't make it. The mighty triple bulwark was too thick.

The ship was still only half built. There would be two years of work yet, and it would be work by fits and starts as the money came in and ran out. She gulped down the $82,000 earned by the *Pegasus,* she swallowed most of W.D.'s savings and she put a mortgage on the house. She kept Jim Ellis hurrying off to Halifax for supplies, and hurrying home to figure out how to pay the bills. And always there was the dismal refrain from the wharves of Halifax to the riverside at Maitland, "She'll never sail" . . . "She'll be too big to handle" . . . "She'll flounder round like a bull playing a fiddle" . . .

By the summer of 1874 the hull was finished. Seams had been caulked, water had been pumped in and out again, and leaks re-caulked. The lower masts, each 41 inches through, had been stepped. Topmasts and topgallant masts had grown above the lower masts, and finally it was time for the yards to go up and the riggers to come aboard. Their forms dwindled and their voices grew faint as they rode 200 feet above the watchers. The canvas followed—800 yards of it, all on credit.

As the launching day neared, W.D. seemed to spend a great deal of time in his study, fiddling in solitude. This meant thoughtfulness and perhaps worry. A bit late for worry, reflected his son-in-law. But Ellis felt a sense of relief the night W.D. opened the door and called him in. It was always best to know how bad a situation was, and face up to it.

W.D. didn't appear worried. The bills lay in a neat pile, untouched beside his fiddle. His eyes were tranquil, though with a little gleam in them, as he looked out at the shadow cast by the ship in the moonlight. He'd made a few decisions, he said, and it was time for Jim to know about them. The vessel was going to be called the *William D. Lawrence*. Jim was going to sail her, of course, and the children would go with him and Mary. The children were getting older, so that would mean shipping a tutor. Also, he added, clearing his throat slightly, this time grandfather was going along.

Ellis, harassed by two anxious years ashore, nearly exploded. Was this what all the fiddling had been about? Every cent they had was sunk in that hull outside, and W.D. was talking about tutors and pleasure trips. What if the ship turned out to be a bad sailer? And what if they couldn't find the huge cargoes they'd need to make money with her?

W.D. smiled and produced a charter from Dreyfus Frères et Compagnie of France for a cargo of guano. The *William D. Lawrence* would go to Liverpool with timber and then take coal to Aden. From there she would go to the west coast of South America and load guano for France. The cargoes would pay the bills, there wasn't any worry about that. This wasn't a pleasure trip, it was a business trip. And business or pleasure, he concluded, it was a trip round the world and he was going to make it in his own ship.

Oct. 27, 1874, was launching day. W.D. was a teetotaller, so a bottle of cider was smashed against the bow; the keel blocks were split, and at two in the afternoon the hull began to move down the ways carrying her 400 tons of stone ballast. The shadow of the bow drew away from the house, the fields and woods reappeared, and the ship rode easily out onto the red waters of the Shubenacadie.

Two months later, with her holds full and her deck piled to the rail with timber, she moved out of Saint John Harbour for England. Jim Ellis still had no way of knowing how the ship would sail on the open sea, yet there was no denying the happy excitement stirring in her. The family was all together, and after two years there was stout timber under his feet again, lifting with the sea.

274

In the pilot house Ellis stood with W.D. beside the helmsman. His face began to clear a little as he got the feel of the vessel, and he gave a course to the helmsman that caused W.D. to look at him with surprise. The wider channel lay down the Bay of Fundy off Digby Neck and Brier Island. Ellis was going between Grand Manan and the Maine shore. It was a faster route because of the tides, but the channel was narrower, and only a master who was sure of his ship would risk it. W.D. said nothing, but a small, complacent gleam came into his eye.

The gleam was a glow by the time they reached Liverpool, and the enthusiasm of the builder was shared by the master. For all her size the *William D. Lawrence* handled like a yacht. She would never be a fast ship, but she hadn't been designed for speed. She would travel any sea comfortably and surely, and she would probably earn her keep. Her bottom still required copper sheathing for a voyage to southern waters, but the freight on her enormous timber cargo would pay for that.

W.D. left his son-in-law in Liverpool to supervise the sheathing work. He was off with Mary and the children to see London. He was still away as the ship left dry dock and the torrents of coal came tumbling into her hold. The decks, the sides, the rigging and the captain himself were covered with black dust, but W.D., in immaculate linen and broadcloth, was inspecting art galleries and museums and concert halls. Hatch covers had gone on again, holds were sealed, tarpaulins battened down, and the *William D. Lawrence* was sluiced, scrubbed and painted before he returned.

The ship had her papers for Aden, and everything about her except the monstrous, money-making cargo holds was fresh and sparkling on the night of the farewell party. Twenty Bluenose ships were in Liverpool and all the captains and their wives had come to say good-bye. They had dined regally and sung songs round the piano in the saloon, and W.D. was scraping his fiddle for them when a knock came at the door. An urgent letter had arrived for Mr. Lawrence from Dreyfus Frères.

It was necessary, the letter said, to cancel the charter for the guano. The firm had a surplus on hand, and new synthetic fertilizers threatened to destroy the market. Dreyfus Frères regretted the necessity of their action, but Mr. Lawrence would understand.

Mr. Lawrence understood very well. The guano charter was the backbone of his voyage, the only source from which he could pay the debts on his ship. He also understood that a charter was a binding contract. There would be no reply to the letter, said W.D. The ship would

For all her size she handled like a yacht.

sail as planned, and she would return with a cargo of guano. Jim Ellis was not so sure. Charters had been broken before, he knew, and luckless carriers had been left to hold the bag.

They moved out of the Mersey next morning. W.D. had nothing more to say about the charter. He was concerned only with the voyage ahead and with the sailing qualities of his ship. She stood out into the Irish Sea, turned down St. George's Channel and into the Atlantic. Her course lay south, round the Cape of Good Hope, and up through the Indian Ocean to blistering Aden at the mouth of the Red Sea. As the links with shore parted, the tangle of debt and worry retreated into the back of Ellis' mind as well. The vessel shouldered cleanly into the long rollers. With thousands of tons of coal settled in her belly, comfortable and secure, she was a giant in her element. The weather held fine. The deck watch would gather at the rail, smirking complacently as passing vessels hailed and admired the mighty product of the Maitland yards. A man forgot about business as he stood under the sighing cloud of the canvas and read those admiring signals.

W.D. was becoming almost too much of a seaman. His pride in the *William D. Lawrence* was open and unblushing now, and his questions and suggestions came in an unending stream. You couldn't keep the owner out of the forward quarters as you could a small boy, and W.D.

276

was everywhere about his vessel, chatting with the men, absorbing sea lore, returning to the saloon with bright ideas.

W.D. was always properly deferential to his son-in-law. Ellis was master of the ship, and Ellis gave the orders. The suggestions from the owner continued, however, and one in particular grew more urgent: "Let's see what she'll do with all her clothes on." It irritated Ellis, partly because he was a sober and responsible master, and more because he wanted to know as badly as W.D. He postponed and evaded as a sop to his conscience, but in his heart he was only waiting for the right day.

When it came it was a day for sou'westers and sea boots and oilskins, a day for a seaman to forget the charters and bills and balance sheets that governed his comings and goings about the world. It was the great, boisterous South Atlantic weather that lifted a man's heart. It made Ellis a bit reckless.

From early morning, with a guilty throb of excitement, Ellis had begun to pile sail on the *William D. Lawrence*. By noon even the skysails were set. The great hull which had seemed so monstrous and unwieldy on the stocks at Maitland lifted with the crested surges and clove them away in graceful furrows. With each lunging roll the lee rail dipped until it was racing almost level with the foaming backwash. The timbers from beside the Shubenacadie were earning their shillings now, at the impressive speed of 14 knots.

W.D. shouted with excitement as he read off the log. Ellis was grinning in spite of himself. For three hours he held the *William D. Lawrence* to it. Fifteen knots came up on the log count, and he knew it was time to rein in. The high-pitched moan in the rigging told of enormous strain. You could almost see the great fist of the wind driving into that mass of canvas overhead. The mate was eyeing the captain and the look in those eyes said, "Shorten down."

Ellis gave the order, and the mate started for the deck, but W.D. was beyond the proprieties now. He grabbed the mate's arm and turned to the captain, pleading like a boy. Let her run for half an hour—15 minutes—she'd go to 16 knots, he knew she would. Ellis looked up at the rigging again, shrugged with hypocritical reluctance and told the mate to stand by. He was pretty sure himself she could make 16.

She came up to 16 knots, passed it and began to edge toward 17. W.D. was sure she'd reach it, but beads of sweat were standing on the mate's forehead and Ellis had had enough. He was turning to call in skysails and royals when there was a warning shout from the deck. The ship had fetched up on the back of a huge surge. She paused for an instant, quivering in every timber at the sudden check. Then the great spars towering to the clouds splintered like match sticks and the whole head of her upper canvas was sheared away at a stroke. Yards, spars and sails, the three topmasts and the three topgallant masts came thundering down onto the lower shrouds and backstays, bounced off and plunged over the side. A vast mess of rope, wire, timber and canvas spread round the ship, tangling and battering her with the heave of the sea.

It wasn't a disaster. Three days of backbreaking work salvaged most of the gear and sent the *William D. Lawrence* on her way. But she went round the Cape and up through the Indian Ocean a limping cripple faced with a repair bill that would eat up most of her coal freight. The dreary bunkering port of Aden came in sight at last, and the ship dropped anchor on Aug. 1, 1875.

The captain had been aloof and irritable since the accident, and the owner subdued and contrite. W.D. knew that the thing had been a sore blow to a master's pride, and it had been his—the owner's—fault. But he judged that the air was clear enough now to make another suggestion. They were going to need new spars and they couldn't get them at Aden. Somebody would have to go to Bombay for them, and it might as well be W.D. With Mary and the children, of course.

Ellis looked at him and laughed, the first good laugh in quite a while. A spot of sea air was turning a sharp old businessman into a boy and a tourist. But it would be good to have Mary and the children away from the heat and coal dust, and it might be nice to prepare the ship for her new spars without W.D. forever at his elbow. He didn't mention the cost of repairs or the fact that they had no outward cargo. The family went off to Bombay, and the captain was left to unload his coal.

For days the ship sweltered at the heart of a choking black cloud. Then, as she rode high and empty, the scrubbing and painting parties went to work. The riggers followed, bringing new and costly tackle to replace the damaged gear. The spars arrived from Bombay at last, just ahead of the family. They were up and ready by the time W.D. had finished his tales of India, and on Sept. 13 the *William D. Lawrence* put out for Callao, Peru.

She was a sound ship once more, but she was sailing with profitless ballast in her hold and nothing but a dubious guano charter ahead. This time it was harder for Ellis to shake himself free of his worries but W.D. still wouldn't talk about business. The spell of new lands and waters claimed him as they nosed east through the Indian Ocean and turned into the Timor Sea. It was hard to get him to meals. He stood more watches than the captain as they passed the northern coast of Australia and crossed the breadth of the South Pacific.

Callao lifted on the horizon in the first days of December, and as they neared the Peruvian coast W.D. seemed to grow a little more thoughtful. Ellis hoped he was brooding on guano. But when he spoke at last it was of Lima, the lovely city on the coast, a day's journey from Callao. He'd heard of its wonders, and he and Mary and the children ought to see it.

Now at last the captain exploded. They'd come to Callao to get a permit from the Peruvian government to load guano. Had W.D. forgotten about that charter? No, W.D. hadn't forgotten. He'd arrange for the permit all right, but first he'd see Lima.

There was a great festival in Lima, with dancing and bright costumes and lovely women. W.D. came back to Callao enchanted with his visit. He talked about it all the way to the government offices, but his son-in-law was not listening. He had already called at those offices and he had talked to other masters around the docks. He knew what W.D. would hear. So far as the Peruvian government was concerned it was quite in order for the *William D. Lawrence* to go down the coast to Pabellón de Pica. There she could take guano if she could get it. But 20 or 30 ships were already waiting, and the agents of the guano importers, who held a monopoly, refused to load them. The thought of paying freight on an unsalable cargo was most repugnant to such companies as Dreyfus Frères.

As they listened to the polite official, Jim Ellis saw a change come over his father-in-law. All at once the eager tourist was a businessman again. His face wasn't exactly hard, but it wasn't soft either. The official would kindly complete the permit. The *William D. Lawrence* was sailing tomorrow.

At long last the desolate, gray-white headland of Pabellón de Pica lifted on the southern horizon. When the ship dropped anchor the waiting vessels lay in careful order ahead of her. Their barnacled sides and blistered paint, and the grim faces of the men idly watching from their decks, told of a long stay.

Gulls, pelicans, gannets, terns and cormorants covered the rocky, sun-baked shores and swooped overhead. A few miserable shacks housing officials of the guano monopoly clustered on the treeless slopes. Near them were half a dozen tumble-down bunkhouses for the coolies, brought

279

here to labor till they dropped. The large wooden chutes reaching out over the water from the steep brows of the hill were idle.

The bored clerks ashore had one reply for every captain who came to them. They gave it to Ellis and W.D.: there was no guano to load. The gray mountain towering outside their door gave them the lie, Ellis pointed out. Weren't they weary of their idiotic story? Very weary, they agreed, but their instructions from France were definite.

Many of the ships in Pabellón de Pica were Bluenose ships, and their masters came aboard the *William D. Lawrence* that evening. Some had been waiting for a month and were ready to give up. W.D. listened with polite interest and announced that he would stay.

A month went by, and the *William D. Lawrence* swung to her anchor with the other ships. A second month passed, and five of the ships gave up and sailed. Four later arrivals sized up the situation and turned away. Barnacles began to grow on the clean sides of the *William D. Lawrence*. Her paint cracked in the heat. The crew leaned on the rails muttering as screaming birds crossed and re-crossed the gray mountain. A steamer came up the coast bringing fresh provisions, and Ellis eyed his crew dourly. Some of the men were ripe to jump ship.

He was looking in the wrong direction. It was the owner who came to him as the steamer prepared to sail. The famous port of Mollendo was only a little way up the coast, and from there a railway led into the Andes. Mary and the children were looking a bit pale, and W.D. was of no particular use at the moment in Pabellón de Pica. He thought he'd take the trip. Ellis looked at his father-in-law unbelievingly, shrugged and turned away.

W.D. returned to Pabellón de Pica refreshed by mountain air, lyrical over sunsets in the high valleys, and aglow with tales of exploration. The tired man waiting on the hot deck in Pabellón de Pica found it hard to appreciate them.

His father-in-law seemed to have forgotten, Ellis suggested, that they had come for guano and were not likely to get any. He seemed to have forgotten the bills in Maitland, and the new bills that were growing round the ship every day along with the barnacles. W.D. had not forgotten the bills, he replied mildly, but there was perhaps one thing that the captain had overlooked. A ship kept waiting through no fault of her own was entitled to demurrage charges of $150 a day. Demurrage had now been accruing to the *William D. Lawrence* for about three months. He thought perhaps he'd go fishing in the harbor with the sail-

280

ors. The fourth month went by and the steamer came again. The festival of Chilean independence was to be celebrated in Valparaiso. A sight like that shouldn't be missed when a man was so near. W.D. went off for Valparaiso.

By the time he returned, the fifth month was wearing away. The sixth, seventh and eighth passed. Twelve of the ships had gone now. The barnacles were a thick crust on the *William D. Lawrence*'s sides and bottom; the crew was growling openly. Departing captains had laughed sourly at W.D.'s talk of demurrage charges. A ship that couldn't get a cargo would certainly not be able to collect demurrage. Ellis believed them. Mary's cheerfulness was failing at last, and the children were dull and listless. The family was bankrupt and it was time to go home and face the music. Instead, there was music to be faced in Pabellón de Pica. W.D., immovable as rock, had turned to his fiddle again.

He pointed out that there was a condition attached to the guano monopoly at Pabellón de Pica. The company was compelled by the Peruvian government to load at least one ship a year. He would stay that year, if necessary, and he would collect demurrage for the wait.

The ninth, tenth and eleventh months went by. The crew's sulky fury had begun to change to a kind of dull amusement. They were sorry for Mary and the children, and they didn't blame the captain. He was as helpless as they were, and as bored with the heat and smell and everlasting clamor of the birds. They'd even stopped blaming the old man. It was interesting in a grim sort of way to find just how stubborn he was.

The ships ahead of the *William D. Lawrence* had given up and departed now, except for one. She was the *Antoinette,* a ship with a stubborn master too, and a Bluenose. On the night of Dec. 1, 1876, the *Antoinette*'s master climbed into a boat and went ashore. It was a night like any other of the 330-odd that had gone before, hot and airless, with the men of the two crews trading bored grumblings across the water. But in the morning there was a change.

Shouts from the deck brought Ellis tumbling out of his cabin. He looked toward shore. The *Antoinette* had moved in under the chutes, there were coolies on the hill above, and guano was charging down into her hold.

W.D. ordered out a boat. In half an hour he and Ellis were in the office ashore. The *Antoinette* was being loaded, the clerk agreed, but she would be the only ship. His instructions were definite. W.D.'s reply was equally definite. The operation proceeding outside had demonstrated first that there was guano to be had, and second that the loading gear was in order. The *William D. Lawrence* would be under the chutes within an hour of the *Antoinette*'s departure, and she would be loaded–either by the staff at Pabellón de Pica or by her own crew.

A week later the big ship, deep in the water with all the guano she could carry, was swinging off for the Horn. She rounded it with all sail up, because that was the way W.D. wanted to make the famous journey. With her bottom fouled by a year in tropic waters she made a slow passage, but it was quite fast enough for the unwelcoming Dreyfus Frères in Le Havre. They had cancelled the charter, they protested, they did not wish the cargo and they refused to pay demurrage.

In France the suit of W.D. Lawrence vs. Dreyfus Frères dragged on interminably. But time did not drag for W.D. He saw the opera, the circus, the masked balls, Versailles and the lovely countryside. He stored his memories of France with all his other mental souvenirs, and brought them home at last when the weary mutterings of the lawyers reached their conclusion.

To W.D. Lawrence of Maitland, Nova Scotia, Canada, was awarded the sum of $59,433 in freight, plus demurrage charges of $50,984. On a memorable day in Maitland the old man stood with Ellis surveying a great pile of golden sovereigns heaped on his study table. Then he swept them all into a huge handkerchief and walked down the street in his shirt-sleeves to pay the debts on his ship.

The Captain's Boat

Captains' wives, with their children, risked sickness, shipwreck and death to accompany their husbands on long voyages in the sailing vessels of the late 19th century. When calamity struck Capt. Henry MacArthur's ship in the Pacific in 1881, the Nova Scotia skipper began an heroic battle for the lives of his wife and sons and his crew. Based on accounts by survivors, this is the story of MacArthur's struggle.

By ARCHIBALD MACMECHAN

WHEN THE FULL-RIGGED SHIP *Milton* was launched near Maitland, N.S., at the head of the Bay of Fundy, Kate MacArthur was already on board. She was no ordinary woman, this devoted wife and mother. She was strong in body and mind, fair of face, educated and musical, and she took her religion to sea with her along with her Bible and her Prayer Book.

A sea captain's daughter, she had married a sea captain at 18 and spent her honeymoon at sea. The man of her choice was Henry MacArthur, like her born and brought up in Maitland. He was rather under middle size though powerfully built, and he had remarkable strength of character.

283

On Aug. 9, 1881, the *Milton* sailed from Shields, England, with a cargo of coal for San Francisco. It was a dangerous cargo, inevitably generating heat and gas in the ship's hold. With MacArthur and his wife were their four-year-old son Archie and his brother Frankie, aged two. Charles Carroll of Windsor, N.S., was first mate and 18-year-old Edwin Anthony of Maitland, who had already spent five years at sea, was second mate. There were 17 hands before the mast, for the *Milton* was one of Nova Scotia's biggest and finest ships.

The voyage through the Atlantic, round the Horn and into the Pacific was as pleasant as any in Kate MacArthur's experience. With good weather and favorable winds it stretched into an endless succession of peaceful days.

On Dec. 22 the *Milton* was just north of the equator, having completed three quarters of her course. Lunch was over in the cabin when First Mate Carroll hurried in with the dread news that smoke was coming up the main hatch. The coal was on fire—and at sea there is no greater terror than fire.

MacArthur was in bed, crippled with rheumatism, "hardly able to move a finger." His wife had to help him dress, but he was soon on deck. He got the pumps working and organized a bucket brigade. All that afternoon and far into the night the crew fought the fire but the hold was a furnace under their feet. At 2 a.m. MacArthur gave the order to lower the three boats.

The weather was calm and there was time to get stores together. Into each boat went bedding and enough water, tinned goods and biscuits for 25 days. MacArthur took the ship's register, compass, and log for measuring distance, as well as his sextant and his chart of the North Pacific (which Kate MacArthur carried in the bosom of her dress). He also took the ship's red ensign, to be flown upside down as a distress signal, and Mrs. MacArthur took a chest of linen she had bought in Belfast.

The captain's boat was 24 feet long, 7½ feet wide and 3½ feet deep. She was fitted with two masts carrying spritsails and a jib. Into this roomy boat went Mrs. MacArthur and the two boys. She had no fear, or even nervousness, although she was soon to bear another child. The carpenter, Johansen, two foremast hands, Anderson and Annesitt, and the boatswain, George Ettinger, went with them.

First Mate Charles Carroll's boat had two spritsails but no jib. The boat of Edwin Anthony, the second mate, had only one spritsail but was long and narrow and went as fast as the others. By 3 a.m. the *Milton* was abandoned.

They rowed about a mile to windward of the ship–MacArthur feared an explosion of gas–and for the rest of the tropic night they watched the *Milton*, like a huge torch, lighting up leagues of ocean. At daylight the fire burst through the deck. The danger of an explosion past, they rowed back to the ship where MacArthur wanted to increase his stock of provisions. Carroll was ordered on board but could not get at the stores for the smoke and heat.

Throughout the whole of Dec. 23, and until the next morning, the boats stood by as the *Milton* burned to the water line. Kate MacArthur later explained the reluctance to part from a ship they could not save:

"She seemed company to us out there on the Pacific. She was a fine ship and we loved her as our home. It seemed such a pity to see her go to ruin right there before our eyes." Another reason for waiting was the chance of the fire attracting a passing vessel.

The *Milton* was a smoking, glowing hulk when the three boats started north for Cape St. Lucas, at the tip of Mexico's Baja California. The captain's boat was in the lead, and at night burned the *Milton*'s port (red) light astern. The second mate's boat followed, showing the starboard (green) light over the stern. The first mate's boat came third. Neither of the first two boats could be certain that the next astern was following and keeping station.

The starting point was not favorable. Cape St. Lucas was 1,200 miles due north, across both the equatorial current, which would carry them eastward, and the counter-equatorial current, pushing westward. After that there would be a long, disheartening beat against the northeast trade winds. Navigation of a small vessel with a simple rig means continual vigilance because conditions of sea, wind and weather vary from hour to hour. MacArthur had to determine a course that would take advantage of favorable winds, lose the minimum of time and cover the shortest distance possible. It was a problem for an experienced navigator. MacArthur solved it triumphantly.

On Christmas Eve, in the third boat, Carroll luffed up alongside Anthony in the second. He passed the usual good night, and a Merry Christmas, and dropped astern. "I supposed he was following," Anthony recalled later, "but when daylight broke on Christmas morning nothing could be seen of his boat. We cruised about all day but did not sight the boat again. He was a fine fellow and a good seaman but in a careless

Like a huge torch in the black tropic night.

moment must have held her in the trough and filled her or turned her over. The breeze was fresh and one had to be looking for combers all the time." [The boat was never seen again.]

The two remaining boats resumed the voyage. The weather was fine. An awning was rigged over the after part of the captain's boat so that Mrs. MacArthur and her children could have shelter and privacy. Often she would ask the captain to leave the awning aside so she could lie and watch the stars. She wondered if she would ever see the folk in Maitland again.

There was no suffering from cold, though all were frequently wet to the skin in rough weather. The morning sun drew thick white steam from the bedding and it soon rotted.

On the ninth day after the fire Anthony awoke to find he had lost sight of the captain's boat. "By inquiry from the seaman who steered the last trick, I found that he had not passed the captain's boat but had

allowed it to get out of sight dead ahead. There was nothing to do but crowd on sail and overhaul it if we could, which we did in a few hours as the captain had missed us and lay to for us to come up. He hailed me and asked me to come on his boat as he wanted to talk. I reluctantly went over and the steward stepped in my place. He was a Dane, an experienced seaman and navigator though one who had seen better days. When it came night the captain said, 'You can go on your boat in the morning, but stay with me tonight; my wife and the boys want to talk with you.' So I did, and when day broke there was no second boat in sight." The captain's boat looked all day for her missing consort and gave up only at dark.

On the 23rd day after the fire the men in the Danish steward's boat were picked up by the British ship *Cochin* and taken to San Francisco, bringing the first news of the disaster.

In Anthony, MacArthur had a good man to relieve him at the tiller, one who understood navigation and could take his place in case of accident or help in the event of other trouble.

On the morning of Jan. 4 MacArthur made a startling discovery. "The provisions and water were becoming scarce and from this day I put all hands on short allowance," he recorded. Behind this unemotional statement was the ugly fact that the hands were pilfering food and water in the night. Foreseeing the dangers of thirst, MacArthur had taken no salt provisions except one ham for each boat. Everything else was in tins. But the sailors would purloin a tin of tomatoes, for instance, pierce it with a nail, drink off the liquid, and replace it. When the time came to open the tin the contents had rotted. Henceforth the captain and Second Mate Anthony kept watch over their scanty stock by day and night.

MacArthur steered his boat ever northward. The bearded figure was badly sunburned now, his eyes bloodshot and painful from the dazzling brightness. Aloft flew the ensign, signalling distress. Under the rude awning were his wife and children, and forward the cowed and treacherous sailors. MacArthur kept his revolver at the ready.

The Pacific, a vast and empty ocean, was traversed at that time by few ships. Not until the morning of Jan. 16 did the castaways sight a sail. The vessel was six miles to the north and sailing eastward. The captain's boat was on the opposite tack. MacArthur came about in order to cross the stranger's track, but there was a rough sea and little wind. To help the boat along he put the men at the oars, and to strengthen and encourage them he gave them two gallons of water out of the scanty store. The captain had no doubt that they were seen and would be picked up, so he could afford to be lavish. He watched the sail try to come about, fail, then come round in the opposite direction as if she had seen the boat and was heading directly for it.

Then, at the critical moment, a squall blurred sky and sea. The stranger turned again with her head to the northwest and quickly disappeared. The castaways stood up and waved and shouted till their voices failed. MacArthur, with the chivalry of the sea, recorded his conviction that the stranger did not see the *Milton*'s boat.

It was a cruel disappointment. Weakened by the short allowance of food, worn out with pulling at the oars, the men "lost heart," as their captain wrote, "and gave up."

Not MacArthur. He was of the breed that fights on with the scabbard when the sword is broken.

On Jan. 18 the last drop of water was gone and the dreadful tortures of thirst began. Hunger is easier to bear than thirst. After three or four days of slow starvation, the feeling of hunger passes. The body falls back on its reserves, consuming first its fat, then its muscle. It wastes to skin and bone. Weakness comes on, and listlessness increases as strength fails. But thirst is agony, always intensifying, and culminating in madness.

Kate MacArthur later told a little of what she endured: "My tongue got thick and stuck out between my cracked lips, and I seemed burning for water. I used to get a little relief by binding my head and throat with cloths dipped in the sea, but still the thirst kept raging worse and worse."

She knew that to drink of the sunlit, sparkling brine—as the four sailors now were doing—was madness. Rain fell all around the horizon from time to time, but no shower blessed the baked lips of the castaways.

Memories thronged on the captain's wife:

"As I lay in the bottom of the boat with the little sufferers, and heard the swish of the sea against the side, the memory of every drink I had ever enjoyed came back to tantalize me. To look at all that water around us, so blue and clear and cool when we dipped our hands, it seemed very strange that we should be dying of thirst." Sleep brought no relief. One dream haunted her—of standing by a well of cold water and putting a cup to her lips. Her children were moaning for water. And there was no water.

MacArthur and Anthony, "after a great deal of trouble," made a condenser. It consisted of a covered tomato can in which sea water was boiled, and a tube fitted into the can and running through a second can of cold water, which condensed the steam. The tube and the fuel were problems.

Forty years later Anthony wrote: "That tube I remember well. It was made from a tin can cut in a long strip, as when you pare an apple round and round without breaking the peel; and spirally constructed, as you would wrap a strip of paper about an inch wide around a pencil, with a half-inch lap. The diameter of the tube was about one quarter or three eighths of an inch. This tube was wound with cloth and marlin [tarred cord]."

The cover of Mrs. MacArthur's metal trunk was torn off for a fireplace. For fuel MacArthur literally burned his boat under him. He whittled up all the oars but two. Then he attacked the planking, the gunwales and the thwarts. The central thwart was the only one spared. Every particle of wood that could be taken without weakening the boat was used to feed the fire. The condenser produced between a pint and a quart of water every 24 hours. Henceforth there was always fine, acrid hardwood smoke drifting to leeward.

"We used to sit and count the drops as the condensed water dripped into the tin," said the captain's wife. A mouthful of water in 24 hours barely held life in the body, but all shared alike.

One night Anthony was at the tiller when he saw one of the sailors worming his way aft on his stomach, evidently bent on securing food or causing trouble. Anthony touched the sleeping MacArthur with his foot. "He understood immediately," Anthony recalled later. "A club we had near for just such an emergency was used immediately and the sailor was stowed away unconscious in the bow. We also discovered that he had a very vicious-looking knife."

All through the voyage Kate MacArthur denied herself for her children, merely nibbling at her rations and giving what she could to the wailing boys. Soon there was nothing at all: the provisions so carefully shared and so insanely pilfered came to an end. On Jan. 28 a big flying fish rose out of the sea and fell into the boat. It was cooked and eaten, affording each a mouthful. That was the last food.

Death entered the boat on Feb. 2. The youngest was the first to go. Said the captain's wife: "My two-year-old baby Frankie lay moaning out of his parched mouth, and died in my lap of hunger and thirst. It was too much . . . too much."

The mother could not bear to have the wasted little body dropped into the sea. Sharks were dogging the boat. MacArthur sewed up his child's body in canvas and placed it in a tin box, to be taken ashore and given Christian burial. For her surviving child, to the end, the mother hoarded a morsel of hard biscuit, in case of an emergency.

On Feb. 5 Johansen the carpenter died.

Early next morning, 46 days after taking to the boats, MacArthur made his landfall near Cedros Island, nearly 500 miles up the Baja California coast from Cape St. Lucas. He had used the northeast trade winds to work west and north. Then, reaching the region of variable winds, he was able to make a much more advantageous slant for the coast. The boat had been held on course for 2,619 miles. The man who had risen from a sickbed to fight fire, who had endured the extremity of hunger, thirst and pain, who bore the whole weight of responsibility, was, at the end of the ordeal, the strongest man in the boat. Anthony was so weak as to be hardly fit for duty. The three remaining sailors, mere skin and bone, were lying helpless in the bottom.

290

Though land was in sight the castaways still had much to suffer from disappointment. The coast was bold and rocky. MacArthur headed the boat south in search of a harbor, but no landing could be effected.

Evening fell. Then, in the gathering dusk, MacArthur sighted a schooner about five miles to the east. He made every endeavor to reach the stranger, but the wind failed and he could not come up with her. The night closed down and the sail of hope was lost to view. For the second time rescue had seemed close at hand and, for the second time, it had vanished like a dream.

Kate MacArthur's brave heart failed her. She begged her husband to pull the plug from the bottom of the boat and end their agony. MacArthur answered, "We will wait a little longer."

Two hours passed. MacArthur lowered his sails and waited, pitching and tossing on the rough sea. His bloodshot eyes peered through the darkness for a glimpse of the vanished schooner. And then he made out the dim shape. In the two hours of waiting she had drawn much nearer to the boat. The wind dropped. Both craft were becalmed. MacArthur set his living skeletons rowing toward the schooner.

For a whole hour they toiled, at the same time shouting to attract the attention of the schooner's crew. The last remnants of their strength went into these frantic efforts.

No answering hail came from the schooner until the boat was within a length of her. Then someone shouted in Spanish, and MacArthur replied, "I have lost my ship and have been cast away for 46 days in the boat. We are perishing for water and food."

The schooner captain flung a line by which the boat was hauled alongside. Then, suddenly, he slacked off the line, dropping the boat some 40 feet astern. The breeze freshened, the schooner's sails filled, and she began to tow the boat in her wake.

Next, without a word of warning, the line was cut and a gun was fired from the schooner, which forged ahead while the boat drifted rapidly astern.

These seemed the acts of madmen. Hope of rescue died again. A whole hour passed. It was now near midnight.

Then occurred another strange incident in this nightmare experience. Two men in a skiff rowed alongside. They had come back from the schooner with a small cask of water which they passed into the boat. They could give no explanation, speaking only Spanish, but their intentions were evidently friendly. Mrs. MacArthur and her little boy got into the skiff and then, to her consternation, the men rowed away with them into the darkness.

Soon the skiff reached the schooner and the two passengers were taken on board. The captain gave Mrs. MacArthur a little wine to restore her. Speaking Spanish, she made him understand, more by tears perhaps than words, that she wanted to be taken back to her husband.

The captain hesitated. He talked with his men, and Mrs. MacArthur caught the drift of what they were saying. They knew that pirates were lurking around Cedros Island, whither they were bound, and when the castaways' boat appeared from nowhere, hailing them frantically in the darkness, they thought they had to deal with a gang of cutthroats attempting to seize their vessel.

Mrs. MacArthur's Spanish was sufficient to make the captain understand the true situation. The mysterious boat was manned not by pirates but by shipwrecked sailors at the point of death. As soon as he understood, he sent the skiff off again. It made fast to the boat and towed it back to the schooner, where all the castaways were taken on board. The vessel was the *Thor*, captained by Christobal Sosa, with a Mexican crew, bound up the coast for a cargo of dyestuffs.

Worn out by his long vigil, his privations and suffering, MacArthur sat on the deck of the *Thor* and leaned against the cabin. For the first time since the alarm of fire on board the *Milton*, the burden of responsibility slipped from him, and he fell asleep.

He had warned his men against drinking freely of the water in their exhausted condition, but the one named Anderson, mad with thirst, crawled to the water cask, worried the bung out and drank his fill. He died the next day.

For three days the survivors remained on board the *Thor*. The kindness of the Mexicans made ample amends for their previous mistakes, but the poor fellows had little to share. There was nothing to eat but black bread. On Feb. 9 they were a few miles south of Cedros Island when they sighted the smoke of a steamer. MacArthur raised his ensign, upside down, and the steamer immediately changed course.

When she came within a mile, MacArthur placed his sick charges in the boat, and the crew of the *Thor* rowed them to the waiting steamer. She proved to be the American passenger vessel *Newbern*, in command of Capt. Thomas Huntington, coming from San Francisco and bound for the Gulf of California. It was the first time she had taken that particular route past Cedros Island. The survivors were taken on board and received every kindness. Annesitt and Ettinger could not rise from the bottom of the boat and had to be lifted on board. Ettinger died a few hours afterward.

One week later, as the *Newbern* entered the Mexican port of Guaymas, Kate MacArthur gave birth to her third son, who weighed only three pounds. He was named Newbern Huntington after the steamer and her captain, and eventually became a distinguished physician.

Captain MacArthur's eye trouble had been caused in part by the strain of taking sights with the sextant in a pitching, tossing boat. There was inflammation and great pain. He went to an oculist in San Francisco for the necessary operation. Refusing to take chloroform, he gripped the arms of the chair he sat in and endured the pain without wincing, while streams of blood and pus ran down his cheeks. When it was all over MacArthur asked about the fee.

The answer was, "Nothing, to a man like you."

Death on the Ice

One day in 1914 more than 120 seal hunters from the ship NEWFOUNDLAND *realized they were hopelessly lost on the ice in a savage blizzard. Bungling and misfortune had put them there: terrible suffering was to be their fate, and only stubborn courage kept some of them alive. This is the story of the great* NEWFOUNDLAND *sealing disaster.*

By CASSIE BROWN
with HAROLD HORWOOD

NATURE HAS NOT BEEN KIND to Newfoundland. Surrounded by the hostile North Atlantic and attacked by the frigid Arctic Current, the island rises gaunt and forbidding out of a cold, gray sea. No Gulf Stream warms its rugged coastline; few men can scratch a living from the shallow soil. For generations, Newfoundlanders have relied mostly on the sea.

Here Nature has been generous. The island's continental shelf, the Grand Banks, is the richest fishing ground in the world. After 1610, when the first permanent colony was established, settlers from the west of England, and from France, Scotland and Ireland, seafaring men all, trickled to the island, and settlements grew.

For a century these self-reliant people lived almost entirely in the south where St. John's was situated. Then, as the settlers spread north in the early 1700s, they discovered an additional resource. Seals! Millions of seals floating by the northern part of the island, lying on the edge of the ice field that was annually swept out to the Grand Banks.

In early March each year hundreds of thousands of young seals were born on the ice within a week. The settlers discovered that these fat young whitecoats were easy prey, since the parents usually didn't remain to defend their young. As the pups could not swim, they simply lay still while the men scrambled over the ice and dispatched them with a blow to the nose. It was not very "sporting"—clubbing fluffy white baby seals—but that thought had no place in the mind of a hungry man with a hungry family on shore.

By the 1850s as many as 13,000 Newfoundlanders went to the seal hunt, landing more than half a million pelts a year—in a season measured in weeks, not months. The merchants of St. John's grew wealthy and lived in mansions, sending their children to the best schools in England. But the children of the settlers hardly knew what schooling was. Boys of 10 were fishing in open boats with their fathers; at 14 they were men who knew they could expect hard, unceasing labor and bitter poverty to the end of their days. They would see little hard cash in their lifetimes, since they usually got in debt to the local merchant, who gave barely enough credit to feed and clothe a family during the winter.

As a consequence, the men actually looked forward to the seal hunt. They knew what they were heading for—a rough voyage, and long days of messy, bloody work on heaving, cracking ice—but they cheerfully volunteered, in fact competed, for berths on the ships going "to the ice." This was their best chance to earn money.

And so in the harsh winter of 1914 men left their outport homes and came flocking to St. John's, eager to join the seal hunt. To the townspeople they looked strange: poorly dressed in rough, worn clothing, with boots of rawhide or sealskin on their feet, gunnysacks over their shoulders and sculping knives belted around their middles. Before they sailed to the hunt there would be almost 4,000 of them.

The S.S. *Newfoundland* ground her way through the ice of St. John's Harbour on March 9. It was the old wooden steamer's 42nd year and her fourth under 29-year-old Capt. Westbury Kean.

Wes Kean was not exactly in love with his ship. To put it bluntly, she was a tub; ancient, underpowered, too long and narrow to manoeuvre safely in an ice field without danger of breaking in two. But he was a young man with a name still to make for himself, and he had had a good voyage in her the year before.

Wes had an additional incentive to make good: his father. Abram Kean, or Captain Abe as he was generally called, was the commodore of the sealing fleet, already a legend at 59, with an unequaled record for getting seals. His enemies accused him of intolerance, harshness and a ruthless lack of regard for human life, particularly the lives of common fishermen and sealers. But none of them cared to say this in his austere presence, and none could point to a career as successful as his.

Wes Kean stopped at Wesleyville, on the northeastern tip of Newfoundland, to take aboard the last of his crew. The men were divided into four watches, each under the command of an experienced sealer known as a master watch. Wes found "old hands" in Wesleyville apprehensive about the weather. That winter was already being called "the winter of storms," and almost every week there were reports of ships lost at sea.

The sealers, however, were optimistic. They always were. Every year, every sealer expected that *his* ship would find the "main patch," as the big herd was called. By 1914, of course, everyone knew that the great herds of the past were gone. In recent years the annual crop of whitecoats had averaged little more than 200,000. But everyone knew, too, that when a ship was "burned down in the fat"—stopped in the middle of the main herd—there was money to be made. Most set their sights on the "crew's share" of $148 that Captain Abe's men had made in 1910. They forgot that the average on his ships was only $51 a year.

The *Newfoundland* left Wesleyville on March 12. Regulations did

297

not allow the newer steel ships to depart until the 13th. Nevertheless, by 10 a.m. March 14 Wes could see his father's ship, the *Stephano*, approaching with the rest of the steel fleet strung out behind him. By noon both the *Stephano* and the *Florizel*, skippered by his elder brother Joe, had passed him.

Wes would have liked to exchange messages with the other ships, but the *Newfoundland* had no wireless. Believing it was not paying for itself, the owners had ordered it removed. Wes had talked about this with his father, and they had agreed on a signal.

"Westbury, me b'y," the Old Man had said, "kape as handy to me as ye can, an' when we reach the swiles [seals] I'll let ye know by raisin' the afterderrick." This sort of deal between members of the Kean family was not regarded as dishonorable, even though they were working for competing firms. But as Wes saw the *Stephano* disappearing to the northwest he thought ruefully that by the time he caught up with the fast icebreaker most of the seals would already be in her hold.

March 15 was the official day for the hunt to begin, but on St. Patrick's Day the steel ships were in such heavy ice that four of them, including the *Stephano*, had to use dynamite to free themselves. Finally, by March 20, all ships except the *Newfoundland* and two others were into the seals. That day the *Beothic* killed 5,000, the *Stephano* 6,000. But as the days went by there was still no sight of the main patch—and the *Newfoundland* was still stuck in the ice.

Wes was growing desperate. The season for whitecoats was three weeks at most. After that they took to the sea, and you could kiss good-bye to a paying voyage.

Finally, on March 27, the ice loosened enough to let the *Newfoundland* work northwest, and soon it was in a small patch of whitecoats. "Get 'em," Wes ordered.

In a few minutes the men had killed about 20 seals, all there were. The captain's patience could stand it no longer; he knew there were seals out there somewhere. Running the *Newfoundland* against the edge of the ice field, he ordered all four watches over the side. Heading northwest, they soon vanished among the peaks and pinnacles of rough ice. Before nightfall they returned, towing some 300 pelts. They were indeed getting close.

But on this day, far to the southwest, a killer storm was spawned. An enormous high-pressure area, centred near Bermuda, was feeding winds into the Gulf of Mexico, from which warm, humid air was sweeping north. At the same time a second high was pushing cold, dry air out over Manitoba and into the United States. A deep low developed between the two systems; a whirlpool of warm, moist air, slowly contracting upon itself, drawing water enough to deluge half a continent, rising and spreading.

The night of March 30 Wes Kean ate a gloomy supper. That morning he had at last sighted the ships skippered by his father and brother. And as luck had it, that afternoon the Old Man, spying to the northwest from the crow's-nest, had spotted seals. They lay in a swath at least half a mile wide, extending for miles to the north and south. The ice was alive with them; here was the main patch. True to his word, he hoisted the afterderrick to inform his son.

The news gave Wes Kean little comfort. The animals were too far away for the *Newfoundland*'s crew to work, and she had come to a dead stop in thick ice again. The chance of reaching the seals seemed small indeed.

After supper Wes retired to the cabin to think things over. Master Watch Thomas Dawson was there getting a mug-up before going on duty.

"Tom, if we can't get ahead tonight, the b'ys will have to walk to the *Stephano* tomorrow."

Dawson nodded. It was no earthshaking news. Many of them had walked greater distances over the ice in their time.

"Father will tell ye where to go when ye get there," Wes continued. "If there be lots o' swiles ye'll be killin' all day an' it'll be too far fer ye to come back. So two watches will go aboard the *Stephano* an' two will go aboard the *Florizel* fer the night."

"Sounds all right, Cap'n." Dawson knew that Abe and Joe Kean would accept the *Newfoundland*'s men without a murmur.

The sun rose in a blood-red sky. It was the last day of March and the air was soft with spring. Five or six miles northwest of the jammed *Newfoundland* whitecoats were bawling, and by 5 a.m. the *Florizel, Bonaventure* and *Stephano* had men on the ice.

Reviewing his plan of the night before, Wes wondered about the younger master watches. How well could they co-operate at such a distance from the ship? If only George Tuff was in charge of the hunt.

Though he was only 32, Tuff had 17 years' experience as a sealer. But now, as second hand, he was in charge of the ship's operation and did not have to go on the ice with the men.

Tuff had his eye glued to the spyglass, trained on the ships to the northwest. The ice between them, he noted, was swarming with men, a sure sign that they were into a big patch of seals.

"No trouble to walk to 'em, Cap'n," Tuff said. "I've walked farther than that many a time."

"Ye mean ye'd go an' lead the men?"

"Gladly, Cap'n."

Wes breathed a sigh of relief. "Make straight fer the *Stephano*, George," he said. "From there ye'll be able to find out exactly where the swiles are. Father will send ye to 'em. I can't give ye any orders as to what ye'll do when ye get there. I'll leave it all to ye." Then he cautioned, "In case ye get into the swiles for any length o' time, ye reckon on the *Stephano* fer the night."

A few old hands squinted up at the veiled sun and noted with distaste twin reflections, like minor suns, one on either side of it. "Sun hounds," remarked Ice Master Stephen Jordan. "Never boded no good, sun hounds." But most sealers had more important things to think about. The *Newfoundland*'s wooden deck was beginning to steam in the sun, and some were removing heavy jackets and extra guernseys, and ducking below to tuck them into their bunks. Walking in this weather was going to be warm work.

Tuff, complete with snow goggles, led off. Soon the bustle and confusion died away as the men fell in, one behind the other, for their winding trek across the rough ice. Tuff was a careful man. He charted his course by a compass. He also ordered those men who had been working in the coal bunkers to rub their coal-blackened mittens on ice pinnacles to mark the trail.

The ice field was far from flat. Strong winds drove it tight to the land; when the pressure became too great, huge pans of ice buckled and reared out of the sea, forming "pressure ridges" like small mountain ranges. In between were ice floes that had "rafted"—piled up on each other in tiers. These were easier to negotiate, but still formidable. And, depending on the weather, there could be stretches where the men had to leap across open water from one pan to another.

Some of the young men, exhilarated at the prospect of action, climbed the pressure ridges, using their hooked gaffs like mountaineers' picks. It was so warm that some stripped to the waist. But the wind kept backing a little easterly, bringing a touch of rawness, making some of them uneasy.

"If the wind comes from the east, 'tis good fer neither man nor beast," someone quoted.

To 20-year-old Cecil Mouland, his cousin Ralph and several of their friends, the excursion seemed wonderfully exciting. They were to stay the night on the distant *Stephano*, the finest icebreaker in the world. To young men from a little cove in Notre Dame Bay the prospect was almost overwhelming.

Cecil Mouland, a cheerful lad and the leader of his informal group, was filled with love for the girl he had left behind—Jessie, a young school-teacher whom he had vowed to marry. He was also filled with good advice from his grandfather. "Cecil," the old gentleman had warned, "if ever ye gets caught out on the ice be sure to keep yer face in motion. Chaw on somethin' all the time, an' yer face will never frostburn."

Cecil had no intention of being caught out on the ice, of course, but he had no intention of returning to Jessie with parts of his face missing either, so he took his grandfather's advice and carried plugs of chewing tobacco.

Cecil and his friends were in the middle of the long line of more than 160 sealers snaking among the floes. It was the roughest ice they had ever seen, and all along the line heavy flagpoles, intended to mark batches of dead seals, were being surreptitiously dropped. Gaffs were kept, of course. No man could walk over such ice without his gaff.

By 10 a.m. the sealers were well strung out, with Tuff in the lead and a trail of blackened pinnacles and discarded flagpoles behind. The sky was now obscured by haze.

The uneasiness that had dogged some of them from the beginning now came out in the open. Ice Master Stephen Jordan remarked to his friend William Evans that he had seen the sun hounds and a dark cloud bank on the horizon at dawn. "Sun hounds never brought no good, an' the cloud bank says fer an easterly wind," he declared.

Evans agreed. "Let's go back to the ship," he suggested.

"Go back?" Jordan privately thought it a good idea, but he was an ice master, in charge of a small group of sealers, and somewhere ahead in the line he had a young brother and two nephews. "I don't know," he said dubiously.

But soon the idea of returning to the ship was being tossed around openly. The men had walked about four miles and were still miles from the *Stephano*, which was slowly moving off northwest. Chasing a retreating ship might take all day. Besides, there seemed to be no seals.

"What in hell are we doin' here?" they asked each other. Even the young men were beginning to lose their nerve, seeing their weather-wise elders so uneasy.

A Bonavista Bay fisherman, Tobias Cooper, was the first to turn around and head back for the *Newfoundland*. William Evans quickly joined him. Then Jordan made his decision. His brother and nephews would have to take their chances. He, too, turned his face toward the ship. He noted uneasily that she was enveloped in a dancing haze that played tricks on the eyes.

There were catcalls and shouts of "Cowards!" but before long 34 men had turned back.

At 10:40 a.m. Capt. Abram Kean on the *Stephano* saw that the *Newfoundland*'s crew was trying to reach him, and he ordered his ship to turn about. Shouting for the chief cook, he told him to prepare lunch for the men.

"We'll pick 'em up, give 'em some grub, an' take 'em back to that patch of swiles we left on our port side," he told his second hand.

Meanwhile, the storm was tearing across the centre of the Grand Banks, sucking in furious winds as it came. A few short flurries fell over St. John's, and then, with amazing suddenness, the city was wrapped in a raging blizzard. Over the ice field, 100 miles north of St. John's, the first flakes began to fall.

The *Stephano* didn't stop. Kean merely slowed her to a crawl to let the *Newfoundland*'s men grab the crude sticks that served as ladders. Agile as monkeys, the sealers swarmed up the side and over the railing. Captain Kean was in a hurry. Within minutes the *Stephano* had turned and was steaming west to get around a bulge of heavy ice. Deckhands were already directing the *Newfoundland*'s crew below to the holds.

In the captain's dining room George Tuff removed his snow goggles and greeted the captain. The two men got down to business while Tuff ate the meal put before him. He told the Old Man about the *Newfoundland*'s difficulties since leaving Wesleyville, and about the lamentable lack of seals. "Well," said the Old Man, "I left a little spot o' 1,400 or 1,500 swiles which ye can pan, an' I've instructed me second hand to steam out there while yer men are eatin'. We'll steam to where we struck a flag for a mark last evenin'. It'll be a fine guide for ye. Ye'll then be two miles nearer yer own ship than when I picked ye up, me son, and ye can get aboard yer own ship afore night."

This was totally unexpected. Go on board their own ship? Tuff had fully expected that he and his crew would remain on the *Stephano* for the night. But the Old Man apparently had other ideas, and Tuff knew well that subordinates did not oppose the Old Man's ideas. He said, "Well, sir, Cap'n Wes told me that 'e wouldn't give me any instructions, but I should come t'ye an' ye'd tell me all about the swiles an' where to go."

"An' I will, George."

Tuff followed Kean to the bridge. The ship had steamed around the bulge of heavy ice. It was still mild, though getting rawer, and the snow had thickened, limiting visibility. Tuff looked vainly for the *Newfoundland*. "Where's our ship, sir?" he asked.

The Old Man pointed. "There she is, George, due southeast."

Tuff still couldn't see her. Maybe it was because he'd been wearing goggles all morning, he thought.

The Old Man called to the second hand, Fred Yetman, in the crow's-nest, "Fred, can ye see the flag we left here yesterday?"

Yetman called back, "There 'tis, Cap'n, jest a little on our port bow."

Still visible through the snow, a flag of the *Stephano* fluttered in the breeze. But Captain Kean and his second hand were unaware that it was a second flag, planted that morning and never recovered. Kean was taking the men almost a mile farther west than he thought.

"All hands out," George shouted, and went to the deck, hurrying his men over the side. He was one of the first on the ice. The men went willingly, confident that Tuff had made arrangements for their welfare. All were looking forward to returning to spend a night on the big, beautiful *Stephano*.

Tuff noted with growing apprehension the thickening snow. He called up to the Old Man, "It looks fer weather, sir."

The Old Man shouted back, "My glass don't show fer weather, George. Now ye go southwest a couple o' miles, track me carcasses, and ye'll find about 1,400 swiles. Kill 'em an' go on board yer own ship."

The sealers heard these orders with great uneasiness. They murmured among themselves, "We'll never see the *Newfoundland* this night." But no one raised his voice against the all-powerful Captain Kean. Some 130 of them watched the stern of the *Stephano* disappear in the swirling snow. Bewildered, they crowded around Tuff, and a fierce argument ensued, many of the men insisting that they return to the *Newfoundland* at once. "If we got to walk aboard," said one, "there's no time to kill swiles."

But Tuff's orders from his own captain were clear: get instructions from Abram Kean and follow them, and this was what he intended to do. There were five hours of daylight left; the men had been brought two miles closer to their ship, or so they believed; they should have time to kill seals and return to the *Newfoundland* before nightfall.

The sealers fell into line with much muttering and discontent, and in less than a mile they came upon the whitecoats. Tuff had expected to walk another mile at least. Surely this didn't mean they had mistakenly been dropped off a mile too far west—a mile farther from the *Newfoundland?* Surely not. Tuff dismissed the idea.

"We're on the swiles, b'ys," he shouted. "Kill 'em and stick some flags!"

There was, however, no great number of seals, so Tuff continued southwest for 100 yards or so until he came upon another patch of animals. But it was a very small patch, and Tuff halted indecisively. The wind was beginning to gust and the snow was thickening—the earmarks of a full-blown blizzard. He had closed his ears to the grumblings of the men, but now he began to come around. "We'll have to forget the swiles an' make fer our own ship," he concluded.

"It'll take us six hours to get back," one sealer growled.

"How're we goin' to find the *Newfoundland* now?" asked another.

Tuff explained. Captain Abe had said that their ship was southeast from where he had dropped them. They had now come less than a mile southwest. Travelling southeast by east, they should intersect their own path of that morning within a mile or so of the *Newfoundland.* It was as simple as that.

Tuff turned to Master Watch Thomas Dawson. "Ye lead, Dawson. I'm goin' to stay with the hinder men in case they drop too far behind."

It was getting rougher, and the snow was beginning to drift, as the last of the great column of men moved ahead. In spite of the storm the men were cheerful; it was still mild and perhaps the snow would turn to rain. The time was approximately 12:45 p.m.

They walked for nearly two hours, and suddenly it was not just snowing and blowing: it was a savage blizzard, roaring out of the southeast. Finally, above the noise of the storm, a cry came back from Dawson: "Here's the path!"

Among the *Newfoundland*'s men there was jubilation. Now all they had to do was retrace their steps! Soon they would be on board, gulping kettles of hot tea. The *Newfoundland*, they believed, was only a mile or so away. With perhaps two hours of daylight remaining, and a well marked path, their task would be easy even in the blizzard.

But they had walked only a few hundred yards when they received a nasty shock. Beside the path was a crimson flag with the number 198.

The flag belonged to the *Stephano*—and they all remembered having passed it that morning when they were a good four miles from the *Newfoundland*.

"Lard Jesus! Ye sartin 'tis the same one?"

"Yah! 'Tis the same number."

"We won't be gettin' aboard accordin' to *that*!"

There was really great alarm now. They were dog tired, lashed by a blizzard, and had at least four hours to go over some of the worst ice in the world. If the *Stephano* had actually brought them a couple of miles nearer their ship, she would have brought them to this point, even a mile or so south of it.

Could Abe Kean have taken them to the wrong flag? Tuff's suspi-

cions, first aroused when the patch of seals had appeared earlier than the Old Man had predicted, were confirmed. "Well, b'ys," he said grimly, "it looks like Cap'n Kean took us farther west than 'e thought 'e did. No use frettin' about it now. We're on the path at any rate."

No one, apparently, thought of staying there for the night, even though they had seal pelts that they could burn, carcasses nearby that they could eat, ice cakes and wet snow to build a shelter. They started for the *Newfoundland* without a murmur, even though they knew they could not reach her before dark.

In the small Salvation Army school at Doting Cove, far to the north of St. John's, Cecil Mouland's bride-to-be was teaching. The snow had been heavy since noon, and around three o'clock a sudden gust of wind struck the door, driving it open with a crash that startled the whole class. Jessie, with a shiver, hurried to close it, and just then Cecil's cheerful face seemed to come before her eyes. She tried to go back to her duties but the face of her husband-to-be kept haunting her, filling her with alarm.

The *Florizel* and *Stephano* had continued sealing into the afternoon. But as the weather worsened, they began to pick up their own men and each other's.

It was late afternoon before the ships met to exchange crews. Joe Kean, on the *Florizel*, hailed his father. "What about the *Newfoundland*'s crew?" he called through cupped hands.

Abe Kean raised his right hand and called back, "All right."

Joe accepted this assurance with relief. But below decks on the *Stephano*, crew members were not so confident. At 5 p.m. Master Watch Garland Gaulton went to the bridge and put the question that was worrying everyone except Abram Kean.

"We heard, sir, that the *Newfoundland*'s crew was aboard us today while we was on the ice. D'ye think they got back to their own ship?"

"I do," the Old Man answered with authority. "Most decidedly."

On the *Newfoundland* the wind shrieked through the rigging, and the timbers groaned in the ice. The 34 sealers who had turned back had reached the ship without incident, to be angrily dressed down by Wes Kean. Later, in the hold, the depleted crew huddled around a tea kettle and discussed the companions they had deserted.

"The cap'n said they got on board the *Stephano*," someone said.

"Yah! So 'e said," muttered Stephen Jordan. "But I've got a feelin' they're out on the ice, an' me brother an' nephews with 'em."

Boatswain John Tizzard was also uneasy. In the late afternoon he went to the cabin. "It's wonderful starmy, Cap'n," he said. "Can't see a hand afore yer face. Will I blow the whistle?"

"There's not much need fer the whistle," Wes decided. "All our men are aboard the *Stephano*. But ye can give it a blow or two if ye like."

Tizzard interpreted Wes literally. He gave the whistle two blows, several minutes apart.

Wind and currents now began to play havoc with the ice. The smaller pans started to wheel and circulate, moving the sealers' trail and making it hard to follow. The heavy snow was too wet to drift much, but in places it lay knee deep and it was exhausting to walk through.

At the rear of the column an inexperienced sealer, William Pear, began to fall behind, and finally he sank to the snow. Tuff ordered a halt and helped Pear to catch up. But no sooner had they started again than Pear began to drag once more. With appalling swiftness the daylight was fading. Tuff called another halt.

"Two or three volunteers stay with me and the sick man," he said. "The rest of ye will go on to the *Newfoundland* for help. We'll need a stretcher."

Sidney Jones, one of the master watches, took charge of the main party bound for the ship. But it was impossible to make any speed. They couldn't see. More and more often they were off the path.

Under their weight small pans dipped, and many feet felt the ominous trickle of icy sea water in leather boots. One of Cecil Mouland's young friends fell in up to the waist. His cry of fright roused Cecil from a trance, and he and another man hauled the boy up on a pan. He was soaked. Shivering with cold and shock, he staggered a few steps and then gradually fell behind. Cecil did not realize until later that the boy was missing. He was never seen again.

The wind gusted heavily, increasing in force. Their faces ached from it. The air was growing cold; snow, not sticky any more, was drifting freely, obscuring the trail.

Suddenly, those up front were electrified by the sound of a ship's whistle. "Shout, men!" Jones ordered. "Shout as loud as ye can!"

All cupped their hands and hollered together into the storm, "Hoy-y-y-y! *Newfoundland*!"

Only the wail of the wind came back to them.

They slogged on, straining their ears, expecting every minute to see the black shape of the ship looming through the storm. A few minutes later the whistle blew again, somewhere to the southeast.

And suddenly they were in a trackless waste. All signs of the path were gone, obliterated by the snow. Knee deep in drifts, the men closed around Tuff, who had by now caught up to them. He said simply, "We're lost, men. It looks like a night on the ice."

Most of them took it gamely enough. They formed three groups on three large pans, within hailing distance of one another. "All hands set to and build shelters," was the order.

To build even simple shelters was a monumental chore for the exhausted men. It meant chopping at the ice hummocks with their gaffs until they had enough loose blocks to build a crude wall, then plastering the wall with snow until it would serve as a windbreak.

In Arthur Mouland's group (an older man, Arthur was no relation to Cecil) only a handful of men made half-hearted attempts to bring ice blocks to the place he indicated, and his voice crackled with annoyance.

"*All* hands will bring ice to build a wall," he snapped. Mouland drove them relentlessly, and after a long time they had a wall 30 feet long running across the pan. Mouland made them keep at it until it was a foot higher than their heads.

"All right," he said. "Now I want the ends turned in." The men grumbled but complied.

On the other pans, however, the men stopped when the walls were shoulder high; they refused to work any more. Little fires flickered and glowed as the men dug into their meagre rations—hardtack for most, rolled oats and raisins or a tin of molasses for a few.

The ice walls gave only partial shelter, and the weather was getting worse. The wind backed from the east to the north, whistling across the ice field and adding to the sealers' cold, damp misery. They clustered around the flickering fires made from their poles, trying to draw warmth from them. But little by little the fuel ran out and the fires died. The cold and all-enveloping darkness returned.

It was nearing midnight when the warm air generating all the fury of the storm finally condensed its moisture and torrential rain replaced the snow. Down it came, a cold cloudburst, soaking them to the skin.

The men huddled close for protection and warmth, but those by the shoulder-high walls couldn't keep even partially dry. Only Arthur Mouland's group had any real shelter. Their wall was snug and tight, but beneath their feet too the snow turned to slush that soaked through boots.

There was a stir in the crowd. "Get a move on, fellers. Gotta get exercise and kape warm."

There was pushing and prodding as they started shuffling round and round, so weary they barely realized they were moving, and each foot seeming to weigh a ton.

For more than an hour the rain beat down. Then, without warning, the wind chopped around to the north-northwest, the temperature dropped sharply, and the rain froze into pellets of sleet.

The wind chill was the equivalent of well below zero, and the sealers' sodden clothing turned to ice.

"*Move*! Kape movin'!" was the order, but many no longer had the vitality to stand. Ice crusted their clothing, their eyebrows, the stubble that bearded their faces; their mittened hands were unwieldy lumps that had lost all feeling. To keep on the move took teeth-gritting determination. It was much easier to let the numbness creep up one's limbs and into one's brain.

A veteran sealer, Jesse Collins, emerged as a leader. On his pan it was to him the younger men turned, rather than to Tuff. "Don't give up, fellers, kape on the move," Collins commanded. "Get yer jiggers ready."

They caught on. Everyone went through the motions of preparing lines and tackles. Jesse Collins next commanded them to throw their imaginary lines over the sides of their imaginary boats, then to haul in the lines, hand over hand. With great seriousness they obeyed.

"Catch anythin', fellers?"

"Naw, Jesse," they chorused.

"We'll kape tryin', then."

They went through the motions time and again. But it became wearying after a while, and Jesse roared above the biting wind, "Time to go on parade, b'ys."

They lined up single file and marched round and round the pan; not so fast as to sap their vitality, just a slow, shuffling movement to keep the blood circulating.

Numb and exhausted, young Cecil Mouland still remembered his grandfather's advice. He was obediently "chawing" his tobacco: it would never do to go home to Jessie with a frostburned face.

Men almost too exhausted to help themselves helped one another. They danced, boxed and wrestled; they coaxed, wheedled and rough-housed those who lay on the ice. Edward Tippett gathered his two sons to him and, with an arm protectively around each, did his best to shield them from the cold. But the first gray light revealed many still bodies. Edward Tippett was among them, his arms frozen around his sons' bodies, still huddled to him in death. They stood like a piece of sculpture planted solidly on the ice, the snow swirling past them.

With the lightening of day the men began to hobble over the pans in a hopeless search for better shelter. There could be no question of wandering in blinding snow to find their ship; to be alive and on their feet was miracle enough.

Most of the living owed their lives to Arthur Mouland and Jesse Collins. Dawson's overcrowded pan was like a morgue. White mounds littered it from end to end. From the mounds a boot, a hand, a leg extended grotesquely. Sometimes a sealer, kicking at a hummock to restore life to his feet, discovered to his horror that he was kicking a frozen body. The wind, frost and drifting snow wore away at the senses, numbed the spirit and dulled the mind. Hunger added to the misery.

But frightful as the situation was, some were kept alive by the certainty that the whole fleet was scouring the ice field for them. Hope burned brightly that at any moment a ship would come crunching through the floes. It was a dream, but it kept them going.

Jesse Collins was still at work keeping men on their feet. Cecil Mouland was still chewing tobacco, grimly determined to keep his face in motion. Since he couldn't reach into his pocket—it was frozen shut—he had stuffed the tobacco inside his mitt. When he felt the need for a fresh chew he worked the plug up the palm of his hand to his wrist, took a bite and let the plug fall back into the mitt again. His chief concern, besides staying alive, was his cousin Ralph.

"Cec, I gotta rest," Ralph mumbled, "jest fer five minutes."

But Cecil would not let him. Ralph's mother and dad would blame *him* if anything happened to Ralph. "Ye kape movin', b'y," he croaked.

The snow squalls finally stopped, but the bitter wind still blew fiercely and the drifting continued. Faces were now blistered with frostbite.

Finally, Ralph Mouland gave up and lay on the ice. "I can't stick it no longer, Cecil," he said.

Cecil clumsily hauled out one of his cakes of hardtack. "Eat some," he urged. Ralph hadn't the strength to bite into it. "I'll chew it fer ye," Cecil coaxed. He bit into the hardtack, chewed until it was sufficiently thawed, and transferred the softened morsel to his cousin's mouth. In this way he gave Ralph enough strength to stagger to his feet and carry on.

Once, in their shuffling around the pan, Cecil found himself face to face with Tuff. "Well, Skipper George, what d'ye think of all this?" he croaked. It was as close to an accusation as Cecil's nature allowed.

Tuff told Cecil, "B'y, I don't think there'll be a man left to tell the tale."

Jessie's face floated before Cecil's eyes. "Well, I'm not goin' to die," he said, and walked away dragging Ralph with him.

About midafternoon the skies cleared and the sun broke through so piercingly bright it hurt the men's eyes. With renewed hope Tuff searched the horizon, and his voice tore through the cold air: "We're saved! There's a steamer comin' fer us!"

Sure enough, a couple of miles to the northwest, looming through the drifting snow was a big steel ship, the *Bellaventure*. She was steaming at random, picking up scattered families of seals—but she was steaming directly for them.

With Jesse Collins, Tuff at once set out for the vessel. Arthur Mouland, whose pan was closest to the ship, had seen her too. He enlisted his cousin, Elias Mouland, and also headed for the *Bellaventure*.

By the time Tuff reached the Moulands' pan Arthur and Elias were well over a mile away approaching the ship, which seemed to have stopped.

They could even see a man on the bulwarks. But they ran into loose ice a quarter of a mile from the ship and had to halt. To get nearer they would have had to swim.

"We're handy enough to signal at any rate," Arthur said.

Elias had a flag of the *Newfoundland* wrapped around his neck. Arthur tied the flag to his gaff and waved it vigorously from the top of a high ice pinnacle. Elias, on another pinnacle, waved his arms. Both shouted, but the wind carried their voices away.

The *Bellaventure*, broadside to them, maddeningly close, was putting men on the ice over the far side. No one seemed to be looking in the direction of the two men trying frantically to attract attention. Soon the big ship turned her stern to them and steamed away. She left behind three sealers. They were less than a quarter-mile away across open water but they did not once look toward the Moulands.

Watching from Arthur Mouland's pan, Tuff realized for the first time that *nobody was looking for them*. Every soul of them might die before anyone knew they were missing!

Then, with all hope gone, Tuff finally saw the *Newfoundland*. She was about four miles away, still jammed in the ice. They had about two hours until dark. Resolutely, he set off once again with a small band of men. The wind knifed at them from behind, and the ice was rough.

Tuff, in a desperate hurry, misjudged his footing several times and slipped into the water. But by now a wetting seemed only an inconvenience.

They made two miles, and the sun was dying. Their chances of being seen from the ship were just about gone. "Never mind," Tuff said. "If the ship keeps her lights up we'll have no trouble reachin' her."

But suddenly the *Newfoundland*, belching heavy black smoke, began to steam away from them. The impossible had happened! After all this time jammed in the ice she had finally broken free, just as they needed her so desperately to stay where she was! No one would see the little cluster of figures two miles away on her port beam. Her course would not take her near the dead and dying sealers on the pans. It was the end. George Tuff sat down on the ice and put his head on his knees and wept.

The first night on the ice had been a nightmare. The second was torture. Men lost their reason, began seeing visions, heard voices. Some sank into mindless torpor, others went raving mad and died. A few stepped off their floating pans into the sea and disappeared forever.

Hunger and thirst increased their misery under the frosty moon. One man, desperately craving a warm drink, gashed his own hand with a sculping knife, sucked the blood, then lay on the ice to die.

The indomitable Jesse Collins seemed utterly spent. He had coaxed, pleaded with and forced less able men to live. Now he seemed to have nothing left with which to save himself. "We can't live through this night," he told a friend, then fell to his knees to make his peace with God. Others had prayed, died, and remained grotesque statues frozen in the posture of prayer. But Jesse was not one of them. He rose from the ice with renewed strength.

The will to live burned fiercely in those still staggering around. They reeled and weaved in a ghostly dance, ice encrusted caricatures of men.

Cecil Mouland had not stopped moving for two days and nights. Until this night he had kept the image of Jessie, his fiancée, continually in mind. Now he began to see other things. Once, before his unbelieving eyes, the *Newfoundland* was coming toward him soundlessly. "Come on, b'y, let's go fer her!" he shouted to Ralph. He came to his senses to see only the empty ice field around them. Much later, Cecil found himself and Ralph pounding on a door, pleading to be let in. The vision faded. He was pounding on an ice pinnacle.

The unspeakable cold did not relent, and the great majority of the survivors' minds were now hopelessly wandering. Men, claiming they were "turning in" to their bunks, lay down on the ice and died quietly. Some died singing. Some died walking, and their bodies froze in the middle of a step.

The night went on. It was one long dirge of keening wind and remorseless cold, and it was never going to end; it was hell, and they would go on forever living in it.

Daylight revealed a litter of dead men. Most of those still alive were unable to move under their own power. Some could see only a few yards. Many were blinded.

At dawn, still comparatively strong, Arthur Mouland could make out the *Stephano, Florizel, Bellaventure* and *Newfoundland.* Hard frost had cemented the ice pans together, and walking would be easier.

"I think the best thing is to travel to our own ship," he reported to Tuff. "She looks like she's froze in a pan of ice."

Tuff now had only limited vision but was still able to walk. These two and several other sealers gathered their last resources and prepared for the final march. Mouland picked the easiest path, working into open ice where they could be seen from the ship. But about a quarter of a mile from the *Newfoundland,* Tuff finally gave out. "I got to rest," he mumbled, and fell to the ice.

Mouland climbed an ice hillock up ahead. There was their ship. He waved and went on waving, but there was no answering signal. Then a slight movement caught his eye.

"There's a swile!" he called to Tuff. "Just one swile!"

"You've got a gaff, Arthur," croaked Tuff. "*Kill it!*"

Mouland stalked and killed the seal, and carried the heart and some strips of meat to the others. The starving men ate ravenously. "How are ye feelin' now, George?" asked Mouland.

"First rate, Arthur. I believe I can make it to the ship."

Tuff could still see no farther than his own feet. A man took either arm, and they continued toward the *Newfoundland.*

The *Newfoundland* was jammed again. As dawn lightened Wes Kean could see a handful of men on the *Stephano.* Where, in the name of God, were his men? Almost involuntarily, he swung his glass around the ice field. And there, to the southwest, it caught and held the small group of men being led by Master Watch Arthur Mouland.

Wes was paralyzed with shock. These men—the thought struck him like a physical blow—had been on the ice for *two days and two nights.*

"My God!" Wes Kean almost fell down in his haste to get to the

316

bridge. He went to the chart room and found a flag. It would not be enough. He needed a black ball—the international sign of distress—to hoist above the flag. His eye lit upon a coal bucket. It was black enough. Staggering to the flag halyards, he hoisted bucket and ensign together. Then he rushed off to look for Navigating Officer Charles Green. His voice was hysterical: "Green ... me men ... somethin' ... somethin' terrible has happened!"

Alerted, the crew began hurriedly picking up rescue gear—blankets, rum, food, kettles of hot tea, kindling. As they climbed over the side of the ship they were as pale as their captain, staring toward the reeling party on the ice.

Aboard the *Stephano* a deckhand informed Captain Abe that the *Newfoundland* was flying a distress signal.

"Send a couple of men across," Abe Kean said.

Two sealers hurried across the ice and were shortly within hailing distance.

"Is anything wrong?" they shouted.

"Are any of my men aboard you?" Wes called back. There was a dreadful pause.

"No, sir," they answered. "They was aboard Tuesday, but they left again 12 o'clock that day."

"My God! They're all lost," Wes wailed.

The men took off across the ice with their ill tidings.

The rescuers, meeting Arthur Mouland and Tuff and the others, were directed to those still out of sight. Stephen Jordan anxiously pushed his face close to that of Mouland: "What about the men from my family, Arthur?"

"All dead," Mouland told him bluntly.

As the survivors came aboard, Wes Kean turned to sealer John Hiscock. "John," he faltered, " 'tis a shockin' affair."

" 'Tis," Hiscock said grimly. "If ye'd blowed yer whistle, or if yer father hadn't ordered us off 'is ship, it never would have happened."

Wes, seeing the grim, accusing faces before him, cried out, "What has Father done?"

Meanwhile men from the *Bellaventure*, the nearest vessel, picked up other survivors. The appalled rescuers could hardly believe the scene that confronted them. Many a tough sealer wept as he hurried about his mission of mercy. Even as the sufferers were being fed some died.

Those not ministering to the living were ordered to pick up the dead. The bodies of the frozen sealers were stacked on the ice like the seals they had so often "panned," one on top of the other so the ship could pick them all up at once. Many had to be chipped loose.

Cecil Mouland and his cousin Ralph were still alive. Ralph, like most of the survivors, was a stretcher case. Cecil walked to the ship with the help of two men, but as he was being lifted aboard his vision began to go. Bright spots of color floated before his eyes and he had to be led inside. Someone placed two orange halves over his eyes. They stung fiercely and tears streamed down his face, but the home remedy worked and his vision returned quickly.

The *Bellaventure* finally reached the disaster area, steaming slowly into the middle of the pitiful shelters the men had erected. Her winches began lifting the frozen bodies aboard. They were laid out until they covered the forehold hatch, then a second and third layer were added. The living were in agony as their frozen limbs began to thaw. Capt. Robert Randall walked among them, mute with pity.

The *Stephano* and the *Florizel* also picked up scattered survivors and bodies.

It was a gray midmorning the next day when the *Stephano* reached the *Newfoundland* and Captain Abe climbed aboard. If father and son had much to say to each other, it was said in private. When the *Bellaventure* joined them about 11 a.m. the Old Man was even more stern-faced than usual. On board the *Bellaventure* he called the roll, ticking the names of those who answered, then counting the known number of dead. At the end he announced, "There's eight men missin'."

"Ye won't find 'em all, sir," a survivor volunteered. "A goodly few went foolish and walked into the sea. They're gone, sir."

The Old Man made some calculations. "We got 69 bodies and eight men are missin'. Ye wireless that information to St. John's," he directed.

Then the captains returned to their ships, and the *Stephano*'s watches were alerted to be ready to continue the seal hunt. The men had expected all ships to escort the *Bellaventure* to St. John's. Continue the seal hunt? What sort of man could give such orders?

Other ships also continued the disrupted hunt. But by the following Monday, the *Stephano* was having trouble. When Captain Abe ordered the men over the side, one of them, sealer Mark Sheppard, refused to go. Sparks flew from the Old Man's flinty blue eyes as he glared at Sheppard.

"I'll put ye on the log if ye're man enough to give me yer name,"

318

Survivors blamed Abram Kean and George Tuff (right) for the tragedy. Wes Kean (centre right) was captain of the NEWFOUNDLAND. *Lower right: Cecil Mouland.*

he roared. Being logged meant that a man would get no pay for the voyage, and would be blacklisted.

Sheppard stepped forward. "Ye'll find me man enough."

For the record, the Old Man put the formal question: "Why do ye refuse duty?"

"After what I seen o' this disaster through neglect o' yers," Sheppard replied, "I don't think ye're competent to look after me."

An enraged roar came from the Old Man. Never had anyone dared to stand up to him like this, or cast doubts on his ability.

"I wouldn't wonder, sir," Sheppard continued, "if yer career as a master isn't very nearly ruined."

The Seamen's Institute in St. John's, where the victims would be placed, was humming with activity on April 4 as undertakers arrived with wooden coffins. The sight of so many coffins, covered in black cloth, sent a shudder through the crowd that jammed the main street.

As dusk was falling the *Bellaventure,* her flag at half-mast, slipped quietly through the Narrows and eased to the wharf. Doctors, nurses and volunteers boarded the ship, and the severely injured survivors were brought off on stretchers. The rest walked to the Seamen's Institute for treatment, hearing sympathetic whispers as they limped along.

Then, one by one, the frozen dead emerged, limbs stiffly extended. They were taken to the Institute basement, where their frozen clothing was cut away and they were placed in hot water to thaw.

Simply and plainly, the survivors told their harrowing stories to the press. It was of little consequence to them that messages of sympathy, headed by one from the King and Queen, were pouring into the port. They had been to hell and back. And in all their stories one fact stood out—Abram Kean had put them on the ice, miles from their ship, at the onset of a bad storm.

On Monday, April 6, the St. John's *Evening Telegram* stated gravely: "The question arises whether Capt. Abram Kean is to be held morally responsible for the great loss of life among the men sent out by the *Newfoundland.* Was there an error of judgment by Captain Kean, who sent men away from his ship to join their own some miles away . . . ? What were his grounds for expecting moderate weather to continue long enough to permit these men to rejoin their ship . . . ? At the hour when these men left the *Stephano* the weather is said to have been threatening. Is that a fact? The investigation will decide it. . . ."

At the investigations—there were two—survivors laid blame squarely on Abe Kean's shoulders. And they blamed Tuff for not making arrangements with Kean to have them picked up.

Abe Kean's mood on the witness stand was one of righteous indignation. He insisted on testifying to courses and directions that were flatly contradicted by almost all other witnesses. He declared that his only error was one of compassion—taking the men of the *Newfoundland* aboard and feeding them. If he had ignored them, he said, they would have turned back of their own accord and reached their ship in good time.

320

Of the three commissioners who reported on the disaster, two decided that Abram Kean had made a "grave error of judgment" by putting the men on the ice at the beginning of a blizzard. The other commissioner disagreed, saying that the disaster was "an act of God."

The only result of any great consequence to come out of the inquiry was an amendment to the Sealing Law requiring all ships to carry wireless equipment. The "Permanent Marine Disaster Fund," another outgrowth of the catastrophe, paid crippled survivors and widows and orphans a trifling amount. Not a cent of damages or liability was assessed against the companies that had sent the men off without proper clothing, food, survival gear or signalling equipment for their ships.

Of the 55 survivors, most were more or less crippled for life. But many returned to sea, some even to the ice fields. George Tuff continued to go to the seal hunt for another 10 years until, as his wife expressed it, he "wore out like an old engine" and retired. Wes Kean became a successful ice skipper and steamship captain.

Cecil Mouland and Jessie were married in the autumn of 1915. As they cruised along the north shore of Bonavista Bay in a steamship, the people of every community they passed turned out to welcome them with gunfire, for their love story and Cecil's heroism on the ice were known everywhere along the coast.

Many of the *Stephano*'s crew refused to sail with Captain Abe again, but it did not hurt the Old Man's career. For 20 years after the disaster he continued to hunt seals, and in 1934 was made a member of the Order of the British Empire for having killed a million—more than any other man in history.

The *St. Roch*
and the Northwest Passage

*She was a clumsy, round-bottomed but robust
104-foot wooden schooner that bucked and heaved
like a bronco—the most uncomfortable ship he
had ever known. He was an RCMP sergeant,
a quiet and modest man with deep affection
for the North and its people, a veteran
seaman-policeman with a sound knowledge of
ice and what it could do—and what could be
done about it. Together the* ST. ROCH *and
Henry Larsen were to make history, writing
final chapters in the story of the long search for the
Northwest Passage, a quest that went back to
Sir Martin Frobisher's first voyage in 1576.
First to sail the passage had been the Norwegian
Roald Amundsen, who went from east to west
in the* GJOA *in 1906-09. Now, in 1940, with
Sergeant Larsen her skipper, the* ST. ROCH *would
attempt a passage from west to east.*

By HENRY A. LARSEN

I T WAS MY GREAT MOMENT. Ever since joining the *St. Roch* in 1928, the year she was built for the RCMP, I had looked forward to getting away from the familiar western Arctic coast. I had spoken to Commissioner Sir James MacBrien about this when he visited the ship at Cambridge Bay in 1937. He reminded me that we were policemen not explorers, but he hoped I would get my wish.

It was imperative that we get under way no later than June. The naval dockyard at Esquimalt was working to capacity because of the war, and I had to pull strings to get the *St. Roch* ready. We bent new iron sheathing on the bow, making it very sharp. Now we would be able to split fairly heavy ice floes, which was something I had wished for ever since joining the ship.

We sailed from Vancouver on June 23. Only the engineer, Cpl. Jack Foster, and the first mate, Const. Fred Farrar, were informed of our destination: Halifax. Others in the eight-man crew were Albert "Frenchy" Chartrand, a veteran of 16 years with the RCMP, most of them in the North; and two newcomers, Pat Hunt of Winnipeg, who became one of the best sailors I ever had with me, and Ed Hadley, our wireless operator. All eight were good fellows, and what some lacked in experience they made up in enthusiasm.

We sailed through Bering Strait into the Arctic Ocean, then east across the Beaufort Sea to Coppermine—where we took on seven powerful husky dogs for the sled patrols and census-taking that were part of our assignment. We got as far as Cambridge Bay, at the south end of Victoria Island, without a hitch. But by then it was September and too late to attempt the Northwest Passage. We returned to Coppermine, acquired four more dogs, then sailed north and anchored in Walker Bay on the west coast of Victoria Island. We were soon locked in by ice but all that winter we patrolled the surrounding area.

We celebrated Christmas alone in the midst of a terrific storm. Christmas dinner consisted of ookpiks, Arctic owls which taste quite a bit like turkey.

On May 17 Chartrand and I went on the last patrol of the winter, looking for anchorages we might use if we sailed up Prince of Wales Strait between Banks and Victoria islands. We camped at the Princess Royal Islands, setting up our tent in the dark in a heavy fog. I woke in brilliant sunshine and spotted a seal weighing at least half a ton sleeping on the ice. We needed meat, so I woke Chartrand, dressed quickly and we stalked and shot the animal. I was set to run up to it when I realized there was blue water rushing under the crust of snow I was stand-ing on. We had pitched our tent on snow that was honeycombed with running water. We moved it in a hurry.

Now I didn't dare retrieve the seal without a safety line, so I tied one end of a long line to the dog team and the other to myself. Crawling on my stomach, not even noticing that I was soaked to the skin, I got within a few feet of the seal. The line was too short. I took off my heavy leather belt and fastened one end to the line and the other to slits I cut in the heavy lips of the seal. With a jump I straddled the seal and shouted to Chartrand to pull away.

A sharp flick of his whip and a mighty shout of "Mush!" sent the dogs off with the heavy seal sliding easily across the ice. The meat was most welcome and the liver was delicious. Perhaps the meal tasted even better for the two of us knowing we had been so close to losing our lives on the weak ice.

That spring of 1941, close as we were to the Northwest Passage, we were ordered back to Tuktoyaktuk, at the mouth of the Mackenzie River, and from there to move supplies to various RCMP posts. With the war there was an acute shortage of transport.

The only way to moor a ship in the swift current at Tuktoyaktuk is quickly to fasten a stern line onto heavy chains dug into the shore. Chartrand and a couple of other men were put on the beach to grab the line. Chartrand, strong as a bull, ran into the water and dragged the heavy line up the beach before anybody could help him.

He had just fastened it when he collapsed, perspiration pouring from his face and hands. He recovered quickly, but sat up visibly shaken. I got him aboard and suggested he see a doctor who was expected shortly. But no: he feared the doctor might send him south. In a couple of days Chartrand was his old self and the incident was forgotten.

The weather was calm during June and July, so the ice failed to break up and drift away. When we reached Coppermine on our return from the supply trip we realized we had small chance of making the Northwest Passage that year either—certainly not through Viscount Mel-ville Sound north of Victoria Island. I decided to head east, south of Victoria Island, and through Queen Maud Gulf.

This was a familiar area and when we reached Gjoa Haven on the southeast coast of King William Island I felt new optimism that we would get to Halifax that year. But now we had to head north and after only a few miles we ran into snow, hail and a wall of ice. It was no place to get stuck, so we headed for shelter in Rae Strait and dropped anchor as close to shore as possible. We wondered if the curse of Niviassiaq had caught up with us.

Niviassiaq was an old Inuit hunter whose suicide near here I had investigated in 1937. His closest friend had built a fine sled, apparently from a spar from one of Sir John Franklin's ships which had been wrecked in the area nearly 100 years before. When the friend died Niviassiaq stole the sled from his grave. From then on he ran into bad luck. His hunting was poor and he became sick and depressed, finally hanging himself.

I had to exhume Niviassiaq's body so I could make my report. Shortly after, although it was April, a terrible storm broke. My guide was convinced that Niviassiaq had sent it because I had disturbed his sleep. The storm raged for three days and nights, and the temperature dropped to an abnormal −40°. People were surprised we made it back to camp. They too were convinced I had been cursed by Niviassiaq. And it is true that a year later, when I passed the grave on another patrol, almost all my dogs took sick and many of them died.

Finally the weather let up a little. With one man constantly sounding for shoals, we headed north into James Ross Strait. In the narrowest part of the strait the current was very strong, and ice started to surround us. I backtracked to shore and anchored by a rocky islet as a strong snowstorm came up from the northeast. Huge ice floes were crashing down on us, but with both anchors out and the 150-hp diesel engine running most of the night we managed to hang on.

Next morning the wind began driving the ice and us north. After another hard day and night some of the men favored returning to Gjoa Haven for the winter. This did not appeal to me, the weather being what it was, and I did not want to give up any of our hard-earned miles.

Heavy ice from the McClintock Channel now surrounded us and I headed for Pasley Bay, halfway up the Boothia Peninsula, for protection. But even there we were soon locked in drifting ice, dragging our anchors. The engine didn't help. The wind came up strong again, with driving snow. It was almost impossible to keep one's eyes open. The elements seemed bent on our destruction.

Around four on the morning of Sept. 6 the ice carried us toward a big shoal. The ship struck, then listed so far to port that the rail was under the ice. More ice was climbing over the starboard side, now high

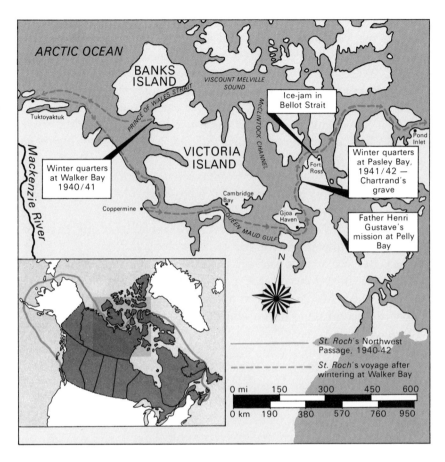

out of the water, and it looked as if the *St. Roch* was going to topple. Suddenly a larger floe came crashing through the darkness and hit the starboard side, making the ship list even more. She was practically on her beam-ends. But it was our luck that the pressure did not let up just then; it held us, as if by a miracle, until the ship was finally pushed upright and over the shoal. Moments later she floated on an even keel in deep water. Incredibly, the *St. Roch* was still in good shape, neither the rudder nor the engine being damaged in spite of the terrifying ice bombardment and the slide across the shoal.

But now the ice started pushing us toward shore, and only the floes between the ship and the shore kept us from being shoved up on land. Then we were carried backward, parallel to the shore and about 100 feet out. Our starboard anchor was out to the last link when I noticed a huge

327

boulder on the shore. Shouting to Chartrand, Hunt and Hadley to get down on the ice, I loosened the end of a cable reeled on our forward deck. The boys on the ice grabbed it and fastened it to the rock while the mate and I snubbed the other end at our bow. The wire tightened with a jerk, and the ship hung as though in a bridle between the anchor and the rock. The great floes now swung out and floated past us.

As if it suddenly conceded it could not push us ashore, the wind dropped. The floes became stationary, with new ice quickly binding them together.

Next morning the weather cleared. From a slope behind the ship we could see that our inlet was packed with heavy, blue polar ice. Here were our quarters for a second Arctic winter.

Although we were disappointed, and wondered if the curse of Niviassiaq was responsible for our recent ordeals and our being stuck in Pasley Bay, we at least knew that we had come too far to think of turning back. In October I made a dogsled trip up the coast of Boothia Peninsula. Heavy old ice had been pushed up along the shore and it was obvious that continuing north would certainly have meant the end of the *St. Roch*.

We got in touch by radio with the Hudson's Bay post at Fort Ross on the east side of Bellot Strait, some 150 miles away. Bill Heslop, the post manager, told us that the company ship *Nascopie* had been to Fort Ross and had encountered no problem with ice. Somehow we had the feeling that the master of the *Nascopie*, Capt. Thomas Smellie, an old hand in the eastern Arctic, thought we were real fools for not making it.

At the end of November we were joined by an Inuit guide named Ikualaaq, the same man who had shown me to Niviassiaq's grave in 1937. On Jan. 5, 1942, Chartrand, Ikualaaq and I took a trip to establish a food cache at Gjoa Haven for longer census patrols later. During the trip we passed near where Niviassiaq was buried. When we returned to our ship we busied ourselves with routine tasks.

Chartrand loved the sled dogs and always looked forward to cooking their food. This he did in a 10-gallon drum on deck.

On Feb. 13 he complained at breakfast of a slight headache, but then went on deck to light the stoves. When I joined him, however, he was far from well and complained of being chilly. I sent him below to rest but he soon felt better and joined the rest of the boys in the cabin. Suddenly he collapsed. Then once again he was on his feet, rolling a cigarette.

Less than five minutes later, Hunt shouted up to me, "Hurry, Skipper, Frenchy's dying!" Chartrand was flat on his back, his hands flailing around. He was unconscious. A moment later he died.

There was nothing any of us could have done and we were stunned. During my 14 years on the *St. Roch* we had been spared any form of human tragedy or even serious accident. I recalled how Chartrand had collapsed the previous summer at Tuktoyaktuk but it was impossible to say whether this had been the first warning of a heart condition.

He had been the only Roman Catholic in the crew and all the others shared my opinion that he should receive the last rites of the Church. The nearest priest, Father Henri Gustave, was more than 400 miles away at Pelly Bay in the Gulf of Boothia. We decided I would go and get him. In the meantime we made a coffin and stored it in a snowbank.

On Feb. 24 Hunt, Ikualaaq and I left with provisions for the dogs and ourselves for two months.

About mid-March we neared a large Inuit camp on Athol Island. We spotted a new igloo a little away from the others, and when we moved closer we could hear noises from inside. I got down on my hands and knees and crawled in through the long narrow tunnel, with Hunt and Ikualaaq on my heels. Then I heard a familiar hymn being sung in Inuit to the accompaniment of what sounded like an accordion. Pushing the door open, we found the igloo packed with people standing around a giant of a white man. He was dressed in a great pair of polar bear pants and a white Hudson's Bay parka. He was pumping away on a concertina, playing "Shall We Gather at the River?" We were witnessing an Anglican church service. I could almost hear the white man's jaw snap shut as the singing stopped. Both Hunt and I had long, bushy beards, and we were taken for Roman Catholic priests. Quickly we introduced ourselves as policemen, and the big man informed us that he was Canon John Turner, the Anglican missionary at Pond Inlet. He was on his annual tour of his enormous parish.

The service continued. Every hymn in the Inuits' books was sung, some up to 15 times. Members of the congregation were in heavy winter clothing and sweat poured down their faces. I stole a glance at my watch; it was 2 a.m. Canon Turner was visibly tiring. Suddenly the roof of the igloo fell in on us. We were in total blackness except for two flickering blubber lamps, and the crowd roared with laughter. The service was over and it was time for the feast that followed every Inuit service. The last guests left around five in the morning.

On the last day of March we reached Father Henri's mission. He lived in a stone house, about 16 by 24 feet, fitted together with clay he had dug himself. As he had no tea or coffee he offered us a glass of wine, but when the little keg was brought out it was frozen solid; after a while he had it thawed. We were tired after our long trip and one glass put us to sleep while the father was saying his Midnight Mass.

Next morning we woke after the morning service. As his Anglican counterpart had done, he was making breakfast for us. When we tried to apologize for sleeping through his service, the father just laughed that it seemed right we should sleep like good Protestants while he prayed for us.

We told him about Chartrand's death and he agreed to come to Pasley Bay in May. The seals would be on the ice then, so he and the Inuit he would take along could hunt for food on the way.

We had a strenuous trip back. I had a bad cold and Hunt caught the flu, so we were pretty weak when we reached Gjoa Haven. We waited there for a mail plane which was due in a few days, but once again old Niviassiaq made his presence felt. The plane crashed, burning all the mail and killing Paddy Gibson, the Hudson's Bay Company district inspector and a former member of the RCMP.

We returned to the *St. Roch* on May 6, having covered 1,200 miles in 71 days.

About two weeks later Father Henri arrived and on May 19 he conducted the Requiem Mass for Chartrand on the deck of the *St. Roch*. Then we buried our friend on a hill overlooking Pasley Bay and Father Henri blessed the grave.

During the summer, our third since leaving Vancouver, we built a cairn over the grave, on top of which we placed a cross and a brass nameplate. Chartrand always liked everything neat and orderly and I think this monument in his memory, not far from the North Magnetic Pole, would have pleased him.

Shortly after midnight Aug. 3 I noticed a faint movement in the ice. We quickly gathered dogs and equipment and took on board a young Inuit hunter and his 16-year-old bride who wanted to go to Fort Ross for an Anglican marriage ceremony.

We started the engine and heaved anchor. Very slowly we began to move along the shore between the big floes. Conditions were about perfect. From the mouth of Pasley Bay we worked our way about 15 miles north before the wind changed to northwest and heavy old floes stopped us completely. The ice shoved the ship from side to side. After two hours an alarming increase in pressure tipped her heavily to port, and she righted herself only to be lifted by the stern so sharply that her bow was level with the ice. A floe had been forced under the keel, the rudder was jammed hard over; the propeller hub, normally about eight feet under water, was exposed. Should rudder or propeller be damaged we would be in serious trouble.

We went over the side with gunpowder to break up the ice, and the blasting formed a cushion of broken pieces around the hull. Some of us got busy with axes and ice chisels to hack away chunks from the rudder and propeller. But the floe underneath us was solid as rock. Now it started to snow heavily.

The situation was so serious that I had the boats loosened in case the *St. Roch* should sink, and ordered each crew member to get spare food and clothing.

The wind increased and so did the pressure. A large floe split from the bow with a tremendous crash, and I thought the end had come. Instead, however, the *St. Roch* settled on an even keel and shot ahead three or four ship's lengths into a patch of open water. To our amazement she floated, apparently undamaged. There was no water in the bilges, the propeller turned when we started the engine, and the rudder worked normally. A weaker ship would never have survived!

But it was still impossible to advance. For over two weeks, often wrapped in fog and rain, we waited for a wind that would break up the ice and let us free. All this time currents carried us south into the area where Sir John Franklin had been trapped with his two ships, never to be released again. On Aug. 12 our diesel engine's Number One cylinder head cracked. Our power hadn't been too great with six cylinders; now we were reduced to five. We had spent over two years trying to get to Halifax and now the best part of the third summer was past.

On Aug. 20 there was a slight slackening in the ice. We started up and covered a mile. The next day we made a few more miles, taking advantage of every patch of water we saw. After two more days of heavy rain and fog a strong north wind came up. It increased to gale force during the night of Aug. 25 and I saw a black line in the white expanse ahead. The ice had split almost directly to the ship and by daylight the opening extended north as far as I could see.

Soon we were going ahead at our top speed of about five mph. It was like a miracle. The leading passage was not very wide but it was

At Halifax in July 1944, before the return voyage. Larsen is far right, front row.

almost clear of ice. By noon we had reached the end of the lead, right against the Tasmania Islands. After 23 days of struggle we were 60 miles north of Pasley Bay.

Finally, on the morning of Aug. 29, we could see small pools of blue water among the floes. We worked various small leads and gradually

conditions improved. By seven that night we were abreast the entrance to Bellot Strait.

It was like peering into a canyon. The 18-mile-long strait is only a mile wide, with high cliffs on both sides. There was no ice in sight, and the water was deep except for one spot halfway through. At the other end was Fort Ross with its Hudson's Bay post. Bellot Strait was a short cut I had not intended to take, but I fell for it.

We went in with the tide and the current, followed by ice floes. As we neared the halfway point we were on the verge of congratulating each other—but the ice gods, frost giants, or whoever were not through with us yet.

I sighted a solid white line across the water. A huge old floe was aground on the shallow spot, with thousands of tons of broken ice pressing against it. Behind us more ice was pouring in with the tide and current. We were being carried rapidly against a solid place and it was impossible to turn around. If we hit, it would be the end.

I rang full speed ahead and swung the ship toward loose, floating ice at the southern tip of the floe, where we crashed to a stop.

In no time we were gripped by ice under terrifying pressure. Tides from both ends of the strait were pushing against each other, and one could almost hear the timbers of the *St. Roch* groan.

I ordered all hands on deck. It was near dusk but there was light enough to see huge cakes of ice spinning in whirlpools produced by the clashing tides. In some whirlpools, lost and bewildered narwhals stood almost upright, their long spiralled horns waving in the air. It looked bad for the *St. Roch*, and I couldn't help admiring our two young Inuit passengers, who stood on the forward deck and sang hymns at the tops of their voices.

After 50 minutes, during which we could have been crushed like a matchbox, the piece of ice which held us broke under the pressure. The current started to run to the east and we moved with it.

The people from Fort Ross had been watching our ordeal from a hill, and as we approached the settlement they came out in boats to meet us. All of a sudden our troubles and hardships were forgotten, and we felt we were practically in Halifax.

At Pond Inlet we put ashore our spare arctic gear and our remaining dogs, who set up a frightful howl when they saw the ship leave without them. No sooner had we reached Davis Strait than a strong southeasterly gale came up and visibility dropped to zero. The sea was studded with fragments of broken icebergs. The smaller ones were almost submerged in the heavy swell, and now and then bobbed up like giant sea monsters. One dark night one of them knocked out a piece of our hardwood guardrail. Had it struck lower down it would have gone through the bottom of the ship.

A naval officer at Corner Brook, Nfld., ordered us to proceed south with a slow convoy. We left on Oct. 5, but even the slowest of the ships was too fast for the *St. Roch*. I set the sails and headed offshore, and with the help of the engine we made slow progress. Submarines had been reported in the vicinity but I doubted that any of them would waste a torpedo on us.

Three days later off Sydney, in Cape Breton, a young naval patrol officer stopped us for identification. I don't think he believed at first who we were or how we had arrived. The *St. Roch* certainly looked disreputable, with almost all the paint scraped off her sides, and our men in their nondescript clothing looked like anything but Mounted Policemen.

The next day we continued through the Bras d'Or Lakes, and at 3:30 p.m. Oct. 11 we arrived in Halifax—two years and 110 days after sailing from Vancouver.

It had not been an easy trip. The short Arctic summers from 1940 to 1942 had been the worst consecutive three I had experienced, and I never saw their like again. Most ships encountering the conditions we faced would have failed. Had we missed that single opportunity to get out of Pasley Bay, we would probably still be there, in small bits and pieces.

In 1944, following an extensive refit, the ST. ROCH—*still commanded by Henry Larsen—made the return voyage through Viscount Melville Sound, the more northerly, deepwater route, in 86 days. In 1950 she sailed under a new skipper from Esquimalt, B.C., to Halifax through the Panama Canal, becoming the first ship to circumnavigate North America. Larsen was promoted to the rank of inspector in 1944. He died in 1964. The* ST. ROCH, *fully restored as a national historic site, is on permanent display in Vancouver.*

War

and Warriors

*... a nation tempered by the fires of sacrifice
and hammered on the anvil of high adventure.*

Lord Byng, 1922

The Battle for Hudson Bay

*For years France and England had waged a bitter
struggle for the Hudson Bay fur trade.
By 1697 England was in full control. But five
French ships were assembled in Newfoundland
that spring to capture York Fort, a key post
on the west side of Hudson Bay where today stands
York Factory. Commanding the fleet was
Montreal-born Pierre Le Moyne d'Iberville—
soldier, seaman, privateer and fierce patriot.
This pugnacious 36-year-old adventurer, making
his fifth expedition into Hudson Bay, would
soon be heading into the most gallant action
of his career.*

By Nellis M. Crouse

THE FRENCH BASTION of Fort Royal, overlooking Placentia Bay on the west side of the Avalon Peninsula, clattered with activity as Iberville, having ravished many of England's colonies in Newfoundland, prepared for the assault on York Fort—2,300 miles away in Hudson Bay.

The fleet had arrived from France in mid-May under the command of Iberville's younger brother, Joseph Le Moyne de Serigny. Its passage had been difficult. Two ships had collided during a storm, suffering heavy damage. But now all five lay safely at anchor. Command had been transferred to Iberville.

The *Pélican, Profond, Palmier* and *Wesp* were frigates—fast, medium-sized warships with three square-rigged masts. The fifth ship was too damaged to make the voyage to Hudson Bay, so Iberville added a smaller, two-masted brigantine, the *Esquimaux.* While his crews made last-minute preparations, Iberville hoisted his flag in the 44-gun *Pélican,* the largest of the fleet.

On July 8, led by the *Pélican,* the ships set sail to a favoring breeze, rounded the Avalon Peninsula and cruised up the east coast. For two weeks they enjoyed a smooth passage. Then a northerly gale bore down on them, burying decks and riggings with ice. When the weather cleared they were off Hudson Strait.

On Aug. 3 they started through the strait, but heavy ice made it a treacherous passage. Caught between the *Palmier* and a gigantic ice floe, the tiny *Esquimaux* was crushed and quickly sank. Her crew were rescued and distributed among the remaining ships.

At the mouth of Hudson Bay, off Digges Island, ice held the ships for nearly three weeks. Finally an opening appeared. But scarcely were they under way again when dense fog spread over the water. Strong currents carried the other ships back into the strait, but Iberville steered the *Pélican* into a small ice-free bay. Three days later he set sail for York Fort, leaving the others to follow as best they could.

When the fog lifted on Aug. 25, the crew of the *Profond* saw three ships bearing down on them, British ensigns fluttering at their mastheads. Two ships belonged to the Hudson's Bay Company—the 32-gun *Royal Hudson's Bay* and the 36-gun *Dering*—and escorting them was H.M.S. *Hampshire,* a 46-gun man-of-war.

The British ships gave chase and the *Profond* headed for the ice. She carried nearly all the expedition's munitions and supplies and her captain preferred to lose her in the ice rather than surrender. The *Palmier* and *Wesp* crowded on all sail to come to the rescue, but a solid barrier of ice blocked them.

Next morning the *Profond* opened fire on the *Dering* and *Royal Hudson's Bay,* but the ice held her firm and she could bring only two guns to bear on her enemies. At day's end four of her crew were dead, 40 were wounded, and she had been hit so many times that the British headed for York Fort, thinking the French supply ship would surely sink.

Iberville had sailed 600 miles west across the bay. He anchored the *Pélican* below Marsh Point—the peninsula separating the mouths of the Nelson and Hayes rivers—and dispatched 26 men to search for Indians who could tell him about conditions at York Fort, nine miles upstream on the north bank of the Hayes.

At dawn Sept. 5 Iberville saw three ships tacking in. He raised anchor and set sail in their direction, but had scarcely cleared the point when he saw British ensigns. It was H.M.S. *Hampshire* and her consorts.

The *Pélican* had only 44 guns against 114 in the three British warships. With 26 men ashore and 40 down with scurvy, she had fewer than 150 men for active duty. But Iberville knew he must prevent the British from entering the Hayes River and saving the fort.

Every able man was assigned to a post. The decks were cleared, hammocks stowed, ammunition served out, and matches lighted for the guns. Iberville took his position on the quarterdeck as the enemy advanced in battle formation: the *Hampshire* followed by the *Dering* and the *Royal Hudson's Bay.*

As the *Pélican* bore down, the *Hampshire* slid out of range. Then the *Pélican* fired a broadside that carried away the tackle of the *Dering's* mainsail. Her next volley destroyed almost all the rigging on the *Royal Hudson's Bay.*

The *Hampshire* came about and delivered a volley of musketry that swept the *Pélican's* forecastle. Artillery shots hit the *Pélican* at the water line, carried away her spritsail and damaged her forward rigging.

For three hours the British ships hammered at her but the *Pélican* fought back. Stripped to the waist, her gunners served the cannon. Soldiers on the upper deck poured musket fire into any Englishman who showed his head above the bulwarks.

Capt. John Fletcher of the *Hampshire,* exasperated at his failure to get a decision, bore down on the *Pélican.* As the ships drew together Fletcher called on Iberville to strike his colors. Iberville refused. In admiration, Fletcher took a glass of wine, drank to Iberville's health and invited him to dine on board the *Hampshire* after the battle. Iberville returned the toast.

These amenities over, Fletcher loaded his guns with grapeshot and fired a broadside that tore away the *Pélican*'s rigging and strewed her upper deck with wounded men. Now the *Hampshire* could drop men on deck to overwhelm the *Pélican*'s crew.

But Iberville made one last effort. The *Pélican* turned and let loose a broadside into the *Hampshire*'s hull. Water poured into her hold and she quickly sank—probably not because of the one broadside, more likely because she hit a submerged reef. Whichever, the suddenness of their victory stunned the French.

The *Pélican* was in sad condition. The lower battery alone had 14 men wounded; seven cannon balls had pierced the hull at the water line; several others had passed through the ship. The foremast was drilled with musket balls for 10 or 12 feet above the deck.

But there was little time to contemplate the damage. The *Royal Hudson's Bay* was nearing the river mouth. Iberville gave chase and Capt. Nicholas Smithsend struck his colors at once, evidently terrified by what had happened to the *Hampshire*.

Iberville started in pursuit of the *Dering*, now retreating out of gunshot range. But the *Pélican* was hampered by a broken main yard and a hull that leaked faster than the pumps could empty it. Leaving the *Dering* to make her way to England, Iberville put about and brought the *Pélican* alongside the *Royal Hudson's Bay*.

Fifteen men were sent to the prize and temporary repairs were made to the *Pélican*. Iberville steered toward the *Hampshire*, hoping to rescue some of her crew. He found the ship grounded on a shoal but winds prevented him from lowering his boats.

At nightfall the northeast wind increased to a gale and snow swept over the bay. The temperature dropped below freezing and the *Pélican*'s rigging became encrusted with ice.

Next morning the gale continued as Iberville entered the mouth of the Hayes River. Here he found the 26 men he had put ashore. Their news: York Fort was held by only 35 Hudson's Bay Company employees.

A mortar and 50 bombs were transferred from the *Pélican* to the *Royal Hudson's Bay*, which was ordered to wait for the rest of the French fleet. Then Iberville rounded Marsh Point and beat to windward, hoping to anchor the *Pélican* offshore for the duration of the storm.

Iberville takes his position on the PÉLICAN'S *quarterdeck as the British advance.*

But the wind grew more violent and he anchored in shallow water off the south bank of the Nelson River—dangerously exposed to northeast winds that bore across Hudson Bay. At eight in the evening, the main anchor cable parted. Sail was made and the *Pélican* stood out to sea.

At 10 the *Pélican* lost her rudder and the rising tide dragged her relentlessly toward shore. Trying vainly to keep their footing, the crew hauled and belayed the ice-coated ropes. Below in the hold lay the wounded, many delirious, tossed by the rolling of the ship. In the light

343

of a few lanterns, officers made their way among the stricken men, attempting to quiet them with a confidence they did not feel.

At dawn Iberville sent a handful of men ashore to find a landing spot. When the water became shoal they leaped in up to their armpits. Their feet sank into the muddy bottom but at last they scrambled onto a snowbank. They warmed their half-frozen bodies around a fire, then returned to the *Pélican* with news that the others could land.

More boats were launched and a crude raft was constructed for the wounded, but so terrible was the short journey from the sinking ship that 18 men perished. The survivors moved to a more sheltered spot and spent the night around a huge fire.

Next day the French force—now about 100 men—marched four miles south across the peninsula and at the mouth of the Hayes River saw the *Profond, Palmier* and *Wesp* at anchor. The time had come to strike at York Fort.

After pitching camp Iberville dispatched a messenger to demand surrender. At the palisade gate the French emissary was blindfolded. He was solemnly led to a council of war, a meeting dominated by Captain Smithsend, who had escaped with 17 of his men from the *Royal Hudson's Bay*—she had been wrecked in the gale which sank the *Pélican*. Smithsend claimed Iberville and many of his men had been killed in the naval engagement. He said the attack on the fort was the last resort of desperate men; the demand for surrender was bluff.

When the messenger returned to camp, the French brought forward a mortar and concealed it among trees 200 paces from the fort. Scarcely had they finished when the British opened fire. The French spent the afternoon landing more supplies, including another mortar from the *Wesp*.

That night fires were lighted to draw the attention of the English while the French reconnoitred along the Hayes River. Now that reinforcements had arrived from the *Royal Hudson's Bay*, the fort was well manned and had two mortars, 34 cannon, seven small pieces and several swivel guns.

Next morning, after two or three volleys, the French summoned Gov. Henry Baley to surrender. He replied that he would rather have his post burned to the ground than haul down his flag. Iberville renewed his attack but Baley served his pieces with precision, though he had only the sounds of the camouflaged French mortars as targets.

At four in the afternoon a third summons promised that this would be the last opportunity to negotiate terms of capitulation; the French were planning an assault.

Governor Baley replied that he would give an answer in the evening. He had more artillery and was entrenched behind a stout palisade. But in an assault the great superiority of Iberville's manpower would be the deciding factor. The garrison were beginning to lose heart, and if Iberville took the place by assault he could dictate harsh terms.

Baley offered to surrender if he could retain all beaver pelts belonging to the Hudson's Bay Company. This request was refused; Iberville had his own expenses to meet.

The following day Baley decided to give up the fort if he was allowed to evacuate with the honors of war—a suggestion which, as it cost nothing, was promptly granted. The governor was to keep the company papers; officers and men were to keep personal property, and all were to be fed as well as the French and to be sent to England.

Baley marched out at one in the afternoon with drums beating, flags flying, muskets loaded, his men carrying their arms and possessions, and made his surrender.

Ice was forming in the river and Iberville now turned his attention to getting back to France. The *Palmier* was left with Serigny, his brother, who took command of the fort. The furs and miscellaneous plunder, and 300 sick and wounded men from both sides, were placed aboard the *Profond* and *Wesp*. French sailors from the *Pélican*, English sailors from the *Royal Hudson's Bay*, and men from the defeated garrison also crowded on board.

On the afternoon of Sept. 24 Iberville headed out to sea under a southwesterly breeze. His action off the Hayes River had placed him on a footing with the great naval captains of France. During Iberville's lifetime, York Fort and much of the Hudson Bay fur trade would remain in French hands.

The War of 1812 had barely begun when British troops
captured Fort Michilimackinac, a key post on
Mackinac Island in the strait between Lake Michigan
and Lake Huron. The Americans were determined to
recapture it, and in July 1814 five ships manned
by 800 soldiers and marines sailed from the southern
tip of Lake Huron, near present-day Sarnia.
Near Sault Ste. Marie they captured two British
ships—one the supply ship MINK from Michilimackinac.
As the Americans prepared to attack the fort, only one
British ship remained on the Upper Lakes.
She was the schooner NANCY—240 miles away in
Georgian Bay.

Lieutenant Worsley's Revenge

By C. H. J. SNIDER

THE AMERICANS LANDED for the attack on Aug. 4, 1814. Fort Michilimackinac's commander, Lt.Col. Robert McDouall, marched out to meet them with 100 men of the Royal Newfoundland Fencible Infantry, 50 militiamen and 350 Indians. He placed two field guns at the edge of a clearing in the thick woods, and when the Americans came within range he opened fire.

The enemy tried to outflank him, but the flankers were ambushed by a crowd of whooping Indians. Showing nothing but the smoke of their rifles, the Indians picked off man after man. The Americans tried to charge, but the elusive Indians were everywhere.

Finally the troops reached a height of land, only to find their position commanded by another ridge, where more artillery checked their advance. When several of their officers fell the Americans began to retreat. A field gun, dragged up from the landing place, failed to clear the woods

Alone on the Great Lakes—and 240 miles away.
Could the NANCY *save Michilimackinac?*

of the unseen Indian sharpshooters with their bloodcurdling war cries. The retreat became a rout. Fearing a massacre, the American commander, Lt.Col. George Croghan, embarked his terror-stricken troops as fast as they returned to the beach.

Not one of the fort's invisible defenders had been wounded; American losses were 22 killed and 44 wounded. Retreating through the woods, the Americans stumbled across the bodies of their own dead—and many had been scalped.

The Americans moved offshore to plot their next move.

"A bad business, colonel," said Capt. Arthur Sinclair, commodore of the American fleet. "We'll keep you near this island if you wish, but I fear you'll never take it. Mackinac is a very Gibraltar in front. And from the rear—well, no one can get by the Indians in those woods."

Silence descended on the council of war in the cabin of the brigantine *Niagara,* flagship of the fleet. She and her men were accustomed to winning. The year before she had led the fleet to victory at the Battle of Lake Erie, in which six British ships surrendered. But the defeat on Mackinac Island had shaken them.

Colonel Croghan spoke: "I felt sure the task was too heavy for us, but it would never do to go back to Detroit without making another try." His voice was heavy with dejection. Then, looking at the commodore, "What do you advise?"

"Gently does it," said Sinclair. "Starve 'em out."

"But we'll starve ourselves in the process," said Croghan. "We've no supplies nearer than Detroit—and you say your fleet cannot keep the lake with the autumn gales threatening."

"No, we can't," said Sinclair. "But listen. Here's the plan. Mackinac's cupboard is bare. They've been drying fish to help them through the winter. And they sent part of their provisions to Fort William [present-day Thunder Bay] in the *Mink.* We've that under hatches and there's only one way they can get more.

"The *Nancy* is the only British craft left in these waters. Before we attacked here, she sailed to load stores at the Nottawasaga [River, at the bottom of Georgian Bay]. Capture her and we'll have a fine prize—"

"That's all very well for you," interrupted Croghan, "but all I'll have to show will be the bodies of my men."

"No, listen," said the commodore. "With the *Nancy* captured, the British will starve to death on their rock or march away over the ice.

"Capture the *Nancy* and Mackinac falls as sure as the law of gravitation—and, with Mackinac in our grip, we can cut off the main fur trading route of the North West Company. What say you, sailing master?"

The *Niagara*'s sailing master, a wise old seaman, shook his head.

"Your plan's good, sir, but I doubt the *Nancy*'ll ever fly the Stars and Stripes. She's a wonderful lucky vessel, and the men in her are tigers."

"You know her?" asked the colonel.

"I saw her launched 25 years ago," said the old man. He told them the *Nancy* had been built in Detroit for the North West Company. Only the best white oak and red cedar had been used. Her figurehead was of a woman in full costume with hat and feathers.

"The lady's gear may be out of style now, but the *Nancy*'s sound as a nut. And her crew! I don't know much of Miller Worsley, the young Navy man in charge of her now, but her old sailing master, Alexander Mackintosh, fears neither man nor devil."

The old man recalled what had happened about a year before when the *Nancy* was on her way to Amherstburg [south of present-day Windsor] to take on supplies for Mackinac. Mackintosh—not knowing that the whole British fleet had been captured in the Battle of Lake Erie, and that the town had fallen into American hands—anchored the *Nancy* in the Detroit River, near Amherstburg. When an American raiding party opened fire from shore, Mackintosh raised anchor and tried to make sail. His crew took cover above decks and returned fire with muskets and light cannon. Mackintosh stayed at the helm as enemy fire splintered the wood around him. When the *Nancy*'s mainsail caught fire the crew doused the blaze with buckets of water.

The old man continued: "While they were passing Detroit that night the only light aboard was a fuse in the fist of Mackintosh. He stood by a powder keg at the mainmast and vowed he'd blow the *Nancy* to Kingdom Come before an American foot should touch her deck. *That's* the ship and crew you've got to catch."

"Well, Sinclair," said Colonel Croghan, "let's catch her."

"Aye, aye," said Sinclair. "Our course'll be straight for the Nottawasaga." He ordered the schooners *Scorpion* and *Tigress* to steer east with the *Niagara;* 350 soldiers and marines would remain with the expedition. The two other vessels were sent back to Detroit.

On Aug. 13 the three bloodhounds hove to off the pine-clad sandbanks at the mouth of the Nottawasaga. They lay far offshore, for the water was shallow. Lookouts at the mastheads searched the shore with spyglasses and reported nothing but some deserted wigwams at the river's mouth. "Perhaps the *Nancy* hasn't arrived," said Croghan. "Could we ease into the river and surprise her?"

"She's too wary for that," said Sinclair, "if all the sailing master says is true. But we'll have a closer look."

They sent their boats ashore. The wigwams had been occupied recently but there was no sign of a vessel. The patrol reported that the sand formed a high ridge where the river entered the bay, but two miles southwest the shore was lower, good camping ground.

A landing party went to prepare the campsite. Scouts crossed a small ridge, then stared in amazement. There, a few hundred yards behind the beach, was the river again, parallel to the shore. Among the pines, gilded by summer sunlight, were the topmasts of H.M.S. *Nancy*.

She had been towed up the winding stream and moored against the higher south bank. On the ridge above her was a blockhouse of fresh-hewn logs. The scouts could see 26 white men and 10 Indians strengthening their defences and hauling the *Nancy*'s two 24-pounders and one six-pounder into the fort. The scouts stole back unobserved—as they thought.

That night there was no camping on the beach for the ship-weary soldiers; at dawn the American vessels were moored opposite their foe behind a ridge of trees.

Sunrise was saluted with the thunder of the *Niagara*'s 10-gun broadside and the lesser concussions of the schooners' long guns. Prompt as an echo came the answering roar of three guns from the blockhouse, and for hours the treetops and sand ridge were torn by cannon balls.

The lively replies from the blockhouse proved that the defenders were suffering little damage, so the Americans landed soldiers, dragged artillery to the crest of the ridge, and opened a destructive fire on the schooner and blockhouse.

The spirited defence suddenly ceased. There was silence, then a deafening crash and a burst of flames as the British magazine blew up. American soldiers ran cheering down the ridge, followed by marines dragging a boat. They pushed across the river, but before they could board the *Nancy* she too was in flames, and small explosions frightened them away. She burned furiously, for her cargo contained wooden barrels of pork. The river suddenly swallowed her hissing hulk.

The attackers found the fort in ruins; a trail of scattered articles marked the flight of its defenders. The Americans would have followed, but rifle fire held them back. Among the litter was the desk of Lieut. Miller Worsley, commander of the *Nancy*. In it was a letter from Robert McDouall at Michilimackinac, warning of the American fleet and advising Worsley to conceal the *Nancy* and build a fort.

"With the *Nancy* out of the way," said Colonel Croghan, "McDouall will soon be starving, and Mackinac will be ours when we return in the spring."

There was still a chance the British might try to get provisions to Michilimackinac in bateaux so, before sailing for home in the *Niagara,* Sinclair ordered the *Scorpion* and the *Tigress* to blockade the river mouth until fall gales made it impossible to remain on the lake.

But Lieut. Daniel Turner of the *Scorpion* had better ways of passing the time. He knew that North West Company canoes were bringing furs down the north shore of Georgian Bay. [See *The Birchbark Brigades,* p. 70.] It began to blow so hard that the vessels had a good excuse for leaving the bleak wilderness around the Nottawasaga. Turner dispatched the *Tigress* to cruise for fur canoes off St. Joseph Island, below present-day Sault Ste. Marie, and followed in the *Scorpion*. Before leaving, he felled trees to blockade the river mouth.

At sunset on Aug. 31 a great birch bark canoe filled with a score of wild-looking warriors approached Mackinac. They were as red as copper from the sun. At the helm, in a tattered blue and white uniform with brass buttons and epaulettes, was a Royal Navy lieutenant.

"It's Worsley!" shouted McDouall, running to the beach. "Where's the *Nancy?*"

"In the Nottawasaga, colonel," said Worsley, "but she'll never leave there. They shelled us out—two schooners and a brig. We fought 'em for hours—three guns to two dozen—but their howitzers made it too hot for us. I blew up the blockhouse and the *Nancy*. We walked with our wounded and dying for 36 miles, up the Nottawasaga and Willow Creek. We arrived at Willow Depot with nothing but what we stood upright in."

At the depot [nine miles west of present-day Barrie], Worsley had found two bateaux and a canoe belonging to Robert Livingston, a fur trader and Indian agent. After delivering McDouall's warning to Worsley while the *Nancy* was loading supplies at the mouth of the Nottawasaga, Livingston had hurried to York [Toronto] and Fort Erie, and returned with 10 Indian reinforcements, just as the Americans appeared.

Worsley continued: "After two days at Willow Depot we loaded 67 barrels of flour and three barrels of pork and dropped down the Nottawasaga with the bateaux and the canoe. We lifted the trees the Americans had felled at the mouth, and passed into the bay. Then we rowed and rowed, with some help from the bateaux lugsails—north to Manitoulin Island and along the North Channel. We've been rowing and paddling day and night for a week—380 miles!"

"But where are the bateaux?" asked McDouall.

"Fifty miles back, safe with Livingston and the other men on a little island," said Worsley. "When we got near St. Joseph Island we sighted the very schooners that sank the *Nancy*. Indians told us the Americans were hunting for fur traders. The bateaux couldn't slip past so I hid them and came on with the canoe. We paddled within 100 yards of one of the schooners last night."

"Well, welcome, boy, welcome to what we've got," said the colonel. "You rest tonight, and tomorrow we'll send for those bateaux."

"Tomorrow," said Worsley, "I'm going for those schooners!"

Next day four large bateaux and some canoes left Mackinac carrying Worsley and his men, 57 soldiers of the Royal Newfoundland Fencibles, and a party of Indians. They reached the food-laden bateaux, then Worsley and Livingston set out in a light canoe. Before long, satisfied as to the whereabouts of one of the American vessels, they returned to the island rendezvous and planned their attack.

At midnight on Sept. 3 the schooner *Tigress* lay at anchor in False Detour Channel, her 31-man crew asleep on deck.

Four bateaux containing 78 men—seamen from the *Nancy*, soldiers and three Indian chiefs—noiselessly surrounded the schooner. Their rowlocks were padded and they slipped to within 10 yards of the ship before they were challenged.

Receiving no answer, the lookouts aboard the *Tigress* fired her 24-pounder swivel gun. Then over both sides swarmed the force from Mackinac.

The outnumbered defenders fought desperately. Amidships, one of the schooner's crew crammed the barrel of the swivel gun with a bag of slugs, and the flash of a pistol showed him about to pull the lanyard. Alexander Mackintosh, the *Nancy*'s old sailing master, sprang forward, whirling his cutlass, and beheaded the man.

The *Tigress'* commander was wounded, two other officers fell, and her seamen were driven into the hold, where they surrendered. Four dead Americans were found, and another three had been thrown overboard. Two British seamen had been killed.

Next morning, feeling much like a man who peruses his own obituary, Worsley read the entries in the log of the *Tigress* telling of the *Nancy*'s destruction.

"Last night," he said to Livingston, "there was not a masthead left to fly the British flag on the Upper Lakes. This morning we're as strong as we were before the *Nancy* was lost. Surely we can balance the account completely."

"Then don't be in too great haste to see the good flag flying," said Livingston.

Worsley looked at him, then at the American pennant which still streamed aloft. "I understand!" he said. "The *Scorpion* can't have heard the firing."

Livingston laughed, then put off in his canoe and in two hours returned with news that the other schooner was heading slowly toward the *Tigress*.

No time was lost. The four bateaux, loaded with the captives and a strong guard, were started for Mackinac; and all day the *Tigress'* pennant waved a fatal welcome in the light breeze while her anchor gripped the bottom.

Next evening the *Scorpion* slowly rounded the last intervening headland. The wind failed altogether at sunset and she let go her anchor two miles from the *Tigress*.

"Smarter than this one, and heavier in metal," said Worsley. "At the Nottawasaga she was throwing 12-pound and 24-pound balls. We'll have to take her by boarding. I'm glad she didn't try to exchange messages."

At dawn the American ship's unsuspecting gunner and six-man watch were washing down the decks when they noticed the *Tigress* hoist jib and foresail and stand toward the *Scorpion*.

"Pass the word below," the gunner called to the boatswain.

"The old man says it's about time," said the boatswain, emerging from the cabin.

"Look at them in their greatcoats while we shiver around in our bare feet," complained one of the deck swabbers as a dozen muffled figures showed at the *Tigress'* rail.

"Look out, you lubber!" called the gunner. "You'll foul us!"

CONFIANCE *and* SURPRISE *(ex-*SCORPION *and* TIGRESS*) beating up for Mackinac.*

Suddenly the *Tigress,* only a dozen yards away, turned into the wind, fired her swivel gun full at the *Scorpion*'s hull, and ranged alongside. Fifty fighting men poured up through her hatches and came leaping over the *Scorpion*'s bulwarks as the two vessels touched. Two deck swabbers were killed and four wounded by the first volley from the boarders' muskets; and the 30 men who formed the balance of the *Scorpion*'s crew were penned below decks with her commander.

The ship was a much easier prize than the *Tigress* had been: only two attackers were wounded. And aboard her were many articles plundered in raids on British buildings and vessels—including goods from Livingston's wharf and stores at St. Joseph Island.

On both vessels now the Stars and Stripes came down—and rose again under the Union Jack. In the first winds of September the *Tigress* and *Scorpion* came thrashing home to Mackinac, the gladdest sight Robert McDouall had seen for many a day.

The *Tigress* became H.M.S. *Surprise,* in memory of what had befallen her. The *Scorpion* was renamed H.M.S. *Confiance.* The ships sailed back, with their original crews in their holds, to the mouth of the Nottawasaga. From there the prisoners were sent to Quebec for internment.

On the return trip to Mackinac, the schooners brought enough provisions to keep McDouall and his men in plenty for a twelvemonth. And so the British held Mackinac, the Gibraltar of the north, for as long as the war flags flew.

In 1927, more than a century after the NANCY *was sunk, a battered wooden hull was recovered from the Nottawasaga River. The hulk, believed by many historians to be the remains of the* NANCY, *is now on display at the Museum of the Upper Lakes at Wasaga Beach, Ont. The museum also exhibits a 12-foot model of the schooner and a replica of her figurehead.*

*John O'Neill recruited
Henri Le Caron (right).
One result: a Fenian
defeat at Eccles Hill.*

Confessions of a Secret Agent

*Their first raid, at Ridgeway in southern Ontario in
June 1866, had been a fiasco. Two years later, however,
militant Irish nationalists in the United States—
members of the Fenian Brotherhood—still hoped
to invade Canada and strike a blow against the
British Empire. But the Fenian ranks had been
penetrated by an adventurous 26-year-old Englishman
named Thomas Beach, who also went by the name
Henri Le Caron. Here he describes the espionage role he
played as the second Fenian conspiracy began to unfold
in the summer of 1868.*

By HENRI LE CARON

I HAD FIRST INSINUATED MYSELF into John O'Neill's confidence while we were comrades-in-arms in the Northern Army during the War Between the States. He was a fine-looking man, nearly six feet in height, possessing an admirable physique and a distinctive Celtic face. His military bearing, combined with a rich, sonorous voice, lent to his presence a certain persuasive charm. He was also the most egotistical soul I ever met.

Bit by bit I had learned of O'Neill's determination to lead a Fenian invasion of Canada. Indignant as I was at learning what was being done against the interests of my native England, but not knowing how to prevent the conspiracy, I did nothing but communicate the news in letters to my father, who relayed my information to the British authorities.

It was not until some time after the first Fenian raid had ended in failure, and the Fenians had begun gathering their forces for a second invasion that, at the request of the British government, I agreed to spy on Fenian activities. O'Neill by this time had attained the presidency of the Fenian Brotherhood, and when I offered him my services as a military man in case of active warfare, he was delighted and promised me a position in the near future.

His telegram arrived in July 1868. "Come at once, you are needed for work." That was all it said.

Here was the opportunity I had been waiting for. I resigned my position as hospital steward in the state penitentiary at Lockport, Ill., and hurried to New York, where on Aug. 5 I presented myself to O'Neill at the headquarters of the Fenian Brotherhood, in a mansion at 10 West Fourth Street. I found the 34-year-old O'Neill, surrounded by his staff, transacting his duties with great pomp and ceremony.

The evening of my arrival I was commissioned a major in the Fenian Army and invited to accompany O'Neill to a Fenian gathering in Williamsburg, a suburb of Brooklyn. Several thousand persons greeted us with enthusiasm and gave us the seats of honor. I was in a state of excessive excitement and greatly feared what was coming, for if called on to speak, I should be found quite ignorant of Irish affairs. There was nothing for it, however, but to keep a brave face, for in the lexicon of espionage there was no such word as fail.

Seated next to O'Neill, I could hear him tell the chairman on whom to call, and how to describe the speakers, and at each pause between the speeches, I hung with nervous dread on O'Neill's words, fearing my name would be next.

The meeting proceeded, and I was beginning to think that the evil hour was postponed and that for this night, at least, I was safe. All but O'Neill and myself had spoken when, to my painful surprise, I heard him call on the chairman to announce Major Le Caron.

The moment was fraught with danger; my pulses throbbed, my heart seemed to stop beating, my brain was on fire, and failure stared me in the face. With almost superhuman effort I collected myself and, tickled by the chairman's error in announcing me as "Major McCaron"– and by the vast cheat I was playing on the lot of them–I rose to the occasion.

Proud and happy as I was at taking part in such a magnificent demonstration, they could not, I said, expect me to detain them long at so advanced an hour. All had been said that could be said upon the subject nearest and dearest to their hearts. (Applause.) If this night was indicative of Irish patriotism in America–(tremendous cheering)–then there could be no fears for the result. (Renewed plaudits.) They were all impatiently waiting, I knew, to hear the gallant hero of Ridgeway, General O'Neill– (thunders of applause)–and I would simply beg of them as lovers of liberty and motherland–(excited cheering)–to place at his disposal the money necessary to the success of our holy cause–the liberation of dear old Ireland from the rule of a tyrant which had blighted and ruined her for 700 years!

These last words worked my audience up to the highest pitch of enthusiasm. Amid excited shouts and cheers I resumed my seat, thinking that if it took so little as this to arouse the Fenians, I could play my role with little difficulty.

Several days later I accompanied O'Neill to the White House. We succeeded in the object of our visit, which was to secure President Andrew Johnson's influence in the return of Fenian arms seized by the American government after the first Fenian raid, which had ended on June 3, 1866, with the loss of eight Fenians dead and about 700 prisoners taken into custody by the American authorities.

Johnson received us cordially. "General," he said, addressing O'Neill, "your people unfairly blame me for the part I played in stopping your first movement, but remember that I waited five days before stopping you; and then, as President, I was compelled to preserve the neutrality of the United States, or be denounced on every side. I want you to understand that my sympathies are entirely with you, and I am willing to do anything in my power to assist you."

Dismayed by this political chicanery but all the more determined to nip Fenian schemes in the bud, I entered with a will upon my duties, travelling through the eastern states, visiting and reorganizing the various military units attached to the rebel society, and addressing public meetings in support of the cause of Ireland's "liberation." Winning the confidence of almost every Fenian I met, I obtained important information for the authorities in London.

In November my espionage career nearly came to an abrupt end. While visiting Troy, N.Y., I met John Roche, one of the shining lights of Irish nationality in that city.

When I learned that Roche had lived in Montreal, I explained that I had been instructed by O'Neill to visit and study the enemy's country, and asked Roche for the names of a few Fenian sympathizers whom I could visit. The truth was that Canadian authorities were anxious to learn the extent of the Fenian organization, which they knew existed in several cities, notably Montreal, Kingston and Toronto.

When Roche furnished me with several names, I foolishly wrote the particulars down in a notebook, arousing his most intense suspicions. On Nov. 24 at the annual Fenian convention in Philadelphia, he formally charged me with carelessness, dangerous conduct and questionable acts. I denied the allegations and demanded an inquiry.

A committee was appointed to investigate the charges, and Roche was duly heard. Friends rallied to my defence and a letter from John O'Neill was presented, demonstrating that I was authorized to visit Canada and acquaint myself with the situation there. Soon a unanimous verdict was reported back to the convention, asserting that the charges were scandalous and without foundation.

But I did not let matters rest even here. I wrote out my resignation, feigning injured innocence and couching my letter in indignant terms. As I hoped and anticipated, the assistant adjutant-general in the Fenian war department responded warmly, saying it was O'Neill's wish that I should remain an officer of the organization. "Your services," he said, "have been thoroughly appreciated ... therefore you should not notice the innuendoes or taunts of parties who cannot value your services."

This placed me on a surer footing than ever and brought me into even more confidential relations with the Fenian leadership. Soon after, I was promoted to inspector-general.

The Philadelphia convention had unanimously ratified O'Neill's plan to invade Canada a second time. His chief object, extravagant as it may seem, was to obtain possession of Canada, not as the permanent seat of an Irish republic, but as the base for operations against England. His theory was that from the ports and shipyards of the Dominion, the Fenians could dispatch privateers to prey upon English shipping. O'Neill anticipated that, possessing Canadian territory, the Fenians could claim and obtain formal U.S. recognition as belligerents.

The situation was now critical where the interests of the British Empire were concerned, for O'Neill had convinced many men who had fought on the side of both North and South during the War Between the States, to enrol themselves under the Irish banner.

After communicating with Lord Monck, the Governor General of Canada, I visited Ottawa and planned a system of regular communication with Magistrate Gilbert McMicken. As commissioner of police for the Dominion, McMicken supervised a small detective force secretly formed by the Canadian government to spy on the Fenian movement. From now on I was to act in concert with him.

The year 1869 saw me fully engaged inspecting units of the Fenian Army and directing the location of arms along the Canadian border. I distributed 10,000 rifles and almost two million rounds of ammunition in the care of the many Fenians stationed between Ogdensburg, N.Y., and St. Albans, Vt. Many of these guns were breechloaders, remodelled from U.S. Government Springfields. Now promoted assistant adjutant-general with the rank of colonel, I was able to obtain the originals of every document and campaign plan, and specimens of Fenian army commissions, all of which I conveyed to the Canadian government.

Successful as I was in evading detection, those assisting me did not always share my good luck. On one occasion I was shipping arms at Malone, N.Y., accompanied by one of the men secretly placed at my disposal by the Canadian government, for personal protection as well as the transit of documents requiring secrecy and dispatch. This man, John C. Rose, was a trusted Canadian agent. For months he followed me along the border, stopping at the same hotels and keeping in constant communication with me. No suspicion was aroused until his identity was inadvertently disclosed by a visitor from Ottawa.

Men began watching Rose without my knowledge, found him always tailing me and concluded that he was spying upon my actions. A few nights later Rose was waylaid, robbed and brutally beaten. He was brought back to the hotel and I was advised by my Fenian friends as to his dangerous character. Though shocked and embittered by the treatment accorded the poor fellow, I had to applaud the assault and denounce Rose, who was suffering in silence and with a splendid spirit. For months poor Rose was quite prostrated, and I was deprived of the services of as faithful and capable an ally as ever was given me.

By the winter of 1869 the Fenian leaders had completed plans for the invasion. The annual convention, in New York, was followed by a council of war. Financial pledges were called in and orders were issued to prepare the military organizations.

O'Neill's plan was to cross the border and to capture the towns of Saint-Jean and Richmond, south of the St. Lawrence River. From Rouses Point and Malone, N.Y., and from Franklin, Vt., Fenian forces were to converge by railway upon the occupied Canadian towns. Diversionary raids were planned in the Buffalo, N.Y., region and the Red River colony in Manitoba.

This second invasion of Canada differed in two important respects from that of 1866. Then the raid was loudly advertised for months before it actually took place. This time secrecy (as it was supposed) covered every move and intention, and this second raid was better prepared, with war material for at least 10,000 men actually on the ground.

On April 28, 1870, came an order to be "in readiness to move at a moment's notice." Fenian military commanders were ordered to report at given points and instructions were issued for the placement of arms at secret depots near the border at Franklin and Malone. The probable date of the attack was May 24–Queen Victoria's birthday.

Fearing that my real chiefs–the Canadian authorities–would be unprepared, I telegraphed Ottawa at once. Fortunately I had already made sure they possessed full details of the plan of action.

Having been summoned by telegram, I hurried to Buffalo where I found O'Neill on May 22 giving orders for an immediate movement on Canada which "no power on earth could stop." That day, we left for St. Albans–he full of enthusiasm and the belief that the Canadians would be taken by surprise, I laughing to myself at his coming discomfiture.

Men began arriving at St. Albans on the 23rd in squads of a dozen or 20, and during the night cartloads of rifles and ammunition were moved toward the frontier, about 18 miles to the north.

On May 24 we arrived at Franklin, a village less than three miles from the border. Prompt action had been taken by those in charge of munitions, and sufficient war material was now ready at the appointed places. But only 200 Fenian soldiers had shown up.

Though still hopeful that as many as 1,500 Fenians would soon arrive, O'Neill decided to abandon his strategy of occupying Saint-Jean and Richmond, and to concentrate his small force for a move toward Eccles Hill, just across the border, near Frelighsburg, Que. I viewed the situation calmly, for my agents had already departed for Canada with further details as to the time, the exact points of crossing and the number of Fenian invaders.

At 8 a.m. May 25 O'Neill left the Franklin Hotel to place himself at the head of the Fenian Army. All available invaders were mustered on the roadside at Hubbard's Farm, the Fenian camp and rendezvous about halfway between Franklin and the border.

All the men were armed but few were properly uniformed. Here and there a piece of Fenian attire caught the eye. The green and gray coats faced with gold and the pants of dark gray or light blue stood out in contrast with the surrounding garments of more sombre hue. Most men wore the usual accoutrements—cross and waist belts with ammunition pouches.

O'Neill was disappointed at the small size of his force, but the appearance in the camp of U.S. Marshal George Foster dispersed all thoughts of a possible delay. Gen. Ulysses S. Grant had replaced Andrew Johnson in the White House in 1869, and now Washington had a different attitude toward the Fenians. Ottawa had got prompt co-operation after passing on some of my information to the U.S. administration.

Foster threatened to arrest "all persons within the territory and jurisdiction of the United States ... aiding, countenancing, abetting, or taking part in such unlawful proceedings" as were being undertaken along the frontier. Shortly before noon, O'Neill decided to commence the attack.

Sentries had gone to the brow of a hill overlooking the frontier. From here to Eccles Hill was nearly a mile. A valley ran east and west and on the Canadian side was Groat Creek. The road from Franklin led down into the valley, past iron posts that marked the boundary, and across a wooden bridge over the creek.

An advance guard of 40 Fenians marched to within 100 yards of the line, halted and loaded their guns. They presented a formidable appearance, marching with the steadiness of regular troops, in column, with rifles at the shoulder, fixed bayonets shining and glistening in the noonday sun.

General O'Neill addressed them: "Soldiers, this is the advance guard of the Irish-American army for the liberation of Ireland from the yoke of the oppressor. For your own country you enter that of the enemy. The eyes of your countrymen are upon you. Forward, march!"

The advance was then resumed and O'Neill entered a house to view the engagement from an upper window. Having been instructed to follow with another 400 men as soon as they arrived from St. Albans, I watched from the hill on the American side.

With a wild cheer, convinced that nothing was known of their coming, the advance guard swept across the boundary line into Canadian territory. They had just crossed the bridge at Groat Creek when rifle fire was heard. One Fenian fell dead on the road, another was badly wounded.

Hidden among the rocks and brush on Eccles Hill and on both sides of the road were about 100 Canadian riflemen. Some were local farmers, but most were militiamen sent out from Montreal and from neighboring towns and villages in the Eastern Townships. From their commanding positions, the Canadian defenders continued firing on the Fenians, wounding several.

The Fenians returned the fire, but halted, undecided whether to advance. The sight of redcoats and the shower of bullets disconcerted the invaders. Instead of lying down, as ordered, to escape the fire of the Canadians and at the same time keep their position, the Fenians turned and fled, seeking shelter wherever cover could be obtained. A second Fenian soldier was killed and two others wounded in the scramble.

For a moment the Fenians rallied to fire a volley on their almost invisible enemies, but they soon retreated up the hill, still under fire, leaving their dead comrades to be buried by the Canadians.

By now the contingent from St. Albans had arrived and was arming. While supervising these men I was startled by the cry "Clear the road, clear the road!" and was almost knocked down by a furiously driven team of horses and a covered carriage. As it flashed by I caught a glimpse of O'Neill seated between two men.

I understood the situation in a moment, but said nothing. U.S. Marshal Foster had made good on his threat and arrested O'Neill right at the battle scene for breach of American neutrality. O'Neill had at first refused submission and threatened force, but when Foster placed a revolver at his head, he gave in, and was lodged in jail at Burlington.

When news of O'Neill's arrest reached us later in the afternoon, a council of war met under Patrick O'Reilly, a veteran of Fenian military expeditions. Contingents were arriving by the hour, and an attempt was made to get O'Reilly to take command and lead the attack at some other point.

Shortly after four, more shots were fired from the brow of the American hill and raked the base of Eccles Hill. But more Canadian troops, including a cavalry unit, had now arrived on the scene. The Fenians openly refused to obey orders, and in small squads fell back upon Hubbard's Farm, where O'Reilly attempted to rally them, but in vain.

By sunset the Fenians had disappeared; they retreated during the night to Franklin and St. Albans. The Battle of Eccles Hill was over and the victorious Canadians had suffered not a single casualty.

Next morning, Gen. Samuel P. Spear, the Fenian secretary of war, arrived at St. Albans seeking to continue the invasion. He appealed to me to supply him with 400 or 500 stands of arms and ammunition within 24 hours. But the arms, hidden in the woods near Franklin, were difficult to get at; and Canadian troops continued to watch the border. Any further attempt at war operations was out of the question.

To avoid arrest for breach of American neutrality, the Fenians had to disappear. I hurried with the rest of them to Malone. Here, too, the arrest of O'Neill and the unexpected determination of American authorities to enforce their country's neutrality had demoralized the Fenians. Soon the Fenian soldiers were planning to return to their homes and families.

On May 27, claiming that I was going to Burlington to see about O'Neill, I succeeded in leaving the Fenian camp at Malone without arousing suspicion. My intention was to report to Canadian headquarters, but it would be dangerous to go direct to Ottawa. Instead, I crossed the border at Rouses Point and spent that night in Montreal.

Next morning I boarded a train bound for Ottawa. At Cornwall there was a half-hour delay for dinner. I was enjoying a hearty meal when I heard a commotion at the door of the station dining room. I looked round to see two men advancing toward me, one remarkable for his tall, military appearance and the other for his clerical attire. All eyes turned upon them. "That is the man," said the clerical-looking person, pointing at me.

The taller man advanced and took a firm grip on my shoulder. "You are my prisoner," he said with a Scottish accent. I imagined there was some mistake and laughed as I turned to resume my dinner. "You are my prisoner," he repeated. "You must come with me at once."

"But won't you let me finish my dinner?" I said.

"No," was the sharp reply, "come."

"For what reason?" I protested. "Why am I arrested?"

"You are a Fenian," came the reply, the words falling clearly and distinctly on the hushed dining room.

I hurried out with my captors and was taken to a room adjoining the ticket office. The tall man turned out to be the mayor of Cornwall. The other was a wandering preacher who had been in the Malone area when I was hiding arms there—I had been pointed out to him as the leading Fenian agent. He had recognized me.

I surrendered my luggage and everything on my person, then asked the mayor for a private conversation. Suspicious and yet curious, he brought me into the ticket office, where we were left alone. Here I told him the exact situation.

True, I was a Fenian, I said, but I was also a Canadian government agent on my way to Ottawa to see Judge McMicken. To delay or expose me would mean serious difficulty for the government. Let him send me on to Ottawa with a guard, if he liked, and then my statements would be verified. Did he want immediate proof? Then here were my papers and a telegram advising McMicken of my coming, which the mayor himself could dispatch.

My manner must have impressed the mayor, for he took my suggestion and let me continue my journey under the escort of a lieutenant and three soldiers returning from Eccles Hill. They would not even allow me to raise the window. News of my arrest as a Fenian quickly spread among the passengers and preceded me on the route. Crowding round our carriage, bystanders hissed and hooted at me, with cries of "Hang him! Lynch him!"

At Prescott, 50 miles south of Ottawa, news of my capture had created a sensation. A special correspondent of *The Globe,* a Toronto newspaper, had travelled to meet me and find out who I was, but he was disappointed, for I refused to speak.

At Ottawa my telegram to Judge McMicken had brought his representative to the station. My guards and I were taken to the judge's office. I smiled and broke out laughing when brought into his presence. But my friend the judge remained stern and solemn as he heard the details of my capture and gave a formal receipt for my custody. Only when my guards left did the old man's genial nature assert itself. I remained in his office till nightfall. Then we took a cab to his club, where I spent the night.

Next day came arrangements for my departure. I was about to leave when I discovered that I had not sufficient money to bring me home to Illinois. Judge McMicken wrote out a cheque, but of course I could not cash it. The amount—$350—was beyond the resources of the club at the moment, so the judge called on the club porter to obtain the needed funds.

The porter knew I was the Fenian prisoner, although nothing more. He soon let out the secret, and the Canadian press published the fact that an important Fenian had been in Ottawa immediately after the raid and received a large sum of money from a government official, adding that the Fenians must have been nicely duped all through!

This was bringing danger very near again. Yet, marvellous to relate, suspicion never rested upon me in Fenian circles in connection with the news item. During the night I was driven by carriage to Arnprior, on the outskirts of Ottawa. Travelling the rest of the way by train, I got home safely to Lockport and was never troubled further by my visit to Judge McMicken. But for a long time I treasured very unchristian feelings toward that porter.

The militia played a major social role in eastern Canada in the 1880s.
Officers were in demand at snowshoe, skating and toboggan parties.
Their colorful uniforms embellished dances, band concerts and theatricals.
Parades were popular entertainment. But in the spring of 1885 Indian
and Métis discontent flared into rebellion in the Northwest, and
the part-time soldiers of the militia found themselves parading in earnest.
Long before reaching the Saskatchewan battlefields, they faced a
harrowing journey along the unfinished route of the Canadian Pacific
Railway—through a desolate, icy wilderness.

Van Horne Moves the Troops West

By PIERRE BERTON

I N THE DARKLING MIDNIGHT of Easter Monday, 1885, a long column
of soldiers inched through knee-deep slush on Lake Superior's frozen
surface. Numbed by wind, snow, water and ice, racked by coughing
and wheezing, the men of the 10th Battalion, Royal Grenadiers, of
Toronto, stumbled through the shrieking storm. Every few minutes some
luckless grenadier sank to his thighs in a hole left by a passing mule train.
Exhausted men dropped out and flung themselves onto the snow, to
be picked up by baggage sleighs that followed.

This terrible trail across frozen Nipigon Bay, bridging the last of
four gaps in the CPR track along Lake Superior's north shore, was only
seven miles long. But it took the troops nearly six dreadful hours to reach
Red Rock, on the west side of the bay. Men by the thousands were being
shuttled, trundled, sledded and marched along the uncompleted route
of Canada's first transcontinental railway that April. They came from
Halifax, Quebec, Montreal, Toronto and half a dozen smaller communities and were off to fight Louis Riel's rebels out on the Prairies. They
left to the music of brass bands and cheering crowds, with adventure
in their hearts and patriotic phrases on their tongues. But when the comfortable passenger coaches of the new railway were exchanged for open
sleighs or flatcars, adventure gave way to misery.

It was an ordeal of epic proportions. Col. George T. Denison of the Governor-General's Body Guard, a crack cavalry regiment, wrote that "a great deal has been said about [Napoleon's] passage of the Alps in 1800 . . . but as far as the hardships and difficulties and exposure to the men were concerned I am satisfied that our trip was much the worst." One of Riel's biographers, Joseph Kinsey Howard, said "it is conceivable that no troops anywhere, with the exception of Russia or Siberia, have undergone a worse ordeal."

The north shore of Lake Superior put more men out of action than the rebels did in Saskatchewan a month later. Some men went insane, some tried suicide, many more endured snow blindness. Scores suffered pneumonia, rheumatism, bronchitis, pleurisy and tonsillitis. On one day 22 men of the Halifax Battalion reported sick with sore throats. The Governor-General's Body Guard reached Winnipeg with a third of its men down with rheumatism and diarrhea.

But most men recovered quickly and all survived the ordeal. When the job was done the nation and its leaders awoke to the real significance of the railway.

Fifteen years before, when Louis Riel had first set the West aflame, it had taken Gen. Garnet Wolseley almost 14 weeks to move troops from Toronto to Fort Garry, Man.–by rail and steamship to the lakehead, then by canoe and on foot. This time roughly the same distance was covered in little more than a week, under the watchful eye of William Cornelius Van Horne.

The general manager of the CPR was born a Yankee and died an Imperial knight. His talents, abilities, enthusiasms and idiosyncrasies seemed endless: he was a poker player, conjurer, caricaturist, geologist, gourmet, art collector, practical joker, gardener, telegrapher, engineer, executive and financier.

A CPR engineer wrote of Van Horne: "He was the kind who would go out to the side of a mountain and say: 'Blow that down!' He wouldn't ask if it could be done; he would just say, 'Do it!' "

In 1885 Van Horne was driving track at breakneck speed, flinging trestles across gloomy crevasses in the Selkirk Mountains of British Columbia, levelling the prairie roadbed with monstrous scrapers, and blasting through the Canadian Shield north of Lake Superior with dynamite manufactured on the spot. There were 15,000 men on the Superior section alone and it took 300 dog teams just to supply them with food.

This section was being finished on faith and pledges, for the financial position of the CPR was desperate.

A single mile of track could cost $300,000. By January 1885 the company had a floating debt of $7 million. In February, using their personal assets as collateral, the company directors obtained a $1 million bank loan to ward off bankruptcy. In the first three months of 1885 the CPR's expenses exceeded its revenues by $342,000 and CPR stock dropped at an alarming rate.

To the public, goaded by an alert Liberal opposition, CPR coffers looked like a bottomless pit into which government money was endlessly shovelled. Further grants or guarantees were politically impossible.

Louis Riel chose this moment to raise a revolt among the native peoples of the Northwest.

First intimations of trouble in Saskatchewan had appeared in fragmentary reports in Ontario newspapers on March 23. But it was not until the Duck Lake massacre on March 26—when Riel's brilliant general, Gabriel Dumont, attacked and decimated a North West Mounted Police detachment—that the government realized the seriousness of the situation. That same day J. P. R. Adolphe Caron, the Minister of Militia and Defence, contacted the CPR about the possibility of moving troops to Winnipeg over the uncompleted track.

Van Horne heard about the government's request while on a business trip to Toronto. A thought flashed through his mind: How could the government refuse to aid a railway that sped troops to the West, to take the Métis by surprise and crush a rebellion?

He acted immediately, promising an astonished and unbelieving government that on 48 hours' notice he would move troops from Ottawa to Fort Qu'Appelle, Sask.—in 12 days. He made one stipulation: he and not the army was to control food and transport.

By March 27 Caron had issued a call to arms, and within 24 hours militia units throughout eastern Canada were mustered and ready.

As promised, Van Horne had cars at the Ottawa station within 48 hours. Nine days later, three short of the promised 12, the first troops disembarked at Fort Qu'Appelle.

Most of the men set off badly equipped and in considerable disarray. The 7th Battalion, Fusiliers, of London, Ont., didn't have enough fur hats and had to make do with some very unmilitary tobogganing headgear. The Governor-General's Body Guard found its water bottles were leaky; the government neglected to supply saddlebags, so the men had to wrap their kits in blankets. There was scarcely a fully equipped man in Montreal's 65th Battalion, Mount Royal Rifles: some lacked tunics, others trousers, others rifles. The Toronto Grenadiers used a gun—the nine-barrel Gatling—which, though still deadly, was first used in the Crimean War, 30 years before.

Some deficiencies in kit were made up by enthusiastic civilians. A Montreal firm supplied 25 pairs of warm mittens to the 65th. The Belleville town council voted a shirt and two pairs of socks to every volunteer the town sent to the Midland Battalion, and the ladies of Lindsay donated a suit of underclothing to each of *their* volunteers. Contributions to support the volunteers' dependants were common.

And so, with bands blaring, flags rippling and crowds roaring, the men boarded trains in Peterborough, London, Kingston, Quebec and all the other towns, day after day, from March 28 to April 13, heading northwest.

Van Horne, a lover of good food, determined that the troops should eat well whenever possible. At Dog Lake, near present-day White River, midway between Sault Ste. Marie and Thunder Bay, the Queen's Own Rifles of Toronto were treated to a dinner that included beef, salmon, lobster, mackerel, potatoes, tomatoes, peas, beans, corn, peaches, currants, raisins, cranberries, prunes, fresh bread, cakes and pies, and all the tea and coffee they needed to wash it down.

But here the ordeal began, for the Dog Lake camp squatted at the end of track. Between here and Red Rock, some 250 miles west, lay four uncompleted gaps totalling about 85 miles.

For the 36-mile gap between Dog Lake and Birch Lake, Van Horne had commandeered 300 teams and sleighs. Eight to 12 men tumbled into each sleigh, sitting on cross seats with their kits tucked beneath them. The trip was endurable as long as they travelled the graded roadbed, but at an unbridged ravine a tortuous tote road took them over boulders, stumps and windfalls, often flinging men and equipment into deep snow.

The horses were changed at Magpie, halfway to the next section of track. The men, jostling around a fire, were refuelled with pork, molasses, hardtack and tea. Back in the sleighs they found that their kits were freezing and that the roadbed was rougher than before.

Forced to detour at the unbridged gaps, the horses stumbled along narrow forest trails, often locking harness against stumps and tree trunks and dumping their passengers. Caps, mitts, mufflers and side arms were lost. One man was buried under a mountain of luggage; another found himself lying in the snow under a horse. Finally the teams pulled into the camp at Birch Lake where, if the men were lucky, flatcars awaited them.

Birch Lake to the troops was Camp Desolation. Fire had swept through the scrub timber, and the only shelter was one small, tattered tent. The temperature fell to almost 40 below but some troops had to remain outside for 17 hours for the flatcars that would take them the next 96 miles to Port Munro, another construction camp.

In daylight, an unexpected problem arose: the glare from the snow burned the men's faces until the skin peeled. Some men became hysterical in their suffering.

In the flatcars the men were packed onto benches arranged lengthwise, squeezed together like sheep as much for warmth as for efficiency.

The track was washboard rough. The ties had been laid on top of the snow, much of which melted in the noon sun. Derailment was common and the trains crept along at six mph. To get horses in and out of the flatcars the troopers built makeshift ramps from old ties and covered them with their personal blankets to keep the horses from slipping.

Port Munro, where the track ended again, was a deep, natural harbor dominated by a sheer 1,000-foot crag. The troops were quartered in the hold of the motor launch *Breck*. Here many enjoyed their first real sleep since departing civilization.

There were only enough teams and sleighs at Port Munro to carry baggage; the men were forced to march 20 miles across the lake's treacherous glare ice. Most men had goggles to prevent snow blindness, but some had to make eye shields out of birch bark. Groping along a narrow track in the ice, their eyes swollen, their feet often cut and their knees and shins bruised from repeated falls, some men did indeed go blind. Others went temporarily mad.

Yet still the men could sing as they stumbled along, strung out for seven miles across the ice, and the sounds of "Hold the Fort" echoed against the dark cliffs that brood along this section of the north shore.

The next stop was McKellar's Harbour. After sandwiches, salt pork and more of Van Horne's strong coffee, it was another 20 miles in open flatcars to Jackfish Bay and potatoes, pork, tea, hardtack and blackstrap molasses. The lucky ones went the next 22 miles to Winston's Dock by sleigh; the rest marched.

At Winston's Dock the bone-weary troops piled into flatcars. On the 52-mile run to Nipigon Bay they began to gain some understanding of Van Horne's tremendous feat. For miles on end the roadbed had been blasted from the billion-year-old schists and granites. Van Horne had constructed three dynamite factories along this section. He had chipped the roadbed into sheer cliffs; he had cut giant troughs directly through barriers and when cuts didn't suffice he had punched long tunnels through precipices.

Now came the final ordeal—the seven-mile trail across Nipigon Bay to Red Rock, which took nearly six hours to negotiate. A private in the 12th Battalion, York Rangers, recorded: "On the way across, one of the boys was so fagged out that he laid down on the sleigh. Captain Thompson asked him to move to one side but not an inch would he stir, so he caught hold of him like bag and baggage and tossed him to one side to let us pass."

At Red Rock a welcome sight awaited the exhausted marchers: comfortable, well-heated railway coaches and, for those who could stay awake, bully beef and hot tea. Scores preferred sleep, sprawling like dead men while the train rattled west.

By mid-April the entire force, save for the Halifax Battalion, was in the Northwest. The swiftest time for a unit to travel from Ottawa to Winnipeg was seven days. It never took more than nine.

But by now the railway was bankrupt. On April 16, after learning that Van Horne planned to stop all construction because there was no money for wages, CPR President George Stephen telegraphed Sir John A. Macdonald's secretary. "Please inform the premier and the finance minister," he said. "Do not be surprised or blame me if an immediate and most serious catastrophe happens."

It took two weeks for Sir John to sway the Conservative caucus, but sway it he did. On April 30, with the militia now in action against Riel's Indians and Métis, the Tory caucus gave its support to a bill authorizing an immediate loan of $5 million to the CPR. The proposal became law on July 20.

Meanwhile events moved swiftly, the rebellion grinding to a halt and the railway speeding to completion. On May 15 Riel surrendered at Batoche. On May 26 Poundmaker surrendered at Battleford. On May 28 the last rail was laid on the CPR's Lake Superior section. By July 2, when the last Indian rebel, Big Bear, gave up, most troops were travelling home in relative comfort, to the grateful plaudits of the populace.

Van Horne made sure the officers got sleepers, even though these

Craigellachie in the Rockies: Donald Smith poses before knocking home the CPR's last spike. Van Horne (black beard) is just left of Smith.

weren't in the contract, "as it is most important that the report of officers as to the treatment of troops on our line should be most favorable."

Less than five months later, on Nov. 7, 1885, Van Horne, with hands plunged deep into his pockets, posed for the most famous of all Canadian textbook photographs as financier Donald Smith hammered in the CPR's last spike at Craigellachie, B.C. Five hundred miles to the east, the man who had unwittingly helped to make it possible sat in a Regina death cell, praying and penning a final testament. Eight days later Louis Riel was hanged.

Far away in Berlin, members of the German General Staff, amazed and impressed by Van Horne's feat, continued to study in their methodical way the detailed report on the movement of the troops which the Kaiser's consul in Winnipeg had prepared at their specific request.

Some 60,000 men of the Canadian Expeditionary Force were killed during the Great War of 1914-1918. Another 170,000 were wounded. One soldier who recorded something of the horror of the Western Front was Charles Yale Harrison, who enlisted in the Royal Montreal Regiment at 18, served for eight months in France and Belgium and was wounded in 1918. This excerpt from his 1930 novel GENERALS DIE IN BED portrays the life of soldiers under almost constant shellfire in muddy, rat-infested trenches.

Bombardment

By CHARLES YALE HARRISON

W E ARE BACK IN THE LINE. This is a noisy front. It is in constant turmoil. There is no rest. The enemy rains an endless storm of fire upon us. At night the barbed wire is hammered by the artillery and we live in perpetual fear of raids. There is talk of an offensive. Out on rest we were human beings; here we are merely soldiers.

Camaraderie, *esprit de corps,* good fellowship—these are words for journalists to use, not for us. Here in the line they do not exist.

The morning rations come up. The food is spread out on the rubber sheet and we start to divide it among ourselves. Bread, the most coveted of all the food, is the bone of contention today. A private named Cleary is sharing it out.

Broadbent, another enlisted man, suspects that his piece is smaller than the rest. An oath is spat out. Cleary replies. In a moment they are at each other's throats like hungry, snarling animals.

They strike at each other with their fists, they kick with their boots. We tear them apart and push them into separate corners of the dugout. Blood streams from Cleary's cheek. Broadbent is alive with hate.

"You bloody rat."

"Aw, shut up, Broadbent. Leave him be."

"Who's a rat?"

"You."

"Come on, come on, cut it out."

"Any man that'll steal another man's bread . . ."

They rush at each other again. Again we pull them apart. Cleary wipes the blood from his face. He scowls and holds his hunk of bread in his hands like an animal. Then slowly he begins to gnaw at it.

We never become accustomed to the shellfire. Its terror for us increases with each passing day. The days out on rest ease our harried nerves, but as soon as we are back in the line we are as fearful and jumpy as the newest recruit. With the first hiss and roar of a shell we become terror-stricken as of old. We look at each other with anxious, frightened faces. Our lips tighten. Our eyes open wide.

Talk of the coming offensive continues. The sector becomes more tumultuous. The guns rage all night. We "stand to" long before dawn and wait at the parapets, expecting an attack, until long after sunrise.

The fatigues are innumerable. Every night there are wiring parties, carrying parties, sapping parties [in which trenches are dug to approach the enemy's position]. We come back exhausted from these trips. We throw ourselves down in the dugouts for an hour's sleep.

But we do not rest. There is no time for rest. We stagger around like drunken, forsaken men. Life has become an insane dream. Sleep, sleep—if only we could sleep.

Our faces become gray. Each face is a different shade of gray. Some are chalk-colored, some with a greenish tint, some yellow. But all of us are pallid with fear and fatigue.

It is three in the morning. Our section is just back from a wiring party. The guns are quiet. Dawn is a short while off.

We sit on the damp floor of the dugout. We have one candle between us and around this we sit chewing at the remains of the day's rations.

Suddenly the bombardment begins. The shells begin to hammer the trench above. The candlelight flickers.

We look at each other apprehensively. We try to talk as though the thing we dread most is not happening. The sergeant stumbles down the steps and warns us to keep our battle equipment on.

The dugout is an old German one; it is braced by stout wooden beams. We look anxiously at the ceiling. The walls tremble with each crashing explosion.

The air outside whistles with the rush of oncoming shells. The German gunners are "feeling" for our front line.

The crashing of the shells comes closer and closer. Our ears are attuned to the nuances of a bombardment. We have learned to identify each sound. The shells land on the parapet and in the trench itself now.

We do not think of the poor sentry, a new arrival, whom we have left on lookout duty. We crowd closer to the flickering candle.

Upstairs the trench rings with a gigantic crack as each shell lands. An insane god is pounding it with Cyclopean fists, madly, incessantly.

We sit like prehistoric men within the ring of flickering light which the candle casts. We look at each other silently.

A shell shatters into fragments near the entrance of the dugout. The candle is snuffed out by the concussion. We are in complete darkness.

Another shell shrieks into the trench near the entrance and explodes. The dugout is lit by a blinding red flash. Part of the earthen stairway caves in.

Shellfire! In the blackness the pounding and thudding over our heads sounds more malignant, more terrible. We do not speak. Each of us feels an icy fear gripping at the heart.

With a shaking hand Cleary strikes a match to light the candle. The small flame begins to spread its yellow light. Grotesque, fluttering shadows creep up the trembling walls.

Another crash directly overhead! It is dark again. Fry, another enlisted man, speaks querulously: "Gee, you can't even keep the damned thing lit."

At last the flame sputters and flares up. Broadbent's face is green.

The bombardment swells, howls, roars. The force of the detonations causes the candlelight to become a steady, rapid flicker. We look like men seen in an ancient, unsteady motion picture.

The fury of the bombardment makes me ill at the stomach.

Broadbent gets up and staggers into a corner of our underground room. He retches.

Fry starts a conversation. We each say a few words trying to keep the game alive. But we speak in broken sentences. We leave thoughts unfinished. We can think of only one thing—will the beams in the dug-out hold?

We lapse into fearful silences. We clench our teeth.

It seems as though the fire cannot become more intense. But it becomes more and more rapid. The pounding increases in tempo like a noise in the head of one who is going under anaesthetic.

The explosions seem as though they are taking place in the dugout itself. The smoke of the explosives fills the air.

Fry breaks the tension. "The lousy swine," he says. "Why don't they come on over, if they're coming?"

We all speak at once. We punctuate our talk with vile epithets. That instant a shell hurtles near the opening over our heads and explodes with a snarling roar. Clods of earth and pieces of the wooden supports come slithering down the stairway.

It is dark again. In the darkness we hear Anderson speak in his sing-song voice: "How do you expect to live through this with all your swearing and taking the Lord's name in vain?"

Unlike most of us, who are in our late teens or early twenties, Anderson is middle-aged, and slightly bald. He comes from somewhere in the backwoods of northern Ontario. He was a Methodist preacher in civilian life. For once we do not heap abuse and ribaldry on his head. We do not answer.

We sit in the darkness, afraid even to light the candle. It seems as though the enemy artillerymen have taken a dislike to our candle and are intent on blowing it out.

I look up the shattered stairway and see a few stars shining in the sky. At least we are not buried alive!

The metallic roar continues.

Fry speaks: "If I ever live through this, I'll never swear again, so help me God."

We do not speak, but we feel that we will promise anything to be spared the horror of being buried alive under tons of earth and beams which shiver over our heads with each explosion. Bits of earth from the ceiling begin to fall.

Suddenly, as quickly as it began, the bombardment stops. We clear the debris and go to the top of the broken stairs. It is quiet and cool.

All night long the artillery to our left up north booms and roars. A ration carrier comes in with a rumor that the Germans have broken through up in Belgium. We are unmoved by this piece of news. We only speculate how it will affect our futures. The enemy victory does not fill us with either fear or hatred. We are tired.

We lie in the dugout talking. Cleary says that the breakthrough will cause our withdrawal from this sector and that we will be sent to fill the gap up north.

"We're bloody shock troops, that's what we are."

"Yeah."

"Whenever the Imperials [English troops] cave in, up we go."

"The lousy bastards won't fight unless there's a row of Canadian bayonets behind 'em."

"But look at all the glory: 'Canadians saved the day'."

"It's beer we want. To hell with the glory."

We talk of when the war will end. On nights when there is little doing this is a good topic of conversation.

"It'll last for at least 20 years."

"They're making sure about reinforcements. They give the WAACs [Women's Auxiliary Army Corps] 10 days' leave and 10 quid for every kid they get."

"War babies."

"It'll all be over by Christmas."

"Like hell. First they said three months, then six, then a year. It's two years now and it's only started."

"It won't be over until every officer has an M.C. [Military Cross]."

"Why the hell should they want the war to end? They got lots of damn fools like us who'll enlist, and when they stop enlisting they'll drag 'em in."

Anderson speaks up. He is cleaning his rifle in the corner of the dugout: "The war will end on Aug. 1, 1917."

"Got it all figured out, eh?"

"No. But the Lord has figured it out for me: 'And the beast which I saw was like unto a leopard, and his feet were as the feet of a bear, and his mouth as the mouth of a lion . . . .' Now what does that mean?"

"Well, what does it mean?"

"It's all in the Book of Revelation."

"But what does it mean? It sounds like Greek to me."

"The leopard is France, the bear is Russia and the lion is England."

"Where's Canada in this deal?"

A sleepy voice from the corner of the dugout answers: "Canada is under the lion's tail."

Anderson continues: " 'And I saw one of his heads as it were wounded to death; and his deadly wound was healed: and all the world wondered after the beast. . . .' That was the first year of the war. 'And power was given unto him to continue forty and two months. . . .' Now 42 months is three and a half years and that means that the war ends on the first of August next year."

"Yeah, but do the generals know it? That's what I wanna know."

"Better write 'em a letter about it. They might forget the date."

Anderson lapses into a martyred silence as he always does when we jolly him about his biblical revelations. There is no shellfire now and he is not taken seriously.

The conversation drifts, lags and rambles on until it reaches the ultimate point of all trench conversations—the discussion of women.

"Well, one night I was with a tart in London and she says . . ."

There is a call for volunteers for a brigade raid. A hundred men are to go over. Some of our section offer themselves, I among them.

There is a rumor that the volunteers will receive 10 days' leave in either Paris or London.

We stand in the dugout which is battalion headquarters. We feel quite important. The colonel is giving us last instructions.

The raid is to take place shortly after midnight. We are to destroy the enemy's trenches and bring back prisoners. We are to have a two-minute preliminary bombardment in order to smash the enemy wire and to keep the sentries' heads down. We are to rush the trenches as soon as the fire lifts and drop depth charges into dugouts. At the end of five minutes red flares will be lighted on our parapets. This will signal that it is time to return and will show us the direction.

We are each given a sizable shot of rum and sent back to company headquarters. The rum makes me carefree and reckless. I feel fine.

At midnight we start on the way up to the front line. We each carry a pocketful of ammunition, a few grenades and our rifles.

All our letters, paybooks and other means of identification are left behind. I have left my papers with Cleary. . . .

We are lying out in front of our wire, waiting for the signal to leap up. It is quiet. Now and then a white flare sizzles into the air and illuminates the field as though it were daytime.

We lie perfectly still. Over in the German lines we hear voices – they are about 50 yards from where we lie.

I look at the phosphorescent markings on the face of my watch. Two minutes to go.

MacLeod, the officer in charge of the raiding party, crawls over and gives us a last warning. "Remember," he whispers, "red flares on our parapets is the signal to come back."

That instant the sky behind us is stabbed with a thousand flashes of flame. The earth shakes. The air hisses, whistles, screams over our heads.

They are firing right into the trenches in front of us. Clouds of earth leap into the air.

The barrage lasts a minute and then lifts to cut off the enemy's front line from his supports.

In that moment we spring up. We fire as we run.

The enemy has not had time to get back on his firing steps. There is no reply to our fire.

We race on: 50 yards – 40 yards – 30 yards!

My brain is unnaturally cool. I think to myself: This is a raid, you ought to be excited and nervous. But I am calm.

Twenty yards! I can see the neatly piled sandbags on the enemy parapets. Our guns are still thundering behind us.

Suddenly yellow, blinding bursts of flame shoot up from the ground in front of us. *Hand grenades!* Above the howl of the artillery I hear a man scream as he is hit.

We race on. We fire our rifles from the hip as we run. The grenades cease to bark.

Ten yards! With a yell we plunge toward the parapets and jump, bayonets first, into the trench.

Two men are in the bay into which we leap. Half a dozen of our men fall upon them and stab them down into a corner.

White flares soar over the trench, lighting the scene for us. We separate, looking for dugouts and prisoners.

Depth charges are dropped into underground dwellings and hiding places. The trench shakes with hollow, subterranean detonations.

Somewhere nearby a machine gun comes to life and sweeps over our heads into No Man's Land.

The enemy artillery has sacrificed the front line and is hammering the terrain between their lines and ours.

Green flares sail into the black sky. It is the German call for help. The whole front wakes up. Guns bark, yelp, snarl, roar on all sides.

I run down the trench looking for prisoners. Each man is for himself. I am alone. I turn the corner of a bay. My bayonet points forward—on guard. I proceed cautiously.

Something moves in the corner of the bay. It is a German. I recognize the helmet. In that second he twists and reaches for his revolver.

I lunge forward, aiming my bayonet at his stomach. It is a lightning, instinctive movement. The thrust jerks my body. Something heavy collides with the point of my weapon.

I become insane. I want to strike again and again. But I cannot. My bayonet does not come clear. I pull, tug, jerk. It does not come out. I have caught him between the ribs. His bones grip my blade. I cannot withdraw.

Suddenly I hear him shriek. It sounds far-off as though heard in the moment of waking from a dream.

I have a man at the end of my bayonet, I say to myself.

His shrieks become louder and louder.

We are facing each other—four feet of space separates us.

His eyes are distended; they seem all white, and look as though they will leap out of their sockets. There is froth in the corners of his mouth, which opens and shuts like that of a fish out of water.

His hands grasp the barrel of my rifle and he joins me in the effort to withdraw. I do not know what to do. He looks at me piteously.

I put my foot up against his body and try to kick him off. He shrieks into my face. He will not come off. I kick him again and again. No use.

His howling unnerves me. I feel I will go insane if I stay in this hole much longer. Suddenly I let go the butt of my rifle. He collapses into the corner of the bay. His hands still grip the barrel.

I start to run down the bay. A few steps and I turn the corner. I am in the next bay. I am glad I cannot see him.

Out of the roar of the bombardment I think I hear voices. In a flash I remember that I am unarmed. Only my rifle stands between me and death—and it is in the body of him who lies there trying to pull it out.

I am terrified. If they come here and find me they will stab me just as I stabbed him—and maybe in the ribs, too.

I run back a few paces but I cannot bring myself to turn the corner of the bay in which he lies. I hear his calls for help. The other voices sound nearer.

I am back in the bay. He is propped up against a bank of earth. His rifle is in such a position that he cannot move. His neck is limp and he rolls his head over his chest until he sees me.

Behind our lines the gunfire lights the sky with monstrous, dull orange flashes. In the flickering light this German and I enact our tragedy.

I move to seize the butt of my rifle. Once more we are face to face. He grabs the barrel with a childish movement which seems to say: You may not take it, it is mine. I push his hands away. I pull again.

My tugging and pulling works the blade in his insides. Again those horrible shrieks!

I place the butt of the rifle under my arm and turn away, trying to drag the blade out. It will not come.

I think: I can get it out if I unfasten the bayonet from the rifle. But I cannot go through with the plan, for the blade is in up to the hilt and the wound which I have been clumsily mauling is now a gaping hole. I cannot put my hand there.

Suddenly I remember what I must do. I turn around and pull back the bolt on my rifle. The click sounds sharp and clear.

He stops his screaming. He looks at me, silently now. He knows what I am going to do.

A white flare soars over our heads. His helmet has fallen from his head. I see his boyish face. He looks like a Saxon; he is fair and I see white down against green cheeks.

I pull my trigger. There is a loud report. The blade at the end of my rifle snaps in two. He falls into the corner of the bay and rolls over. He lies still.

I am free. But I am only free to continue the raid. It seems as though I have been in this trench for hours. Where are the red flares? I look toward our lines and see only the flickering orange gun flashes leaping into the black sky.

The air is full of the smoke of high explosives. Through the murk I see two heads emerging from the entrance to a dugout. The heads are covered with the familiar pot-shaped helmets—we use a more vulgar term to describe them. Apparently this was a dugout our men had overlooked.

I raise the rifle to my shoulder. The first one sees me and throws his hands high into the air. *"Kamerad! Kamerad!"* he shouts. His mate does likewise. The word means comrade. It is the international word for compassion and mercy.

Suddenly the sky over in the direction of our lines becomes smudged with a red glow. The flares! The signal to return!

"Come with me," I shout. I start to drag them with me. They resist and hold back. They stand with their backs glued to the side of the trench and look at me with big frightened eyes. They are boys of about 17. Their uniforms are too big for them and their thin necks poke up out of enormous collars.

"Nicht schiessen!—bitte—nicht schiessen!" the nearest one shouts, stupidly shaking his head.

I search them for weapons and then sling my rifle over my shoulder as evidence of good faith. We start down the trench toward a sap—a narrower trench which leads out into No Man's Land.

We are back in the bay where he with my bayonet in his ribs lies in the corner. I pass him quickly as though I do not know him.

The one nearest to me throws himself on the dead soldier. I spring upon him.

The red flares color the sky. It is the signal to return, and here this maniac is trying to keep me in this trench forever! I grab him by the slack of his collar and start to tear him away.

He looks up at me with the eyes of a dog and says: *"Mein Bruder—eine Minute—mein Bruder."*

The red flares grow brighter. The other prisoner looks at me with sad eyes and repeats: *"Ja, ja, das ist sein Bruder."*

"Schnell!" I shout into the kneeling one's ear. He nods and takes a few letters and papers from his brother's pockets and follows me into the sap.

The earth leaps into the air on all sides of us. I do not see any of our men. We are alone. I point toward our lines and we begin to run. The field is being swept by machine gun fire.

We run and stumble over stray bits of embedded barbed wire. We pick ourselves up and run again. It is miraculous how we can live, even for a moment, in this fire. A shell explodes about 20 yards from us. The brother falls. We pick him up and carry him into a discarded communication trench that runs from the German lines to ours.

The fire grows fiercer. We can distinguish shells of every calibre. The air begins to snarl and bark over our heads. They are using overhead shrapnel.

We stop and feel in the darkness. We find a dugout in the side of the trench and wait there while the storm of living steel rages about us. It is black inside. The unhurt prisoner pulls a stub of a candle out of his tunic pocket. I light it; it flickers with the force of the nearby detonations.

The brother hugs his wounded leg and rocks to and fro with pain. We examine him. He has been hit in the calf of his right leg. We take the emergency dressings from our tunics and pour iodine into the open wound. He winces and then shrieks as the stuff eats into his flesh. I apply a gauze and his mate starts to bind the wound with bandages.

By signs and with my meagre German I make them understand that we will wait here until the barrage abates. I pull out a package of cigarettes and offer them one each. We light up from the candle and sit smoking.

I point to the wounded one's leg and ask him how he feels. He shakes his head, points back toward the German lines and moans: *"Ach, ach, mein Bruder."*

He begins to weep and talk rapidly at the same time. I cannot understand. I can distinguish only two words—*"Bruder"* and *"Mutter."*

The other prisoner nods his head solemnly, affirming what his comrade says: *"Ja, ja, das ist wahr—das ist sein Bruder, Karl."*

We sit silently, waiting for the storm of steel to die down. The wounded one's cigarette goes out. I move the candle toward his mouth. He puts his thin hand to mine to steady it. The cigarette is lit. He looks into my eyes with that same doggish look and pats my hand in gratitude.

"Du bist ein guter Soldat," he says, his eyes filling with tears. With his hand he describes a circle. The motion takes in his trenches and ours, the thundering artillery, the dugout, everything. In a little-boy voice he says: *"Ach, es ist schrecklich—schrecklich."*

The explosions die down. We decide to move. I motion to them that we are to go forward. We crawl out of the dugout. We support Karl's brother, one on each side of him.

There is no shellfire here. To the rear they are shelling our artillery batteries, but here there is only a steady sweep of machine gun fire. In this discarded trench we are in no danger.

At last we reach the sap that leads to our trenches. The sentry challenges us and we are allowed to pass.

Clark is waiting, checking off the names of those who return. He looks with approval at the two prisoners. I am ordered to take the prisoners down to battalion headquarters.

In the headquarters dugout about 50 men are congregated. I am greeted with shouts of approval by the officers. It seems that mine are the only prisoners brought in.

The colonel slaps me on the back. I ask that the prisoners be treated nicely. "Of course—of course," says the colonel in a gruff voice.

They are taken into a corner and given some food and rum—to warm them up and make them talk.

One of the men in our company comes up to me and whispers: "They're talking of giving you an M.M. [Military Medal]."

I watch the noisy scene quite calmly. The officers and men are flushed with the freely flowing rum. The colonel calls me to his table and offers me his bottle of whisky. I take a drink. I am amazed that I do not tremble and shake after the experiences of the night.

They are talking of the casualties of the raid. MacLeod was killed by a grenade as we leaped into the trenches. Forty men are missing out of the hundred who went over.

One of the captains in another company takes the little red and black striped fatigue cap from the wounded prisoner and gives it to me. I refuse to take it.

"Here," he shouts boisterously, "here, take it and send it home to your mother as a souvenir." He stuffs the cap into my pocket.

Outside an occasional shell screams over our heads and explodes, shaking the dugout.

The terrific noise is gone. The raid is over.

Forty men—a young officer—two prisoners—and Karl. I think about this calmly but sadly.

The raiders are excused from duty for the remainder of the term in the line. We are sent back to the reserve dugouts. They are spacious.

The effect of the rum begins to wear off. I lie on my blanket and think of the raid. I am proud of myself. I have been tested and found not wanting. I feel quietly sure of myself. I went through all that without breaking down.

I feel colder now that the rum no longer acts. I begin to shiver. I draw my greatcoat over my head.

"Cold," I say to myself, "cold." My hands shake—my whole body. I am trembling all over.

"Fool," I say to myself, "why are you trembling? The raid is over. You're safe. You'll get an M.M.—10 days' leave in London or Paris."

I try to decide where I'll go, to Paris or to London, but the thoughts do not stick. The image of Karl, he who died on my bayonet, seems to stand before my eyes.

The shaking becomes worse. The movements are those of one who is palsied. I begin to sob.

I am living through the raid all over again, but I cannot relieve myself with action now.

389

I do not think things now; I feel them. Who was Karl? Why did I have to kill him? Forty men lost—why? MacLeod killed—why?

I do not want to lie here. I am frightened at being alone. I get to my feet and start up the stairs leading to the communication trench.

An officer comes stumbling down the stairs. He recognizes me. He sees my frightened eyes. "Here, here," he says, "what's the matter?—where are you going?"

I mumble something. He offers me his flask. It is filled with rum. I take a long swig. It burns my insides.

I stumble along the trench looking for my section. It is dark, there are no lights in the sky. No moon, no stars.

I reach the front line. I recognize faces. My name is called. Fry grasps my hand and shakes it heartily. His face is serious. "You did fine, I hear," he says. "They're all talking about it. You're going to get the M.M."

"Where's Cleary?" I ask.

"He got it," Fry replies.

"Where? How?" I ask.

"Right over here." He points a finger. "As soon as the barrage started they sent over a couple of heavies. A hunk of shell caved his helmet in. He's down at the M.O.'s dugout."

I dash down the trench. I begin to cry. Tears stream down my face.

It begins to rain. The drops fall on my steel helmet, making a tick-tock noise. The water splashes my face. It trickles down the collar of my tunic.

The trench becomes muddy and I slip and flounder in the dark.

The front is quiet. Not a sound rips through the silence. I see a lone figure looming out of the darkness. It's a company runner. I ask where the medical officer's dugout is. He directs me. I stagger on.

Odor of chemicals. The M.O.'s dugout. I stumble down the stairs.

Wounded men are lying all over the earthen floor. The M.O. sees me. He's an elderly man. He smiles. "What is it, son?"

"Cleary—Cleary, 'A' company," I stammer.

"Pal?"

I nod my head.

He puts his arm on my shoulder. "I'm sorry—he won't live."

I stand still. I say nothing.

"Do you want to see him?"

"Yes," I say at last.

He takes me to a corner and points to a blood-soaked bundle. It is Cleary. His head lies on a small pile of sandbags. His chin rests heavily on his collarbone. His face is yellowish green. His eyes are closed. The eyelids flutter slightly. Over his right eye there is a gaping wound. Part of his jaw is ripped off. He is breathing heavily, half snoring. His face is twisted.

I turn to the doctor. "Is he conscious?"

He shakes his head. "No, he's out of it. Knocked out. Bad fracture of the skull. He'll soon pass out."

As we talk Cleary gives a loud snort. His legs and arms convulse and jerk spasmodically. Then he lies still.

"He's dead."

I explain to the M.O. that some of my papers are in the tunic of the corpse. I ask permission to take them. He nods assent.

I stuff the papers into my pockets and run out to the slippery trench.

I walk back to the reserve dugouts. I throw myself down on the blanket. I cannot sleep.

I am calm now. It is quiet. I think of all that has happened, of Karl, the prisoner's dead brother, and of Cleary, dead with a hole in his head, with his jaw shot away.

Questions press on my brain, cry aloud for answers. I toss and turn in my searching.

It is better, I say to myself, not to seek answers. It is better to live like an unreasoning animal. Better not to ask questions. Better not to think.

I pull my coat over my head. I feel warm and drowsy. At last sleep comes, mercifully.

The Courage of the Early Morning

William Avery Bishop made his first kill as a Royal Flying Corps pilot March 25, 1917, scored a second victory the same month, and added 12 more kills in April. He had left Owen Sound, Ont., two years earlier as a reckless 21-year-old, a ladies' man and a crack shot with his .22 squirrel gun. Now an ace, with a reputation for rough flying but straight shooting, Billy Bishop was invited by Albert Ball, the highest scoring British pilot, to join him in the first-ever attack on enemy planes at their own field. Before they could try, Ball was killed. Bishop was now the top Flying Corps ace. But what would happen to Ball's plan?

By WILLIAM ARTHUR BISHOP

ETURNING FROM LEAVE in England on May 22, Billy Bishop
rejoined 60 Squadron at its airdrome, Filescamp Farm, some 10
miles back of the front line and not far from Vimy Ridge and
Arras. Ball's plan kept nagging at him. Perhaps it was still possible; perhaps he could do it alone.

Four days later, in his old silver Nieuport—"fixed up better than
new," he was assured—Bishop shot down a single-seater Albatros scout
plane near Vimy Ridge. It was his 20th victory. He bagged a German
two-seater reconnaissance plane the day after that.

But the enemy had a new tactic. Reconnaissance planes roamed
at 3,000 feet just on the German side of the line. When British fighters
attacked, the Germans dived, leading the British into heavy ground fire.

Bishop cornered the squadron commander, Maj. Jack Scott, after
one nerve-wracking day. "If I've got to shoot at Hun planes practically
at ground level I'd rather do it at one of their airdromes where at least
the anti-aircraft wouldn't be ready and waiting. What do you think?"

Said Scott: "Just let me know when you're going to do it."

Next afternoon, to relax, Bishop went for a lone flight at 10,000
feet. He sighted two Albatros scouts spiralling down toward their airdrome. He engaged one, hit the German pilot and watched the plane
crash at the edge of the enemy airfield.

Although the fight had been near an enemy air base, no plane had
risen to help the Albatros—presumably, Bishop reasoned, because no
British plane would be expected at such a place. He decided to attack
as he and Ball had planned.

Next day, June 1, 60 Squadron continued its futile and hazardous
chases of the German two-seaters. "What a complete waste of time,"
Bishop complained to Scott. "My mind's made up. I'm going after those
airdromes tomorrow morning, rain or shine."

"Good luck," said Scott.

All afternoon Bishop practised his shooting. Then he checked each
round that went into his two ammunition drums. He oiled his Lewis
gun. He pored over maps, checked every detail. His mechanic, Corp.
Walter Bourne, checked the Nieuport's engine and controls.

That evening Bishop scrawled on the mess blackboard: "Early call—
Capt. Bishop—3 a.m."

At 3 a.m. there was a light drizzle, with heavy cloud at 500 feet. Bishop
gulped tea and pulled his flying suit over his pyjamas. Corporal Bourne,

the only other man out at that hour, had the Nieuport engine running. Bishop climbed into the cockpit, still sleepy. Bourne pulled the wheel chocks away and waved. Bishop smiled and waved back.

The drizzle became rain as he climbed, and he could hardly see. Over Arras, six miles from the front, the ceiling was higher. He turned right, saw he was headed along the road to Cambrai—inside the German lines—then climbed to just under the clouds. He experienced a loneliness he had never known before.

Bishop lost his way in the cloud and flew farther into enemy territory than he intended. When he descended he found himself over a deserted airdrome. He hunted for another airfield and minutes later sighted the shadowy shapes of hangars. This was Estourmel, near Cambrai, although he did not know it at the time. He came down to 200 feet.

Before first light six Albatros scouts and a two-seater had been wheeled out of the hangars. Now their engines were warming up. One pilot was ready in his plane. The others were straggling across the field from breakfast.

Bishop went into a shallow dive. His Nieuport streaked over the hangars, spraying bullets among the waiting planes. His first burst carried him to the far edge of the field, where he pulled into a tight climbing turn. He could see men running onto the field and a machine gun opened fire from the ground. Bullets ripped his wingtips. He swerved to dodge more bullets. The Albatros pilot, already in his plane, was gaining speed for take-off. Bishop went after him.

The German was only 10 feet off the ground when Bishop pressed the firing button from 60 yards' range. Without speed to dodge the attack, the Albatros took the full blast of 15 rounds, sideslipped and crashed.

Another Albatros started to roar across the field. Bishop fired from 100 yards and missed, but the attack so unnerved the pilot that he crashed into a tree, tearing off the right wings. Bishop hauled back on the control stick and climbed.

Two more planes started to take off in opposite directions. One Albatros flew away and hovered at a safe distance but the other made straight for Bishop, who turned as the German pilot closed behind him. The enemy tried to follow, firing a short blast. Bishop saw an opening and fired. Twice the machines circled each other, but neither pilot could get in position for a decisive burst.

The Nieuport's manoeuvrability came to Bishop's rescue. He got underneath and at a slight angle to the Albatros, and finished his first drum in a long burst. It struck the fuselage just in front of the pilot and put the engine out of action. The Albatros crashed 400 feet from the airfield.

Bishop was now intent on escape. No doubt the Germans had sent an alarm to nearby airfields, and heaven knew how many fighters were swarming toward the scene. At least no more planes were attempting to take off from the airfield.

For the moment he had forgotten the fourth enemy plane, which had stayed clear of the fighting but now was bearing in. The German pilot opened fire at 300 yards. Bishop saw the flashes from its twin guns and turned away sharply. His own ammunition drum was empty.

Changing a drum while flying was tricky and to do it while dodging the bullets of a skilled and tenacious pursuer was most difficult. Bishop had practised endlessly—minus the enemy plane—and somehow he managed it now without giving the Albatros pilot a fatal advantage.

To escape he must either shoot down the Albatros or chase it away. He pointed the nose of his plane in the direction of the other machine, pressed his thumb on the firing button and kept it there. The German had undoubtedly never had all 99 rounds of a Lewis gun's drum thrown at him in one burst. He broke off the fight.

Bishop did not wait to see his opponent land. He turned toward home and climbed with all the power he could coax from his engine. His smoking gun was now dead weight. When it cooled he hurled it overboard.

The overcast had broken and Bishop kept a wary watch. Three miles west of Cambrai he sighted four enemy planes cloud-hopping in the same direction he was flying—2,000 feet above him. Farther west the clouds disappeared and the five planes were in a clear sky.

The Germans did not appear to have seen him. But at any moment one might look down—and four planes with eight guns blazing would dive on the slower, unarmed Nieuport. Bishop tried to keep directly under the enemy formation in what he hoped might be a blind spot. As they turned, he turned. The general direction of the formation was taking him south. He knew he would soon have to make a break west. He counted 10 slowly, then dived in the direction of the front lines at full power. When he looked back the German planes were continuing their patrol—the pilots still unaware of his presence.

To Billy Bishop from the general: "The greatest single show of the war."

His dive brought Bishop down to 1,000 feet, and as he crossed the enemy lines anti-aircraft fire straddled the Nieuport. He dived, climbed and swerved. He heard sharp snapping sounds of shrapnel ripping the fabric of his plane. One of the lower wings, already damaged in the attack on Estourmel, now looked like tattered clothing flapping on a clothes line. The barrage suddenly and mercifully ceased as he crossed into Allied territory.

Bishop turned northwest toward Filescamp Farm. It was 5:15 a.m. The sky was calm and clear and oddly haunting. The exhilaration of the early morning battle was gone. "I flew in a daze," he said later. "The excitement and the reaction had been too much. My head was going around and I thought I would suffer from nausea any minute. Nothing mattered except the struggle to bring the plane safely to earth."

At 5:30 Bishop was over Filescamp and feeling better. The airdrome was still asleep, just as he had left it an hour and a half before.

Jubilantly, he fired off flare after flare from his Very pistol. Ground crewmen led by Corporal Bourne ran to greet him as he climbed out of the cockpit holding up three fingers and calling out rather incoherently, "Three of them, taking off."

By mid-morning the news had spread across the Western Front. Gen. John Higgins, the brigade commander, sent congratulations. The commander of the Flying Corps, Gen. Hugh Trenchard, wired Bishop that the raid was "the greatest single show of the war."

The exploit won Bishop the Victoria Cross. Before the investiture at Buckingham Palace that September he ran his string of victories to 47 — three more than Albert Ball had scored.

Bishop was to receive from George V not only the VC but also the Military Cross and the Distinguished Service Order he had won earlier. He arrived late at the palace and was not sure where to go. An equerry shunted him into an anteroom with those who were to receive the MC. A call came that a DSO appeared to be missing and Bishop, feeling conspicuous, had to admit he was a DSO. He was escorted to a second room. Then it was learned that a VC was missing. Once more he was identified and was led to a third room where he was admonished by a staff officer for delaying the proceedings.

What happened next he described in a letter to his father: "I had learned the investiture drill thoroughly — 10 yards across the middle of the room, then turn left and bow. Imagine my consternation when during those first 10 paces one of my boots began to squeak."

His embarrassment mounted when the King instructed a staff officer to show the medals around the room, since this was the first time all three had been awarded to one man at the same time.

"It was too awful for words," Bishop wrote. "For 15 minutes the old boy talked to me in front of a huge crowd. I nearly died."

A week later Bishop was notified that he had been awarded a fourth decoration, a bar to his DSO. The citation read: "For conspicuous bravery and devotion to duty while engaging hostile aircraft. His consistent dash and fearlessness have set a magnificent example to the pilots of his squadron. He has destroyed no less than 45 hostile machines within the past five months, frequently attacking enemy formations single-handed."

Again Bishop was acutely embarrassed. The newspapers conferred on him various titles, including one that made him wince most painfully: the Lone Hawk.

Bishop returned to Canada on extended leave and received a hero's welcome. He married his fiancée, Margaret Burden, and was assigned to the British War Mission in Washington. But his public frankness about the lack of preparedness of the U.S. Air Force got him into hot water. He returned to England, was arrested, reprimanded—and secretly commended. And he was authorized to form his own squadron.

Bishop, now a lieutenant-colonel, hand-picked his men, the Flying Foxes. Their list of kills grew impressively, and so did Bishop's. When he had left France in August 1917 his score was 47 kills. In the last five days of May 1918 he pushed his total to 55. By June 18 he reached 67.

But Bishop had become too valuable a symbol to risk further in battle. He was ordered to a desk job in England. The Flying Foxes said farewell at a party in the mess the night of June 18.

June 19 dawned in a gloomy drizzle. It had rained all night. The field was soaked. It was as rotten a day for flying as Bishop had seen. His head pounded from the festivities of the night before and he had to leave for England at noon.

One last flight? Why not? At 1,000 feet it might be clearer to the east—the wind was blowing from that direction.

Bishop sloshed across the field to his new plane, a gaudily decorated S.E. 5a. At 9:30 a.m. he climbed into the cockpit. As he headed east toward battered Ypres visibility improved and Bishop could see the ground. At the trench lines he climbed into the clouds at 1,800 feet to hide from the ground fire.

He decided to fly to Passchendaele, seven miles east of Ypres, before coming down from the clouds to cut a wide arc to the north. After 10 minutes he dropped out of the clouds to check his position. He had not paid enough attention to his compass, and his plane had veered off course. And he was not alone.

To his left, flying away from him, were three Pfalz scouts. The German fighters began to turn as Bishop swept in behind them. From 150 yards he took aim but his gunsight fouled with oil. He shifted to the less accurate auxiliary sight but he was too late. The scouts had come around and now dived head on at him. Ugly orange flashes blossomed from the muzzles of their guns and Bishop heard the bullets streak past. There was a rending crunch as his left lower wingtip was shredded by tracer bullets. Bishop got away only a short return burst as the enemy fighters slipped by underneath. He banked left to get behind them again, taking a quick look to the rear. It probably saved his life. Two more Pfalz scouts were diving out of the clouds.

The three enemy planes in front were now only 400 yards away. Bishop decided to risk a quick attack before the two others could join in. He had no time to get at close range, and opened fire at 120 yards. The burst was brief but destructive. It struck the rearmost plane and killed the pilot. The machine turned over and fell nose forward but Bishop had no chance to see it crash. The second pair of Pfalz scouts began to fire at him.

He slammed the left rudder control and pulled into a steep turn. His attackers slipped past below.

The other Pfalz machines had begun to climb. Bishop knew they intended to hide in the clouds until he was fully occupied, then pounce. But they never made it. Just under the clouds, where it was misty and hard to see, they drifted too close to each other, locked wings with a splintering crash and for a moment hung there. Then they fell apart. Bits of wing, fuselage and tail fluttered away, and they joined the first Pfalz, which was burning on the ground.

It had all happened in three minutes. The remaining pair of enemy fighters now tried to climb into the security of the clouds. One escaped but the other was too slow and he presented a perfect target. Bishop had a dead shot from 50 yards. He watched his tracers tear a gaping hole in the wings. The plane nosed forward, went into a spin and crashed.

Bishop, now alone in the sky, noticed the clouds had dropped lower. His compass had been shaken out of kilter and he had only an approximate idea of his location.

As he flew in the misty drizzle, the outline of another plane emerged. It was a two-seater with German black crosses.

It wallowed in shallow turns and the observer in the rear seat peered over the side. Both pilot and observer were obviously unaware they were pursued. Bishop easily slipped into the ideal position—the blind spot, behind and beneath. When he got within 40 yards he tilted his nose upward and took aim. Ten rounds from both guns tore into the enemy plane. It wobbled for a second, then skidded violently. One wheel fell off and spun past Bishop. Then the two-seater fell earthward. Bishop could see the pilot fighting to keep control while the observer was slumped in his seat. Seconds later the plane crashed into a hillock and burst into flames.

Bishop circled, watching smoke rise from the hillock. The sky was now clear of planes. He was barely aware he had achieved his greatest triumph—five planes within 15 minutes.

Billy Bishop's final tally was 72 kills—25 in the 24 days between May 27 and June 19. He was the Allies' third greatest ace, behind only France's René Fonck and Britain's Edward Mannock, who destroyed 75 and 73 enemy aircraft respectively.

But none surpassed my father in raw courage.

When he died in 1956, aged 60, the tribute that moved me most, perhaps because I felt it would have secretly pleased my father, too, even while it embarrassed him, was written by John Bassett, publisher of the Montreal *Gazette*:

Death came to Billy Bishop in the early morning. He died at that chill hour before the coming of dawn—an hour when he must often have been making ready for his solitary flights.

Perhaps the very core of his courage lies in this very fact—that he showed it most at an hour when men feel it least. For his courage was not a thing of sudden inspiration, the surge of the moment, needing the support and cheer of others. It was a solitary thing, lonely as the dawn itself.

Perhaps if he had a choice, this would have been the hour he would have preferred. For he had that courage which Napoleon once said was the rarest—*the courage of the early morning*.

'Bonjour, tout le monde à la maison d'Alphonse'

Sgt.Maj. Lucien Dumais of les Fusiliers Mont-Royal was captured in the Dieppe raid on Aug. 19, 1942, but escaped the next day and got back to England by way of Spain and Gibraltar. British Intelligence asked: Would he return to occupied France to help other men escape? Dumais said no; he'd had enough of life on the run behind German lines. He got battle experience in North Africa and in mid-1943 was back with his unit in Britain, commanding a platoon and awaiting the inevitable invasion of Europe.

By LUCIEN DUMAIS

Ray LaBrosse (above) and Lucien Dumais delivered escaping airmen to the "Channel Ferry Service."

I WOULD HAVE BEEN part of the invasion if it had not been for the arrival, fresh from Canada, of a new platoon commander. He knew it all, and after a week or two of his airs and ignorance I found myself remembering the Intelligence major who had interrogated me. In due course I was granted an interview.

We sat on a bench in St. James's Park in London on a sunny summer day in 1943 discussing in the most prosaic terms the possibility of undertaking an assignment of blood-chilling risk.

"You do realize," said Major Langley, "what you're letting yourself in for if you're accepted?"

I said I did.

"And if things go wrong, and you're caught?"

"I'll be shot."

"Eventually, yes, but only after the Gestapo have finished with you."

Three days later I reported to Canadian Military Headquarters and was granted a two-week leave. But this, I discovered, was so the major and I could continue our alfresco conversations. He asked a great many ques-

tions, some very strange indeed. Gradually I came to realize that my whole life, every hole and corner of it, was being closely scrutinized. Nor did it stop with the past.

Strangers would come up to me in pubs, press drinks on me and try to pump me. On one occasion the military police accused me of having a forged pass. They overdid it. I got angry and insisted on laying a charge against them. Langley told me to forget it. Like everything else that had happened, I realized it was a put-up job designed to test my reactions.

One morning I was told to report to Free French HQ and ask for a certain captain. Langley was there and introduced us, then strolled away, leaving us talking. The French captain asked me a number of loaded questions, and then, staring at my chest, snapped:

"And may I ask why you are wearing a medal to which you are not entitled?" [Dumais had won the Military Medal at Dieppe.]

I lost my temper.

"If you weren't in uniform," I said, "I'd fill you in"—and a lot more on the same lines. I was seething. The major returned from examining the pictures on the far wall.

"Cool down, Lucien. I just wanted to find out how good your French is. Now I know." He turned to the captain. "What do you think?"

"The accent could be that of central France—say the Nivernais. I suggest his background be constructed accordingly."

Toward the end of the two weeks the major gave me an out: men of my experience (I was 38 and had been a soldier for nine years) were needed to train the youngsters; there would be no disgrace in going back to the FMRs.

But I had no intention of backing down now, and I said so forcibly.

"Fine," said Major Langley. "Glad to have you with us."

Next day we went to fetch my things from Canadian HQ. I was given civilian clothing and packed my uniforms in my military bags; then we drove to the Canadian Records Office. When my bags and rifle were registered, the major casually reached over, picked up the receipt and slipped it in his pocket. It was as good as saying there was very little chance of me collecting my gear in person. In fact, I was about to cease to exist: my name was posted on the "Q" list—people about whom no information was available. There was only one stage after that, the "X" list, and those on it were dead.

My room-mate in the quarters Major Langley found for me was Raymond LaBrosse, like me a French-speaking Canadian. He had lived in Ottawa and been a sergeant in the Signal Corps, attached to the Canadian Artillery.

He was reticent at first, but when I told him I had been on the Dieppe raid and how I had escaped, he opened up. He and a partner had parachuted into France in March 1943 to form a network to recover Allied airmen. After five months the Gestapo got onto them. They caught Ray's chief and a lot of others.

Ray escaped, only to find himself with a faulty radio, no cipher, no money and 27 airmen on his hands. Most people would have got out of there fast, and alone. Not Ray. He dragged his party of escapers through France and across the Pyrenees to Spain.

Major Langley left Ray and me strictly alone for a week. Then he asked if we would like to work as a team. We said yes. Ray accepted me as chief; he would be my assistant and radio operator.

In going back to France, Ray was running a greater risk than I. He would be known to the Gestapo and they would have his description, if not his photograph. Because of his youth and physique, he would always be in danger of being picked out for forced labor in Germany, as happened to so many young Frenchmen.

I would be safer, not only because I intended to increase my age on my identity papers, but also because I was growing a moustache and would wear neutral glasses. Moustache and glasses could be taken off quickly if necessary, a better dodge than growing a beard, which takes time, and putting on dark glasses, which tend to be conspicuous.

Now our work started in earnest. Ray, being a qualified parachutist, did only a few jumps to keep his hand in. I had to start from scratch. I was sent to a parachute school in company with a lot of other "civilians." Everyone had a different accent and we realized we were all prospective agents, earmarked for different countries.

From parachute jumping we turned to security. One important aspect of this discipline, the most vital of all to an agent, was the question of women. Too many agents owed their capture and death to women who had, perhaps, become jealous and given them away. There was only one safe rule, our lecturer said: "Have nothing to do with them. But if you must have a woman, don't tell her about your work."

We also had to learn our cover stories. The story they made up for me was plausible. I was Lucien J. Desbiens, Administrator of Funeral Enterprises, living at 40 rue Violet, Paris XVe.

Obviously it was not possible to stop being Lucien Dumais, just like that, as I was continually meeting people I knew. But as I tried to assume my new personality and live with it, my contact with my old, true self began to grow weaker. And, of course, once I stepped out of England, I would cease to be Lucien Dumais and become Lucien J. Desbiens, the Amiens-born undertaker, not just in name but in person, and would have to act and live like him.

All this left me with a strange feeling of not having existed before, and sometimes I seemed to be searching for myself. At the same time, my new personality was something I wasn't yet sure of, something made up, that had never existed before. It felt as if it only half belonged to me, like a suit of clothes I had borrowed.

It was almost time to go. We were given a code, microphotographed on cards so tiny you needed a magnifying glass to read them, and we had a long session with the navy, planning a number of pick-ups by sea. We had false papers, old Paris Métro tickets, two small compasses, maps, metal saws and escape ropes made up into the soles of house slippers.

We were each given a money belt. I gave Ray a quarter of a million francs and kept half a million. I would need more cash as I would be paying the operating expenses. The major said: "Don't be stingy, and keep no accounts. They're dangerous. We're not interested in money, but results."

Last of all he gave us our password and our contact address in Paris, a hairdressing shop in rue des Capucines.

We had been given the choice of parachuting into France or being landed by aircraft. I preferred the latter course. All that remained now was to wait for a suitable moon. Every morning we rang the office, to be told "call tomorrow." Then it came. "Stand by. You will be picked up at 1830 hours."

Right on the dot, two staff cars driven by astonishingly beautiful women swept up to the door. All our officers were there and they looked after the luggage. Ray and I were the VIPs.

After an hour's drive, we came to the airfield. Guards on the gate checked the drivers' papers, but not the passengers'. With time still on our hands we made ourselves comfortable in a Nissen hut. Drinks were handed round, and the girls took off their jackets and on a small stove cooked us ham and eggs—a rarity in England then. We knew this was the condemned men's last meal.

At last the cars took us across the airfield to a parked Lysander—a light, single-engine aircraft built for short landings and take-offs.

"Let's hear from you soon," said Langley. We kissed the girls passionately. It was a symbolic leave-taking: we were kissing *all* our girl friends good-bye and leaving the world we knew.

We squeezed in behind the pilot. Then the hatch closed, the engine revved up, and we were away, bound for central France, where a Resistance committee was to receive us.

Above the French coast we ran into fog–too much for a landing. I heard the pilot talking over the wireless and then he banked. We were heading back to England.

As we recrossed the French coast we saw a shadow behind us: a German night fighter, coming in fast. Our pilot put the Lysander on a wing tip and we saw a burst of gunfire to our left and astern. It was over. We flew too slowly and turned too fast for that night fighter, especially at night when he could hardly see us.

It was a dejected group that landed back at the airfield, climbed into the cars and returned to London.

Ten days went by before the message came again. Down to the airfield we drove once more. Again we kissed the girls good-bye.

There were three planes on this trip and we flew together to Poitiers. We circled while the first aircraft put on its landing lights, started its approach and landed. Our pilot straightened out to go in, but just then the radio crackled and a voice yelled: "Don't land! Don't land! It's too soft. I'm bogged down."

Reluctantly we climbed away. There was nothing we could do. Again we headed back to England.

As we approached the French coast the Jerries opened up with ack-ack. The first shot was above us and the second underneath, so close that we felt the plane lift. The pilot pushed the nose down and gave her the gun. There were three more shots, but behind us. Then we were clear.

Now the waiting started again. We were very depressed and wondered whether we would ever get to France. I even said we would go in by parachute. But in the end there was no need for this.

This time we were in the lead plane and as soon as our pilot saw the ground landing flares he started to lose height. He made one tight circuit and landed. As the aircraft stopped rolling, we opened the hatch and drew our guns, just in case we had the wrong reception committee.

A Frenchman appeared out of the darkness; everything was all right, and now, after all the weeks of frustration, we were on our own.

We climbed into a truck waiting in a small clearing 300 yards from the landing field. After several miles the truck turned into a farmyard and was driven straight into a shed. The door was shut, the engine was switched off, and we were told to stay where we were and be quiet. The silence lasted several minutes. Then someone hissed at us from a dark doorway leading to the house, and we went in, I hanging on to my briefcase, Ray to his radio.

People were looking out in all directions from the darkened windows. This group was wary and I liked that.

Drinks were poured and we saluted one another. We were talking over a much-needed breakfast when an elderly man came in and was introduced as the chief. He was the director of a sugar factory and he took us to an empty part of his house, across the road from the plant. He assured us we were perfectly safe as he had told his staff we were the hated Vichy government police. Everyone would shun us—good!—but it occurred to Ray and me that some patriot could well put rat poison in our food!

We stayed with the director for two days before word came that it was safe to go on to Paris. Ray and I travelled by train in the same coach, but behaved as if we were strangers.

In rue des Capucines we found the hairdresser's shop. A young woman came forward and said she was Christine Georges. I gave the password and she answered correctly. She put on a coat and we went to a park to talk.

"I have just come in from London; they told me to contact you," I said.

"Good. I hope you have some money and a way to send parcels." (A parcel was an escaper; it had to be rewrapped and stamped—that is, given other clothes and false identity papers.)

Christine had been sending parcels south to Spain but many had failed to get across the border or had ended up in Spanish jails. She had had to borrow to keep the operation going and now owed 40,000 francs.

That, at least, could be put right at once, and Christine went to telephone Suzanne, her assistant, who worked as a nurse at a nearby clinic and who would take us to her house in Rueil-Malmaison, a western suburb of Paris.

Suzanne rented the second floor of a two-storey house. As soon as we entered the building Ray and I inspected it for escape routes. We had hardly started to unpack when the doorbell rang. Suzanne assured us it was Christine, but this did not prevent us from drawing our pistols. It was Christine, and she was taken aback at being received at pistol point. Suzanne told her jokingly: "They've been behaving like that ever since I met them; it must be the fashion in London."

Christine told us what had been going on: "We were asked by a man we had known for a long time to help get airmen to Spain. We lodged them in Paris and then sent them south."

"Did he have any money to speak of?"

"No, he was always trying to find fresh supplies."

"Then he had no radio contact with London?"

"He sent messages to London, but I think it was through another man. He was always expecting money but it never came. He was arrested two months ago, and since then I've been trying to carry on by borrowing."

It was plain they had no idea about security. I explained as gently as I could that we would need a safer set-up. We would organize our own escape routes without anybody else knowing about them.

Next morning Ray started to set up his radio to inform London of our safe arrival. I put my message into cipher, not forgetting an intentional mistake, so that I would be identified. Every operator has his personal touch, so Ray would be recognized by his key work. The dangers inherent in the work could be minimized by certain precautions. Ray never transmitted at the same hour, from the same place, or on the same wavelength. This had all been arranged beforehand in London, so they would know when and on what wavelength to listen for him.

Everything for our broadcast was ready on time. I kept watch from the windows as Ray sent his call letters. He listened intently. No response. Again he sent his call letters. Time stood still and so did I, listening with Ray. No answer. What had gone wrong? Every few minutes Ray called until the half-hour allowed us went by, but there was no answer.

Ray put away his set and we held a post-mortem. Perhaps we were in a silent zone; perhaps the transmitter was not powerful enough, although it had been checked thoroughly before we left.

"We must make contact," Ray said, "or we're wasting our time." We decided to change sectors and get closer to England in time for the next radio rendezvous three days later. We selected Normandy, where I had contacts from my escape days. Before then, however, another shock awaited us.

The next day was a Sunday. Christine and Suzanne were not coming to Rueil; they had to go to the Gare St-Lazare to get the last of their own evacuees on the train to the Spanish border. They would join us in the early evening, when we would draw up a plan for our new network.

Ray and I went to a restaurant for a quiet lunch. Afterward we walked at a leisurely pace back to the house. We felt well-fed and relaxed.

I opened the flat door; there was a note on the floor: "Christine and Suzanne have been *arrested,* you had better get out fast."

Presumably there were no Germans in the house or they would have picked up the note, but they might arrive at any moment. We went into the bedroom and got our guns. I went to a front window, Ray to a rear one. Everything seemed normal; nothing moved in the deserted street. There was no question of leaving our stuff behind; we needed it too badly.

While Ray packed, I kept watch. My mind was groping for an explanation. Who had brought the note? It must have been a friend, but only Christine and Suzanne knew of our existence. Had they told one of their friends about us, despite our warnings? Whoever it was must have seen them arrested, to be here so soon.

The trouble was we didn't have a clue where to look. There was no question either of taking refuge in a hotel, as the police regularly checked the identity papers of the guests.

Ray suggested we meet Paul Campinchi, who had been one of the main helpers of Ray's former chief. While a lot of others had been arrested, Campinchi had got away. This was enough to make him suspect in London. Had he been lucky, or had he betrayed the others?

Ray was certain that London was wrong, that he could trust Campinchi. Well, it was his life as well as mine, and Ray went to get him.

Campinchi was a middle-aged Corsican with brown hair and a moustache, of good height but heavyset. He told us how, by sheer luck, he had missed being arrested; he had spent the past six months in hiding. When he had finished his story, I asked him whether he would consider taking up his previous work again.

"You're asking a lot," he said. "It's been no fun hiding out like this. My chief was a nice fellow, but he would talk about his mission to anybody. The only thing he didn't do was put an ad in the papers, asking for agents for British Intelligence work."

"Things will be different this time," Ray promised. Paul was still unconvinced, but the upshot was that the friend who had been hiding him agreed to put us up as well.

410

This friend was called Guette. Though well over 50, she had the looks and the vivacity of a much younger woman. When she was angry or excited, her dark eyes would flash, and she was given to tossing back her vividly hennaed hair. I put her down as the kind of person who would do anything in the world for you if she liked you.

We now had a base again, but there was still the problem of contacting London. We stuck to our plan to go to Normandy, where I would contact Mme Francine Bellenger at Bourgtheroulde-Thuit-Hébert. She was one of those who had helped me when I escaped after Dieppe.

The train journey to Bourgtheroulde took all night. Then we found that Mme Bellenger had some visitors she felt she could not trust; she could not risk putting us up. But she said: "The hotel keeper is a friend of mine; go to him. Tell him I sent you."

Ray said he could broadcast from a hotel room without anybody knowing about it, and there was no reason to mention her name unless the proprietor refused to let us have a room. In the event, he gave us an upstairs room which suited us admirably.

Ray ran his aerial round the room. He was ready in good time, and I stood by at the window, watching for any strange arrivals.

Right on the dot, Ray sent out his call letters . . . and then it came, that beautiful sound of London answering. I could have yelled with delight, but did a skip instead. We had done it. We were in contact. In a few minutes London knew of our safe arrival, of the arrest of Christine and Suzanne and of our meeting with Campinchi. I had to tell them this, no matter how foolish it might look. If things went wrong, they would know why.

The return to Paris was a nightmare. One train was so full that we could not get on—until, just as it started to pull away, a door opened and out jumped a civilian. Ray and I scrambled in—into a coach reserved for German army personnel. The military police had got rid of one civilian; now they had two. An NCO demanded our papers, examined them briefly, and told us we must get off at the next stop. When at last we were left alone, a soldier who spoke fair French told us not to worry: the next stop was Villeneuve-St-Georges; we could get off there and move down the train.

It felt very queer, standing there talking to an enemy soldier as if he were simply a casual acquaintance, when all the time I could feel the weight of a rifle in my hands and imagine ramming the bayonet into his belly.

Back in Paris, I resumed my interrupted discussion with Paul Campinchi. I found him an intelligent and wary man. This was what I was looking for–someone who would talk only when it was necessary.

Eventually he agreed to take control of the Paris region and its suburbs. He would choose a man who could organize a group of guides to go into the country and bring in baled-out airmen and others whose presence was required back in England. These guides would convoy them to whatever destination we selected.

In addition, Paul agreed to try to find someone to supply lodgings and food for the evacuees in and around Paris and a printer to manufacture false identity papers. He would also need a sort of quartermaster to search for food and clothing. We agreed to look for a suitable English-speaking person to act as interpreter and work with the lodging master.

Rules on security were laid down as follows:

1. All agents to keep their addresses secret.
2. Chiefs to meet their inferiors only when necessary, and never to give them information not absolutely essential.
3. Work through accommodation addresses.
4. Agents to avoid friendly meetings with one another.
5. Contacts between guides and lodgers to be carried out by prearranged signals.
6. Evacuees to be passed along the line without their guides meeting one another.
7. Nobody to talk about his chief, or admit to having one.
8. The head of the network to remain completely unknown.
9. Evacuees not to be told of the existence of a network.
10. All evacuees to be interrogated as soon as taken in charge.

The purpose of laying down rules was twofold: first, to impress on the members of the network the idea that they were professionals, and were not therefore at liberty to gab as they pleased; and second, to prevent the enemy from infiltrating our network with bogus airmen.

Stopping careless talk was not an easy task, especially where Frenchmen were concerned. They liked to expatiate on the fact that they were doing something for their country; and after that it only needed one of their friends to talk in front of an acquaintance who was a *collaborateur*.

Although it was necessary to shut off agents and sections from one another, it was difficult to achieve. Everyday life had to go on. But it was vital; in the event of an arrest, such ignorance could save a lot of agents' lives.

The infiltration of false airmen was a real headache. The enemy would place an English-speaking man, dressed in a captured flying suit, near a farm—usually one suspected of having helped airmen or at least of being pro-British—and he would ask for help. He would be passed along from one hide-out to another; and when he had gone as far as possible he would come out and report to the nearest German post. In this way a whole network could be busted.

It was possible to prevent this happening by insisting on confirmation of the identity of any evacuee taken in charge. This was not difficult; most of the airmen came in batches, from one plane; they knew one another well, and they tried hard to stick together.

The fighter pilot, on the other hand, was usually alone. But he could nearly always be identified by his accent, and his knowledge of England and of recent events there, such as shows, films and race meets. With British airmen we could check on their knowledge of cricket; with Canadians and Americans it was baseball.

Soon Campinchi was carrying out the plans we had discussed, recruiting personnel among his friends and acquaintances, on the assurance that they would be working for the Allied cause, that money was available and that security would be strict.

The next big step was to set up an organization on the coast. In London we had agreed to look at a spot near Plouha in Brittany. First of all, though, we needed a contact. In this we were lucky. Ray remembered that in Paris during his first mission to France he had met a medical student named Le Balch, who had been from the Côtes-du-Nord—in Britanny.

Ray learned that Le Balch, now a full-fledged doctor, had just bought a practice in Plouézec, some 20 miles from Plouha. We arranged to visit him as soon as he moved there.

Paul Campinchi had already picked up some parcels and was getting them together in Paris, but as we still had no way out of France this was jumping the gun.

In the meantime, the fact that Paul, Ray and I lived in the same apartment was a risk; if one got into trouble the other two were bound to be involved, so we separated. We found a place to store all the dangerous equipment we had with us, including our money, and at least I knew that I was "clean."

Guette had a friend who managed a hotel close by, and I took a room there. This was not the best solution—she, as well as Campinchi, his wife and Ray would all know where I lived—but it was an improvement on all of us living together. At the same time Ray rented a room from some friends. He did not give his new address to Guette or Paul, and he and I would meet only for essential business.

Plouézec, where Dr. Le Balch was taking up practice, was in a restricted zone. Many residents had been moved out, and to visit the area it was necessary to procure a temporary permit from the German authorities. We had no intention of revealing anything about ourselves to the enemy, so I asked Campinchi to organize *Ausweise* [permits] for Ray and me. His printer did a good job. We made reservations on the train to Saint-Brieuc, where we would catch a local train for Plouézec.

The journey passed without incident. Our permits withstood the scrutiny of the German police at Saint-Brieuc. The luggage that contained the wireless, which had been our main worry, was not examined.

The local train was a real museum piece, so enfeebled by age and poor coal that the passengers had to get out and push at the inclines.

At Plouézec we found the doctor waiting for us. His family were still in Paris and he had his spacious house to himself. This simplified the problem of lodging for us.

Through Henri Le Blais, the local wheat controller, I was introduced to François Le Cornec, who ran a café in Plouha and was the head of the local Resistance. He was just the man I was looking for to take charge of the beach operation and we went together to inspect the spot that had been discussed in London.

It was about five miles north of Plouha, and the beach itself was fine: shingle and then sand that would be uncovered for 50 yards at low tide. The snag was that behind it was a sheer cliff 100 feet high. But by taking it at an angle, sliding down more or less on our backsides, this was not a serious handicap.

Everything was falling into place. The escapers would arrive at Saint-Brieuc, where Le Blais would take charge of them. Le Cornec's group would escort them in the old local train and hide them in farmhouses around Plouha. Le Cornec would supply all guides and arrange lodgings. We set the first operation for the next moonless night, Dec. 15.

By now, Campinchi had assembled 15 parcels in Paris and they were dispatched north without a hitch. They were taken to the Gare

Montparnasse and handed over to guides who put them on the train. They were instructed to play the part of exhausted workers slumped in deep sleep. Toward the end of the journey, the guides slipped each man new identity papers and an *Ausweis* prepared by the Paris printer.

At Saint-Brieuc they passed through the gate like other passengers. Then they were moved to Plouha, a few at a time and mostly at night; otherwise the number of strangers appearing in a small town might have aroused suspicion.

Ray and I moved into Le Cornec's place. He locked the door leading into the café, and as long as we did not make too much noise we could remain there undetected. Above, we had a room with two beds.

The weather was bad, with a gale blowing. It was bitterly cold, and next morning was no better. There was nothing to do but sit and talk, and sometimes take a look at the weather vane on top of the church.

At six o'clock we switched on Le Cornec's old radio, and listened to the BBC program *Les Français parlent aux Français*. After the news came "personal messages" that were in fact instructions to networks such as ours. Toward the end we heard one of our three prearranged messages: *"Yvonne pense souvent à l'heureuse occasion."* Not the go-ahead message. We were disappointed but did not show it because we had not told Le Cornec about the system. Because of the gale, I said, the operation was postponed for 24 hours.

In fact, we spent nine miserable days in those rooms, freezing in the daytime, freezing at night, and chasing fleas in our beds. How we would have welcomed some good flea powder!

On the ninth day we got a message finally calling off the operation. It hardly came as a surprise, for the gale had been blowing all the time.

I arranged with Le Cornec and Francis Baudet, his assistant, to leave the parcels in Brittany until the next attempt, on Jan. 28. They would be less trouble in the country. Le Cornec arranged to move them out of the town into farmhouses where they could play mute farm laborers or aliens.

Ray and I could do little more at Plouha, so back to Paris we went. It was time I moved from the hotel, where I could be traced via Campinchi, and I set about looking for a flat. They were hard to find, but the fact that I was able to pay top prices helped, and after a time I was offered exactly what I wanted in avenue Charles-Floquet.

At the end of January Ray and I travelled back to Brittany—with a supply of flea powder.

415

The weather was fair but we tried to keep our hopes down. At six o'clock the night of Jan. 28 we tuned in the BBC in the small room next to the café. *"Bonjour, tout le monde à la maison d'Alphonse."* That was the message we had been waiting for. The operation was on.

We had to wait for confirmation on the nine o'clock news, but if all was well then the guides would move the parcels, by separate routes, to the rendezvous we had picked, Jean Gicquel's house, known from now on as *la maison d'Alphonse.*

At nine the confirmation came; it meant the boat from England had not turned back. I said: "Let's go."

Le Cornec and I travelled together, avoiding the main street and using footpaths as soon as we were in the open. We could follow the progress of the different groups by the barking of farm dogs. Everyone got to the rendezvous in good time. Le Cornec checked the furtive entry of each lot and Baudet, his assistant, sorted them out.

The airmen had been living for a month in twos and threes in farmhouses without a clue as to what would happen next. Now all 17 had been brought together to this room on the coast; little wonder they were bewildered.

Up to this point I had been just another Frenchman. Now I spoke English, without a French accent. "Well, fellows, this is the last lap of a long journey. We're about a mile from the Channel; if everything goes well, you'll be in England by nine in the morning."

At midnight we turned out the light, opened the door, and were confronted with inky darkness. We waited for two minutes to let our eyes get accustomed to it, then moved off to the beach in single file.

From the cliff-edge we could see the waves far below. I was one of the last to slide down and although I was careful to lean back, I could feel myself trying to roll forward headfirst.

The code letter B was flashed at one-minute intervals on a flashlight masked by a cardboard tube.

Suddenly we saw three dark spots on the sea. We watched intently. They were not an illusion, they were moving slowly toward the shore. I waded out to the centre one, pistol drawn, ready to fire, and called out the password:

"Dinan!"

"Saint-Brieuc!" came the reply.

What a relief! It was the Royal Navy. Our helpers quickly unloaded incoming stores, then brought the men out. In 12 minutes the sailors

Dawn on the beach north of Plouha: Dumais' 17 parcels are now safe in England.

were rowing back to their motor torpedo boat, 17 very happy parcels with them.

We were wet to our shoulders and the water was so cold that, even with the excitement, it choked the breath out of us. We hauled and dragged the cases of stores up the cliff and wasted no time in marching back to *la maison d'Alphonse.*

We had some hot coffee with cognac but, although the kitchen was warm, we went on shivering for a long time.

Six cases had come in; they were all alike, all beautifully packed. I was so elated that the operation had gone off smoothly that I made a silly mistake and opened them in front of the operators. They contained not only weapons but also ammunition, a wireless set, chocolate, cigarettes, coffee, whisky and many other items—virtually everything I had asked for—together with four million francs. The money was all in one case—good, worn 10,000-franc notes, pressed (not ironed) into tight bundles, and I felt a stir of expectancy round me.

417

I gave the guns and ammunition to Le Cornec and distributed some of the luxuries to the operators. Then I closed the cases, remarking that the rest was for other members of the organization. I had discussed with Le Cornec how much he would give to each person, and he had paid them accordingly; but, seeing all this money, they imagined I was going to dish it out by the fistful.

I could not pretend, even to myself, that they were getting paid adequately for the risks they were taking; those were beyond computation. But we did not want anybody working purely for money. We paid a good wage, plus expenses; to overpay had its own dangers. Some people lose their heads when they get a bit of money, start drinking heavily, and then start talking. In addition, if a number of people in a small town suddenly appeared flush, the word would quickly get around and suspicions might be aroused.

Le Blais had managed to arrange sleepers for us the next night on the Paris train, and as I turned in to the rhythmic clack of the wheels, I looked back over all that had happened. I saw no reason why the network shouldn't repeat the operation. There was always the possibility that it might come to an abrupt end, but even if Ray and I were killed we would still be in credit on the deal. Those 17 lives could not be taken away from us, and whatever they achieved in the future would be partly due to us. With such complacent thoughts running through my mind, I drifted off to sleep. My mood might have been very different had I known what was awaiting me in Paris.

At Montparnasse all was well. Ray and I went our separate ways and I took the *Métro*. As I stepped out at my station I ran straight into police who were searching all bags. I had two, one full of money.

I had come across these snap searches before, and I knew that plain-clothes policemen mixed in the crowd watching for people who turned back. These would be picked up for special attention.

I had a good story, but no matter how expert false papers are they cannot withstand a thorough investigation. In any case, an honest man does not cart four million francs in cash about in a suitcase. There was just one chance. The police were not working in pairs, as they usually did; if I could find a young one, I might be able to scare him into letting me through. Some gendarmes had been killed by the Resistance for helping the Germans. Better still, I might hit on an anti-German one.

I chose my gendarme carefully. He was young and did not look too tough. When my turn came, I handed him the keys to the bags. He lifted a handful of clothes out of my personal case, then picked up a shirt from the other one and saw the money.

"Where did you get it?" he demanded.

"It's Resistance money," I said.

"Go on. Clear out," he told me.

I doubted whether my legs would carry me to the nearest bench. If he had so much as lifted a finger, my goose would have been cooked.

The sky now was full of Allied planes every night, and airmen were bailing out all over northern France. At one time Paul Campinchi had 75 hidden in Paris and found it difficult to supply them all with food and clothing.

It was urgent that I find more escape routes—or I might end up with my own air force in France. Then came news about smugglers in the south who had already taken a party of airmen across the Pyrenees to Spain.

In the past, paying these men in advance had led to some double-crossing. I decided to give them the price they asked for before leaving and promised to double it on the safe arrival of the airmen at the British Embassy in Madrid. I specified that we would check with Madrid by wireless. The smugglers accepted this arrangement, and guided 24 airmen into Spain.

On Feb. 26, 1944, we also ran a second Plouha operation—to try to clear the backlog. Twenty parcels went this time without a hitch. This was the start of what became known as the Cross-Channel Ferry Service.

I sent a message to London telling them to put on three more operations for March 15, 19 and 23. They must have thought I had gone crazy, and asked for a repeat. I gave them the dates again, and they agreed.

To prepare for the March 15 operation Ray and I, as usual, went to Plouha in advance. The first thing we saw was a convoy of nondescript vans going around town at a snail's pace. We knew at once what they were doing—locating illicit broadcasters. Le Cornec told us that the whole coast was on alert, although nobody seemed to know why.

This was serious. It might be possible to send out a message cancelling the operation, but it would be extremely hazardous. It would take me over an hour to code it, and then Ray would have to call London on the emergency wavelength. With the detector vans prowling round, the Germans would be onto us at once.

419

I decided instead to send Ray back to Paris to radio from there to cancel the second operation, if not the first. He had little time to do it, for the first was due the following night.

I did not say anything to Le Cornec, but held my breath and hoped that the BBC message to *la maison d'Alphonse* would put off the operation. But when it came, it was confirmatory. There was nothing for it but to keep our fingers crossed and go ahead. The guides dispersed to muster the parcels and lead them to the beach.

I switched on the walkie-talkie that had arrived on the previous operation, and once again the call came:

"Dinan!" I waited a few seconds and answered:

"Saint-Brieuc!"

The navy was right on time and moving silently toward the shore. Suddenly the silence was broken by a loud explosion. The boats were being fired on. They pulled out. Would they be back? We could only wait and see.

Two hours later, when my left arm was numb from holding the walkie-talkie to my ear, a faint noise came over it.

"Dinan!"

"Saint-Brieuc!"

"We're on our way back."

We strained our ears for the sound of the MTB, for the sound of oars, for more firing. Even the airmen stopped whispering, but all we could hear were waves lapping on the beach.

Then out of the darkness the small boats appeared. It was getting late and we bundled the parcels aboard in double-quick time.

When daylight came a few minutes later, the MTB was still visible, but well out to sea and getting rapidly smaller. Mercifully, the Germans, after their earlier performance, must have been off guard, for no shots followed her. She had not been seen—which was just as well for us. This was confirmed next day when the Germans called off the alert.

I was sorry I had cancelled the second operation, but there was still time to organize the third, and perhaps advance it a day or two. To do this, I had to get back to Paris by the first train to contact Ray.

For once, however, radio problems had worked in our favor. He had not been able to send off the first message, so everything remained as originally planned.

The operations on the 19th and 23rd went ahead without trouble. This meant we had successfully shipped out 75 useful fighting men in eight days. No wonder London referred to us as the Cross-Channel Ferry Service!

One of the messages we got soon afterward took me 45 minutes to decipher but it was worth the effort:

> HEARTIEST CONGRATULATIONS FROM DIRECTOR OF MILI-TARY INTELLIGENCE ON RECENT SEA OPERATIONS STOP YOUR HAZARDOUS WORK FULLY APPRECIATED ESPECIALLY IN VIEW OF PRESENT LARGE-SCALE TIGHTENING UP BY ENEMY STOP . . . GOOD LUCK FOR THE FUTURE

And to show they really appreciated the work we were doing, they had promoted both of us. I became a captain, Ray a lieutenant.

On the morning of June 6 I switched on the radio for the news. It was 11 o'clock and there was a special announcement: "Early this morning the Allies landed in Normandy."

At long last it had come! I knew that this was no Dieppe; this time it was the real thing.

The next day a message came from London:

"Get to Brittany and stay here."

This meant that they intended to cut off the Brittany peninsula, and we had better be behind the Allied lines. But getting there was more easily said than done.

For a month or so a good part of the Allied air forces had been paying particular attention to the French railway system. Now, with the invasion as well, there were only two ways to get to Brittany—on foot or by bicycle.

So Ray and I equipped ourselves with bikes. Mine, bought in the black market, was monstrously heavy and pedalling it was like shifting a five-ton truck.

Louisette Lorre, my liaison agent who came from Saint-Brieuc, was going back with us, and we all left Paris early in the morning of June 11. We had quite a trip in front of us—over 400 miles on roads that were far from safe. Allied fighter-bombers patrolled day and night and strafed everything that moved. I was also suffering from a severe attack of boils on my posterior.

We reached Chartres that night and found a boarding house. The proprietress was a talkative woman from Quebec, of all places, and throughout dinner she regaled us with information about Canada. We played the part of interested Frenchmen, curious about the strange ways of the new world across the Atlantic.

When we set out again the next morning, we heard bombing ahead of us, and all along the road were scenes of destruction: here a burnt-out German truck, there a crater where an ammunition-carrier had blown up, its bits scattered over the nearby fields.

At one point we came to a bridge that had been blown up, but a farmer rowed us across the river in his boat. Later, as we were free-wheeling downhill toward another river, aircraft came over to bomb the bridge there. Time and again they tried to hit it, and failed. Eventually, after one near-miss, they sheered off in disgust. We took our chance and nipped across before they came back.

In the suburbs of Laval a school had been turned into a reception centre. When the woman in charge saw me getting off my bicycle she asked whether I had been wounded. I had, but only in my pride. I told her of my condition and she sent for a nurse. Afterward, with my "wounds" dressed, I felt better. Cots had been set up in the classrooms, and we had a good night's sleep.

We were now on the last leg to Saint-Brieuc. We had about 75 miles to go and we wanted to make it before nightfall. In spite of everything, the journey was going well. Then, just after we had crossed a small bridge, a German sergeant by the side of the road yelled at me to halt. I was in the rear, and paid no attention.

He shouted again, and this time he drew his revolver. I was 15 yards away by then, and I doubted whether he could hit me. I stood on my pedals to sprint off, but he yelled at a soldier next to him. This fellow brought up his rifle and aimed at me. He could hardly miss, so I dismounted and waited for them to come up to me. The sergeant motioned that he wanted my bicycle. I hung on to the handlebars and refused to let go. I knew that he had no right to requisition it, but there was little I could do but protest. The soldiers stripped the bicycle of my things, which they handed to me, and wrote me out a receipt for it.

I gave my baggage to Ray and Louisette to take to Saint-Brieuc, and told them to press on. I would get there somehow. I tried to sound confident, but in truth I had not the faintest idea how I was going to manage it.

I sat on the curb for a while, feeling dejected and at a loss. Then an idea struck me. They had no right to take my bicycle; therefore, I would go to the German authorities, lodge a complaint, and demand that they give me transport.

In my pockets were some identity papers showing that I was Jean-François Guillou, a stonemason working for the Germans, and I played the part of an angry and voluble *collaborateur*.

Was it my fault if the English decided to invade while I was on a business trip to Paris? I had co-operated with the occupying forces and this was what I got in return.

The major who saw me begged me to calm down. Unfortunately he had no bicycle to give away, but he was sure the captain of the Feldgendarmerie, the military police, would look after me.

"You will be reimbursed in full," the captain, to whom the buck had been passed, assured me.

But I told the captain money was no good. I wanted transport to Saint-Brieuc. He almost fell over backward. French civilians in German army vehicles? Preposterous!

Finally, with ill grace, he signed a transportation order. Perhaps he was afraid I might take the matter further. After all, it had been a case of outright theft.

My papers were returned to me and I was taken back to the crossroads to await a vehicle. There was little traffic. German army transport had learned to wait for dark before travelling on the open road. Around six o'clock a small staff car appeared and was flagged down. The young Luftwaffe officer in the back said he was going to Loudéac. Although it would still leave me 25 miles to go, I accepted the lift.

It was dark and after curfew when we got there, and I had hardly gone 50 yards from the car when I was stopped by a German patrol. The NCO did not understand French, but when I showed him my travelling orders he took me to his post. I was questioned in French; a truck would be leaving for Saint-Brieuc at 10 o'clock in the morning, and I was issued with a sleeping pass for the local hotel.

At the hotel, I knocked for a solid 20 minutes. At last a window opened, and a grumpy voice asked me what I wanted. When I replied that I had a lodging ticket, I was told that I could go and sleep with the people who had given it to me, or with the cows if I preferred.

There was nothing else for it; I found a hayfield and made myself a bed under some bushes, having first made sure that I hadn't been followed by a German-hater. It was a mild night and I slept well.

Next morning I found a café. Several peasants were standing about,

423

eating or drinking, and as I entered there was a lot of whispering. I asked for bread and coffee but was told there was none, despite the fact that several customers had both in front of them.

I was famished. I went to the counter where I could see four hard-boiled eggs and grabbed them before anybody could stop me. I asked for cider, but, of course, the Germans had drunk all their cider, so I had a drink of *eau non potable* from the washbasin.

When I asked them how much I owed them, I was told that nobody had served me with anything. I put some money on the counter. The barman began wiping up the bar and brushed the note to the floor. The implacable loathing these French country people felt, and expressed, for everything connected with the Germans was, of course, merely another aspect of the courage of people like Le Cornec. I could feel it all round me, not only in the café, but even in the street as I made my way to the military police.

At about 10:30 I was ordered into a small truck. It took us to the Gestapo headquarters nearby. Soon several burly men in civilian clothes came out. I couldn't see much but it seemed that a man was being half-carried to a car.

We set off in convoy, but soon stopped at a crossroads where several Resistance attacks had taken place. Everybody got out of the vehicles as a motorcyclist went ahead to reconnoitre, and I did the same.

I wanted to see who they were taking to Saint-Brieuc. I pulled out a cigarette, and before anyone could react, I was almost at the car, asking for a light. They blocked my view at once; but not before I had a glimpse inside. Between two of the plainclothes thugs was a young man, unconscious and almost naked, his head lolling, covered in blood from head to foot. He was handcuffed, and they had certainly given him a mauling.

As we started up again, I began to formulate a plan to rescue him, but I soon realized it was hopeless. Not only would I risk getting killed to no purpose, but if I were captured the whole network might be endangered. I had no right to take such a chance. But the sight of the tortured young man, propped up between those two bullyboys, made me see red.

When the convoy stopped in the centre of Saint-Brieuc to let me off, I went straight to Louisette's place, our rendezvous. I got the key from under a flagstone in the back yard, and let myself in. I had a good wash and a hot meal, and after a time the others slowly pedalled up the hill. They looked tired and worried. At the gate they stopped and stared at me incredulously.

"How did you get here?" they almost shouted.

I could not resist answering: "By courtesy of the Wehrmacht, the Luftwaffe, the Feldgendarmerie and the Gestapo."

London now began sending us all kinds of people who needed passage back to England. We had to go out and fetch some of them ourselves, under directions from London; others made their own way in.

Among our distinguished customers was a general, who was no trouble at all, thanking us warmly for everything we did, and a French major who sent word that we were to fetch him by car from his Resistance unit. We replied that he would do better to walk, as the Germans were searching all vehicles. This did not suit him at all; indeed, from his answer, I thought he must be sick, so I sent a horse and cart for him.

It was 50 miles each way, and when he arrived he was beside himself with the indignity of his mode of travel. I let him rave on for a time; then I turned to the driver of the cart and asked him why he had brought this lunatic in instead of shooting him. The major put his hand on my shoulder, intending to spin me round. I spun around all right and, drawing the Colt .45 at my belt, I fired one shot at his head. I missed intentionally, and he vanished into the bushes, never to be seen again.

Toward the end of July, we put on another operation and, though we did not know it then, it was our last. We had only a few airmen, but several important officers whose presence was urgently required in England. With so few, it seemed pointless to go to all the trouble of hiding them in farmhouses until the evening of the operation; instead, they were to go directly to *la maison d'Alphonse*, where they would stay with Jean Gicquel, the owner, until it was time to be taken to the beach.

It was around two o'clock in the morning when we left them there. We had barely gone 200 yards when we heard shots coming from the house. We turned back to find out what was going on, creeping silently through the fields at the rear where we could see over the wall.

Several German soldiers were standing in front of the open door engaged in violent argument. One was lying on the ground, apparently wounded in the leg. While we watched, the others carried him inside. There was no sign of the parcels, and we wondered who had shot the soldier.

With mounting impatience we waited for the Germans to depart and Jean Gicquel to contact us at a nearby house where we knew he would look for us.

425

La maison d'Alphonse, *burned by the Germans in July 1944.*

When he finally appeared, he told us what had happened. The Germans had knocked at the door, ordering him to open it. Jean did so and had started to move forward when he noticed shadows on either side of the door. He drew back quickly, and the two Germans fired at the same time, one hitting the other in the leg. Jean said that the soldiers appeared to be the worse for drink, and that while they were in the kitchen, bandaging the wounded man, they kept pointing toward the ceiling and muttering:

"Tommy, Tommy, terrorists."

A Tommy was a British soldier, and a terrorist was a French Resistance fighter. Did the Germans know there were British servicemen concealed in the house, or, seeing a ray of light and hearing people talking, had they jumped to that conclusion? The regular ambushing of German units was undoubtedly having its effect on the nerves of the occupying forces, and they were seeing the Resistance everywhere.

As soon as the Germans left, Jean sent the parcels into a wheat field 200 yards away and told them to stay there, as the enemy was likely to come back in force. He then took his wife and baby to a neighboring farm and came to report to us.

In the morning the Germans arrived early and set fire to the house. As it was built of stone, it did not burn very well, and they had to use a lot of incendiary bombs to get it going. We moved Mme Gicquel and her baby to the home of one of our helpers, much farther away, and everybody who heard of their plight brought in clothes.

Later in the afternoon Le Cornec and I went to find our parcels. Their track through the corn was quite obvious, and in the next field we could see the grass moving, not because of the wind. We did not want to be shot at, so we called to them from a safe distance. We had brought them food and drink, and arranged to meet them later.

The final operation went well, and without further trouble, of which we had had our fill. All in all, we counted ourselves lucky to have escaped without casualties—one house burnt down was the sole cost.

After the liberation of Paris, I returned to my apartment. I was officially attached to M.I.5, but no fewer than three times the *concierge* reported that an impostor who had lived there before the liberation, a black market operator, had now turned up again, claiming to be a Canadian officer. So insistent was she that, one morning, a party composed of a French *commandant de gendarmerie,* a British major from the military police, a Canadian lieutenant from the Provost Marshal's department, and a British corporal and four men, all armed to the teeth, appeared on the doorstep and demanded that I identify myself.

As I was wearing French riding boots and breeches, an American army windbreaker, a German leather belt with *Gott mit uns* on the buckle, an American woollen shirt, a British beret adorned with a Canadian badge, and was carrying a Luger and a commando dagger, they had reason to be curious.

I would like to end this story by saying that, after months of giving the Gestapo the slip, I finished up being arrested by a Canadian policeman, but I must admit it wasn't like that. They simply took me to our HQ for identification.

The most difficult part was giving them my real name. I had almost forgotten it!

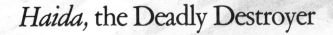

Haida, the Deadly Destroyer

Pound for pound, she was as successful as any Allied fighting ship in World War II. Commissioned by the Royal Canadian Navy in August 1943, HAIDA *was a brand-new, lean and powerful Tribal Class destroyer, designed primarily to attack surface ships. She first spent four months escorting convoys to and from Murmansk in arctic Russia. Early in 1944, as the Allies completed plans for the Normandy invasion,* HAIDA *joined the 10th Destroyer Flotilla of the Royal Navy in Plymouth, England. She sailed on 19 missions without encountering a single German warship. Then, on April 25, 1944, her luck changed.*

By WILLIAM SCLATER

THE WIND WAS FRESHENING that evening as *Haida* slipped her moorings at Plymouth. Ahead were the darkening seas of the English Channel. With three other Tribals, the Canadian *Athabaskan* and *Huron* and the British *Ashanti,* and the British cruiser *Black Prince,* she had been ordered to intercept three German destroyers expected to sail from the French port of Saint-Malo, 150 miles to the southeast.

The shrill pipe ordered: "Port watch to defence stations." Guns and firing circuits were checked. "Darken ship" was piped and every man off duty headed below to get what rest he could while deadlights were screwed down on portholes, hatches were closed and thick canvas blackout curtains were drawn. "Action stations" would be sounded at 10:30 if no enemy contact was made earlier. From then on *Haida*'s entire crew of 250 would be on duty till after dawn.

Ten o'clock passed and the men below began to struggle into heavy underwear, thick socks, sweaters, life jackets, ear protectors, steel helmets and "lammy" coats. Promptly at 10:30 the buzzers sounded and along the decks running figures moved to their stations. Swiftly and surely, *Haida* was readied for action.

It was quiet up on the open bridge under the stars. Visibility was good, about two miles. There was no moon. *Haida,* with *Athabaskan* close astern, formed the starboard subdivision. To port was *Black Prince* and beyond, screening the cruiser on the other side, were *Huron* and *Ashanti.*

The five ships were nearing the French coast and lookouts swept the seas and the skies through binoculars, alert for a flicker of light, a movement, the sound of aircraft.

Two hours passed and then the flash of gunfire was observed from shore batteries. A few minutes later there was more. The senior officer, in *Black Prince,* ordered a slight alteration of course and the cruiser picked up radar echoes dead ahead. In a few minutes the contacts were confirmed by the four Tribals: four or five echoes that appeared to be turning away. The time was 2:10 a.m.

"Increase to 30 knots," the cruiser signalled. *Haida*'s turbines hummed higher and the plot reported to the bridge that the enemy contacts were being held and closed. They appeared to be destroyers.

The cruiser opened fire with star shell. Her role was to provide illumination while the destroyers closed in to engage. *Haida* increased speed again, her turbines rising to a high whine as she raced through the seas

430

with *Athabaskan* right astern. Her bridge crew watched a star shell light the sea to the right of the bearing of the enemy ships. Nothing was visible.

"More left . . . more left," *Haida* signalled. The cruiser corrected and fired again. Another long, tense moment and then a star shell burst, flooding the horizon with sudden light above the indicated bearing.

Half a dozen voices blurted at once: "There they are! There they are!" Low on the horizon, five miles ahead, several dark objects could be seen under the spread of star shell.

"Three, possibly four enemy destroyers, making to eastward under cover of smoke screen," reported the bridge observers.

"Open fire!" ordered *Haida*'s captain, Comdr. Harry G. DeWolf.

The tracers of four shells from *Haida*'s two twin forward mountings arched across the skies. The cruiser was firing steadily and so were the other destroyers.

Answering flashes came from the German ships and star shell burst along the horizon away over to port. The enemy seemed bewildered by the guns which had lashed at them so suddenly.

The ships swept on in formation, surprised to discover that they were gaining on German destroyers reputed to be much faster than the Tribals, whose top speed was 36 knots. *Haida* was abeam of the enemy smoke screen now. It was a light, whitish color, about 100 feet high and some 500 yards to starboard. Then the enemy's searching star shell found the bearing of the outer subdivision and caught *Huron* and *Ashanti* and the whole area between them in a greenish, ghostly brilliance.

Voices cried "A hit!" as flame burst on an enemy ship and showed through the smoke screen. Moments later the cry came again and, as the Tribals raced all out, the range slowly but inexorably decreased.

The illumination died suddenly and there was only darkness ahead. *Black Prince* signalled that her B gun turret was out of action and could fire no more star shell. Two minutes later her lookouts sighted a torpedo and her captain ordered "hard aport." The torpedo passed up the starboard side. More enemy torpedoes were observed and, since her B turret was out of action and in any case her role had been solely to supply illumination, *Black Prince* disengaged. The time was 2:48.

Command of the destroyers devolved upon the captain of *Haida* and, by prearranged plan, illumination was provided by the second destroyer in each of the two subdivisions. At 3:01 two enemy destroyers were observed emerging to windward of their smoke screen, then turning back in again. A warning was sounded to watch for torpedoes.

431

"E-boat at red two-five!" called a bridge officer, and every man on deck looked 25 degrees off the port bow. A fast-moving object, throwing up a wide bow wave four or five feet high, could be seen approaching on an opposite course. In the light of an enemy star shell, it swept past *Haida's* port side, about 400 yards off, then was lost to sight as the shell dropped into the sea. It was not an E-boat but a British motor torpedo boat. Returning from a secret mission to France, it had stumbled into the action by mistake.

Following the coastline as tightly as they could, *Haida* and *Athabaskan* found themselves close to the enemy smoke screen and drawing ahead of *Huron* and *Ashanti*. All four Tribals were making the same swift speed but the inside ships had the advantage of position as the coast veered south.

Heavy fire arched over the smoke screen from inshore, passing well above *Haida* and *Athabaskan* and seemingly directed toward *Huron* and *Ashanti*. All four Tribals were sending a furious crescendo against the enemy ships ahead, destroyers against destroyers now in equal numbers.

There was a mine field in this area but the German ships simply fled through it and the Tribals followed. The shooting from the landward side was far astern now and seemed to be dying out. Ahead, too close, were the islands called Sept Iles.

Tense and alert, *Haida's* bridge watched for a sign that the German ships would try to break off the engagement. Enemy smoke floats could be seen at regular intervals, smoke pouring from them and being carried back in the wind. Farther ahead the smoke screen looked more irregular and then the bridge caught a glimpse of something at its edge, something that might be a ship trying to double back. It was a momentary glimpse, followed by a pause in which no star shell fell. *Haida* altered course to allow her rear gun mounting to fire star shell. The first burst, directly over the target, revealed a destroyer streaking clear of the smoke. Every detail of her long hull with its high foredeck was visible; the silhouette was unmistakable to trained eyes.

"Elbing Class destroyer!" *Haida's* guns swung and steadied on the target. In the eerie light, the Elbing was speeding along, apparently unmarked. *Haida's* guns crashed salvo after salvo.

The first was a direct hit. It caught the Elbing amidships, about 10 feet below her main deck, and crumpled through her plates. Another crashed in aft, below deck level again, then one below the bridge, another just abaft the first.

Geysers of steam rose from the enemy midships. She slowed and stopped dead, red flame licking hungrily up from where the salvo had gone home. Three fires joined rapidly to make an inferno of her main deck.

Now *Athabaskan* was hitting her too. One salvo smashed through the high bows, then another. More fires broke out until only the Elbing's upper bridge and afterdeck showed black in a sea of red.

As *Haida* and *Athabaskan* closed for the kill, the roar and hiss of steam escaping from the enemy ship could be heard across two and a half miles of flame-lit water.

Ahead, to seaward, were *Huron* and *Ashanti*. Having lost sight of the ships they'd been pursuing, they turned back to the battle.

Survivors could be seen trying to get clear of the Elbing on a life raft but her guns were still being served and *Haida* had no alternative. A salvo, intended to strike below the water line, crashed into the enemy's hull and sent raft and occupants hurtling skyward.

The German's guns appeared to be silenced. There was only the roar and crackle of the flames and small, intermittent explosions. Circling like Indians, the Tribals sailed round her, close in.

Some men were still alive aboard the doomed destroyer. As the Tribals passed, two streams of tracer spat unexpectedly from high on her bridge and far back on her quarterdeck. They swept along *Haida*'s after superstructure, spattered *Athabaskan*'s length and beat on *Huron*'s bridge.

A stream of colored tracer spurted from *Haida*'s Oerlikons and swept the enemy's decks, ricochetting over her bridge and after structure. The Elbing fired no more.

She still floated. Aflame from bow to stern, she seemed unsinkable. The Tribals closed again and more salvos rocked her, smashing into the hull and sending up showers of sparks against black masses of oily smoke billowing to leeward.

Then, as they watched, she rolled to port. Her bows dipped and she slipped swiftly under the sea. From *Haida*'s foredeck came hoarse cheering as the gun crews watched her go. The time was 4:20.

Flashing their fighting lights, the Tribals formed up and stood away to seaward on course for England. The stars came out again and the night wind was fresh and sweet after the reek of cordite. The damaged enemy ships had probably made some French port. They would have to be left for another night. Dawn was near and it was time to go.

As *Haida* sped toward Plymouth, the ship was checked. There were several splinter holes through the hull and the rear gun deck; the forward messdecks were a shambles; the sick bay and the captain's day cabin, an emergency operating theatre during the battle, had been swept by close-range fire. Several men had suffered wounds, all minor.

Sailing up harbor they were the subject of interested scrutiny. The word had got around, in the mysterious way it does in naval ports, and ship after ship saluted them. *Haida*'s crew was happy and proud: she had acquitted herself well.

Two nights later *Haida* and *Athabaskan* were ordered out again. Mine-laying craft were to operate inshore in French waters and the two Tribals were to cover them to seaward.

The order "action stations," delayed by Commander DeWolf until midnight to allow *Haida*'s crew as much rest as possible, brought all hands tumbling out. This was E-boat weather: the moon would not go down for another two hours and the Tribals could be seen easily from a long way off. *Athabaskan,* looking like a ship of silver as she cruised astern, was plainly visible. Like *Haida*, she was in the first degree of readiness.

An hour dragged by, then a second and a third. Around 3:30 a.m. a signal was received from Plymouth. Radar reconnaissance had discovered two enemy destroyers making to westward, close in on the French coast.

DeWolf, as senior officer, decided to steam an intercepting course and close them. At the point of interception, his ships would be at the western end of their area. He hoped to turn the enemy and drive them eastward along the coast to prevent them escaping round the corner to Brest at the top of the Bay of Biscay.

Less than 48 hours since the Tribals' last action, the chance had come again. Heeling over as they turned, *Haida* and *Athabaskan* angled in toward the French shore, every man on the qui vive.

The moon had gone down and a slight haze made observation difficult. The range of the enemy ships was 7,000 yards.

"Ignite," said the captain.

"Three stars, spreading left, fire!" ordered the illumination control officer, and the rear guns fired.

"There they are . . . two of them!"

"Red five-oh, two enemy destroyers."

"Open fire!" barked the captain.

Haida rolled with the recoil of her guns. *Athabaskan* was firing too, with star shell and main armament.

"Enemy making smoke and turning to eastward."

Haida and *Athabaskan,* according to plan, turned toward the German ships to make themselves smaller targets for any torpedoes.

Through binoculars, *Haida*'s bridge studied the smudges in the enemy smoke screen from which his gun flashes were coming. Enemy star shell was bursting overhead and between them. Other shells whistled overhead as the Germans brought their main armament into action.

A cry: "*Athabaskan*'s hit!"

Every head on *Haida*'s bridge turned. From somewhere aft of *Athabaskan*'s bridge a column of flame was shooting up, outlining her fore section in bold relief. As they looked, her B gun fired.

From the enemy ships came a frenzy of gunfire as they turned all their guns on the burning destroyer.

A stoker crawled out on *Haida*'s afterdeck and opened a valve which turned on the chemical smoke producers. They soon put a dense curtain between the stricken ship and her enemies.

Below: HAIDA, *the most famous Canadian warship of World War II. Inset:* ATHABASKAN, *sunk off the French coast.*

In *Athabaskan* there was no panic. The propellers had ceased to function and she was being carried forward by her own impetus. The first report reached the bridge.

"Torpedo hit near the gearing room. Heavy damage aft the apron and Y gun collapsed. Steering gear out of action."

"Damage control party on the job?" asked *Athabaskan*'s captain, Lt. Cdr. J. H. Stubbs.

"After pump is gone, sir. The forward pump is being taken back and rigged now."

"Try the after steering position," ordered Stubbs. "Better hoist out the sea boats but don't lower them yet. *Haida* is making a smoke screen and will try to take us in tow later."

There was feverish activity on *Athabaskan*'s decks. Up forward the bosun's party rigged the towing hawser. Amidships, others hauled the 70-ton portable pump into position and started to get it ready to fight the flames rising behind them.

"After steering position out of action and ship settling by the stern, sir."

The young captain nodded. "All hands stand by abandon-ship stations," he said.

The crew started to file off the bridge; the captain remained.

There had been no power failure and down on the main deck the men worked desperately to bring the emergency pump into action. It was almost ready. Suddenly a roar of flame blasted skyward. The after part of the ship became a holocaust. The deck tilted crazily, then collapsed. Chief Petty Officer Charles Thomas Burgess, the torpedo gunner's mate, was flung forward from the pump. Dazed, thinking he had landed in the forward stokehold, he staggered to his feet.

Great blobs of burning oil were falling everywhere. Men standing by the boats covered their heads with their arms and dashed blindly forward, trying to find shelter under the boats. Many plunged into the sea. More oil came down. The ship lurched violently and most of those who were left went over the side.

"Abandon ship!" Burgess, the torpedo gunner's mate, heard the shout. He tried to grasp the rail to go over but his arm wouldn't move. Unaware that it was broken in two places and that blood was streaming from his gashed and broken head, he looked dumbly at the rail. The ship heeled and he sat down heavily. He felt himself sliding. He went under the rail and into the sea. The water revived him and he turned on his side and swam with his good arm. The ship was sinking and he knew he had to get clear of the suction. He was a well-built man, in excellent condition, and a good swimmer.

About 50 yards from the ship, he looked back. *Athabaskan* was going. She had righted and now the bow was rising. Up, up it came until it was nearly perpendicular, clear of the surface almost back to the first funnel. She seemed to poise there a moment and then she slipped swiftly into the sea.

While *Athabaskan* lived her last moments, *Haida* came under fire from the two German destroyers. Yet she continued to press her attack. Her gunners had been fast before, but now they fought desperately. Far below them the lights in the forward magazines snapped out as a splinter hit. In the dim light of a couple of flashlights the supply parties continued to pass heavy shells to feed *Haida*'s guns.

"A hit!" The glow of fire broke out amidships on the first German destroyer and smoldered through the smoke.

The second enemy ship appeared to be slowing and was falling behind the first. Commander DeWolf swung his guns to train on her. One salvo punched out, another and another. Then a hit. High amidships, flames mounted on the German destroyer's superstructure. Another salvo thudded into her and the flames spread. Then suddenly she let loose a vicious burst of close-range fire—but it was directed at the other fleeing German destroyer. The fire was returned. The enemy ships were attacking each other. In the confusion they seemed unable to tell friend from foe.

Haida was surging toward one of them when a warning cry came from the officer of the watch: "Reefs ahead!"

"Port 20," snapped the captain, and *Haida* heeled over and swung away from the shore. One enemy destroyer, burning furiously, had driven up on the beach, out of control. Swinging round, *Haida* let her have it again and again. When the shooting stopped, intermittent explosions burst through the smoke and flames.

Daylight was close now, too close for a long chase after other enemy destroyers up a hostile coast. *Haida* turned back toward where *Athabaskan* had gone down. Smoke from the screen *Haida* had put out was still drifting, though thinner now. "Star shell over that bearing," Commander DeWolf ordered. "Let's see if there's anything left on the surface that we might bump."

Under the star shell, black clusters of survivors could be seen—three or four groups and numbers of small, separated figures. *Athabaskan* had left no other trace. As *Haida* closed, the flashing lights of survivors' life jackets could be seen more than a mile away.

The captain let the ship glide to a stop among the largest clusters. "All gun crews remain at their posts," he ordered. "Every man who can be spared from other positions will go to the main deck and help survivors inboard. Lower all boats that'll float. Drop all life rafts. We'll wait 15 minutes. Get as many on board as you can."

It was an eerie scene. Life-jacket lights were flashing; survivors were shouting and blowing their whistles. Inshore a red rock-buoy light was flashing. Behind that rose the low shore, a rocky promontory. And above it, a lighthouse flashed steadily.

Her engines stopped, *Haida* drifted sideways with the light wind. Survivors on the starboard side could be seen and heard, but the ship was drifting downwind faster than they could swim.

To port the wind was a help to the survivors. Lining the rail, *Haida*'s men encouraged them to swim in. The sea was heavy with fuel oil and those who reached the ship's side were covered from head to foot. Few had strength to climb up the scramble nets or the ladders and *Haida*'s people went over the side and helped them. Six men formed a rescue line on one scramble net, pulling and pushing the survivors on board. Soon rescuers and rescued alike were filthy with oil. It was difficult to get a grip on the survivors since there was no handhold on the life jackets. To leave their arms free, the rescuers hooked themselves to the scramble nets with the clasps of their life preservers.

Haida's whaler went away. It was damaged but would float. The starboard motor cutter was not lowered—it had been shot full of holes. The port cutter was serviceable and three *Haida* men manned it, although they knew the ship could not wait for them.

After 15 minutes Commander DeWolf started calling warnings: five minutes, four minutes, three, two, one minute. Then: "We are going ahead *now*." But he waited another few moments before giving the order: "Slow ahead." Men working over the side to rescue *Athabaskan* survivors kept right on as *Haida,* alert for possible air attack, started up. The captain's first responsibility was the safety of his own ship and her company.

It was lighter now; the coast could be plainly seen. They were off Ile de Vierge. A raft came alongside with officers and men on it, and others in the water clinging to its life lines. "Quickly now," said a voice on deck, "the ship's ready to go."

438

"Take the wounded first," said a man on the raft. The wounded were helped up. It was slow work for they could not help themselves. Many were burned. As *Haida* moved gently ahead, the men on the nets worked desperately to get the survivors inboard.

From the back of the raft someone was calling, "Get away *Haida*, get clear!" A sailor said later it was the young captain of *Athabaskan*. Other survivors said Stubbs had swum to the raft, resting his arms on it as if they were burned, and had encouraged them to sing.

A line parted with a snap and the raft swung away from the ship. One of the men on the net tried to hook it with his foot but missed, and it drifted astern. Unaware that the raft was alongside, the bridge had ordered the ship to move ahead and all men back to their stations. Daylight was imminent. It was time to go.

Unhooking themselves from the net, the rescuers scrambled up on deck. But two, on the lowest level with water sweeping past their legs, couldn't make it. An officer climbed back down and tried to free them, but the sea was catching the boom at the foot of the scramble net and sweeping over their thighs so that they had to use both hands to hang on.

From the deck, another officer tried to haul the scramble net up. Just as others were coming to help him, the two seamen on the net let go. Torn loose by the seas sweeping past, they disappeared into the propeller-churned vortex of waters astern.

Dawn was coming up when *Haida* cleared the land. As she sped swiftly seaward, every man was at his action station and lookouts searched the skies.

Below decks, in the dim light of the battle lamps, survivors seemed everywhere. Every blanket and "lammy" coat and sheepskin had been requisitioned to wrap them in. In the after flats the air reeked with fuel oil. Heaps of soaked clothing lay where it had been stripped off.

The surgeon and his assistants worked ceaselessly, administering morphine, treating burns, and doing a blood transfusion for a serious case in the captain's bunk. It was cold and many of the half-frozen men shivered in their blankets. All electric radiators and heating pipes had been shut off to reduce fire hazards when the ship went to action stations. Now, with everything battened down and the reek of oil everywhere, not even smoking could be permitted.

Most of the men were quiet, glad to be free of the cold, oily sea.

But they couldn't forget that back off the French coast were others, drifting on rafts and clinging to a few pieces of wreckage—all that remained of a good ship and her company. With them, too, were three members of *Haida*'s crew in the ship's motorboat, men who had put other lives before their own.

Both the sailors swept off *Haida*'s scramble net had gone under as the wash of the sea along the hull sucked them down. They turned end over end in the churning water above the propellers, but their life jackets brought them up. When they surfaced they were in the wake of the ship.

They had survived almost certain death. Above them the stars still shone in the paling night sky. Inshore, France was in plain view. England and safety were over 100 miles away. They decided to float until they got their bearings.

Some distance away another man watched *Haida* go, a man with a badly broken arm and a gashed face—Charles Burgess, the torpedo gunner's mate of *Athabaskan*. Swimming away from the sinking ship, he had come across *Athabaskan*'s coxswain in the water. They knew that if the survivors were grouped in life rafts together, there might be a better chance of survival. They set to work bringing the isolated survivors, clinging to bits of wreckage, to the life rafts.

When *Haida* returned, they were helping a young seaman get to a raft. In the semidarkness they looked at each other, one thought in their minds. Both knew they could reach *Haida* on their own, but they would have to abandon their burden.

As if sensing their thoughts, the burned, half-conscious lad muttered, "Don't leave me." That was that. They continued toward a raft and by the time they reached it, *Haida* was preparing to go. They brought others in and then, worn out, sought refuge themselves.

The coxswain found a handhold on one raft but there was no place for Burgess. He swam to another but it, too, was full. Everywhere it was the same grim story. Tiring fast, Burgess swam slowly away and, with a last effort, turned over on his back and floated.

Things were getting hazy. He didn't feel the cold chill of the Channel any more. Warm slumber seemed to be creeping over him. It was pleasant and he had no strength left to fight it. Then, dimly, he heard voices far back in his mind and a big shadowy thing seemed to loom over him. He felt strong hands haul him clear of the water. They laid him gently down by the shelter of the engine of *Haida*'s motorboat.

440

"What ship?" he muttered.

"It's *Haida*'s boat."

"Good old *Haida*," said Burgess, and he passed out.

The motorboat had been busy. The coxswain, Leading Seaman William Maclure, with the stoker, William Cummings, and the bowman, Able Seaman Jack Hannam, had decided first to pick up men who had been unable to reach a raft. They had hauled in four shivering sailors when they saw *Haida* getting under way. To line up her course so they could follow later, they swung a quarter mile astern and ran in her wake. They were about to turn back toward the *Athabaskan* survivors when Hannam heard a voice hailing him.

He stared at the dark water, imagining he had heard the voice of a chum. It must be hallucination; his friend was in *Haida*. But the voice sounded again and this time it was stronger, and unmistakable. "Hi, Jack," it called. "How about a hitch?"

The astonished bowman saw a dark blob. There, grinning up at him, was his friend from *Haida*.

It was a vigorous ghost. "Give me a hand up," it ordered. "This water's cold." It was one of the seamen swept off the scramble net. Feeling cold, he had decided to swim and had sighted the motorboat. Once aboard he quickly directed them to the other *Haida* lad, 200 yards ahead. Both were in good shape.

With that, their good luck deserted them. The boat's engine spluttered and stopped. Helpless, they drifted with the wind and tide. On the port side they discerned another floating figure and, ripping up floorboards for paddles, manoeuvred the heavy motorboat toward it. They hauled in another survivor, a far-spent signalman.

It was heavy work handling the improvised paddles and they were about to give up when Hannam sighted yet another figure, floating on his back. At first they thought he might be dead, but then they saw an arm move feebly. It was Burgess, the torpedo gunner's mate.

The men in the motorboat could see the German destroyer still burning furiously on the beach. There came a sudden flash and then a violent explosion; the flames had reached a magazine. In the motorboat the crew and those survivors who could stand got to their feet and cheered.

Precious minutes were slipping away. To the eastward they could see *Athabaskan* survivors on rafts. It was daylight now. They wondered if they could get the engine started in time to rescue some of the men

441

on the rafts before the enemy spotted them. But the stoker, Cummings, was having a difficult time. Those who were not helping him watched the sky and the land. The wounded Burgess lay unconscious.

"Something's coming up round that headland," said Maclure. There were ships, three of them, in line not more than four miles away.

"Minesweepers!" said Hannam.

They watched the German ships stop near the other survivors some three miles east. Two seemed to be going closer to pick them up and then, with sinking hearts, they saw the third minesweeper get under way and steam directly toward them.

Cummings lifted a hammer and, in a last frantic effort, smashed it down on the engine intake and pressed the starter button.

It caught. Coughing and spluttering, the engine started. "Give me a hand," yelled Cummings. "Hold this ruddy plug in place." Half a dozen hands reached to help him as the engine steadied into the sweetest music they had ever heard. The motorboat surged ahead, the coxswain steering directly away from the approaching enemy.

Their first quick elation was momentary. The German ship was slowly but steadily overtaking them. The original lead of 2,000 yards had been reduced to almost half that. Tensely, they waited for a shot to come whistling overhead. But the minesweeper suddenly altered course and headed away. Why, they did not know. Whatever it was, they thanked Providence and kept on going.

Seven miles offshore the engine spluttered and died again, but they were in better condition than they had been to start with. Sun and wind were drying their clothes. Their cigarettes had been soaked but they spread them out to dry on the engine cover. Someone produced a pipe and when the tobacco was ready, they filled it up and passed it from one to another. Then Cummings and two assistants went back to work on the engine.

It was about nine o'clock. The stoker stopped, listening. The others heard it too. Faint and distant—the sound of aircraft. They could see them now, two fighters flying low. They stood up, waving and shouting. Maclure fired a red flare into the sky. The two planes thundered toward them.

Sweeping in, about 12 feet above the surface and 100 yards off, they went past on each side. The men in the boat could see the pilots looking at them.

A seaman suddenly stopped waving. "Krauts!" he yelled, ducking down by the bulwark. Faces grim, they watched the Messerschmitts go.

At first they thought the planes would circle back to machine-gun them but the fighters made directly for land. They knew, however, that they would be reported. Without a word, they all turned impulsively toward the engine.

Cummings had done a good job. The engine started. It was a bit ragged but the motorboat started to forge ahead.

They were tired and hungry. They needed food and medical supplies. There was little they could do for the unconscious Burgess but try to keep him warm. They were a long, long way from a friendly harbor, yet they were hopeful and cheerful. *Haida,* they knew, would report them. They held course toward England.

Around noon the motor failed again, but they got it going. This time it ran steadily. About 6:30 in the evening they saw two planes coming from the direction of France. Believing they were the German fighters, they ducked for cover and it was not until they were almost overhead that they saw the RAF markings. They went a bit crazy, waving and signalling "Canada" with semaphore flags.

They were spotted. The fighters stayed above them for an hour and then were relieved by two more fighters and a bomber. About 10 o'clock one plane came in close and circled. Then they saw a ship coming, a rescue launch.

In all, 44 of *Athabaskan*'s crew had been saved and 83 had become prisoners of war. But *Athabaskan*'s captain, Lieutenant Commander Stubbs, and 128 men were lost.

By the end of 1944, when HAIDA *sailed home for a major refit and a warm welcome in Halifax, she had sunk two destroyers, a U-boat and 15 other ships. Her name had become famous throughout Canada. When it was announced long after the war that* HAIDA *was to be sent to the scrapyard, a public subscription was started to save her. Today, with her motorboat still aboard, she is berthed at Ontario Place on the Toronto waterfront, a monument to the nearly 100,000 Canadians who served in the Royal Canadian Navy during World War II.*

The Two Jacks

*On June 7, 1944, the second day of the great Allied invasion
of France, the North Nova Scotia Highlanders were trapped
far forward of supporting artillery and were overrun by waves
of German troops. Many of the 128 Canadians taken prisoner
were killed in cold blood. Lieutenants Jack Veness, 21, and
Jack Fairweather, 20, both from New Brunswick, were among
the survivors. Two weeks later they found themselves aboard
a packed and fetid prison train.*

By WILL R. BIRD

T HE DOORS WERE BOLTED and padlocked, the small windows heavily wired. Day after day, trapped men huddled helplessly in the straw of stinking boxcars as bombs rained down from high-flying aircraft bent on destroying the Germans' transportation network. The bomber crews were Americans, Britons and Canadians. So were the men in the long train below.

Veness and Fairweather were among 31 officers and sergeants in one boxcar. With hundreds of other Allied prisoners, they had been moved well away from the beachhead. For days they'd been sealed into

the boxcar, with inadequate food and little exercise and so many air raids that they wondered how long their luck could last. On the sixth night, the train was on a siding near Tours, 125 miles southwest of Paris.

Veness wakened to the hum of aircraft, groped his way to a window and saw flares drifting slowly earthward, lighting everything for miles. The earth seemed to shake as German anti-aircraft batteries opened up. Soon shrapnel was striking loudly on the boxcar roof. Above the racket rose the mighty sound of many bombers, a thunder that struck terror to the heart.

"We're done!" someone screamed. "This is it!"

Men grovelled on the floor. One chanted "Our Father . . ." An officer attacked the end of the car like a maniac, striking and kicking at the boards, then trying to tear them loose.

There came the crump-crump-crump of falling bombs—far in the rear. A calm voice: "They're after the railway yards, not us." Another five minutes of explosions, then the din ended and the sound of bombers faded. Relief.

But in each man's mind was a heavy dread: could he take another attack? Escape was the only hope. Fairweather and Veness found that where the crazed officer had attacked the wall, a board had been damaged and could be removed easily. If the hole could be enlarged . . .

After several days on the siding, the train began to move. Maj. Don Learment of the North Novas and an American pilot, William R. Fredenberg, pried and pounded away at the hole with two spoons, a pocketknife and a hammer. The train rolled on through the night. Men drifted off to sleep.

When Veness woke it was very dark and there was no pounding. He found Capt. Joe Trainor of the North Novas beside the hole. Through it came cool air and a clatter of train wheels. "Where are Learment and Fredenberg?"

"Gone!" said Trainor. "And five others have crawled out."

Veness turned quickly to Fairweather. "Wake up!"

Fairweather crawled to the 18-inch hole, remembering what a paratrooper had told him: "Keep your legs together with your knees slightly flexed, and roll when you fall."

"We'll jump five seconds apart," said Veness. "I'll go first."

He crawled headfirst through the opening, onto the buffers between the two boxcars. The buffers were low, the track was rough and the cars were bucking. One slip would be his last. Three other men on the buffers clung to the cars, reluctant to jump, leaving little room for anyone else. Veness lunged when the train was on an upgrade and landed spread-eagled across the buffers. He caught hold of the car and gained his footing.

Fairweather, thick and broad, got stuck in the opening and for a moment felt relief: now he wouldn't have to risk his life. But he squeezed through and dropped onto the buffer.

The first three men took off, one by one. It was strange to see them fling out into space and to have not the slightest idea where they landed. Suddenly Fairweather saw Veness had one hand on top of a buffer pad with his fingers extended downward. The train had climbed a long curving grade and now began to straighten out on a level stretch. Fairweather kicked Veness' hand away just before the colliding buffers would have squashed it.

"Here goes," said Veness. He stood, and in an instant vanished. He skidded a few feet and crashed hard on his chest and hands, then rolled into a shallow ditch, face down in mud and weeds. A spasm of dizziness faded and he rose gingerly and watched the red tail light of the train disappear. His chest was badly bruised. His hands were bleeding.

Now Fairweather crouched and hurled himself outward. He struck heavily and pitched head over heels into a ditch filled with nettles. A bit lip and numerous nettle stings on his face and hands were his only damage. As the train's tail light vanished, he stood, stretched and grinned. He was free again. He turned and walked along the track.

Veness heard footsteps on gravel, someone walking with care. German patrols? He slowed and waited. The footfalls became quicker and steadier. Veness stood.

"Jack?"

"Yeah."

"Hurt?"

"No. You?"

"No. Let's go."

Veness pointed south. "That way."

The air was cool and fresh. "It sure is a nice night," said Veness.

It was about 2 a.m. July 22. They moved with caution, remembering what they had been told of minefields, anti-aircraft batteries and German patrols trying to curb the French underground. Above all they feared being hunted by the fierce dogs such patrols used. Stars shone faintly but the night was misty. Then all at once they were on the bank of a river about 150 yards wide. They recalled escape maps they had studied on the train.

"It's the Cher (a tributary of the Loire)," said Veness. They swam it, scrambled out hungry, weak and exhausted. They ate what they could of their soggy German bread and threw the rest away. Veness wanted to hurry but there was no hurrying Fairweather. They were to prove a good combination: Veness kept Fairweather stirred to action; Fairweather restrained the impulsive Veness.

They passed through vineyards, a grainfield, more vineyards, checking their direction by the Big Dipper. About four o'clock they found an orchard and devoured a few green and very sour apples.

At first light, looking for a place to hide, they spotted a little copse across a field from a farmhouse. There they stripped and spread their clothes to dry. They tried to sleep but their nerves were taut. Intermittent rain became a steady drizzle. They were wet and miserable.

"Let's go to the farm," said Veness.

"Okay," said Fairweather. "They can only turn us in."

In the barn was a man pitching hay. Veness explained as best he could in French that they were escaped Canadian officers. The man kept on with his work.

"We're Canadians," Veness shouted in English.

The man looked frightened and mumbled, "Madame." He led them to the kitchen door where a middle-aged woman beckoned them in. She sent her small daughter for an interpreter, then fetched a bottle of wine. The two Jacks were sipping and trying to question her when they heard footsteps. It was a postman. The Canadians were conscious of his quick scrutiny. It made them nervous.

They heard men running and braced themselves as the door was flung open. Two Frenchmen rushed in, kissed their bearded cheeks, jabbering a welcome. One with fiery red hair announced he was an agent of the underground and said they must take every care because the Germans were combing the country.

As others crowded in, Madame put food on the table and asked Veness and Fairweather if they wanted to eat. "No thanks," said Veness. The ample Fairweather groaned, and agreed—they had heard the French were nearly starving. But Madame brought two loaves of bread and a pot of meat paste and two bottles of red wine and forced them to eat.

They were asleep in the barn when the door opened and a voice said in English: "Hello, boys!" A tall man came in and shook hands.

"I'm the interpreter," he said. "My name is Raimond." He had the red-haired man with him and said he was in touch with the Maquis resistance. "We'll get you in their hands as soon as possible. They'll look after you. But caution is vital. The Germans are determined to find all who escaped from the train."

Raimond left but returned at dark with the redhead and another man. They brought clothing and two bicycles. But the two Jacks decided not to discard their uniforms; if captured in civilian clothing they would be shot as spies.

Raimond said nothing. Then Fairweather and Veness recognized their selfishness: if it was dangerous for them to pose as civilians, it was doubly dangerous for Frenchmen to be caught with escaped soldiers in uniform—they would be shot without trial. The two Canadians accepted jackets and caps as partial camouflage.

Raimond said they must move quickly; the postman was under suspicion and there must be protection for Madame. Only French was to be spoken. Fairweather hopped on the crossbar of one bicycle, Veness on the other. Via country roads and crooked lanes they came to another farm, stayed there and the next night were taken to another. A woman and a young man emerged from the shadows.

"You cannot enter the house," said the young man. "The Germans were in this village an hour ago and fought with the underground. A hundred at least came in armored cars. We did not know they had such strength. Many of our Maquis were killed and our force has been dispersed, and we have no communications. The Boches are searching houses everywhere."

The woman led them to a small tool shed. There they hid.

The next night the shed door opened and three more escapees from the train were squeezed in. After midnight the five soldiers slipped out and a guide led them along a field path into a small town called Luzillé, a dark, silent, ghostly place.

At a church a curé came forward and silently embraced them, a small man in black surplice and cassock. He poked at a wall until a panel slid back to reveal a narrow doorway. The escapees followed him up circular stone steps into a room 15 feet square, seven feet high. The priest placed a candle on the floor and the men saw that they were right under the beamed roof.

The floor was covered with dirt but two wide mattresses were laid on it. The priest brought out bars of chocolate and later returned with two French women who would bring food daily. The two Jacks climbed a ladder into the belfry and found they could watch people in the street.

They chilled as six German soldiers entered a shop, then emerged, curtly dismissing a terrified shopkeeper. They saw several persons asked for identification papers—and the priest casually pass the Germans. Much later they were to learn that he had saved 21 Allied servicemen and been awarded the American Medal of Freedom.

The women fed them well—omelettes, chicken, custards, *pâté de foie gras,* bread, plus the inevitable wine. They said on their second visit that a large party of German troops had arrived and every building in town was being ransacked. But the patrols never questioned the priest or entered the church.

Raimond came after dark. "You're lucky," he said. "The Germans were at the tool shed one hour after you left. They've guessed you're in this town." The whole group—now there were seven escapees—was to be moved that night. The risk of remaining in Luzillé was growing too great.

"There will be guides here shortly after·midnight," they were told. "You will be taken to a rendezvous where a truck will pick you up just after daylight and take you to Loches, 18 miles from here."

But no guide came that night. When the priest arrived with breakfast he indicated—he could not speak English—that greater caution than ever was needed. From the belfry Veness and Fairweather saw German soldiers everywhere, in and out of shops, stopping people and vehicles. Five stood beside the church for an hour, delaying the women bringing the noon meal.

"What happened to our guide?" asked Veness when they did come.

"He was almost caught," said one woman. "The Germans pursued him but he got away."

At the church door that night a man gave a signal and two guides and seven Canadians moved off in sock feet. At the outskirts of town they put on their boots. They halted at a wooded slope overlooking a highway. "The truck will come along this road," said a guide.

But the truck did not arrive, though they waited until long after daylight. The guides became very nervous. Something had gone wrong, they muttered.

"We will go from here," said one.

"Where?" asked Fairweather.

"The only place I know is a small deserted farm less than three kilo-

Veness (left) and Fairweather served in le groupe Le Coz, *a Maquis force led by Capt. Georges Le Coz, a one-time Foreign Legion officer.*

metres away." Crouching, running, hiding in fields, the group got there. It was a place grown up in shrubs and vines and tucked in under a thickly wooded hill.

Here they were picked up by eight Frenchmen and two more escapees— Learment and Fredenberg—all armed to the teeth, grinning and wearing the armband of the French Forces of the Interior, the Maquis. In two cars displaying the French tricolor they made a hair-raising drive down country roads, through villages and at last into a forest with roadblocks and sentries.

Cheering, laughing young Frenchmen came out to embrace them. Learment took his fellow North Novas to meet the captain. "He's a wild

451

man," he said, "but a good soldier and strong for us Canadians. Be sure to address him as 'mon capitaine.' "

At a long table of boards laid across wooden horses, Veness and Fairweather met Georges Le Coz, a tall, lean, cold-eyed man with authority written in his lined, sallow face and in his swagger. He wore the ribbons of the Croix de Guerre and Légion d'Honneur.

Le Coz greeted them in French, boasting that he would do great things for them.

They discovered that of 40 Frenchmen in camp only one spoke English: Tony, an aristocrat who had served in the French army. Le Coz disliked him but kept him on his staff as an interpreter.

Fairweather and Veness had never thought there would be so large a group at one place. A lieutenant beside them as they ate tried, in French, to identify everyone.

"The woman with the captain is his mistress," he murmured. "He's a very jealous man. Remember that." She was an attractive woman about 30. "She's a new one," the man whispered. "When he tires of one he sends her to the kitchen. The man and wife along the table are prisoners. He was chief of police in Loches but it was said he was giving information to the enemy. So Le Coz captured him."

After meat came fruit and pastry, wines and liquor of all kinds. Everyone seemed to be toasting somebody or something. The Marseillaise was sung many times. Then Le Coz shouted: "Georgette! More Armagnac!" A deposed mistress hurried in with three bottles captured from the Germans. The dinner ended at 10 o'clock. The two Jacks were taken to a large tent with expensive mattresses and sheets of snowy white.

Fairweather found the next day that practically all the weapons in the camp were English, the majority Sten automatics designed to take German ammunition. There were three Bren light machine guns and 20 British rifles.

Veness sensed that most of the men were at loose ends and in search of excitement. About half were around 20, some younger. Nearly all wore blue coveralls and a red, white and blue armband. The officers were in civilian clothes with a red, white and blue ribbon at the lapel. Le Coz wore a natty gray business suit with the armband plus his ribbons; the story was that he had won them in North Africa with the Foreign Legion. This Maquis band—*le groupe Le Coz*—appeared to function entirely on its own.

The French called all the escapees "Americans." They were not

452

required to do anything unless there was an attack or an "expedition." Then it was hoped they would do their share.

The two Jacks went on their first expedition that day—and came back with a pig for a banquet. The tables fairly groaned with food and drink. Lanterns shed light over everything. The women were dolled up in their best, laughing shrilly at everything their officer-lovers said.

There was a sudden commotion. Sentries burst from the bushes, forcing five young Frenchmen toward Le Coz. A sergeant accused them of attempting to desert.

Le Coz raged up and down before the culprits, kicking and striking them, screaming hatred. There was no court; he was judge and jury. The police chief from Loches protested. Le Coz shouted an order and three of the five were dragged to the table. The captain said he had sentenced them to die. They were dragged away.

One, no more than 17, threw his arms around a large tree. Guards tore him loose and hauled him toward the woods. He wrenched free and ran. A dozen Sten guns were fired and he fell dead.

Everyone at the tables sat rigid, watching. The guards, at a sign from the captain, put pistols to the heads of the other two condemned men and shot them. Le Coz raised a glass. "Vive la France!" he shouted.

The gaiety went on—forced at first—and an hour later all were singing under a full moon. Then he shouted that the remaining two accused were to be beaten.

A sister of one screamed protests but Le Coz ignored her. The night was filled with her cries, the oaths of the guards and the groans of the pair being beaten.

Next day Tony told Fairweather one had died. The sister's face was swollen, her eyes blackened, her head shaved—like a collaborator's. Veness saw Le Coz and a woman viewing the bodies. The woman was crying, the captain trying to console her. Tony said Le Coz now had proof that the boy who had clung to the tree was innocent of desertion.

Le Coz took the two Jacks and others on a supply raid that day. When they got back Tony told them: "The chief of police has vanished. Wait till Le Coz knows!"

Soon Le Coz was shouting. "He's gone to tell the Boches where we are. We must move, quickly!"

They set up camp in another wood. At dusk a messenger reported that 30 tanks had attacked the one they'd left. The Germans were preparing to attack the new position.

Le Coz called for 15 volunteers; Veness and Fairweather were among them. They got to the main road, heard German half-track vehicles—but saw none and eventually learned they had left. Everyone knew, though, that the Germans had full information about the Le Coz group. At dawn Germans were reported coming up the wood road.

"Carry all ammunition," screamed Le Coz. As they ran, the two Jacks heard the German machine guns. They ran faster when mortars began exploding. The firing gradually ceased as the Germans discovered the vacated position. A mile away the fugitives staggered to a halt.

"They won't dare follow us," said Le Coz. "No need to worry."

Nevertheless, they had now been reduced from affluence to mere existence. When the two Jacks bedded down in a barn that night, at another temporary headquarters, their world once more seemed upside down.

Next morning Le Coz chose Fairweather, Veness and four others to steal a vehicle and some food. They marched in bright sunshine, singing everything from the Marseillaise to Tipperary, to the turreted Château Montpoupon, a well-known beauty spot and tourist attraction. Le Coz took prisoner the owner, his wife and daughter and everyone piled into a huge Daimler to return to the farm. The car ran on gas produced by burning charcoal and wood.

Some of the Maquis fell ill. Le Coz seized mattresses, sheets and quilts from another château and moved the patients into a hay barn in the middle of a field. A doctor quickly began injections. "Diphtheria," he muttered.

Soon they moved again, to a château surrounded by beautiful open woods, lawns and hedges, a huge white stone mansion with large rooms and reception halls.

There were many newcomers now. Two Italian opera singers entertained at a banquet in the great hall. Seven Ukrainians would salute Fairweather each morning: "Good morning, Mistaire Lootenant Jack," then sing like a Cossack choir.

There were also German prisoners. The Maquis, guns blazing, attacked a German road convoy, killing 11, capturing 17, including two officers and their wives. The weapons of the convoy were a good catch but the two Jacks did not like it when the German dead were arranged in a semicircle, propped up with wine and bread in their hands, cigarettes in their mouths. The Maquis danced gleefully around the dead until checked by Le Coz, who sensed the Canadians' revulsion. "I like you very much," he told the two Jacks. "You're men I can depend on." They had told Le Coz they would fight as soldiers but wanted no part of robbing châteaux and mistreating prisoners.

Though he said bitterly that the enemy had killed his wife and children and beaten him savagely, Le Coz was ambivalent toward Germans. When two North Africans raped the wives of the two German officers, he had the rapists shot, then showed their bodies to the women. When he found that one German officer had been given black bread instead of white, he slapped the responsible Frenchman's face a dozen times. He feared capture and was determined to be able to prove that he had treated prisoners well.

He sometimes used escapees to loot farms, sometimes to attack Germans—as when word came that the enemy had ordered one village to provide 50 horses. Le Coz attacked, cleaned out the Germans and came away with a great booty of arms. There were free drinks at the cafés and the afternoon ended like a great picnic.

Expeditions became more frequent. One day two cars raced into Loches, a town of about 6,000, in which the Germans had a headquarters, and drew up at a building where hundreds of tires were stored. Le Coz led an orgy of destruction, then the cars raced away without a shot being fired at them.

The Milice—the secret police of the collaborationist Vichy government—were active and the danger of German attack was great; Maquis from another camp were caught on the highway and not a man escaped. But Le Coz became more daring. He shot up a German convoy, killing seven and securing two cars crammed with arms. Then on Aug. 12 an agent reported that the Germans were preparing to attack his headquarters. He moved again, to a three-storey château.

An F.F.I. major parachuted in and said he had come to take charge. Le Coz talked furiously and the major, with one look at Le Coz's men, backed off, saying mildly there was no need of his taking command. His main errand was to bring the group into line with the Grand Strategy.

"Hell take the Grand Strategy," yelled Le Coz. "I have already done more than any other group. I am dedicated to fighting the Germans and the Milice. My ambition is to free Loches of German domination."

But the Jacks were glad to see the major stay. They felt his presence would restrain Le Coz from brazen looting.

There were more skirmishes and evidence pointed to strong German reinforcements in the area. Information was received that their assignment was to eliminate Le Coz. He ordered that no one was to venture out by day, that sentries were to be doubled. Shots were heard frequently, and an expedition for meat barely escaped when three carloads of Milice closed in on a Maquis car.

Germans surrounded the château on Aug. 14, blocked every road and attacked with mortars. With no way of countering mortar fire the Maquis had no choice but flight. The Germans rushed the château and ransacked it. About midnight they marched away as the Maquis watched from cover in woods a few hundred yards away.

Le Coz led his party to yet another château. But the attack had shown that much had changed. The Germans had mortars. They moved in strength. There could be no more hit-and-run raids; Le Coz wanted to lead a general attack on Loches.

Twelve escapees decided to leave and search for a secret airfield in the area. Veness and Fairweather were among five who elected to stay. They felt as safe with Le Coz as in country infested with the enemy.

On Aug. 15 he called the group together and said that the next day he would lead a movement against Loches. The F.F.I. major protested but Le Coz said they were going in no matter the cost.

Le Coz and 150 heavily armed men were nearing Loches when a large number of persons approached, shouting and laughing. The German garrison had fled.

Le Coz shouted for Veness and Fairweather to march with him, seized a tricolor and entered the town amid a tumultuous welcome. Soon there was scarcely room to march through the crowds. When a man shouted defiance Le Coz killed him. Then he rounded up alleged collaborators. The march ended in the town square, where people wept as they sang the national anthem.

A hush came over the crowd as Le Coz began to kick and spit at those held as collaborators. One man shouted his innocence, attacked Le Coz, was thrown to the ground, scrambled up and attacked again. There was a shot. A great gasp from the crowd. As an officer stepped forward to deliver the coup de grâce, the man stirred, jumped up and grappled with him. Two men hurled him to the ground. One discharged his rifle into the writhing body. A long sigh quivered through the crowd.

Hundreds hurried off as if ill, and there were ugly looks at Le Coz. "That was rotten," murmured one Frenchman. "There'll be a reckoning."

"We'll hope so," said another. "That captain is a madman."

The other prisoners were marched off to the Château of Loches and placed in cells. The two Jacks were taken there for a fine dinner.

Next morning they explored the picturesque, ancient town. They were welcomed into many homes and offered food and wine. They wrote postcards home. (The one Veness mailed never got there but Fairweather's was received in New Brunswick three months later.)

The Germans, Le Coz boasted, would not dare attack. "They know their losses would be too heavy. I'm sending word for other Maquis to join me. When they arrive I'll lead an attack against the Boches wherever we find them."

Two hundred Germans were advancing from the southwest. Le Coz told Fairweather to lead six men to a small hill 300 yards from the road and to the right of where a strong Maquis force had concentrated to defend the entrance to Loches.

The hill commanded about 1,200 yards of open ground on which Fairweather saw a squadron of German tanks. His men seemed paralyzed with fear. "The first man who tries to run will be shot," he said. "My orders from the captain."

The tanks in fact took no part in the attack because the Germans wrongly thought the Maquis had antitank weapons. But repeated infantry attacks came in, were repelled, came in again with mortar support.

Fairweather made deadly use of a Bren. But after hours of battle he saw that the entire Maquis force was in retreat. His men were practically isolated and the enemy was close. The one avenue of escape was narrow and almost without cover.

Fairweather vaulted a fence amid a hail of bullets. He saw his men reach the first houses, swerved and dodged as bullets whined around his ears. A glance showed him the Maquis were in full flight. He ducked into a ditch and ran. When he reached shelter he saw some Maquis standing hesitantly by a street corner. Fairweather began to set up his Bren.

"Where are the others?" he asked.

"Gone. Like scared pigeons."

One of Le Coz's drivers ran by, beckoning to them to follow. On another street he wrenched open a garage door. Inside stood a 1928 Chevrolet, now little more than a wreck. The driver cranked it into life. There was one open road from the town, he said; Le Coz had already used it.

The car died at three intersections in a row; the driver got it going again each time. It rolled through the silent, shuttered town and out into the country until it caught up with other Maquis.

"Out!" shouted the driver. "There are more to get."

The men piled out and the old Chevrolet headed back into Loches. Fairweather trudged gloomily along a country road. It seemed a tragedy, losing Veness, when they had been so near to freedom.

Veness and 20 men had crawled through a field with bullets singing overhead and had reached a forward slope within 200 yards of the Germans. They formed a long line and Veness set up a Bren behind a bush. Bullets sizzled in. They had been spotted.

The Château of Loches was in full view and suddenly they saw mortars bursting around it and heard the boom of artillery. Then vehicles could be heard directly in front and they knew enemy reinforcements were arriving.

A French officer said the Germans numbered over 600 and were the vanguard of an armored division. A German officer under a white flag had told Le Coz that if the division could pass through Loches there would be no reprisals and the Maquis could reoccupy the town. Le Coz had laughed in his face. "Come and get us!" he had challenged.

The German officer left in a rage and the German mortars fell with new fury. When the withdrawal order came, the 20 men in the field left at top speed, every man for himself. Veness and four others reached the town safely, then dived aboard a truck just as it roared away. It took them to a group of Maquis sitting by the road. Fairweather was among them.

The Germans had not won Loches easily. Various groups of defenders had fought like tigers until at last the German commander sent an ultimatum: if Loches was not immediately abandoned by the F.F.I., his artillery would blast every building to rubble.

Le Coz had had nearly 300 men; there were scarcely 50 with him now. At least 20 had been killed, more than 50 wounded. A few had been captured. The rest had gone into hiding. The majority would escape.

Le Coz, discouraged, asked endless questions of surviving officers. A farm was selected as a headquarters, and two salvaged trucks were unloaded. The two Jacks slept in a barn.

Next morning the men sat numbly in the sun. At noon Learment arrived with the others who had left before the attack. He reported finding an F.F.I. headquarters and a British major who had direct contact with London. He had promised them a flight to Britain but they had tired of waiting and now were going to try to reach the Allied lines.

The two Jacks declined to join them but the talk strengthened their decision to leave Le Coz and strike off on their own. When they told him, he gestured wildly and stamped away. When they said good-bye, Le Coz wished them luck. But he obviously was not pleased.

They and an American pilot were picked up by a car that took them to a clearing where a man wearing the insignia of the Welsh Guards introduced himself as "Major Crown."

They told him of their experiences. "*Groupe Le Coz!*" he exclaimed. "We've been looking for him for weeks."

"Do you want him for anything special?" asked Veness.

"To hang him, of course."

It was evident that Le Coz and his ways were well known.

"Is it true," asked Fairweather, "there's a secret airfield near here?"

"It's true," smiled Crown.

"Could we get back to England by plane?"

"As soon as the weather clears."

Two days later the major said that aircraft were due that night but air force personnel had priority. The American pilot and an RCAF navigator would go first.

Veness put on a headset and listened to the BBC newscast from London. Suddenly the French radio operator thumbed through his code book. Veness heard nothing but the news in English but the Frenchman leaped up and tried to embrace both Jacks at one. "Two planes at 11:30 tonight," he shouted. "You go with the second."

In London a military policeman stood speechless at the sight of two hatless, unshaven, long-haired tramps as they crossed Trafalgar Square on their way to Canada House. Veness had no tunic, only a German shirt. The only marks of rank were two lieutenant's pips clinging precariously to one shoulder of Fairweather's tattered jacket. The policeman saluted.

The two Jacks rejoined the North Nova Scotia Highlanders and saw a lot of action. Both were wounded. Both became majors.

Later, as they awaited repatriation to Canada, a letter came from friends in France: Le Coz had been arrested and tried as a criminal. There was plenty of evidence from the relatives of those he had killed. Le Coz was executed.

Fortune

Seekers

Yet somehow life's not what I thought it,
And somehow the gold isn't all.

Robert W. Service, 1907

Search for the Coppermine

In the early 1700s the Hudson's Bay Company,
intrigued by Indian tales of rich copper mines beside
a mysterious river flowing far into the Arctic,
commissioned several sea voyages which searched in vain
for the "Coppermine River" and the fabled
Northwest Passage. Then, in 1769, a 24-year-old
HBC clerk named Samuel Hearne set out on foot from
Fort Prince of Wales, at present-day Churchill, Man.
In an epic quest across 5,000 miles of barren tundra,
Hearne found no fortune. But he won everlasting fame
for his courage and endurance.

Excerpted from Adventurers of the Far North
By STEPHEN LEACOCK

Samuel Hearne, in later
life governor of Fort
Prince of Wales, was a
young clerk when he made
his heroic trek across
the northern wilderness.

SAMUEL HEARNE TRAINED in a rugged school. He joined the Royal Navy as a midshipman and at 12, during the Seven Years' War, saw his first sea battle against the French. Later he was a mate on Hudson's Bay Company ships. Arriving at Fort Prince of Wales in 1767, he worked in the fur trade north of the Churchill River and gained a thorough knowledge of the Hudson Bay coast.

Now Governor Moses Norton instructed Hearne to make his way west to Lake Athabasca, then find Northern Indians who could guide him to the "Coppermine River" and trace it to the Arctic Ocean. He was to note the position of any mines, prepare the way for trade with the Indians, and determine whether there was a water passage through the continent. With him went a sailor and a landsman and, as guides, a chieftain named Chawchinahaw and a small band of Chipewyans. The party set out Nov. 6, 1769, saluted by seven of the fort's cannon.

Hearne was headed for one of the most inhospitable regions on earth. The northern limit of forest ran roughly in a line northwest from Churchill to the mouth of the Mackenzie River. East and north of the timber line were the Barren Grounds, a desolate wasteland broken by precipitous watercourses and wide lakes, with little vegetation except mosses, short grasses and small flowering plants, which supported great wandering herds of caribou. A few spruce trees and shrubs struggled to survive but even these died early in the bitter climate. Hearne would see little but barren rock and water, or in winter an endless mantle of ice and snow.

But the Chipewyans were convinced the journey would be futile. They knew the best route to the Athabasca territory, but had little knowledge of the country beyond, to the northwest. When supplies started to run out, they quickly lost interest and wanted to return to their families. Hoping to discourage Hearne, they deliberately kept north of the woods, along the edge of the Barrens, exposed to the intense cold. At night only a few poor shrubs could be gathered to make a campfire, and they had to scoop holes in the snow for shelter. The Indians provided little game; Hearne and his two white companions were each reduced to a ration of half a partridge a day.

But Hearne struggled on, and the party trekked westward over 200 miles of snow-covered wilderness. Then some of the Indians made off in the night, carrying with them a good part of the supplies. The next day Chawchinahaw and the rest departed, mockingly inviting Hearne to get home to the Hudson Bay coast as best he could. The three white men trudged back through the snow to Fort Prince of Wales. Hearne's first expedition had lasted five weeks.

Neither Governor Norton nor Hearne was discouraged and in less than three months Hearne was off again. He set out Feb. 23, 1770, accompanied only by six Indians. This time there was no salute from the fort; the cannon on the ramparts were buried deep in snow.

Hearne's little party went west along the Seal River, then struck north over the Barrens. By June the snow was beginning to melt and progress grew more and more difficult. Snowshoes became useless and even the sleds were abandoned. Every man staggered under a heavy load. Hearne's pack included a bag of clothes, a box of papers, a hatchet and other tools, and the clumsy weight of his quadrant—a navigational instrument too precious to be entrusted to the Indians.

The party carried no poles and in that treeless land could not use their one wretched tent; they lay shelterless at night in bitter cold and sometimes drenching rain. They depended on such fish and game as could be found; most they ate raw, as they had nothing with which to make a fire. Late in June, the party tramped northward, making 80 miles in four days, with no other sustenance than water and an occasional pipe of tobacco. In one seven-day period the party had nothing to eat but a few wild berries, some old leather and some burnt bones. On such occasions the Indians would examine their clothing to see what part could best be spared and would stay their hunger with a piece of rotten deerskin or a pair of worn-out moccasins.

But in July, as the travellers moved farther north deer became plentiful and roving bands of Indian hunters joined them. Hearne's guides claimed it would be impossible to reach the Coppermine before winter. (The truth was that they preferred to remain with the hunters.) Knowing it was useless to protest, Hearne drifted west with the hunters, so numerous by the end of July that about 70 deerskin tents formed a little village of nearly 600 persons. Hearne wrote that each morning as they broke camp, "the whole ground seemed to be alive with men, women, children and dogs."

The hunters moved southwest, rounding the western shore of Dubawnt Lake. Hearne now had little chance of reaching the Coppermine. Its headwaters were [almost 400] miles distant; the season was late, the guides unmanageable.

Then came an accident that compelled Hearne to abandon his enterprise. After taking his noon observations, he left his quadrant standing and sat down to eat. A sudden gust of wind smashed the delicate instrument on the rocky ground. No longer able to ascertain his exact whereabouts, with guides who could not be trusted, and no winter supplies or equipment, Hearne turned back south.

The return trek was three and a half months of hardship. On the very first day, a band of Chipewyans from the north plundered Hearne of almost all he had. From his Indian guides the marauders took everything except their guns, some ammunition and a few tools.

Hearne and his followers resumed their journey home. Their only shelter was a blanket thrown over three long sticks which one of the guides had managed to salvage. They had no winter clothing, snowshoes or sleds, and no food except what game they could find on the way. Winter set in and the party suffered intensely from the cold, the want of snowshoes making their march increasingly difficult.

The marvel is that Hearne ever reached Fort Prince of Wales; he probably would not have succeeded had he not fallen in with Matonabbee, a Chipewyan chieftain of strange and exceptional character, who was crossing the Barrens on his way to the fort with furs.

As a young man Matonabbee had lived for years among the English; he understood that a certain merit would attach to rescuing Hearne from his predicament. Moreover, Matonabbee had been to the Coppermine River, and it was partly owing to his account of it that Governor Norton had sent Hearne across the Barrens.

Hastening to relieve the young explorer's suffering, Matonabbee provided Hearne with warm deerskins and prepared a great feast. After an orgy of eating, the Indians sang and danced around their campfires.

Matonabbee travelled with Hearne for several weeks. As they drew near the fort their ammunition was almost spent and the game had almost disappeared. By Matonabbee's advice, Hearne and four Indians went ahead. The days were now short but the moon and the aurora borealis cast a brilliant light upon the waste of snow. Hearne and his guides reached the fort Nov. 25, 1770. Matonabbee arrived a few days later.

In less than a fortnight Hearne set off on his third quest for the Coppermine. He had by this time formed a great opinion of Matonabbee: "the most sociable, kind, and sensible Indian I had ever met with." The chieftain offered to lead Hearne to the great river of the north, and Governor Norton willingly furnished ammunition, supplies and trading goods.

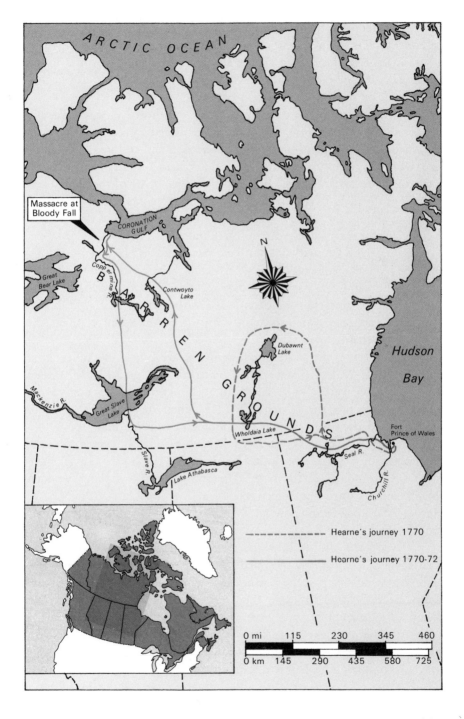

Massacre at
Bloody Fall

ARCTIC OCEAN

CORONATION GULF

Great
Bear Lake

Coppermine R.

BARREN GROUNDS

Contwoyto
Lake

N

Dubawnt
Lake

Hudson

Bay

Mackenzie R.

Great Slave
Lake

Wholdaia Lake

Fort
Prince of Wales

Slave R.

Lake Athabasca

Seal R.

Churchill R.

— — — — — Hearne's journey 1770

——————— Hearne's journey 1770-72

| 0 mi | 115 | 230 | 345 | 460 |
| 0 km | 145 | 290 | 435 | 580 | 725 |

December was spent toiling over the Barrens, Hearne and his companions trudging under heavy loads. At best they made only 18 miles a day. Intense cold set in and game seemed to vanish. Christmas found the lonely party plodding farther each day from the little outpost of civilization back on the shore of Hudson Bay.

At the end of December, in a thicket of stunted pine, poplar and willow at the edge of a frozen swamp, they joined a group of Matonabbee's band, two men and more than 20 women and children. The chieftain, who had eight wives, did not consider them a hindrance. "Women were made for labor," he told his English friend. "One of them can carry or haul as much as two men; they pitch our tents, make and mend our clothing; and, as they always stand cook, the very licking of their fingers is sufficient for their subsistence in scarce times."

January and February of 1771 were spent trekking farther west along the tree line. The cold was intense, especially when, exposed to the full force of the wind, the travellers crossed a frozen lake or river. But game was plentiful; at intervals the party killed caribou in such quantities that four days were sometimes spent in camp in a vain attempt to eat the spoils of the chase.

On March 2 the party reached Wholdaia Lake [300 miles from Fort Prince of Wales]. They pushed on northwest, pausing for 10 days in mid-April to gather poles and bark to be used for tents and canoes when they reached the Barrens. In May, when they stopped again to build canoes, they were joined by about 200 Indians, many of whom eagerly agreed to accompany them to the Coppermine. It seemed an excellent opportunity for an attack on their enemies, the Inuit [Copper Eskimos] at the mouth of the river. The Indians began making wooden shields and assumed the appearance of a large war party. On May 22 Hearne, Matonabbee and about 150 Indians began the long march across the Barrens.

Toward the end of June the ice was breaking up and the braves used their canoes (which they had carried) to traverse a series of lakes and rivers which led past the northeastern tip of Great Slave Lake. Farther north, near Contwoyto Lake, they met more Northern Indians, also delighted to learn of Matonabbee's plans. They too joined the war party, celebrating with a great feast. These Indians had never seen a white man and examined Hearne with great curiosity, frowning at the color of his skin and comparing his hair to a stained buffalo tail.

The party moved on through alternating sleet and rain, along a broken and difficult path. July 4 found them at a rugged and barren set of hills which Hearne called the Stony Mountains. Nine days later, from the low hills that rose above its east bank, Hearne looked down upon the Coppermine River, at a point some 35 miles south of the Arctic Ocean. The river plunged over its rocky bed in a series of foaming cascades; fringing its banks were scattered shrubs and trees—so crooked and dwarfish that they merely heightened the desolation.

Matonabbee and his Indians prepared for their attack on the Inuit. Spies were sent toward the sea. The remaining Indians bustled about hunting, building fires and roasting meat so they might carry a supply so large as to make it unnecessary to alarm the Inuit by the sound of hunters' guns. Hearne, sick at heart at the thought of the bloodshed ahead but powerless to dissuade his companions, occupied himself with surveying the river.

Two days later, the spies brought word that five Inuit tents had been seen 12 miles northwest on the other side of the river. Matonabbee and his braves hurried across to the west bank; there, under the brilliant light of the midnight sun, they painted their shields with rude daubs of red and black. Then, noiselessly they snaked among the rocks along the river bank, to avoid being seen from higher ground.

The Indians stealthily approached a broad ledge of rock where the Coppermine, between lofty cliffs of red sandstone, roars over a narrow cataract some 300 yards long. From their ambush among the rocks, they could look out upon the tents of their sleeping Inuit victims.

The Indians paused to make final preparations. They cast aside their outer garments, bound back their hair and painted their faces with a hideous coating of red and black. Then, with weapons in hand, they rushed forth.

Hearne was compelled to witness the awful slaughter: "The poor unhappy victims were surprised in the midst of their sleep, and had neither time nor power to make any resistance. Men, women and children ran out of their tents stark naked, and endeavored to make their escape; but the Indians having possession of all the land-side, to no place could they fly for shelter. The shrieks and groans of the poor expiring wretches were truly dreadful."

Then followed a revolting mutilation of the corpses; the Indians viewed it as a proper custom of tribal war, and Hearne's protests only drew their contempt.

After the massacre the Indians tore down the Inuit tents and recklessly threw them and great quantities of food into the cataract. After a feast, they announced to Hearne that they were ready to accompany him to the mouth of the river. The desolate scene was left behind, the broad rock ledge strewn with mangled corpses. (Fifty years later, in 1821, explorer John Franklin—see *Franklin's Last Voyage,* p. 207—saw the skeletons of the Inuit. One of Franklin's Indian guides said he had witnessed the massacre.)

From the height of land beside Bloody Fall, as the cataract is now called, the Arctic Ocean can be seen some eight miles away. Hearne followed the river till he stood upon the shore [of Coronation Gulf]. Before him lay nearly a mile of open water, studded with rocks and little islands. Beyond, the clear white ice pack stretched to the horizon. While Hearne lingered on the shore, thick fog and drizzling rain rolled in from sea and shut out the bright sunlight of the northern day.

For the sake of form, as he said, he erected a stone cairn and took possession of the Arctic coast in the name of the Hudson's Bay Company. Then he turned south to begin the long march home.

On the second day of the return journey, Hearne's guides finally led him to their northern "Eldorado." It lay among the hills east of the Coppermine River, roughly 30 miles inland from the sea. Some mighty force seemed to have rent asunder the solid rock and strewn it in a confused heap of broken boulders. Here, said the Indians, was so much copper that it could be gathered as easily as one might gather stones on the shore of Hudson Bay.

Hearne searched eagerly among the rocks, but after four hours found only a few small pieces of native copper. One piece weighed about four pounds, and Hearne kept it, convinced now that the wealth of the district had been highly exaggerated by the Indians.

The return march lasted nearly a year, during which Hearne was exposed to the same hardship, famine and danger as on his way to the sea. In October, with great gales and deep snow, snowshoes and sleds were made for traversing the many small lakes and rivers, now frozen. By mid-November the party had reached the northern edge of the tree line. Here they had better shelter from the wind, and firewood was abundant. The party carried dried meat, and as they passed into thicker woods they killed a few rabbits and wood partridges, and caught some fish through a hole in the ice of a river. During the two-month trek only two deer were seen.

Christmas Eve found Hearne [near present-day Yellowknife] on the north shore of Great Slave Lake. He and his party, crossing its vast frozen surface, found deer and beaver were plentiful on the lake's many islands. Great quantities of fish abounded under the ice.

From the south shore, the party entered a fine level country over which wandered great herds of buffalo and moose. They followed the Slave River for about 40 miles, then struck east, plunging into a forest so dense that at times hatchets had to be used to clear the way.

At the end of March the first thaws began, and walking through the bush became difficult. Traversing open lakes, the travellers were often exposed to violent gales. By mid-April flocks of waterfowl were seen flying north. In May it became so hot that the party could barely march 12 miles a day. By May 25 they were clear of the woods and out on the Barrens. On June 30, 1772, after an absence of more than a year and a half, Hearne arrived at Fort Prince of Wales.

Hearne was not left without honor. Within three years the Hudson's Bay Company made him governor of Fort Prince of Wales. He returned to England in 1787 and was chiefly busied with revising and preparing his journal until his death in 1792, aged 47.

No better appreciation of his work has been written than the words with which he concludes the account of his safe return after his years of wandering: "Though my discoveries are not likely to prove of any material advantage to the Nation at large, or indeed to the Hudson's Bay Company, yet I have the pleasure to think that I have fully complied with the orders of my masters, and that it has put a final end to all disputes concerning a North West Passage through Hudson's Bay."

Privateering was practised with gusto and profit by many Nova Scotians in the 1790s and early 1800s. They turned to this legalized piracy because Nova Scotia's trade with the West Indies was threatened by war between the big European powers—England on one side, France and Spain on the other. Some privateers ventured as far as the Caribbean. Among them was the ROVER, a 16-gun brigantine that sailed from the town of Liverpool in July 1800, bound for the Spanish Main and an adventure that Nova Scotians would long remember.

The *Rover*, Private Ship of War

By THOMAS H. RADDALL

THE VOYAGE WAS FILLED with work and drill under the stern orders of Capt. Alexander Godfrey. He knew that in a fight or a storm it would be vital for every one of his 55 men and boys to do the right thing quickly when the moment came. Godfrey was lean, big-shouldered, well over six feet. He looked in his early 30s but was 41. He could bellow an order clear to the masthead in a gale.

Godfrey kept well out to sea and passed east of Bermuda, but not a sail appeared. He went on to the Virgin Islands for water and provisions, cruised along the north coast of Puerto Rico and kept a careful watch in the Mona Passage into the Caribbean. All for nothing. The French and Spanish merchants in the West Indies were holding their ships in port, hoping for news of the rumored peace.

In late August, Godfrey headed for Barbados. Then, off the coast of Venezuela, he had a sea look at the port of Cumaná and steered west along the Main, slipping into a deserted bay for water and wood. At the foot of the high mountains beyond lay La Guaira (near present-day Caracas) and Puerto Cabello. The *Rover* was running a great risk cruising between these busy naval ports, but if the Spanish merchantmen would not put to sea Godfrey had to seek smaller fry, the coasters stealing along the Main by night.

The water was deep and the *Rover* could run close to the cliffs. Her lookouts could see the town and batteries of La Guaira and watch the ships lying there.

Each night Lieut. Ludovic "Lud" Harrington and 10 armed seamen went out in the *Rover*'s cutter, sailing and rowing in the black loom of the cliffs. Most of the sloops they captured were laden with cocoa. He put their crews ashore, loaded the cocoa onto the *Rover* and sank them. One night he captured something bigger, the *Nuestra Señora del Carmen*, a schooner whose cargo of salt would be useful in the Liverpool fishery. The vessel itself would fetch a handsome sum at auction, so Harrington and his 10 adventurers steered for home.

From the height of land the Spanish had watched the *Rover* running in close to drop a boat in the evening and again to pick it up in the morning. The governor at Puerto Cabello was eager to capture the bold little brigantine, and he had a squadron suited for such work: the schooner *Santa Rita* and three galleys, called *guarda-costas*.

The *Santa Rita* had 125 seamen and marines, and she carried 10 six-pounder cannon and two 12-pounder carronades. Each galley carried a single six-pounder mounted in the bow, and was manned by 25 marines and a crew of Negro slaves who pulled the oars. Apart from the gun platform at the bow and a short raised deck for the marines at the stern, the galleys were open. Each had two big lateen sails and a sharp timber snout for ramming.

On Sept. 9, as the *Rover* cruised slowly west toward Puerto Cabello, the governor prepared his trap. The bait was a trading schooner which slipped out in the night and showed herself next morning. The *Rover* headed for the strange sail at once and followed the Spaniard toward the coast. Close to shore, with the *Rover* coming rapidly downwind, the Spaniards ran their craft aground and scrambled into the steep woods.

The *Rover* backed her main topsail, then lowered a boat to examine the wreck and see if her cargo was worth salvaging. Suddenly the wind fell calm and the privateer's sails hung lifeless from the yards. The boat's crew found a hulk, empty except for stone ballast. They set it afire and returned to their ship in disgust.

Not even the *Rover's* fore-topmast lookout had kept an eye seaward. Suddenly there was a shout. A schooner and three galleys were coming from Puerto Cabello, and the galleys with their powerful oarsmen were towing the schooner at a good speed.

Even if Godfrey managed to fight off the Spaniards his masts and sails were bound to suffer damage. The *Rover* carried sweeps—long oars for turning in a calm anchorage or moving into a wharf, and they could move her ahead or astern too—but would be slow compared with the speed of the Spanish galleys, even with the schooner in tow.

To give the crew free room and a clear view during the fight, the *Rover's* lower sails would have to be furled; Godfrey was about to give the order when he saw a ruffle of wind on the sea. As the squall filled her sails, the brig began to move seaward.

Soon the breeze reached the *Santa Rita.* She hastily slipped the tow-lines and let her own sails fill. The galleys hoisted their canvas and came on rapidly.

The breeze carried the *Rover* a mile or two to seaward, then the air fell calm again. The brig rolled in the glittering Caribbean swells and flapped her empty canvas. The breeze favored the Spaniards for some time longer, bringing them almost within gunshot. Once more the galleys took the *Santa Rita* in tow. They approached the *Rover's* stern, where she had only two cannon. Godfrey clewed his lower sails.

The seamen stripped to their trousers—for freedom in action and so no shreds of cloth would fester in their wounds. Each man untied the handkerchief about his throat and knotted it over his head, to keep the sweat out of his eyes. Under the orders of master gunner Ebenezer "Eben" Harrington (Lud's brother) the cannon were cast loose along the waist of the ship. Powder monkeys laid out cannon balls and canisters of grapeshot, and placed swab buckets along the deck, each half-full of water. Over each bucket rim hung lengths of match—slow-burning fuses which gave off wisps of smoke reeking of saltpetre and sulphur. Each man wore a cutlass at his belt. Muskets were loaded and primed. Long, sharp boarding pikes were slung under the boom of the spanker.

Godfrey stood on the poop with Harrington and his cannon crews. Both guns poked through ports in the stern bulwark. Muskets and pistols lay loaded on the skylight, held in place by loops of yarn.

"Time to take in the waistcloths," said Harrington, nodding at the painted canvas screens that disguised the *Rover* as a merchantman. "The cloths are no use now—they know what we are."

"They don't know how few we are," Godfrey said. With Lud Harrington and his 10 seamen gone the *Rover* had 45 men and boys, some ill with fever. There would be only about three dozen on deck, barely enough to work one broadside and the two stern guns.

Harrington shaded his eyes and peered at the oncoming Spaniards, guessing their distance. "We could try a shot or two now."

"We'll wait and see what metal they've got," Godfrey said. Now the gunboats ceased towing the schooner and steered clear. The *Santa Rita* swung slowly until her larboard guns faced the *Rover*'s stern. Five flashes ran along the *Santa Rita*'s side. Five spouts of white smoke followed. Five jets of water leaped from the sea. Then came the delayed clap of the guns.

"Short!" snapped Godfrey.

"They fired on the down roll," Harrington said. "They'll wait for the lift next time. It's chancy, shootin' in a sea like this. They sounded like six-pounders. If they've got no bigger we stand a chance."

A long wait. Then five spurts of fire and smoke again, and a tearing and screaming in the air. The men at the *Rover*'s stern crouched instinctively. Five splashes leaped from the water beyond the brig. One struck the slope of a sea, skipped a short way, and sank.

"She carries half a dozen guns a side," Godfrey observed, "yet they only fired five, both times."

"Then she carries two carronades, one each side, heavy ones probably. They'll save 'em till they close the range."

A puff sprang from the bow of each gunboat. All three shots went wide. "Sixes again," Harrington said. "We're well in their range."

The galleys were moving in to tow the schooner again. "What d'ye make of 'em, Eben?"

"*Guarda-costas*," said Harrington. "They work inshore, mostly. They ain't used to a sea swell. Notice how long it took 'em to reload? We could fire two broadsides in that time and shoot better in the bargain. We ought to get our sweeps out and try a broadside."

"Not yet."

"Let 'em work that schooner much closer and she'll swing again and rake us proper, cap'n."

"If she tries that again we'll swing and give her the rough side of our own tongue, Eben. See how the Spaniard takes care to come up astern? He'd like to know what guns we've got but he won't offer us a broad mark to find out. He calculates we've got no sweeps or we'd have swung ship afore this."

"Look, cap'n!" said Harrington. "There's a mob o' men on that schooner, and a squad o' *soldados* in each galley, not countin' the blacks at the oars. Let 'em get closer and they'll run in and board us!"

"Ah!" Godfrey said. "That's what I want."

"But it's four, maybe six men to one!"

"Better than a gunfight at this range. They can afford to lose a spar. We can't. Not on a lee shore 2,000 miles from home." Godfrey stabbed a finger west toward Puerto Cabello. "That's where we'll drift if we lose a spar and the trade wind comes on again. Or if we drift past Cabello there's a bight in the coast where we'd be caught nicely. They call it Golfo Triste–Sorrowful Bay."

"But s'pose the wind comes off the land again," said Harrington. "It'd carry us out to sea, and those *guarda-costas* daren't follow us far. A wind might bring another privateer or maybe a British warship."

"That," Godfrey said, "is why the Spaniard wants to make a quick job of us where we are, Eben. He can see himself strutting up the *embarcadero* with what's left of us chained two-and-two."

"You're goin' to let 'em board us?"

"I'm going to let 'em *think* they can. Now listen to me, Eben . . ."

As Godfrey talked, the two leading galleys fired again. One shot skipped past the *Rover* like a flying fish. The other made a neat hole in the maintopsail.

"Well, is all that plain?" said Godfrey.

Harrington nodded, then spoke to the men crouching by the two stern guns: "Aim for the bows o' those two galleys towin' the schooner. Their gunners'll shoot worse with a ball or two nipping past their ears."

Godfrey stepped down to the main deck and the *Rover*'s crew clustered about him. "Lads," he said, "those Spaniards think they've caught us in a sling, so you've got to move smart and shoot straight to get us out. So far they don't know we've got sweeps. Without wind they reckon we can't swing ship and give 'em a broadside – that's why they're keeping us stern-on."

"What d'ye reckon they'll do, cap'n?" a seaman asked.

"The Spaniard's got a choice. He can stand off at easy gunshot and hammer us. If he tries that, we'll swing ship and bang it out with him. But a gunfight'd take time, and time's precious. The Spaniard knows this calm won't last forever – that's why I reckon he'll try to close in and board us. He's got men enough to overrun us in two minutes."

Suddenly there was a double clap as Harrington's gunners fired their stern four-pounders. Then the rumble of greased trucks on the planking as the cannon were hauled back for swabbing and reloading.

"Now, lads," Godfrey said, "get those sweeps handy so you can run 'em out smart. When I give the word you've got to claw this brig round as you never clawed afore. I want her to spin like a tub. And you gunners – Eben Harrington will give the word to fire and mind ye wait for it! When you've fired, then out sweeps, swing her round and man the other broadside. If they get aboard you'll have to fight like wildcats if ye hope to see Nova Scotia again. Keep down, shoot cool, and reload fast." The captain smiled. "Who'd want to be jigging a cod-line on the Grand Bank this fine afternoon?" Shouting and laughing, the crew trotted back to their stations.

The *Rover*'s stern guns barked again as Godfrey stepped down the companionway and passed along a short alley to the magazine. The door was hooked open and the gleam of the battle lantern at the window fell upon his 13-year-old nephew, Henry Godfrey, sitting on a powder keg, clad in nankeen breeches, with his hands in his pockets and wiggling his bare toes. Sweat ran down his tanned face and body.

"Harry," the captain said.

The boy sprang up. "Sir?"

"There should be a man with you but I can't spare one. It's your job to pass out powder and shot as the other lads run down for 'em. If the cartridges get low, pass the word and I'll send some hands to help make up another lot."

Godfrey paused and the boy flinched under a look he had never seen in his uncle's eyes. The captain's face was grim.

"Harry, when you asked to come to sea with me I said you could, on one condition – that you obey my orders smarter than any man or boy aboard."

"But I have, sir!"

"So you have. Well, here's another—maybe the last you get from me. Harry, lad, the ship's becalmed, with four Spanish craft coming down on us hand over hand with oars. You heard the man that got away from the Spaniards last year. That was no old seaman's yarn. It was true, every word. D'ye want to die like his shipmates?"

"No," the boy said.

"Nor do any of us. So we'll fight it out the best we can. You'll hear a lot o' noise. Every time our guns go off it'll feel like a big hammer beating you over the head. Just be smart with the powder and shot and pay no heed to anything else—except one thing. If the Spaniards get aboard you'll hear men running about and yelling, muskets and pistols going off, thumps on the deck, a rattle and clash like drunken men loose in a tinker's shop. Still, it may be we can beat 'em off. In that case things'll get quiet, and I'll send someone to tell you how things are."

"What if you can't beat 'em off?"

"In that case things'll get quiet, too. But then you'll hear people at the hatch yelling Spanish—yelling for you to come up and surrender. If you hear that, there's one thing left to do." Godfrey pointed to the magazine window. "Then you must slip out there for the lantern. Bring it in here. Smash it and drop it into the nearest open keg."

"Why, that'd set the powder afire and blow us all up!"

"Aye, and a lot o' Spaniards too."

"But Mr. Harrington warned us—"

"Never mind. I'm captain of this ship, and when I want something done I want it done—no questions."

The boy's eyes went to the pane, to the lantern, to an open keg where gunpowder glistened like evil black salt, and back to his uncle's face. He nodded slowly.

"You'll do what I say?"

"Yes, sir."

"And don't mention this to anyone. It's between you and me."

"Yes, sir."

The captain turned away, paused, and looked back. "Remember, boy, one Spaniard calling down the hatch and you'll know it's all up. Then—" He made a sweeping gesture with his big hands, and was gone.

The sunlight was blinding. Through half-shut eyes Godfrey saw his men stooping at their posts. The Spaniards, firing only their bow guns as they approached, had shot five holes in the maintopsail. One ball had grazed the topmast. The same shots had probably gone through the fore-topsail as well. Some rope ends dangled.

A bullet whined past Godfrey's head as he moved to the poop steps and raised his head and shoulders above deck level. It startled him, the bullet, and the fact that the Spaniards had got within musket shot so soon. One galley had dropped back but the others were still towing the schooner. Their sharp rams poked within 100 yards of the *Rover*'s stern, and from their bows came the spit and puff of musket fire. Driven away from their two stern cannon, Harrington's men lay on the deck, four of them bobbing up over the bulwark to fire their muskets, the others reloading. The Spaniards had also retreated from their cannon.

Godfrey crawled along the deck, hearing bullets thud into the stern timbers, and now and then a sharp flick as higher shots went through the topsails. A cannon shot shattered the binnacle and the steering wheel was nicked and splintered by musket balls.

Harrington turned to the captain. "Will you swing ship, Alec, you madman?"

"Hark!" Godfrey snapped. The firing had ceased. He raised his head cautiously and saw the Spanish commander, in white uniform and broad-brimmed hat, standing at the *Santa Rita*'s bow shouting orders to the galleys through a tin speaking trumpet. The commander did not seem to care that men in the *Rover* might hear what he said, or that some might have learned Spanish during peacetime trading in the West Indies.

Godfrey listened intently, then slid back down to the main deck. "Now, Eben," he said. "They're going to board us. The schooner'll steer for our starboard quarter. One galley's to steer for the larboard waist. The second's to work round to our larboard bow. The third—she's to keep off and watch for a wind. They'll keep up their musket and pistol fire as they close."

Godfrey shouted to the men and boys in the waist. "Now's our time! In with those waistcloths—sharp!" A leap and a quick scrabble of hands, and the canvas camouflage vanished from the bulwarks.

"Now, lads," Godfrey snapped. "Out with your sweeps to larboard! Heave her round, fast as you can! But your backs into it! Make that sea boil if ye want to see home again!"

The strongest 24 men in the *Rover*'s crew tore at the sea, three men at each long oar. Slowly at first, then gaining momentum, the privateer turned to starboard.

480

From the *Santa Rita*'s quarterdeck, the Spanish commander could not see the oars sliding out on the *Rover*'s larboard side; his view was blurred by the smoke of his own marines' muskets. When at last he saw the *Rover*'s starboard side growing longer by the moment, he screamed to his helmsman. But it was too late. His own ship, without the towing way of the galleys, answered her rudder sluggishly. At each of the starboard cannon Harrington's gunners waited.

Godfrey shouted: "Way 'nough! In sweeps! Get 'em across the deck and stand by!"

Harrington was already at the aftermost starboard cannon. As both ships danced on the long seas from the east, he waited for his moment. "Fire!" Then he trotted forward along the deck, pausing at each gun, giving the order again, and passing to the next.

As each gunner put his linstock and its smoking match to the powder at the gun's touchhole, there was a light flare and then a stunning thunderclap, the gun jumping back against the breech tackles. A spout of white smoke spread, rose and eddied lazily off the *bover*'s starboard, completely shutting off the view.

Godfrey's voice came quickly. "Out sweeps to starboard! Never mind those guns—we've got no time to reload now! Heave, lads! Round with her on the other tack!" As Godfrey leaped up the poop steps, the sharp rams of the two galleys poked within 15 yards.

Suddenly the commanders of both galleys cried out to the oarsmen, and at once they began to back water. The white-clad Spanish marines on the afterdecks were all staring open-mouthed at the *Santa Rita*. Something there appalled them. The flagship was hidden from Godfrey's view by his own gun smoke, but he could hear a wild commotion there.

The *Rover* was coming round swiftly with the furious working of her sweeps. Harrington ran over to larboard, passing from gun to gun with a word of warning and, as before, taking his station at the aftermost four-pounder.

The two retreating galleys made easy marks, their crews exposed from bow to stern every time they dipped on a sea. As the first galley came into view, Harrington called "Fire!" to the gunner beside him, and moved on to the next. At the third clap he held up a hand to the men at the four guns beyond. "Hold, lads! We've got another to deal with."

The *Rover* was still swinging under the pull of the starboard sweeps. The first galley had vanished behind a wall of smoke. The second was backing away from the *Rover*'s stern. On each swell the galley tipped forward and Harrington could see the gunners frantically reloading their six-pounder at the bow, the rows of oarsmen all glistening with sweat, the *soldados de marina* clutching their muskets and swords on the afterdeck.

Harrington waited at the fourth gun until the galley began to dip her bow again. "Fire!" And so to the other three gunners. Gun smoke leaped from the muzzles, gradually changing from pure white to dingy gray. Only the *Santa Rita*'s upper masts could be seen, with their square topsails and topgallant dangling loosely.

As Harrington's gunners feverishly reloaded the larboard cannon, a breath of air came out of the east and soon swept away the smoke, revealing all four Spanish craft. The two galleys that had attacked the *Rover* were crawling away to join the third, now out of gunshot to the west. Some of their oars were working, others trailed in the water.

The *Santa Rita* had been badly mauled, but the Spanish commander was working his ship round with a pair of sweeps over the stern. His seamen dragged the wounded below and tossed dead men over the side. Some bodies floated, others sank at once. There was an ominous thrashing in the water along the schooner's side: the sharks were busy.

The two ships were parallel, 150 yards apart, rising and falling on the swells, their mastheads scratching the sky in long slow arcs. Harrington judged his moment, watching the ship's roll. "Fire!" All seven larboard guns crashed off together. At once the gunners fell upon them, heaving at tackles and handspikes, plying their swabs and rammers. As soon as the smoke curtain drifted away, six jets spat from the *Santa Rita*. The volley screamed high over the *Rover*'s bulwark and there were tearing sounds aloft.

Again Harrington waited for the ship's roll. "Fire!" Again the scurry of reloading. This time the Spaniards took longer to reply, and their broadside was raggedly spaced. One shot struck the keel of the *Rover*'s longboat, lashed upside down on the main hatch. The rest went high.

"They're still after our spars and rigging," Harrington said. Godfrey glanced aloft. The topsails and topgallants showed many holes and slashes. The canvas could be replaced and his sailors could mend the cut rigging, but a broken topmast could be fatal. This was not Nova Scotia, where you could find masts growing on the slopes of almost any cove.

The *Rover*'s larboard guns fired again, and Godfrey caught the master gunner's arm. "Better shift our aim, Eben, and try for his top gear."

Harrington made a stubborn mouth. "That broadside we gave him caught his boardin' party on the bow. Must ha' shook up his gunners as well. Let me pepper his deck a few more times and ye can count your top gear safe, barrin' a lucky hit."

"It's the lucky hit I'm thinking about," Godfrey said.

The *Rover* rose on another sea. Harrington stooped and squinted over the bulwark. "Fire!" The larboard guns bellowed and leaped back on the breechings. The smoke rose and thinned again. The Spaniard replied and there was another slapping and tearing at the *Rover's* topsail canvas, and this time a hard crack overhead and the sound of wood rending. A wild Spanish cheer came across the water. The larboard end of the *Rover's* maintopsail yard had snapped a foot or two from the mast.

Godfrey swallowed his anger. "Eben, you see? I don't question your judgment, man. Knock me down one of his topmasts—or cut his mainsail halyards—and ye can hammer his deck as much as ye like. Or try one broadside low and the next high, with a few chain shot to cut up his rigging. This is going to be a long fight, my friend. The Spaniard's got his blood up."

Harrington shrugged. "You're the master." He trotted along the deck, yelling to the gunners.

Thunder and the sharp scream of shot were spaced with silence. At times the faint movement of air from the east died away, and smoke hung between the ships for what seemed an eternity.

In one of these silences Godfrey, pacing barefoot on the hot planks, noticed a boy sitting against the poop bulkhead, watching a sandglass. This lad's watch was over, but nobody had relieved him and he was still there, turning the glass every half-hour and ringing the ship's bell.

This led Godfrey below to the magazine, where he found Henry, still alert, his face and hands blackened with powder and sweat.

"How are your cartridges?" Godfrey asked, running an eye over the casks.

"I've been filling fresh ones, sir, fast as I could, whenever the guns stop firing."

"I'll send a couple o' hands down to help you, by-and-by."

"What's happened, sir? The boys can't tell me much . . ."

"Well, we cut up the galleys when they tried to close with us. Our lads are working their guns well, but it's chancy in a sea like this. We got one good broadside home at the start o' things, but the Spaniard's got a big crew and he's full o' fight. I dare say his governor is up there

483

on the high land, with a spyglass. The *comandante* has got to take us or find a mighty good reason why not."

On deck Godfrey went to the boy at the sandglass. "How long since the fight began?" he said.

"A glass and a half, sir."

Three quarters of an hour. Godfrey looked at his broken topsail yard and the tattered canvas. The yard could be mended, but those sails would soon be nothing but rags. As he watched, another Spanish broadside put two more holes in the maintopsail.

Harrington called "Fire!" Again the seven guns cracked and jumped. Godfrey moved over to the master gunner. "How goes it?"

Harrington ran a powder-blackened hand over his face. "Well, we're cuttin' up his sails and riggin', though we ain't hurt his spars. Can't tell what we're doin' to his deck people. Some of those gunners aim well but they're slow—we're giving 'em two shots for every one we get."

The gunners were calling out. "Loaded!" Then, "Primed!"

Harrington studied the heave and roll of the two ships. "Fire!" he snapped. Godfrey watched through his spyglass but the *Rover*'s broadside had put only a few more holes in the schooner's canvas. Then through the ringing in his ears he heard the stirring of dry canvas aloft.

"Wind at last!" said Harrington. The *Santa Rita*'s ragged topsails pressed flat against the masts. At the schooner's gaff the naval flag of Spain lifted and blew out in the new breeze. Now was the time to make for the open sea.

But suddenly Godfrey noticed the *Santa Rita*'s fore-topmast. It bent away from the wind, leaning back more and more until it reached an incredible angle. Finally it snapped near the butt and swept down in a long arc, taking with it the topgallant yard and its sail, which drooped into the sea at the schooner's starboard bow.

The *Rover*'s gunners uttered a hoarse cheer. Harrington was triumphant. "There she is, cap'n! She can't steer, she can't even move till they clear that raffle away, and she can't catch us anyhow, not with a wind like this in our sails!"

Godfrey had taken the telescope from his eye but he was still gazing toward the Spaniard. "Aye," he said. "There she is. We could rake her now. We could wreck her. But why?"

Harrington blinked, incredulous. "Cap'n," he growled, "now's our chance to get away—"

"And let the Spaniard get away too?" Godfrey snapped. "What d'ye think we came here for, gun practice? All we've got is a few tons of cocoa and that schooner o' Lud Harrington's loaded with salt! And yonder's a good prize—look at the lines and the room of her—and built o' tropical woods that live forever. She'd fetch a smart price at Halifax."

"That's a long way from here," said Harrington.

"But what about our commission, Eben? We're not on a pleasure jaunt. We're here to make war on the King's enemies."

"We're not a man-o'-war," Harrington grumbled.

"And I'm not a frigate captain hard bent on promotion," said Godfrey. "But Eben, think how many lads have suffered and perished here on the Main the past four years or so. We owe them something. And here's this Spaniard caught in his own trap!"

He glanced over the *Rover*'s rigging, estimating the damage, and turned to the men and boys in the waist. "We're going to take that schooner, lads! Aloft, a few hands, and loose the foresail. Master-at-arms, serve out the pikes and muskets. Eben, man those stern cannon and keep up a hot fire. Grape—all grape, mind! I want his foredeck swept clean—but no more damage to his hull and spars. Now, move!"

Though riddled with holes, the *Rover*'s foresail still held wind, and she began to move, stern first, toward the schooner's bow. Harrington's four-pounders on the poop fired rapidly. The *Rover*'s best marksmen perched aloft with muskets, aiming at the marines trying to cut away the *Santa Rita*'s dangling topmast. The *Rover*'s boarding party, armed with cutlasses and pikes, crouched behind the stern bulwark.

As the wind slowly carried both ships toward Puerto Cabello, the *Santa Rita*'s marines frantically loaded and fired their muskets and pistols.

Almost at the moment of collision the *Rover* lifted on a sea while the *Santa Rita* lay in the trough beyond. At the stern, Godfrey and 25 of his men looked down at the schooner's foredeck. Several men sprawled there, apparently dead. Other Spaniards were running aft, away from the menace of that high black stern. As the sea passed under her the *Rover* dropped, the schooner came up, and the two hulls smote together with a mighty thump.

"Boarders away!" Godfrey leaped onto the schooner's bow with his cutlass uplifted. His rovers yelled and followed. Two of them hooked grapnels under the schooner's bulwark. From these a pair of stout ropes ran back to the *Rover*'s stern bitts. Harrington, standing at the *Rover*'s stern, anxiously watched the wild dance of the hulls.

Godfrey in the lead, the rovers ran aft along the schooner's deck, shouting as they came. But the Spaniards were crying out and throwing down their muskets and cutlasses with a great clatter on the deck.

The only officer to be seen was a marine on the quarterdeck. His men still held their muskets but made no attempt to shoot. The officer, a slim man with a mustache, held an elegant long sword. He looked at it, put it back into the sheath, slipped the whole thing from his belt and stepped forward with his eyes on Godfrey. "*Misericordia*," he said, offering the sheathed sword, hilt first.

A rover drew back his pike for a thrust and Godfrey grabbed the haft. "Hold hard," he said. "It's mercy they're asking for." He stepped forward and took the sword, saying in Spanish, "Tell your marines to throw their weapons overboard." The officer turned and cried out to his men; their muskets and swords splashed into the water.

Godfrey pointed to the Spanish flag streaming from the schooner's gaff. "Strike that!" A sailor ran aft, pushed aside the *soldados de marina*, and hauled down the flag. The Spaniards huddled together while the rovers tossed more muskets and cutlasses over the side.

Godfrey called across to Harrington. "The galleys—how close are they?"

"A bare gunshot," Harrington answered. The three galleys were tacking against the wind toward the two ships.

"Then give 'em shot—any gun you can bring to bear." Hardly a dozen men remained aboard the *Rover* but soon her four-pounders boomed, and the galleys turned away.

"Where is your *comandante*?" demanded Godfrey. The officer pointed to a crumpled figure on the deck. Nearby were 13 other dead.

"How many men have you lost?" asked Godfrey.

"*Señor*," said the officer, "your first *salva*, when you turned your ship and caught us with many men forward ready to board you—that was terrible. You won your battle then. The fight with the cannon since—that was bad, but nothing so bad as the beginning. *Señor*, we have thrown 40 men to the sharks. I am the only living officer."

Godfrey was surprised. Including the wounded, 71 Spaniards were prisoners; 54 had perished. "*Señor*," said Godfrey, "I shall do something for you that you would never have done for me. You shall have mercy and fair treatment."

The Spaniard shrugged. Then, looking over the rugged Nova Scotians and inspecting Godfrey from head to foot: "Who you are? You speak Spanish like an *Americano* but we are not at war with the *Estados Unidos*. Are you a *pirata?*"

"You see the flag we fly," Godfrey answered angrily. "This is a privateer under a commission from the governor of *Nueva Escocia*."

"*Nueva Escocia?* What is that?"

Godfrey smiled sourly. "*Señor*, when you are at war with England you are at war with all her colonies, including *Nueva Escocia*. Your own *corsarios* seem to know that well enough—my people have suffered much at their hands."

Godfrey summoned two of his men. "Get below and secure the magazine—clear out anybody you see." And to the Spanish officer: "*Señor*, tell your men to go down there." He pointed to the fore hatch.

"And I?" the officer asked.

"You also, *Señor*. Later you shall be my guest aboard the brig."

Godfrey walked forward, watched his chance as the ships lurched together, and leaped back to the *Rover*.

Harrington was staring west at the galleys retreating toward Puerto Cabello. "They'll not be back," he said.

"How many men have we lost, Eben?"

"None."

"What about wounded?"

"None, I tell you. Not so much as a splinter cut, man or boy. It'll make a pretty yarn to spin at home, and a good thing we've got the schooner to show and prisoners to speak for us."

"Why?"

"Why! Who'd believe us? A fight like that. Four ships to one—and us coming out top dog and not a man hurt. It don't make sense."

Godfrey laughed. "Well, Eben, we need luck yet if we're to get clear o' trouble. We must make for Eves [a pair of small islands off present-day Curaçao] and patch up the ships in some sort o' safety. Now, go below and see that our magazine's secure. And send up young Henry."

Harrington started for the companion hatch.

"Eben!" Godfrey called.

"Yes, cap'n?"

"As you go down there, whistle a tune—I'm not joking—whistle a tune at the top o' your pipe—something familiar, A Stout Heart, or something o' that sort."

Harrington was mystified but he went, whistling like a robin all the way down the dim steps to the magazine.

Overland to the Cariboo

*Most came from present-day Ontario and Quebec,
a few from as far as Britain. Some 200 men,
three children and one pregnant woman struggled
1,000 miles across the Prairies, climbed into
the Rockies, and ran the treacherous rapids of the
upper Fraser River on log rafts. They were drawn
by the Cariboo Gold Rush of 1862.*

By BRUCE HUTCHISON

THAT SPRING the British Columbia Overland Transit Company was offering its prospective customers transportation "over the Grand Trunk Railway and continuous lines of railway to Chicago and St. Paul and, via the Red River settlements, in covered wagons, to British Columbia."

This, the company advertised, "is the speediest, safest and most economical route to the gold diggings. The land transit is through a lovely country unequalled for its beauty and salubrity of climate. . . . About 1,000 carts annually trade along this line. There are numerous

posts, missions and trading stations from the Red River settlements along the Saskatchewan, now discovered to abound in vast gold deposits, to the Rocky Mountains. The route is constantly travelled with perfect safety."

B.C. Overland's customers were to cross the mountains by the Yellowhead Pass, reach the headwaters of the Fraser, and drift pleasantly down to the gold fields. Clerks and apprentices were to undertake—without experience, proper equipment or knowledge of the terrain—an expedition as arduous as Simon Fraser's [see *Down the Roaring Fraser*, p. 172].

Early in May the Overlanders started by rail from Toronto, bound for St. Paul, Minn. Some were English and Scottish, the majority were Canadians. Many were leaving farms, shops or careers behind in a headlong rush for gold. They expected to reach the Cariboo in 60 days. Sponsors of a group from St. Thomas, Ont., proudly declared: "The young men composing the party are highly respectable and belong to some of the best families in town."

At St. Paul a few turned back. The rest started north for Fort Garry (Winnipeg) by oxcart or on foot; one group made part of the journey in a steamboat on its maiden voyage down the Red River.

At Fort Garry the travellers were welcomed by the cannon of the Hudson's Bay Company fort. Dancing, feasting and religious services followed. The worst, they felt, was over: only the easy wagon route lay ahead through "lovely country unequalled for its beauty."

For $40 the travellers could buy a Red River cart, the creaking of its two wooden wheels audible for a mile. An ox to pull it cost the same, a horse $25, and pemmican—buffalo meat and berries—16 cents a pound. Having bought these essentials, the first Overlanders started across the Prairies in early June.

Each party organized itself under a captain. Discipline was strict, morale high. At nine in the evening the carts were arranged in a triangle and scouts were posted to guard against Indians. Camp was broken at two in the morning, the carts were strung out in line and the march resumed. It halted for breakfast at six, dinner at two, and supper at six. Every Sunday there was a pause for rest and worship. Even oxen could cover 50 miles in a day; a few weeks should bring them handily to the Cariboo. The largest party, captained by Thomas McMicking of Queenston, Ont., numbered 150. Among them was Mrs. August Schubert, who had three children with her and expected a fourth before autumn.

The Prairies were soaked by heavy rains, the wagon track was deep in mud, the rivers high, the fords dangerous. But at its beginning the route was at least well marked. Factors of Hudson's Bay posts sold the travellers supplies and sometimes ferried them across swollen rivers.

But when the expedition moved out of the flat central plains into rolling brush country, the trail became harder to follow. Carts bogged down to the wheel hubs, oxen sank to their bellies in muskeg. The pace dropped to a few miles a day.

Desperately men chopped down poplars and laid them in corduroy bridges across the swamps. Where streams were too deep to ford they swam out into the current and threw together floating bridges, anchoring them with ropes, then pulling the lightened carts across, making the oxen swim. Most of the men had been soft when they started out—the Britons had never handled an axe or pitched a tent—but they were hardening now under the hot prairie sun.

Supplies began to run short. A few buffalo were shot but not many, for they ran at the sight of humans. There were ducks and prairie chickens, curiously tame, and one diary recorded that a meal of young eagles "tasted delicious." The first party reached the high banks of the North Saskatchewan River on July 21, and saw Fort Edmonton. Hudson's Bay men there warned that the trails ahead would be narrow; most of the gold seekers traded carts and oxen for pack horses. But a few kept the beasts that had pulled them this far.

On July 28 most of the Overlanders headed into the timbered foothills of the Rockies. Though advance parties cleared away the windfall, the expedition made only 10 miles a day. Summer was waning and the local guides looked west, where no peaks were yet to be seen, and counted the days left before the first snow.

Early on Aug. 15 as the clouds lifted, a serrated line of rock and snow stood out suddenly against the sky. The travellers cheered, threw their hats into the air, and rejoiced that the Fraser lay just beyond.

Through a valley of wild flowers and rippling streams, such as they had seen on post cards, the Overlanders would stroll blithely to the Fraser and gather gold nuggets from its sand. The guides did not argue. They had been paid to lead the party to the source of the Fraser, beyond which they knew no trail.

On reaching the Athabasca River the expedition paused a week, built a great raft and ferried to the west bank. This brought them to the Yellowhead Pass. Their troubles, surely, were finished.

Pass there might be, but there was no path. The guides climbed

Swamp country: animals flounder in muskeg, the pace slows, soft men learn to survive.

the sheer hills, blazing a trail. The expedition was now strung out 10 miles, a day's march between the guides and the last stragglers. Soon the last oxcart was abandoned. Many horses and oxen slipped on the narrow ledges and plummeted into the chasms below, taking their loads of food with them.

492

The expedition had brought food for only two months: 168 pounds of flour and 50 pounds of pemmican to the man. Now, after nearly three months, most of the grub was gone. The travellers shot chipmunks, birds and porcupines. Thomas McMicking dined upon roasted skunk, "a dish so delicate and rare that it might have tempted the palate of Epicurus himself." But soon not even skunks could be found, and the travellers began to kill their starving oxen and horses.

On Aug. 22 the expedition camped on the reedy shore of Cow Dung Lake. Seeing that the lake emptied into a little creek which ran westward, they surmised they were finally over the continental divide, and that this was the beginning of the Fraser. They feasted heartily on roasted ox that night. Now they had only to follow the creek to the river and it would lead them to the Cariboo.

Progress was rapid at first but soon the creek swelled into a torrent and drove them high up onto the hills again. There was no trail, no blaze on any tree. The guides had never been here, their contract was almost complete and the sharp night frosts warned them autumn was beginning.

At Moose Lake [30 miles west of Jasper] the Overlanders found a band of Shuswap Indians, who traded salmon and berries for ammunition, bits of clothing, needles and thread. The salmon had struggled 700 miles from the sea, had eaten nothing on the way, were half-rotten and heavy with spawn, but they tasted good to the Overlanders. Dried in the sun, or mixed with berries in the Indians' cakes, they would yet save the expedition from starving.

On the sand the Shuswaps drew a crude map that seemed to show a white man's trail which led south. But already, they said, this road was a foot deep in snow. And the Fraser was not flowing west, but north—away from the Cariboo. McMicking looked long at the Indian map. If he followed the river he would reach the gold fields somehow, but how to navigate a river which at every mile widened, deepened and flowed faster? South must lie the headwaters of the Thompson River and beside it the white man's trail. One route or the other must be followed—and soon.

After two days' march [to Tête Jaune Cache] McMicking left each man to decide for himself. Most could bear no more foot travel and elected to run the Fraser. The others, seeing the fury of the water, chose to herd 130 horses and cattle overland to the Thompson. With this group went Mrs. Schubert.

Frantically, with an eye on the weather, the river party cut down cottonwoods, bound them together with withes [tough, easily bent twigs] and made six rafts, each 40 feet by 20. Railings held the remaining oxen, and fireplaces of stone and clay made it unnecessary to stop even for cooking. Crude dugout canoes were hollowed out of larger cottonwoods, and one man made an even lighter craft by stretching green oxskins over a framework of saplings.

494

On Sept. 1 the rafts were ready and a captain was chosen for each. First the *Scarborough* was pushed into the current. It spun for a minute and drifted slowly north. The crew cheered, the oxen bellowed, and the Shuswaps watching from shore sadly shook their heads.

Now the *Ottawa* was launched, then the *Niagara*, the *Queenston* and finally the giant *Huntingdon*—two rafts lashed together, 85 feet long. The Overlanders lay down on their logs and watched the riverbank glide by. No rapids or whirlpools had been mentioned in the prospectus of the Overland Transit Company. Surely the river ahead could not be so bad as the trail behind.

The first autumn rains were falling, and every man was soaked. "Rainy all day," said the diary of John Hunniford, "very uncomfortable, diarrhea very bad on board, meat badly tainted—our flour about done." Still, it was delicious to lie on the cottonwood logs after the labor of the trail, drifting even in the darkness while they slept.

Ahead the dugouts moved faster. The first, carrying three men from Toronto, reached a series of violent rapids in two days. At first sight of the maelstrom the paddlers beached the canoe, then tried to lower it on a rope. The canoe bobbed for a moment in the current, was sucked down and swept away. The three men were stranded on the shore for two days without food or shelter. One of them, named Pattison, was near death when the first raft caught up.

Meanwhile three men from Goderich, Ont.—Robertson, Warren and Douglas—had lashed two canoes together and tried to run the rapids. Their clumsy twin craft immediately capsized and broke apart. Warren and Douglas clung to one canoe as it hurtled through the rapids; Robertson swam for shore. Looking back, he could see the canoe dragged under the water, but when it surfaced his companions were still with it. Robertson shouted to them to hang on. Finally the canoe was thrown up on a sandbank, and when Douglas and Warren crawled ashore Robertson had disappeared. He was never seen again.

The two men lay exhausted and helpless on the sand bar. There they would have died if the *Huntingdon* had not reached the upper end of the rapids a few hours later. Two of the giant raft's crew launched a canoe, somehow ran the rapids, and rescued Douglas and Warren.

By Sept. 6 two more canoes had been lost in the rapids. Could the rafts get through? The *Queenston*, its crew asleep, was almost into the rapids before the lookout shouted the alarm.

"At half past five in the morning," McMicking recorded, "we were suddenly startled by an unusual roaring noise that broke the silence of the morning. We had reached the big rapids and were already so near them and were being swept toward them so rapidly that we barely had time to row ashore and make fast.

"After landing we went some distance along the shore to examine the place before trying to run it. We found that the rapids consisted of three distinct stretches with small bays or eddies of comparatively quiet water between. . . . We saw no alternative: we had either to run the rapids or starve where we were."

It was decided to take the raft through the water with only 10 men, just enough to work the oars. The others of her crew would portage. McMicking continues: "Onward they sped like an arrow, rushing, it seemed, into the very jaws of death. Before them, on the right, rose a rocky reef, threatening instant and unavoidable destruction, and on the other side a seething and eddying whirlpool was ready to engulf in its greedy vortex any mortal who might venture within its reaches. With fearful velocity they were hurried along directly toward the fatal rock. . . .

"Not a word was spoken except the necessary orders of the pilot, which were distinctly heard on shore above the din and tumult. Now was the critical moment. Everyone bent manfully to his oar. The raft shot closely past the rock, tearing away the stern rowlock, and glided safely down the eddy below. The agony was over. The gauntlet had been run and all survived."

The crew of the *Queenston*, except one lookout, slept all the next night while the raft gathered speed. At daylight they awakened to find themselves in a new series of rapids. For 15 miles, all hands at the oars, the raft tossed from one side of the river to the other. The men clung to the railings and their oxen were swept overboard as the raft sank in whirlpools, but always it lurched to the surface again and moved forward until it stuck fast on a submerged rock. Three men swam ashore and managed to pull the craft clear with a rope. After that it was plain sailing.

The *Queenston* reached Fort George at 8:45 a.m. Sept. 8. The other rafts followed during the next two days.

Meanwhile the Overlanders who had left McMicking's party at Tête Jaune Cache had reached the Thompson River. Unable to hack their way through the huge cedars and firs that lined its banks, they killed most of their oxen, let all but seven horses loose, built themselves two rafts and a dugout, and entrusted themselves to the river. With the exception of one man who was drowned when one of the rafts overturned, all eventually reached Fort Kamloops. Mrs. Schubert floated in with the last arrivals on Sept. 13 and gave birth to a baby girl the next day.

In the last week of September, back at the headwaters of the Fraser, other Overlanders were still straggling into camp through the Yellowhead Pass and building more rafts. Their first raft hit a rock seven miles from its starting point, and dumped all the supplies. The crew clung to it for a day until one man swam ashore and brought rescuers from the camp. This prompted the rest of the travellers to kill their oxen, dry the meat, buy salmon and dried groundhog from the Indians, and take to canoes.

The last party of Overlanders to get through before winter—two men in one canoe and three in two canoes lashed together—reached the rapids on Sept. 30. There the double craft was swamped and one of its crew drowned. Another, a young Scotsman named Alexander, narrowly escaped: "After swimming a distance of about three quarters of a mile, I touched shore but was so benumbed with the cold I could not hold on to it but drifted off again. Soon, however, I made the shore again and dug my hands among the pebbles and pulled myself out of the water and lay there."

Having swum the rapids, Alexander had to swim back to rejoin his comrades. The four survivors let the remaining canoe down the river on a line but it broke loose and disappeared. Now it was walk or perish. They started for Fort George with a diet of one groundhog a day among them. Crawling through the dense underbrush along the bluffs, they made only a few miles, but the next day they spotted one of their canoes beached on the opposite side of the river. The canoe was too small to hold all four men and their supplies, so they took turns riding in it while one man struggled along the bank.

Alexander had shot a brace of ducks and two squirrels. Just as these and the last groundhogs were eaten, and the first snow began to fall, the four men heard voices on shore. Heading in, they found a camp of Indians. In exchange for a few shirts and some tobacco the Indians fed the white men on beaver and guided them to Fort George.

Everybody save those lost in the river was safe at Fort George now, sheltered, fed and clothed. The sick man, Pattison, had died on arrival, and was well buried under a pile of stone to keep the wolves away. (A few Overlanders had straggled so far behind the march that winter caught them in the mountains. Before spring they tried to run the river. In the summer their bodies were discovered on the sand bar below the rapids.)

From Fort George the canoes and rafts drifted 60 miles down to Quesnel, where the huddle of log cabins on the bank must have appeared an odd gateway to the land of gold. But a few miles away lay all the glittering promises of the Overland Transit Company. Why, even on the banks of the river by the town a few men were panning and rocking the gravel. With a shout the Overlanders leaped ashore.

That was the last shout. From the townsfolk of Quesnel they soon heard that there was gold at Barkerville, but not enough to go around. For every man who found any, nine found nothing. The Overlanders noticed hundreds of ragged men walking into Quesnel from Barkerville and hurrying down to the coast before winter blocked the trail.

Three thousand miles on foot, on rafts and in canoes, five months of travel and the wastage of their savings, had brought the Overlanders to a country where, in the words of one man from Huntingdon, Que., people merely "stayed and starved."

A few sanguine spirits walked 40 miles east to Barkerville, but quickly returned. One party reached the Pacific at Bella Coola. The rest of the Overlanders stopped in Quesnel for a day or two, then floated farther downriver to Alexandria. There, after selling their rafts, canoes and a few last skinny oxen, they began the 240-mile journey to the coast, where a few found work on the new Cariboo Road to Barkerville.

Most of the Overlanders remained in British Columbia. None found gold, but all found the "lovely country unequalled for its beauty and salubrity of climate." At least that part of the Overland Transit Company's promise had been fulfilled.

McMicking, who settled in New Westminster, had set down his expenses in detail. For the journey from Queenston to Quesnel he had spent $97.65. Noting the equipment he had brought, he added: "Our mining tools were the only articles in the above list that we found to be unnecessary."

The Stampeders

Mountains stood between the stampeders and the Klondike gold—and the chief route through was the treacherous Chilkoot Pass on the Alaska/British Columbia border. Swept by banshee winds and sudden blinding snowstorms, its icy slopes were an awesome challenge. Yet in the bitter winter of 1897-98, some 22,000 gold-crazed men and women set out to scale the Chilkoot—not just once but the 40 times it took to backpack a ton of supplies to the summit. This is the story of their ordeal, an incredible testimony to human ability to endure when the stakes are high.

By PIERRE BERTON

The Chilkoot in '98, a place of terror, hardships and yearning.

OR MANY the story of the Klondike gold rush is evoked by a famous photograph of a solid line of men, a human chain hanging across the white face of a mountain rampart. Each man, bent almost double under the weight of his burden, seems frozen in an attitude of supplication. It is a mirror of all the terror, hardships and yearning of '98. The Chilkoot Pass has come to be a symbol of the stampede.

The gateway to the Chilkoot was Dyea, Alaska, a feverish little town almost identical with its rival, Skagway: a jungle of frame saloons, false-fronted hotels, log cafés, gambling houses, stores, real estate offices and flapping tents. Until the summer of 1897, Dyea had consisted of a trading post. But by midwinter barques were dumping as much as eight million board feet of lumber on the beach in a single day, and hotels rose almost hourly (not to mention a three-storey opera house).

A liquid stream of humanity gushed through Dyea's narrow streets day and night, so that the air was never still from animal cries and human curses. Only the natives remained silent, and, of all the thousands who attacked the Chilkoot that winter, none profited more than they. The Tlingits worked as packers. Over the mountains they trudged, squat and swarthy and taciturn, tumplines taut around their flat foreheads, packs balanced upon their massive shoulders. They were shrewd bargainers: they worked for the highest bidder, refused to labor on Sundays and continued to raise their fees as the fervor of the rush increased.

The first arrivals at Dyea found their outfits had to be lightered from steamer to beach, where they were dumped helter-skelter. Each man had quickly to move his gear above the high-tide mark. One 1898 arrival wrote: "We saw grown men sit down and cry when they failed to beat the tide. Their limited amount of money had been spent to buy their stuff and get it this far. With their flour, sugar, oatmeal, baking powder, soda, salt, yeast cakes, dried potatoes and dried fruits under salt water, and without time or money to replace them, their chances of getting to the gold fields were gone. A terrible blow to the strongest of men." They used dogs, horses and oxen to push or pull their outfits across the glistening sands. One old man, unable to pack his outfit on his shoulders, rolled the boxes as best he could, barely keeping ahead of the waves.

For a few brief months the horse was king. Pack animals were so scarce that even poor ones sold for $600 or $700. And although feed ran as high as $150 a ton, each animal could earn $40 daily in packing fees before he collapsed. "Every horse that lands at Dyea may be considered as dead," wrote one stampeder. "They mostly die of starvation, as no one brings enough feed, not anticipating so much packing."

The first few miles of the Dyea Trail were a pleasant wagon road through meadow and forest. Then piece by piece the telltale symbols of the stampede appeared—a litter of goods thrown aside by men who had already begun to lighten their burdens. Each stampeder learned that trunks were useless, and the only practical containers for his outfit were stout canvas bags 50 inches long. Weary men kicked off their heavy rubber boots and left them behind. Two enterprising Alaskans retrieved this mountain of footwear and took it to Juneau for sale to newer arrivals; hundreds of pairs of boots came back over the passes time after time.

Five miles from Dyea the trail reached Finnegan's Point, a huddle of tents surrounding a blacksmith shop, a saloon and a restaurant. Here Pat Finnegan and his two husky sons tried to charge $2 per horse for the use of their corduroy bridge, until the mounting tide of stampeders brushed them aside. From here the trail led toward the canyon of the Dyea River, a slender crevice cluttered with boulders, torn-up trees and masses of tangled roots. Through the slushy thoroughfare of Canyon City the steady stream of panting men trudged on. At the far end of the canyon, in a strip of woods, a third wayside settlement sprang up, called Pleasant Camp because it came as such a relief after the gloom of the gorge. Now each man felt the tug of gravity as the grade began to rise slowly until Sheep Camp was reached at the base of the mountains. This was the last point on the trail where it was possible to cut timber or firewood; everything beyond was naked rock and boulder, sheathed in ice and snow during the winter.

Sheep Camp lay in a deep basin which seemed to have been scooped by a giant paw out of the encircling mountains. In one mountain was a small notch: the Chilkoot. On most days the peaks were shrouded in fog, but when the sun was out and the sky clear, the pale light glinted on glaciers which hung from the rim of the mountain wall. The summit was only four miles distant, but it was a long way up—3,500 feet above Dyea.

From Sheep the new arrival could see ahead and above a vast panorama framed by the grimy hovels of the camp and set against the alabaster backdrop of the sharp-edged peaks. The once-immaculate slopes were spattered by fly-speck figures of men. The newcomer, already smarting under the tug of his pack, saw the dimensions of the task that faced him. Within a few days he would be another midge on the mountain inclines.

501

Sheep Camp, last stop before the big climb. Hotels were huts—or tents.

There were seldom fewer than 1,500 people in Sheep Camp. The tents and shacks were wedged so closely that it was difficult to squeeze between them, the only open space being the semblance of a street which curled haphazardly along the bank of the narrowing river. At times the camp seemed like a giant dry-goods repository. Canvas emporiums offered groceries, hay, rifles and laundry service. The biggest store of all, a log building, offered everything from drugs, cigars, tobacco, candy, nuts and stationery to "first-class beds."

There were 15 "hotels," none more pretentious than a hut. The best known was the Palmer House, named after its owner, a Wisconsin farmer who had been driven north by hard times just before the stampede began. He had come this far with his wife and seven children and, having only $8 left, had gone no farther; now, in a one-room dwelling, he was reaping a fortune. He and his family fed 500 people a day and slept 40 each night, jamming them so tightly on the plank floor that it was impossible to walk through the building after nine in the evening. But until freeze-up the Palmer House did boast running water: a brook rippled through one corner of the building.

By the time the snow began to fall, early in the autumn of '97, Sheep Camp had become a bedlam of sweating men, howling dogs and abandoned horses. Cut adrift by their masters, who could not get them over the pass, these starving creatures hobbled about the camp, stumbling into tents, seeking food, shelter and companionship. In the end they were rounded up and shot and their bodies hidden under the swiftly falling snow. All that winter the snow continued and was packed down by the trampling men, so that the valley floor rose slowly and no man knew how far the ground lay beneath him. In midwinter one party punched a hole in the snow with a pole to test the depth, forcing it down for seven feet before it hit bottom. The pole struck something yielding. "Bottom" was a dead horse.

From Sheep Camp the trail rose sharply until in the last assault on the pass it reached more than 35 degrees and a man could drop to his hands and knees and still seem partially upright. There were only two points on this four-mile stretch where a climber could properly rest. The first lay beneath a huge overhanging boulder known as the Stone House. The second was a flat ledge only a few city blocks square at the very base of the ascent, known as the Scales because everything was reweighed here and the packers' rates increased to $1 a pound. Loaded animals could go no farther, though one or two horses did make the climb; even sleds and dogs had to be packed over on men's backs. Thousands of tons of supplies, half hidden by the falling snow, were piled here, waiting for their owners to gather stamina for the last climb.

All winter long, from Sheep Camp to the summit, for four weary miles the endless line of men stretched up the slippery slope. From first light to last, the line was never broken as the men inched slowly upward, climbing in that odd rhythmic motion that came to be called the Chilkoot Lock-Step. All individuality seemed to end as each man became a link in the chain. Even separate sounds were lost, merged in the single all-encompassing groan which rose from the slow-moving mass and echoed like a hum through the bowl of the mountains.

To any alpinist the ascent of the pass would have seemed child's play. But the men of '98 were not mountaineers. Poorly attired in heavy furs and wools, rather than in light practical hooded parkas, the novices alternately sweated and froze. Unable to disrobe or bathe, seldom free of the winds that were the terror of the trail, bent double under their packs by day and by the need to curl up for warmth at night, half-nourished by cold beans and soggy flapjacks, plagued by dysentery and stomach cramps—filthy, stinking, red-eyed, and bone-weary, they still forced themselves upward. The delays were interminable. Blizzards and gales made the slopes impassable for days. Mishaps on the trail caused the line to move by fits and starts. One 35-mile trip from Dyea to Lake Bennett was no great hardship, but the gold-seekers had to suffer it over and over again. It took the average man three months or more to shuttle his ton of goods across the pass, and by that time the word "stampede" seemed a cruel misnomer.

As the winter progressed, enterprising men began to hack steps out of the ice wall above the Scales. The first stairs were chopped out of the last 150 feet of climb, where the going was so steep that one stampeder compared it "to scaling the walls of a house." Two partners cut the steps out with axes in a single night and collected more than $80 a day in tolls, and then, after six weeks, went on a tear and blew it all. But others cut more steps until there were 1,500 in the mountainside, with a rope balustrade alongside and little shelves where men could step out of line and rest. Yet few stepped out, because a man might have to wait all day before being able to slip back in.

Up the "golden stairs" they went, men from farms and offices, climbing into the heavens, struggling to maintain the balance of the weight upon their shoulders, occasionally sinking to their hands and knees, sometimes breaking down in near-collapse, sometimes weeping in rage and frustration, yet always striving higher and higher, their faces black with strain, their breath hissing between their gritted teeth, unable to curse for want of wind yet unwilling to pause for respite, clambering upward from step to step, hour after hour.

The packers took the ascent more casually. While 50 pounds was as much as the average stampeder could handle, most packers carried 100 pounds. One Indian managed to reach the summit with a 350-pound barrel on his back. An Iowa farm boy on a wager carried a 125-pound plough up the final slope. On a bet, a Swede named Anderson and a Siwash Indian called Jumbo each made one trip from the Scales to the summit with 300 pounds. They returned in a dead heat, whereupon the Swede immediately hoisted a second 300 pounds on his shoulders. The Indian stared at him in dismay and retired from the contest.

If a man was too poor to hire a packer, he climbed the pass 40 times before he got his outfit across. A representative list of groceries required for one man, to be lugged over the mountains, suggests the magnitude of the task:

400 lbs. flour	36 yeast cakes	50 lbs. onions
50 lbs. corn meal	15 lbs. salt	50 lbs. potatoes
50 lbs. oatmeal	1 lb. pepper	24 lbs. coffee
35 lbs. rice	½ lb. mustard	5 lbs. tea
100 lbs. beans	25 lbs. apples	4 doz. tins condensed milk
40 lbs. candles	25 lbs. peaches	5 bars soap
100 lbs. sugar	25 lbs. apricots	60 boxes matches
8 lbs. baking powder	25 lbs. fish	15 lbs. soup vegetables
200 lbs. bacon	10 lbs. plums	25 cans butter

But this was not all. There were a steel stove, a gold-pan, three nests of granite buckets, a cup, plate, knife, fork, two spoons, two frying-pans, coffee pot, pick, handsaw, whipsaw, whetstone, hatchet, two shovels, three files, drawknife, axe, three chisels, 20 pounds of nails, butcher knife, hammer, compass, jackplane, square, Yukon sled, 200 feet of rope, 15 pounds of pitch, 10 pounds of oakum, and a canvas tent.

And there were clothes: three suits of heavy underwear, a mackinaw coat, two pairs of mackinaw trousers, a heavy rubber-lined coat, a dozen pairs of wool socks, half a dozen pairs of mittens, two overshirts, two pairs of shoes, two pairs of blankets, four towels, two pairs of overalls, a suit of oilskin clothing, and five yards of mosquito netting.

When he had dumped his day's load on the summit and marked it with a pole, each man turned back down again, for there was no shelter at the top. The return trip was swift and precipitous; the stampeders simply tucked their boots beneath them and tobogganed down the slope on their rumps, gouging deep chutes in the snow, and hitting the bottom in a matter of minutes.

Inevitably, human ingenuity won over nature. By December 1897 the first crude tramway—an endless rope wound around an upright wheel and turned by a horse moving in a circle—was opened by a sourdough named Archie Burns. It set the pattern for more ambitious devices. By

May there were five operating over the pass. One consisted of an endless chain of buckets—hundreds of them—each carrying 100 pounds. These soared a mere 50 feet over the line of struggling men. Another, worked by a gasoline engine and a rope wound around a drum, dragged sled loads of equipment up the ice of the pass directly beside the climbers.

By far the most ambitious tramway, built by the Chilkoot Railroad and Transportation Company, opened in the spring of 1898. Its 14 miles of copper steel cable, supported by towering tripods anchored in concrete, enabled goods to be transported aerially all the way from Canyon City to the summit. Steam engines at each end supplied the power, and men struggling along the trail could gaze up and see carloads of goods hurtling through the snow-filled air 1,800 feet above them. The cars, each loaded with 300 pounds, were dispatched at the rate of one a minute, day and night, so that by spring freight was being dumped on the summit at the rate of nine tons an hour.

On top of the pass a silent city took shape. The "buildings" were towering piles of freight; the "streets" the spaces between. The blizzard that rarely ceased covered the goods soon after they were dropped, making it necessary for the owners to leave poles or long-handled shovels marking their property.

The piles of freight provided the only shelter. Firewood was priced at $1 a pound to cover the cost of hauling it seven miles by sled from the timber line on the Canadian side. Those who could afford it paid $2.50 for a stale doughnut and a cup of weak coffee (five times the price of a three-course meal in Seattle), gulped it down, and were away, for no one wished to tarry. Only the North West Mounted Police held fast to their post. The presence of these men in their huge buffalo coats marked the summit as the international border. The sight of a tattered Union Jack fluttering in the storm, and the blurred outlines of a sentry with a Maxim gun, always on duty, was the first indication the stampeders had that they had reached Canadian territory.

Here, every man was required to pay duty on the outfit he had hauled across from the Alaskan side. The levy ranged from three quarters of a cent on a pound of corn syrup to 60 cents on a barrel of flour.

One storm raged for two months, stopping almost all movement on the trail, but still the police clung to their post, their hut dripping as the snow was melted by its warmth, while supplies, blankets, documents and records were slowly coated with a creeping fur of mildew.

The detachment once was driven from its post by the shrieking

The summit: Canadian territory, the Union Jack, the Mounties, the "customs house."

gale. The Mounties retreated into the lee of the mountains, pitching tents on the ice of Crater Lake, an old volcanic hollow just below the peak of the pass. Here in a below-zero blizzard they crouched while the water rose six inches above the ice, soaking their bedding. Unable to move their tents in the storm, they pulled their sleds inside and slept on top of them. Then, when the wind abated, they returned to their perch on the mountain.

The police checked 22,000 men across the pass that winter—Scots and Canadians, Yanks and Greeks, Swedes and Australians, Japanese and Hawaiians. There were women, too: stocky soubrettes heading for the dance halls of Dawson . . . lithe Indian girls who carried 75 pounds on their backs and scaled peaks more nimbly than some of the cheecha-kos . . . a German woman, almost 70, in a full dress and a lace apron . . . Capt. Jack Crawford, the "poet scout," met "a handsome girl, straight as an arrow, blue eyes, curly blond hair, dressed in boy's clothes—blue shirt, no coat, with a belt with a .44 Colt pistol strapped around her waist." Her brother walked ahead of her, carrying a guitar.

Among the real gold-seekers were fake stampeders—confidence

men–sent up from Skagway by Soapy Smith. They mingled with the endless line of plodding figures, tugging sleds behind them or carrying authentic-looking packs that seemed to bulge with Klondike gear. The packs were stuffed with feathers, hay, or shavings; the sleds were dummies built for a quick getaway.

It was difficult for many a weary climber to resist the blandishments of Smith's gang along the trail. The con men built fires and put up tents where men could warm themselves, and constructed seats or ledges for tired packers to rest on. On a single mile of trail one observer counted four shell games in operation, each surrounded by an eager knot of players.

Old Man Tripp, a saintly looking sinner, was in his element, working with a younger colleague, Frank Brown, nicknamed "Blue Jay." One carried a cane which unfolded into a three-legged support, the other a book which opened into a counter 12 by 18 inches. Thus equipped with the traditional con man's "tripe and keister," Tripp ran the game with Blue Jay as shill. Tripp could slip a rubber pea out from under a shell so deftly that no one could tell it was gone. Nobody but Blue Jay could win and the two made daily clean-ups. One pioneer wrote that it was not uncommon for Soapy's gang to realize $2,000 a day.

Every variety of the human species had a representative on the pass that year. There was an English nobleman, fastidiously dressed in tweeds, with a valet who, in the late fall, fed him morsels of food while he reclined beneath a net to protect his skin from insects. There was Wilson Mizner, wit, bon vivant and gambler, later famous as a Broadway playwright and owner of Hollywood's Brown Derby restaurant. Mizner's ton of goods on the Chilkoot included certain luxuries; his main item of baggage was a dance-hall girl from San Francisco.

Like Soapy Smith and his men, Mizner was interested not so much in finding a gold mine as in finding a man who had already found a gold mine. Many others had the same idea. A newsboy struggled up the slopes with a sackful of old newspapers which he hoped to sell at high prices to miners starved for information. One man managed to lug a grindstone over the summit; it had occurred to him that by spring most of the picks in the Klondike would need sharpening. A Buffalo man took 10,000 bottles of mosquito lotion across the slopes. He had bought them for 20 cents each and hoped to sell them for $10 to insect-maddened prospectors in Dawson. Arizona Charlie Meadows carried a portable bar which he set up on every possible occasion, raising the price of the drinks in direct ratio to the height of the trail. At Canyon City he served whisky for 25 cents a shot, but at Sheep Camp the price was doubled, and by the time the Scales were reached every drink cost 75 cents.

The singleness of purpose with which the stampeders flung themselves at the mountain, time and time again, would have astonished a dispassionate observer. The harsh trials of an English couple named Rowley illustrate the intensity of the common desire to reach the Klondike.

The Rowleys' first misfortune occurred when the S.S. *Corona*, on which they were Dyea-bound, was shipwrecked. The couple lost their entire outfit but, rather than turn back, they attempted to earn enough to keep going by freighting goods across the pass. The effort was too much for Rowley, who took sick at Sheep Camp, but this only caused Mrs. Rowley to redouble her efforts as a packer. She managed to move 1,300 pounds of goods as far as the Scales, often working 20 hours at a stretch and seldom leaving the trail before two in the morning. The strain was too great, and before her husband was fully recovered, she herself was worn out from fatigue. Rowley resolved to send her back to San Francisco. Her brother wrote that he had sent her $100 to the Dyea post office, but she did not receive the money. This was too much to endure. Distraught and enraged at the supposed theft, Mrs. Rowley bought a gun and tried to shoot the postmaster. She was ordered taken to Sitka on a charge of attempted murder. En route she leaped from the steamer, but her husband pulled her from the water and she was shortly released from jail on grounds of insanity. While all this was going on, the Rowleys' entire second outfit, purchased with money earned from freighting, was stolen at Lake Lindemann. Did this deter them? Not in the least. As the Rev. J. A. Sinclair of Skagway wrote to his wife: "You can imagine the intensity with which the gold fever possesses these men when I tell you that Rowley still intends to go on to Dawson."

There were hardships on the trail, certainly, but comparatively few deaths and, considering the circumstances, little major crime. That year, progress across the Chilkoot was marred by only two natural disasters, but both were spectacular.

The first occurred in September 1897. For years, travellers had been fascinated by a glacier that hung like a brooding monster over the pass. Harry de Windt, a British explorer who crossed the Chilkoot in the mid-'90s, saw it suspended insecurely between two granite peaks, looking "as though a child's touch would send it crashing into the valley below."

The face was 300 feet high, "indescribably beautiful" because of the shifting light—turquoise and sapphire on dull days, dazzling diamond-white in the sunlight, delicate mauve, pink and green in the twilight. From this scintillating mass there issued occasional reports like the distant rumble of cannon, sometimes faint, sometimes so deafening that the watchers below expected the entire ice sheet to tumble into the valley below. That is what happened.

Warm summer weather and heavy rains had caused a lake to form within the heart of the glacier. Then the autumn winds, whistling through the mountains, tore half an acre of ice from the edge of the mass. With a noise like a thousand cannon, a wall of water descended upon the pass. The reverberations woke 25 campers who had pitched their tents on the dry ground of an old gorge, and they raced for the hills as a wave 20 feet high tore down upon them. The roaring waters picked up the Stone House as if it were a pebble and moved it a quarter of a mile down the valley, smashing to pieces about 40 tents and outfits, including the entire gambling casino and liquor supply of Arizona Charlie Meadows. But there were only three deaths.

The second tragedy occurred April 3, 1898, and it was far crueller. For two months an intermittent storm had been raging, making travel impossible on most days. On Saturday, April 2, the blizzard increased and six feet of wet snow fell; the peaks and glaciers were top-heavy with it. The pass was now at its most treacherous and those few who dared to climb it did so only in the cool of the evening. The Indians and experienced packers refused to go up at all.

In spite of their warnings, large numbers took advantage of a lull in the storm to make for the summit. The first hint of impending tragedy came early on Sunday. A bent old man, groaning and waving his arms, hammered on the door of a restaurant at the Scales and cried out that several people had been buried alive by a snowslide up the trail. A dozen men dug frantically through 10 feet of snow and rescued all but three. Now every person was thoroughly alarmed, and a headlong race began for Sheep Camp, two miles below.

Higher still in the mountains, the guttural rumble of avalanches could be heard. A group of tramway workers had made their way in at midmorning to report that enormous mounds of snow, piled high along the peaks, were starting to slip down the smooth glaciers. This lent wings to the retreat. Downward the fleeing men and women scrambled, in single file, while clinging to a rope that had been strung along the way.

They did not follow the main trail but went by way of a ravine which had long been considered treacherous by knowledgeable guides.

At noon it happened. One of the survivors, J. A. Rines, recalled: "All of a sudden I heard a loud report and instantly began to feel myself moving swiftly down the hill and, looking round, saw many others suddenly fall down, some with their feet in the air, their heads buried out of sight in the snow." Rines braced himself, kept to his feet, and let himself be carried along. He was caught by the snow and buried instantly 30 feet deep.

Others had similar experiences. Some grasped the rope that was used to haul freight to the summit. Some, feeling themselves buried hip-deep by the weight of loose snow which struck them first, struggled with it only to be smothered by the main force of the avalanche which followed.

The avalanche had tumbled from a peak 2,500 feet above the trail. It covered 10 acres to a depth of 30 feet. Within 20 minutes 1,000 men from Sheep Camp were on the spot digging parallel trenches in an effort to locate the victims. The scene was a weird and terrible one. Small air holes sometimes appeared in the snow to mark the spot where a man or woman had been buried, and somewhere beneath them the searchers could hear muffled cries. Those who still lived beneath the snow (and only a few had been killed by the slide) could hear one another talking, and conversations were carried on between them. Relatives above called out their last good-byes to those entombed below. One old man could be heard alternately praying and cursing until his voice was stilled. But even the strongest could not move a muscle, for the snow was packed around them as tightly as cement.

As the hours wore on, those not rescued at once began to feel drowsy and drifted into sleep from which few awoke. Their corpses were lifted out later, many of them still in a running position, as if forever fleeing from the onrushing avalanche.

More than 60 perished. A handful were rescued alive, including a man named Joppe, whose recovery was Lazarus-like in its drama. When he was lifted from his frozen tomb, apparently dead, his sweetheart, Vernie Woodward, was beside herself. She was a resilient young woman who had been packing on the pass since the previous summer, first carrying freight on her back like a man and later working with horses. She flung herself hysterically upon Joppe's limp figure, begging him to return to her, manipulating his arms and legs, rubbing his back, breathing warm air into his lungs, and crying and praying by turns. For three hours she continued. Then Joppe suddenly opened his eyes and spoke her name. It was as if a dead man had miraculously come alive again.

Some of the victims were buried in a little hollow in the mountains not far from the scene of the disaster, and even as the services were held, the long line of men resumed its inexorable grind across the mountains. The sun increased its arc as the days lengthened; wild flowers soon spattered the mountainside; sedges and grasses began slowly to creep over the debris of the previous winter's rush. The hollow where the bodies rested became a lake, and when summer arrived the last stragglers following in the wake of the main wave of stampeders came upon the grisly spectacle of dozens of floating bloated corpses.

Thus was the epitaph to the story of the Chilkoot written. The following winter a railway was pushed through neighboring White Pass, and the mountains that had resounded to the groans and the shouts of thousands were as silent as the graves of those who had perished beneath the snows.

The Lost Treasure of *Le Chameau*

*For 236 years the cold and treacherous Atlantic near
Fortress Louisbourg hid a fortune in gold and silver coins.
The treasure—pay for the French army in Quebec—had been
strewn over the rocky ocean floor in 1725 when the 48-gun
naval transport* LE CHAMEAU, *seeking refuge from a sudden
gale, was wrecked on a submerged reef less than a mile
offshore. In 1961 a skindiver found a silver coin with the bust
of Louis XV and the date 1724. The treasure hunt was on.*

Condensed from CANADA ILLUSTRATED

FROM THE MILITARY PORT of Rochefort on the west coast of France, *Le Chameau* set sail for Quebec in early July 1725. On board were 316 persons, including the newly appointed intendant at Quebec, the governor-designate of Trois-Rivières, and several high-ranking military officers. In addition to livestock, spices, clothing, arms and other supplies, *Le Chameau* carried a staggering 116,050 livres in gold and silver coins (worth more than a quarter of a million dollars in today's currency).

Louis XV had entrusted this mission to a capable and prudent captain, Jean-Charles Percheron de Saint-James. The navigator, one Chaviteau, although occasionally accused of recklessness, was an experienced seaman who had made numerous transatlantic voyages. *Le Chameau* was 133 feet long, 30 feet in the beam and armed with 48 cannon. She was seaworthy, her crew experienced; the voyage would be routine.

No record remains but there must have been trouble, for the crossing took longer than usual. It was late August before Saint-James sighted the rocky coast of Cape Breton Island. Quebec was still more than 700 miles distant.

On Aug. 25 villagers along the coast took refuge from a violent southeast gale. On into the night the storm raged and Saint-James apparently decided to head for the nearest safe harbor. *Le Chameau* attempted to beat her way to Fortress Louisbourg, 10 miles south along the coast.

At dawn Saint-James saw the small, rocky Portnova Islands, near the entrance to a small bay [Kelpy Cove]. The lee of the islands would offer temporary refuge from the gale winds and mountainous seas. Saint-James veered toward the cove. Moments later *Le Chameau* struck a submerged rock (known to this day as Chameau Rock). The impact ripped open her hull. Spars came crashing down, cannon broke free and careered to starboard, smashing through the side and tumbling into the water.

Badly holed, *Le Chameau* capsized and began to sink, taking with her all on board. The battered hulk, considerably lightened and aided by empty water and wine casks, bobbed back up, righted itself and lurched toward the beach of Kelpy Cove. *Le Chameau* drifted, striking more submerged peaks and spilling her lower-deck guns.

Finally her starboard side disintegrated, then her upper decks and parts of her port side. Through the smashed hull of the stricken ship dropped the chests of gold and silver coins.

By 10, as the storm waned, inhabitants of the villages of Baleine and Little Lorraine ventured out. They saw wreckage along the beach. On one spar was a pulley marked with the fleur-de-lis. The news was hastily carried to Louisbourg: one of the king's ships had been lost.

The governor and military commandant of Louisbourg set out to inspect the area. Beaches and coves were strewn with wreckage, including a figurehead identified as that of *Le Chameau*. Part of her starboard side, with the mainmast and its rigging, was found on a rocky promontory. Her port side was washed up on another beach. Bodies were found in Little Lorraine harbor, and at Kelpy Cove it became apparent that the calamity was complete. The gravel beaches were strewn with bodies and debris. About 180 battered corpses were recovered.

The authorities sent word of the tragedy to Quebec and arranged to send gunpowder, lead shot and money from the supplies at Louisbourg until replacement stores arrived from France.

Louisbourg was convinced that most of *Le Chameau*'s guns and treasure were still salvageable from the after part of the ship. It had not washed ashore but, as the rock upon which the ship had foundered was covered by only a few feet of water at low tide, it was felt divers could do the job.

The salvage contract was granted to Pierre Morpain, the captain of the port of Louisbourg. He would be assisted by two French navy divers from Quebec—Antoine Frustier and Pierre Poittevin. Poittevin's nickname was *Tempête* (Storm).

The salvagers were hindered by severe weather and bad diving conditions. In October, after weeks with no success, operations were called off. The divers had located cannon, anchors and cables from the wreck—all in the vicinity of Chameau Rock—but they found no trace of the treasure. The after part, which had contained the chests of gold and silver coins, had vanished.

This was the only French attempt to recover the treasure. For nearly two centuries *Le Chameau*'s remains lay undisturbed.

But local lore kept the story alive until the turn of the 20th century, when several expeditions tried in vain to locate the lost coins. Strangely, the existence of gold coins among the treasure was usually discounted by the treasure hunters and residents of the area.

Interest was revived in 1961 and for a few months a flurry of activity centred on Chameau reef. Most of these expeditions were outfitted to recover materials from more recent wrecks, but the divers knew they were working in the area where *Le Chameau* had met her fate in 1725.

In mid-June, while searching for a modern wreck, skindiver Alex Storm came across cannon from *Le Chameau*. Intrigued, he swam over the entire area and noticed clusters of eroded cannon balls and more cannon. By the time he surfaced, he had decided to try to solve the mystery of *Le Chameau*.

Storm, a Dutch-born draftsman who had taken up diving as a hobby, persuaded the salvage vessel skipper to try for the treasure. On his very next dive, Storm retrieved a silver coin from a clump of fused cannon balls. The coin was in remarkably good condition and examination revealed the bust of Louis XV—and the date 1724!

Storm's initial good luck did not hold; although many dives were made, no more coins were found. The skipper of the craft called off the coin-hunting and ordered Storm and the other divers to shift their attention to salvaging cannon—in demand for the federal government's recently begun restoration of Fortress Louisbourg. A series of hazardous and time-consuming dives did yield a number of cannon from the site, but the guns were relatively valueless—salt water had corroded the cast-iron barrels. The skipper suspended operations.

But Storm's appetite had been whetted. If there was one coin, wouldn't there be others somewhere in the depths of Kelpy Cove?

News of Storm's find reached a group of local divers who had also been interested in *Le Chameau*. They contacted Storm and agreed to join forces with him.

The wreck site was a diver's nightmare. Jagged Chameau reef extends almost 4,000 feet offshore, from the gravel beach of Kelpy Cove to the barely submerged pinnacle of Chameau Rock. The ocean swell continually breaks over this rock, and powerful tidal currents rush in and out over the reef each day.

Contending with cold water, fog, storms, and even sharks, the salvagers dove for weeks with no tangible results. Finally, in December 1961, the diving tender was pulled ashore and the group separated.

In 1962 Storm worked as a diver in the underwater survey of Louisbourg harbor. There he learned techniques of underwater archaeology from an American expert employed on the project. Storm convinced him to look at the site. But because the wreckage was scattered along the 4,000-foot reef, the American claimed it was "of no archaeological value." Storm was back where he started and the treasure seemed more unobtainable than ever.

Two years passed with little activity at the site, but Storm continued to brood over the possibilities. Finally, convinced that a well-planned attempt could succced, he recruited two new partners who he felt would persevere despite the difficulties: David MacEachern, diver-surveyor, and Harvey MacLeod, engineer-navigator.

A boat was found, the *Marilyn B II,* and at Little Lorraine, the group's operations base, she was outfitted for salvage work. Then came research into *Le Chameau*'s exact specifications—important in determining where the coin chests had been stored. Archives in France supplied the missing information.

Now the main question remained: exactly what had happened to *Le Chameau* after she struck the rock?

In June 1965, the *Marilyn B II* sailed into Kelpy Cove. The area was marked with underwater markers. It was painstaking and tedious work but the divers hoped that, after exploring each section of their grid, they might establish a pattern indicating the trail the wreckage had taken.

The first sections were searched, and it became apparent that the wreck had not settled close to Chameau Rock. One of *Le Chameau*'s anchors was found in much deeper water. Another puzzle remained: 26 cannon had been located but where were the other 22? Obviously the entire armament of the lower gun deck was missing.

The trio persevered and the clues led them steadily into deeper water. At 75 feet the conventional search methods had to be abandoned. They decided to rig up a special towing device which would enable a diver to be pulled underwater, scanning bottom features on the ocean floor in deep water where skindivers had never been. Their first attempt was a success; cannon not previously sighted were spotted on the dark bedrock.

The divers were beginning to feel confident again, when the trail of clues came to an abrupt end. Storm and MacEachern diligently searched the shoreline, but found no more relics. They re-examined the broad cove but it, too, revealed nothing significant. Returning to the area where they had found the last pieces of ironwork, they worked out in a new direction. Finally they discovered another anchor, then the last of the missing cannon. They were closing in on their goal.

On Sept. 19 a routine dive to check out more ironwork yielded the results they had dreamed of. Lying on the bedrock was a cluster of coins—silver *écus*! Jubilant, they picked up the pace. Find after find began turning up: a watch, a miniature 16½-inch cannon, lead sounding weights, cannon balls and lead shot.

Three days later they struck the bulk of the treasure; the wooden chests had long since disintegrated, but a staggering concentration of slate gray coins remained. The divers excitedly began gathering the coins. Then they noticed an unmistakable glitter among the gray *écus*–gold!

Harvey MacLeod, David MacEachern, Alex Storm with treasure from LE CHAMEAU. *Inset: at Fortress Louisbourg, salt-corroded cast-iron gun barrels from the treasure ship.*

Within minutes Storm and MacEachern had filled their canvas bags; they could barely drag them to the salvage basket. A tug at the line and MacLeod, the man at the top, began hoisting it out of the depths. Breaking the surface a few minutes later, both divers gesticulated wildly to MacLeod who was still hauling the basket to the surface, unaware of the riches it contained.

The trio opened the canvas bags and watched breathlessly as hundreds of silver and gold coins came tumbling out. It was unbelievable; after over two centuries at the bottom of Kelpy Cove, most of the coins were in good condition!

The divers went down again and again, and the number of coins grew from hundreds to thousands. Week after week, the *Marilyn B II* rode at anchor above the site. Each day, on the return trip to Little Lorraine, the trio sorted the coins into separate piles of gold and silver.

Hijacking was now a distinct possibility and the utmost secrecy had to be maintained; the coins and other artifacts, including sword hilts, broken pottery, silver forks, spoons and buckles, were carefully stowed in diving-gear bags and smuggled ashore as diving equipment.

At the end of October operations were suspended and the treasure tabulated. The three men had amassed 11,000 silver *écus,* more than 900 gold coins (called *louis d'or*), and many valuable artifacts. It was the largest underwater treasure find in Canadian history—with an estimated value of $300,000.

The restless Atlantic still washes over Chameau Rock, and the Portnova Islands preside over the area where the king's ship went to her grave in 1725. The first Storm, the French navy diver known as *Tempête,* narrowly missed a king's ransom then, but the second Storm, 240 years later, did not, and the once illusive *Le Chameau* treasure is a mystery no more.

The Supreme Court of Canada ultimately awarded Alex Storm and his associates 75 per cent of the treasure. Storm's original partners, who gave up in 1961, claimed he had entered into a binding agreement with them and the court awarded them 25 per cent. Both parties were required to hand over 10 per cent of their respective treasures as royalty payment to the Province of Nova Scotia.

Most of the coins and artifacts owned by Storm and his associates were auctioned in New York for about $200,000. Some of LE CHAMEAU*'s armament and cannon balls, and part of Nova Scotia's share of the coins, are displayed at Fortress of Louisbourg National Historic Park.*

Law

and Order

*What is more indicative ... of a country
than the style of its laws, the manner
in which they are observed and ...
the manner in which they are enforced?*

L. H. Nicholson, 1954

The Damnedest Man That Ever Came Over the Cariboo Road

*Judge Matthew Begbie brought justice to British Columbia's
lawless Cariboo gold fields in the early 1860s.
Starting with 15 poorly paid constables and a shaky
knowledge of the law, he quickly cowed and disciplined
gangs of rowdy miners up from the murder and banditry of
the earlier California gold rush. He became known as
the Hanging Judge but was regarded with such awe that few
hangings were necessary. One old-timer described
him thus: "Begbie, by God, was the biggest man, the
smartest man, the best-looking man, the damnedest man that
ever came over the Cariboo Road."*

By BRUCE HUTCHISON

A TOWERING YOUNG STRANGER from England stepped ashore at
Fort Victoria on Nov. 16, 1858. His top hat was cocked rakishly
on the side of his head. His dark mustache was waxed to fine
points, his beard trimmed in a neat wedge. His look was handsome, proud
and theatrical.

In this self-confident figure Governor James Douglas (with some
secret Scottish doubts) beheld the most incredible figure in the history
of British Columbia, one of the makers of the Canadian nation, the au-
thentic stuff of national myth.

Matthew Baillie Begbie had brought with him the law of Britain, very vague and muddled in his head. He had arrived just in time. Thousands of American miners from California were swarming in to mine the gold of the Fraser River sand bars. If they fought with the Indians and appealed for aid to the U.S. government Douglas foresaw an American push northward. The desperate governor of British Columbia had no military power to defend his colony against the expansive, trigger-happy movement called Manifest Destiny which had turfed the British out of Oregon and was now observing the whole Pacific coast with an envious eye. Douglas' only hope was to prevent violence from the start, by enforcing the law.

Begbie, the first judge west of the Rockies, didn't understand the law very well: unable to make a living at the London Bar, he had been reduced to reporting the courts for the *Law Times*. But fortunately, in legal matters, he had an inventive imagination. At 39, with no prospects, he had jumped at the chance of a judgeship at £800 a year on the other side of the world. Anyway, his sweetheart had just run off with his brother and he was glad to get out of England.

It was not necessary that he know law. The British colonial secretary, Sir Edward Bulwer-Lytton, asked only that the new judge be a man who could "truss a murderer and hang him from the nearest tree." Begbie was such a man and much else besides.

The trails were hardly open in the spring of '59 when Begbie and his staff walked up the Fraser from the gold rush centre of Yale. To his surprise, and doubtless to his secret disappointment, the new judge found the miners strangely peaceable. They were taking gold by the sackful out of the Fraser and they seemed uninterested in international politics. There were no murderers to be hanged from the nearest tree. It was not a promising start for a man who would be remembered as the Hanging Judge.

With time on his hands Begbie inspected mines, tramped the interior ranges, mapped the country, wrote Douglas enthusiastically about its future, advised him to open it with a road—the famous Cariboo Road was rushed through three years later—and quickly came to regard himself as a builder of the British Empire.

Douglas was impressed but Col. R.C. Moody, chief commissioner of lands and commander of the Royal Engineers, resented such interference. His palace guard called Begbie the "archenemy" and intrigued against him continually. As it turned out, the judge outlasted his enemies and became himself a pillar of the oligarchy, shouting down charges against his honesty and surviving a final attempt to ruin him.

After his first quiet season he found more congenial work. As gold was discovered in the uplands of the Cariboo and the second rush of miners headed overland from the Fraser to the creeks of Barkerville, killings, thefts and claim-jumping kept the judge agreeably occupied.

Now began the most extraordinary series of trials ever held in British North America. Travelling with a string of 12 horses Begbie would gallop to the scene of a crime, don his robes and wig, and hold court in a settler's cabin, in a barn, or still mounted in an open field. A court order scribbled in the saddle might be questionable law and was nearly always misspelled, but his writ ran through the Cariboo and he was seldom far behind it. He slept wherever night found him, often in a tent, summer or winter.

Begbie acted as prosecutor, defence counsel and judge. This kind of one-man litigation was rough, often technically wrong, but generally just. If the crime was serious the judge gathered in anyone who happened to be handy and impanelled a jury. Since most of the miners were Americans who had no right to act as jurors in British Columbia many trials were probably illegal, but a little point like that never worried Begbie.

He worked on the simple assumption that if a crime had been committed someone should pay for it. Once he threatened to punish a man who had been found not guilty, and actually assumed that he had the power to do so, although he finally cooled off and let the prisoner go. There were no lawyers in the country. An appeal had to be taken to England, which no man could afford.

But whatever he might get away with, the judge was impotent against the jury system. In his shrill nasal voice Begbie could shriek and threaten as if his juries were the criminals but the jurors often retorted with a verdict of not guilty to spite him, even if the prisoner's guilt had been proved to the hilt. Sometimes a jury would find that a murdered man had accidentally "fallen off a cliff" or "died of fever." On such occasions Begbie was left gibbering with rage.

When, in a plain case of murder, a jury brought in a verdict of manslaughter, the judge screeched from the bench: "Prisoner, it is far from a pleasant duty for me to have to sentence you only to imprisonment for life. Your crime was unmitigated, diabolical murder. You deserve to be hanged! Had the jury performed their duty I might now have the painful satisfaction of condemning you to death. And you, gentlemen of the jury, are a pack of horse thieves, and permit me to say it would give me great pleasure to see you hanged, each and every one of you." This was the kind of oratory the miners could understand and they would come from miles around to hear it.

Another jury brought in a verdict of not guilty against a man who, as the evidence showed, had sandbagged a companion in a Victoria bar-room brawl. Looking out coldly from under his massive wig, Begbie snarled his most famous dictum: "Prisoner at the bar, the jury have said you are not guilty. You can go, and I devoutly hope the next man you sandbag will be one of the jury."

Begbie's brand of justice was crude and gaudy, but the miners came to know that it was usually fair and they were awed by it. They began to call Begbie the Hanging Judge and he never lived down that name in British Columbia.

It was a false name. When Begbie had to pass the death sentence he was so shaken that he kept a chaplain by his side to support him at the awful moment. Often he secretly advised Douglas to commute the sentence to life imprisonment.

In the case of an Indian named Quahook he wrote to the governor: "The Indian & the murdered man had been getting drunk together; and in this there was some misunderstanding about a female. I am quite aware that if 2 men engage in a burglary or any other crime & kill the other, even by accident, it is murder! but surely, when it is the seducer and the far more guilty party (as to the original crime) who is killed it wod not be irrational to modify the punishment of the murderer."

Concerning another condemned Indian who had been held for a long time in the jail at Lytton, Begbie advised Douglas: "I cannot but think that the sentence ought to be commuted to penal servitude. It is scarcely right to keep a poor fellow on the tenterhooks for so long & hang him at last."

Begbie's methods achieved precisely the result that Bulwer-Lytton and Douglas wanted—the rule of law, a friendly, firm hand on the Americans and the steady enforcement of British ways against the northward pressure of Manifest Destiny.

Between the Rockies and the sea one hard-riding, hot-headed man—government and justice in the same saddle—directed the police, managed local magistrates, and settled the disputes of miners, settlers and towns-folk. Single-handed, he established law-abiding habits.

He did not introduce the law. He *was* the law over the whole sprawl-

Barkerville, "capital" of the Cariboo, in 1869.

ing terrain of British Columbia. And in a colony where there was considerable pressure for union with the United States, Begbie, perhaps even more than the abler Douglas, organized a native society which could resist the pressure and finally consign its future to Canada. Douglas at Victoria was governing a British colony. Begbie, in the interior, was laying the foundations of a Canadian province.

Up to about 1863 it was easy for the judge. He could make up the law to suit the occasion. There was no one to question him. But as towns sprang up, as miners, homesteaders and storekeepers acquired property, the population became annoyingly prone to launching lawsuits. And in civil cases Begbie was helplessly at sea. Worse, lawyers who knew the law had settled in the colony and Begbie could not shout them down.

For months he refused to allow George Walkem to practice before him because Walkem was merely a lawyer from Canada and not "a Gentleman from England."

Having set up a court to deal with estate litigation in the existing English fashion, Begbie once reversed a decision he had rendered already in his own supreme court. In civil cases, where juries determined only facts, Begbie, like a modern judge, could set aside their findings and he often did. But he could not get away much longer with his abuse of

527

lawyers and litigants: that pestiferous growth called democracy was flourishing, and it showed scant respect for English gentlemen.

After one of Begbie's more perverse decisions 500 miners held a mass meeting beside the Richfield courthouse. They resolved that "the administration of the mining laws by Mr. Justice Begbie is partial, dictatorial and arbitrary in setting aside the verdict of juries," and that the judge should be removed or an appeal court established above him.

Begbie rode off with his little retinue, taking no notice of such protests. He was used to criticism and, lately, to threats against his life. One day, sunning himself on the upper balcony of the Clinton Hotel, he heard some men on the street below plotting to shoot him. He went to his room, fetched out the chamber pot, emptied its contents on the heads of the conspirators and resumed his siesta.

So far he had feared no man and carried his honor high. He had become a chief pillar of the oligarchy. When at last his honor was openly impeached Begbie knew fear for the first and last time in his life.

On Nov. 26, 1862, New Westminster's paper, *The British Columbian,* published a letter signed "A" accusing Begbie of accepting land from a man named Dud Moreland who wanted a questionable Barkerville-area homestead title approved. For months Begbie had borne in silence the criticism of the paper's angry editor, John Robson, chief enemy of the Victoria family compact and a fighter for responsible government. Now the judge had the editor where he wanted him—in contempt of court.

Begbie summoned Robson before him in New Westminster and demanded an apology. Although he conducted the case in his usual high-handed style the judge obviously was worried. He denied in laborious detail the charge by "A." He said he had acquired 20 acres of land from the homestead in question on which to build a house where he intended to recuperate from rheumatism. He had paid 10 shillings an acre for the land and, quite properly, had confirmed Moreland's title to the rest of the homestead.

Robson listened unmoved. A grim man, with the face of an eagle and a gift for flamboyant invective, he hated Begbie and sought to strike at the family compact through the ruin of the judge. Granted a day to think it over, the editor refused to apologize and Begbie ordered him locked up.

Martyrdom was just what Robson sought. The cheers of the crowd at the courtroom door assured him that his cause was popular. While

The British Columbian.

NEW WESTMINSTER, SATURDAY, DEC. 6.

A VOICE FROM THE DUNGEON !

Fellow colonists ! We greet you from our dungeon. Startled by the wild shrieks of a dying maniac on the one hand, and the clanking of the murderer's chains on the other, while the foul and scant atmosphere of our cell, loaded with noxious effluvia from the filthy dens occupied by lunatics, render . . . . . able, our readers will o . . . . . or want of connected . . . .

British Colum . . . . been aimed at . . . great bulwark . . . you have nob . . . of the act. . . . fortunate vic . . . the absolute . . . change the p . . . adopted coun . . . but small imp . . . comparatively . . .

Editor John Robson: up from a dungeon, a man with the face of an eagle.

529

500 people held a mass meeting to denounce Begbie as the Tyrant Judge and to petition the British government for his dismissal, Robson sat down to write the most celebrated editorial in British Columbia history. It was headed "A Voice from the Dungeon!" and began:

> Fellow colonists! We greet you from our dungeon. Startled by the wild shrieks of a dying maniac on one hand, and the clanking of the murderer's chains on the other, while the foul and scant atmosphere of our cell, loaded with noxious effluvia from the filthy dens occupied by lunatics, renders life almost intolerable, our readers will overlook any incoherency or want of connected thought in our writings. . . .

Brave words, but the jailed Robson couldn't get them in print. He soon tired of martyrdom and asked to be taken before the court again. The judge was glad enough to hear him. Robson's apology was not quite complete but it was good enough to vindicate Begbie and extricate the government from a threatening clash with democracy.

When released Robson published "A Voice from the Dungeon!" on his front page. It was a little late, but the prose was too fine to waste. On page three appeared a brief note of explanation: "Liberated. Since writing the article on our first page we have been discharged from custody. Further particulars in our next."

The incident has a look of comic opera now but Robson, who later became a premier of British Columbia, had dealt a deadly blow to the family compact. He left around Begbie's name a cloud of suspicion and doubt which has lasted to this day.

The British Columbian continued to publish evidence on Begbie's land deal, while other writers frantically sought to vindicate the judge. Finally Moreland said he had given Begbie the land for nothing: it was a flat repudiation of the judge, who did not answer.

In a few more years he had no need to answer. British Columbia entered Confederation in 1871 and Begbie, as chief justice, enforced the law of Canada. He was knighted in 1875. His black whiskers turned white and he became quite genial. Sir Matthew was now, in his own lifetime, British Columbia's great folk figure, the man on horseback who had carried justice from the sea to the mountains.

Having established his legend, Begbie lived long enough to enjoy it. He built a rambling house with a spacious garden on the edge of Victoria. He strode about the city with a pack of spaniels at his heels. He shot ducks out of season on the Fairfield marshes near his home. He gave weekly tennis parties in the summer, his servants tying ripe cherries on bushes so players could pick them conveniently. Every Saturday night he entertained the clergy at dinner. They debated theology until nine o'clock, then the parsons were dismissed and the bloods of the town arrived to play poker until dawn.

On Sunday mornings Sir Matthew sang in a church choir in his high, obnoxious voice, and at noon he invariably burst into the house of a friend named Peter O'Reilly, greeted his host in the Indian tongue of the Cariboo and sat down to a huge rice pudding.

In the spring of '94 the clergy and the town bloods were no longer invited. Sir Matthew had learned he was dying. The following weeks were long and painful for he would take no drugs "lest they dull my mind." On June 11 he died.

The Hanging Judge, it turned out, was not the man that British Columbia imagined. His fortune—so small as to destroy any charge of dishonesty—was left to a group of poor, unknown men and women whom he had been supporting secretly for years. To each of his clergy friends he left $100 and a case of claret or sauterne "at their choice," and to the wives of two other friends "a dozen potted plants and a dozen roses at their choice."

And the Tyrant Judge, the blusterer of the courtroom, the terror of the mining camps, ordered that his grave be marked by a wooden cross bearing only this inscription:

"Lord, be merciful to me, a sinner."

The March West

*In the early 1870s, with the buffalo vanishing, starving Indians
on the Prairies were at the mercy of greedy American traders. Coming
from Fort Benton in Montana, the traders built forts with such
names as Whoop-Up and Robbers' Roost, sold bad whiskey, and
cheated the Indians of furs and horses. But in late 1873 a small
force, predecessor of the Royal Canadian Mounted Police, was finally
formed to establish control over the vast, barely populated area
known as the Northwest. In 1874 the force marched west. The trek
across the Prairies came close to breaking
the Mounted Police, but in fact it helped
make them.*

By RONALD ATKIN

PRIME MINISTER JOHN A. MACDONALD had specifically requested "as little gold lace, fuss and feathers as possible." The government wanted the North West Mounted Police to be more a civil than a military organization.

But on July 8, 1874, there was at least plenty of fuss in Dufferin, Man., as the scrubbed and glittering police assembled to carry law and order onto the Prairies. Their first objective: Fort Whoop-Up, near present-day Lethbridge, Alta., the most important of the whiskey forts.

Certainly Dufferin, a Boundary Commission post south of Winnipeg, had never seen anything like it. George Arthur French, a combative Royal Artillery officer on loan to the Canadian government, was commissioner of the Mounted Police but still a soldier of the Queen. His men, in scarlet tunics, white gauntlets and pith helmets, were also unmistakably servants of Victoria. Red coats, to the Indians, were synonymous with friendship and fair dealing; they were also believed to be dyed with the blood of the Queen's enemies. Swords, buttons and brass chinstraps dazzled in the sun.

With a keen sense of occasion, Commissioner French had mounted each of his six divisions on horses of different colors—dark bay, light bay, dark brown, bright chestnut, gray and black.

Behind the 275 officers and men were 73 wagons and 114 Red River carts with supplies and ammunition, 93 cattle for slaughter, and mowing machines to cut fodder. The baggage included two nine-pounder field guns, two brass mortars, field kitchens and portable forges. Even when closed up for the start the column stretched a mile and a half.

With a rousing cheer they were off. As one of the policemen noted in his diary, "It was a splendid sight, destined to last but a short time."

The column was as noisy as it was imposing, mainly because of the Red River carts. Axle grease wasn't used because it collected dust that would eventually seize the hubs on the axles, so each hub rubbed with an ear-stabbing screech.

French ordered what was known as a "Hudson's Bay start" that day; the force travelled only two miles before making camp, a measure designed to check that everything was working satisfactorily, all goods were correctly loaded and nothing had been forgotten. The commissioner sent two wagonloads of "luxury articles" such as syrup back to Dufferin, and two loads of oats were sent in replacement.

Next morning several officers were unhappy about French's use of quality bloodstock as cart horses. A team had bolted after being harnessed to a mowing machine, and a row between French and Insp. Theodore Richer ended with Richer shouting at his commander, "If you don't put me under arrest you are no gentleman!" French offered to retain Richer if he apologized, but the inspector refused. He returned to Dufferin threatening that he would make things hot for French back in Ottawa.

The following day's march did not start until the afternoon because of straying oxen and stampeding horses. By the time it had covered six miles – through clouds of dust borne on a strong wind – three broken wagons had been abandoned and one horse had died. No water could be found so the column had to turn back two miles. At night a dozen men took advantage of the proximity of the United States to desert.

On Sunday, July 12, a start was made at 5 a.m. Sub-Insp. Sévère Gagnon, who sported a beard almost to his waist and balanced his forage cap over his right ear without benefit of a chinstrap, noted dryly in his diary: "Orangemen Day. They are easily noticed, for they are all displaying yellow flowers on their hats or on the heads of their horses." The column travelled only three hours before camping for the day near good water at the foot of the Pembina Hills. Gagnon commented that this was "a day of rest – i.e. we worked as hard as usual but we did not travel; we did our washing, cleaned our kit, got our horses shod, greased our wagons etc. etc."

In the hills the going became tougher and progress was painfully slow. Stragglers stretched the column for miles over the countryside. E. H. Maunsell, an Irish constable who was relegated to the position of cattle drover for falling asleep on guard, criticized French for thinking that cattle could keep up with mounted men. The supply wagons too began to fall behind, and there was often no food for the exhausted men at the end of the day. The diary of Const. James Finlayson for July 14 read: "Camped on the open plain near a swamp. No water, no wood, no supper. The [supply wagons] did not get in till after midnight." Two days later his diary told of "one flapjack per man for breakfast, lucky to get that. Supper the same as I had for dinner. Namely nothing! Hunger and thirst is two of the worst complaints among the boys."

One young constable, Pierre Lucas, became so terrified when his exhausted horse lagged far behind the column that he shot it, made his way into camp on foot and breathlessly explained that he had been forced to abandon the animal when he was attacked by a Sioux war party. The commissioner commented, "I do not believe his statement," but took no action.

Hordes of mosquitoes left the flanks of the animals and faces of the men streaked with blood. The police dangled nets from their helmets, but in their anxiety to find water they often invited even heavier mosquito attacks by pitching tents near swamps.

The Montreal artist-journalist Henri Julien described the insects as "simply dreadful. Your eyes, your nose, your ears are invaded. If you open your mouth to curse at them they troop into it. They insinuate themselves down your collar, up your sleeves, between the buttons of your shirt.... You can brush them off your coat in layers.... Often in the evening when we went to the nearest brook to water our horses, the mosquitoes would rise in columns out of the spongy soil. Our horses would rear, pitch and kick. We would be covered with scratches and blood. Our only refuge was to run our horses to their pickets, then throw ourselves on the ground and cover [up with] blankets."

One day a swarm of grasshoppers descended on the camp, devouring even the paint from the wagons. The men were also drenched by thunderstorms and once were showered with hailstones the size of walnuts.

But the heaviest blow to their dignity came when French ordered them to take turns driving the ox teams. According to 16-year-old bugler

Fred Bagley, "This was the most severe jolt Romance had been dealt since we left Toronto." The duty did have its benefits though, since the carts often contained food and "it was sometimes possible . . . by careful selection to get enough for a substantial meal."

Jean d'Artigue, a former mathematics teacher, considered it "more than discouraging" to see uniformed police driving oxen with sticks. He wondered, "What military commander who respects his men would have placed them on the same footing as those who work for mercenary motives?" D'Artigue was one of the unfortunates placed in charge of an ox team and, like the others, he fell miles behind the main column. One night he reached camp just before midnight: "Who goes there?" a sentry called out. "A famished man," replied d'Artigue. He was allowed to pass without further explanation.

However, d'Artigue, known as The Professor, was swift to adjust to the food shortage, catching frogs with a whip and sharing the feast with some initially dubious friends. One of them, Maunsell, recorded that "I soon lost my prejudice against the French for eating frogs."

Despite the discomforts there was still great rivalry between the divisions to see which could get away first each morning, and after 16 days the expedition staggered up to Roche Percée, 270 miles from Dufferin and the first main objective. This outcrop of wind-eroded rocks near the Souris River, venerated by generations of Indians and covered in animal carvings, was "the very place for a picnic," according to Sub-Inspector Gagnon.

French set up a four-day rest camp for his bedraggled column. D'Artigue reported that the force "resembled a routed army corps. For a distance of several miles the road was strewn with broken carts and horses and oxen overcome with hunger and fatigue. Was it in this manner that the Canadian government had intended the Mounted Police to be managed and directed? Certainly not. Could Colonel French have done better than he did? Certainly yes."

Sub-Insp. Cecil Denny, an aristocrat known as Texas Jack, considered that "prospects for a successful termination to the journey [begin] to look none too rosy," and French shared his opinion. So the commissioner decided to split the column, sending one division and what became known as "the barnyard contingent" of cattle, weak horses and surplus wagons directly to Fort Edmonton, 900 miles northwest.

July 26 was a Sunday, and the first church service was held since the departure from Dufferin. French took the Church of England party,

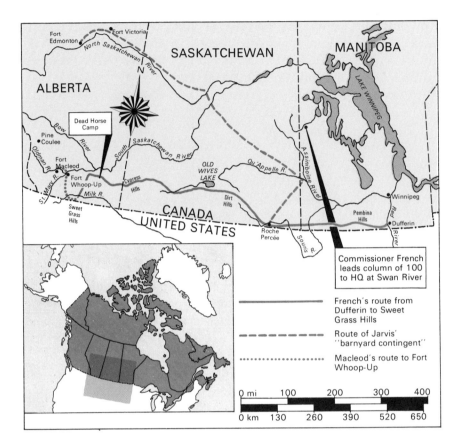

and the senior Roman Catholic, Presbyterian and Methodist officers were in charge of their denominations. "Some held their meeting on the hills, others in the valley," wrote d'Artigue. "It was a grand sight to see [the] men standing in the wilderness giving thanks in different manners and offering prayers to their Creator." Gagnon noted that the Roman Catholics sang the Ave Maria Stellis "rather badly," while French confessed he was "much pleased to hear many of the men singing hymns; unfortunately the language of a great many is by no means Scriptural."

At Roche Percée letters and news from Dufferin caught up with the force. French learned of reports in American newspapers that the column had been exterminated by Indians, and of prayers that had been said in churches throughout eastern Canada for the men's safety.

Both horses and men benefited greatly from the rest by the Souris River, and songs and music enlivened the evenings around the campfires.

537

Sub-Const. Bill Latimer led the tunes on a fife, accompanied by Const. Frank Parks on a drum improvised from a tin dish and tent pegs. The favorite songs were *Home, Sweet Home* and *God Save the Queen*, the latter rewritten by Const. Frank Norman to end thus:

> *Confound their politics*
> *Frustrate their knavish tricks*
> *Get us out of this damned fix*
> *God save all here.*

On July 29 French's five divisions moved off again, turning northwest, away from the U.S. border. The country was rougher, and Henri Julien noted, "Our skin felt as if on fire from the effects of hot winds, dust and mosquito bites.... There was no use washing, which I am afraid was a great relief to many...."

When they got to the Dirt Hills the men had to help the horses tow the cumbersome nine-pounder guns up the inclines. Julien said the guns "were always in the way, retarded our march, took up the time of several men and the service of several good horses.... But I suppose they looked military and had therefore to be dragged along, as much for show as anything else."

By some extraordinary oversight no water bottles had been included in the equipment, and water from stagnant sloughs caused widespread dysentery; 22 men reported sick on Aug. 2. Bugler Bagley's lips became so swollen and blistered he was unable to produce a note.

French wrote to his superiors in Ottawa, "If you saw the delight with which we hail the sight of a swamp you would be astonished, and if the relatives of some of the Ottawa boys saw their hopefuls standing in a swamp till enough water ran over their boots to get a drink, they might not turn up their noses so much at Ottawa's turbid stream."

Sugar had disappeared, bread was strictly rationed and there was little fat or grease. One man who found a tin of machine oil left behind by boundary surveyors sprinkled a few drops on his food at every meal and refused to share it.

There was a flurry of excitement on Aug. 12 when scouts reported a small Sioux camp ahead at a place called Old Wives Lake, and a pow-wow was arranged for the following morning. The police were looking forward to their first sight of the noble red man. The disappointment was immense. The Indians were a dejected and verminous bunch, with dangling, matted hair and filthy blankets wrapped about them.

Pulling the nine-pounders through the Dirt Hills.

Henri Julien described the reception given the group of about 30 men, women and children: "They were conducted to a kind of pavilion made by putting two large square tents into one. We at first met them with closed lips as we did not know what to say. The usual 'How-do-you-do' would have sounded ridiculous and the 'Happy-to-see-you' would have been a lie on our lips. However, we soon got into using the 'How' of our red brothers."

Police outside the door of the tent elbowed one another to get a glimpse of what was going on inside. The traditional smoking of a pipe was followed by a conference and the distribution of gifts. French, trying to impress the Sioux, succeeded only in amusing them when he told them that the Great White Mother whom he served had "red children, white children and black children."

The Indians managed to leave a lasting impression on their hosts in the form of fleas and lice. "Within a week every man, from the colonel down, was infested," wrote Maunsell. There was much suffering and cursing until the force was paraded naked and each policeman rubbed down with juniper oil. The men also learned how to get lice out of their clothing by placing it on ant hills.

Near Old Wives Lake French left behind another 14 wagons, 28 of the poorest horses, seven sick men and some footsore cattle, as well as provisions for that part of the force which would be returning to winter headquarters in Manitoba. Then as quickly as possible ("I grudged the loss of a day, even an hour") French pushed his expedition west again. Free of most of the cattle and the worst of the horses, the column made brisk time and on Aug. 24 sighted the Cypress Hills. Here the men managed to kill several antelope and deer, and enjoyed their first fresh meat since leaving Dufferin 47 days before. There were other luxuries: "We got better water and gorged ourselves on berries," said Maunsell. The police were also warned about possible Indian raiding parties, and French ordered them to wear their scarlet tunics and ammunition belts whenever travelling.

As they left the Cypress Hills on what they thought was the last leg to Fort Whoop-Up, travelling was made doubly miserable: the fine weather had broken and many of the horses were too exhausted to be ridden. Finlayson noted in his diary, "Raining again this morning. Mud sticks to our feet so that we are scarcely able to lift them."

On Sept. 2, amid great excitement, the first buffalo were sighted. Cecil Denny described what happened: "Most of us joined in the hunt; guns popped in every direction. I remember seeing one man riding alongside an old bull, in his excitement beating him with the butt of his empty gun until someone came to his assistance and brought down the game." Five buffalo were killed, one of them by French. When dressed, it produced 953 pounds of meat. Each policeman received two pounds but the anticipated feast was from tough old bulls and it defied their teeth.

The farther west the police travelled, however, the more plentiful buffalo became. Denny wrote that "there were places where untold thousands were in sight, the country black with them. Many times we killed them from the saddle without going out of the line of march." The marksmen soon learned to search out the fat young cows which provided the best meat.

Maunsell commented on the new diet: "For some weeks our only food was buffalo. I cannot congratulate our cooks on the scientific manner in which they prepared it. They would just cut it into chunks and boil it. . . . Straight boiled meat soon palled on the palate. We were all attacked with diarrhea, which greatly weakened us."

Although the buffalo herds produced badly needed food they also swept away vegetation and trampled water holes. Thirsty police had to dip their water cans into a foul mixture of urine and mud, boil the evil-

"Sept. 9: We called the place Dead Horse Camp."

smelling liquid they collected, add tea and attempt to drink it. As Maunsell pointed out, "When one is without water for perhaps 24 hours one will drink almost anything."

By early September the weather was turning chilly and tempers were growing short. French suspected the Métis guide who was supposed to be leading them to Fort Whoop-Up of deliberately going the wrong way, and grumbled that he was "the greatest liar I have ever met." In fact the guide was just following an erroneous map given him by the police. Finlayson's diary showed the perilous position of the expedition:

> Sept. 9: Last night it was very cold and eight horses died. We called the place Dead Horse Camp.
>
> Sept. 10: B Troop refused to leave camp until they had had breakfast. . . . The reason was very good, namely we had no dinner or supper yesterday. The weather getting very cold, I have put on drawers.
>
> Sept. 11: We are lost on the prairie. No one knows where we are . . . horses and oxen dying fast, provisions getting scarce, things looks very dark.

541

And French's diary for Sept. 10 noted, "I had a blanket taken from every officer and man last night so that each horse was covered and protected from the cold rain and wind. I began to feel very much alarmed for the safety of the Force. If a few hours' cold rain kills off a number of horses what would be the effect of a 24-hour snowstorm?"

That same day the creaking column reached the junction of the Bow and South Saskatchewan rivers where it was expected to find Fort Whoop-Up, bristling with cannon and full of heavily armed desperadoes. But three dilapidated, roofless log huts were the only sign of man's presence. The land, far from being the luxuriant pasturage the police had been told to expect, was parched and poor. There was not a tree in sight.

The police halted, lost and bewildered. Nobody seemed to know how to find Fort Whoop-Up, which was actually 75 miles west at the junction of the St. Mary and Oldman rivers. The men did know they were 800 miles from Dufferin and the weather was steadily deteriorating.

French urgently needed to find a camping area with grass, wood and water. He sent scouting parties along the Bow and South Saskatchewan rivers but the country there was even more desolate. It was decided to head 80 miles south to the Sweet Grass Hills, just below the American border.

Painfully the column readied itself for another march. In the first 36 hours nine horses died. Maunsell wrote, "This march had all the appearance of a retreat. . . . It was well for us that the Indians did not prove hostile. None of us would have returned."

It took five days to reach the hills, already dusted with the first snow of the season. By then the men were a pathetic sight. According to Bagley, "The sentry in front of the commissioner's quarters had gunny sacking wrapped around his feet [and] his rags of clothing were fluttering in the breeze." Bagley felt the police looked like the outlaws they were supposed to be chasing. When Finlayson decided to wash his uniform he had to shiver in his underclothes and shirt until it was dry. His diary complained: "If the people of Canada were to see us now, with bare feet, not one half-clothed, picking up fragments left by the American troops and hunting buffalo for meat, I wonder what they would say of Colonel French."

French had no time to wonder. He decided to strike out at once for Fort Benton to get both supplies and news. With a small party and empty wagons, French and James Macleod, the assistant commissioner, reached Fort Benton, 80 miles away, in three days.

542

French now decided to split the column a third time, leaving 150 men under Macleod (whom he described as "a capital fellow, my right hand") to find Fort Whoop-Up and build their own fort nearby, while he led 100 men back to Swan River, Man., where the Department of Public Works was building permanent headquarters for the Force. Fresh horses, warm clothing and wagonloads of supplies were bought on credit from the Fort Benton merchants, who also promised to help the police find Fort Whoop-Up even though some of them had active business interests there. French hurried back north with supplies for his eastward-bound column.

Macleod quickly organized supply lines with the leading Fort Benton trader, I. G. Baker, and sent word for his men at the Sweet Grass Hills to move west along the border to await his arrival. After four days' march they struck the well-beaten Whoop-Up Trail, which linked Fort Benton and Fort Whoop-Up, and pitched their tents along the nearby Milk River to await Macleod. But the first man to reach them was an enterprising Fort Benton merchant, John Glenn, who loaded a wagon with sugar, flour, syrup and canned fruit, headed for the police camp and sold out in minutes to the luxury-starved men.

To guide Macleod and his force to Fort Whoop-Up, I. G. Baker loaned the services of a short, bow-legged, monosyllabic Métis scout named Jerry Potts. Thus was forged a bond between Potts and the Mounted Police which was to last 22 years.

Potts' father had been a Scot who worked as a clerk for the American Fur Company; his mother was a Blood Indian. When Potts was only a year old his father was murdered in a case of mistaken identity, and the boy grew up dividing his time between Indian camps and white settlements. He fought in Blackfoot, Blood and Peigan war parties, and worked at the whiskey forts where he developed an ardent and lifelong addiction to liquor. (One police corporal said that Potts had "an unquenchable thirst which a camel might have envied. He drank whiskey when he could get it. If he could not get it he would take Jamaica ginger, or essence of lemon, or Perry Davis' painkiller, or even red ink.")

Potts was hired for $90 a month as both a guide and an interpreter, but it was as a guide that he served the police so well. The word laconic might have been invented for Jerry Potts the interpreter. After one meeting between some Blackfoot and the police Potts was asked to interpret the lengthy speech of a chief. He shrugged his shoulders and muttered, "Dey damn glad you here." And on the march from Fort Benton, as

Macleod's group approached a hill Potts was asked, "What's beyond that hill?" "Nudder hill" was the reply.

Potts' value was quickly demonstrated after Macleod rejoined the men at the Milk River. On the first day of the renewed march to Fort Whoop-Up Potts rode ahead of the column, selected a stopping place and killed and dressed a fat buffalo cow for the policemen's lunch. The next day Potts led them to the best springs they had drunk from since leaving Dufferin.

Eventually, on Oct. 9, Macleod and his men topped a rise and looked down on Fort Whoop-Up. The field guns and mortars, dragged from Dufferin at such cost, were unlimbered and trained on the fort. Macleod and Potts rode forward, dismounted and hammered on the main gate. It was opened by a tall, goateed American, Dave Akers, who disconcerted Macleod by inviting him to dinner. So, instead of fighting, the police sat down to eat fresh vegetables from a flourishing garden inside the fort. Akers explained that his partners were "away on business." In reality they had received ample warning of the arrival of the police and had removed themselves and their liquor.

Macleod was so impressed by the solid construction of Fort Whoop-Up that he tried to buy it as a winter headquarters. But Akers refused, and with the need for shelter becoming daily more urgent, Jerry Potts led the column 28 miles west to a fine spot on the Oldman River. The place had ample pasture, water and wild game, and groves of cottonwood trees provided timber. Here Macleod started building the Force's first fort in the west. By the unanimous wish of his officers and men it was named after him.

A heavy snowstorm blanketed the area at the end of October and Macleod's main concern was for the ailing horses. They were herded into the shelter of the woods, wrapped in blankets and fed liberally on oats and corn. He wrote to French, "I have made up my mind that not a single log of men's quarters shall be laid till the horses are provided for, as well as a few sick men. The men's quarters will then be proceeded with, and then the officers'." Gradually the little fortress took shape. By the beginning of December everybody was out of tents and by the middle of the month the work was complete. Twelve-foot logs placed upright in trenches formed both the stockade and the outer walls of the buildings, all of which faced inward. Roofs were flat and covered with several inches of earth. Floors were bare earth, and running across the officers' mess was the indentation of a buffalo trail.

Scout Jerry Potts led NWMP's James Macleod (seated, centre, in army days) to Fort Whoop-Up.

I. G. Baker, who had negotiated a year's contract to supply the police, promptly built a store alongside Fort Macleod. According to Cecil Denny, "after the long march on short rations no price was begrudged for luxuries."

While construction was going on Macleod's men struck their first blow at the illegal liquor traffic. A minor Indian chief, Three Bulls, reported that he had exchanged two of his ponies for two gallons of fire-water supplied by a man named William Bond. Three Bulls guided a

10-man detachment under Insp. Leif Crozier to Pine Coulee, about 50 miles north of Fort Macleod, where Bond traded. Two days later they were back with Bond and four other men. The patrol also confiscated two wagonloads of alcohol, 16 horses, rifles, revolvers and a pile of buffalo robes. The liquor was spilled and the traders received heavy fines of up to $200. Unable to pay, they were put in custody until a Fort Benton merchant named J. D. Weatherwax arrived to pay for the release of all but Bond, who managed to escape.

Soon, it was the turn of the cool and polished Weatherwax to be arrested. A patrol commanded by Cecil Denny and guided by an Indian informant trekked in bitter cold from Fort Macleod to an isolated trading cabin where they found Weatherwax and another man known as Diamond R. Brown. The police also uncovered a hoard of liquor and hundreds of valuable robes and furs. Macleod later fined the pair $240 each, confiscated their furs and property and ordered the liquor destroyed. Weatherwax threatened to "make the wires to Washington hum." Instead, he spent a week cutting wood and mucking out stables until his fine was paid.

The incident provoked an outburst in the *Fort Benton Record*, edited by John J. Healy, who turned to journalism after his own whiskey enterprise at Fort Whoop-Up was terminated by the police: "We knew from experience that wherever the English flag floats might is right, but we had no idea that the persons and property of American citizens would be trifled with." But Macleod wrote smugly to Ottawa, "I am happy to report the complete stoppage of the whiskey trade throughout this section of the country."

Meanwhile, nearly 300 miles north of Fort Macleod, Insp. William Jarvis and his "barnyard contingent" had staggered into the Hudson's Bay Company post at Fort Edmonton at the end of an arduous 88-day march.

When the division was left behind at Roche Percée toward the end of July, both officers and men were downcast. Jarvis had only three officers, 27 other ranks, a dozen Métis drivers and a guide to look after 57 Red River carts, 26 wagons, nearly 100 cows and calves, 63 oxen and 60 horses in varying stages of decrepitude. Fortunately, much of the route was frequently used by traders and trappers, and there were rest points and supply posts.

Most of the men shared the opinion of Jean d'Artigue about being away from French and his main column: "Jarvis was as fond of short marches as French was of long ones, and he was right. . . . Since we were detached from the main column we were living together like a family. If Jarvis had asked us to follow him to the North Pole, not one of us would have refused."

Though water was occasionally scarce, a regular supply of ducks, geese, prairie chickens and the occasional skunk varied the monotonous diet. A constable once brought down 11 geese with one shot.

By mid-September, however, there was regular frost and occasional snow. The horses began to fail at an alarming rate. When they lay down to rest they became so stiff they had to be raised with poles passed under their bodies, and their joints had to be rubbed before they could move off. By Oct. 19 the column was at Fort Victoria, 60 miles from Fort Edmonton. The horses were dying at the rate of one a day, and all the surviving cattle and most of the oxen were left behind. For the final 12 miles of the trip some horses were carried bodily on poles.

The two divisions which returned with French to winter at the new headquarters at Swan River enjoyed Indian summer weather for much of their march. With freshly purchased horses and plentiful supplies—and free of the encumbrances of cannon and cattle—they averaged 25 miles a day, enough to assuage even the anxious French.

On Oct. 21, as the column approached Swan River, the commissioner rode ahead, eager to see the fine new headquarters. What he saw horrified him: the barracks were being erected on top of a snake-infested, treeless hill covered with massive granite boulders. Instead of being grouped in a fort-like pattern the buildings were strung out in a line, fully exposed to the north wind. A prairie fire had burned to within 20 feet of the barracks and half the hay cut for the winter had been lost.

Furious that such a wretched place had been picked without his knowledge, French posted only one division there and took the other on to Winnipeg. It was time to have words with the politicians. [The headquarters was eventually moved, but not until after French had been replaced as commissioner.] By Nov. 7, a day under four months since he had left Dufferin, French was in the Manitoba capital.

The march west had been an epic of endurance and determination. Avoidable blunders had caused unnecessary hardship, and survival had become the main aim of the expedition. Yet the Mounted Police had passed their first great test with flying, if tattered, colors. French was extremely proud of his men and paid them sincere tribute in his official report. Privately he confessed, "I was not sorry when it was all over."

Wild and Woolly Days

*One of the first to join the newly formed North West Mounted Police
in 1873 was a cool, tough 24-year-old ex-soldier named
Sam Steele. During the next 30 years he became a legendary hero in a force
famous for facing down cutthroats, rebels and outlaws. Steele, with
a character to match his name, was "erect as a pine and quick as a cat,"
according to one friend. He had joined the militia at 17 and
served in the Red River Rebellion of 1870. Later he would lead a cavalry
unit during the Northwest Rebellion, help police the Klondike gold rush,
take another cavalry unit to the South African War, and
command the 2nd Canadian Division during World War I. Here he
describes some of his earliest experiences as a Mountie.*

By SAMUEL BENFIELD STEELE

I N AUGUST 1873, while posted to Kingston, Ont., with the Royal
Canadian Artillery, I first learned of the North West Mounted
Police. I obtained my discharge and a few days later was sworn in
as a Mounted Police sergeant-major. I was sorry to leave the army but
now I had the Great Lone Land before me where it is a man's own fault
if he fails while he has health and strength.

It was decided to dispatch three divisions of 50 men each to Lower
Fort Garry so they might arrive before winter. At the Stone Fort, as it
was called, we were soon settled fairly comfortably in the store buildings
which had to answer for barracks. The officers were quartered in the
Hudson's Bay Company officers' mess in the centre of the square.

I took over the breaking of the horses and instructed the NCOs
and men in riding. Our work was unceasing from 6 a.m. until after dark.
I drilled five groups per day the whole of the winter and the orders were
that if the temperature was not lower than 36 below ($-38°C$) the riding
and breaking should go on.

With very few exceptions the horses were broncos which had never
been handled, and none but the most powerful and skillful riders dared
attempt to deal with them. Even when we had them "gentled" so as
to let recruits mount, the men were repeatedly thrown with great violence
to the frozen ground. But no one lost his nerve. When spring opened
the men were very fine riders, laying the foundation of Canadian horse-
manship in the wild and woolly west.

There were amusements such as balls, parties and rifle matches,
but with the thermometer far below zero there was little pleasure in
shooting. There was a Quadrille Club for the NCOs and men but I never
attended; I much preferred an evening with the old settlers who could
tell me something about the country, or attending their dances and wed-
dings. I took notes of all the information I received, and became pretty
well acquainted with the customs of the Indians, hunters and traders.

On June 7, 1874, we left the Stone Fort, with considerable regret
but high hopes, for Dufferin, south of Winnipeg, where we were to
join three divisions from Toronto before starting our march west. [See
The March West, p. 532.] On the 19th the Toronto group camped beside
us. It was composed of fine, carefully selected and well-educated men
with exceptionally good horses. These were all over 15½ hands with
almost perfect forms. The horses were corralled inside a ring of loaded
wagons, where they were secured to pickets. Our horses, mostly broncos,
were kept at a distance, a fortunate circumstance as was afterward proved.

About 10 o'clock the following night a terrific thunderstorm burst upon us. I was riding near the large corral at the time, and the incessant flashes of lightning made every object visible. A thunderbolt fell in the midst of the Toronto horses. Terrified, they broke their fastenings and made for the side of the corral. The six men on guard were trampled underfoot. The maddened beasts overturned the huge wagons, dashed through a row of tents, scattered everything, and rushed for the gate of the large field in which we were encamped. In their mad efforts to pass the gate they scrambled and rolled over one another in a huge mass. A constable named Colman had just gone out the gate with his team, and it ran away with utmost speed.

The stampede continued south over the bridge on the Pembina River. The powerful Colman hung on to his reins and brought his team to a halt in about half a mile, but the other crazed horses were between 30 and 50 miles into North Dakota before they were compelled by sheer exhaustion to stop.

I shall never forget that night. The unceasing flashes of lightning, the rolling of the thunder, the loud shouts of the troopers as they vainly attempted to stop the horses, and the mad gallop of Colman's team gave it a weird and romantic complexion typically suggestive of the wild west.

We started after the runaway horses the next morning, using our own broncos and horses, and covering over 100 miles during the following 24 hours. The fugitives were brought in with only one missing. When they reached camp several of them lay down and rested for some days. For the remainder of the summer they were ready to repeat the performance on hearing the slightest unusual sound.

The winter of 1878-79 in the Northwest was exceptionally severe. Blizzards were common. After Christmas I was detailed to take a census of the Métis in the vicinity of Fort Macleod and Calgary. I left Fort Walsh, in the Cypress Hills, on the afternoon of Jan. 3, taking with me two constables and a fine old Métis plains hunter named Foley as an interpreter. Foley and I were riding and the two men, Henry Holtorf and George Mills, drove jumpers (small sleighs with shafts), each drawn by a pony. We took eight days' rations and forage.

The weather was extremely cold and our provisions and the forage ran short. To make matters worse, the ponies showed signs of playing out. We got into a maze of very deep coulees so I decided to leave the sleighs and baggage and mount Holtorf and Mills on the ponies. Foley said he did not know the way any longer so I took the lead and we struggled through the deep snow for some hours. Darkness and a blinding blizzard came upon us, and presently my horse halted and refused to go. I dismounted and found that the wise brute was within a yard of the high steep bank of the Belly River. Another step would have launched us onto the ice at least 100 feet below.

Next morning the blizzard still raged; the snow was too deep for the ponies to walk, and as Foley's horse and mine were very strong and in good condition the men were mounted behind us. In the teeth of the storm we rode up the valley until we reached abandoned Fort Kipp, where we had hoped to light a fire. The effort was in vain, however. There was no fuel, and the dry cottonwood logs of the old buildings were so smooth and hard that had we tried to set the place on fire we would not have succeeded. There was no help for it but to push on to Fort Macleod, 17 miles distant.

The blizzard became worse as we mounted the hill to the west, and there was no sign of a trail, but with a good idea of the right direction I led the way until Foley cried out, "The man behind you is freezing to death!" I dismounted and found that Holtorf was going into the death sleep. I pounded, shook and slapped him, saying, "A nice fellow you are, to try and steal off in this way! You must wait a while, you are too young to die yet!" These exhortations had the desired effect, and we pushed along for some time at a slow walk until I had to call out to Foley, "The man behind *you* is freezing to death!" Thereupon Mills was dragged off the horse, shaken, cuffed and reproached for his apparent willingness to leave this world of care and cold.

This sort of thing had to be repeated several times, and I began to have misgivings as to our chances of bringing the poor fellows through. Four miles east of Fort Macleod I had Holtorf dismounted for what seemed to be the last chance for him, when I saw a ranch belonging to a man named Joseph Macfarland. Letting the horse follow me, I supported the man to the door, where we were met by Mrs. Macfarland with a kindly Irish welcome. We had been nearly four days without food, but neither Foley nor I felt any ill effects from this or the storm.

During the winter of 1880-81 when I was at Fort Qu'Appelle I suffered for the first time from snow blindness. I found that the first symptom is the desire to rub one's eyes as if sand or some other irritating substance was beneath the eyelids; the next sensation is to see the snow a bright yellow. The pain is so severe that the slightest light causes agony. Even indoors a handkerchief has to be tied over the eyes and the blinds must be drawn until the room is in total darkness.

In my case I got some medicine and applied tea leaves with no apparent effect, and was sitting wondering what would turn up next when there was a knock at the door. I bade the visitor enter. When he had seated himself he said, "Oh, sir, are you snow blind?" I answered in the affirmative, and he asked me what I was using. When I told him he remarked, "Let me give you an old plains hunter's remedy. Get a pot of strong black tea made, cover your head with a silk handkerchief so as to let no steam escape, and look into the kettle."

I took his advice, got instantaneous relief and was quite well in a couple of days.

On Sept. 13, 1882, I was sent to Regina to lay out the ground for the portable buildings which were to be NWMP headquarters for a long time to come. I was also to act as magistrate and remain in charge of detachments along the Canadian Pacific Railway as far as Swift Current.

There was much secret gambling in Regina, and it was a common thing for half a dozen gamblers to be brought before me, but one of the cases had a most amusing side. The senior partner of the construction company building that section of the CPR had two nephews working for him. The older one, careful and staid, was paymaster; the younger and livelier was his quartermaster. This latter was fond of a game of poker whenever he could indulge in it although his uncle had an intense objection to gambling.

One dark, wet night the nephews were in Regina after finishing some business and were planning to join their uncle on his westbound train which was expected hourly. Near midnight I was busy writing in my tent when the younger nephew burst headlong through the door followed closely by the bright young corporal who was in charge of the town station.

"For God's sake, Cap, how much is it?" the nephew shouted. "The corporal has just caught me in a poker game and has the pot. Do try me now! If I miss the train the old man will know what has happened and I shall lose my job. Do try me, Cap!"

By this time the elder brother had entered in a more orderly manner and was standing behind with the corporal. When the younger brother had finished, the elder said, "I wish you would try him, sir. His uncle will be very angry with him if he hears of this scrape. The amount of the fine matters little." These requests had their effect. When the corporal had laid the charge and sworn to it, and the prisoner had pleaded guilty, I inflicted the usual fine, which was promptly paid, and confiscated the pot. The brothers, thanking me for my generosity, made their best licks to the station in time to catch the train.

This episode has been the subject of a magazine article, which states that I was roused out of bed to try the case. A Mounted Police officer roused out of bed at midnight! He might be at 4 a.m., but until the small hours he would be, as I was that night, booted and spurred, ready for the trail. The whole case did not take above 10 minutes. The young man often said to me afterward when we met, "By Jove, Cap, you did me a good turn then!"

In November 1883 I went to Calgary to take temporary command of the district. Total prohibition, under the Northwest Territories Intoxication Act, had proved excellent for preserving peace during the railway construction and keeping the Indians from deterioration, but it should not have been forced upon the rest of the community. We soon learned that compulsion will not make people sober. Liquor was brought in by every conceivable trick. Eggshells were emptied of their contents and alcohol substituted, tin imitations of the Holy Bible were filled with intoxicants and sold on the trains, and metal kegs filled with alcohol came concealed in the centre of barrels of kerosene.

We had one brutal murder during the winter. The victim, a fine young fellow, had a store near us. He was found lying near his desk with his throat cut from ear to ear and the whole place bespattered with blood. I learned that on the same evening the cook of a neighboring restaurant had been in the store and had disputed in a hostile manner an account which had been rendered to him by the proprietor; the cook had even gone behind the counter to give vent to threats.

I turned out several mounted parties assisted by numerous civilians. About midnight James Christie, an ex-member of the Force, arrested the suspect near some Indian lodges about a mile from our barracks. Blood was found on his right fingernail, and a dark oblong stain in his right trousers pocket. We noticed that the right leg of his trousers, being lower than the other, was frozen at the bottom from being in contact with the snow after being wet. The man had overshoes and his stockings were very damp.

Inspector Sam Steele and a Mounted Police detachment in 1885.

The snow round the store had been trampled over but next morning, at the front window of the store, the marks of the toes of the overshoes were very distinct. The tracks, and those of stockinged feet, were with great difficulty traced to the inside of the store and then through deep snow to a haystack.

The haystack had been disturbed, as if a hand had been thrust into it, and a search revealed about $20 in notes which had been crushed in a bloody hand. The tracks showed a semicircle behind the right heel, apparently made by a frozen cuff. They led to where the suspect had been arrested, and thence to the guardroom.

The accused was taken out and led through some snow, and it was seen that the bottom edge of his trousers made the same sort of mark which had been perceived by the trackers. It was fortunate that the tracking was commenced at daylight for, soon after it was finished, a chinook took off every particle of snow. The following day the suspect was committed for trial. A strong defence was made but the jury found him guilty without leaving the box. Before sentence was delivered he confessed his guilt. On the scaffold some weeks later he stated that drink was the cause of the crime. This was the first execution in the Northwest of any person other than an Indian.

The murder caused a great deal of excitement, and when it was first reported a mob of citizens, headed by a very decent but excited individual, came to find out what I was going to do about it. There were threats of lynching the perpetrator. But I said to the leader, "You lads are all tenderfeet and have visions of taking part in a necktie social. There never has been a lynching in Canada, nor will there be as long as our Force has the police duties to perform. Go away like sensible men. Any attempt at lynching will be bad for those who try it!" This settled the matter, and from that date the man was one of our best friends.

During the spring of 1884, while I was still in Calgary, I got proof that there was trouble before us in the Northwest Territories [present-day Alberta and Saskatchewan]. My orderly room sergeant, who understood Cree and spoke Blackfoot, had been on leave at High River, south of Calgary. On his return he reported that he had seen a Cree Métis talking with some Blackfoot Indians, traditional enemies with whom he seemed to be on very friendly terms. The Métis had come from Montana with Louis Riel and told the Indians they had a right to kill settlers' cattle, that the country belonged to the Indians and that the whites should be turned out. I caused a complaint to be laid against the Métis, charging him with vagrancy. When he appeared in court he admitted he had come over with Riel and that he had suggested that the Blackfoot had the right to kill cattle. The magistrates sentenced him to one month's imprisonment and cautioned him against any further misconduct.

Some weeks later Magnus Begg, the Indian agent for the Blackfoot, came to Calgary and reported that the formerly friendly demeanor of the tribe had changed to one of sulkiness and hostility since the arrival in Chief Crowfoot's camp of a visiting Métis. Begg's description of the man convinced me he was the one who had come from Montana with Riel. I had no great faith in Crowfoot but could not quite understand his sudden change toward Begg, who had been very kind to him. There was nothing for it but to arrest the Métis.

The Blackfoot were holding their Sun Dance. The ceremony included an initiation for warriors which was an important indication of the tribe's future fighting strength. The initiation took place in a large tent supported by a post. Candidates had sharp skewers of hardwood driven through the thick muscles of the breast, and these were secured by rawhide thongs to the upper part of the post. Young braves, to the low, deep chant of assembled warriors, the rhythmic sound of whistles and drums, and unearthly shrieks of women, threw their weight back until the skewers were torn from the flesh. The braves' teeth were set and drops of agony stood in beads on their foreheads, but there was nothing more to indicate they were in pain. This ordeal made them warriors.

I sent Sgt. Frederick Dann and a constable to Gleichen, a station near Crowfoot's camp, where they arrested the Métis after Begg got a friendly Indian to decoy him to the station. Next morning Dann and the constable had their handcuffed prisoner in the mail car of the train to Calgary. The train was making about 30 miles an hour and the sergeant was brushing his clothes when the Métis slipped his handcuffs, which were too large, and sprang to his feet. He seized Dann's rifle, jumped from the train and ran at top speed in the direction of Crowfoot's camp. Dann and the constable followed, but Dann put his knee out of joint and the constable could not run fast in his long boots.

The train stopped to pick up the two men. After they arrived in Calgary I informed Commissioner Acheson Irvine and Supt. William Herchmer of what had occurred, and was asked by them to arrest the Métis. Herchmer expressed great anxiety and seemed to think the behavior of the Indians serious.

I left with two constables, one driving a buckboard: I thought it was important to make as little display of force as possible. We scouted east for nearly 40 miles, and at dark turned into a ranch where we were received with hospitality. We waited until 1 a.m., then rode to a Blackfoot camp to get both the Indian who had decoyed the Métis to Gleichen, and Jean L'Heureux, an interpreter.

L'Heureux was a man of great experience and equally great timidity. He had lived with the Blackfoot for many years, often sharing Crowfoot's lodge [tent], and advising him when any question came up between him and the whites. When I told L'Heureux that he must come with me to get the Métis at Crowfoot's Sun Dance camp he showed palpable signs of fear, and I am convinced that he knew what was the matter. I told him there was no cause for alarm, that Crowfoot and I were good friends, and that the police were not going there to fight but to make an ordinary arrest. Then we all went to the outskirts of the Sun Dance camp where we waited in torrential rain for morning.

It rained all the time we were there, a fact which I welcomed, for the Indians would not be wandering about the camp as they would in fine weather. At daybreak the friendly Indian pointed out Crowfoot's lodge. I entered with the interpreter, leaving the others outside. The

leading men of the tribe were seated in a circle round the lodge. Crowfoot sat at the back facing the door. The Métis occupied the place of honor on his right, sitting there without a movement or sign. Crowfoot gazed fiercely at me and showed every indication of hostility.

I spoke firmly to him but in a friendly way. I said that the Métis had been making mischief, had to be tried for his offences, and must come with me now. The Métis understood English and I told him in that language that he must come at once, but he still showed no sign of moving.

Crowfoot spoke with great vehemence in what I understood to be defiance of me, and the Indians expressed approval of what he was saying. All this time L'Heureux was as pale as death with his knees knocking together in fright. I told him to tell the chief I was in earnest and would stand no nonsense. I said to L'Heureux that he was not telling the truth to Crowfoot, that he was temporizing with the chief, and I would not permit it.

He braced up a bit then and told the chief what I said to him. Crowfoot then sprang up and came at me in a hostile manner, but I waved him back. I told him not to make an offensive move or it would be the

worse for him, and that if the worst came he would be the first to suffer. I spoke sternly, straight at him, and moved close to him, and when he stood back I ordered L'Heureux to open the flap over the entrance of the lodge. Holding my right hand on the butt of my revolver I seized the Métis by the back of his collar with my left hand. I whirled him round through the door and had him outside before he had time to resist. I gave him over to the constables, who placed him in the buckboard and secured him to the seat. I found the lodge surrounded by hundreds of Indians, all of whom looked sullen and hostile.

559

I made the interpreter tell the assembled warriors that when the Mounted Police came for an Indian or a white, then that person had to come, and anyone who interfered would suffer. I told Crowfoot to come out of the tent so I could speak to him. I then said that I had to have the Métis dead or alive and that he, Crowfoot, had behaved badly although he had always received fair play from the Mounted Police and the Indian Department. I had expected his assistance as the chief of a great tribe.

Then I spoke to the other Indians to the effect that anything the Métis had said to them or the chief was false. I wrote a note to the CPR agent at Gleichen to let Crowfoot have a return ticket to Calgary, saying to the chief as I handed it to him, "You may go up to Calgary and hear the Métis tried by Ho-mux-a-stamix (Irvine). If you think the prisoner is not fairly dealt with, then perhaps you may explain your conduct in the tent. In future, I should advise you to assist maintaining the law as you promised to do."

In Calgary next day the charge against the Métis was dismissed. Ten months later the Riel Rebellion began.

In April 1884 I had received orders to select from the division a strong party to go with me to British Columbia, where I was to have sole charge of the Mounted Police on the CPR construction line through the Rocky Mountains.

The whole division volunteered to a man and, to resolve the dilemma, I selected the best shots with rifle and revolver. I went to the end of track at Laggan [now Lake Louise] with a number of the men and posted them where they were most needed. Large numbers of gamblers, whiskey men, in fact almost every type of criminal, who had been plying their trade on the Northern Pacific Railroad, were establishing their dens on every little creek along the line.

The belt over which we had jurisdiction was 20 miles wide, with the surveyed line of the railway in the centre. The sale of liquor was prohibited by federal law, but possession and consumption were not. Liquor could be confiscated only if there was a bar in operation, and persons caught selling were liable only to a fine of $40 for first and second offences; for the third they might be imprisoned, but they avoided that by transferring the goodwill of their dives to others, who went on in the same way. In any case the belt was so narrow that the laborers could go out after they received their month's wages and spend every dollar on prolonged sprees. This delayed work and caused no end of annoyance to the contractors.

The greatest obstacle in our way was the determination of the government of British Columbia not to be deprived of its internal revenue. It issued licences to all comers to sell "spirituous and fermented liquors" within the 20-mile belt. This gave courage to the liquor men, and many sold who would not otherwise have attempted it.

We had right on our side, however; the building of the great work must not be retarded. I therefore made up my mind to enforce the laws to the limit and to make an example of anyone under the influence of alcohol. I also recommended that the federal government widen the belt to 40 miles, and after this was done the workmen found a 20-mile walk too long for the sake of a spree.

Railway supplies were moved along what was called the tote road. Above the Kicking Horse River it was cut into the side of solid rock for several miles, and generally it was not wide enough to let teams pass. A skittish or shying horse on that trail was impossible. Horses are seldom afraid of a precipice; they fear the rocky wall, and the shying kind keep working away from a wall and toward the brink.

Not long after the tote road was built above the Kicking Horse some fresh mounts were sent to me from Calgary, and I selected a fine looking animal to take me to Golden. At the high and precipitous part of the tote road I met a workman with his bundle of blankets and he, as was then the custom, planted himself against the wall of rock. At the sight of him my horse whirled in fright and I was just saved by hurling myself to the road. The animal's hindquarters were over the brink but I hung on to the reins and collar. My companion, who rode a steady horse, ran to my assistance and we dragged my animal back on the road. I returned the horse to Calgary with a letter to the effect that if the commanding officer there valued our lives he would keep such brutes on the plains.

After Christmas I transferred my headquarters to the Beaver River within a mile of the new end of track. We had a great deal of trouble with gamblers and toughs. They built cedar log saloons, dance halls and disorderly houses at the other end of the bridge from our post. From there they preyed upon the workers.

During February and early March of 1885 many of the workers complained to me that they had not been paid for some time, and that the money was much needed for their homesteads. I counselled patience, but in spite of my advice a strike was on the point of being arranged.

Meanwhile, there had been mutterings of rebellion in the Northwest Territories. This did not surprise me, but it was plain that I should have no help from that quarter in the event of a strike. Nonetheless I was confident that with the assistance of the railway staff and other well-disposed persons I could control the situation. I warned James Ross, the manager of CPR construction, that a strike was likely but I could not convince him of the danger. I telegraphed the Prime Minister and warned him that the results of a strike might be serious. I then made arrangements with George Hope Johnston, commissioner of police for British Columbia, to go up the line and assist in maintaining order in case I was attacked by the illness which I felt coming on. The next day I was down with fever and was ordered to stay in bed.

The workers struck on April 1 and talked openly of their intention to commit acts of violence upon the staff of the road and to destroy property.

I was on the mend, but very weak, when the lieutenant-governor of the Northwest Territories telegraphed me to come out of the mountains with all my men because the rebellion had broken out. I was obliged to reply that the strike made it impossible. I did not report my illness, for I was aware that there was no relief for me. My inclinations were the very contrary to what I felt was my duty, but it would have been sheer madness to leave. Some days later I had an urgent wire from the mayor of Calgary to this effect: "For God's sake, come; there is danger of an attack by the Blackfoot!" I replied: "Cannot leave; telegraph the lieutenant-governor."

A deputation of strike leaders came to see me, and I managed to sit up in my chair to receive them. I assured them that they made a great mistake in striking, and warned them to be orderly in the strictest sense of the word. They also saw James Ross, who promised to do the best he could if they would return to their camps. Several hundreds were satisfied and agreed to return to work. Many remained at the Beaver, however, where a large number of loose characters was ready to urge them to any mischief. Those who remained were apparently very quiet but I learned that about 300 of their number, most armed with revolvers, were to watch the end of track and prevent any work from being done.

I had only eight men at the Beaver as I had sent detachments to other threatened points. A small party under Sgt. Billy Fury proceeded

Beaver River: "I will open fire and mow you down!"

to the end of track with instructions to use the strictest measures with any who tried to stop the work.

A trainload of tracklayers had been paid and sent out but, intimidated by the strikers, had been driven back to the yards. Ross then mounted the engine and the train went out again. When it came to the strikers' position Ross directed the engineer to put on all steam and run past the crowd. Several shots were fired but no one was hurt.

The strikers followed the train, making a great uproar and firing their revolvers, until they came to a narrow cutting which was only the width of the roadbed. Sergeant Fury had drawn his party across the canyon, and upon the strikers' arrival he stepped to the front and announced that he would shoot anyone crossing the line. The strikers made a great noise and started a hostile demonstration, but seeing the futility of their position they gradually broke up and retired to the Beaver, allowing the tracklayers to finish their day's work.

Later that day I rose as best I could and sat in a camp chair awaiting the return of Const. John Kerr, who had gone to the end of track for a bottle of medicine for me. Shortly after I had risen George Johnston came in to see how I was and to ask if there was anything he could do. A few minutes later Sergeant Fury returned, stating that Constable Kerr

563

had seen a desperate character inciting the strikers to attack the barracks, had attempted single-handed to arrest him, but had been overpowered and forced to leave the ground. After hearing the sergeant I remarked, "It is a pity that he attempted the arrest without sufficient assistance, but as he has done so we must take the man at any cost. It will never do to let him or the remainder of the gang think they can play with us. Take what men you require and arrest him."

Fury went off at once with Constables Fane, Craig and Walters. After a long interval they returned with Fury's jacket torn and other evidence of a struggle. The sergeant said as he entered, "They took the prisoner from us, sir." I replied, "That is too bad. Take your revolvers and shoot anyone who interferes with the arrest!"

He started off again, and Johnston went to the window and watched the party cross the bridge and disappear round some buildings. In a few minutes we heard a shot and Johnston said, "There is one gone to hell, Steele." I went to the window and saw Craig and Walters dragging the desperado, fighting like a fiend, across the bridge while a woman in scarlet followed with wild shrieks and curses. Fury and Fane were in the rear, trying to keep off the crowd.

I rushed out, calling upon Johnston to get the Riot Act and come with me. Seizing a Winchester rifle from the constable on guard at the jail, I ran to the bridge as the crowd was on the point of rushing it. I covered them with the rifle and called upon them to halt or I would fire. They answered with curses and cries of "Look at the — ; his own deathbed makes no difference to him!" but they halted. The prisoner was still struggling fiercely but Walters raised his huge fist and struck him on the temple. The two constables then dragged him by the collar, as insensible as a rag. The woman passed, screaming "You red-coated — !". I said "Take her in too!" and went forward over the bridge.

By this time Johnston had joined me with the Riot Act, which he had to get by kicking the orderly room door open because the key was with Constable Fane who was busy in the riot. Johnston and I stood before the rioters. He opened the book and I said, "Listen to this and keep your hands off your guns. I will shoot the first man who makes a hostile movement." Johnston then read the Riot Act, and when he had finished I said, "I warn you that if I find more than 12 of you standing together I will open fire upon you and mow you down! Now disperse at once and behave yourselves!" By this time a considerable number of engineers, respectable merchants and contractors, all well armed, had assembled at the barracks to back me up. The eight Mounted Police stood at the head of the bridge under Fury with guns loaded. Johnston and I remained where we were until the rioters had dispersed. The man Fury had wounded was sent to the CPR doctors for treatment.

Darkness came on soon and, as there was danger of an attack on the jail to rescue the cause of the trouble, I obtained a locomotive from James Ross and sent the prisoner to the end of track whence he was taken to my detachment at Palliser. Next morning was as quiet as a country village on Sunday. The strike had collapsed and all the laborers were paid that day.

On Nov. 7, 1885, I was one of those picked up at Revelstoke by a special train which took us to where Donald Smith drove the last spike of the CPR.

James Ross had arranged for an excursion to Victoria, and at Kamloops I joined James Dickey, a government engineer, in the private car of a CPR traffic manager. Dickey knew the man well, which ensured a warm welcome. The train rushed along at 57 miles an hour, roaring in and out of the numerous tunnels and whirling our short car round the sharp curves as if it was the tail of a kite. When dinner was served, Dickey, the manager and I were the only men in the car who were not suffering from train sickness. I think this was one of the wildest train rides that any of us had taken; had the train left the rails it would have plunged a couple of hundred feet into the wild waters of the Fraser. The next morning when the train rushed out of a tunnel a handcar loaded with section men was seen on the trestle bridge in front; the men jumped off and clung to the sides of the bridge in the nick of time to save their lives; their car was hurled to the torrent below.

That memorable journey to the coast on the first train through was the exultant moment of pioneer work. Yet on our return to the Prairies, as our train emerged from the Bow River Pass and we saw again the magnificent expanse, there were cheers of delight, and one stalwart engineer shouted at the top of his voice, "Hurrah! Civilization at last!"

Memoirs of a Master Detective

Murder, theft and fraud were getting out of hand in Ontario in 1873, but criminals in the rough, fast-growing province felt the grip of a new master that year. John Wilson Murray, the fearless son of a Scottish sea captain, had become a detective after joining the United States Navy and cracking a major Confederate plot during the War Between the States. He moved to Canada at 32 as head detective of the Canada Southern Railroad, but spent most of his career tracking down wrongdoers on behalf of the Ontario government. During those 31 years his relentless determination solved thousands of crimes and his unflinching audacity in making tough arrests won the admiration of his enemies. What follows is from his memoirs.

By JOHN WILSON MURRAY

THE CANADA SOUTHERN ran between Fort Erie and Windsor. Soon after I joined it in 1873 my attention was drawn to robberies from cars which passed over the line on their way from Boston or New York to the western states. All the railways over which the cars passed had to pay a share of the losses. I went to Boston and started over the route of the goods. I saw the cars go through unbroken to Black Rock, the American border point outside Buffalo, N.Y., where customs officers and sealers inspected and resealed the cars, after which they went on west through Canada. After following the route of the goods several times I became convinced that the robberies were perpetrated at Black Rock, and that car sealers and railway employees were in collusion. They alone could have the necessary knowledge and opportunity.

The customs officer at the International Bridge and I drew up a fake manifest showing boots, shoes, silks and clothing, making a fat car. We included the number of a car and sent the manifest out as usual,

then had the car placed at the yards. On the night of July 12, 1874, three Buffalo policemen and I lay in wait by a fence which ran near the track. It was blazing hot, breezeless, suffocating. We crouched silently for several hours. About 1:30 in the morning we saw two lanterns dodging in and out among the trucks. Three fellows slipped along, looking for the car listed in the fake manifest. "Here it is," said one of them. They broke the seal, slid the door open, climbed in and began to open boxes. When they were well along with their work we made a break for the car. Two of the three fled with the three policemen after them. I grabbed the third fellow, a powerful giant in a cotton shirt and overalls. We grappled in the car and fell among the boxes, his clothes coming off like the peel of a banana. In his fury he tore my clothes off, but neither of us spoke a word. Even naked, we were drenched with sweat in the stifling darkness. I finally recognized the fellow as one of our employees named Sweetman. He tried to strangle me – and this so deliberately that I had to

567

admire his coolness. I broke his hold. He tried to jam me behind some boxes where he could shove a packing case to crush me, but I forced him over by the door. We heaved and strained until we fell to the track.

There was no letup. Whichever man got the chance banged the other's head on the rails, jammed his face in the cinders or thumped his bare body on the ballast and ties. A free hand meant a stunning blow. We fought under the car and out onto the next track. My gun was gone.

We came to a momentary stop, straining and gasping between the rails, neither of us on top. As we lay we heard a creaking and crunching. Instinctively both of us looked down the track. An engine had backed some cars in and they were bearing down on us. Sweetman was a game man; he never flinched. "You first!" he gasped, as he strove to roll me nearest the approaching cars. My answer was a heave that turned him prone between the rails and there I held him, panting and desperate, not daring to relax my hold. Nearer and nearer came the cars. We could hear the grind of the flanges. Sweetman writhed and strove to drag me down and force me over.

"Give up?" I gasped.

Sweetman shook his head and butted me full between the eyes. Together we reeled back on the track. The trucks of the nearest car were not 30 feet away when one of the policemen came running up from the chase after the other two men, dragged us back and snapped the handcuffs on Sweetman. The policeman had captured one man but the other had escaped. I was somewhat disfigured and had to borrow some clothes, but I was mightily relieved when I saw the trucks of the freight cars go by and felt my bones safe beyond their reach.

When I returned to my headquarters at St. Thomas I found complaints of train tapping. Cars laden with grain would lose bushels in transit. Frequent weighing of the cars narrowed the territory where the thefts were committed to the vicinity of Amherstburg, near Windsor.

The train tappers would crawl under a grain car at night, bore holes in the floor, fill as many bags with grain as they could cart away, then plug the holes. The car would bear no visible sign of having been robbed. One night a single train was rifled of enough grain to make two wagon-loads. The amount stolen satisfied me that a gang of six or seven had done the job, but I was puzzled to learn what became of the grain, for I could find no trace of unusual sales.

I arranged for a string of grain cars to be laid out on a siding near

Amherstburg, and on the first night I spotted a figure sneak under some of the cars, bore holes and put in plugs. No attempt was made to steal any of the grain; evidently the cars were being prepared for the next night. I decided to follow the fellow. The trail led to the home of the Thrasher family, a father, mother and three sons, whose constant companions were two fellows named Johnson and Fox.

I went back to town and told two constables to meet me in the yards, but they failed to appear so I went to the house to arrest the five Thrashers. I knocked at the door but no one answered. I knocked again with no response, so I shoved against the door and walked in. No one was in sight. I was in the kitchen when a screech like the high quavering note of a calliope came from an adjoining room. I shoved open the door and entered. Sitting upright in a big, old-fashioned bed surmounted by a mosquito net was one of the ugliest women I ever saw. She glanced at me, then threw back her head and screeched just as a coyote howls at the moon. She was Mrs. Thrasher. I bade her get up. She answered with a series of earsplitting screeches. I spent about 10 minutes trying to persuade her to get out of bed. When words were of no avail I laid hold of the mosquito netting and pulled it out of the way.

"I am palsied!" shrieked Mrs. Thrasher. "I am paralysed and cannot be moved!"

I approached the bed and she dealt me a thump on the head with her clenched hand such as no paralytic was ever able to manage. I sought to take her out of bed but she buried herself in the bedclothes. I pulled the tick [stuffed cover] off the bed and was preparing to take the bed apart with her in it, when she sprang out and fled through the kitchen. I knew I could get her later, and the tick had seemed very heavy in my hands. I slit it open and found it filled with new boots and shoes. While I was emptying them out I heard a stealthy step behind me, and whirled just in time to see Mrs. Thrasher swing an axe at me. I dodged and laid violent hands on her ankles, landing her on the floor with a thud. Before she could regain the axe I rolled her in the emptied tick and fastened her by one of the tall bedposts, where she kicked and screeched and probably well-nigh suffocated while I was searching the house.

They had a number of bed ticks all filled with wheat. They also had a big unused chimney stuffed with bags of wheat. Old man Thrasher came out of a closet and I arrested him. I went to the place of their friend Fox nearby, and arrested him after finding more of the stolen stuff on his premises. I also arrested Johnson.

That broke up train tapping. Mrs. Thrasher averred that after she was bagged in the tick she experienced a sensation similar to that caused by someone smiting the outside of the tick with an open hand. I suggested that perhaps she had wriggled and kicked so much as to bump herself against the bedpost, but she clung to the idea she had been spanked. What could a woman named Thrasher expect?

Premier Oliver Mowat, increasingly concerned about the crime rate and anxious to help overworked local constables, hired Murray away from the Canada Southern in 1875 and made him the first "Detective for the Province of Ontario." Murray's narrative continues.

On a cold night in March 1875 two men in Toronto slipped noiselessly along Yonge street to Bloor, which marked the city limits in those days. There stood the house of three rich brothers—Joseph, James and Major Dain—and their mother. The brothers carried large sums of money for their business as cattle dealers.

The two men went to the rear where one took off his overcoat, handed it to the other, and jimmied the door. He entered. The second man moved to the doorway to stand watch.

Upstairs Joseph Dain was asleep in his room, his trousers on the chair beside his bed. He stirred, opened his eyes, and saw a tall figure rifling the pockets. Joseph Dain was a powerful, fearless man; he leaped out of bed and grabbed the burglar. The man broke away and fled downstairs and thence outside with his pal. The burglars separated as they ran.

Although there was snow on the ground, and Dain was barefooted and clad only in a nightshirt, he gave chase to the man who had rifled his trousers. Block after block they ran. Dain's feet were bleeding but he was gaining on his man when the burglar shouted over his shoulder:

"Turn back or I'll shoot!"

Dain leaped forward and was still closing in when a shot rang out and he fell with a bullet in the abdomen. The burglar escaped. Dain was carried indoors, surgeons were summoned, and he rallied after an operation. The second burglar, meanwhile, had tripped on the overcoat he was still carrying. A baker going to work held him until a policeman came.

I did not take up the case until later, when I looked the captured burglar over and recognized him at once as an American named Charles Leavitt. In the overcoat I found the mark of a Cleveland tailor. While looking up Leavitt's record in the States I found that one of his friends was Frank Meagher of Cleveland, a fine-looking, well-educated man, but a burglar and one of the ablest and worst rough-ones at large. His description tallied in general with Dain's description of the burglar at his bedside. I started for Cleveland, where I found that Meagher also matched the description of the man for whom the tailor made the coat. I was satisfied that Meagher and Leavitt had crossed to Canada on a burglary tour and had picked the Dain house for their first job.

Dain died from his wound a year and a couple of months after he was shot. An attacker cannot be convicted of murder if his victim lives for a year and a day after the crime, so Dain died too late to hang his murderer. But I determined to find Meagher.

Another year passed. Whenever I made a trip to any big police centre I made special inquiries. I examined every description I could obtain of every prisoner sentenced in Canada or the States. In 1877 I came across a description that fitted Meagher in almost every respect. It was of a man named Armstrong, sentenced to seven years in the Northern Indiana Penitentiary for burglary. I prepared extradition papers, and started for Indianapolis on June 1.

The moment I saw Armstrong I was satisfied he was Meagher, and on June 19 he was ordered into my custody.

It was long after midnight when I had all my papers signed and ready. I went with Cleveland Detective Lou Muncie, who knew Meagher well, direct to the Indianapolis jail where he was being held. A train left at 4:35 in the morning and I had decided to get away on it because I knew Meagher was clever and daring, and had admiring friends who would probably make plans to rescue him. Two or three times in his career he had escaped, and had shot and killed a deputy on one occasion.

We arrived at the jail about three o'clock.

"Mr. Sheriff," said I, "I am here after Meagher. Here are my papers."

"I'm afraid we're going to have trouble with Meagher," said the sheriff. "He's armed, and he's got up to the top tier of cells and threatens to kill anyone who goes near him. He's a desperate man, Mr. Murray; a desperate man."

"Sheriff," said I, "I want the prisoner. My papers call on you to produce the prisoner."

"But how am I to produce him?" exclaimed the worried sheriff.

"That is for you to determine," said I. "Please produce the prisoner."

"Well then, come this way please," said the sheriff, and we went to a gate in the main part of the jail. The cells rose in four tiers, with

571

iron stairways leading from tier to tier. There, at the top, sat Meagher. He had a baseball bat in one hand and a revolver in the other.

"Meagher, come down!" called the sheriff in a nervous voice.

Meagher's answer was a volley of oaths. "Come up and get me!" he yelled. "I'll kill the first — that sets foot on these stairs!"

I saw that the sheriff would not get Meagher. I saw also that Meagher was playing for time, probably expecting an attempt to rescue him. From the fact that he had the revolver and club I knew that some of his pals were at work. I decided that I must take him on the 4:35 train at all hazards.

"Open that gate," I said to the sheriff. "I want to speak to him."

I stepped in and walked upstairs. When I reached the landing below Meagher he said:

"Stop, Murray! Don't you come near me!"

He had the gun pointed straight at me. I stopped.

"I am not coming up, Frank," I said as I stood on the stairs. "I want to talk to you so everybody won't hear."

He had risen and we stood eyeing each other.

"Come down or I'll shoot!" shrilly cried the sheriff below.

I heard Detective Muncie sternly tell the sheriff to shut up.

"Shoot and be — !" yelled Meagher to the sheriff without swerving his glance. "I'd rather be shot here than hung in Canada."

"Shut up, sheriff," I said, with my eyes still on Meagher. "Frank," I continued, "you won't be hung. You know that. The man lived over a year. You know you've got to come. You could try to kill me, but you would go just the same."

While I was speaking I mounted the stairs step by step until I stood within 10 feet of him, the revolver pointed full at me.

Neither of us spoke. My hands were empty; my revolver was in my pocket.

"Murray," he said suddenly, but without shifting his eyes, "I have no fit clothes. I am not going like a pauper to Canada. I am a gentleman."

"The sheriff has a suit of clothes for you, Frank," I said. "It's a pretty good suit, but if it is not good enough I will wait until you can get one."

His eyes lighted with satisfaction. I was sure then that he was playing for delay, and I was doubly determined to take him on the 4:35 train.

He began to curse Muncie, possibly hoping a row would break out then and there. I realized he could kill me as easily one way as another, so I turned my back half to him and sat down on the stair. If he had glanced away I could have slipped out my gun. He watched like a hawk. I yawned and turned my back full to him.

There was a long silence. I wondered if he would reach down and smash me with the bat. I thought I heard a catlike tread on the step, but I kept my eyes front although I have done easier things in my life. Finally he spoke – softly, and in almost a whisper.

"Murray," he said, "you're a game man. Get me a suit of clothes and I'll go with you, but not with Muncie."

He handed me the bat.

"Give me the gun, Frank," said I.

He handed me the gun. We walked down the stairs and into the office side by side. He spat at the sheriff and swore at Muncie, and his glance flew to the clock as we passed it. It was four o'clock, and a smile flitted over his face. He donned the suit of clothes, and he really looked like a prosperous gentleman. I put handcuffs and leg irons on him and, with him swearing all the way at Muncie, we drove at a gallop in a closed carriage to the station.

As we alighted the train was making ready to go. A second carriage galloped up and out jumped four friends of Meagher's including Red Jim Carroll. They climbed on another car.

Meagher was very nervous. I sent for the conductor and brakeman, and told them I expected trouble.

"Well, I and my crew are not on this train to get shot, but I'll do what I can," said the conductor. Most of the other passengers hastened into other cars.

We put Meagher in the middle. Muncie was facing the rear and I the front with our revolvers in our hands, well beyond Meagher's reach.

"Frank," I said, "if there's any break here someone will get killed before we do." I think he knew what I meant.

An hour passed. No one entered the car. Then suddenly the forward door swung open and in stepped Red Jim, the others of his crowd behind him. Muncie and I jumped up, revolvers in both hands.

"Stop there, Jim!" I ordered.

He stopped in the doorway, and it was a wise act.

"Good morning, Mr. Murray," he said. "Good morning, Mr. Muncie."

"Are you looking for trouble, Jim?" said I.

"No, Mr. Murray, I am not looking for trouble," he answered with a grin. "Will you allow me to speak to Frank?"

"Speak to him from right there, Jim," said I.

When Red Jim halted, Meagher's face grew sullen.

"Go to hell!" he shouted at Red Jim.

Jim was about to put a hand in his pocket when I stopped him, for I did not know what he might draw forth, and Meagher's rage could easily have been feigned.

"What did you want to get, Jim?" I said.

"I wanted to give Frank a couple of hundred dollars," he said.

"Go to hell with your money!" roared Meagher, who seemingly was in a terrible rage over the failure, thus far, of the plot for his rescue.

Still keeping Red Jim covered, I told him to go no lower than his breast pocket with his hands, and to count out the money where he stood. I would take it and see Frank got it. Meagher shouted that he wanted none of the dirty money of a gang of cowards that would stand by and see a friend dragged away.

Red Jim answered with a touch of dignity. "Sometimes the worst comes to the worst, Frank, and nothing can help it just at the time. This man Murray is a gentleman; he will give you a fair show."

So saying, Red Jim tossed the money toward my feet.

"Good-bye, Jim," I said pointedly.

He hesitated, glanced at me and my revolvers, then nodded.

"Good-bye, Mr. Murray," he said. "Good-bye, Frank. Good-bye, Mr. Muncie."

He backed out and closed the door. Meagher was beside himself with wrath. I picked up the money and later I gave it to him. He found it of real use in his defence although he was eventually sentenced to 18 years for robbery. The train stopped at a junction. I had the brakeman bring our breakfast aboard. As the train pulled out Red Jim stood on the platform and waved good-bye.

Wild Dobbin was a name given by some to 50-year-old John Dobbin of Bracebridge. He won it by his habit of flying into a rage and chasing those near him with club or gun or whatsoever he laid his hands on.

In 1883 he skipped out of the Muskoka district after swindling a Scotchman named John Breckenridge. The Scotchman had settled in Bracebridge and bought a farm from Dobbin, paying part cash and giving a note for the balance. When the note came due Dobbin swore he had lost it, was paid by Breckenridge, and disappeared. But instead of losing the note he had sold it, and the new owner got a judgment against Breckenridge. The Scotchman complained to the government and was directed to me.

I went to Dobbin's old home at Bracebridge. I could find no trace of him. I nosed around until I learned that his sister had gone away some time before and had bought a ticket to Winnipeg. Through a friend of the sister in Winnipeg I learned that she had gone to Morris, 35 miles south of Winnipeg, at that time the end of a branch of the Canadian Pacific Railway. There she had disappeared. I got my warrant and went to Manitoba. I arrived in Morris on a stifling hot day in July. I inquired right and left for a trace of John Dobbin, but no one seemed to know of him. I walked four miles down the river asking at every house. Finding no way to cross the river I sat down in the shade to cool. The river was not wide, so while I sat I bellowed at the top of my voice at frequent intervals. I became interested in the echoes; then I whistled and finally I screeched and roared.

Suddenly I heard an answering screech. On the opposite bank stood a woman screaming to know what was the matter.

"I want to cross the river," I shouted.

"How much will you give?" she screamed.

"I'll give you a dollar," roared I.

"All right! I'll call my man from the field!" she shouted.

Presently a funny little man, burned almost black by the sun, pushed off in a boat and paddled over. He stood offshore about 15 feet.

"Give me the dollar," he said.

I took out a bill and was about to walk down the sandy shore when he let out a terrific whoop and waved me back.

"Quicksand! Quicksand!" he yelled.

I climbed out on a tree limb overhanging the water and tried to hand him the money. The limb broke and down I went in the quicksand. My ankles disappeared and my knees were vanishing. The little man rescued the dollar, then backed his boat over just beyond my reach.

He smiled with a sweetness born of the angels.

"How much will you give?" he asked.

I was sinking well up to the hips but I had to go down in my pocket, dig up another dollar and toss it to the little man. He whirled his boat around and shot it in to where I could reach it. I kicked and heaved while the little boatman paddled valiantly, then I came up like a cork out of a bottle and the boat shot into the stream with me dragging behind. I clambered in. The little man folded one bill in a tiny wad and tucked it in his left ear. The other he rolled in a ball and, as he was about to hide it under his tongue, he smiled to me and said, "Please do not tell her," nodding to the woman.

I smiled, and he paddled us to shore, took the dollar out of his ear and gave it to the waiting woman. She shouted at him to give her what was in his mouth but he darted beyond reach.

"I understand a man named Dobbin lives near here and has a farm to sell," I said to the woman.

"The only Dobbin I know is four miles back cutting hay," she said.

"Can your man show me?" I asked.

"For $1.50," she said.

I paid her. She shouted to the little man and away we started. After an hour's trudge in the blazing sun we came upon a man cutting hay.

"Are you John Dobbin who lived near Bracebridge?" I asked.

"Yes, why?" said Dobbin.

"Dobbin," said I, "I have a warrant for your arrest."

"Arrest me!" exclaimed Dobbin, and then slowly he turned on the little man. "And you brought him here to arrest me? You — !"

With a roar Dobbin went after the little man with his scythe.

They ran themselves to a standstill, the little man unable to escape and Dobbin unable to overtake him. I came up and caught Dobbin and started him back toward his house. I heard the little man crying after me piteously. I turned back to see if he were hurt.

"The dollar!" he lamented. "I swallowed it!"

Dobbin's wife was out when we arrived so we sat down in the kitchen, he in one corner, I in another. She came in presently with her sister. She was a terror. The moment she spied the handcuffs on her husband she made a break for the woodpile. The sister ran down in the cellar. In a moment in marched Mrs. Dobbin, axe in hand, and up from the cellar came the sister with a cleaver.

"What does this mean?" said Mrs. Dobbin to me, even though I had drawn my revolver. "Explain yourself or I'll chop you into mincemeat."

She was the kind of woman who could have made first-class mincemeat out of a man. I carefully changed my revolver to my left hand and began to reason with her but she advanced toward me with the axe. I drew a second gun.

"Dobbin," I said, "call off your wife. I dislike to shoot a woman. I can take her to Winnipeg and send her to prison. She's a fool."

The woman stopped in the middle of the floor. There she stood, with her sister guarding the door, while the twilight fell and darkness came. Finally a clock struck nine.

"Time's up," I said, rising. "Strike a light!"

There was silence. I turned to Dobbin.

"I've had enough of this," I said. "Axe or no axe, woman or no woman, this stops now. Call her off."

Mrs. Dobbin burst into furious ragings.

"I'll die before Dobbin crosses the Red River tonight," she shouted.

She raised the axe and planted herself to strike. I stepped forward, and with my left hand holding a revolver and my right hand free, I feinted to draw her blow. Dobbin, who had watched it all, saw the beginning of the end. He stood up and called his wife aside and tried to pacify her.

"Be quick," I said to Dobbin. "I've dallied too long. I'll get a boat three miles up the river."

"I own a boat on the river," said Dobbin sullenly.

"It's mine, not yours," said Mrs. Dobbin.

I thought of the commercial instinct. "You can make some money out of your boat," I said to her. "Dobbin must go over the river with me. Someone will make the money."

"What will you pay?" she asked.

"I'll give you a dollar," I said.

I dropped four quarters on the floor, one by one. She leaped for a candle, lighted it, and gazed at the silver.

"For $1.50 I'll do it," she said.

I took Dobbin away; we hired a team and driver at Morris and drove to Winnipeg, getting a midnight meal on the way. Dobbin employed a lawyer in Winnipeg, the famous Fighting Mackenzie [probably barrister Frederick Mckenzie], but a writ of habeas corpus was dismissed and Dobbin was ordered into my custody.

I had to take him by way of the Sault Ste. Marie Canal, and our boat would pass on the American side where I would have no papers authorizing me to hold him in American territory. I learned that Fighting Mackenzie had told Dobbin to keep quiet until the boat was in the canal, then to yell and demand protection. Mackenzie would telegraph the American sheriff to be there, and he would compel me to liberate Dobbin.

We embarked on the steamer *Campana* at Port Arthur [now Thunder Bay]. The crew and officers were all my friends, and I told the captain of the plan to save Dobbin.

The captain suggested we should lock Dobbin up before we got to the American side. He, the steward and I talked it over and the captain selected a room on the port side farthest from the American shore. I was to get Dobbin in there and the steward would lock the door.

Dobbin was all primed for the planned escape. As we drew near the locks he even cleared his throat for the yells he was to pour forth. The steward came to me.

"Mr. Murray," he said, "would you like a little good whisky?"

"Yes, indeed," said I. "Dobbin, want a drink?"

Dobbin smacked his lips. He had time before the boat entered the locks. "Why, yes," he said.

We went down to the room. It was a cubbyhole of a place with only one little porthole. A decanter of whisky and glasses were on the table. We went in. The steward stepped out and slammed the door.

"What did he shut the door for?" asked Dobbin with suspicion.

I eyed him. "Why don't you holler, Dobbin?" said I.

He glared at me. I could see the crimson dye his face, the veins swell, the eyes grow small. He grabbed the decanter. I flipped out my revolver. We stood face to face with the little table between us.

The boat was in the locks.

He looked at me, at the locked door, at the porthole; then he sank into a chair.

"Murray, I've lost my voice," said Dobbin.

He sat with eyes closed for an hour or more. When we were through the locks and out into Canadian waters the steward unlocked the door and said, "Dinner, gentlemen."

Dobbin awoke as if from a dream.

"I'm hungry as hell," he said, and went in to dinner.

Early in 1885 a conspiracy had been hatched to defeat the Mowat [Liberal] government. Several cash offers were made, the government got onto it, and there was great excitement in the House. Warrants were issued for the arrest of parties alleged to have tried to bribe members. I was instructed to serve papers on one of the members, R.A. Lyon [Reform], who was at his home on Manitoulin Island. Time was limited. I went by rail to the end of the line at Gravenhurst, arriving March 3 in a raging blizzard.

I hired a pair of horses and a sleigh with buffalo robes, and struck out for Sufferin, actually just a farmhouse and a barn with a giant tree beside it, 45 miles away. The snow was whirling and blowing and drifting, and the trail was hid for long distances. As night was falling I got stuck in a drift a few miles out of Gravenhurst, but I found a fence nearby: I appropriated one of the rails to help me get out, and took it with me.

About midnight I suddenly came upon the end of the road, a deep drift in a pocket of dense forest. No house was in sight. I could move neither forward nor back, and the snow drifted up against the sleigh. I tumbled out and floundered around. I discovered I had missed the main road and gone up a blind timber trail. I got my fence rail and laboriously broke a road. Then I unhitched the horses and tied them to a tree. I dug the snow away from the sleigh with the rail, and finally got underneath the sleigh and lifted it around. In doing so I stuck feet first in the snow underneath it. I struggled to get out but was caught as if in a vice. The rail lay just beyond my reach and the wind was whirling the snow about me.

I grimly calculated my chances of escape. I was up an abandoned, blind trail so I could expect no passers-by. As I thought it over I was dealt a stinging blow across the face. It seemed to come from nowhere, yet I felt the burn of the welt. I began to dig with my hands to free my body when a second smashing slash in the face made me turn in time to see the reins from the horses fly past in the wind. I waited, watching them. They whirled up again and came swishing down. I grabbed them.

Then I began to pull and call to the horses to back up. They plunged a bit then drew back, snapping the strap that tied them to the tree. I drew them close by me, then fastened the reins through the traces and wrapped them around me. I shouted to the horses and pelted them with snowballs, and wriggled and kicked as best I could. They leaped forward, and at last I felt myself coming up out of the drift.

I hitched the team to the sleigh again and beat my way back to the main road. Every big tree that loomed up caused me to stop and alight and stumble through the snow in search of the house or barn of Sufferin. At 1:30 in the morning I heard a long, loud howl. I drove forward, listening, and saw in the night another big tree. I alighted and a dog rushed through the drifts to me. I followed him and found the farmhouse of Sufferin. A woman answered; the man was ill. I stabled the horses. They were too hot to feed, and I had to wait up with them until three o'clock. Then I took the buffalo robes into the house, lay down on the floor by the stove and slept two hours.

At 5:30 in the morning I started for Parry Sound, 30 miles away.

It was afternoon when my exhausted team dragged its weary way into town. With great difficulty I found a man who would travel the remaining 150 miles to Manitoulin Island by dog-sled. Lyon was served with his papers but the bribery cases dwindled to nothing.

On the road to Sufferin was the only time in my life when I was grateful for a slap in the face, repeated on the other cheek.

A singsong-voiced, jet-black-haired, sanctimonious rogue named J. K. Herres lived in the county of Waterloo. His father kept a country store and was reputed to be fairly well off. When young Herres was not teaching a little school, or singing German songs, he was gallivanting about the country. He had a profuse rush of hair to the upper lip, and he developed a fondness for twirling the drooping ends of his black mustache.

Herres frequently went to Galt [now Cambridge]. In the summer of 1887 he walked into the Imperial Bank there and presented two notes to be discounted. One was signed by Peter Leweller, a neighbor of the Herres family, and the other by Herres' father. They totalled $900, and Herres vanished with the money. Peter Leweller and old man Herres pronounced their signatures forgeries. The case came to me, and on Sept. 22 I went to Galt, saw the bank manager and thence went to Berlin [now Kitchener], the county seat of Waterloo. There I prepared extradition papers and obtained a description of Herres from Chief Constable John Klippert of Waterloo. Klippert was one of the best constables in Canada, a shrewd old German.

"Shon," he said to me, "you vill know him two vays, vone by his shet-black hair and vone by his ding-dong mustachees. He has some of ze lofliest mustachees you efer see. Zey flow down like Neeagara Falls, only zey too are shet-black."

I telegraphed all over the country for a trace of Herres and found none. I learned that he had a cousin who was a lawyer in St. Cloud, Minn. Shet-Black Herres, as I always called him after Klippert's description, had been in correspondence with the cousin, whose address was found in an old coat belonging to Herres.

I went to St. Cloud where I learned from neighbors that the cousin had had a visitor some time before, a dapper fellow with a remarkably fine mustache. He had tarried only a few days. I set out to find him. I travelled all around the country. I saw more smooth-shaven men and more men with beards than I had ever imagined were in that part of the country, but not one man with "ding-dong mustachees" did I see.

Then I learned of a settlement of Germans at Little Falls, 30 miles away, where Herres' cousin was reported to have a relative. I arrived there Oct. 4. It was a place of about 1,000 people, and I think I saw everybody. I found no trace of Herres and was about to give up the chase, when I remembered Herres' school teaching.

The clerk of the school board told me two teachers had been appointed to little rural schools. Both teachers were strangers to him. Neither was named Herres.

"One was smooth-shaven, one I did not see," he said.

I decided to look at the teachers. I told a big fellow named Richardson, a sort of town constable who had been born in the area, that I was going shooting, and he agreed to show me around. Prairie chickens were thicker than flies. I hired a splendid team and a light wagon. The liveryman lent me his shotgun, shooting jacket, cartridge belt and two valuable dogs. It was dark when we trotted out of Little Falls. After we were well on the road I told Richardson the real purpose of my trip. It seemed to make him solemn as an owl. He was a jolly hunter but a solemn policeman.

Well after daylight we came to the first school. The teacher was a little fellow, clean-shaven, who could not speak German. But he told me that the teacher at the next district school had a fine, long mustache.

When we came in sight of the other school I unhitched the horses and tied them.

"If this is the fellow I will nod to you and you arrest him," I said to Richardson.

"I have no authority," he said, "and I will not arrest a man without authority."

"Richardson," I said solemnly, "I am a United States Marshal. I hereby declare you my deputy. You must obey the law and serve."

"But I must be sworn in," said Richardson.

I pulled out a bundle of papers, ran over them, selected one and told him to kneel down. He knelt amid the briars. I mumbled the form of an oath, ending with the question, "Do you so swear?"

"I do," he answered solemnly.

Then we went to the schoolhouse and walked in. There stood a dapper teacher with "ding-dong mustachees," but instead of being "shet-black" his hair and mustache were brown. "It looks like him," said I to myself, "yet is it?" Just then he twirled his mustache. That settled it. He was a bleached Herres.

There were about 30 children, mostly girls, in the room. They eyed us curiously.

"Teacher, how long have you been here?" said I.

"For some time – since school opened," said he, and his voice had a little singsong.

"What is your name?"

"John Walker," he replied.

"Are you German?" I asked.

"Yes," said he.

"John Walker is not a German name," I said.

He smiled.

"You are from Canada!" I said abruptly.

"I am not!" he exclaimed, and turning to the astonished children he told them to go and get their fathers. "Tell them to bring their guns," he said in rapid German. "There are robbers here."

I understood him clearly, and I told Richardson to keep the children in. Deputy Marshal Richardson obeyed by standing against the door. The children began to cry, then to scream.

"Come with me," said I to the teacher.

"I will not," said he, and he whipped off his coat.

I leaped for him and down we went, upsetting the table and rolling on the floor. He was an active fellow, and I had to drag him out of the schoolhouse.

I tied him to a wheel, handcuffed, while I hitched up the horses. Then I lifted him into the wagon. Richardson came running. The screaming children streamed out of the schoolhouse and rushed in all directions.

"Drive to the nearest railway station," I said, and away we went to Royalton, a German settlement of perhaps 1,500, 11 miles south of Little Falls.

We got there late in the afternoon and drove to the station. The telegraph operator was German. When the teacher spied him he began to yell in German to send a message saying he was kidnapped by robbers.

A crowd gathered. It grew rapidly. The teacher kept yelling and the crowd began to murmur. I moved back against the side of the station, keeping the teacher beside me and holding the shotgun.

"Richardson, keep the crowd back," I said, but Richardson decided he wanted nothing more to do with the affair.

"I resign as deputy marshal," he said.

The crowd drew closer. I could see men galloping into town and

I knew they were farmers who had been roused by their children's tales of the struggle in the schoolhouse. They dismounted and told the story given by the children. I discarded the shotgun and drew a second revolver. All the while the teacher kept haranguing the crowd, inciting it to rescue him and hang me.

"Give up that man," demanded a sturdy fellow not 20 feet away.

"The first man of you who touches him or me dies in his tracks," I said.

The crowd surged closer. I gripped both revolvers and decided that the bleating teacher, now at my feet, would be one of us on the other side when they picked up the bodies.

"Stand back! Stand back!" I shouted, one man standing off a whole town. I flourished the guns then levelled them, and just as I expected the crash a big fellow burst through the crowd.

"What's up?" he said as his hands flew to his hip pockets. Out flipped two guns. He sprang beside me and backed up against the wall.

"A thousand to one," he chuckled. "God, but you're a game man." He looked out of two fearless blue eyes at the crowd. "Come on, you villains!" he shouted. "Come on! Who'll be the first to die?"

It was superb. The man was a whirlwind in his way.

"I'm Quinn, sheriff of the next county," he said to me rapidly. "What's it all about?"

"I am an officer from St. Paul, and these people are after my prisoner," I said.

"So ho!" said Quinn. "Well, they don't get him."

He eyed the crowd. "Get back! Back up!" he shouted. "Back up or I'll back you up! One . . . two . . ." he started.

The crowd began to give, and the space in front of us grew as Quinn counted. He laughed and I laughed.

Richardson came up then, and I gave him the shotgun and money to pay the liveryman. Quinn stood by until the train arrived, and rode with me to the third station beyond. He left with a hearty handshake and a laugh when I thanked him. The teacher had subsided. He may have realized how close to death he was on that station platform.

After a three-month legal battle, during which Herres' identity was established, I was able to bring him back to Canada. He was convicted of forgery and sentenced to seven years in Kingston Penitentiary, where the "ding-dong mustachees" he had lightened with butternut dye finally vanished before the razor of the prison barber.

The Mad Trapper of Rat River

*Those who encountered Albert Johnson remembered best his
cold blue eyes and unsmiling face. Nobody could claim to know him.
For 48 days in the winter of 1931-32 he fought a running
battle with Mounties, trappers and Indians across hundreds of miles
of wild, Arctic terrain. He became known as the Mad Trapper
of Rat River but mad was the least accurate way to describe him.
Resolute, tough and almost superhumanly resourceful,
he was so wily that two trackers once met
head on as they followed his trail. This epic
manhunt, in which pursuers too
needed infinite courage and stamina,
has been called the Arctic Circle War.*

By DICK NORTH

THE BEGINNING OF July 1931 was warm even in the Northwest Territories. Fort McPherson, on the banks of the shimmering Peel River, dozed in the still humidity of the short Arctic summer. The air buzzed with mosquitoes and black-flies.

On July 9 a stranger came drifting down the river on a raft made of three large logs. He was about five feet, nine inches tall and 35-40 years old, with light brown hair and a snub nose. Three miles above Fort McPherson the powerful but slightly stooped figure made for shore. He had no dogs and virtually no outfit, and that evening he walked to the Northern Traders supply store at the settlement.

Apart from his withdrawn manner the stranger was an ideal customer, owner W.W. Douglas noted later: "He knew what he wanted and appeared to have plenty of cash." Douglas also commented on the stranger's "cold blue eyes."

The quiet man returned upstream and set up a tent across the river from an Indian named Abe Francis. During the next three weeks he spoke several times to Francis but seemed nervous and reluctant to show his face. One day there was a storm and the stranger was offered shelter at the Hudson's Bay post in Fort McPherson. He refused.

Another day he visited the post and bought $700 worth of supplies, paid for with cash from a tobacco tin. He allowed that he planned either to establish a trapline on the Rat River, flowing into the Peel from the Richardson Mountains to the west, or to cross the mountains into the Yukon via the Rat River Pass. He also returned to the Northern Traders store, where he bought a single-barrel shotgun.

In a settlement as small as Fort McPherson such a mysterious visitor did not go unnoticed. Const. Edgar "Spike" Millen of the nearby Arctic Red River detachment of the Royal Canadian Mounted Police was ordered to interview him on his next trip to Fort McPherson.

The 30-year-old Irish-born Millen was popular in the Mackenzie Delta, mixing easily with the local people and treating them fairly. A Mountie since 1920, he had volunteered for northern service and was famous for his abilities as a pastry cook and a step dancer.

On July 21 the two men met while the stranger was buying more supplies.

He identified himself as Albert Johnson and said he had come from the Prairies by the Mackenzie River. Millen knew he had come down the Peel River but he did not press the matter. Many men in that part of the country, especially trappers and prospectors, were reticent about their travels. Johnson told Millen he wouldn't be staying in the community because he wished to live alone. The constable reminded Johnson that he would need a licence to trap in the area.

A week later Johnson bought a 12-foot canoe from Abe Francis. The same day he broke camp and went back to the Northern Traders store for some final supplies. The clerk asked if he'd like to buy a small outboard engine for his new canoe. "No," Johnson replied, flexing his arms, "these are good enough for me. I'm not crazy yet." He walked to the river, launched his canoe and paddled downstream.

Within a few days he was ascending the Rat River, a notoriously difficult route. The channel was crooked, the current increasingly rapid, and the banks were a jungle of Arctic willows: travellers normally had to haul their craft much of the way with ropes from the bank. Johnson went 15 miles upstream until he came to a promontory which afforded

Spike Millen touched off the Johnson investigation.

a good view in three directions. There he spent the rest of the summer building a cabin and hunting for his winter food supply. The eight-by-twelve-foot cabin was made of foot-thick spruce logs and had a two-foot-thick sod roof.

Little more was heard of Johnson until Christmas Day. The holiday was a colorful one at the Arctic Red River RCMP post, Indians and whites putting on their finest clothes and joining in a series of parties and dances. But when an Indian named William Nerysoo arrived from the Rat River area he complained to Constable Millen that a man believed to be Albert Johnson had been springing his traps and hanging them on trees.

The next day Millen ordered Const. Alfred King, a rugged, five-year veteran of the Force who had volunteered for northern duty, to mush to Johnson's cabin and question him. King was to be accompanied by a peace officer, Special Const. Joe Bernard.

It was 40 below when the men set out with two dog teams. A raw wind nipped at them as they raced 30 miles west to Fort McPherson.

They stayed the night with Hudson's Bay trader John Firth, who threw the finest parties in the North and who invited them back for New Year's Eve.

Next morning King and Bernard turned their teams northward down the frozen Peel River. It was even colder than the day before, with a north wind. The men journeyed 25 miles to the mouth of the Rat before making a brush camp and rolling up in their sleeping bags with the northern lights for a ceiling.

They reached Johnson's cabin at noon the following day. King noticed snowshoes in front of the small dwelling and smoke coming from the stovepipe. In the time-accustomed manner of the North, he shouted a greeting. Receiving no acknowledgment, he snowshoed up to the four-foot-high door and knocked.

"Mr. Johnson, my name is Constable King," said the Mountie. "I have received a complaint about you interfering with a trapline and would like to ask you a few questions." He received no answer. Puzzled, King looked toward the 12-inch-square window immediately to the right of the door and observed Johnson staring at him. Johnson dropped a burlap sack over the window.

King sensed trouble. It was unnatural for an individual living in such isolation to ignore a greeting or a knock on the door. Normally a traveller could expect to be asked in for tea and to spend the night. The constable thought Johnson might be wary because he represented the law so he patiently explained his mission again. He waited almost an hour but the trapper refused to appear or say a word.

King decided he would have to go to Aklavik, 80 miles north, where he could report the incident to Insp. Alexander Eames, commander of the Mounties' Western Arctic sub-district, and get a warrant and reinforcements.

King and Bernard reached Aklavik the following day. Eames issued a warrant and assigned Const. Robert McDowell and Special Const. Lazarus Sittichinli to go back to the cabin with the other officers. The four left early on Dec. 30 and travelled fast, hoping to take care of the Johnson call and celebrate New Year's Eve at Fort McPherson. They broke camp on Dec. 31 without any breakfast.

They arrived at Johnson's about noon. King left McDowell and the other men by the river bank and walked to within hailing distance of the cabin. Smoke was coming from the stovepipe. "Are you there, Mr. Johnson?" King shouted. There was no answer. King shouted again, explaining that he had a warrant and would have to force the door if Johnson did not open it. Johnson remained silent.

Expecting trouble, King approached the door from the left side, away from the window. He turned partially sideways, extended his left arm and knocked with the back of his left hand. Immediately a shot rang out, shattering the frigid stillness. It came through the door, hit King in the chest and knocked him to the snow. Painfully he crawled to the river bank where the other men pulled him to safety while exchanging shots with Johnson. They lashed King to a sled and started a dash for Aklavik to save his life.

The dogs were tired, having already run for half a day, and the winding trail went continuously up and down the steep banks of the Husky River, crossing and recrossing from one portage to another. King's sled had to be patiently lowered or hoisted over every brink. The exhausting work of breaking trail had to be repeated too because 20-mph winds had drifted snow over the tracks made only hours before.

The winds and 40-below cold slashed at the men's faces. King's comrades had to stop repeatedly to rub his face, to keep fluid from freezing in his nostrils and ice from forming on his eyelids. It had to be done but they fretted at the delay.

Soon darkness enveloped the trail. All night, mile after mile, the men and dogs bent their heads into the biting winds. Dawn came and finally, 20 hours after leaving Johnson's cabin, the exhausted party reached Aklavik. King was rushed to the settlement's small hospital where it was found that the bullet had missed the heart.

Inspector Eames now organized a force of nine men, including himself, to go after Johnson. He sent a message over Aklavik radio station UZK, of the Royal Canadian Corps of Signals, for Constable Millen to leave Arctic Red River and meet him at the mouth of the Rat. On Jan. 4, 1932, Eames left Aklavik with Constable McDowell, Special Constables Bernard and Sittichinli and trappers Karl Gardlund, Knud Lang and Ernest Sutherland.

Two days later the posse met Millen and an Indian guide named Charlie Rat. By the following night the party was camped seven miles up the Rat River. They decided to circle Johnson's cabin and approach it from upstream because they feared the trapper might ambush them in the tangles of willows and brush along the river. At dawn they set out on an Indian trapline trail. They carried 20 pounds of dynamite.

The posse tramped all day. When it came time to make camp, Charlie Rat assured them they were only a few miles above Johnson's cabin. Next day they found they were miles off course, and had to return to their previous day's starting point. They had wasted two days and had used up most of their supplies. It was colder than ever.

Next morning, Jan. 9, the posse advanced up the river to the bank which extended in a half-circle around the trapper's cabin. Eames shouted for Johnson to come out, explaining that King was still alive: at least Johnson would not be up on a murder charge.

Ominous silence greeted Eames' words. The inspector decided to break down the cabin door. Six men rushed it but they were met with such heavy gunfire from eight loopholes around the building that their attempts could not be sustained.

During one sortie Lang slammed the butt of his rifle against the door, jarring it open. He saw in amazement that the floor of the cabin was a pit three feet below ground level, from which Johnson was firing "two hand guns." These later proved to be a sawed-off shotgun and a .22 Winchester rifle with the stock sawed off. The cabin, reinforced with extra logs and frozen sod around the base, was a virtual fortress.

As the hours went by, the cold began to tell on the posse. The men couldn't keep moving to stay warm, but had to remain posted along the riverbank watching the cabin. Only two days' dog food was left and supplies for the men were critically low. Eames knew he would have to break through Johnson's defences soon or retreat. He ordered the dynamite thawed, since it would not explode when frozen. The men held it next to their skin for the required five hours—avoiding sudden movements as it warmed.

The siege had begun near noon. Now it was 9 p.m. and quite dark. Eames ordered flares lit, figuring the glare might blind Johnson, and began throwing dynamite sticks at the cabin in hopes of dislodging some of the logs, the door or the roof. He had no success.

Midnight came. The flares had long since gone out. Knud Lang volunteered to propel his lanky six-foot-four-inch frame over the bank and throw dynamite onto the roof of the low cabin. The resulting explosion blew a hole in the roof and knocked off the stovepipe. Lang found himself staring at Johnson but he froze and failed to shoot. Johnson recovered quickly, ducked away, and when the smoke cleared continued firing. Lang withdrew.

It was nearly three in the morning when Eames decided on one last effort. He bound up the remaining four pounds of dynamite and heaved them across the 20-yard clearing. The resulting blast ripped the roof off the cabin and partially caved in the walls. Expecting Johnson to be stunned, Eames and Karl Gardlund charged across the clearing. When Gardlund reached the cabin he held a flashlight at arm's length and shone it through the wrecked door. The besieged trapper shot it out of his hand. Eames and Gardlund retreated to the riverbank.

Eames, realizing that Johnson could outwait the posse in the relative comfort of his cabin, decided to go back to Aklavik. One tough man had defied nine others for 15 hours.

In the meantime word of Constable King's shooting and the resulting expedition had been flashed to the outside world over Station UZK. Johnson, as the underdog, was an object of some sympathy. Newspapers played up the story, and for days people stayed close to radios awaiting developments. The drama has been credited with changing radio from a curiosity to an important news medium.

Somewhere along the line the label Mad Trapper of Rat River was given to Johnson and it stuck. But Eames wrote in his official report that "on the contrary, he showed himself to be an extremely shrewd and resolute man, capable of quick thoughts and action, a tough and desperate character."

On Jan. 14, while another posse was being formed, Constable Millen and Karl Gardlund returned to the Rat hoping to keep an eye on Johnson. They found his cabin empty. Then, searching through the wreckage they could hardly believe he had survived the last dynamite blast. Later there was speculation that he might have had special police or military training or experience, possibly in the 1914-18 war. The men scoured the area for clues to the trapper's real identity but found none. His tracks had been buried by fresh snow.

On Jan. 16 Eames led the new posse out of Aklavik. It included two soldiers from the signals unit, with a radio transmitter and a receiver: Staff Sgt. Earl Hersey was a former Olympic runner and a good northern traveller; Quartermaster Sgt. R.F. Riddell was one of the great bush-men, equally adept at mechanical repairs and wilderness survival. Their radio proved nearly useless, however, because its batteries wouldn't work properly in the cold.

The posse made it through a blizzard and camped nine miles east of Johnson's cabin, where the men were joined by Millen, Gardlund and 11 Indians. An intensive search over the next few days failed to turn up any trace of the fugitive.

By Jan. 21, Eames again faced the problem of diminishing supplies. He could maintain the large posse for four days or cut it to a minimum to continue the search for 10 days. He chose the latter course and selected Millen as leader, accompanied by Gardlund, Sergeant Riddell and trapper Noel Verville.

Millen and his party now had to concentrate their efforts and choose one direction in which to search. They surmised what they might have done in Johnson's position, and decided to continue up the Rat. Although they had dogs, travel was slow and wearying. Johnson had the entire wilderness to run in, and one day he might not run, choosing instead to ambush his trackers.

The men combed the valley. From dawn to dusk they scanned the snow for telltale signs. They struggled through tangled brush, broke up dog fights, chopped ice for water, and lay ambushed for hours in the piercing cold.

On Jan. 28 the temperature was again bitter. The trackers had put in another long, frustrating day. They were trail-hardened men, used to long hours in temperatures where every movement was an effort, but they were becoming exhausted. Their supplies were down to a little tea, hardtack and bacon, and they were almost out of dog food. They had stopped near the Bear River to build a fire and boil tea. While they were waiting, the ever-curious Riddell circled their resting place looking for a sign of Johnson.

He spotted the faintest trace of a trail on glare ice and latched onto it like a bloodhound. He followed the trail to the top of a ridge and suddenly lost it. But a man with Riddell's years of experience is not easily discouraged. He set off in a wide circle in an attempt to pick up the trail. He found it again in a small creek, and examined it closely in the growing darkness. It was probably two days old.

Riddell straightened up to snowshoe back to the others when a sharp crack behind him split the northern silence like a thunderclap. He dived into a snowbank, then levered a shell into the chamber of his rifle. Stoically he waited for the inevitable second shot. Then he realized that the sound was nothing more than a tree snapping in the cold. He shook his head as he pulled himself erect and walked back to tell his companions of his find.

Next day the temperature dipped even lower as the men followed Riddell's trail of the previous evening. They traced it through several old camps but finally lost it completely. However, they were getting

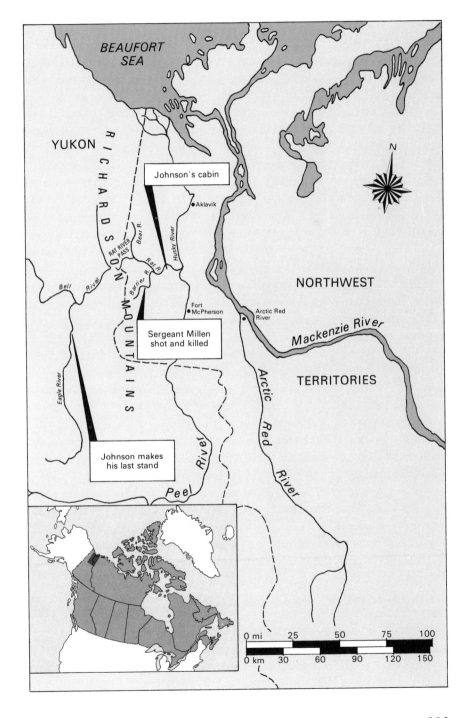

to know Johnson's habits. He never crossed a creek except on glare ice. Like a wolf, he travelled the ridges where the snow was packed and a trail was hard to find. He often made a long zigzag pattern, enabling him to watch the men pursuing him from one side of the Z as they proceeded up the other. Johnson's stamina seemed almost superhuman. On snowshoes and carrying a heavy pack, he was travelling two miles to every one by his pursuers, who had the benefit of dog teams. To avoid detection he could build only small fires under cover of a snowbank. He had to take time out to snare squirrels and rabbits; rifle shots for bigger game would give away his position. He spent long, arduous hours climbing cliffs, trotting through spruce forests, and crawling among seemingly impenetrable clusters of willows. He expertly travelled such a maze of trails that at one point two of the trackers met head on.

The searchers now found themselves far up the Rat. They were conferring on which way to turn when an Indian came mushing upriver to tell them he had heard two shots from the vicinity of the Bear River, where Riddell had first picked up Johnson's trail. Johnson might have taken a chance on shooting a caribou to replenish his food supply, figuring that his trackers had lost the trail and the shots would not be heard. It was a slim lead but Millen decided to follow it. Then, by continued circling, they picked up the trapper's tracks and followed them out of the Bear, down the Rat and five miles up a creek which emptied into the Rat about a mile from where it joined the Barrier River. They found quarters of caribou, confirming the food theory. They climbed a ridge running parallel to the creek but lost the trail again. Then one of the men looked down into a ravine formed by the creek and spotted a wisp of smoke through the thick woods. It marked Johnson's camp.

The searchers followed the ridge until they were almost above Johnson. They could see a fire and the edge of a tarp, and although they could not see Johnson, they could hear him puttering and whistling among the trees. The trackers stayed for two hours but they never did see him. Waiting so long in the cold took its toll: frost collected inside the men's fur clothing. At dusk they headed back to their outcamp.

The temperature had moderated slightly but a blizzard was raging next morning, Jan. 30, when the four trackers set out to apprehend Johnson. Riddell and Gardlund descended unnoticed into the ravine and took up positions only 15 yards from their man, hemming him in against a steep wall. They could hear him coughing. Verville and Millen then started down the ridge to the creek bed. However, one of them slipped, making enough noise to alert Johnson, who racked a shell into the breech of his rifle. He spotted Millen, and his 30-30 Savage barked. Millen and Verville dropped to the snow and fired back. Johnson, apparently wanting better cover, leaped across his fire to an overturned tree, but Gardlund, a Swedish army veteran, was ready for him. He fired as Johnson leaped, and the trapper seemed to collapse behind the tree. Gardlund thought Johnson had been hit.

Millen yelled for Johnson to give up but there was no answer. The four men did not dare approach immediately: while the trapper might be disabled, his position in the hole left by the uprooted tree had the advantage of elevation and was almost invulnerable.

Minutes went by and nothing happened. An hour passed. No sound came from Johnson's direction. Another hour went by and darkness was approaching. If Johnson was unhurt and the men tried to outwait him he might get away in the night. Millen decided to end the stalemate.

"Git down, Spike," Verville warned, "Git down or he'll kill you." But Millen, joined by Riddell, began moving toward Johnson's hiding place. Verville and Gardlund covered them anxiously. The men had walked about five paces when Riddell suddenly shouted "Watch it!" and went headlong over a bank as a shot cracked and a bullet whistled above his head. Millen spotted the movement of the trapper's rifle, dropped to one knee and snapped off a shot. Johnson replied with his Savage, and the gunfire echoed through the ravine. Both men had missed. Millen fired again and the trapper returned two shots so quickly that they came almost as one. Millen rose, whirled and fell face down in the snow, his rifle falling beside him. He did not move. Gardlund crawled to him and, under covering fire from his companions, tied Millen's mukluk laces together and dragged him out of Johnson's range. He had been shot through the heart.

The three remaining trackers decided to send Riddell back to Aklavik with the news. Gardlund and Verville built a raised cache to keep Millen's body out of the reach of animals, then retired to their campsite. There they met Staff Sergeant Hersey, who had been sent from Aklavik with supplies.

Next morning Hersey retrieved Millen's body. Johnson had escaped by climbing the steep hill behind his camp. He had chopped handholds in the ice, and on reaching the top had cascaded snow over his escape route in an effort to hide the trail.

Riddell reached Aklavik at noon on Jan. 31. Inspector Eames took the unprecedented step of asking for an airplane to help in the search. On Feb. 5 a ski-equipped Bellanca monoplane, piloted by W.R. "Wop" May, flew into Aklavik. May, a World War I ace who had become one of the North's most famous bush pilots, was about to become the first pilot directly involved in an RCMP manhunt.

Scoffers doubted that a plane would help much in the adverse winter conditions, but Eames was hoping it would not only provide aerial surveillance but also solve his supply problem. Dog teams in the hunt were eating 50 pounds of food a day.

Meanwhile, on Feb. 2, Eames led a new posse back to the site of Millen's death. By the time it got there, on the same day that May flew into Aklavik, it numbered 11 men including Eames and Riddell. There was no new trace of Johnson. On Feb. 8 the party was joined by Const. Sidney May (no relation to the pilot) and several more men, who had trekked through the Rat River Pass of the imposing Richardson Mountains after hearing about the manhunt.

The previous day Wop May had landed near Eames' camp with the first airborne supplies, and on Feb. 8 he ferried 700 pounds. He was a fearless pilot. Once, when heavy snow clogged his take-off path, he had the searchers tie the plane's tail to a tree. He gunned the engine and signalled for the taut rope to be cut. The plane surged ahead, cutting a swath through the snow: momentarily it threatened to bog down but at the last instant May got it into the air seemingly with his own body-English.

Now, with Riddell aboard, he quickly picked up Johnson's trail, saving the ground party days of tracking. The trapper had spent a week working his way up the Barrier River, craftily setting up blind leads to delay and confuse his pursuers. Upstream, where the channel ran parallel to the Richardson Mountains, he made several wide circles into the foothills, backtracking to rejoin his old trail. He may have been visiting old food caches or hoping to get behind the search party, but he was so far ahead that he kept coming back to the trail before the posse had got that far.

Inspector Eames ordered Constable May and three men to scour the headwaters of the Barrier, and others to watch the passes through the mountains. And from all directions an enormous ring began to close in on the fugitive. Patrols and surveillance flights went out from Dawson, Mayo and Whitehorse, hundreds of miles to the west and south, and extended along some 600 miles of the Mackenzie River to the east.

Johnson had now been living off the land, through a series of blizzards, for a month. Breaking trail with homemade snowshoes that weighed 10 pounds each, weary, hungry and cold, he knew he had to break for freedom.

His best escape route lay west to the Yukon and Alaska, over the Richardson Mountains, and he knew that the deep, soft snow on their western slopes would slow his pursuers' dog teams. But the craggy, barren range, an Arctic extension of the Rockies, was a formidable obstacle. The mountains were swept almost continually by howling blizzards; Indians in the search party told Inspector Eames that nobody could cross them alone.

On Feb. 9 a blizzard whipped among the rocky peaks and down the Barrier and Rat rivers. All over the Mackenzie delta planes were grounded and patrols called off. Yet during this raging storm, shunning the passes which he knew would be watched, Johnson clambered to the high ridges of the mountains and crossed into the Yukon. He descended a creek to the Bell River, carefully skirted the trading post of La Pierre House, and snowshoed on to the Eagle River and turned south on it.

But now the whole north country was on the alert. Several Indians spotted strange snowshoe tracks east of La Pierre House. A trapper mushed through the Rat River Pass with the message, and on Feb. 13 Eames, Riddell, Gardlund and a constable flew to La Pierre House in the Bellanca. Sid May, Hersey, Noel Verville's brother Joe and five more men followed on foot through the Rat River Pass.

Immediately after landing Eames and his party, Wop May flew off in search of Johnson's trail. He soon found it leading up the Eagle River, then lost it at a point where Johnson had removed his snowshoes and walked in the tracks left by a herd of caribou.

Flying conditions the next day were poor but May managed to pick up Johnson's trail again 20 miles up the Eagle.

The following day fog closed in and the plane was grounded, but Eames and his party set out after Johnson on foot. Soon Sid May and his men arrived from their trip through the mountains and set out after Eames. Within a few hours the groups were united and ascending the winding Eagle River past low, scrubby hills.

Fog was bad again the next day, but on Feb. 17, as the posse started out, skies were gradually clearing.

Johnson was not far away. He had ascended the Eagle until he came across ski tracks of local trappers. Johnson knew that Gardlund had been using skis, and thought the tracks were his. Believing the posse to be upstream, he started to backtrack down the middle of the river. Suddenly, shortly before noon, he saw Earl Hersey come round a sharp bend. The men were about 200 yards apart, heading directly for each other.

Both stopped, astonished. Johnson quickly put on his snowshoes and ran out of sight behind the steep bank. Hersey snatched a rifle and ran ahead to where he saw Johnson trying to climb the bank.

Hersey kneeled and fired. Sid May and Joe Verville came running up and also fired. Johnson whirled and snapped off a shot at Hersey, who fell wounded in the snow. The others were coming up now, and May signalled for them to break into two groups.

Johnson couldn't make the climb, and ran back toward the easier slope on the opposite bank. Then he fell or threw himself to the snow, wriggled out of his pack and settled behind it. Gardlund and three men climbed the bank, coming out above the outflanked Johnson. Riddell led four men to the other bank, and now Johnson was caught below the two groups.

The men kept up a barrage of fire, which the trapper returned. Eames joined Sid May on the river and shouted for Johnson to surrender. A shot hit ammunition in Johnson's pocket and he jerked when it exploded. Another bullet slammed into his shoulder and still another into his side but he kept on firing.

Eames called again for Johnson to surrender but his only answer was the bark of a gun and the wave of an arm.

Meanwhile, Wop May and his mechanic had been photographing the battle from their plane. It was so cold they could hear the rifle shots above the roar of the engine. Said May later: "I circled back upriver. As I flew over the fugitive's lair it seemed as though he was lying in an unnatural position. Swinging back, I nosed the Bellanca down till our skis were tickling the snow. Johnson was lying face down, his right arm outflung grasping his rifle. I knew he was dead."

May waggled the wings of his plane to indicate the news. About the same time, rifle in hand, Sid May walked up to Johnson, ready for anything. He hooked the barrel under Johnson's body and turned him over. The emaciated Mad Trapper had nine bullets in him, one through the spine.

Wop May landed the plane. Hersey, who had been hit in the left elbow, left knee and chest, was taken aboard and flown to Aklavik.

Before taking off, the pilot walked over for a look at Johnson. "As

Albert Johnson after death: 'The awful grimace of hate.'

I stooped over," said May later, "I got the worst shock I've ever had. Johnson's lips were curled back from his teeth in the most awful grimace of hate I'd ever seen—the hard-boiled, bitter hate of a man who knows he's trapped at last and has determined to take as many enemies as he can with him."

Among his possessions Johnson had $2,410 in bills, three guns, five pearls worth $15, gold dental work worth $3.20, a jar containing gold worth $9.36, an axe, a pocket compass, a razor, a homemade knife with moose-skin cover, sewing materials, fish-hooks, nails and matches wrapped in tin foil, a lard can and lid used as a tea pail, a dead squirrel and a small dead bird.

Johnson's origins remain a mystery. His appearance and habits were strikingly similar to those of a trapper named Arthur Nelson who had appeared in the north country in 1926 and vanished shortly before Johnson came floating down the Peel on his raft. But Nelson too had apparently come from nowhere.

Johnson's possessions included no written clues to his identity: indeed, when the manhunt was over, his pursuers realized that during the entire episode he was never heard to utter a word.

Doomsday Flight 812

It was 1971 and airline hijackings were at their peak. Air Canada Capt. Vern Ehman's eastbound DC-8 had been air-borne 45 minutes from Calgary when his purser passed him the note. "Welcome aboard the original doomsday flight," Ehman read. "I have just boarded your plane with 54 sticks of dynamite and one shotgun." This was Canada's most sensational hijacking, a bizarre seven hours of madness and heroism.

By PAUL KING

A T 4:30 P.M. ON NOV. 12, 1971, Flight 812 from Vancouver left Calgary with 115 passengers for Toronto and Montreal. Among the first-class passengers who boarded in Calgary was 27-year-old Paul Joseph Cini. He wore an oversized, beige trench coat and clutched a Woolco department store shopping bag bound with tape.

Purser John Arpin, an Air Canada employee for 25 of his 48 years, pointed him toward a seat. Cini sat down, placed his parcel on the floor between his feet, and scratched the backs of his hands.

The 15 other first-class passengers wondered what he was doing in their section. "Shabby," they said of him later. "Shabby and rude."

After take-off Arpin went through the section taking orders for drinks. Cini ordered a screwdriver (vodka and orange juice) which he drank in a gulp. Then he scratched his hands again.

When Arpin returned with a second tray of drinks, Cini asked where the washrooms were. Arpin pointed to a door in the front of the section. "It's occupied," Cini said.

Arpin turned and opened the washroom door. "No sir," he said, "it isn't."

"Well, there's another one, isn't there?"

"Yes, just ahead of the curtains – in the lounge."

Cini went into the lounge washroom.

Arpin then served hot hors d'oeuvres. It took him 30 minutes. A woman asked for a gin and tonic. Arpin went to the bar in the lounge and was just reaching for a bottle when he heard a voice behind him saying, "Over here."

He turned and saw a man sitting in the rear lounge seat beside the window. He was wearing a black satin hood over his head, with slits for the eyes, nose and mouth. On top was a black wig. In his hands was a double-barrelled, 12-gauge sawed-off shotgun pointing at Arpin's head.

"Where the hell did *you* come from?" Arpin asked. Then he recognized Cini's trench coat.

"Get over here and sit down," Cini ordered.

"You're kidding!"

"When I blow your head through the side of the plane you'll know I'm not kidding."

Arpin sat down in the centre seat of the row facing Cini, separated from him by a small table.

Cini handed Arpin a note written on yellow paper the size of a stenographer's notebook. Arpin started to read it.

"Don't you look at that," said Cini. "Take it to the captain."

At that moment stewardess Mary Dohey, 38, a registered nurse and 17-year Air Canada veteran, walked in to get wineglasses for the dinner trays. She started to speak when Cini said, "Sit down."

Mary turned and saw the man in the black hood. "Sit down," Cini repeated.

"Sit down, Mary," said Arpin. "It's for real."

Mary sat beside Arpin, and Cini placed the barrels of his gun at her forehead.

"Don't be long," he told Arpin, "or I'll blow her head off. And don't make any plans up there."

As Arpin walked into the cockpit, Cini told Mary: "Get over there by the window. Put your back against it and stare straight ahead. If you turn your head I'll blow it off."

Mary did as Cini told her. From the corner of her eye she saw him flicking a butane lighter and lighting a cigarette. He chain-smoked furiously from then on.

Three officers sat in the cockpit guiding the jet at 37,000 feet across Saskatchewan. They were First Officer Nelles Hagenson, 30, of Vancouver; Second Officer Noel Belanger, 28, of Montreal; and the captain, Vern Ehman, a handsome 43-year-old Montrealer who had flown with

Air Canada for 17 years. All were drinking tea that Mary Dohey had taken them.

"Captain," Arpin said, "there's a man back there with a gun." Ehman thought he was joking. Arpin has a reputation as a joker. Then the captain looked at Arpin's face. "Is it for real?" he asked.

"It's for real," said Arpin.

Ehman started to read the note, written in a misspelled scrawl on both sides of the paper.

When Arpin returned Cini asked him, "Did the captain get the message?"

"Yes," Arpin said. For 60 seconds they sat in silence. Then Cini said, "Go back and see that they understand."

Arpin returned to the flight deck.

"Just a second, John," said Ehman. "It's written on both sides. I read the wrong side first. Tell him to wait just a minute."

Arpin went back and told Cini. "Get back there," Cini said, "and tell them I want the note back. Now. And *hurry*."

As Arpin left, Mary Dohey heard paper tearing. She turned her head slightly and saw Cini pulling two wires out of his package. "Oh, God," she thought, "he's got a bomb, too."

"Come over here," Cini told her, pointing to the seat beside him.

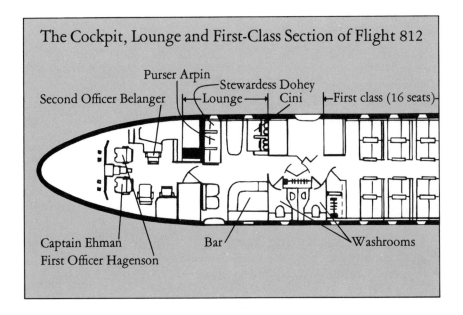

The Cockpit, Lounge and First-Class Section of Flight 812

603

Then he handed her the two wires. "Lady," he said, "I don't want to frighten you."

"I know, dear," said Mary.

"Okay," said Cini. "Now hold those wires apart in your left hand." She tucked one against her thumb, the other next to her baby finger.

"If you want to die now," said Cini, "put the wires together. If you don't, keep them apart."

On the flight deck, Ehman was telling Arpin: "Okay, I think he wants us to go to Great Falls, Montana, pick up a million and a half dollars, and proceed to Regina."

He started into a slow turn to the south, just short of the Manitoba border. It was 5:15 p.m.

At that second a blast shook the plane. Shattered fibreglass from the partition separating the lounge from the cockpit flew past the pilots. Shotgun pellets hit Noel Belanger's shoes.

Mary Dohey had just placed the wires in her hand when the shotgun blasted a hole in the cockpit wall. "I'm sorry," Cini told Mary. "I didn't mean to do that."

"I know you didn't, dear," Mary said. "Would you like me to hold your hand?"

Cini shoved a new shell into his shotgun, then looked at Mary and said, "Yes."

John Arpin dashed in, expecting to see Mary dead.

"Sit down," Cini said.

"They understand the message," Arpin said. "We're to go to Montana, pick up the money, then go to Regina, release the passengers, load the aircraft full of guns and ammunition, and head for Ireland, right?"

"Right," said Cini.

"There's just one thing," Arpin said. "Who do we get the money from?"

"Air Canada supplies the money."

"Okay," said Arpin, and went back to tell the captain.

When he left, the stewardess said to Cini, "My name is Mary. Please call me Mary."

"Mary," said Cini. "That's a nice name."

"And what's your name, dear?"

"Dennis." Cini had a cousin named Dennis Monroe in Kearny, N.J., and was carrying identification papers with that name.

"May I call you Dennis?"

Cini nodded as Arpin returned. "His name is Dennis," Mary told Arpin.

"That's fine," said Arpin. "Dennis, may I tell the passengers what the blast was about?"

"Tell them a light-bulb blew," Cini said.

"But Dennis, sir, I . . ." Arpin's sentence was cut off by Cini screaming.

"Sir? *Sir?* I knew it. You're FBI or RCMP aren't you? They all say sir. And I'm going to kill them all. All the FBI that come to the airport in Great Falls. And all the RCMP in Regina. And you're *one* of them."

"No, sir . . . I mean, Dennis," Arpin said. "I'm not a policeman. I'm a purser."

Cini stared at him. "What nationality are you?" he asked.

"French Canadian," said Arpin.

"Okay," Cini said finally. "You're safe. But I'll kill every Englishman on this flight."

Arpin said nothing.

"Don't worry," said Cini. "I like you. When I get the money and we land in Ireland, I'll take care of you. Now go and tell the passengers whatever you like."

"Thank you," said Arpin. First he told Ehman that no one was hurt in the blast. Then he went back to tell the first-class passengers, "Ladies and gentlemen, we're being hijacked."

Most accepted the news calmly, except for two who ran back to the economy section.

"Now," said Arpin. "Who'd like a drink?" Five passengers raised their hands.

In the lounge Cini was telling Mary: "You know, I have a mission. I have to help the Irish."

"Oh Dennis, *I'm* Irish," Mary said.

"You are?" Cini said. "That's good."

"Do you have any family?" Mary asked.

"No," said Cini. "None."

"There are 14 kids in mine," Mary said. "I'm the youngest."

"That's a lotta kids." Cini laughed for the first time. (Mary made a mental note: "The man likes kids.")

Then Cini started talking again about his mission. He had to help the Irish Republican Army. "I went to chapel this morning and prayed about it," he added.

605

Arpin returned and sat in his seat. Then Phillip Bonné, 22, the assistant purser in charge of the economy section, walked in. "Sit down," Cini ordered.

Bonné sat beside Arpin.

"What nationality are you?" Cini asked.

"French Canadian," said Bonné.

"I'll blow your head off. The FLQ [Front de Libération du Québec] would be proud of me, and de Gaulle would turn over in his grave."

Nobody knew what he meant.

Then Cini told Bonné to pull the curtain shut between the economy and first-class sections. Bonné got up and went back.

"Why should he do that, Dennis?" Mary asked.

Cini pulled two bundles of dynamite from his coat pocket. There were five sticks in each bundle. Fuses stuck from the ends.

"Because I'm going to light one of these and throw it inside," Cini said.

"Oh, Dennis. Why would you do that, dear?" pleaded Mary. "You're going to hurt all those people. Do you *know* those people, Dennis?"

"No," said Cini. An instant later he told her, "Call him back."

"PHILLIP," Mary screamed.

Bonné returned.

Cini said he was hot under his hood. Arpin adjusted the temperature control and within minutes the lounge grew uncomfortably cold. Arpin asked if he could put on his jacket. Cini nodded. Then he saw the gold braid on Arpin's sleeves, and started to yell again.

"Now I *know* you're the FBI," he shouted. He shoved a stick of dynamite into Arpin's mouth, then raised his shotgun and pressed it against Arpin's temple. "Now move your head toward the hole," he ordered, pointing to the shattered section of the cockpit wall. "I'll show you how big a hole I can make." Arpin leaned his head back, but gently pushed the barrel of the gun away from his forehead with his right hand.

"Dennis, dear," said Mary. "Why don't you put the safety catch on the gun?"

Cini turned to her. "You," he said. "Lean over the table." Then he told Bonné, sitting opposite, "Now take her hands."

Mary and Bonné grasped hands across the table. "I want to see the whites of your knuckles," Cini told them.

Arpin sat with the dynamite in his mouth. After 10 minutes he reached up slowly and removed the stick.

"Who told you to take that out?" Cini snapped, and shoved it back in. Then, impulsively, he grabbed the stick and handed it to Mary. "Smell that," he ordered.

"My darling, I don't know anything about dynamite," she said.

"I didn't think you did," Cini said. He put the stick on the table. Then he asked Arpin, "What's taking so long?"

"We can't land until the money is ready, you know," Arpin said. "You insisted on that, remember? It's going to be hard to raise a million and a half with all the banks closed."

"Yeah," said Cini.

Suddenly he turned to Mary. "You want to be the stewardess of the year?"

"Why, Dennis? What do you want me to do?"

Cini held the shotgun in front of her. "I want you to take this and shoot me," he said.

"Oh, Dennis. Why would I hurt *you*, dear? *You're* not going to hurt *us*."

"How do you know?" Cini said.

"Because you told me and I believe you."

Cini shoved the gun toward Arpin. "Shoot me," he ordered.

"I can't, Dennis," Arpin said.

"Well, if you don't kill me I'll shoot you."

"Then you'll have to," Arpin said, "because I can't kill anybody." He was lying. At that second Arpin would have loved to fire both barrels at Cini's head.

Cini nodded. "Good," he said. "You're a lucky man. If you'd grabbed for the gun, I'd have put the wires together."

In the cockpit Captain Ehman received a message from Great Falls: "Okay, we've got the money. Come in on runway 03." Ehman started down.

As they descended, Cini placed his bundles of dynamite on the table with the fuses facing him. He pulled out a butane lighter and waved a four-inch flame in front of the fuses. The plane touched down at eight o'clock.

Cini put his lighter away and handed Mary the package with the wires. She placed the wires in her left hand and Cini once more put the shotgun to her head.

Ehman taxied the plane past the terminal building so Cini could see the Great Falls sign. There was sudden consternation in the economy section, where some of the passengers realized for the first time they were not landing in Toronto.

No one could see the dark figures of FBI men lined up on either side of the runway. The control tower had asked Ehman if he wanted the FBI to intervene.

"No way," Ehman shot back.

When the DC-8 stopped and turned at the end of the runway, huge tank trucks raced up and started refuelling it. A black, unmarked police car drove to within 200 feet of the cockpit and a briefcase was carried toward the plane.

Bonné, following Cini's instructions, had cut a long strap and dangled it out the door. The briefcase was tied to the strap and Bonné hauled it in. But the door was designed so it wouldn't close without being opened all the way first, and Cini had said not to open it more than six inches. He was afraid sharpshooters might be hidden outside.

Arpin explained about the door.

"I don't care," Cini said. "Just tell him to shut it."

Mary knew Bonné's problem. She asked Cini if he would hold the package of dynamite for a minute – she had to blow her nose.

Cini turned his head to look at her. At that instant Bonné opened the door wide and swiftly slammed it. Cini turned to Bonné: "Did you get it?"

"Yes," Bonné said.

They had been on the ground for five minutes. They sat for 10 more while the refuelling continued. Then Cini said, "Okay, we take off *now*."

Ehman took the plane to 37,000 feet and aimed it northeast to Regina.

"Where are we going, Dennis?" Mary Dohey asked Cini.

"I have a plan," he said, "but I'm not even going to tell *you*." Then he turned to Arpin: "Count the money," he said.

Arpin opened the briefcase and noticed bundles of $5, $10 and $20 bills. Each bundle was wrapped in elastic bands, and strips of paper marked the total in each bundle. Arpin made a show of counting each bill separately, but he'd added up the marked amounts in his head. They came to only $50,000.

"How much is there?" Cini asked.

"One and a half million," Arpin lied.

"Count it again," said Cini.

Arpin counted the bills again, very slowly. Then he looked up. He *knew* now that they totalled only $50,000.

"How much?" asked Cini.

"A million and a half," Arpin said. Then, for some reason, he took off his tie and tossed it across the money. "Old tie," he said, "you've never been closer to so much money in your life."

Cini started to laugh, but Mary was praying silently: "Lord, it looks as if you want me to die. I will, but please, Lord, not in vain. First save the passengers, Lord. And then the crew."

Cini was still chuckling when she stopped. She looked at him and suddenly remembered that he had seemed to like children. "Oh, Dennis," she blurted, "I hear the children crying." She didn't even know if there were any children aboard.

"You mean," Cini said, "there are kids on this flight?" He sounded sincerely concerned.

"Yes, Dennis," said Mary. "And the dear little souls are so tired and hungry they don't even know what's going on."

Cini turned to Arpin. "Turn this airplane around. We're going back to Great Falls. And I want the passengers to get off."

"*All* the passengers?" Arpin asked.

"Yes."

"And how many of the crew?"

"The crew at the back can go."

Arpin went to the flight deck and told Ehman. It was 8:35.

When Arpin returned to the lounge Cini reached into his pocket and pulled out a baggage slip. "I've got a light blue suitcase aboard," he said. "Everything I own is in it. When we land I'll give you 10 minutes to get it."

The DC-8 touched down again at 9 p.m. and taxied to its previous position, ready for take-off. Buses and fuel trucks were waiting. Ehman shut off two engines but left the other two running. Cini had insisted on this, even though it made the refuelling considerably slower.

Arpin jumped up. "You've got 10 minutes," Cini reminded him. "If you're not back I'll blow Mary's head off."

Arpin went to the economy section and started to open the galley door. A truck with a ramp was having difficulty lining up with the door, and Arpin had to wait and direct the driver before he could dash under the plane. Two baggage carts had already been filled.

"Who's in charge here?" Arpin screamed.

"I am," said a man.

Arpin gave him Cini's baggage slip. "Find this suitcase," he said, and started looking himself. Eight minutes had gone by.

After a few minutes Arpin found a bag. It was navy blue not light blue, but it bore the number of Cini's slip. Or did it? Arpin wasn't sure now. He yelled for the supervisor. Nobody answered. Arpin looked at his watch in the lights of the fuel trucks. "God," he thought. "I've been gone 11 minutes already!"

The supervisor appeared.

"Where's the slip?" Arpin shouted. "What's the number?" The supervisor showed him. It was the right one.

The bag weighed 70 pounds. Arpin lugged it to the ramp and started to shoulder up the steps past passengers coming down. "It's too late," he kept thinking, "Mary's dead."

He pulled the suitcase into the plane. There were a dozen passengers still inside, cramming the aisle. "Thank you," they said to Arpin, grabbing his hand. "We all feel sorry for you . . . . What's going to happen to you?"

Arpin just kept struggling down the aisle, his arms aching from the weight.

Inside the lounge, when the 10 minutes were up, Cini had looked at his watch and said, "I'm sorry, I have to kill you."

Mary thought, "My God, the passengers aren't all off yet." She said, "May I turn and look at you, dear?"

"Go ahead," said Cini. Mary turned. The gun barrels pointed at her eyes. Cini's fingers were on the triggers.

"Dennis," Mary said, "do you want to kill me?"

"No."

Mary placed a hand on Cini's knee. "Well then, dear, will you please wait just a little while longer? John will be back with your suitcase. It's dark outside. The engines are running. And he's looking for a suitcase he's never seen."

Then she prayed. "Please, God. Please send Johnny."

At that second Arpin burst into the lounge and dropped the suitcase beside Cini. "Thank you, God," Mary whispered.

At the galley door Bonné saw the last passenger leave the ramp. He shut the door and went to the lounge.

Then Mary heard Cini whisper in her ear: "Do you want to get off, too?" She thought, "The second I go he'll kill the rest." She said, "Dennis, what do *you* want me to do, dear?"

"I want you to stay."

"All right, I will," said Mary. "But please, may I go to the bathroom?"

Cini said, "Go ahead." While Mary was gone he made Arpin get on his knees in front of him, and aimed the shotgun at his head.

Mary returned and sat beside Cini again. She had put on a blonde wig and brushed her teeth.

"See," she said, "I told you I'd be back. Do I look gorgeous?"

"I thought you looked gorgeous before," Cini said.

"See, John," said Mary. "Dennis says nice things to me. Why don't you?"

Arpin laughed weakly. Cini looked at him and raised the gun. "Tell the captain to hurry up," Cini ordered.

Arpin went into the cockpit and Ehman said he wanted to talk to Cini. Arpin relayed the message. "All right," Cini said. "Send him in."

Ehman walked into the lounge with his hands high above his head.

"Where do you want to go?" he asked. "To Cuba?"

"No," Cini said. "I'll give you your destination in the air."

"It will still take a little while to get a full fuel load," said Ehman.

"That's okay."

"We'll do everything you ask," Ehman said. "Just don't harm the crew."

"Go back to the cockpit," Cini said. Ehman turned, his hands still up, and returned to the flight deck.

In a few moments Cini suddenly barked at Arpin: "Tell the captain we're leaving."

"Right now?" Arpin asked.

"Right *now*."

"But we're not finished fuelling."

"Do as I tell you."

Arpin went to the cockpit and Ehman called the control tower to order the fuel trucks away. They roared back down the runway. It was 9:45.

When Ehman reached 37,000 feet Cini ordered him to fly to New York. Two minutes later the destination was changed to Phoenix, Ariz., and Ehman was ordered back to the lounge. He entered with his hands in the air, and Cini told Arpin, Bonné and Mary Dohey to go sit at the front of the economy section.

To Ehman Cini said, "Okay, Captain, I want to go back to Calgary, pick up a friend and get a full fuel load."

"Fine," said Ehman. "But if we don't shut down all the engines to refuel, it will take about an hour. If we do, it will take only about 30 minutes."

"I'll let you know," Cini said.

Ehman returned to the cockpit.

In the economy section the stewardess and two pursers were sure Cini would now count the money. When he found only $50,000 he would go berserk and come through the doorway with his shotgun blasting. But when the black hood did appear it was with an order for Bonné to get the captain again. Bonné took the message and returned to his seat.

When Ehman stood up and turned around Cini was in the cockpit, his gun pointed. He took all the microphones and headsets and ordered Ehman into the lounge again.

"I want to bail out from the rear main door," he told the captain.

"It's impossible," Ehman said. "You can't open the door against the slipstream."

"Okay," said Cini, "then I'll blow the tail off."

"It won't work," Ehman said softly. "First of all, you might blow up with it. Second, the aircraft will go into a dive and you won't be able to scramble out the hole. The best thing to do is go out an emergency window over a wing."

"I'll hit the tail," Cini said.

"No you won't. The tail's well above the wing."

"All right," Cini said. Ehman went back to the cockpit and started to descend. Then he heard a noise behind him. It was Cini. "I'll need help opening the window," he said.

Ehman turned the controls over to the first officer and gave him instructions to drop to 3,000 feet and slow to 120 mph. Then he went back to the lounge. Cini was sitting shooting his lighter flame toward the dynamite fuses.

"You have a knife?" Cini asked.

"No."

"I have to cut the twine on this parcel."

"All we have is an axe in the cockpit."

"Get it."

As Ehman went to the cockpit he decided to jump the hijacker.

He didn't know how, but he knew he had to. He returned to the lounge and handed Cini the axe, handle first. "What's in there?" he asked pointing at the parcel.

"A parachute," Cini said, and handed the parcel to Ehman. "Now carry this down the aisle." Cini followed, holding the mikes, earphones and axe in one hand, his shotgun in the other. He waved his gun at the seated crew members. "You three get out," he said. "Go back front." Bonné and Mary left but Arpin ducked on the floor between the seats in Row 6.

Ehman set the package on a seat in Row 9 and stepped back three feet. Cini tossed the mikes and earphones beside the package. He tried to sever the twine with the axe while holding the gun with his left hand. He couldn't do it, and set down his gun on a seat.

Ehman jumped. He grabbed the gun and tossed it down the aisle. Then he hit Cini's arm. The axe fell, and Ehman went for Cini's throat. Cini couldn't believe it. "What the hell?" he said. Ehman stuck both thumbs on Cini's windpipe and started squeezing. Cini struggled, and in his sudden fear had "the strength of three guys," Ehman recalled later. The captain hollered for help.

Arpin rushed up and grabbed Cini's arms. Suddenly Cini quit struggling. Ehman hollered again, and Bonné ran in. "Get some tape," Ehman told him. "We've got to tie him up."

Bonné ran out, and Cini started thrashing again. He wrenched free an arm and dived for his pocket. "I'll blow you bastards up," he screamed. Arpin seized his right arm and Ehman his left. They stripped off the wig and hood. Cini's eyes were circles of terror and his face was soaked with sweat.

Bonné returned with tape but Cini continued thrashing and screaming.

"Hit him, Phillip," Ehman yelled. "Hit him with the axe."

Bonné swung the blunt edge at Cini's head but it glanced off. Bonné struck two more times. Blood gushed out but Cini stayed on his feet, struggling wildly. Bonné flipped the axe over and brought the sharp edge down. Cini kept fighting.

"Use the handle," Ehman yelled. Bonné turned the axe around and smashed the handle against Cini's head. There was a crunch. Cini went limp and fell on top of the microphones and headsets. The three crew members thought he was dead but they kept holding him.

Noel Belanger ran in with more tape.

613

"Tie him up," said Ehman, "and tie him good." He went back to the cockpit. It was 11:30.

Arpin, Bonné and Belanger used 50 feet of tape. They wound it around Cini's arms, ankles and body, then wrapped it around the seat and up to the overhead rack. Cini looked like a mummy.

Only one mike and one headset weren't broken. Ehman plugged

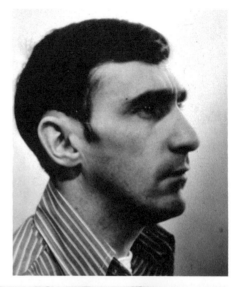

Stewardess Mary Dohey was awarded the Cross of Valour, Canada's highest decoration for bravery, for her handling of Paul Joseph Cini (right). Purser John Arpin (below) received the Star of Courage. Facing page: First Officer Nelles Hagenson and Capt. Vern Ehman. Ehman and Assistant Purser Phillip Bonné were awarded the Medal of Bravery.

them in and called ground control in Calgary: "We've subdued the hijacker," he said, "and want to land."

When the DC-8 came down it taxied to an unused runway because of the explosives aboard. Ehman shut off the engines and looked at his watch. It was midnight. He stood up and said, "Let's get the hell out of here."

He and his crew talked to the RCMP, then were driven to the Calgary Inn where Air Canada had laid on a spread of Chinese food and all the liquor they could drink. They drank a lot.

The RCMP learned that Cini was born in Glasgow, had moved to Canada in 1956, and at the time of the hijacking had been working as a salesman for a Calgary record distributing company. His manager said Cini was the best salesman he'd ever had.

The hijacker was found guilty on seven charges ranging from possession of explosives to kidnapping. He was given four separate life sentences, 14 years on a fifth charge, and five years on two remaining charges. All sentences were concurrent.

After they testified at the trial, the crew of Flight 812 were given a banquet by Air Canada, plus a week's paid vacation, a free flight anywhere for two and $500 each.

Stewardess Mary Dohey took her older sister, a nun, to Lourdes. There she got on her knees and "thanked Our Lady for saving our lives."

The

Human Spirit

To have striven,
to have made an effort,
to have been true to certain ideals —
this alone is worth the struggle.

Sir William Osler, 1896

Martyrs of the Wilderness

*A tiny band of 17th-century French Jesuit
missionaries offered their lives to an enormous
vision: to convert the Huron Indians as a first
step toward spreading Christianity across
North America. But the Huron villages lay far
inland and were vulnerable to roving bands
of Iroquois who wanted the furs that the Hurons
traded to infant French settlements along the
St. Lawrence River. This tale recounts the courage
and the fate of the Jesuits in a primitive world
of superstition, disease and war.*

By FRANCIS PARKMAN

*Saint Jean de Brébeuf was the greatest martyr
of the Jesuits' mission to the Huron Indians.*

THE JESUITS WERE NO STERN EXILES seeking an asylum for a persecuted faith. Rank, wealth, power and royalty itself smiled on their enterprise. Yet their fervor, self-abnegation and self-devotion will scarcely find its equal on the page of human history.

He who set sail for the country of the Hurons left behind him the world and all its prizes. True, he acted under orders, obedient as a soldier, but the astute Society of Jesus knew its members, gave each his fitting task; and when the word was passed to embark for New France, it was but the response to a secret longing of the fervent heart. The letters of these departing priests breathe a spirit of enthusiastic exaltation.

The first among them, Father Jean de Brébeuf, spent the years 1626-29 in the Huron villages, apparently without making any conversions. By 1634, after a period in which New France was surrendered to British control, he was back in the tiny settlement Champlain had founded at Quebec. There he was entrusted with founding and organizing a real mission among this distant native people who had been allies of the French from the beginning. They lived a settled existence at the western terminus of the only route into the interior open to them, via the St. Lawrence, the Ottawa, the Mattawa, Lake Nipissing and the French River to Georgian Bay and the Great Lakes. But Brébeuf, Fathers Antoine Daniel and Ambroise Davost and other Frenchmen who were to go with them found that the Hurons who came to New France that year to trade were not anxious to take them back.

Grievous calamities had befallen the Huron nation. They had suffered deplorable reverses at the hands of the Iroquois, and a pestilence had begun its ravages among them. They appeared at Trois-Rivières—this year the place of trade—in small numbers, and in dejection and alarm. They refused to take the Jesuits. In private, however, some were gained over, then again refused, then a second time consented. On the eve of embarkation, they once more wavered. All was uncertainty, when Brébeuf made a vow to Saint Joseph. At once, he wrote, the Indians became tractable and, amid salvos of cannon from the ships, the Fathers set forth.

They reckoned the distance at 900 miles but distance was the least repellent feature of this arduous journey to Huronia. Barefoot, lest their shoes should injure the frail vessel, each crouched in his canoe, toiling with unpractised hands to propel it. Before him, week after week, he saw the same lank, unkempt hair, the same tawny shoulders and long, naked arms ceaselessly plying the paddle. The canoes were soon separated and for more than a month the Frenchmen rarely or never met. Brébeuf spoke a little Huron but Fathers Daniel and Davost heard only the unintelligible complaints and menaces of the Indians, many of them sick and all terrified, despondent and sullen. Their only food was a pittance of Indian corn, crushed between two stones and mixed with water.

The toil was extreme. Brébeuf counted 35 portages around rapids and cataracts. And more than 50 times they were forced to wade, pushing their empty birchbarks or dragging them with ropes. Brébeuf tried to do his part but boulders and sharp rocks wounded his feet. He and his companions bore their share of the baggage across the portages, sometimes for several miles. The way was through dense forest, encumbered with rocks and logs, tangled with roots and underbrush, damp with perpetual shade, and redolent of decayed leaves and mouldering wood. The Indians themselves were often spent with fatigue. Brébeuf, a man of iron frame and a nature unconquerably resolute, doubted if his strength would sustain him.

Davost's Indian guide robbed him of part of his baggage, threw some of it into the river, including most of the three priests' books and writing materials, and then left him behind among Algonkin Indians. He found means to continue and at length reached Huronia in a state of prostration. Daniel, too, was deserted but was taken into another canoe. A young Frenchman named Martin was abandoned among the Nipissings; another named Baron, on reaching the Huron country, was robbed of all he had except his weapons. With these he compelled the robbers to restore part of their plunder.

Brébeuf, separated from his companions, descended the French River and followed the lonely shore of Georgian Bay, reaching his destination 30 days after leaving Trois-Rivières. The Indians in his canoe left him to his own resources and, without heeding his remonstrances, set forth for their respective villages, some 20 miles distant. Brébeuf knelt, not to implore succor but to offer thanks to the Providence which had shielded him thus far. Then, rising, he pondered what course to take. He had lived three years in the Huron town of Toanché, but Toanché had ceased to exist. Here Etienne Brûlé, Champlain's adventurous interpreter [see *Huronia's Immortal Scoundrel*, p. 16], had recently been murdered. The inhabitants, dreading the consequences, had deserted the spot and a few miles off built a new town called Ihonatiria.

Brébeuf hid his baggage in the woods and began his search for this new abode. He passed the burned remains of Toanché, saw the charred poles that had formed the frame of his little chapel. Evening was near when he emerged from the forest into a wild clearing and saw the bark roofs of Ihonatiria.

A crowd ran out to meet him. "Echon has come again!" they cried, recognizing the stately figure robed in black. Soon the whole population swarmed about him. There was a certain Awandoay in the village, one of the richest and most hospitable of Hurons—a distinction not easily won where hospitality was universal. His large house was amply stored with beans and corn, and though his prosperity had excited jealousy he had recovered good will by his generosity. Brébeuf first made his abode with Awandoay.

All the other Frenchmen eventually reached Huronia and Brébeuf assembled them at Ihonatiria. The Fathers had planned to establish themselves at Ossossané (which they called Rochelle), the largest and most important town of the Huron confederacy, but Brébeuf now resolved to remain at Ihonatiria. Here he was well known and here too, he flattered himself, seeds of the Faith had been planted which, with good nurture, would in time yield fruit.

By ancient Huron custom, when a man or a family wanted a house—as the Fathers now did—the whole village joined in building one. Both Ihonatiria and the neighboring town of Wenrio took part in the work—though not without the expectation of gifts. The house was constructed after the Huron mode. It was 36 feet long and about 20 wide, with strong sapling poles planted in the earth to form the sides, the ends bent into an arch for the roof, the whole lashed together, braced with cross-poles and covered with overlapping sheets of bark. Without, the structure was strictly Indian; within, the priests, with their tools, made innovations which were the astonishment of all the country. They divided it into three apartments, each with its wooden door, a wondrous novelty to their visitors. The first served as hall, anteroom and place of storage for corn, beans and dried fish. The second and largest was at once kitchen, workshop, dining room, drawing room, schoolroom and bedchamber. The third was the chapel. Here they made their altar, and here were their images, pictures and sacred vessels. Their fire was on the ground, in the middle of the second apartment, the smoke escaping by a hole in the roof. At the sides were two wide platforms, after the Huron fashion, four feet from the earthen floor. On these were chests for clothing and vestments, and beneath them they slept on sheets of bark.

There was no lack of visitors, for the house contained marvels whose fame was noised throughout the Huron nation. Chief among them was a clock. Guests would squat by the hour, waiting to hear it strike; they thought it was alive and asked what it ate. At the last stroke one of the Frenchmen would cry "Stop!" and the obedient clock was silent. A hand mill was another wonder; the Indians never tired of turning it. There was a prism and a magnet, a magnifying glass which transformed a flea into a monster, and a multiplying lens which showed the same object 11 times repeated. "All this," said Brébeuf in a report for the Jesuit *Relations*, "serves to gain their affection, and make them more docile in respect to the admirable and incomprehensible mysteries of our Faith; for the opinion they have of our genius and capacity makes them believe whatever we tell them."

"What does the captain say?" was the frequent question, for so the Hurons designated the clock.

"When he strikes 12 times he says, 'Hang on the kettle,' and when he strikes four times he says, 'Get up and go home.'"

Both interpretations were well remembered. At noon visitors were never wanting to share the Fathers' meal, but at the stroke of four all departed. Now the door was barred and, gathering around the fire, the priests compared experiences and took counsel for the future. But their standing topic was the Huron language they sought to master. In analyzing its construction and deducing its hidden laws, these highly cultivated minds found congenial employment.

Daily they went about their chosen tasks. If someone was sick or suffering they were always at hand with assistance and relief, adding, as they saw opportunity, explanations of Christian doctrine. Their friendly offices also included matters widely different. The Hurons lived in constant fear of the Iroquois. At times, on the rumor of an approaching war party, the whole village population would fly to the woods or to one of the neighboring fortified towns. The Jesuits promised them the aid of the armed Frenchmen who had come with them. They advised the Hurons to make their palisade forts not, as hitherto, in circular form but rectangular, with towers at the corners for the men and their arquebuses.

At every opportunity the missionaries gathered children at their house, where Brébeuf, for greater solemnity, put on a surplice and the close, angular cap worn by Jesuits in convents. He chanted the paternoster, translated by Father Daniel into Huron rhymes, the children chanting in their turn. He taught them the sign of the cross, made them repeat the Ave, the Credo and the Commandments, questioned them as to past instructions, gave them briefly a few ones and dismissed them with a present of two or three beads, raisins or prunes. The priests, with amusement and delight, saw the children gathered in groups about the village, vying in repeating what they had learned.

The elders of the people, the repositories of its ancient traditions, were induced—at times to assemble at the house of the Jesuits, who explained the principal points of doctrine and invited discussion. The Indians proved pliant to a fault but when urged to adopt the Faith they had always the same reply: "It is good for the French but we are another people, with different customs."

Despite all their exhortations, the Jesuits in the first year or more baptized no adults except those at the point of death, for with excellent reason they feared backsliding and recantation. They found special pleasure in the baptism of dying infants, changing them "from little Indians into little angels."

The Fathers' slumbers were brief and broken. Winter was the season of Huron festivity and, as they lay on their hard couches, suffocating with smoke and tormented by fleas, a drum resounded all night long from a neighboring house, mingled with the sound of the tortoise-shell rattle, the stamping of moccasined feet, and voices keeping time with the dancers. Or some villager would give a feast and invite the warriors of the neighboring towns. Or there would be some grand wager of gambling with its attendant drumming, singing and outcries.

But these were light annoyances compared with the insane rites to cure the sick, prescribed by the medicine men or ordained by the eccentric inspiration of dreams. One young sorcerer, by alternate gorging and fasting, joined with excessive exertion in singing to the spirits, contracted a disorder of the brain which caused him, in midwinter, to run about naked, howling like a wolf. The whole population sought a cure. The patient had, or pretended to have, a dream in which the ridiculous conditions of his recovery were revealed. The elders met in council and the villagers lent aid till every requisition was fulfilled and the incongruous mass of gifts the dream demanded were all bestowed. This cure failing, a medicine feast was tried, then several dances. Except the masquerades of the Carnival among Christians, Brébeuf said he never saw a folly equal to a final grand dance: "Some had sacks over their heads with holes for the eyes. Some were naked with horns or feathers on their heads, their bodies painted white, their faces black as devils." The village was a pandemonium. "Truly," Brébeuf wrote, "here is nonsense enough, but I greatly fear there is something more dark and mysterious in it."

But all these ceremonies were outdone by the grand festival of the *Ononhara* or "Dream Feast." This madness began at night. Men, women and children, pretending to have lost their senses, rushed shrieking from house to house, upsetting things, throwing firebrands, beating those they met or drenching them with water and taking safe revenge on any who had ever offended them. In the morning they again ran from house to house, demanding the satisfaction of some secret want revealed in a dream, but giving no hint what it was.

The Jesuits Pierre Pijart and François-Joseph Le Mercier arrived in 1635 and in midsummer 1636 came Isaac Jogues, Pierre Chastellain and Charles Garnier. They were received by their brethren with scanty fare but with a fervor of affectionate welcome. Scarcely had the newcomers arrived when they were attacked by a contagious fever which turned the mission house into a hospital. Those who remained in health attended the sick but scarcely had health begun to revive when the pestilence returned with tenfold violence, and with it a new and fearful scourge—smallpox. Terror was universal, and when winter came, far from ceasing as the priests had hoped, the ravages were appalling. The season of Huron festivity was turned to mourning. Suicide became frequent. The Jesuits, singly or in pairs, journeyed from village to village, ministering to the sick and seeking to commend their religious teachings. They had no medicine but a little senna. A few raisins were left and one or two, with a spoonful of sweetened water, were eagerly accepted by the sufferers, who thought them endowed with some mysterious efficacy.

No house was left unvisited. As the missionary entered one of these smoky dens, he heard the wail of sick and dying children and saw adults, their heads muffled in skins, seated around the fires in silent dejection. The Father spoke words of kindness, administered his harmless remedies or offered broth made from game brought in by the Frenchmen who hunted for the mission. Then he addressed himself to the soul. "This life is short and very miserable. It matters little whether we live or die." The patient remained silent or grumbled dissent. The Jesuit passed to the joys of Heaven and the pains of Hell. His pictures of infernal fires and torturing devils were readily comprehended but he was slow of conviction with respect to the advantages of the French Paradise, "I wish to go where my ancestors have gone," was a common reply. Said one

Huron: "Heaven is a good place for Frenchmen, but I wish to be among Indians, for the French will give me nothing to eat when I get there." Above all other obstacles was the dread of starvation in the regions of the blest. Nor when the dying Indian had been induced to express a desire for Paradise was it easy to bring him to contrition for his sins; he would deny with indignation that he had ever committed any.

Thus did the worthy priests, too conscientious to let these unfortunates die in peace, follow them with benevolent persecutions to the hour of their death.

It was clear to the Fathers that their religion was valued solely because it was supposed by many to be a medicine or charm, efficacious against famine, disease and death. At Wenrio, after trying in vain all the feasts, dances and preposterous ceremonies their medicine men used to try to stop the pest, the Hurons called the priests to council. "What must we do that your God may take pity on us?"

Brébeuf's answer was uncompromising: "Believe in Him, keep His commandments, abjure your faith in dreams, take but one wife and be true to her, give up your superstitious feasts, renounce your assemblies of debauchery, eat no human flesh, never give feasts to demons and make a vow that, if God will deliver you from this pest, you will build a chapel to offer Him thanksgiving and praise."

The terms were too hard. They wanted to be let off with building the chapel alone. The council broke up in despair.

But at Ossossané, a few miles distant, the terrified people accepted the conditions and promised to reform. One of their principal sorcerers proclaimed that the God of the French was their master. "What consolation," wrote Le Mercier, "to see God glorified by the lips of an imp of Satan!"

The Fathers' joy was short. Soon a noted sorcerer came to Ossossané, a dwarfish, humpbacked figure with a vicious face. With 10 or 12 other savages he ensconced himself in a kennel of bark. On several stones, heated red-hot, the sorcerer threw tobacco, producing a stifling fumigation in the midst of which he sang boastful yet meaningless rhapsodies of Indian magical songs. Then came a grand medicine feast—and the Jesuits saw that the objects of their spiritual care were bent on invoking aid from God and the Devil at once.

Opinion was divided as to the nature of the pest but most agreed it was a malignant *oki* (spirit) who came from Lake Huron. To conciliate or frighten him, feasts were held and each guest gorged himself. A mystic fraternity danced with firebrands in their mouths; other dancers wore masks and pretended to be humpbacked. Tobacco was burned to the Demon of the Pest. A chief climbed onto a roof and shouted to the invisible monster, "If you want flesh go to the Iroquois!" To add terror to persuasion, the crowd in the dwelling below yelled and beat sticks on the walls of bark.

Amid all this, the irrepressible Jesuits roamed from town to town in restless quest of subjects for baptism. In the case of adults, their efforts, even with the aid of Saint Joseph whom they constantly invoked, were not always successful. Cheaply though they offered salvation, they sometimes failed to find a purchaser. With infants, however, a drop of water sufficed. But the Indians, who at first had sought baptism as a cure, now began to regard it as a cause of death. Scowling parents watched the priests with distrust lest the deadly drop should be applied. The Jesuits were equal to the emergency. Father Le Mercier told his own story:

"Father Pijart baptized a dying child without being seen by the parents, who would not give their consent. He pretended to make the child drink a little sugared water and at the same time dipped a finger in it. As the father called out to him not to baptize it, he gave the spoon to a woman and said 'Give it to him yourself.' She found the child asleep. Father Pijart, under pretence of seeing if he was really asleep, touched his face with his wet finger and baptized him. At the end of 48 hours he went to Heaven."

This equivocal morality, built on the doctrine that all means are permissible for saving souls, and that sin itself is no sin when its object is the "greater glory of God," found far less scope among the Hurons than among the interests, ambitions and passions of civilized life. But when we see these Jesuits in the gloomy winter of 1637 and the gloomier months that followed, toiling on foot from one infected town to another, all for one sole end, the baptism of the sick and dying, we may smile at the futility of the object, but must admire the zeal with which it was pursued.

In May 1637 Father Pijart went to Ossossanë to found a new mission. The Indians had promised to build a house and Pijart found the work in progress. There were about 50 dwellings in the town, each containing eight or 10 families. A new quadrangular fort had been completed under the instruction of the priests.

The new mission house was about 70 feet long. No sooner did the bark cover its top and sides than the priests took possession and began preparations for a notable ceremony. They made an altar and hung decorations throughout the half of the structure that formed their chapel. On the altar was a crucifix with vessels and ornaments of shining metal; above hung several pictures, among them paintings of Christ, and the Virgin, both life-size. There was also a representation of the Last Judgment with dragons and serpents feasting on the wicked while demons scourged them into Hell. The chapel entrance was adorned with tinsel and green boughs. Never had such splendors been seen in the land of the Hurons. Crowds gathered from afar and gazed in awe.

A great event had called forth all this preparation. Of the many baptisms achieved by the Fathers, the subjects had all been infants or adults near death. But now a Huron in full health and manhood, respected and influential, had been won over and was to be baptized in the new chapel. The house was packed: warriors glistening in grease and sunflower oil, wenches in gay attire, hags muffled in filthy deerskin, their leathery visages corrugated with age and malice, eyes riveted on the spectacle. The priests radiant in surplices, the genuflections, the tinkling of the bell, the swinging of the censer, the sweet odors, the mysterious elevation of the Host (for a Mass followed the baptism), and the agitation of the neophyte, whose Indian imperturbability deserted him—all these combined to produce in the Hurons an impression that seemed to promise a rich harvest for the Faith. To the Jesuits it was a day of triumph and hope; light had dawned on the long night of heathendom.

But they overlooked one thing: the Devil had taken alarm at a conversion which threatened to shake his Huron empire to its foundation. In fury and fear, he put forth all his malice and ingenuity. Such, at least, is the explanation given by the Jesuits of what followed. Let us examine the background.

These priests, mysterious strangers, who had made their abode among them from motives past finding out, marvellous in knowledge, careless of life, had awakened in the breasts of the Hurons mingled wonder, fear, respect and awe. From the first, the Indians had held them answerable for the weather, commending them when crops were abundant, upbraiding them for scarcity. They thought them mighty magicians, masters of life and death, came to them for spells, sometimes to destroy their enemies, sometimes to kill grasshoppers. And now it was whispered that it was they who had bewitched the nation and caused the pest which threatened to exterminate it.

Father Jogues first heard this ominous slander. It spread fast and far. The priests' friends looked at them askance; enemies clamored for their lives. Some said they concealed in their houses an infectious corpse, a notion derived from some half-instructed neophyte concerning the body of Christ in the Eucharist. Others ascribed the evil to a serpent, to a spotted frog, to a demon the priests carried in the barrel of a gun. Others said they had pricked an infant to death with awls to kill Huron children by magic. "Perhaps," observed Father Le Mercier, "the Devil was enraged because we had placed a great many of these little innocents in Heaven."

The picture of the Last Judgment became an object of terror. The dragons and serpents were supposed to be the demons of the pest; the sinners they were devouring were its victims. On a spruce tree at Ihonatiria the priests had fastened a small streamer to show the direction of the wind. This, too, was taken for a charm, giving off disease and death. The clock now excited alarm; the Jesuits had to stop it since, when it struck, it was supposed to signal death.

Had the objects of these charges been Indians, a hatchet would have promptly avenged their sorcery and delivered the country from peril. But the priests inspired a strange awe. Nocturnal councils were held, their death was decreed, and whispering children gazed after them as men doomed to die. They were reviled and upbraided. Boys threw sticks at them.

Yet nothing could divert the Jesuits. They penetrated every house. When they heard a sick infant, no menace and no insult could repel them. They pushed in, asked to buy some trifle, spoke of Iroquois forays, of anything except the pestilence and the sick child. They conversed till suspicion was partially lulled; then, pretending to observe the sufferer for the first time, touched it with a corner of a handkerchief previously dipped in water and snatched another soul from the fangs of the "Infernal Wolf."

In August 1637 the Huron chiefs were summoned to a great council to discuss a crisis that demanded all their wisdom. For, while disease threatened annihilation, the Iroquois infested the outskirts of their towns and murdered them in their fields and forests. The Jesuits, knowing their deep stake in its deliberations, attended the assembly.

The first night was spent discussing treaties and alliances with a deliberation and good sense the Jesuits could not help admiring. Later the assembly took up the question of the epidemic. Deputies from three of the four Huron nations were present, the Jesuits sitting with the Nation of the Bear in whose towns their missions were established. The fires cast an uncertain gleam on the wild and dejected throng that filled the platforms and the floor. "I never saw anything more mournful," wrote Le Mercier. "They looked like men who already feel the terror of death. They spoke with sighs, each reckoning up the sick and dead of his own family. All this was to excite poison against us."

"My brothers," said one old chief, "you know that I rarely speak except in councils of war but since nearly all the other chiefs are dead, I must utter what is in my heart before I follow them to the grave. I have seen other diseases ravaging the country but nothing to compare with this. We have suffered for a year and more and yet the evil does not abate. And what is worst of all, we have not yet discovered its source." Then he accused the Jesuits of causing the unparalleled calamities.

Brébeuf rose and exposed the absurdities of the chief's statements, whereupon another accuser brought new charges. A clamor arose and the whole assembly called upon Brébeuf to give up a certain charmed cloth as the cause of their miseries. The missionary protested that he had no such cloth. "Then tell us the cause of the pest," the Hurons cried.

Brébeuf, mingling his explanations with Christian exhortations, was continually interrupted, and he was again called upon to produce the charmed cloth. The debate continued till after midnight. One old chief, as he left, said to Brébeuf: "If some young man should split your head, we should have nothing to say." As the priest continued to harangue those who remained, the chief of Ossossané called out: "What sort of men are these? They are always saying the same thing. They are never done with telling us what their *oki* demands and what he forbids, and Paradise and Hell."

"Here was the end of this miserable council," wrote Le Mercier. "If less evil came of it than was designed, we owe it, after God, to the Most Holy Virgin, to whom we had made a vow of nine Masses in honor of her Immaculate Conception."

The Fathers had escaped for the time but were still in deadly peril. None dared openly take their part. The few recent converts warned that their death was determined. Their house was set on fire. In public every face was averted from them. A new council was called to pronounce the decree of death. They appeared before it with such unflinching assurance that their judges postponed sentence. Yet it seemed impossible that they should much longer escape, and Brébeuf wrote a letter of farewell to his superior, Father Paul Le Jeune at Quebec, and confided it to some converts he could trust to carry it there.

"We are perhaps," he said, "about to give our lives in the cause of our Master, Jesus Christ. It seems that His goodness will accept this sacrifice, as regards me, in expiation of my numberless sins, and that He will thus crown the past services and ardent desires of all our Fathers here . . . Blessed be His name forever, that He has chosen us to aid Him to bear His cross in this land!" He told Le Jeune that he had directed the sacred vessels, and all else belonging to the services of the altar, to be placed in case of his death in the hands of a convert, and that special care would be taken to preserve a dictionary and other writings on the Huron language.

The imperilled Jesuits now took a very wise step. They gave one of those farewell feasts—*festins d'adieu*—which Huron custom enjoined on those about to die, whether in the course of nature or by execution. It was a declaration that the priests knew their danger and did not shrink from it. Brébeuf addressed a packed house on God, Paradise and Hell. The throng listened in gloomy silence and each departed leaving utter doubt as to his feelings. From this time forth, however, the clouds that overhung the Fathers became less threatening. Voices rose in their defence and looks were less constantly averted. They ascribed the change to Saint Joseph.

Whatever the cause, when they went out in the morning it was no longer with the expectation of having a hatchet struck into their brains. Their persecution as sorcerers continued intermittently, however, for years, and several escaped death very narrowly. Yet the belief that these persecutions stemmed from the Devil, driven by them to desperation, was an unfailing consolation. In all the copious records of this dark period, not a line gives occasion to suspect that one of this loyal band flinched or hesitated. As their numbers gradually increased, the iron Brébeuf, the gentle Garnier, the all-enduring Jogues, the enthusiastic Le Mercier, Chastellain, Daniel, Pijart, Paul Ragueneau, François Du Peron, Joseph-Antoine Poncet, Simon Le Moyne, Gabriel Lalemant, Pierre Chaumonot—all bore themselves with a tranquil boldness which amazed the Indians and enforced their respect.

Father Lalemant, in his journal of 1639, drew an evil augury for the mission because as yet no priest had been put to death—inasmuch as it was a received maxim that the blood of the martyrs was the seed of the Church. He hoped that the daily life of the missionaries might

631

From Sainte-Marie in Huronia came six of North America's eight martyr saints.

be accepted as a living martyrdom since abuse and threats, the smoke, fleas and filth of the Indian lodges, and cold, hunger and ceaseless anxiety were a portion to which many might prefer the stroke of a tomahawk.

But the Huron church was not destined to suffer from a lack of martyrdom.

It had been the first purpose of the Jesuits to form permanent missions in each of the principal Huron towns but before the close of the year

1639 the difficulties and risks had become fully apparent. They resolved, therefore, to establish one central station as a base of operations and a focus whence the Faith should radiate through the wilderness. It was to serve as residence, fort, powder magazine, hospital and convent. Hence the priests would set forth on expeditions far and near, and hither they might retire in sickness or extreme peril. Here the neophytes could be gathered safe from perverting influences, and here in time a Christian settlement might thrive, Hurons mingled with Frenchmen.

The site of the new station was admirably chosen. The little river Wye flows from the south into Lake Huron's Matchedash Bay; about a mile from its mouth it passes through a small lake. The Jesuits chose the right bank of the Wye, where it issues from this lake, gained permission to build from the Indians, though not without difficulty, and began their labors with an abundant energy and a very deficient supply of workmen and tools. A house at Teanaustayé and the house and chapel at Ossossané were abandoned. The new establishment was called Sainte-Marie. On one hand, it had a short water communication with Lake Huron; on the other, its central position gave ready access to every part of the Huron territory.

Jesuit pens have told us little of Sainte-Marie, and even this is to be gathered chiefly from incidental allusions in the *Relations* and letters of the priests. The fortified work was in the form of a parallelogram about 175 feet long and up to 90 wide. It lay parallel with the river. On two sides it was a continuous wall of masonry flanked with square bastions adapted to musketry and probably used as magazines, storehouses or lodgings. The sides toward the river and the lake had no other defences than a ditch and palisade—flanked, like the others, by bastions, each displaying a large cross. The buildings within, no doubt of wood, included a church, a kitchen, a refectory, places of retreat for religious instruction and meditation, and lodgings for at least 60 persons. Near the church but outside the fortification was a cemetery. Beyond the ditch or canal which opened on the river was a large area in the form of an irregular triangle, surrounded by a ditch and apparently by palisades. It seems to have been for the protection of Indian visitors who came in throngs and were lodged in a large bark house. Here, perhaps, was also the hospital, placed without the walls so Indian women, as well as men, might be admitted.

No doubt the buildings were of the roughest—rude walls of boards, windows without glass, vast chimneys of unhewn stone. All its riches were centred in the church, which was regarded by the Indians as one of the wonders of the world but would have made but a beggarly show in France.

One wonders, at first thought, how so much labor could have been accomplished here. As the years went by, however, the number of men at the command of the mission increased considerably. Soldiers had been sent up from time to time. Thus 20 men of a reinforcement just arrived from France in 1644 had been sent as an escort and to remain during the winter, lodging with the Jesuits and living at their table. It was not, however, on troops that the Fathers mainly relied for labor or defence. Any inhabitant of Canada who chose to undertake so hard and dangerous a service was allowed to do so, receiving only his maintenance from the mission, without pay. In return, he was allowed to trade with the Indians and sell furs at a fixed price. Many availed themselves of this permission and all whose services were accepted by the Jesuits seem to have been enthusiastically attached to their order and their cause. There is abundant evidence that most of them acted from motives wholly disinterested. They were, in fact, so-called *donnés* of the mission, laymen given heart and hand to its service. It is probable, indeed, that the profits of their trade with the Indians were reaped for the mission. It is difficult otherwise to explain a statement in a letter to the General of the Jesuits at Rome: "Though our number is greatly increased, and though we still hope for more men and especially for more priests of our Society, it is not necessary to increase the pecuniary aid given us."

Much of this prosperity was no doubt due to excellent management of resources and a very successful agriculture. The French raised maize in such quantities that eventually it was thought their provisions might suffice for three years. Hunting and fishing improved and they had fowls, swine and even cattle. How they got cattle to Sainte-Marie is difficult to conceive. The astonishing feat helps indicate a fixed resolve to build up a solid and permanent establishment.

It is by no means to be inferred that the household fared sumptuously. Their ordinary food was maize, pounded and boiled, and seasoned with morsels of smoked fish—in the absence of salt (regarded as a luxury).

At the peak there were in the Huron country and its neighborhood 18 Jesuit priests, four lay brothers, 23 men serving without pay, seven hired men, four boys and eight soldiers. At Sainte-Marie all was method, discipline and subordination. Some men were assigned to household work, some to the hospital; the rest labored at the fortifications, tilled the fields and stood ready to fight the Iroquois. The Father Superior, with two priest-assistants, controlled and guided all. The remaining Jesuits were devoted to their respective missions, spread through the countryside. Two or three times a year all the priests assembled at Sainte-Marie to take counsel and determine future action. Hither also they came at intervals for meditation and prayer.

Besides being a citadel and magazine, Sainte-Marie was the scene of a bountiful hospitality for the increasing number of converts. Every

635

alternate Saturday and on feast days they came in crowds from the farthest villages. They were entertained Saturday, Sunday and part of Monday and the rites of the Church were celebrated with all possible solemnity and pomp. They were welcomed also at other times, and entertained usually with three meals to each. In the later years of the mission prevailing famine drove them to Sainte-Marie in swarms. In 1647 some 3,000 were lodged and fed; the next year the number doubled. Heathen Indians were also received and supplied with food but not permitted to remain at night. Christian or heathen, few left without a word of exhortation. Charity was an instrument of conversion.

Such, so far as we can reconstruct it, was this singular establishment, at once military, monastic and patriarchal. The missions of which it was the basis were now 11 in number; two were in the neighboring Tobacco nation, three among Algonkin tribes.

Gradually but inexorably, over a period of years, a great shadow lengthened over the Huron nation and the mission linked with it. With Dutch traders on the East Coast providing both encouragement and firearms, the fierce Iroquois became the pirates of the fur trade, blockaded rivers, captured convoys, pillaged and massacred in raids on the French settlements on the St. Lawrence. At Ossernenon (near modern-day Auriesville, N.Y.) they put to death by torture Father Jogues and two *donnés,* and their successes led ultimately to a broad and deadly plan: the extermination of a Huron people whose population had been cut by warfare and by the ravages of smallpox, influenza and dysentery, from some 30,000 to 12,000.

By 1647 fear of the Iroquois had become so great that the Hurons sent no furs to Quebec. The following year they resolved at all risks to make the attempt, for the kettles, hatchets and knives of the French traders had become necessaries of life. Some 250 of their best warriors made the voyage in safety to Trois-Rivières and there promptly discovered, attacked and routed a large body of Iroquois, who had been lurking in the forest, watching their opportunity to strike. When their trade was ended, the Hurons returned home in triumph, decorated with the laurels and scalps of victory. It would have been well had they remained to defend their families and firesides.

Teanaustayé, or Saint-Joseph, lay on the southeastern frontier of the Huron country, about 15 miles from Sainte-Marie. It had been the chief town of the nation and was still large, with at least 2,000 inhabitants. It was well fortified with palisades and was esteemed the chief bulwark of the country. Here countless Iroquois had been burned and devoured. Its people had been truculent heathen but many now had surrendered to the *faith*; for four years Father Daniel had preached among them with excellent results.

On the sunny morning of July 4, 1648, you might have mounted the rising ground on which the town stood and passed unchallenged through the opening in the palisade. Within, you would have seen the crowded dwellings of bark decorated with the totems or armorial devices of their owners. Girls chatted in the shade, old squaws pounded corn in large wooden mortars, youths gambled with cherry stones on a wooden platter, and naked infants crawled in the dust. Scarcely a warrior was to be seen. Some were out after game or Iroquois scalps, some had gone with the trading party to the French settlements. The church was full. Daniel had just finished the Mass when voices shrill with terror burst upon the languid town: "The Iroquois! The Iroquois!"

Hostile warriors were rushing across the clearing, toward the opening in the palisade. Daniel hurried to the point of danger. Some Hurons snatched weapons; some rushed to and fro in blind panic. The priest rallied the defenders, promised Heaven to those who died for their homes and their faith, then hastened from house to house, calling on unbelievers to repent and receive baptism. They crowded around him, imploring to be saved. Immersing his handkerchief in a bowl of water, he shook it over them and baptized them by aspersion. They pursued him to the church where he found a throng of women, children and old men, some crying for baptism, some for absolution, and some wailing in terror. "Brothers," he exclaimed as he shook the baptismal drops from his handkerchief, "brothers, today we shall be in Heaven."

Fierce war whoops rose close at hand. The palisade was forced. The enemy was in the town. "Fly!" screamed the priest, driving his flock before him. "I will stay here. We shall meet again in Heaven." Many of them did escape but Daniel would not follow while there might be souls to rescue. The hour had come for which he had long prepared himself. He came forth from the church to meet the Iroquois. When they saw him radiant in his vestments, confronting them with the inspiration of martyrdom, they stared in amazement, then showered him with arrows. A gunshot followed and he fell dead, gasping the name of Jesus. They rushed upon him, stripped him naked, hacked his body and bathed their faces in his blood to make them brave. The town was in a blaze; when the flames reached the church, they flung the priest into it.

When the town was ashes, the victors took up their march with nearly 700 prisoners, many of whom they killed on the way. Many more had been slain in the town and the neighboring forest, where the pursuers hunted them down and where women were betrayed by the cries of their infants.

A neighboring fortified town, part of Daniel's mission, shared the fate of Teanaustayé. Never had the Huron nation received such a blow.

More than eight months passed. The winter came and went. Around Sainte-Marie the forests were gray and bare; in the cornfields the half-thawed soil showed itself in patches through the melting snow.

At nine o'clock on the morning of March 16, 1649, the priests saw heavy smoke over the forest toward the southeast, about three miles distant. They looked at one another in dismay as flames mingled with the smoke. "The Iroquois! They're burning Saint-Louis!" Two Christian Hurons, breathless and aghast, came from the burning town. The Iroquois had entered the heart of the Huron country, undiscovered, through the wide gap created by the destruction of the two towns the previous July. Common vigilance and common sense would have averted calamity, but the Hurons were like a doomed people, stupefied, sunk in dejection, fearing everything yet taking no measures for defence. They could easily have met the invaders with double their force but the warriors lay idle in their towns or hunted at leisure in distant forests. Nor could the Jesuits rouse them to face the danger.

Before daylight of the 16th the Iroquois had approached Saint-Ignace which, with Saint-Louis and three other towns, formed one mission. They reconnoitred in the darkness and found it defended on three sides by a deep ravine and further strengthened by palisades up to 16 feet high. On the fourth side it was protected by unguarded palisades alone. Most of the population had abandoned the town, thinking it too much exposed to the enemy, and there remained only about 400, chiefly women, children and old men. Their defenders were away hunting or on futile scalping parties against the Iroquois. Just before dawn a yell as of devils startled the inhabitants from their sleep. The Iroquois, bursting in, cut them down with knives and hatchets, killing many and reserving the rest for torture. Only three Hurons escaped.

The Iroquois left a guard to hold the town and secure the retreat of the main body in case of a reverse. Then, smearing their faces with blood, they rushed, in the dim early dawn, toward Saint-Louis.

The number of inhabitants here at this time was less than 700. All who had strength to escape, except about 80 warriors, fled in wild terror when the three survivors from Saint-Ignace arrived. Many of the old, sick and decrepit were left in the lodges. The warriors, ignorant of the Iroquois' strength, sang war songs and resolved to hold the place to the last. It had not the natural strength of Saint-Ignace but was surrounded by palisades.

Here were Brébeuf and Lalemant. Brébeuf's converts entreated him to escape but he had no thought of flight. His post was in the teeth of danger, to cheer on those who fought and to open Heaven to those who fell. Lalemant, slight and frail, trembled despite himself, but deep enthusiasm mastered the weakness of nature and he, too, refused to fly.

Scarcely had the sun risen, scarcely were the fugitives gone when the Iroquois rushed to the assault. Yell echoed yell, shot answered shot. The Hurons fought on their ramparts and with arrows, stones and a few guns killed 30 of their assailants and wounded many more. Twice the Iroquois recoiled, and twice renewed the attack. They swarmed at the palisades and hacked with hatchets till they had cut through at several points. There was a deadly fight at these breaches. Here were the two priests, promising Heaven to those who died for their faith—one giving baptism, the other absolution.

At length the Iroquois broke in and captured all the surviving defenders, the Jesuits among them. They set the town on fire and those who had been unable to fly were consumed. Next they fell upon Brébeuf and Lalemant, stripped them, bound them and led them with the other prisoners back to Saint-Ignace, where all turned out to beat the two priests savagely with sticks and clubs.

The victors divided into bands to burn neighboring villages and, in the flush of triumph, meditated a bolder enterprise. In the afternoon, their chiefs sent small parties to reconnoitre Sainte-Marie.

There the priests Paul Ragueneau and François-Joseph Bressani and their companions waited. On one hand they trembled for Brébeuf and Lalemant; on the other they looked hourly for attack. At evening they saw Iroquois scouts prowling the edge of the forest. They had with them about 40 well-armed Frenchmen, but their palisades and wooden buildings were not fireproof. They stood guard all night, praying above all to their great patron, Saint Joseph, whose festival was close at hand.

639

In the morning they were relieved by the arrival of about 300 Huron warriors, chiefly converts, tolerably well armed and full of fight. They were expecting others; meanwhile, several bands took post in the neighboring forest, hoping to waylay parties of the enemy.

At this time 200 Iroquois were making their way from Saint-Ignace, in advance of the main body, to begin the attack on Sainte-Marie. They fell in with a band of Hurons, killed many, drove the rest in terror through the snow to within sight of Sainte-Marie. The other Hurons, hearing the yells and firing, ran to the rescue and attacked so fiercely that the Iroquois in turn were routed, and ran for the gutted Saint-Louis. There the palisade was still standing, though breached and broken. The Iroquois rushed in, Hurons at their heels. Many Iroquois were captured, the rest killed or routed.

The Iroquois who escaped fled to Saint-Ignace. Here they found their own main body, and the whole angry swarm turned toward Saint-Louis to take revenge.

Now ensued one of the most furious Indian battles on record. The Hurons within the palisade did not much exceed 150, for many had been killed or disabled and many, perhaps, had straggled away. Most of their enemies had guns, while they had few. Their weapons were bows and arrows, war clubs, hatchets and knives, and of these they made good use, fighting like devils and driving back their assailants again and again. The scout from Sainte-Marie heard far into the night the howl of battle rising from the darkened forest. The principal chief of the Iroquois was severely wounded and nearly 100 Iroquois warriors were killed. When at length their numbers and fury prevailed, their only prize was some 20 Huron warriors. The rest lay dead around the shattered palisades they had so valiantly defended.

Lamps burned all night at Sainte-Marie and its defenders stood watch till daylight. Not an Iroquois appeared. All the next day, the 18th, there was a stillness like the dead lull of a tempest.

The following day, the festival of Saint Joseph, Indians came with tidings that panic had seized the Iroquois and that they were retreating in disorder, possessed with a vague terror that the Hurons were upon them in force. They had found time, however, to plant stakes in the bark houses of Saint-Ignace and bind the inhabitants side by side, male and female, from old age to infancy, husbands, mothers and children. Then, as they retreated, they set the town on fire and laughed with glee at the shrieks of anguish.

"Noble Death of Certain Fathers" (1660) is a composite of incidents in 1646-50.

They loaded prisoners with their baggage and plunder and drove them southward through the forest, braining with their hatchets any who gave out on the march.

On the morning of the 20th one priest and seven armed Frenchmen set out from Sainte-Marie. In Saint-Ignace they saw a spectacle of horror: the ashes, the half-consumed bodies of those who had perished in the flames—and the scorched and mangled bodies of Brébeuf and Lalemant.

They had already learned the two priests' fate from Hurons who had escaped in the confusion of the Iroquois retreat. Brébeuf, bound to a stake, had addressed his captive converts in a loud voice, exhorting them to suffer patiently and promising Heaven as their reward. The Iroquois, incensed, scorched him from head to foot, whereupon, in the tone of a master, he threatened them with everlasting flames. As he continued to speak, they cut away his lower lip and thrust a red-hot iron down his throat. Still he held his tall form erect and defiant, with no sign or sound

641

of pain, and they tried another means to overcome him. They led out Lalemant, strips of bark smeared with pitch about his naked body. When he saw Brébeuf, he called out with a broken voice in the words of Saint Paul, "We are made a spectacle to the world, to angels and to men." When he threw himself at Brébeuf's feet, the Iroquois made him fast to a stake and set fire to the bark that enveloped him. As the flame rose, he threw his arms upward with a shriek of supplication to Heaven. Next they hung around Brébeuf's neck a collar of hatchets heated red-hot. The priest stood like a rock. A Huron, once a convert but now an Iroquois by adoption, called out with the malice of a renegade to pour boiling water on their heads, since they had poured so much cold water on those of others. "We baptize you," they cried, "that you may be happy in Heaven, for nobody can be saved without a good baptism." Brébeuf would not flinch so they cut strips of flesh from his limbs and devoured them before his eyes. Other renegade Hurons called out to him: "You told us that the more one suffers on earth the happier he is in Heaven. We wish to make you happy; we torment you because we love you; and you ought to thank us for it." Finally they scalped him, laid open his breast and came to drink the blood of so valiant an enemy. A chief then tore out his heart and devoured it.

Thus died Jean de Brébeuf, the founder of the Huron mission, its truest hero and its greatest martyr. To the last he refused to flinch, and "his death was the astonishment of his murderers."

Lalemant, physically weak from childhood, slender almost to emaciation, was tortured all night, then killed with a hatchet.

The two bodies were carried to Sainte-Marie and buried in its cemetery.

All was over with the Hurons. The death knell of their nation had struck. Without a leader, without organization, without union, crazed with fright and paralyzed with misery, they yielded to their doom without a blow. Their only thought was flight. Within two weeks after the disasters of Saint-Ignace and Saint-Louis, 15 Huron towns were abandoned, and the greater number burned, lest they should give shelter to the Iroquois. The last year's harvest had been scanty; the fugitives had no food, and they left behind them the fields in which was their only hope of obtaining it. In bands, large and small, some roamed northward and eastward, through the half-thawed wilderness; some hid themselves on the rocks or islands of Lake Huron; some sought an asylum among other tribes.

The Jesuits, determined to carry on, made plans to re-establish their mission to the west, on Manitoulin Island. Then, fatefully, they were persuaded by the representatives of several hundred Huron families to join them on St. Joseph Island, off the mainland of devastated Huronia. It was a heartbreaking act to "forsake our second fatherland, our home of innocent delights," but the Jesuits burned Sainte-Marie to the ground and floated anything worth saving to their new home.

It was a tragic choice. The winter of 1649-50 brought despair, famine and disease. The Iroquois swept in again, to the shores opposite the island. They killed Father Garnier at his mission among the Petuns. A renegade Huron tomahawked Father Noël Chabanel.

On June 30, 1650, some 300 Hurons and the Jesuits who had come to convert them fled once more, this time all the way to Quebec where the Indians had been promised a place of refuge.

"It was not without tears," wrote Father Ragueneau, the last Superior, "that we left a country which we loved, a country watered with the blood of our brothers."

Nearly three centuries later, in 1930, Pope Pius XI bestowed the titles saint and martyr on eight of the Jesuit missionaries of New France: Jean de Brébeuf, Isaac Jogues, Gabriel Lalemant, Charles Garnier, Antoine Daniel, Noël Chabanel, René Goupil and Jean de la Lande. Today at Midland, Ont., a replica of Sainte-Marie stands on the bank of the Wye River below a hill crowned by the Martyrs' Shrine. Not far away is a reconstruction of the sort of 17th-century Huron village that drew the Jesuits to this land.

A Tibetan Tragedy

*Few 19th-century Christian missionaries ventured
into the remote mountains of Tibet, in southwestern
China. But in 1895 Dr. Susie Carson Rijnhart,
a graduate of Women's Medical College in Toronto,
and her Dutch husband, Petrus Rijnhart,
established a tiny mission near the Buddhist lamasery
of Kumbum. Their son Charles was born in
July 1897. Twelve months later, the Rijnharts set
forth on an expedition into the heart of Tibet,
seeking to spread the Gospel. Their goal was the
forbidden city of Lhasa, not seen by Westerners
in half a century. This excerpt from her 1901 book,*
WITH THE TIBETANS IN TENT AND TEMPLE, *is an
account of that tragic journey.*

By SUSIE CARSON RIJNHART

OUR ROUTE TO THE HOLY CITY of Lhasa lay southwest across the Kunlun Mountains into the strange, hostile reaches of Inner Tibet. Once over the Kunluns, the natives said, travellers were certain to encounter formidable dangers in the shapes of passes, rivers and robbers. But the Lord had opened many doors for us in China, and we were confident He would open others.

Having learned that a party of Mongols were crossing the mountains on their way to Lhasa, we decided to follow them by two days. Otherwise we might miss the trail where it was not distinct. A young lama (Buddhist monk) was travelling with them and he told us when the caravan would leave. The morning after his tent was missing, we made our way to the last halting place on the Tsaidam plain north of the mountains, and camped on the bank of a large stream. All of us—Petrus and I, our infant son Charles, our friend Rahim and our two guides—prepared for the long climb the following day.

Shortly after daybreak we began our ascent along a dry watercourse. Strewn here and there were dead yaks, many reduced to skeletons. We camped some distance from the summit, in a beautiful recess in the hills. As we looked down upon the plain we had just crossed, it seemed to belong to another world.

Our journey soon turned into a series of ups and downs—the road continually ascending or descending, grass and firewood abundant one day, scarce the next. One night the rain fell in torrents, and the next morning the men had to travel 10 miles for firewood. At times yak horns and the roots of small plants were our only fuel—scarcely sufficient to heat the water for tea and to make baby's food.

Travelling southwest, we forded a river barely passable after the heavy rains. The tedious march along the swampy riverbank in search of a camp with good grass and spring water discouraged our guides. They became less and less amiable and one morning we arose and found they had left. My husband and Rahim rode off to try to bring them back, leaving Charlie and me with Topsy, our dog, high in a sheltered nook.

Occasionally a chill would pierce my heart: *what if an accident should prevent their return?* A garment being knitted for baby grew very rapidly under my fingers that day, and great was the rejoicing when, late in the afternoon, the jaded horses bore their riders home, even though they returned without the guides.

After a rest of four days we rearranged our loads and continued our journey. It snowed and hailed at about noon almost every day. We experienced considerable difficulty fording one of the headwaters of the Yangtze, for small sand bars separated the river into several branches. In the first branch our horses sank into quicksand, and had Rahim not been an expert we would have lost several loads; the last branch was very deep and all the horses had to swim. Then we crossed a shaking bog which well-nigh exhausted our animals. It seemed that at every step we would sink into the depths of the earth. Dead horses and camels were strewn along the way.

On Aug. 10 we reached another high water of the Yangtze. We skirted its banks, looking for a place to cross, when in the distance we saw 14 white tents, with about 1,500 yaks and many horses. We rode up and were received in a very friendly manner. The travellers were on their way north, so we sent messages with them back to our friends. Though they wanted us to camp beside them we went on to cross the river.

That night we had the worst storm we had yet experienced, but we steadied the tent poles and in time all danger was past. Later on somebody must have visited our camp, for next morning five of our best animals were gone. They had undoubtedly been stolen. We traced them to a river crossing where we found signs of another horse and a dog. We resumed travel in very short stages.

Wild animals abounded. One day we surprised a herd of yaks which, on seeing us, dashed headlong across a stream, their tails high. Bears and antelope were visible everywhere.

On Aug. 21, after ascending for several days, we found ourselves travelling directly south. In front of us towered the Tanglha Mountains, snow-clad and sun-kissed. Beyond lay the district of Lhasa, where the Dalai Lama exercised supreme power and the teachings of the Gospel were unknown. We hoped to obtain permission to reside in Lhasa, so it seemed that our journey was almost at an end. This hope, and the fact that our darling now had eight teeth shining white above the gums, revived our spirits.

The morning of the darkest day in our lives arose bright and full of promise. Riding along, we talked of the future, of the possibility of going [farther southwest] to India when our stay in the interior was over, and of then going home to Canada and my husband's native Holland before we returned to Tibet.

Suddenly a herd of yaks on a riverbank tempted Rahim away to try a shot, but the animals, scenting danger, ran away. Then across the river we saw other yaks coming toward us. They were tame, driven by four mounted men who quickly crossed our path when they saw us, and disappeared. Carefully we selected a campsite hidden by little hills.

Baby, meanwhile, had fallen asleep. Rahim dismounted and took him from his father's arms so he might not be disturbed until the tent was pitched and his food prepared. Rahim laid him down and, while I was kneeling to cover the infant comfortably, his appearance caught my attention. He was unconscious! A great fear chilled me. I called out to my husband. I loosened baby's garments, chafed his wrists, performed artificial respiration, and prayed fervently to Him who holds all life in His hands, to let us have our darling child.

Our efforts were of no use. The little flower blooming on the bleak and barren mountainside had been plucked and transplanted, to bask and bloom forever in the sunshine of God's love. We lifted our hearts in prayer, we tried to be submissive, but the fact stared us in the face; it was written on the rocks; it reverberated through the mountain silence: little Charlie was dead.

Our drug box, emptied of its contents and lined with towels, served as a coffin, which I prepared while Petrus and Rahim dug the grave. I robed baby in white flannel and laid him on his side. In his hand I placed a little bunch of wild asters and blue poppies which Rahim had gathered. Many of Charlie's belongings were put into the coffin, accompanied by our names written on a piece of linen. Then there was the agony of the last look. It seemed more than we could endure.

The little box was lowered as the three of us stood over the grave. Petrus conducted the burial service and the cold earth of Tibet closed over the body of the first Christian child committed to its bosom: Charles Carson Rijnhart, aged one year, one month and 22 days. Petrus and Rahim rolled a large boulder over the grave to keep animals from digging it up. That night the sky was unusually dark. Thunder rolled, lightning flashed and rain fell in torrents and turned to snow as the wind grew colder. We could not sleep.

How I missed him the next morning! Petrus tenderly placed me in my saddle and, all three of us sobbing, we tore ourselves away. On the bank of a stream we saw some bears with their cubs digging for roots, and we felt thankful for the boulder over the little grave.

After the first sudden descent on the south side of the Tanglha, the road led down gradually for days and was comparatively easy travelling. It was warm when the sun shone but there was almost an inch of frost on the night of Aug. 25 and the firewood was wet. We went supperless to bed and the next day, having had no breakfast, we approached the first encampment of nomads we had seen in Tibet, on the opposite bank of a river. Two heavily armed men came over, rode close behind us, then returned to the opposite bank without saying a word.

No one else came near our camp and we were not anxious to court interference, so we stayed away from their tents. In the night one of our horses died, and the next morning Rahim and Petrus had to take turns walking and riding. After three hours, we met eight armed riders. They asked us what we had and where we were going. Soon two rode on ahead, evidently to report our presence. This was apparently a government patrol from Nagchuka [135 miles northeast of Lhasa]. We pushed on as far as we could that day. But as we neared a river, one of the men told us to camp there until their companions returned with permission for us to proceed.

We camped about 100 yards from where the Tibetans pitched their ragged brown tent. They were friendly but they told Rahim no foreigner had ever passed that place, and they did not intend to allow us to. We resolved to get away. In the dead of night, while they slept soundly, we arose stealthily, packed our loads, took down our tent and rode off.

Daybreak found us descending a stony road, but soon we reached a plain dotted with tents. A man rode up, pointed to his tents, and invited us to stay near him and do some trading. The ground was wet from frost, so we postponed pitching our tent. While we waited for the ground to dry, our "guards" of the previous night came galloping toward us. Dismounting and throwing themselves on the ground beside us, they laughed heartily. We were smart, they told us, to have escaped as we did! So thoroughly do the Tibetans enjoy outwitting their neighbors, it seems, that they can display their approval when they themselves are outwitted.

We spent two days in this encampment doing considerable bartering, for we were in need of meat, butter and milk.

The second day after we resumed our journey we were confronted by nearly 40 soldiers. One of them, dressed in woollens, invited Petrus to enter their outpost tent to drink tea. When my husband laughingly declined, saying we would soon be camping nearby anyway, they said their *ponbo* (chief) was coming to see us. The situation was becoming delicate. Petrus put them in good humor by giving one of the men's prayer wheels a turn in the right direction, thereby showing his knowledge of their ceremonial. Thus, amid politeness on both sides, we went our way, leaving them kindly disposed, yet staring in consternation.

A man soon rode past us on the gallop, presumably on his way to notify the *ponbo* that the foreigners had succeeded in getting by the guard. We were soon overtaken by several of the men, who rode alongside and conversed pleasantly. We saw many camels and yaks and clusters of the nomads' black tents; we knew we were approaching Nagchuka. Toward evening a storm forced us to make camp just short of the outskirts of the village. Some of the men we had seen at the outpost tent came to our fire and informed us that we were to stay put, because in the morning their *ponbo* would see us. My husband replied that we would have breakfast, pack our loads, and then, if the *ponbo* had not arrived, we would slowly make our way to him.

We knew we had not yet met anyone with any real authority to stop us. Surely the *ponbo ch'enpo* (high official) of Nagchuka was too exalted a dignitary to travel any distance to meet such a small caravan as ours.

The hard travelling had prepared us for an undisturbed night's rest, and the sun was shedding its warmth on our tent when there was an excited cry at our door. Peering out, we saw a crowd of people erecting a huge white and blue tent. About 10 o'clock the *ponbo ch'enpo*, accompanied by a large retinue, rode up on a chestnut horse richly caparisoned with red and gold. We were soon invited to visit him; we donned our best clothing and went to the big tent.

We beheld a sumptuous interior: beautiful mats lined the sides, and the far end was covered with rich Turkish rugs. On a dais of mats filled with wool sat the *ponbo ch'enpo*, a handsome lama about 35, with fine features, a small black mustache and a shaven head. He was dressed in richly brocaded silks. At his left sat an elderly Chinese official.

They invited us to take seats behind little carved tables. As a mark of honor tea was poured into our basins from the same pot from which the *ponbo* received his. We gave him a satin *khata* (ceremonial scarf) which he accepted, looking a little surprised at our knowledge of Tibetan customs. He said that no foreigner had ever been to Nagchuka, that he could not permit us to go farther into Tibet, and that we must return the way we had come. My husband replied that he was not a traveller just passing through the country; he had lived among the Tibetans for years, and we would not go back to China proper. The *ponbo* looked perplexed, but replied that he could not forcibly stop us; if he allowed us to proceed, however, he would be beheaded. Petrus laughed and said he knew that in the Tibetans' sacred books a man is forbidden to destroy life, even that of a louse.

How strange it was, the young chief remarked, to meet foreigners who knew the Tibetans' customs, spoke their language, wore their clothes and had even read their sacred literature. He told us that if we went on, he would have to send word ahead, and we would be met by a chief of greater power who would have the authority to stop us. Our conference lasted a long time, but when we rose to withdraw, nothing had been settled. My husband declared that he would rather be beheaded than return by the route over which we had come.

Almost immediately on our return to our own tent some Tibetans brought us a bag of rice, one of flour, two large bricks of good tea, and a skin containing four pounds of butter. A message from the *ponbo* informed us that the gifts were from him, and that as soon as the flocks were driven in, we would also be given a fat sheep. That night soldiers were stationed in front of our tent.

We had pitched it in a low, damp place, so we moved the following morning to a spot in the midst of a large colony of tents. After we were settled, some of the *ponbo*'s men came to inform us that their chief was glad we had moved to a better place, but we were not to move again until we started for China. Evidently the tent dwellers had received instructions not to talk to us; not a soul came to barter or chat. Only the government people visited us.

The whole object of our journey was to come into contact with people. We feared that if we continued south, this object would be frustrated by the orders of the chiefs. Thus we decided either to spend the winter in Nagchuka, if we could gain permission, or yield to the *ponbo*'s desire that we go back toward China—and winter someplace on the road.

But the next time we visited the *ponbo*, we did not find him so polite as before. Our tea was now poured from a different pot. We were denied permission to winter in Nagchuka, and when we requested fresh horses in exchange for our tired ones, the chief said yaks were better. He refused to allow Rahim, a Tibetan, to go to his home in Ladakh, but insisted that all three of us go back to China together. We returned to our tent and decided we would stay indefinitely until the *ponbo* arranged things to suit us.

The next day his *kao-yeh* (secretary) came to ask on what conditions we would journey toward Tatsienlu [more than 500 miles east] in China proper. We replied that we needed three guides who knew the road, and fresh horses. The next day four of our horses were traded and we received two extra ones.

That evening we settled with Rahim who, according to our agreement with the *ponbo*, would be permitted to go on to Ladakh. We gave Rahim 40 ounces of silver, a carbine and cartridges, a horse, and as much food as he wanted. He would travel with us the first day, then branch off on his own.

At 11 the following morning (Sept. 6) our three guides appeared on small, graceful ponies, each leading another pony laden with food and pots. They also had two sheep which, with ours, would provide us with fresh meat for some time. Amid a crowd of spectators, the *ponbo*'s steward instructed our guides to take us to the lamasery of Tashi Gomba where we would seek permission from the abbot to remain all winter. Then the guides were to return home. But if we couldn't obtain permission, they were to accompany us to Jyekundo. Upon arrival there, we would give them food for their return journey and a present of money if they served us well. When all was agreed to, the steward introduced our men to us. The oldest was a *mamba* (doctor) and hence the leader.

The *mamba* was about 40, a short, wiry man with a wizened face. He turned his prayer wheel incessantly as he rode. His companions were both about 20. One was so willing to work and so agreeable that we called him "the nice boy." The other was unwilling to do anything that could be avoided; we called him "the lazy one."

The first morning on the road we arose early and, after tea, prepared ourselves for another heart wrench: it was time to part with Rahim, the last friend we had in the interior of this great lonely land. Words seemed powerless to express our feelings. We could but grasp his hand, then watch with tear-filled eyes as he rode away.

On our fourth day we followed a deep river down a narrow gorge until we reached a ford. Dragging our sheep, we urged the horses on. They had to swim hard to keep from being swept downstream, and it was an enormous relief when we reached the other side.

After crossing an immense plain, we camped on Sept. 15, our fourth wedding anniversary, in a deserted tenting place. The day meant so much to us that we celebrated even amid the silence and desolation. We shared with our guides a feast of rice pudding with sultanas, sugar and butter. Memories came trooping up from the past, of friends at home and in

China, of Charlie, and of all the joys and sorrows that had come to us since we had gone forth to fulfil the mission to which we had been called. The weather was perfect and we enjoyed talking of our prospects at Tashi Gomba where, the *mamba* assured us, we would be allowed to spend the winter.

The following day we crossed another plain and forded a river so clear that every pebble on the bottom could be seen distinctly. Packs of wolves howled around our tent. Topsy the dog chased a bear only 100 yards from us, and a herd of wild cattle were scattered around us. On Sept. 18 we had snow, hail and rain while we crossed a mountain and camped near a large stream. Our guides had never been this far east.

Two days later we crossed the Tsach'u, the last large river to be forded before we reached the lamasery. We followed a bridle path along the bank until we stopped, exhausted, on a level sward. The view was gorgeous. The river valley from which we had just emerged was narrow; the rugged hills and mountains on either side ranged against the horizon in glittering masses, fantastic and multiform in outline. The brilliant green pastures mounted gradually and faded into the delicate purple and gray of the rocky summits. The river in its placid course suggested peace and power.

Toward nightfall we saw, on the other side of the river, two men on horseback. At a spot opposite us, they reined in their horses to talk to our guides. The lazy boy went to the river's edge while Petrus watched through our telescope. They were armed with guns, spears and swords, and one had his face painted red and yellow. While they talked they were looking too closely at us to make us feel altogether comfortable. As soon as they had gone, the guides warned us about their probable intention to rob us that night. The guides took down their tent and slept outside so they could watch their six ponies. We put iron hobbles on our horses and tied Topsy nearby. Petrus, armed with two revolvers, slept at the door of our tent.

The night passed and no noise was heard. In the morning, feeling we had been unduly alarmed, we bent our thoughts and hopes on the lamasery. About noon we reached a spot where the river boiled against a cliff that rose steep and straight from its watery depths. Petrus suggested fording the river and refording farther on, but the *mamba* said our horses were too tired; it would be better to rest and then go over the hills. We agreed, and took the loads off our horses; then the men got stones to rest the pot on, gathered fuel and began preparing our lunch.

We were reclining in the shade of the cliff, waiting until the tea was ready, when Petrus thought he heard men whistling. Suddenly a shot rang out. At the command of the *mamba* the two boys jumped up and ran to drive the horses into the shelter of the cliff. The nice boy was shot almost immediately through the right arm; we all sought cover while bullets spattered around us like rain. Immense boulders were hurled down toward us. Petrus, determined to know where the bullets were coming from, stepped out toward the river's edge and looked up but a bullet struck the ground behind him and drove him back into another nook.

After what seemed an eternity the firing ceased. Then a final volley of quick shots, followed by shouts dying away in the distance. Petrus ran over to me, and we crept along the rocks to where the guides were. Three of our horses had been shot; the others had run off, although the guides had managed to save three of their ponies. A sorrowful, frightened little band we were, huddled in the cover of the rocks, the wounded boy tenderly nursing his arm, his face bearing an expression of hurt surprise. Petrus spotted an old gray horse wandering in the distance and walked off to bring him back. While he was gone, the guides quickly prepared to leave. "Buddha knows that the men will return for our baggage and kill us all," said the *mamba*. I asked them where they were going. "To the monastery for help," one of them replied; then they started across the river. I shouted for Petrus. But when he got back they were halfway across, and it was too late to follow them.

Quietly we dragged our possessions into the shelter of the cliffs, tied our gray horse nearby, and sat down to drink tea. Suddenly we missed Topsy, and remembered that we had last seen her rushing toward the road when the shots were fired.

It was about two in the afternoon. We no longer knew where we were. Evening came on and we saw no one, though we had a strong feeling that we were being watched all the time. The night was long and dark. We heard only the rippling of the water over the stones and the occasional cry of an animal or bird. It rained almost until dawn.

I tried to make light of our misfortune but we were almost certain that the guides had deserted us. Midday came with bright sunshine, so we undid all our baggage and separated from it what we needed most. We kept enough food to last 15 days, bedding, two pots, a change of clothing, the diary of our journey, my husband's Bible, and a few cherished belongings that had been loved and handled by our little boy.

The afternoon wore away, the sun sank behind the hills. Evening brought no guides but did bring an aversion to spending another night in that place. We placed the riding saddle on our horse, and piled on as much baggage as he could carry. Petrus shouldered the remainder and, each of us carrying a tent pole as a staff, we set out.

Soon we were at the top of the cliff, passing the robbers' hiding place of the day before. A beautiful spot it was: a little hollow behind the rocks where they had sheltered their horses. It had grown dark, but we went on as long as we could see a short distance. Finally we stopped, unloaded the horse, tethered him nearby, arranged our food in little packages at our heads, and lay down exhausted—but slept very little. At dawn we were astonished to discover ourselves on the edge of a deep gully, into which we would have fallen had we advanced a few more steps.

After breakfast we followed the river for three hours along its steep bank, until we reached an overhanging ledge where we must either ford the river or branch in over the hills. But the hills seemed to rise endlessly, one tier above another, and we felt utterly unable to do any more climbing. The river, wide and turbulent, was a formidable obstacle, too; however, Petrus said he could swim in any current and was not afraid to try. Opposite a sand bar that divided the river, Petrus loaded the horse, led him through the shallows, then let him go and both swam over.

It began to rain before Petrus returned for me. His teeth chattered as he tied our blankets to the back of the saddle and I mounted. Taking the long rope in his hand and leading the horse as far up the sand bar as he could without swimming, he then let go and stood to watch us. The current caught the rope; the horse, thinking he was being led, turned and began to swim downstream! Instinctively I pulled the right rein. The horse turned suddenly, and the rushing water almost swept me into the river. But I threw myself over to the opposite side and, hanging onto the horse's mane, with my weight in the right stirrup, I kept my balance and reached the bank in safety. The old horse, tired out, sat down in the stream; I had to dismount in the water.

As soon as the rain stopped, we spread the blankets out to dry and roamed some distance in search of fuel. Suddenly we found the fresh footprints of three horses and a dog. Our guides and Topsy? Wet and cold and forsaken as we were, a tremor of joy awoke in us as we thought of the possibility of help from the *mamba* and the two boys.

Next morning we crossed a tributary of the Tsach'u and entered a ravine. We found three stones that had recently served as a fireplace,

Petrus and Susie Rijnhart. "No," he said,
"I cannot leave you here alone."

and a bit of paper and string that we judged had held some medicine used by the *mamba* for the wounded boy's arm. But these were the last traces we saw of our three guides.

As we rested for lunch at a level place on the river's edge, we saw cattle downstream on the opposite side. Through our telescope we could see immense flocks and herds, and tents. Rocks obstructed our way along the riverbank, so a long detour would probably be necessary to reach the tents. But how welcome the sight!

I would have been quite willing for Petrus to cross the river then and there and go to the tents for help. He looked at me, then said: "No, I cannot leave you here alone. When we reach a place opposite the tents, I can watch you while I am gone."

So we left the river, went at right angles to it over steep hills, and reached a limpid mountain stream, which we followed. There were traces of tents in this secluded spot, an admirable place for bands of robbers to hide. At dusk, almost at the source of the stream, we camped. A vague feeling of uneasiness seized both of us; we spoke in whispers while we selected a spot near an old fireplace.

Eight inches of snow fell during the night. A few yards from us a large brown bear with a white ring around his neck prowled and shuffled about. In the morning we crawled out to breakfast on barley meal and snow water. Our horse had already brushed the snow away with his lips in order to reach the luscious grass. With fingers aching from the cold, we fastened on the horse's load, Petrus shouldered his, and off we started again, bruin watching us with interest.

The walking was inconceivably bad. The horse would slip and struggle on the snow and grass, the load would fall off, and all would have to be readjusted. Finally, on the side of a steep hill above the river, the horse slipped and rolled over and over down the hillside; he was stopped on his headlong course before he reached the water. We were not much nearer the tents on the opposite bank than we had been the previous morning, yet we could not possibly go another step. Scraping the snow away from a piece of level ground, we sat down and made a fire with some brushwood.

By now it was too late for Petrus to try to reach the tents; it would be best to spend the night where we were. How sore our faces were from the sun and snow, and how severely our eyes smarted!

We rose on the morning of Sept. 26, had breakfast, and my husband prepared to swim over, hire animals, and find out how to reach the lamasery. Cutting our rubber sheeting in two, he used part of it to wrap dry underwear and trousers, a five-ounce piece of silver, some *khatas*, and my light revolver. He strapped the load on his back and started away cheerfully, telling me not to be afraid, but to use his big revolver if anyone threatened to harm me. He said he would return before dark, if possible; if not, he would call out when near me, so I would not be frightened. When he had gone a few steps he turned to wave and said "ta-ta."

At the river's edge he threw his heavy, dark blue jacket down on the bank and waded into the water. He put out his arms to make the first stroke, but suddenly turned around, waded back to the bank, and shouted something which I did not hear on account of the rushing water. Then he walked upstream away from the tents and followed a little path around some rocks. I thought he intended to try at a spot farther upstream. When he didn't reappear I took the telescope, walked down the hill, and was surprised to see more tents, and flocks of sheep and some cattle just beyond the rocks, on my side of the river. I knew then that when Petrus turned about in the water so suddenly, he had glimpsed these tents nearby and had decided to go to them instead. I expected him back in an hour or so with some of the natives; at least he would not be away until dark. But he did not return. *I never saw him again.*

Eventually the sun went down over the top of the hill, and the shadows grew longer. Four bears gambolled on the hillside until the shade fell on them and they shuffled away. The cattle and sheep across the river were rounded up and driven home to be tethered near the tents. Except for my horse, there was not a sign of any living creature. The flocks and herds toward which my husband had gone had long since disappeared.

Reason told me he had fallen prey to wicked men, but my heart hoped against hope. Dusk settled into darkness, and a desolate solitude reigned, chilling me to the heart as I sat alone. I tied my horse among the bushes and lay down for a slumberless night.

Morning came. The cattle and sheep spread out over the hills across the river, and all nature basked in the sunshine. By evening my undefined fear had shaped itself almost into a certainty, leaving me with scarcely any hope of seeing my husband again. I grew convinced that the tents beyond those rocks belonged to the robbers who had stolen our horses. I concluded that when Petrus suddenly came into their presence, they thought he had come for his horses and would accuse them to their chief; they had probably shot him and thrown his body into the river.

The second night I lay awake watching the stars, praying for some light as to my future. At about 10 the following morning I stood scanning the landscape with the telescope, when suddenly I heard shouts from behind. Two lamas and several armed men were coming down the hill. They asked where my husband was, and I replied that he had gone to some tents and had not returned. Was I not afraid to stay alone? For answer I showed them my revolver. They were travelling, they said, to a place three days' journey away, and as they seemed friendly, I asked them to take me across the river. I would pay them well, I promised. They jumped up and ran back up the hill and out of sight. I waited all day, but saw no sign of them again.

I felt my life would be worthless if I remained there another night. I tried to cross the river on my horse, but he would not venture into the water. Finally I walked downstream toward the tents on the other side. Although vaguely uneasy, I hoped that somebody would take me to the lamasery, or to the chief of the tribe.

At the river's edge I called across so loudly that a man and a boy came to the place nearest me. I held up a piece of silver and they ran away to fetch two yaks and a packsaddle. I stared as they drove the fierce-looking brutes into the water with stones and shouts. They expected me to catch both yaks, put my bedding on one, and saddle and mount the other! All my life, I had had an inordinate fear even of domestic cattle. I shouted over that if the man did not come with the yaks they need not send them, as I could not manage them. They stopped throwing stones and the two unwieldly creatures returned to the other side. The man said I could stay where I was.

At dawn I called again and several women and children came to the river's edge. But they would do nothing for me until I had proved that my horse would not take me across. I put my bedding on him and mounted; the women shouted, threw stones, and waved their hands, while I did my best to persuade him to cross. But the horse knew his weakness and not one step would he take. Finally, about 10 o'clock, a man came over for me. He tied my horse to one yak, put my bedding on another and my saddle on a third.

We arrived on the other side amid the clamor of a crowd of onlookers. I expected to go into a tent, change my clothes and warm myself before a fire. Instead, a man pointed to a spot in the open and said I could put my things there and sleep. I urged them to put up a little shelter for me or let me share a tent with other women. Finally I was led to a narrow cave, and I was soon comfortable in dry clothes and sipping hot tea, the first I had had for three days.

Before long I was on good terms and chatting freely with these people. But deep in my heart lurked the awful fear of my husband's fate, and despair of getting help. They told me that the lamasery of Tashi Gomba was two days' journey away. The abbot had been beheaded, and the people were fighting there, so nothing would induce my hosts to go with me. I did not say what I thought had happened to my husband, but they realized that something was amiss.

They knew I had been robbed—I could not have come there alone. But they would not help me to reach any person of authority; they might then be interfering in their neighbors' escapades and earning lifelong enemies. They simply told me that Jyekundo could be reached in 10 days by horseback, in 15 by yak.

A Chinese official was stationed at Jyekundo; he could send letters for me and dispatch soldiers to find out what had happened to Petrus.

I asked for guides to go part way to Jyekundo with me, but they wanted so much money that it took four days to come to terms.

Meanwhile, people visited me freely in my little cave, bringing me butter and meat for sale. I went one afternoon to the riverbank across from where I had sat those days waiting and waiting. I saw on the opposite bank, just where he had left it, my husband's blue jacket. Two lamas crossed on horseback to get the things I had left there. As I watched through the telescope, my heart sank. Everything was in the same condition as when I had left it; no one had been near the place. My last atom of hope for the return of my beloved was gone.

Finally three men agreed to accompany me toward Jyekundo for five days. They were to receive 10 ounces of silver, and were to arrange with other men to take me the next five days. The oldest, about 50, was very dirty but his manner was full of simple dignity and kindness. One of his companions was the man who had brought me across the river. All three walked, driving along their yaks, one with my things, one for me to ride and the other to carry their food.

The first yak I rode made such sudden lurches going downhill that twice I was thrown off. After the second fall I insisted on another animal and found him much better. Then, much to their satisfaction, my guides succeeded in trading my jaded horse for a fresh one. They took quite an interest in me, showed sympathy, and made me presents of some food. But nothing could induce them to go outside their own district. They were afraid of robbers. That was why they had come unmounted; anyone meeting them would conclude that they had nothing of value, looking as they did like beggars.

On the fifth day we parted on friendly terms, and I was lonely when they were gone. My three new guides were each armed with gun and sword. One was a man of about 40; the youngest was a boy of 17 with a pleasant face; the third was sneaky both in appearance and action, and the only one I feared and mistrusted. We jogged along very harmoniously for three days. Strangely, they avoided camping near other people, though they agreed to find local guides to take me the rest of the way to Jyekundo when they themselves had to return home.

On the morning of the fourth day, as the road led us high up on a slope, we saw a chief's tent at the foot of the hill. I decided to ask for an escort of men with horses because our yaks were so slow. At the rate we were going, I doubted that my money would last. The chief's steward came out to meet us. He told me a woman could not enter into the *ponbo*'s august presence; he himself would act as middleman. I explained that we had been robbed some distance away and that I would pay for an escort to take me to Jyekundo. He withdrew to make my wishes known to his master, and returned to say that another chief nearby would give me what I wanted. I replied that my present guides were not responsible to anyone for my safety, and I would not leave without an escort. This was sufficient to move the chief, but I was to wait until the next day so that the escort might prepare for the journey.

The *ponbo* never forgot his dignity enough to speak to me, but he sent a subordinate to ask for the loan of my telescope. Pleased as a child, he was anxious to buy it. I said that if his escort took me to Jyekundo, I would send it back with them as a present for him. Several times he sent messengers to ascertain if I meant what I said; each time I replied that if my escorts returned without it, it would be because *they* had not fulfilled the agreement. In the evening my two escorts were introduced to me.

I had an easy heart as we set off next morning, thinking that they would be quite an improvement over my previous guides. But the very first day the one who carried my food on his saddle stole half my little supply of barley meal and butter. I spent the night beside the other man's tent, and my soul revolts when I think of the suggestions he made to me. I said that if anything approached me during the night, I would fire my revolver at whatever it was.

In the morning we continued along the caravan road toward Jyekundo. Women were so low and degraded, said my guides, that they were ashamed to be seen travelling with me. When we were near people, I was not to utter a word. They wished to appear very kind and offered to carry my heavy telescope, but I preferred to keep it in the blouse of my gown. As long as I had it, they were to some extent in my power, for they would almost certainly lose their heads if they returned to their chief without the expected present.

About noon the more wicked of the two complained of a severe pain in his stomach, which grew worse until he was apparently unable to proceed. Seeing tents in the distance to the left of the road, he said we would spend the night beside them; there he would secure the services of a lama who could give him medicine and say prayers for his recovery. We started toward the encampment, but soon they had made other plans, and we left the tents behind, my guides claiming that the inhabitants were robbers.

We reached an immense marsh through which we travelled for hours, our horses having difficulty picking their way. We crossed a black little stream, then followed it back into a bend, where we dismounted to camp. We were hemmed in by swampy ground that extended miles away to the base of some hills. I noticed that the men carefully concealed the fire so it could not be seen from a distance. They frequently assured me of the safety of our camp: we could all sleep soundly because the sound of feet plunging in the bog would betray any intruders.

My escorts lay down with their guns ready, and their heads beside the smouldering fire. I spread my rubber sheeting in the driest place I could find and, with my revolver in hand, I spent the night looking at the stars and at the horses—praying for strength to keep awake that I might watch every movement of the two treacherous men beside me. Though they had told me to sleep without fear, they called me very softly six times during the night. I answered promptly each time. When morning came the man's pain had vanished, and with it even the appearance of kindness. They angrily saddled their horses—I had to saddle my own—and before the sun had risen over the hills, we were trotting back to the main road.

At a fork the guides hesitated; they weren't sure which road led to Jyekundo. Eventually we took the narrower one and stopped at some tents for directions. The men were told there was an epidemic of smallpox at Jyekundo. I said I was not afraid, and they must go with me or they could not have the telescope for their chief. They replied that it would be better to be killed by the *ponbo* than to die of the plague. Faint from the long ride and the strain of watching them, and yet afraid of going on alone, I could scarcely restrain my desperation. All my attempts to induce them to go to Jyekundo proved futile, but finally they agreed to guide me along the caravan road until we met a Chinese traveller. I felt certain that one of these merchants, so common near Tibetan towns, would help me.

That night we camped in one of nature's loveliest spots—a little recess among the hills where many tents were pitched on grassy strips; flocks and herds were grazing, and winding brooks babbled. The men said we were approaching the lamasery of Tashi Gomba, where there was an intense hatred of foreigners. We might all be killed, they told me; everything that would betray my nationality must be destroyed. My husband's Bible—his most precious possession—and his diary were buried in a miry stream with stones piled on them.

Next day we went on and when dusk began to fall my escorts led the way high up into the hills, far from some tents in the valley. We found just enough water to make a little tea, and then lay down to rest. Suddenly a voice rang out in the darkness. A stranger appeared by our fire, and I heard him ask the men who I was. They replied that I was a Chinese going to join his companions at the lamasery. The stranger went away, and returned almost immediately with three others. It turned out that we had been taken for robbers and they had been sent by their chief to investigate. They took one of my escort's guns as security that we would molest no one during the night. I was painfully weary but dared not sleep. At daybreak a young lama brought back the gun. I had the seal of silence on my lips, and a straw hat and fur collar concealed most of my face; he believed that I was a Chinese.

How beautiful the country through which we now wended our way! Evergreen trees dotted the hillsides. Was it because hope sang in my heart that nature looked so bright and inviting? Presently we came in sight of a small lamasery. Hundreds of tents were scattered around the lamas' substantial houses. A fair was in progress. My escorts found a Chinese merchant, a man of about 50, who had rooms in a lama's house. It was forbidden for me to enter because I was a woman, so he came out to see me. The guides told him that I was a Chinese woman from Sining; then they made off, telescope and all, while I breathed an enormous sigh of relief.

I addressed the merchant in Sining dialect. But his first sentence told me that he had pierced my identity and knew that I was a foreigner. "How is it that you are here alone like this?" he asked. I poured out my troubles to him and told him of the fate of our caravan, of our little son's death, of our being robbed, and then of the awful separation from my husband. The merchant was touched, "You have eaten much bitterness," he said. "Quiet your heart, for now that you are here, you are all right."

Two months after her husband's disappearance Susie Rijnhart finally reached an outpost of the China Inland Mission at Tatsienlu {now Kangting} in China proper. She spent six months there, trying in vain to find out what had happened to her husband, and the identity of his supposed murderers. At Tatsienlu she also made the acquaintance of a missionary named James Moyes, and six years later she became Mrs. Moyes. Most of her remaining years were devoted to missionary work in Tibet. She returned to Canada and died in hospital in Chatham, Ont., in 1908.

West With Thomas Wilby on the All-Red Route

*In 1912 the automobile had hardly reached
adolescence. Balky, bouncy and noisy, the average
car had no starter, no windows, two-wheel brakes
and just four cylinders. Gas was bought in a
pail at a hardware store and many roads were
literally wagon tracks—rocky and dusty in dry
weather, slippery mud in the rain. A 100-mile
trip was a major adventure: who would dare
to cross the continent?*

By HUGH DURNFORD *and* GLENN BAECHLER

THOMAS WILBY WAS THE FIRST MAN to take a motor car across Canada. A whimsical, aristocratic Briton, he set out from Halifax on Aug. 27, 1912, with a chauffeur and a brand-new 1913 Reo Special touring car. He couldn't drive all the way, of course; road builders had yet to cross the Rockies, and north of Lake Superior lay a wilderness of forest, rock and muskeg. But Wilby, lured by the open road and propelled by a sense of British imperialism, was anxious to promote an "all-red route," a coast-to-coast highway through Canadian territory only. Like the "all-red" CPR, Wilby believed, such a highway would help unite the country.

Wilby's car was loaned by the Reo Motor Car Co. of Canada Limited, then turning out 100 cars a month in St. Catharines, Ont., and eager for publicity. Reo also sent along F. V. Haney, the capable but moody young chauffeur who did most of the driving. Haney showed little appreciation for the Canadian panorama or its challenges; when not behind the wheel he preferred the bright lights of civilization. But Wilby, in baggy tweeds, his battered fedora turned up jauntily at the front, enjoyed every minute. Later, in his book, *A Motor Tour Through Canada,* he told how the great adventure had delighted him.

Thomas Wilby, aristocrat in a battered fedora, and chauffeur F. V. Haney pose with the Reo somewhere on the All-Red Route.

Wilby and Haney first met in Halifax where they had to wait four days while the railway located their car. When it arrived Wilby was more than pleased: "Glittering in her shiny coat of black paint, her fore and aft lines as fine as those of a yacht, she was an ideal tourist car—a guileless thing, apparently unconscious of the long and trying journey before her.

"Rough-shod with anti-skid tires on all four wheels, her spare 'shoes' hanging jauntily behind, she had two speedometers, a horn worked by foot, and two long boxes on the running boards to hold the loose paraphernalia. I knew her for a beauty and forgave her her delay."

On the day of departure the rear wheels were backed into the Atlantic, a flask was filled with ocean water, and then, "leaping gaily over the stones, the car dashed out of the water and we were off." It had been raining for six weeks in the Maritimes, but the road surfaces, while sloppy, had a good base and presented no real problem.

Other problems soon became apparent, the railway crossing for one. "There it was, at every few miles of our way, the most obnoxiously omnipresent thing on the American continent—the level railway track—threading the village and the town, crossing the highway and rushing into the path of pedestrian, motorist and driver where steep banks or winding curves shut it out of sight that Death might reap his grim harvest. These crossings form an intolerable curse and menace, a juggernaut for human sacrifice."

Truro, the first night's destination, was reached at 10 p.m. by the ghostly light of the Reo's acetylene headlamps. The hotel dining room was closed. "There was nothing to do but beat a hasty retreat to the railway buffet, where some excellent sandwiches were unearthed and washed down by a deadly concoction of stewed hay that masqueraded under the name of tea."

The first real trouble came a few days later when the car ran low on gas and stalled on a hill 14 miles below Grand Falls, N.B. "It was already dark, and ahead were bad hills and a swamp paved with logs. To go farther was an impossibility; it was an equal impossibility to descend backward, for the road behind was narrow and would lead us again into an ugly marsh covered with a rank growth to the edge of the wheel ruts. Men from a neighboring farmhouse emerged from the shadows and silhouetted themselves in helpless curiosity in the strong rays of the lamps."

Haney, the professional, discovered that by blowing into the gas tank vent and then quickly plugging it with a matchstick, he could force a little of the remaining gas into the carburetor and get the engine running.

"Two big hills surmounted on a thimbleful of remaining liquid power—it was a miracle," Wilby exulted. "It was a miracle too that the unfortunate chauffeur did not burst his cheeks or succumb to asphyxia, for it fell to his lot to blow into the petrol tank every few moments of the remaining journey. How tremblingly we scanned each succeeding rise in the ground! How joyously we hailed every descent, until swamp and hills were past and the small hotel of Grand Falls stood before us in silent welcome."

In Quebec, just west of Rivière-du-Loup, was a trail that delighted Wilby—"a grassy path, a couple of ruts in the sward with the bare, intervening space marking the tread of the horse's hoofs, a narrow spoor along which the early French may have trekked. Over its unconventional surface the car sped like an arrow. I would not have exchanged my grassy carpet for the best macadam road in the world."

He wasn't delayed until he reached the paved streets of Quebec City and tried to climb to the Upper Town "to the accompaniment of a series of Gatling-gun explosions from the 'cutout.' The car, heavily loaded, realized by some mechanical instinct before we did the absurdity of the unequal contest. It showed the white feather, and halfway up tried to run down again backward. What it actually succeeded in doing was to come to a full stop athwart the line of traffic.

"The situation was ludicrously humiliating. A delighted crowd did not scruple to point sarcastically to the inscription on the tire drum which flauntingly announced the Pacific as our destination. Here we were undertaking the longest road tour ever attempted in Canada, and yet we were unable to climb a paved hill. I sprang out to lighten the load."

Haney whipped the car around and backed it up the hill, a common stratagem of the era when gas was low in the tank.

West of Montreal, at Carillon, Wilby crossed the Ottawa River on a ferry to Pointe-Fortune. Now they drove through pretty farming country, where "the livestock was mostly in the centre of the road. It awaited our coming and necessitated a great deal of skilful manoeuvring to avoid self-immolation by chickens, dogs and ducks, and much descriptive phraseology, for humane reasons, from the irate driver. Now and again a dog rushing along in parallel course with our flight challenged us to a race until the indicator of the speedometer was somewhere among

the 30s. Then, caught by a stump or other obstruction, a sudden somersault would arrest his mad career, and he would make his way back, crestfallen."

The route led through Ottawa, where Wilby was appalled at the taste that pollution gave to the drinking water; down to Toronto, which he found urbane and a little dull; then up toward North Bay to see what prospects were of getting past Lake Superior. On a sandy hill near Scotia, less than 100 miles from North Bay, Wilby's luck ran out.

A first rush at the treacherous hill had failed, and on the second the car stalled again, then slipped into a pocket at the side of the road

and stuck fast. But the attempt was impressive. "This storming of a sand redoubt by a thing of steel and horsepower is something to wonder at and admire. The creature charges joyously, terrible to behold, shattering the great silence of the wilderness with its battery of guns, raging and storming, groaning, moaning, then roaring and whirling again. But her spirit is broken at last. The wheels spin on the same spot in frantic, static dynamics. A tremor only runs through her frame and she ceases to roar impotent defiance. She admits defeat. The silence is piteous, primitive. Only horses can now bring life to the useless, motionless mechanism.

"And it was the big brawny horses of a singularly taciturn Irish farmer on the hill that finally jerked our transcontinental car out of that pothole of sand. Alas for the strength of those well-meaning beasts! The jerk was all but a deathblow. The steel driving shaft was hopelessly twisted; coaxingly, slowly, crawling inch by inch, we pulled her into hospital beneath a crazy shed roof."

Scotia, Wilby decided, was the end of the world, "a fitting spot in which to effectively hide the ignominy of disaster." Finally a new drive shaft was installed and a brave new start was made. There was an hour-long struggle to get the groaning Reo over a 30 per cent corduroy "Jacob's ladder" between South River and Trout Creek. But with the car perched on the muddy crest, it was discovered that the new shaft had twisted and locked the car's transmission into low gear.

Wilby and Haney inched the Reo through the dusk along the over-grown corduroy trail but soon came to a stream with no bridge. At a lonely farm a woman let them "rummage around" for something with which to make a bridge.

"We came upon a pile of lumber. Our prospective bridge was there; it only needed to be transported and scientifically laid across the stream. We commenced to transport it—no need to describe how! It was the most ignominious and the most fatiguing method of transporting a bridge I have ever witnessed." But the span did its job.

In North Bay the road ended. Wilby shipped the Reo 80 miles to Sudbury by rail. From there he drove to Sault Ste. Marie, with only a 17-mile detour on a tug between Algoma and Blind River.

At the Soo Club House "friendly acquaintances mournfully an-nounced that the wilderness to the north of Lake Superior belonged to the locomotive alone." They were right: the only way to drive to Win-nipeg was south of the lake through the United States. Rejecting this route because it was not Canadian, Wilby had no choice but to load his car on a boat for the Lakehead. There he found that a road was being built south to Duluth, Minn., but not west to Winnipeg. Again the Reo went aboard a train.

West of Winnipeg, on the open prairie, Wilby and Haney followed prairie trails "in unrestricted freedom, the car gently bounding along on the finest natural road I had ever travelled.

"It had mystery, it had solitude. The settlers' houses had disap-peared. So had the human milestones, the interminable telephone poles. Green-brown lines marked the swales of the unending sod. The distance was pinkish-purple, the sky blue, the horizon steel and indigo.

"The world was silent, majestic in its hush and sense of arrested motion. It was grand and large, unspoilt and primordial. It was the real West at last!"

The prairie roads, in theory, ran at regular intervals between sections of farmland in a grid. This system worked well where the land was settled but fell apart in the gaps between the settled areas. Much of Wilby's difficulty lay in crossing these gaps and picking up the road on the other side.

For much of the route Wilby had picked up and dropped men who helped pilot or chauffeur. One particularly methodical young co-driver he met in Saskatchewan stayed with them to the coast.

The prairie roads were not bad, except for some gumbo near Winnipeg. Prairie dogs were something else. In Saskatchewan, near the Alberta border, Wilby wrote, "the roads were positively alive with tiny yellow gophers as far as the eye could reach.

"They waited until the rubber wheels were upon them; then they turned tail, scampered to a hole in the rut, stood up and, turning a somersault, catapulted into their subways. Scores appeared to vanish under the wheels, get themselves in the spokes, clamber on to the radiator, leap on to the mudguards, revolve gleefully on the axles, fall off, hit the ground, rebound on the windshield and disappear somewhere in the sky. They always moved one-thousandth part of a second faster than the car."

At other times, "on the open trails of the ranches, a string of horses, their curiosity aroused, would chase us for a long time—to gradually tail off to the pastures again when satisfied as to our harmless eccentricities. Often, however, they would gallop close ahead, playfully hurling huge clods of earth in our faces."

Soon the Prairies were behind. The hills got steeper and a score of times Wilby and the others had to jump out to lighten the load and help coax the Reo over a summit.

At Cranbrook, B.C., Wilby was again advised to put his car on a train but he decided to drive on, a pilot car accompanying him and horses to help him through a swamp. The narrow, twisting mountain road out of Cranbrook proved almost too much for the flagging Reo but at dusk it descended to a little wooden bridge at the entrance to the swamp.

Lamps lit, the car plunged onto a swamp path "littered with stones and roots and fallen trees. Sometimes tree snags covered the track; again it was lost in pools of unknown depths, which we took only after cautious sounding. At times both cars sank to the hubs, listing heavily, grinding and ploughing their way, pounding the tires to rags, while the engines roared and groaned and the wheels angrily shot the water in inky spindrift over men and trees." Then the horses showed up and took the Reo in tow. The rest of the 40-mile journey from Cranbrook to Yahk was uneventful.

At Yahk, in a gloomy hotel, Wilby and Haney had a greasy and unsavory meal. They learned that, although driving along the railway right of way was strictly illegal, a work gang down the line could direct them to a level crossing where they could get on the tracks. No train—barring a possible freight or two—was expected for several hours. Wilby located the work camp, got instructions and found himself "astride the glittering rails." (The Reo's wheels straddled *one* rail.)

"There was a gasp as one felt the first forward plunge of the car and the white path of our acetylene light shot before us into the immense shadows of the forest wilderness. Eyes strove to pierce the distance ahead and behind; every nerve was strained in listening for a possible monster of steel and steam which might dash down upon us at any moment from around a curve, or catch us in its swift career from behind! Muscles were tense, ready for the leap to a precarious safety at first sight of an approaching headlight.

"And yet danger was no greater there than at every turn of the crowded city thoroughfares, where no one knew from what direction it might come. Here every fibre, every cell was ready for it.

"As the wheels crept from sleeper to sleeper there was an incessant jiggling and jolting that shook the teeth and vibrated through the spine. The jaw rattled slightly as when a man shivers with cold. One felt as though there was a danger of biting the tongue at every attempt at speaking. Time dragged interminably as we chased the brilliant light into the forest. The way began to contort and writhe. The track ran sharply downhill. The curves grew sharper and shorter, the contortions more violent.

"When we caught the wheels in the frogs of switches, we hurriedly jacked the car above the level of the rails. Then we filled the roadbed beneath the wheel with stones and shot the car over the obstruction. The spikes in the sides of the rail cut the rubber and very soon our rear tires were in ribbons. But apparently the enemy thought it idle to interfere with fools and their folly, and we reached our haven—a lonely and darkened railway station in the forest—in safety. We roused a sleepy lad, jerked the car off the tracks and through a gate, and commandeered the youth to show us what he called the 'government road' to Creston."

This mountain path led the clattering, straining Reo through more primeval woods and gorges, and finally, at 2 a.m., into the open where the correct fork of half a dozen choices eventually led the weary travellers to Creston.

"Three o'clock! The first motor car that had ever entered Creston from the 'road' stood panting and trembling, while the horn sent out hoarse messages to the sleeping world of our safe, triumphant arrival.

"We clambered down and roused the inmates, and in the dimly lit bar the blinking proprietor served the 'loving cup' wherewith to celebrate the occasion ere we tumbled off to bed."

From Creston it was a short run up a dry lake bed to Kootenay Lake and a log raft to Nelson. There it was back on the train for 20 miles to Trail and finally back on the road to Princeton. From Princeton to Hope was only 65 miles as the crow flies, but Wilby had to make a 300-mile loop north to Ashcroft and Lillooet, then down the Fraser River, because there was no direct road over the mountains.

The Thompson, said Wilby, "buckled and warped and wrenched the path into semblance of a flapping ribbon. Then it dropped us to water level and tried to drown us; next it endeavored to pitch us into a cleft in the rocks, or to shoot us up in the sky again. Failing in these tactics, it threw out a lofty wall of rock and a careful arrangement of trees and bushes as screens. To all seeming, there was an end to the path and the tour! But the path merely lay hidden."

Coming down the Fraser the road was similarly tortuous, dodging mountains and creeks, snaking around slides, hanging seemingly in midair over the chasm. Fourteen miles above Lytton an innkeeper warned Wilby to watch for a couple of freight teams expected from the other direction. With lighted lamps the Reo crept along the unprotected precipices above the river. A high-pitched voice was heard.

"I sprang cautiously down. Nothing could be seen. After some time a light wagon containing an Indian and his squaw appeared round a curve directly in front of us. Gingerly the car backed out upon a jutting ledge to let them by, and they passed us indifferently while we anxiously watched our rear wheels, all but poised over space.

"Again we cautiously advanced. Then came the sounds of bells and our lights flashed upon the huge canvas tops of the expected

End of the line: Wilby empties a bit of the Atlantic into the Pacific.

freighters with their long strings of horses. The wagons carried no lights and one marvelled at the miracle which kept them on the roadway. Had the horses taken fright a catastrophe would have been inevitable.

"We backed again. We stopped the engines. We held our breath. The freighters crawled past, half-asleep.

"We still had 10 more miles to shelter, but our big acetylene lamps went out, leaving us in total darkness on a dangerous curve. We pulled up, lit the lamps again and crept onward. Once more the lights went out; the gas in the cylinder was exhausted. To advance without lights meant certain death, and our small oil lamps were next to useless, being hung too high above the roadway to give us a view of the dangerous ledge."

The extra driver Wilby had picked up in Saskatchewan came to the rescue. "Taking one oil lamp, he stretched himself at full length along the mudguard next to the outer edge of the road, reached out his arm so as to bring the lamp close to the ground, and boldly gave the signal: 'Go ahead.'

"Ten miles on one's stomach, holding a light over a sheer drop

674

of hundreds of feet, is a devilishly unpleasant role. Inch by inch we crept on. Moment by moment the poor fellow grew stiffer. A sudden jolt and it seemed we would throw him down the bank. A flicker of the light and we all, car and passengers, would be over the brink. We were incessantly rounding a series of bluffs, twisting and turning in short, sharp curves that shut out the road ahead. Conversation languished. The unfortunate man on his stomach gave vent to his emotions only in occasional grunts." Thus was the trip to Lytton completed.

From there it was a breeze down to Hope and Chilliwack, where "at long last the mountains we had been facing for so long parted to reveal a broad and pleasant valley. With almost a sigh of relief the car scudded forward. Our difficulties were over—the journey all but finished."

There were stops at Vancouver, Alberni (as far west as they could drive on Vancouver Island) and Victoria. There, 52 days from Halifax, with 4,200 miles on the odometer, the car was guided to the edge of the ocean, and the flask of Atlantic water was emptied into the Pacific.

Frontline Surgeon

*Norman Bethune was a born crusader.
When World War I broke out,
he interrupted his medical studies in
Toronto and enlisted immediately.
He was wounded in France and was
discharged from the army but soon
recovered his health and re-enlisted as a
medical officer. After the war he
interned in British hospitals, practised
and taught medicine in Montreal, and
was an internationally known
chest surgeon when in 1936 he went to
Spain to help the Republican
government against Franco's fascists.
There he revolutionized battlefield
medical care and committed himself to
the cause for which he would die.*

By SYDNEY GORDON *and* TED ALLAN

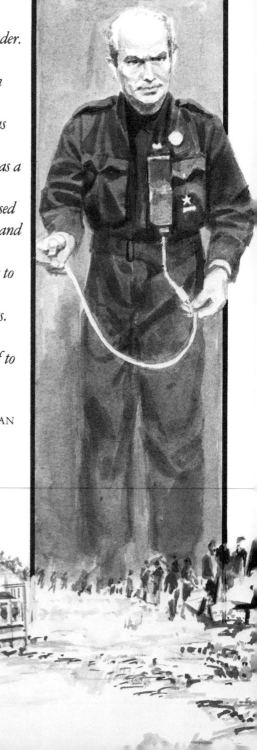

A STATION WAGON manoeuvres along the blacked-out Gran Via, skirting ripped pavement and shell holes. It moves slowly, cautiously, without lights. At the end of the thoroughfare it turns right and crawls through the shattered streets leading to Casa del Campo, the Royal Park.

Suddenly, the air is convulsed. Great sheets of light flash through the sky. The silence is shredded by a deafening cannonade; the pavement trembles. In the orange-red glare of an exploding shell the station wagon lurches to the side of the street, then speeds on. Soon it is roaring into Casa del Campo, heading for the trenches pinpointed in the darkness by the blaze of guns and the sounds of battle.

This is Madrid early in the morning of Dec. 23, 1936.

The city has heard its women weeping, its men cursing, its evacuee children saying good-bye. La Pasionaria, a veteran of the 1934 Asturian miners' uprising, has gone on foot through the streets, lifting her voice

Norman Bethune: not to shed blood but to give it, in the agony of the Spanish war.

with the unspoken hopes of all the inarticulate, putting into simple words the meaning of all the terror, agony and resistance: *Better to die on our feet than live on our knees!* The people of Madrid know that if Gen. Francisco Franco and his fascist troops defeat the government there will be dictatorship. There is a unity of purpose: resistance to the end, death to the enemy, and long live the Republic!

The station wagon in Casa del Campo comes to a jarring stop at a casualty station under a clump of trees, close to the trenches. Two men jump out. They pause to take stock of the figures hurrying about in the dark. There are muffled shouts from the trenches, the chatter of machine guns, and the anguished cries of the wounded lying all around. The moon emerges suddenly from the clouds, making it easier for the two men as they unload paraphernalia from the station wagon.

They exchange documents with a harassed medical officer. They are an unexpected pair: two strangers, speaking little Spanish, suddenly materializing out of the night in the precise sector where government troops have launched a local attack. One is tall, lean, long-faced. The other, the one in command, is not easily classified. He gives an impression of slender height, yet is not tall. His face is strong, showing no definite age, yet his finely shaped head is fringed by thick gray-white hair. He is dressed in a blue, zippered uniform, the insignia of a colonel of the Republican Army on his chest, a Maple Leaf on each shoulder.

The Spanish doctor glances at the uniform, hands back the documents, salutes, says *"Si, comandante,"* and extends his arm in a gesture signifying they can begin.

The comandante kneels beside the first soldier in the line of casualties. He looks into the soldier's face. The features are twisted by pain but the very pain signifies the strength with which life holds fast in the wounded body. The comandante pats the soldier's arm and moves on.

The next man is dead. The comandante unbuttons the soldier's shirt. "Not much of a wound, but much blood lost," he whispers.

He rises again and continues along the line. To some men he speaks words of encouragement; they don't understand the words, but they understand the intent, and smile with the easy grace of children. At one point he nods and says to his tall, silent companion, "This one."

When he has made the rounds he walks back unerringly to a still form covered by a coat. He drops on one knee and gently raises the man's head—but when he looks at the face it is not of a man but of a boy, perhaps 16 or 17. The comandante reads the face easily: the lips slack, the cheeks sunken, the skin clammy. "Bad shock," the comandante murmurs. "We'll begin with him."

He rests the lolling head gently on the ground and sets to work. He rips the sleeve of the lad's jacket, rolls back the shirt, and swiftly explores the exposed forearm. "Ready, now." His companion hands him a slender rubber tube with a needle at the end. In the slack flesh the comandante's fingers find the vein.

There is the whine of a shell, followed by still another before the first explodes. The enemy is extending the barrage closer to the Republican lines. But there is no time to gauge the danger. The comandante tapes the needle onto the arm with adhesive, rises, and runs his hand along the tubing to the squat bottle his companion is holding. "Right, I'll take it," he says. "You can get more bottles out of the car."

He stands erect now, ignoring the bullets that ping into the trees, the flares, the shells that ravish the night, the rumblings that penetrate to his very bones. He holds the bottle above the young soldier, moving to the soldier's head so as to put his own body between the bottle and the fighting.

It is an ordinary bottle, but it stores a precious fluid. Dark, mysterious, life-giving blood—universal in type, thick and cohesive still from the veins of the living donor. The comandante sends the first drops into the depleted veins of the dying soldier. He releases the clamp on the tubing slowly. The lad is far-gone. He shivers, his teeth chatter. The comandante opens the clamp fully. Now the blood flows in a steady stream, and the miracle is near. The comandante has seen it many times before, but it is always new: like a wasted flower suddenly blooming again with rich-hued petals.

The boy stirs. His teeth no longer chatter. He opens his eyes, blankly at first, then with a painful effort to remember. But it is only the beginning. Casting aside the now empty bottle the comandante prepares the second. Soon, after the second bottle, the miracle is complete. The lad smiles: the comandante knows, without being able to see, that the color has returned to his face, that after a few minutes of chill his skin will grow warm again, that after his wounds are tended he will live.

"*Bueno, bueno,*" the comandante says cheerfully. He lights a cigarette and puts it to the soldier's lips. The soldier takes a deep puff. He suddenly realizes he is alive. "*Gracias,*" he murmurs joyfully, but the stranger has already vanished.

Back and forth among the wounded he moves, holding his bottles aloft, opening veins to the salty river that washes life back into the bodies of the near-dead. Soon the containers in the station wagon are empty. There is no more blood to be transfused, but of the men who stormed out of the trenches to seize a strong point from the Moors and Germans one hour or so ago, 12 who would have died are still alive; 12 soldiers of the Republic who will remember this night under the trees, and the man with the gray-white hair and his magic bottles of blood.

"*No más?*" the Spanish doctor has followed the comandante to the station wagon. "No more?"

The comandante shakes his head and makes signs that he will have to return to the city for a fresh supply of blood. The Spaniard raises his fist in the Republican salute. Solemnly, he says: "Dr. Alvarez Ruiz. *Muchas gracias.*"

The Canadian doctor stands erect, his fist raised too. "I am Dr. Norman Bethune. My friend, Hazen Sise. It is we who must thank you."

In the sudden silence Canadians and Spaniards look at each other in a burst of feeling that none knows how to express. Then a soldier points to the lettering on the station wagon: Instituto Hispano-Canadense de Transfusión de Sangre.

He cries out, "*Viva la transfusión de sangre!*"

The response sweeps along the line of wounded: "*Viva!*"

"*Viva el Canada!*"

"*Viva yo!*" a small voice cuts thinly through the bass chorus. Everybody turns. It is the boy who received the first transfusion. He has risen on his elbow, his eyes burning in his young face. "*Viva yo!*" he cries. (Long live *me!*)

There is laughter; they all understand.

"*Viva!*" they cry.

The word spreads swiftly through the lines in Casa del Campo. From somewhere beyond the seas a friend has come with a miracle for the soldiers of the Republic. Tomorrow it will be broadcast to all Madrid and finally to all the world.

For the first time since humans learned to kill their brothers, a man had appeared on the battlefield to give blood, not to shed it.

Dr. Norman Bethune had arrived in Madrid on Nov. 3. With Henning Sorensen, a Canadian newspaper correspondent, as guide and interpreter, he had set out to find the best method of organizing Canadian medical aid for the Republican troops. He made a swift tour of the city's military hospitals, went into the trenches, and visited the fronts outside Madrid. He inspected casualty stations behind the lines and worked with surgeons at several base hospitals. Here he studied the types of wounds the soldiers suffered and kept notes on the percentage of fatalities and the recoveries after surgery.

On Nov. 11 Bethune returned to Madrid. By now he sensed what had to be done and what was missing in the army's medical services. To Dr. Erwin Kisch, one of the chief medical officers of the International Brigades helping the Republican Army, he outlined a project that had taken shape in his mind. In all modern wars, he pointed out, even the most highly organized medical services suffered from a serious defect: some wounded bled to death on the battlefield or on the trip from front to base hospital; others were so weakened by loss of blood or by shock that they were unable to survive surgery. In Barcelona, Dr. Duran Jorda had done great work in storing blood and organizing blood banks. But the main problem had not been tackled. *How to provide transfusion directly at the front, as close to the battlefield as possible?*

Bethune was convinced it was feasible and would result in a sharp decrease in deaths among the wounded. He envisioned a *mobile* transfusion unit that would gather blood from volunteers, store it, make it available to casualty stations and field hospitals, and above all, provide transfusions at the front while fighting was in progress.

For a long time Kisch stared at Bethune. "If you can do it," he said at last, "you will be making medical history."

Officials of the Socorro Rojo, a Spanish trade union relief organization and the only effective medical service in Republican Spain, were sceptical of Bethune's ideas. But eventually he won them over and then sent a long cable to the Spanish Aid Committee in Toronto. He outlined his plans and ended with an appeal for immediate action: "Am leaving with Sorensen for Paris and London to buy necessary equipment. Cable as much money as possible to committee representative in Paris."

The next morning he set out for Paris without waiting for a reply. When he arrived he found $10,000 from the Canadian committee with a message expressing approval of the project and promising full financial support.

He made a quick tour of medical suppliers in Paris, established contacts for future supplies and moved on to London. There, having completed his purchases, he armed himself with all available literature on techniques of transfusion, locked himself in his hotel room and plunged into the study of blood.

On Dec. 6 Bethune was back in Madrid with a station wagon loaded with supplies. With him were Sorensen and his latest recruit, Hazen Sise, a young Montreal architect who had run into Bethune in London and had volunteered to serve with the unit.

In Madrid there was open jubilation. The fascists had thrown the most powerful attacks of the war against the city from the south, but had been stopped. The city flexed its muscles like a young giant who has suddenly been faced with a staggering test of strength and has emerged a little dazzled by his unsuspected stamina.

The Socorro Rojo had selected special quarters for the blood transfusion unit, a palatial apartment formerly occupied by the German Embassy's legal counsel on Principe de Vergara, a wide boulevard in one of Madrid's wealthiest residential sections. "Here," a Socorro official said wryly, "you will not be disturbed by the bombs. Franco is careful with the property of the rich."

Three rooms were to be used by the Canadians as living quarters, the rest as laboratories, refrigerator rooms for storage of blood, and reception and transfusion rooms. Two young Spanish doctors were assigned to Bethune as assistants. The unit was to function along a 400-mile front with Bethune and the two Spanish doctors each in charge of a sector.

Once everything had been installed on Principe de Vergara, small refrigeration units were distributed to the hospitals and field stations in the three sectors. Now everything was ready. Bethune called the members of the unit and Socorro Rojo officials into session.

"Our glorified milk delivery system," he reported, "has been set up—we're ready to start delivering. There's only one thing we need. The milk. Without that we might all just as well go home."

A Socorro representative nodded confidently. "We shall see that you have all the blood donors you need."

"The need for donors will continue as long as the unit is operated. To have a sufficient store of blood on hand for all emergencies, donors will have to come forward every day."

The Spaniard looked baffled, as if he failed to understand why the matter had to be discussed. "You shall have the donors," he said simply.

For three days an appeal went out to the people of Madrid through press and radio. Blood was needed for the men at the front!

On the morning of the fourth day, when donors had been asked to turn up, Bethune was wakened by someone calling him.

Dr. Lopez, one of the Spanish doctors, beckoned him onto the terrace, pointing to the spectacle below.

Over 2,000 people filled the street, with more arriving every minute. They stood close together—men and women, young and old, gaunt and portly, poorly clad workers and well-dressed housewives. They were waiting patiently, silently.

Bethune gazed at the upturned faces, then went inside. His face betrayed nothing of the turmoil he felt; he issued quick orders, the doors were opened, and the first donors filed in.

All morning and far into the afternoon they worked, registering, checking blood counts, filling the bottles—and still the donors came. A militia detachment had to be called out to keep traffic moving outside. From the Socorro Rojo extra clerks were sent to help. And finally there were no more bottles and even the kitchen refrigerator had been used for makeshift storage space.

From the balcony Dr. Lopez announced that no more donors could be taken till the next day. But the men and women who had waited for hours cried out in protest.

"Hombre... camarada... por favor... ahora! You must take the blood now! Our men *need* it now!"

Shouting above the din, Lopez tried to explain that there were no more containers for their blood, and there was no more space to store it. But the protests continued.

With a harassed look Lopez turned to Bethune. "What shall we do? They will not leave!"

Bethune leaned over the balcony railing to look at the shouting crowd below. Turning back to the Spaniard, his face lit up with pride, he said: "If they won't leave, then we'll stay open. We'll admit them all. Let the clerks register them, take their names and addresses. We'll make as many blood tests as we can today, and explain to all of them that we'll be calling them back within a few days."

Ten days later, on Dec. 23, the first transfusions were given from stored blood delivered by the mobile Spanish-Canadian blood unit.

The war was like a flood: blocked at one point, it broke out at another. In November it had swirled round Madrid; now, in the new year, it threatened to engulf southern Spain.

Franco had thrown everything into the assault against Madrid–and failed. A stalemate now would gain the Republicans time to strengthen their defences–and the fascists, a moral defeat. To surround Republican Spain, to cut it off from the rest of the world, to reassure Rome and Berlin–that was now viewed by Franco as a prime necessity. By the end of January massed German, Italian and Moorish troops deployed in the south began heavy attacks northward. Their aim was occupation of the coast and a flanking movement against the Republicans. Standing in their way were the cities of Málaga, Motril and Almería, a string of sunbaked towns, and the poorly equipped troops of the Republic.

At the Blood Institute Bethune tapped veins, kept up his relays to the front, and studied the map of Spain. It was clear that a new phase of the war was opening, and therefore a new phase in the work of the institute. He laid his plans before the Socorro Rojo at the end of January. The decisive thing now, he contended, was to extend operations to the fronts directly in the path of the latest fascist attack. His proposals received immediate endorsement. On Feb. 4, accompanied by Sise, he set out for Málaga, travelling in a new truck fitted with transfusion equipment and special refrigerators loaded with blood.

When they arrived at Valencia on Feb. 6, the news at Socorro Rojo headquarters was sombre. Because of the situation in the south, an official said, it might be more prudent to establish the subsidiary blood bank in Valencia itself. But Bethune and Sise rejected the advice and left for the front the next morning.

For three days they followed the coastline, feeling the tension growing in every town along their route. On Feb. 10 they reached Almería and heard the worst: Málaga had fallen. "You can go no farther," a government spokesman said. "There is nowhere for you to go. We don't know where our troops are. There will be nothing–"

"But wounded," Bethune said. "There will be plenty of wounded."

They drove silently through the town. Under the palm trees gracing the small port below, Sise stopped the truck. They were 105 miles from the front. "Well," he inquired, "what do we do now?"

"Exactly what we set out to do."

Bethune recorded the events that followed:

There was only one road. It circled round steep curves, banked on the right by gray cliffs. Below us the Mediterranean tossed its breakers against the rocks.

Ten miles out of Almería my reveries were interrupted by a strange procession. I peered through the windshield wonderingly. Peasants? Yes, plodding along with the ever-present donkey. Yet as they drew closer they were no longer merely peasants.

Coming toward us, leading a donkey, we saw a man dragging his feet, his head hanging, a child tied onto his back with a shawl. The donkey was heaped high with a mattress, pots and pans, a pair of boots, blankets, a water jug. A boy hung onto the donkey's tail. Behind him came a woman with an infant in her arms, and behind her an old man hobbling with a stick, dragging another child by the hand. They plodded along wearily, their feet scuffing the hard road, their shoulders drooping as if to pull them forward.

Farther down the road another group was filing round the bend. They were like mourners following a hearse. The men staggered under their wide hats, the women trailed haltingly in their traditional dark cotton cloaks, the children wore only short pants or shifts, their half-naked bodies hot in the sun.

Around every bend there were more refugees. At first they came on in scattered groups, then at more frequent intervals—100 yards apart, 50 yards, then following on each other's heels: a thin line flowing without break along the side of the road.

They were of all ages, but their faces were drawn with the same weariness. They flowed past our truck without expression: a young girl, hardly 16, straddling a donkey, her head drooping over an infant at her breast; a grandmother, her old face half-hidden in her dark shawl, dragging along between two men; a patriarch, shrivelled down to the skin and bone, his bare feet dripping blood on the road; a young man with a pile of bedding strapped to his shoulders, the leather thongs cutting into his flesh with every step; a woman holding her stomach, her eyes wide and fearful—a silent, haggard, tortured flood of men and animals.

Sise stopped the car. I got out and stood in the centre of the road. Where were they from? Where were they going? What had happened? They looked at me slowly, sideways. The fascists were behind them, they said. Málaga? Yes, they were from Málaga, and Málaga had fallen. Where were they going? Wherever the road led. The fascists had come to Málaga, the guns had roared, the houses had crumbled, and everyone able to walk had taken to the roads. Turn about, they advised; there was nothing left . . . nothing behind them but more people on the road, and behind them again, the fascists.

How had it happened? But it was no use thinking about that now. What mattered was that somewhere this side of the captured city Republican lines, surely, would be reforming. Somewhere down the road there would be fighting, wounded, needing the blood we had brought from Madrid.

We drove more quickly now. There was a sharp turn away from the sea, a slow climb, and suddenly we breasted a hill falling away to a long, level plain. Sise rammed his foot on the brake.

The scene below held us speechless. The plain stretched as far as the eye could see; across it, where the road should have been, there wriggled 20 miles of human beings, like a giant caterpillar, its many limbs raising a cloud of dust, moving slowly, ponderously across the arid, flat country and up into the foothills.

I shielded my eyes to look down onto the plain. Nowhere was the road visible. It was blotted out by the refugees, thousands upon thousands of them, pressed together, falling against each other, like bees swarming in a hive, and filling the plain with the hum of voices, cries, wailings.

We began to descend slowly, Sise sounding his horn without stop. The refugees paid no attention; they merely flowed around the car with downcast eyes, then spread across the road behind it.

If they were from Málaga they had been walking at least five days and five nights. Was it possible? That old woman with the open ulcers on her legs—could she have survived five days and nights on the road? Yet here she was, her cloak trailing in the dust, swallowed up now behind the truck. And the children, most of them barefoot—could they too have survived?

We drove on through wretched villages emptied by the general retreat; alongside bomb-pits and burnt-out hovels. Then the plodding mass changed imperceptibly, like a spring suddenly filled with mud. I swore under my breath: militiamen!

At first there were only a few, but a mile farther they came on in hundreds, then in thousands. Their uniforms were torn, their weapons gone, their faces covered with stubble, their eyes hollow with defeat. What were they doing among the refugees? Political irresponsibles? Deserters? I had no time to wonder, for behind the militiamen came lines of cavalry. Horses and riders were spent. Some of the cavalrymen slouched along with their boots slung about their necks, leading their mounts, women or children clinging to the saddle. They were no longer cavalry; they were refugees like the rest, silent, grim, in flight.

The Spanish sun was as merciless as the fascists that day. The heat became a tangible, hated enemy. The road swerved back to the sea, and we heard the sound of the surf on the rocky coast again, rumbling like a distant drum beneath the sounds of the exodus.

Now there were more signs of panic and disorder. Stopped momentarily by an obstruction on the road, we were engulfed by shouted pleas, hands reaching out toward us, people begging for water, for transport to Almería. I threw my water canisters out the window and we pushed ahead.

At last the sun began to set. The sky glowed, long tongues of flame trembled in the Mediterranean, then it was dark. We sensed the quickened pace of the refugees about us. Sise switched on the headlights. Immediately we heard angry cries: "*Luz*—lights!" Lights were a menace; only the black night held safety.

Without headlights it was almost impossible to drive. We sounded the horn, we shouted, but it was no good. In an hour we moved a short distance, then we moved no farther. A group of militiamen came up, harassed, but with some semblance of discipline. They asked for our documents, examined them carefully, saluted, and reported the situation behind them. The next town, Motril, was already in enemy hands or would be soon. There was no front; no stand was being made anywhere this side of Almería. It was more than a rout—it was a collapse, with the southern coastal region falling like a ripe plum into the hands of Franco's foreign troops.

The door of the truck flew open. In the darkness a man stood with a five-year-old child in his arms. He held out the child, emaciated, shivering with fever, and began to talk, the words spilling from his mouth, his voice rising till it was like the wail of a desolate flamenco. "*Mi chico—muy malo* . . . My child is very ill . . . He will die before I carry him to Almería . . . I will stay behind . . . I ask for him . . . Take him—leave him wherever there is a hospital . . . Tell them that I will follow . . . Tell them this one is Juan Blas and that I will come soon to find him."

I took the child and laid him gently on the seat. The Spaniard seized my hand convulsively and made the sign of the cross over me. I needed more than Spanish to speak my heart to this stranger, to the faces coming out of the tumult and the night, the faces gathering about me, twitching with fear, to the arms reaching out like a wavering, stricken forest, to the voices beseeching me.

"*Camarada* . . . *por favor* . . . save us," they cried.

"Take our women and children. . . ."

"Have pity, *camarada,* save us, for the love of God. . . ."

"*Camarada, los niños* – the children. . . ."

I bent down to peer at Sise across the shivering body of the child. "They're right," I said. "It's senseless to go farther. There's only one thing we can do – get as many of these people to Almería as we can. We'll unload everything, and send the stuff along with the first ambulance that comes by. We'll take children only. . . ."

We turned the truck about, unloaded the equipment and stores of blood, and when we were finished I opened the back doors. A thrill of excitement ran through the refugees. I calculated the number of people the truck would accommodate, and jumped to the ground. "*Solamente niños!*" I announced, but the words were lost in the hubbub and I was thrown back by the sudden surge of bodies. The doors to safety had opened, and to every refugee it seemed rescue was a matter of now or never. As I fell back under their frantic charge, I flung my arms across

The beseeching voices: "Camarada, save us!"
And the reply from the Canadian ambulance:
"Niños! Children only!"

the open doors. "Children only!" I shouted furiously, holding them off. "*Niños!* Children only!" Sise came plunging to my side to help.

It seemed gruesome now to decide who would go and who would stay, more terrible even than to be a helpless onlooker. "You," I called, pointing over the heads at a woman holding a baby about her neck. "We'll take your child!" Willing hands pushed her toward me. "We'll take the child," I repeated, but the mother merely looked up at me with great, dark, sunken eyes and held the child tighter. Perhaps she didn't understand? I put out my arms, but still she looked at me without expression, and I saw that the child was too young to be separated from the mother. I felt a stab of uncertainty. It was easy to say, "Children only," but this woman's eyes replied: "Take my child alone, and you kill us both." I put my arms about her, opened a way for her to the truck and into Hazen's waiting arms. "Both of them," I said and pushed into the crowd again.

Back and forth I went, grimly turning adults away, carrying the children in my arms.

"How many more?" I called to Sise.

"Two more—with a tight squeeze."

I felt a touch on my arm. I looked over my shoulder and saw an old face, a stooped back, tears, and the unspoken inquiry glimmering through the tears. I looked at the old man, then slowly shook my head. "Your face will haunt my dreams, friend," I thought, but I put aside the hand at my sleeve—an old man's hand at my sleeve like the hand of a child.

Two more to go—and there was a sudden silence as the truth dawned on the waiting refugees. I passed a woman of 50, old before her time, but still too young for death. She could hardly stand erect. Her legs were gigantic, the varicose veins visible in the darkness, knotted like swollen thongs of torture, blood seeping into the cuffs of her linen sandals. I came back to her. What if this were my own mother—how would I decide? I stood before her, touching her bony shoulder. My own mother? But if not my own, then someone else's—a mother of Spain, and therefore my own. I steadied her swaying shoulders, but she looked calmly away, as if she had nothing to ask.

I took the last child for the last precious space—plucking it from the arms of a woman who held it, screaming, then screaming gave it up as if it was issuing once more, in blood and pain, from her very womb. I carried the child, a little girl, through the silent crowd to the truck.

Suddenly a woman pushed in front of me, seized the doorjambs and clambered in. "Get out!" I ordered, holding the child toward her. "It's you or the child! Do you understand? Will you take the place of the child?"

The woman was young. Her long black hair fell about her pale face. She looked at me with haunted eyes, then flung open her cloak and raised her cotton shift high. Her belly was distended with child.

For a moment we looked at each other, I with the child in my arms, she with the child in her womb. She pressed herself down on the tiny space of flooring at her feet, her great stomach between her knees, smiled at me and held out her arms. With her eyes and her arms and her smile she seemed to be saying: "See, I will take the child, and it will be as if I am not here, as if I am taking nobody's place." She placed the girl on her knees, pillowing the little head on her shoulders.

Now it was done. Forty children and two women were jammed together in the truck and the front cab. I banged the doors shut and ordered Sise to take them directly to the hospital in Almería and to stop for nothing and nobody. He was to make sure they got food and medical attention, then inform the governor of the situation, and tell him he must send transport at once or there would be more dead from hunger and exhaustion than from enemy action. Then he was to get the tank filled with gas and come back for another load. He turned, walked to the cab without looking back, climbed in, and started the motor. . . .

The truck was gone. The women wept for their departed children, the men hoisted the packs to their backs, and they moved forward again, the thought of the enemy like a hot wind on their necks.

At the side of the road I found the old woman with the bleeding legs. She was sitting with her head on her knees. She looked up, the same calm resignation on her gaunt face. I took a tube and bandage from my kit and bandaged her feet. "Come," I said. "It's a long way to Almería. We'll walk a while, till it's safe for you to rest." She understood nothing of what I said, but she gave me her hands. I raised her gently, talking to her in the strange language she had never heard before. Together we joined the other refugees on the road. Together, with the others falling in behind, we began the trek to Almería. . . .

Carried along by the stream of refugees I peered at the illuminated dial of my wristwatch. Was it only midnight? Had I been walking only four hours? Four hours seemed like an eternity, yet the others had been walking for days!

I had left the old woman two hours ago when she could go no farther, after making a bed of earth for her in an open field, among the many others who owned nothing now but a bed of earth. Perhaps, I thought, a stray ambulance would pick her up; perhaps, on the other hand, the fascists would reach her first.

I had used up my last bandage, administered my last pill, given away my last chocolate bar, smoked my last cigarette, and thrown away my empty kit. I had only my bare hands now, and my impatience for Sise's return. And then—what? Then it would be like trying to drain the ocean with a thimble.

There was a commotion on the road. I made out our truck, crawling along with dimmed headlights. Sise jumped out, his face haggard but elated. . . .

Back and forth we shuttled, working furiously to evacuate the remnants of a whole city. Sise stayed behind the wheel while I stayed on the road, assembling the next group to be transported. We grew white-faced with lack of sleep. We lost track of time. We lived with the heartbreak of those left behind, and the weary joy of those brought to safety. We worked with the knowledge that every trip might be the last.

On every trip to Almería, Sise stopped at the governor's office to clamor for trucks, carts, for anything movable to speed the evacuation. But there was nothing left on wheels in the city.

On the second day I decided it was no longer possible to take children only: the sight of parents separated from their children became too ghastly to bear. We began to move whole families, giving preference to those with children. On the second day we tasted too what the others had tasted for five days—hunger.

Then, as if to mock our hunger, a man appeared on the road from nowhere, pushing a cart of oranges and shouting his wares in a stentorian voice. In the midst of war, flight, death, an ordinary, prosaic street hawker! I bought the whole cart of oranges, keeping one for myself and distributing the others.

Thus it went, for four days and nights. By day we worked in clouds of dust, under a sun that blistered the skin, our eyes red-rimmed, our bellies rumbling. At night the cold grew unendurable, so that we longed for the tormenting heat once more.

A great silence settled over the refugees. The starving lay in the fields, gripped by torpor. The thirsty sat on the rocks, trembling, or staggered about aimlessly, the wild glassy stare of delusion in their eyes. The dead lay indiscriminately among the sick, looking unblinkingly into the sun. Then the planes swept overhead glinting, silvery Italian fighters and squadrons of German Heinkels. They dived toward the road, as casually as at target practice, their machine guns weaving intricate geometric patterns about the fleeing refugees. . . .

Again I saw the truck return. We piled in as many as we could. This time I got in as well, a child on my lap, moaning, looking at me with hot, feverish eyes. Probably meningitis. After a while he no longer seemed to be in pain. A bad sign. I hoped we would get him to Almería in time.

I dozed, then awoke to find the truck rolling slowly downgrade. This looked like the last mile. But what a mile! From the Sierras into the city tens of thousands of refugees were fanned out like a funnel with a giant spout and a narrow, twisting stem. They swarmed over the hills, the road, the beaches below, some wading into the sea to get to the city sooner.

In four days Almería had become a vast encampment. The streets were filled with refugees who had nowhere to stay and nowhere to go. Several thousands were quartered on the main square. Men and women rose wearily from the pavement to let us through.

At Socorro Rojo we were directed to an old building where a hospital and reception centre for the children had been improvised. We helped the refugees in and put the sick child in a doctor's care. Then I found a cot and collapsed. . . .

I jerked awake. For a moment I thought I was lying out in the hills, beside the road, but my hand slid over the rough floor and I remembered this was no longer the road but Almería. I wondered at the ringing in my ears.

It was the wailing of the siren that had awakened me. I scrambled to my feet, and fell on my knees again as the first bomb went off. The explosion was like a giant mailed fist smashing deep into the earth. I could hear the terrible, frightened screams of the children. In the hallway people were running and shouting. I scrambled up again, the floor still vibrating under my feet. More explosions sounded.

I ran through the dark corridors, jostling against people hurrying in every direction. In the dormitories children were crying with fright. I found my way into the street, and made for the centre of the city, on the run.

The planes kept sweeping in, one after another, the roar of the engines filling the streets till it seemed my eardrums would burst. Then came the bombs, falling up ahead. I caught a glimpse of one bomber banking gracefully in the moonlight, disdaining the protection of height or darkness. The devils could afford to take their time! The occasional burst of anti-aircraft fire merely prettied up the sky like Roman candles.

In a few minutes I reached the densely populated section of the city. Here the streets were no longer dark. Great sheets of flame shot up from the skeletons of buildings, hit by incendiaries. Vast crowds surged about wildly, running from the bombs, going down under toppling walls, falling, crawling, disappearing into bomb-pits, clutching and screaming as they vanished.

There were no sounds of bombing from the direction of the port. The bombers weren't interested in the port! They were after the 100,000 people who had eluded them at Málaga, who had refused to live under the fascists, who were now penned together here in a perfect target. For a week they had let Almería alone. Now that the trek from Málaga was over, now that the refugees were caught in a few city blocks where mass

693

murder required only a minimum number of bombs—now Franco was slaking his thirst for revenge.

I fought my way through the dense crowds, shouting, "*Médico! Médico!*" My voice was lost in the shrieking of the sirens, the explosions, the fearful braying of donkeys.

Then suddenly the bombing stopped and the roar of the planes faded. The flaming buildings lit up the faces of men and women looking numbed, shocked, horror-stricken. The raid was over. My ears ached in the silence. Silence? No. With the bombing over I could hear the voices . . . the raid was over but the dying remained.

I bound the wounds of the injured with strips of cotton torn from their shirts. In a gutted house I found a little girl whimpering beneath a pile of heavy beams. She was perhaps three years old. I pulled the beams away and carried her in my arms till I came across an ambulance. I laid her on the stretcher, thinking it would be kinder if she died, for if the crippled body survived, the light of sanity had gone out of her eyes.

In the centre of the city I came to a silent circle of men and women. Inside the circle was a great bomb crater. Inside the crater were twisted drainpipes, torn clothing, a splattered mass of what had once been human beings.

My body felt as heavy as the dead themselves. But empty and hollow. And in my brain there burned a bright flame of hate. . . .

So went Bethune's journal of his four nights and days on the Málaga road.

Back in Madrid he extended the work of the blood unit to cover the whole of the central front. With the transfusion service working well, he was persuaded to lecture in North America in support of Republican Spain. For seven months he toured Canada and the United States but late in 1937—he was now an avowed communist—he decided his usefulness again lay in direct participation. This time it would be China, whose need for doctors was even greater than Spain's.

Bethune left Vancouver on Jan. 2, 1938. He spent almost two years with the guerrilla forces of Mao Tse-tung's Eighth Route Army, performing front-line operations, setting up training schools for doctors and nurses, and writing textbooks on medical procedures for guerrilla warfare. On Oct. 28, 1939, while operating without gloves, he cut a finger and contracted blood poisoning.

He lived only until Nov. 13. He was 49.

694

Through Nightmare to Freedom

*On the evening of Sept. 5, 1945, a stocky blond 25-year-old Russian
named Igor Gouzenko walked for the last time to his office at the Soviet
embassy in Ottawa, where he had worked as a cipher clerk
since 1943. Gouzenko had decided to seek asylum in Canada and to reveal
the existence of a Soviet spy network in the lower and middle echelons
of the Canadian government. In his 1948 book,* THIS WAS MY CHOICE, *Gouzenko described his frantic attempts to make contact with Canadian
authorities. For him and his pregnant wife Anna,
their first 36 hours of "freedom"
were a nightmare.*

By IGOR GOUZENKO

*Hooded to prevent identifica-
tion, Gouzenko testifies
about the Russian spy ring.*

I HAD TO GO FIRST to the military attaché's on Range Road, ostensibly to complete some work but really to ensure that Lieutenant Koulakov was there, then to the embassy on Charlotte Street where the really important documents were kept.

It was unseasonably hot and sultry as I walked to Col. [Nicolai] Zabotin's. But I knew the perspiration trickling inside my shirt was caused by more than the weather. Tonight was to be the turning point of my life, and the lives of my family, from Soviet slavery to democratic freedom.

The deadline had been forced by Colonel Zabotin's abrupt decision for me to turn over my work to Koulakov in the very near future and act henceforth as advisory onlooker.

I am no hero. Nature seems to allow very few to don the heroic mantle. I was born a very ordinary little man of Russia. I had never excelled in athletics. My triumphs seemed limited to the realm of studies. Dangerous living never had appealed to me. But that Wednesday night of Sept. 5, during the long walk to Range Road, I came as close to becoming a hero as I ever will.

This could be, I was fully aware, my last night on earth. One wrong move could mean the complete ruination of all our plans and, as far as I was aware, the NKVD [Russian secret police] might have been watching me for some time. Perhaps Zabotin's sudden imposition of the deadline was actually the setting up of a trap into which I was now entering. My very roots had been injected with fearful respect for the NKVD's omnipresence and vengeance.

There was an easier, a vastly safer, way out than by going back for those documents. Yet somehow, I managed to freeze my mind into the course Anna and I had mapped out. Come what may, I had to remove the documents tonight.

We had decided that it would be necessary to make my escape during a weekday although a Saturday night would have been ideal, allowing me until Monday morning to make good my getaway. But the newspaper offices would not be open Saturday night and we had decided I should take the documents and my story to a newspaper.

There was no thought of going to the police. That was a natural result of our experience with the thoroughly corrupt NKVD. I naturally thought the local police would sell out to the Soviet embassy. At the same time, we had been impressed with the freedom and fearlessness of the Canadian press.

Other factors were involved in the Wednesday night choice. This was Koulakov's night to sit up on watch at the military attaché's and he would be permitted to sleep until noon next day. This would allow me more leeway because Koulakov would be the most likely one to first report me as missing. Since the cipher work was so secret, the rest of the staff, with the exception of Colonel Zabotin, knew little of the hours I was supposed to be on or off duty. And I knew that Zabotin, who was to attend a show at the National Film Board that night, would hardly turn up before noon.

Finally I turned into Range Road and, curiously, I felt exhilaration. Suspense had put my nerves on edge, but now the moment was upon me I felt strangely relieved. I noted Koulakov had taken his place at the night-watch desk. That was good. A switch in Koulakov's plans would have hurt mine.

Captain Galkin, supposedly a guard but in reality an extremely well trained intelligence operator, appeared as I entered.

"How about coming to a movie?" he asked.

I tried to appear interested. "Which one?"

Galkin mentioned a neighborhood theatre. It occurred to me that this would provide an ideal opportunity to leave, since I had really wanted only to see if Koulakov was on the job.

"Good idea," I said. "It's too hot to work anyway."

Galkin said other members of the staff were coming and we waited outside until they joined us.

We walked to the theatre. There I pretended disappointment.

"Damn it, I've seen that show! You fellows go ahead because it's a good picture. I'll take a streetcar and go to another show downtown."

I walked toward a car stop but veered when they vanished into the theatre. I turned toward Charlotte Street and walked deliberately to the embassy. The guard returned my nod as I signed the book. As I was putting my pen back in my pocket I glanced toward the reception room and my blood seemed to freeze.

There sat Vitali Pavlov, chief of the NKVD in Canada!

Somehow I managed to act naturally and walked by the reception room seemingly concerned with the clip of my pen not fastening into my pocket the way it should. Pavlov apparently did not notice me. I pressed the secret bell under the banister, mounted the stairs leading to the secret cipher room, pulled aside the curtain and stood at the steel door.

The attendant who unbarred it was Ryazanov, commercial attaché cipher clerk and a friend of mine. I noted with relief that he was alone.

We exchanged a few remarks on the weather. Ryazanov asked if I was working late again.

"No," I replied, "there are just a couple of telegrams to do and then I'll catch an 8:30 show."

Ryazanov said I was being sensible and turned to his own work.

I entered my little office and closed the door carefully behind me. I went to my desk, opened it and removed Zabotin's cipher pouch, which I had left there that afternoon. Most of the documents I wanted were there. The others were in the files. All were marked by turned down corners.

Some of the documents were large sheets of paper. Others were small scraps. Later, the police count showed 109 items.

I opened my shirt and carefully distributed the documents inside. Then I completed the telegrams which represented my reason for being there. They dealt with information supplied by Emma Woikin, an agent in the Canadian External Affairs Department.

Originally these "excuse" telegrams hadn't seemed important, but on second thought I saw they fitted in with other data. It was too bad for Emma that I stopped to reconsider them. They cost her a three-year prison sentence.

Once the ciphering task was finished I stood up and gingerly examined my shirt, which to me appeared to bulge suspiciously. However, the evening was so warm I felt a sloppy-looking shirt wouldn't arouse undue interest.

I walked across the corridor and handed the telegrams to Ryazanov for dispatching to Moscow. I also handed him Zabotin's sealed pouch to be placed in the safe.

I watched Ryazanov's face for any evidence that he saw anything unusual in my manner or appearance. He displayed no undue interest. Casually I stepped into the men's room and washed my hands.

While doing so I called out: "It's too hot to stick around here. Why don't you skip out with me to the show?"

Ryazanov grunted.

"Fat chance of getting away with anything around here. Besides, Pavlov is downstairs. Thanks just the same, I'd better stick around."

Mention of Pavlov left me a little weak around the knees. I had momentarily forgotten him. But there was no turning back. I adjusted

my shirt and stepped to the door. Ryazanov opened it and I bade him goodnight.

I was careful walking down the steps, afraid I might disturb the documents and cause an extra large bulge, or that a small document might slip through my belt and drop from a pant leg.

Sweat was standing out on my brow and I felt my chest tightening as I approached the reception room. I didn't dare reach into a pocket for my handkerchief lest the movement might disturb something.

The street door seemed miles away. But now I was passing the reception room. My heart leapt with joy. The room was empty. Pavlov had gone. A good omen. I was very much in luck. I signed myself out, bade the attendant goodnight and walked out. Gratefully I sucked in the humid air.

I took a streetcar downtown and went to the Ottawa *Journal*.

I was trembling like a leaf. I stopped to mop my brow and make sure nobody was following me, then entered and asked the elevator man where I could find the editor.

"Sixth floor," he said, and he slammed the door shut behind me.

At the sixth floor I walked toward a door marked "Editor" but just as I was about to knock something happened inside me. Grim doubts filled my mind. Surely, I thought, every big newspaper must have an NKVD agent working in it. Was I doing the right thing? I decided to think it over and turned back to the elevator. The door opened to let somebody out and the operator yelled: "Down!"

I stepped in. The elevator descended a few floors and stopped to pick up some people. Among them was a girl who looked at me and smiled.

"What are you doing here? Is there news breaking at the embassy?"

I was panic-stricken. Her face was familiar. Where had I seen her before? What would I do?

The elevator reached the ground floor. As the door opened I muttered an apology to the girl, said something about being in a big hurry and walked quickly to the street. I ran to the first corner, then slowed to a fast walk. I walked for blocks as I tried to calm my burning mind. What would I do now? I boarded a streetcar and went home to Anna. We would talk it over.

Anna answered my code knock. Her face was drawn and white.

"Did something go wrong?" she whispered tensely.

I sat down heavily on the sofa. Anna came over and sat beside me. I told her the whole story, finishing up with the account of being spotted by the girl in the elevator.

Anna was absolutely unruffled: "Don't worry about her, Igor. She must be a journalist or she would not have been in the office. Many journalists were entertained at the embassy and that is where she probably met you. They have good memories. But even if there is an NKVD agent in the newspaper office, it needn't matter. What could he do in time to stop you?"

I took renewed strength from her confidence.

"What now?" I asked.

"Go right back to the newspaper office and see the editor. You still have several hours before the embassy learns what has happened."

I opened my shirt and removed the documents. They were soaked with sweat. Anna tried to dry them a bit by waving them. Then she wrapped them in a paper.

Anna kissed me as she opened the door. I squeezed her arm and went out into the night again.

At the *Journal* the same elevator man took me up to the sixth floor. I stepped quickly to the editor's door and knocked. There was no answer. I knocked again. Still no answer. I tried the door. It was locked. I walked to a door leading into the large city room. Nobody paid any attention to me. I saw an office boy hurrying in my direction. I asked him where I could find the editor.

"Gone for the night," he said, dashing past me.

I went to the nearest desk and told a man working at a typewriter that I wished to see whoever was in charge.

"It is extremely important," I said.

He took me to a desk at the other side of the room. An older man wearing a green eyeshade told me to sit down.

I took out the stolen documents and spread them on the desk. As I did so, I explained who I was and that these were proof that Soviet agents in Canada were seeking data on the atomic bomb.

The man with the eyeshade stared at me, then picked up several of the documents. But he looked at them only for a moment. They were in Russian.

"I'm sorry," he said finally. "This is out of our field. I suggest you go to the Royal Canadian Mounted Police or come back in the morning to see the editor."

I hastened to explain that by morning the NKVD might be on my trail and even kill me. I could see he thought I was crazy.

"Sorry," he said. "I'm busy."

He stood up and walked away, leaving me sitting there. I felt helpless and confused. Out on the street I leaned against the wall and tried to collect my thoughts. There was only one thing to do and that was contact a high official. The minister of justice seemed the logical person. I walked to the Justice Building on Wellington Street, where a tall man in RCMP uniform stopped me at the door. I hesitated for a moment but realized things were getting desperate. I said it was most important that I see the minister of justice immediately.

The policeman replied politely but firmly:

"It is almost midnight. You can see nobody until morning. Sorry."

Sorry? That word was getting on my nerves. "But," I repeated, "it is desperately necessary that I reach the minister right away—by telephone at least."

He shook his head. "It can't be done."

I returned home, thoroughly subdued and more than a little frightened. Anna bolstered me again.

"Don't worry about it. You have the whole morning to reach the minister. Have a good sleep and you will feel better."

She tucked the documents in her handbag and put it under her pillow. But neither of us slept that night. We just lay there thinking and talking until the first light of dawn was filtering through our bedroom window. I raised myself on one elbow and looked out. There was a tinge of red in the eastern sky. Somehow, it comforted me immensely to know there was a nice day coming.

"Anna," I said, "we will all go to the justice minister's office as soon as it opens. I might be kept waiting and the suspense would be unbearable if I wasn't certain about your safety. I'll dress Andrei. Do you think you can stand the strain . . . even if you are ill when you get up?"

"I will be all right, Igor," she replied instantly. "We will all go together and you will have nothing to worry about once we are all in the justice minister's office."

I lay back with a sigh of relief. Things were clearing somewhat. The next thing I knew, Anna was shaking me.

"It is seven o'clock, Igor."

I had dozed off into heavy slumber, but the sleep had done me good. I shaved and put on my good brown suit. Anna was feeding Andrei and had a pot of coffee on the stove. It was a bright, sunshiny day. I felt prepared for anything that lay ahead.

But even my immense optimism would have wilted if I had been able to foresee the staggering disappointments in store for us.

Before leaving the house we decided that Anna should carry the documents in her purse, because if the NKVD caught up with us they would go after me. I would try to create a diversion and Anna might have a chance to slip away. The documents would be a passport to protective custody with the Canadian government.

At the Justice Building, I explained to the man at the reception desk that I had to see the minister of justice on a matter of absolute emergency. The man looked at me doubtfully, then spoke for some time into the telephone.

We were escorted to the minister's office, where a courteous secretary asked what was the nature of my business. I did my best to tell him the matter was of such urgency and importance that I dared not speak to anybody but the minister. The secretary glanced from me to Anna to the child. I could imagine what was running through his mind; this man may be off his head but if that is the case why would he bring along his wife and child? I had not thought of that angle in my planning but it seemed a fortunate one.

The secretary went into the inside office and I could hear him telephoning somebody. Then he finally returned.

"The minister is in his other office over in the Parliament Buildings," he said. "I will take you there."

We went to Parliament Hill and through the picturesque halls to the minister's office. But I had to see another secretary first. It was the same thing all over again. I had to speak to the minister personally, nobody else would do. The secretary picked up his telephone and talked to somebody at length—in French. I knew it was about me because I heard my name mentioned, but I could not understand anything else. After some time he hung up the telephone and told the first secretary to take us back to the Justice Building and wait there for the minister.

Back we went and there we sat for two precious hours. Andrei was getting impatient and we had trouble keeping him from crying. The telephone rang. The secretary listened.

"Very well, sir." Then he turned to us: "I am very sorry. The minister is unable to see you."

Sorry? Again that word! I looked at Anna with a hint of panic. She was biting her lip. Poor Anna.

"Let us go to the newspaper office again," she said quietly.

The editor wasn't available, we were told at the *Journal*. But a reporter was sent out to talk to us. She was a beautiful blonde named Lesley Johnstone, kind and interested. She patted Andrei on the head as she invited us to sit down.

I told her the whole story. She listened intently, looking at Anna repeatedly as if seeking confirmation. She studied the documents momentarily, then took them into the editor's office. Within a very short time she came out.

"I am terribly sorry," she said, handing me back the documents. "Your story just doesn't seem to register here. Nobody wants to say anything but nice things about Stalin these days."

It was Anna who spoke first.

"What should we do now, miss?"

"Why not go to see the RCMP about taking out naturalization papers? That should prevent the Reds from taking you back."

In desperation we returned to the Justice Building. An officer at the police identification branch said the RCMP had nothing to do with naturalization and he told us to go to the Crown attorney's office on Nicholas Street.

We had quite a distance to go and the day was getting hot. Andrei was whimpering so I carried him. Anna was obviously growing weary. But these things seemed minor. Through my actions we were now all in an awful predicament and something had to be done.

At the Crown attorney's office we were told the woman who handled naturalization applications had just gone to lunch. I took Anna and Andrei to a little restaurant nearby and as I ordered lunch I noticed it was almost two o'clock. I could imagine what was happening at the embassy. But perhaps they hadn't yet noticed the documents were missing and were merely wondering why I hadn't shown up for work.

Andrei fell asleep at the table. Anna decided we had better take the child to a friend of hers, a British woman in the next building to ours. We got on a streetcar and went back to Somerset Street. The neighbor was most kind when Anna stated she had to do some shopping. The child would be all right until we returned, she said.

Back we went to the Crown attorney's office. The girl gave us forms to fill out, then told us to return next day to arrange for photographs. I looked at her in alarm: "How long will this naturalization take?"

"Oh," she replied, "I can't tell you for sure. A few months, perhaps."

Anna burst into tears. It was the first time her courage had failed her. I put an arm around her and spoke in Russian. Miserably, I looked around the office. There, at another desk, was a woman in a red dress whom we had spoken to when we came before lunch. Just what I saw in her expression I don't know but, on impulse, I moved quickly across the room and poured out my story to her.

She listened in obvious amazement, then stood up and brought over a couple of chairs. She brought Anna to her desk and signalled for us to be seated. I noted a nameplate on her desk: Mrs. Fernande Joubarne.

"This is something the world should know," she said firmly. "I will try to help you."

I felt like crying. Anna grasped my hand as Mrs. Joubarne telephoned another newspaper. I heard her telling somebody there was a "story" in her office of "world importance" and suggesting a reporter be sent immediately. The conversation seemed to run into difficulties. Everybody was busy, it appeared, and couldn't she explain over the telephone? Mrs. Joubarne called somebody else.

In about half an hour a male reporter appeared. He knew Mrs. Joubarne and greeted her by name. She introduced us and, once again, I related my story. Anna handed me the documents and I translated them for him. He asked me to repeat the contents of the documents relating to the atomic bomb. Then I translated the dossier on Labor-Progressive Party organizer Sam Carr. This seemed to impress him, but he finally shook his head.

"It's too big for us to handle—much too big. It is a matter for the police or the government. I suggest you take it to them."

Mrs. Joubarne, Anna and I all started speaking at once, trying to enlist his active co-operation. But he merely voiced his regrets, and left. Mrs. Joubarne sighed:

"There is nothing more I can do. You had better follow his advice." Then, to Anna she said: "And good luck to you. Let me know if it is a boy or a girl."

We walked out into the blazing sun. I stopped at the foot of the stairs, not knowing which way to turn. Anna took my arm.

"Let us go home, Igor," she said, an immense weariness in her voice.

The danger of going home didn't mean anything to me any more. I was near total exhaustion and home, at least, meant rest; somewhere to think, somewhere to plan what to do next.

As we neared Somerset Street I told Anna to go into the next building for Andrei while I went up to our apartment, No. 4. If all was well I would wave to her across the areaway between the buildings.

I went up the stairs quietly and listened at our door. Everything was quiet. I looked inside. Everything seemed in order. I stepped out onto the rear balcony. All was clear. Anna was looking from the friend's window and I waved.

After she returned with Andrei I lay across the bed, but sleep wouldn't come. Every noise bothered me. I got up and walked to one of the front windows. As I looked down, my heart skipped a beat!

Two men seated on a bench in the park opposite were looking up at my window!

I stepped back so as not to be seen. I studied them closely but, from that distance, could not see their faces. They appeared to be total strangers. As I turned to bring Anna from the kitchen, a knock sounded on the apartment door.

I froze in my steps. As Anna came from the kitchen, I signalled for her to remain quiet. There was another knock, louder and more insistent. This was repeated four times.

The person outside apparently then decided to call it a day but Andrei chose that moment to dash across the living room to Anna. The person at the door must have heard the child.

A fist banged harshly on the door. "Gouzenko!"

I recognized the voice. It belonged to Lavrentiev, Zabotin's chauffeur and contact man!

He called my name several times. Then we heard his footsteps going down the stairs. I returned to the window. The men were still on the bench, occasionally looking up.

Anna was sitting in the living room, holding Andrei. Her eyes were fastened on me. I knew that the time for positive action had arrived. The clock said 7:05. That meant RCAF Sgt. Harold Main would be at home next door.

I hurried to the rear balcony. Main and his wife were seated there seeking relief from the heat.

I asked Main if I could speak to him. He said "Sure, go ahead!" I asked if he and his wife would take care of Andrei if something happened suddenly to Anna and me.

The sergeant showed surprise. Then he beckoned me to come over the railing and follow him inside. I felt there wasn't much time to talk so I boiled everything down to the fact that Anna and I expected an attempt to be made on our lives by the NKVD and we were worried about the boy. Main looked at me doubtfully but his expression changed when I pointed out the men on the park bench. As he led the way back out onto the rear balcony, he stopped short. There was a man in the areaway looking up!

Sergeant Main made up his mind promptly.

"Get your wife and boy, Gouzenko, and bring them over here. I'm going to get the police."

The idea of consulting the police no longer alarmed me. I was between the devil and the deep blue sea and the capable, assured manner of my air force friend carried a confident impression that everything would soon be all right.

I climbed back onto our balcony and entered the apartment. The door was open—Anna and Andrei were gone!

Rushing into the hall, I stopped short, somewhat abashed on seeing them in the apartment directly across the way talking to a Mrs. Francis Elliott, who lived there.

After listening to our story, Mrs. Elliott suggested we stay with her for the night because her husband and son were away and there was a day bed we could use. She would find a place for Andrei.

I accepted her kindness gratefully. While Anna and Mrs. Elliott were talking I sat down in the dining room, feeling rather spent. Before long, heavy footsteps sounded in the hallway. It was Sergeant Main, with two Ottawa constables. I told them the story, concluding with our fears of being killed, the men posted in the park and at the rear, and the visit of Lavrentiev.

The constables asked a number of questions, then one spoke to Mrs. Elliott.

"We'll keep this building under observation all night long. The light in your bathroom will show on the front street. Leave it turned on unless something happens, then turn it off. That will be our signal to come up."

Then he turned to me.

"Take it easy, Mr. Gouzenko—you've nothing to worry about now. If we're needed we will be upstairs in a flash. Okay?"

His smile was most comforting.

"Okay," I replied automatically.

"Attaboy!"

With that the constables left.

Around 10 o'clock Mrs. Elliott made up the day bed and suggested we get some rest. Just before I lay down I turned out the light and pulled up the window blind. There was nobody below.

Sometime between 11:30 and midnight Anna and I woke up with a start. There was a sound of knocking on our apartment door across the hallway. I slipped out of bed and over to the door. Through the keyhole I could see our door clearly. Knocking on it was Pavlov, the NKVD chief!

With Pavlov were three others from the embassy. As I watched, I heard another door open. It was Sergeant Main's. I could hear him asking what they wanted. One mentioned my name. The sergeant replied: "The Gouzenkos are away."

Pavlov thanked him and the four went downstairs.

Anna squeezed my arm as I made a motion to move away. "Keep still," she whispered, "they're coming back!"

I looked through the keyhole once more and saw Pavlov working on our door with a jimmy. There was a rasping sound and the door opened. The four entered and shut the door quietly behind them.

Mrs. Elliott tiptoed beside me.

"I've tried turning the light on and off but it doesn't get the policemen. What should I do?"

I told her to call them on the telephone. She dialled central and asked for the police. She reported somebody was trying to break into apartment 4, 511 Somerset Street.

In an unbelievably short space of time, the same two constables appeared at my apartment door. The one who had done the speaking, a Const. Thomas Walsh, didn't wait for any formality. He threw open the door. He and Const. John McCulloch caught the four men rifling my desk and bureau drawers.

We opened Mrs. Elliott's door a crack and listened to what was going on. Constable Walsh had apparently asked for an explanation and Pavlov said in crisp, official tones:

"This apartment belongs to a fellow member of the Soviet embassy, a man named Gouzenko, who happens to be in Toronto tonight. He left some documents here and we have his permission to look for them."

Constable Walsh's tone was just as official.

"Did he also give you permission to break his lock or"–he pointed to the twisted lock–"was this done with your bare hands?"

Pavlov waxed indignant.

"How dare you talk to me like that? We had a key for this apartment but lost it. Anyway, this lock is Soviet property and we can do what we like with it. I order you to leave this apartment!"

Walsh looked at McCulloch, then back to Pavlov. "Constable McCulloch," said Walsh, "insists we remain here until the inspector arrives. I hope you don't mind. Meanwhile, let me see your identification."

Insp. Duncan McDonnell queried the four more extensively. Pavlov was fuming. He charged the constables had insulted them and that Soviet diplomatic immunity had been assailed. The inspector told them to wait while he made inquiries, but after he was gone Pavlov told the other three to leave with him. Constables Walsh and McCulloch made no effort to stop them.

Shortly before four in the morning there was another knock on our apartment door across the hall. Whoever it was left before I could identify him.

In the morning another Ottawa city police inspector visited us. He said the RCMP would like to have a talk with me at the federal Justice Building.

Anna gave a big, deep sigh of relief.

"At last, Igor, at last," she said. "They are going to listen to you. I am so glad!"

As I hurried into my coat, I looked at Anna. She appeared pale and nervous. "What are you going to do while I am at the Justice Building?" I asked. Anna's reply was typical.

"I have a big washing to do. Don't worry about me, Igor."

My reception at the Justice Building was in marked contrast with my two worried visits of the previous day. This time, high-ranking RCMP and civilian investigators were waiting. They treated me most courteously and for almost five hours I answered their questions. The documents aroused considerable interest and discussion after they had heard my translations.

When I described my difficulty in trying to get somebody to listen to me, the RCMP officer in charge smiled.

"You weren't quite as neglected as you thought," he said. One of the civilian investigators added: "That's a fine way to talk, after my partner and I spent so much time sitting in the park watching your apartment."

The two men had been policemen, not NKVD men as I suspected. Actually, during the two hours Anna, Andrei and I had waited outside the justice minister's office, the Department of External Affairs and the RCMP had been pondering what to do with me. Prime Minister Mackenzie King was consulted. It was decided to shadow me for a few days to judge by developments whether I was what I claimed to be or just a mental case suffering from an anti-Red complex.

It was realized, too, that if I was bona fide the case would be an international hot coal to handle.

Since those anxious days there have been many periods of worry in my life of heavily guarded hiding. Anna's pregnancy called for intensive planning, since I knew Pavlov was aware of Anna's condition and would be watching the hospitals for miles around. So it was arranged that, one night in December, an RCMP constable should take her to a hospital, where he posed as the father. By pretending to be an illiterate foreigner he managed to overcome much of the red tape demanded in making out official forms. He said in broken English that he was a Polish farmer and Anna also pretended to be Polish, with but very little knowledge of English.

The baby was a girl, 7 pounds 12 ounces. Two days after the birth, a nurse stopped by Anna's bed and exclaimed: "Why, hello there, you! Don't you remember me? I took care of you in Ottawa when you had another baby."

Anna was petrified with fear but somehow managed to play her role. She was a Polish farmer's wife. She had never been to Ottawa. Then her "husband" appeared and apparently the nurse finally decided she had made a mistake. There was no sequel to the incident, but we were worried.

Life in hiding can never be ideal. I have emerged for the various espionage trials—some 20 of them, I believe—but only under heavy guard. The RCMP are taking no chances with Pavlov's long memory and the equally long memory of the NKVD.

But there has been sunshine, too. I had no thought, in making my break, of any financial returns to be derived from it. But a prominent Ottawa businessman provided me with an annuity for life. An American magazine paid handsomely for a partial story of my disclosures on Soviet espionage activities. Hollywood has seen fit to make a movie involving Anna and me, for which rights they paid handsomely. There will be revenue from the sale of this book. In my leisure hours I have been painting and some of those paintings have already gone on exhibition in a number of cities.

Yes, fate has been kind beyond all expectations. If I had it all to do again, with no hope of financial benefits or even security for my family, I would make the break again.

The greatest gain is the one I feel deep down inside: that I did my duty toward the millions enslaved and voiceless in Russia. Letters have come to me from all parts of the United States, Canada, Europe and even India, which warm my heart.

It was heartwarming, too, to be told by Prime Minister Mackenzie King:

"You have accomplished an historical act. The people of Canada and the world are your debtors."

The opportunity I was given to serve my people will not be granted all sons of Russia, but I think it is promising that such a small cog as myself in the vast Soviet machine could have done so much.

Ironically enough, Vitali G. Pavlov, officially the second secretary of the U.S.S.R. embassy, and unofficially chief of the secret NKVD police in Canada, emerges in my view of the drama as the person immediately responsible for smashing the powerful Soviet espionage ring.

In the mysterious way that small happenings so often lead to big happenings, influencing the lives of individuals and nations, it was Pavlov's jimmying of my apartment door that convinced the authorities Igor Gouzenko really had a story to tell.

A Royal Commission established as a result of Igor Gouzenko's disclosures heard evidence that Russia, through the spy ring, had penetrated the armed forces, atomic research, the National Research Council, the Munitions Department, the External Affairs Department, the office of the British high commissioner, even Parliament itself through Labor-Progressive (Communist) MP Fred Rose, who was among those convicted. But, said the RCMP, more important than punishing those involved—the British physicist Alan Nunn May and a handful of idealistic Canadian Communists or Communist sympathizers—was "the fact that Soviet espionage methods had been exposed."

Two Who Refused to Die

After 24 days the RCAF abandoned the search and gave them up for dead. Even if they had survived the crash, they could not have endured that long in the snowbound wilderness along the border between British Columbia and the Yukon. Their tiny plane had no proper equipment or food to keep them alive in sub-zero weather. And neither the pilot nor his woman passenger had any knowledge of living in the bush.

By Thomas Whiteside

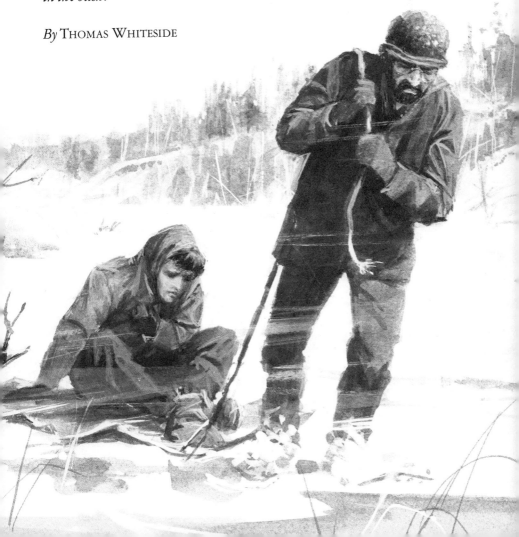

O N MARCH 24, 1963, bush pilot Chuck Hamilton was flying supplies over desolate, snowbound and mountainous country from Watson Lake in the Yukon to a ranch at Terminus Mountain in northern British Columbia. Seventy-five miles southeast of Watson Lake (and well into B.C.) he decided to go in low over Aeroplane Lake—where several months earlier he had flown in medical aid for the baby of an Indian family living in a trapper's cabin on the shore. Now nobody appeared to be there. Hamilton gained altitude and continued his flight.

He was seven miles southeast of Aeroplane Lake when something on the ground caught his eye. In a small meadow at the foot of a heavily wooded mountain, an S O S had been stamped out in the snow.

Hamilton circled, then followed a snowshoe trail that went northeast from the S O S. It led toward a creek and there Hamilton spotted the flash of a mirror. A man was standing in the middle of the frozen creek, and it was obvious he needed help. In a clearing uphill Hamilton saw smoke from a fire, a little tent and another human figure.

Hamilton wanted to land, but the meadow was too small. He decided to fly to Terminus Mountain. Later that afternoon he returned. This time the figure standing by the tent was waving a strip of fabric bearing the identification number of a plane. The other figure was waving from the bank of the creek.

As a landing on the meadow seemed too risky, Hamilton put down at Aeroplane Lake. There he encountered two Indian trappers. They promised to reach the two people and set off by dog team.

Hamilton returned to Watson Lake and notified the RCMP. The Mounties could scarcely believe him. The identification number Hamilton had spotted was that of a small civilian plane reported missing seven weeks before. Aboard had been Ralph Flores, 42, a Mexican-born U.S. citizen, and his passenger, 21-year-old Helen Klaben, a pretty girl from Brooklyn. Almost eight inches of snow had fallen in the seven weeks and the temperature had been as low as 40 below zero. The RCAF, after a long, extensive search, had reluctantly given the pair up for dead.

Now a rescue party was organized, and the next morning Ralph Flores and Helen Klaben were flown to hospital at Whitehorse, Y.T. The man, heavily bearded and wearing a girl's woollen hat, limped badly from frostbitten toes on his left foot. He seemed to take his rescue without great surprise. The girl, thin but still pretty despite a very dirty face, was dressed in layers of sweaters and pants, her feet swathed in hole-riddled sweaters. The toes of her right foot were frostbitten and gangrenous.

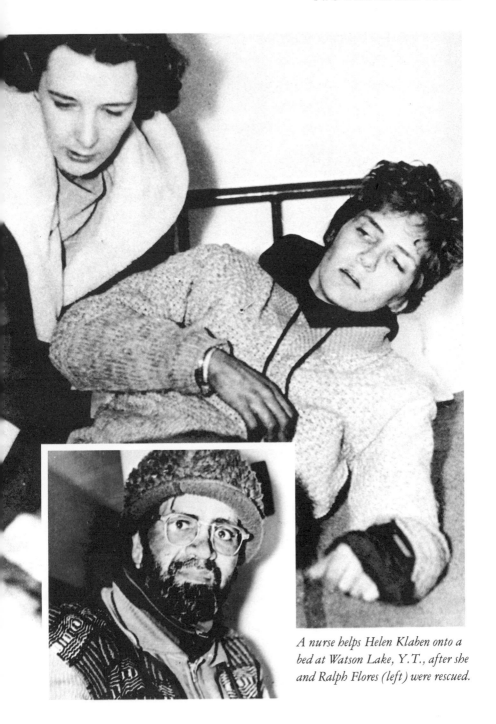

A nurse helps Helen Klaben onto a bed at Watson Lake, Y.T., after she and Ralph Flores (left) were rescued.

She alternately sobbed, talked of her mother and joked with her rescuers. Both spoke fervently of their faith in God and gratitude to Him for their deliverance. They told one of the most extraordinary stories of survival ever known in the Canadian North.

Helen Klaben left high school in Brooklyn in 1959 and qualified for City College. Her family's finances would not permit daytime studies, so she took night courses in liberal arts and worked during the day.

She had always wanted to travel. One day in August 1962 she saw a newspaper advertisement for a "female or couple" who wished to drive to Alaska, sharing expenses. Helen dashed off a reply. She had saved $700 and was ready for anything.

The advertiser was a girl with a Volkswagen. Within a few days the two young women headed north; 17 days later they wound up in Fairbanks. Helen got an apartment, then a job. She took up bowling, skiing, swimming and painting, did some writing and joined a great-books discussion group.

But by mid-winter Helen's wanderlust began stirring again and she decided to go to San Francisco. She planned to leave by commercial airliner on Feb. 1 and was about to get her ticket when she heard that a pilot going to San Francisco was looking for a passenger who would share expenses. Helen jumped at the idea; it would mean saving more than half the commercial fare.

On Jan. 30 she met the pilot—a short, wiry, mild-mannered man with glasses, a mustache and a Spanish accent. She knew nothing about planes or what to ask Ralph Flores about his equipment, but he was a decent, kind-looking fellow.

"He said to me: 'If you don't trust me, don't go with me,'" Helen recalled. "I said to him: 'I trust you.' It came to me that I did. Click. Just like that. There's no halfway business with me. I put my complete trust in him then and there."

Flores had completed an 18-month contract on the Dew line as a $1,100-a-month mechanic, and he was in a hurry to join his wife and six children in San Bruno, Calif. His fellow workers in Alaska regarded him as a nice fellow but something of an odd duck. A Roman Catholic turned Mormon, he did not smoke, swear or drink (even coffee or tea).

In Fairbanks he had become a lay preacher. His salvationism was certainly stronger than his respect for government flying regulations—or even for the common-sense precautions required of anyone flying in the

718

Northern winter. His second-hand aircraft, which he had bought in 1957 for $4,500, was a 1942 Howard single-engine monoplane.

Helen did not realize that Flores was not authorized to fly by instruments in bad weather, or that his motor was not winterized to operate efficiently in very cold temperatures, or that his plane was not equipped with skis for emergency landings. Nor did she know that he did not carry the required winter survival gear—a rifle, an axe, sufficient food for two weeks, 30 feet of snare wire, sleeping bags, fleece-lined flying boots, and waterproof matches.

Before noon Feb. 1, after Helen's baggage had been stowed aboard, they took off from Fairbanks. They landed at Whitehorse late that afternoon, and an hour later the weather worsened and the airport was closed.

They stayed in Whitehorse for three days because of unfavorable weather forecasts. On the night of Feb. 3 Flores told Helen they might be able to take off the next morning. "You still trust me?" Flores asked.

"I said, kiddingly: 'No, I don't,'" Helen recalled. "Then I said: 'We'll probably die tomorrow.'"

Flores told her he was a Mormon priest. He said it was perhaps his mission to see she did not die on the trip with him. He spoke to her of his religion. She told him she believed in God but that, being Jewish, she had not been brought up to recognize in Christ a divine figure. Flores said nothing to this but declared later: "Whenever I hear this I feel a chill going through my whole body."

About mid-morning Feb. 4, when Flores and Helen went to the airport, the temperature was 31 below. Flores had a mechanic warm up the plane's engine. The weather forecaster told Flores that a flight to Fort St. John, B.C., under visual-flight rules would be impossible. He cautioned that a trip to Fort Nelson, B.C., approximately 80 miles north of Fort St. John, might not be possible either, but if Flores wanted to get away he should listen for weather conditions en route and turn back if worsening weather was forecast.

Flores told Helen they were taking off. She took the co-pilot's seat to his right and they began taxiing to the runway. Helen felt conditions were not right for flying but she said nothing. She chewed gum and stared out the window.

The departure is described in an RCAF report: "The aircraft took off from Whitehorse without clearance from the control tower . . . after which the plane disappeared from view in light snow."

719

"I saw the right wingtip hit the trees and I just closed my eyes."

Said Helen: "We went around and around, trying to get above the clouds. I kept chewing gum and thinking *he's the pilot, he's the pilot, I trust him.* But I could feel the tension getting greater."

She helped Flores by pulling maps out of his briefcase in order. She held in her lap a paper on which he had written the frequencies he could use to contact radio stations and control towers.

After three hours the air became increasingly turbulent. Flores kept climbing and Helen sensed he could not locate his position visually. Flores climbed to 11,500 feet to try to get above the clouds, and tried to establish his position by radio, but he could not make contact. He turned to Helen to take the paper with the other frequencies. But, with the turbulence, the paper disappeared from Helen's lap. During the 15 minutes they searched for the paper the plane pitched and bumped around in the clouds. They were hopelessly lost, off route and over terrain as forbidding and desolate as anywhere in the North. Flores was confused and exhausted by the effort of trying to control the plane. Now he tried to get below the weather.

"He wouldn't say we were lost but I knew we were, and I felt so bad about that piece of paper," said Helen. "We were coming down and one fuel gauge was close to zero. We were flying by the side of a mountain and I saw trees below us. He put his hand down to change tanks but the plane stalled. I said out loud: 'Okay, Helen, here it comes.' I saw the right wingtip hit the trees and I just closed my eyes."

Both wingtips must have hit at the same time, for if one had hit a fraction of a second before the other–or appreciably harder–the plane would have tumbled over and Flores and Helen would have been killed.

Helen blacked out. When she came to she found she was bleeding from the chin and her left arm was broken. Flores' seat had been torn loose and knocked forward. He was unconscious. The instrument panel was smashed. "Ralph," she said. No answer. She shook him gently. "Ralph."

"In about five minutes he began to move a little," she recalled. "I told him to put his parka on. I was calm. It's amazing how outside myself I was, and aware of what was going on. It wasn't quite twilight. I figured we would have to get out in the snow and make a fire first thing. I tried to get out but my right foot was stuck. I couldn't feel it. Ralph began to get out through the broken windshield in front of us, and I helped him. He went around the plane to my side to get me out."

Flores had lost his boots in the crash. He could not feel his feet or his fingertips; frostbite had set in. He felt his ribs were broken. He was horribly cut about the face, and blood was pouring from his mouth. He was unable to move his jaws, and could talk only with great difficulty.

By the time he got around to Helen, she had got her foot free and some feeling began to return. The foot felt as though it had been crushed. Flores helped her out of the fuselage through a broken window. As he did so, he said to her through his teeth as blood continued to pour from his mouth: "You know why we are here, don't you?"

"Why?"

"Because you reject Jesus Christ," Flores said. He was struck by a sudden conviction that the crash must have been pre-ordained, and that he was fated to be the instrument of her religious salvation.

It was bitterly cold: the airplane thermometer showed 48 below zero. Helen had also lost her boots and before Flores got her out she wrapped a sweater around each foot. The snow was knee deep and in many spots waist deep.

They dug in the snow, gathered brushwood knocked down by the crash, and made a small fire with one of Helen's matches. She had a few boxes of cigarettes and several books of matches. Papers they used for kindling included a bloodstained map—the one map, it turned out, sufficiently detailed to have let them know where they were.

Ralph's upper jaw was split and part was hanging by the skin. Blood continued to pour from his mouth. He put on a sweater and his parka. They got back into the plane and sat in the broken seat. Helen was shivering and every time she moved she felt the break in her arm.

Flores told her a search would be started when the plane was reported overdue, but it might be several days before they were found. He reminded her of her feeling in Whitehorse that she was going to die, and told her she would not die if she studied the Bible.

Neither slept. In the morning the temperature was still 48 below, and they removed the rear seat to make room for a proper shelter. He had no hat, and she gave him one of hers—a woollen tuque.

Flores was in great pain. He let the blood on his face cake to hold the cuts together. With a rolled sweater he propped his lower jaw against the loose upper jaw; blood soaking into the sweater froze and formed a kind of cast.

Flores made a fire with brushwood and they took stock of their position. The spruce forest was so dense that they could see only a little sky. They were obviously on a mountainside. They had four cans of sardines, two of tuna, two of fruit cocktail, a box of crackers and a part bottle of protein pills. Their other supplies were a box of bandage tape, a few boxes of matches, a pocket knife, a small hunting knife, a putty knife, binoculars, a ball-peen hammer, a cold chisel, a couple of mirrors, Helen's oil-painting set, the clothes in her suitcases—including a number of sweaters besides those she and Flores were wearing—and some books, including Flores' Bible.

Early on the second morning, with his broken jaw, battered ribs and frostbitten fingers and toes, Flores dragged himself out of the fuselage, made a fire and, using a gallon can that had contained paint thinner, melted snow and heated water for their breakfast. They ate nothing.

To protect Helen's feet from the snow and to keep them dry—the toes on her right foot had turned black from frostbite—Ralph made foot coverings from canvas he ripped from the rear seats. He dressed her injured foot with strips from one of her dresses. He hobbled off into the snow to retrieve pieces of the wing, and with these made splints for Helen's broken arm, bound with strips torn from a dress.

For Helen's lunch, Flores heated a can of fruit cocktail. He, unable to open his mouth, could take only a little juice between his lips. For dinner she ate tuna and he mixed mashed sardines with water and, using a twig, poked the food into his mouth. With crackers and water he made a soup in the paint-thinner can. In this manner they made their sardines and tuna last a week.

On the seventh day Helen found two small chicken legs, the forgotten remains of a couple of fried chickens they had bought to eat on their journey from Fairbanks to Whitehorse. They made the chicken into a half-gallon of soup. But now they had only one can of fruit cocktail, some crackers and the protein pills. Helen was very weak and spent most of her time lying in the plane.

The weather remained very cold. Nearly every clear day they heard an airplane and once even saw one through the broken trees where the plane had crashed but they were all far away.

Flores' fingers and the toes of his right foot were badly swollen from frostbite. He could move only a few feet from the plane, and that very painfully. He wore a rubber overboot on his right foot but could not get one on his left foot, so kept it wrapped in a sweater.

On the ninth day they shared the last can of fruit cocktail. Helen took one of the protein pills and later her frostbitten foot seemed more painful. Flores advised her to take no more pills. From then on, apart from the few crackers—which were used up in a few days—they existed on melted snow.

Helen read books from her great-books course—excerpts of works by Thoreau, Tolstoy, Adam Smith, Shakespeare, Milton and others.

Flores talked of religious matters and she read to him aloud from St. Matthew. Then she started reading from the Old Testament while Flores worked to repair the plane's standby radio. On the 11th day he turned it on to try to make contact with an airplane they heard passing on the other side of the mountain. A tube blew. He had no replacement.

His next project was to make an S O S where aircraft might see it. With red paint from Helen's set, he painted an S O S on a piece of the white aileron from the plane's wing. Then, using his cold chisel and hammer, he cut down three young spruce trees. He spliced them together with wire, fixed the sign on top, rigged up a pulley and tried to raise the S O S in among the broken trees where the airplane had come down. Even with Helen's help, he could not raise the tailpiece. He abandoned it in favor of a small metal spar from the plane. On it he painted S O S and together they managed to raise that.

On the 14th day Flores got his mouth open for the first time—by prying his jaws apart, on the unbroken side, with a strong stick. Helen asked him to celebrate. Sitting on a log in the snow, he sang a Spanish song, and Helen hummed along with him.

About the time he put up his S O S, Flores started to repair the plane's very-high-frequency radio. It took a week but he got it working— except for the distress frequency.

On the 18th day Flores decided they needed a better distress signal. He cut down and trimmed a slim, 25-foot spruce and tied to it a strip of fabric with a few numbers from the fuselage. Then, his jaw broken, his fingertips and toes frostbitten, his ribs and chest terribly bruised, he climbed a 60-foot spruce with the 25-foot pole. He raised the pole and distress flag above the top of the tree and secured it with pieces of wire and string. But the tree was no higher than surrounding trees and he realized the distress sign had little chance of being seen from the air.

The next day he decided to make some sort of snowshoes to enable him to travel and find a clearing where he might be able to attract the attention of passing planes.

Flores tied his hunting knife to a length of spruce and tried to spear rabbits. But he had no luck. He tried making traps, again without success.

He fashioned a slingshot, using a strip of rubber from a wheel of the airplane, leather from the pilot's seat, and the fork of a willow branch. He had no small stones for ammunition but found a rock near the fire where the snow had melted to the ground. He broke it up with the hammer, but the pieces were so irregular that they would fly off to one side of his target. He never succeeded in hitting a rabbit.

Because of the snow and his frostbitten toes, Flores could go only a short distance for firewood. He took his chisel and hammer and, with astounding persistence, cut down whole trees, some a foot or more in diameter, then trimmed them into lengths suitable for burning.

They worked, waited and drank snow water. "We were not terribly hungry, mostly weak," Helen said. But they thought about food constantly. "What did you dream last night, Ralph?" Helen would ask. And Flores would describe great platters of roast chicken, of tamales—a whole tableful of food. Some mornings, while making the fire, Ralph would ask Helen what she wanted for breakfast. "Bacon and eggs," she would sing out. "Coming right up!" he would say, and she would get her hot water.

A couple of weeks after the crash, Flores came across a half tube of toothpaste. He tasted it and found that it lubricated his mouth. Helen found her toothpaste, too. While the two tubes lasted, they ate a little each day for the flavor, sometimes stirring it into their hot drinking water.

Planes continued to fly over when the weather was clear, but Flores and Helen seldom saw them. On March 1, unknown to the downed pair, the search was called off.

By then Flores had completed one snowshoe. That day he cut out of an airplane tire a rubber sandal for his right foot, so he could expose his frostbitten toes to the fire. He knew he had to improve the condition of his foot before he could venture from the camp.

On the 32nd day he completed the second snowshoe. He was ready to try to find a clearing from which he might attract the attention of a passing plane. If he didn't get help he would probably return in three days. He had accumulated firewood which he estimated would last Helen for more than a week. She gave him one of her coats, honey-colored with an imitation leopard collar.

Flores set off about noon, padding downhill on his snowshoes. He carried the airplane's six-pound compass, his spear and a pack made of Helen's coat and containing his chisel and hammer, a can in which to boil water, and matches. Binoculars hung from his neck and he had a small mirror in a pocket.

"For the first time in my life I found myself *really alone*," said Helen. "And it wasn't too bad. I never got bored. I thought of that Tolstoy story in which Ivan Ilych, when he is dying, looks back on his life. I did on mine. I reflected on what I had done. I couldn't think of anything desperately bad I had done except that I felt guilty I hadn't gone straight back to New York from Fairbanks as I had promised my mother I would. I thought about my mother all the time. I talked to her: 'Ma! Listen to me, Ma! Ma, I'm alive! Ma!' And I would talk to my younger sister: 'Linda! I love you! I'm alive, Linda!'"

When after three days Flores did not appear, Helen began to worry. Icy winds were blowing, and the skies remained leaden. Helen fed on hot snow water and continued her reading of the Bible.

After eight days of waiting, late one afternoon she heard Flores calling from the woods, and she burst into tears. She was overjoyed to see him, perhaps a little hysterical.

Flores made a fire—hers had gone out—and sang her songs in Spanish. He had found a clearing he thought was about two miles downhill (actually it was only half a mile) and had made a shelter and waited in vain for airplanes. He had returned because he was worried about her and in particular about her wood supply. Helen's frostbitten toes had turned gangrenous and she was in no condition to go hunting for wood.

On Monday, March 18—the 42nd day—they set off for the clearing, Helen on a toboggan that Ralph had constructed from a metal section taken from the airplane. Helen had mixed some red paint and lettered a sign on the fuselage:

WENT
2 MI.
DOWN HILL
3/16/63

(She apparently had slipped up a couple of times in marking days off the calendar she kept in the airplane.)

They were confident they would be rescued. Helen took her comb and make-up kit, Flores his shaving things. The toboggan was so heavy that after going only a short distance Flores could not pull it. Helen had to walk. She pulled and he pushed. The terrain was extremely rough, with steep gullies, fallen trees and thick brush.

The canvas foot coverings Flores had made for Helen became loose and full of snow. After a while she lost them and had to struggle along with sweaters around her feet. Sometimes the toboggan would overturn and they would have to stop and load it again, Helen doing what she could with her one good arm. Sometimes they had to manoeuvre down hills so steep that, Helen said, "I would have been afraid to go down on skis." Altogether they descended about 1,000 feet from their previous location on the mountain. The trip took five hours.

Darkness was coming on as they got within sight of the clearing, which was on a knoll. Flores was in agonizing pain from abdominal cramps but he made a fire and hot water for Helen. "I just sat on the cushions in the snow, unable to move. That trip knocked the hell out of both of us. My feet were wet and bad. Ralph took the sweaters off and dried them at the fire, then bound rags around my feet from a cotton nightgown he got from the toboggan and ripped up."

During his previous stay at the clearing, Ralph had made a lean-to of spruce boughs against a fallen tree trunk. They turned in about 11:30.

The next morning Helen got her first real look around the knoll. "It was a very eerie place. There obviously had been a forest fire there once. All around were these dead trees standing out of the snow against this gray sky. There was a range of mountains, very desolate, to the southwest of us. It gave you a scary, kind of like a death, feeling. But it was a good spot for some plane to see us."

Flores made a tent with tarpaulins. At one end he placed the toboggan upright as a wall; the other end he left open and there he built a fire. He made a rough floor of timber and covered that with green branches. Not far from the fire they laid out, as a disaster signal, the strip of canvas bearing the plane's identification number.

On March 21, 45 days after the crash, Flores set out in search of a snow-covered meadow, found one some four miles away, and stamped out a huge S O S, each letter 75 feet high, and an arrow pointing to the camp where Helen was. He slept there that night on a bed of green branches on the snow.

The next day he headed northwest in an attempt to skirt the mountain range to the west of him. That night he slept in the hollow of a tree and the following day he climbed a 70-foot tree to try to get his bearings. The effort exhausted him and he slept again in the tree.

The next day he sighted a creek and followed it. That afternoon, as he was crossing the frozen creek, an airplane came in sight. He took out his mirror and began to flash.

Pilot Chuck Hamilton circled low around Flores. Then, up the mountain, he sighted Helen by her tent at the clearing.

"I sensed the pilot had seen me," Helen said, "but I had to struggle with myself not to get my hopes up too high. I went back to the Bible, which I had been reading ever since Ralph left. I had finished the New Testament and had turned back to the Old and was reading Isaiah. I

Flores made this tent in a clearing where he hoped he and Klaben would be spotted.

told myself, *Got to finish that chapter—got to*, and read on. Later in the afternoon the plane came back. It circled around again. I was so excited! I was standing there and waving, and my feet were hurting so much from standing, and when the plane waggled its wings to show that I

had been spotted, I just fell down and cried, and it was so wonderful! Just cried and cried, and was so thankful!"

About 6:30 the next morning, on the 49th day after the crash, she was awakened by the noise of a small plane—a different plane. This one was piloted by Jack McCallum, a mechanic at the Watson Lake airport. He was accompanied by Ed McNeill, who worked at the airport weather station. McCallum dipped his wings to indicate he had sighted her.

She saw the plane descend—it came down in the S O S meadow—and after a while "this man came out of the woods toward me on snowshoes. I lay down and again I just cried and cried, saying over and over, 'Thank God, thank God, thank God!'" She asked McCallum to heat some snow water for her. Then McNeill came up.

After some time, Chuck Hamilton arrived. Helen said to him: "You must be the pilot who spotted me yesterday. I'd like to come over and kiss you, but I can't walk." Hamilton, a big brawny man, sat beside her on a log and gently put his arm around her. She was wearing a plaid wool shirt of Flores over layer upon layer of sweaters, and her hooded sweat shirt. Over her legs she had long underwear, tights, black corduroy pants, magenta woollen slacks, brown woollen pants belonging to Flores and another pair of blue service pants, also his.

On top of all the sweaters she wore her parka—"and with all that I was still cold," Helen said. The rags and sweaters around her feet were reeking. But, said Hamilton, "she was very pretty." After a few minutes of talk she said to Hamilton: "Well, I didn't get my kiss, did I?" He kissed her. Then he carried her piggyback through the snow and the forest to his plane at the S O S meadow.

Hamilton flew her to Aeroplane Lake and she was carried to the trappers' log cabin. Inside, sitting on a rough wooden bed, was Ralph. Helen hobbled over and kissed him. He had been found the previous evening by the two Indians.

The trappers offered them food. They took a little moose meat sandwiched between a couple of crackers. Then they were flown, separately—Helen sometimes laughing, sometimes crying, sometimes calling out: "Ma, I'm alive!"—to Watson Lake and then to hospital at Whitehorse.

Doctors found them well apart from malnutrition and the condition of their frostbitten toes. Ralph's toes were healing but the gangrenous toes of Helen's right foot were beyond saving. Her broken arm had healed nicely in its splints of wing spar. Ralph's broken jaw had set solidly. It was only slightly out of position and, after a couple of back teeth had been filed a little to adjust to this, his jaws were working normally.

Helen's brother Arthur flew to Whitehorse and took her to the Columbia Presbyterian Medical Center in New York. There the toes on her right foot were amputated. Helen was matter-of-fact about it: "It won't interfere with my walking. They tell me I'll even be able to dance."

Near her bed was the Bible that Flores had given her in the crashed plane. Far from being converted to Christianity, she felt stronger now in her Jewish faith. "I know that my God put me in that crash for a purpose, but I don't know that it was a religious purpose," she said.

"People expect me to *tell* them something about what I learned when we were alone. To give them some sort of a message. But I can't really. I'm the same person I was before it all happened, although I've learned so much. People also talk of the terrible time I must have been through out there in the wilderness. But I don't think of what happened to Ralph and me in that way at all. It was tough, it's true, but what the two of us went through in those 49 days was a really amazing, a *wonderful* experience together."

Ralph Flores' licence to fly was suspended, then reinstated in 1966. He continued to live in San Bruno, Calif., working as a mechanic for an airline, flying only as a hobby. Helen Klaben worked as an editor for a publishing house, then for a stockbroker, and later took over operation of a tennis workshop in Vermont. She and Flores were technical advisers for a movie about their experience.

Acknowledgments

The editors acknowledge with thanks the assistance of Kenneth Conoley, Alexander Farrell, Douglas How, Herb Rutherford, Charles W. Smith, Adrian Waller.

Thanks is expressed also to the Canadian Permanent Committee on Geographical Names, the Department of National Defence (particularly the Canadian Forces), the National Library, the National Museums of Canada (particularly the National Aeronautical Collection), the Public Archives;

And to the following individuals and organizations:

Arctic Institute of North America
David Armour, Mackinac Island State
    Park Commission
Ruth Matheson Buck
Glenbow-Alberta Institute
Neils Jannasch, Nova Scotia Museum
S. W. Horrall, Historian, RCMP
Omar Lavallée, Canadian Pacific
    Railway
Lawrence A. Learmonth
Maritime Museum, Vancouver
McGill University Libraries
Dr. Eric Morse

W. S. Neidhardt
Robert Oleson, Historian,
    Hudson's Bay Company
Ontario Provincial Police
Maj. Frank Riddell (RCMP, retired)
A. L. Ringlet, Meteorologist,
    Environment Canada
Eric Ruff, Yarmouth County
    Historical Society Museum
Simcoe County Archives and Museum
Westmount Public Library
Prof. Richard Wilbur,
    Concordia University

Story Credits

HURONIA'S IMMORTAL SCOUNDREL From *Etienne Brûlé: Immortal Scoundrel* by J. Herbert Cranston. Copyright 1949. Reprinted by permission of McGraw-Hill Ryerson Limited, Toronto.

THE EPIC FEUD OVER ACADIA Adapted from *The Old Regime in Canada* by Francis Parkman. Published 1893 by Little, Brown and Company, Boston.

ESCAPE FROM MICHILIMACKINAC Adapted from *Travels and Adventures in Canada and the Indian Territories* by Alexander Henry. First published 1809 in New York. Edited by James Bain and published 1969 by M. G. Hurtig Limited, Edmonton.

JOHN GYLES' AMAZING ORDEAL Condensed from *The Ordeal of John Gyles* by Stuart Trueman. Copyright © 1966 by Stuart Trueman. Reprinted by permission of The Canadian Publishers, McClelland and Stewart Limited, Toronto.

Picture Credits